# MARKETING

## THE CORE

Fifth Canadian Edition

**ROGER A. KERIN**
*Southern Methodist University*

**STEVEN W. HARTLEY**
*University of Denver*

**CHRISTINA CLEMENTS**
*Humber College Institute of Technology & Advanced Learning*

**ARSENIO BONIFACIO**
*University of Guelph*

**CAROL BUREAU**
*Sheridan Institute of Technology and Advanced Learning*

McGraw Hill Education

# MARKETING: THE CORE
## Fifth Canadian Edition

The Internet addresses listed in the text were accurate at the time of publication. The inclusion of a Web site does not indicate an endorsement by the authors or McGraw-Hill Ryerson, and McGraw-Hill Ryerson does not guarantee the accuracy of the information presented at these sites.

ISBN-13: 978-1-25-926926-4
ISBN-10: 1-25-926926-4

5 6 7 8 9 10 11 12 TCP 22 21 20 19

Printed and bound in Canada.

Care has been taken to trace ownership of copyright material contained in this text; however, the publisher will welcome any information that enables them to rectify any reference or credit for subsequent editions.

**Portfolio Director, Business & Economics, International:** Nicole Meehan
**Portfolio Manager:** Sara Braithwaite
**Director, Portfolio Marketing:** Joy Armitage Taylor
**Content Developer:** Amy Rydzanicz
**Senior Portfolio Associate:** Marina Seguin
**Supervising Editors:** Stephanie Gibson/Janie Deneau
**Photo/Permissions Editor:** Derek Capitaine
**Copy Editor:** Michael Kelly
**Plant Production Coordinator:** Michelle Saddler
**Manufacturing Production Coordinator:** Sheryl MacAdam
**Cover and Interior Design:** Lightbox Visual Communications, Inc.
**Cover Image:** © Yobro10/Dreamstime.com
**Page Layout:** MPS Limited
**Printer:** Transcontinental Printing Group

# Author Profiles

**Roger A. Kerin** is the Harold C. Simmons Distinguished Professor of Marketing at the Edwin L. Cox School of Business, Southern Methodist University in Dallas, Texas. Professor Kerin holds a B.A. (magna cum laude), M.B.A., and Ph.D. from the University of Minnesota. His teaching and research interests lie in marketing planning and strategy, product management, financial aspects of marketing, and marketing research. Professor Kerin is a frequent participant in executive development programs and is also an active consultant on matters of marketing planning and strategy. Professor Kerin has published and authored several texts and many articles on marketing. He also serves on numerous journal editorial review boards and is currently a member of the Board of Governors of the Academy of Marketing Science.

**Steven W. Hartley** is Professor of Marketing in the Daniels College of Business at the University of Denver. He holds Bachelor of Mechanical Engineering, M.B.A., and Ph.D. degrees from the University of Minnesota. Dr. Hartley was formerly the chair of the Department of Marketing at the University of Denver, and has taught at the University of Colorado, the University of Minnesota, and in several executive development programs. His teaching interests include principles of marketing, marketing research, and marketing planning. Dr. Hartley's research has appeared in many leading marketing publications. He is an active consultant to several prominent U.S. corporations and is active in many professional organizations, including the American Marketing Association, the Academy of Marketing Science, and the Marketing Educators' Association.

**Christina Clements** is an award-winning professor from the Business School at Humber College Institute of Technology & Advanced Learning in Ontario. She is renowned for the creativity and knowledge she brings to the field of marketing education. She is a recipient of the Leadership in Faculty Teaching Award, honouring Ontario's best university and college faculty, from the Ministry of Training, Colleges and Universities, and the Distinguished Faculty award from the Humber College Institute of Technology & Advanced Learning. She holds an M.B.A. from the Bradford University Management Centre in the U.K. and a master certificate in Internet marketing from the University of San Francisco. She has

a wealth of experience in marketing and advertising—from both client and agency perspectives—in consumer packaged goods, cosmetics, food service, and personal care. She now channels her practical experience, knowledge, and creativity into the field of education, by teaching, managing social media sites, and developing written materials, online resources, and educational tools. Her passion lies in teaching marketing communications and Internet marketing courses. She is frequently called upon to mentor others in the field of education.

**Arsenio Bonifacio** teaches marketing in the Department of Marketing & Consumer Studies at the University of Guelph. He also taught courses in the Pilon School of Business at Sheridan College applying experience as a investment industry marketing executive to the classroom. Arsenio holds an M.B.A. from Wilfrid Laurier University and a B.Sc. from McMaster University. His career in marketing involved leading teams and initiatives in Canada, the United States, and the United Kingdom. Arsenio gained practical experience in sales, advertising, public relations, direct marketing, market research, and recruitment marketing. Aside from his teaching, Arsenio is an executive at one of Ontario's largest credit unions and is responsible for wealth management strategy within the organization.

**Carol Bureau** is a Professor of Marketing at the Pilon School of Business at Sheridan College and is also the Program Coordinator for the marketing diploma and degree programs at Sheridan. She is active with student activities, including acting as faculty advisor for the Student Marketing Association, coaching Ontario Colleges Marketing Competition teams, and coordinating internal case competitions. She obtained her M.B.A. from the Ivey Business School at Western University where she worked on several innovative projects, including customer satisfaction measures, selling to the seniors' health care market, telemedicine in Canada, and the development of strategic planning models. Carol graduated with a Bachelor of Business Administration from Wilfrid Laurier University. During the course of her marketing career, she held progressively senior positions in sales and marketing, mainly in the pharmaceutical industry. In addition to teaching, Carol enjoys consulting in her areas of interest, including strategic planning, product launches, and business development.

# Brief Contents

# Contents

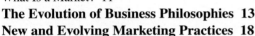

## Chapter 6 Segmentation, Targeting, and Positioning 136

# Part 3 Designing Marketing Strategies and Marketing Mix Elements

## Chapter 7 Products and Brands 160

## Chapter 8 New Product Development 182

## Chapter 9 Pricing 206

## Chapter 10 Marketing Channels and Supply Chain 236

## Chapter 11 Retailing and Wholesaling 262

## Part 5 Putting It All Together

# Preface

Welcome to the exciting and dynamic field of marketing! Boosted by technological change, this fast-paced environment continues to quickly evolve, challenging marketers to stay informed and knowledgeable on new marketing approaches, regulations, and ideas. New digital approaches, especially, continue to advance social media marketing, mobile marketing, and customer relationship management programs, as well as in other Internet marketing pathways that may be integrated into offline or online marketing practices.

Real-time marketing and content marketing approaches are used in increasingly creative ways to reach consumers, businesses, and organizations. Conventional marketing approaches reach target markets, and new regulations ensure a smooth transition into this new marketing reality. In all instances, marketing messages compete in a sea of information that floods people's daily lives, and challenges marketing programs to be noticed, relevant, and engaging. This marketing reality uses metrics to monitor and measure marketing performance and analytics to reveal insights and areas of improvement.

The fifth Canadian edition of *Marketing: The Core* reflects this new marketing reality with its standard features as well as new elements and content that are designed to engage. There is an expanded focus on digital marketing channels with a chapter called "Digital Marketing Communication," as well as a focus on financial fluency that has been integrated into the chapters on pricing and strategic planning in a way that students can understand. Each chapter is boosted by new content, examples, and features to ensure the text reflects the very latest online and offline marketing approaches in Canada.

The fifth Canadian edition of *Marketing: The Core* returns with its popular magazine-style format that engages with its visual appeal, direct writing style, sound pedagogical features, and fresh new content. Chapter elements include *Chapter Features* and *Chapter Outlines*, which open each chapter, flagging interesting topics and helping students navigate chapter content. Pedagogical elements include *infographics*, as well as critical-thinking *end-of-chapter* features that help apply and bring the material to life. These elements are in addition to the highly rated chapter-opening vignettes, Marketing NewsFlash boxes, and Focus on Ethics boxes that are all new and interspersed throughout each chapter.

The fifth Canadian edition of *Marketing: The Core* is designed so that students enjoy learning about marketing. It is current. It is real. It reflects marketing in Canada.

## TEXT ORGANIZATION AND CONTENT

*Marketing: The Core*, Fifth Canadian Edition, is divided into five parts:

Part 1, "Understanding Marketing," looks first at what marketing is and how it creates customer value and customer relationships (Chapter 1). Chapter 2 analyzes the major environmental factors in our changing marketing environment.

Part 2, "Understanding Markets and Their Behaviour," first describes, in Chapter 3, how individual consumers reach buying decisions. Chapter 4 examines the marketing research function, metrics and analytics, and how information about prospective consumers is linked to marketing strategy and decisions. Chapter 5 looks at industrial and organizational buyers and how they make purchase decisions. The process of segmenting and targeting markets and positioning products appears in Chapter 6.

Part 3, "Designing Marketing Strategies and Marketing Mix Elements," covers the four Ps of marketing: product, price, place, and promotion. The product element is divided into two chapters. Chapter 7 looks at the way existing products, services, and brands are managed. Chapter 8 discusses the development of new products and the product life cycle. Pricing is discussed, focusing on the way organizations set prices (Chapter 9). Two chapters address the place aspects of marketing: "Marketing Channels and Supply Chain" (Chapter 10) and "Retailing and Wholesaling" (Chapter 11). Chapter 12 discusses offline marketing communications and how to integrate communications to maximize their impact.

Part 4, "Focusing on New and Evolving Areas," includes a refreshed chapter covering the rapid changes in digital marketing communications (Chapter 13). Chapter 14, "Customer Relationship Management," takes a deeper look into technological innovations that are improving how companies meet consumer needs and grow consumer experience.

Part 5, "Putting It All Together," provides an overview of the strategic marketing planning process that occurs in an organization (Chapter 15) and includes a new marketing plan example in Appendix A.

## WHAT'S NEW?
## *MARKETING: THE CORE*

The fifth Canadian edition of *Marketing: The Core* builds on the strengths of the previous editions, adding new and exciting elements that make the material even more interactive and engaging. Our authors go to extreme lengths to interview respected Canadian marketers so that content is fresh and accurately reflects current marketing practices. The authors also turn to the teaching environment so that each chapter includes solid pedagogical features that help students learn and faculty teach. The freshness of this new edition is reflected in the following:

- **Enhanced magazine-style format:** The popular magazine-style format returns with its fresh visual appeal, direct writing style, and active-learning techniques that challenge students to understand and enjoy learning about marketing. Many features are included to enhance learning, as noted below.
- **Chapter features and outlines:** Each chapter opens with these elements to highlight newsy features within the chapter and create a path that guides readers through the chapter and its content.
- **New opening chapter vignettes:** The popular chapter-opening vignettes return with all-new content that provides a glimpse into real marketing situations, with advice from senior business professionals in Canada. The discussions centre on many exciting brands that will be familiar to students, such as PUR Gum, Canada Post, Chevrolet Cruze, and the Toronto Raptors, as well as many other stellar brands and companies.
- **New Marketing NewsFlash and Focus on Ethics boxes:** These popular features return with all-new content, meticulously researched to provide perspective on the latest marketing approaches. Examples are

tentree's social responsibility branding, the Interac "Be in the Black" campaign, Mountain Equipment Co-op's corporate social responsibility, and Uber.

- **Sections on metrics, analytics, and big data:** Marketing requires students to understand the metrics and analytics used by the industry. Sections in the text explain this topic and discuss the issues surrounding big data.
- **Updated sections on forecasting, budgeting, financial analysis, and profit-and-loss statements:** Marketers are involved in forecasting and budgeting, and use financial analyses and profit-and-loss statements to evaluate programs and brand success. These areas are enhanced in the fifth Canadian edition through discussions in the pricing chapter (Chapter 9) and the strategic planning chapter (Chapter 15).
- **Updated marketing plan appendix:** A revised marketing plan example and template has been built into the text. This example was developed in collaboration with marketing consultant Glenn Cressman, from Share of Marketing, to ensure that it reflects current marketing planning approaches.

## CHAPTER-SPECIFIC ADDITIONS

In addition to an updated narrative for each chapter and all-new opening vignettes, Marketing NewsFlash and Focus on Ethics boxes, databoxes, and infographics, the following new topics have been added:

### *Chapter 1: Marketing Fundamentals*

- Role of the marketing function
- Experiential marketing
- Marketing regulations and ethical considerations
- Personal/career SWOT analysis

### *Chapter 2: The Marketing Environment*

- New Statistics Canada demographic data from the latest census
- Generational and ethnic diversity
- New media-viewing trends
- Canadians' use of technology
- Updates to regulatory practices in Canada
- The Competition Bureau's *Little Black Book of Scams*
- Real-world example of the steps in a marketing environment scan

## Chapter 3: Consumer Behaviour

- Insight into how Canadians are using their phones
- Updated PRIZM5 clusters, courtesy of Environics Analytics
- Expanded content on Canadian subcultures

## Chapter 4: Market Research, Metrics, and Analytics

- Rules of marketing metrics
- Updates to key marketing metrics
- Four Vs (velocity, volume, variety, and veracity) of big data
- Segmentation using recency, frequency, and monetary value analysis (RFM)
- Market research sources
- Writing survey questions

## Chapter 5: B2B Marketing

- Small business insights in B2B marketing
- Expanded content on content marketing
- Additional sustainability considerations in B2B marketing
- Update to the largest global companies

## Chapter 6: Segmentation, Targeting, and Positioning

- Enhanced figure on segmentation strategies: mass, segment, niche, and individualized strategies
- Examples of personas
- Updates on the segmentation analytics platform PRIZM5
- Simplified six-step process for segmenting a market

## Chapter 7: Products and Brands

- Enhanced graphic for the total product concept
- Interbrand's *Best Global Brands* study
- New product mix width, product line length, and product line depth
- Ipsos' *Most Influential Brands* study

## Chapter 8: New Product Development

- Brandspark's *Best New Products* award winners
- Why new products and services fail

## Chapter 9: Pricing

- Enhanced examples of pricing strategies in practice
- Enhanced sections on forecasting and financials

- Enhanced sections on legal and ethical considerations, including price fixing

## Chapter 10: Marketing Channels and Supply Chain

- Multichannel marketing to the online consumer
- Ethical considerations in supply chain management

## Chapter 11: Retailing and Wholesaling

- Enhanced examples of retail forms of ownership
- Sustainability in retailing

## Chapter 12: Marketing Communications

- Updated data on media usage
- Updated data on advertising expenditures
- Top magazine readership in Canada

## Chapter 13: Digital Marketing Communications

- Online marketing landscape
- Display ad formats
- Comparing social media with traditional media
- Benefits of social media marketing
- Canadian brand and consumer usage of social media
- Facebook page components
- Best practices for Facebook, Twitter, YouTube, Instagram, and LinkedIn
- Social media metrics
- Canadian use of smartphones and apps

## Chapter 14: Customer Relationship Management

- Enhanced examples of customer relationship management (CRM) in practice
- Enhanced examples of loyalty programs

## Chapter 15: Strategic Marketing Planning

This chapter on strategic marketing planning has been placed at the end of the text so that students can gain a greater understanding of marketing before embarking on this more complex topic. The following new content has been included:

- Enhanced examples of small business strategy
- Enhanced marketing budgets and financials

# A Student's Guide to *Marketing: The Core*

*Marketing: The Core* offers an array of features to help readers learn and apply marketing concepts.

Each chapter opens with a **vignette** on a Canadian marketing situation or program, featuring current facts, real approaches, and tangible examples from interviews with marketers in Canada. **Chapter Features** and **Chapter Outlines** give an overview of the key features and provide an outline of each chapter. Clear and precise **Learning Objectives** help students preview chapter content and study effectively. **Reality Check** questions appear at the end of each vignette.

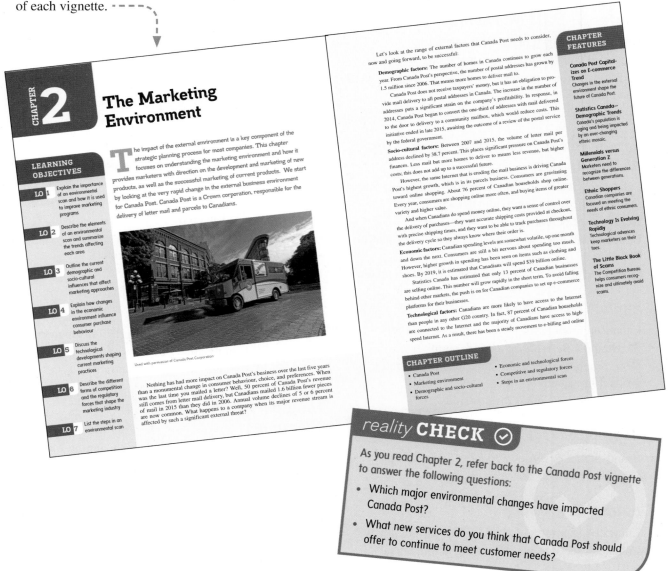

**Infographics** are used to draw attention to metrics that relate to a topic within the chapter and to help students become familiar with this visual approach to presenting marketing information.

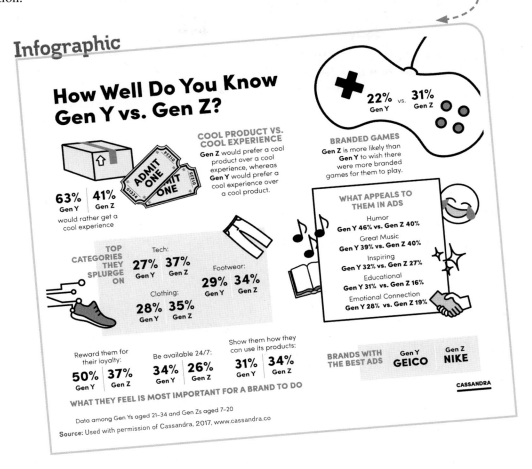

## Infographic

### How Well Do You Know Gen Y vs. Gen Z?

**22%** Gen Y vs. **31%** Gen Z

**BRANDED GAMES**
**Gen Z** is more likely than **Gen Y** to wish there were more branded games for them to play.

**COOL PRODUCT VS. COOL EXPERIENCE**
**Gen Z** would prefer a cool product over a cool experience, whereas **Gen Y** would prefer a cool experience over a cool product.

**63%** Gen Y | **41%** Gen Z
would rather get a cool experience

**TOP CATEGORIES THEY SPLURGE ON**
Tech: **27%** Gen Y **37%** Gen Z
Footwear: **29%** Gen Y **34%** Gen Z
Clothing: **28%** Gen Y **35%** Gen Z

**WHAT APPEALS TO THEM IN ADS**
Humor
Gen Y 46% vs. Gen Z 40%
Great Music
Gen Y 39% vs. Gen Z 40%
Inspiring
Gen Y 32% vs. Gen Z 27%
Educational
Gen Y 31% vs. Gen Z 16%
Emotional Connection
Gen Y 28% vs. Gen Z 19%

Reward them for their loyalty:
**50%** Gen Y | **37%** Gen Z

Be available 24/7:
**34%** Gen Y | **26%** Gen Z

Show them how they can use its products:
**31%** Gen Y | **34%** Gen Z

**BRANDS WITH THE BEST ADS** Gen Y **GEICO** Gen Z **NIKE**

CASSANDRA

**WHAT THEY FEEL IS MOST IMPORTANT FOR A BRAND TO DO**

Data among Gen Ys aged 21–34 and Gen Zs aged 7–20

**Source:** Used with permission of Cassandra, 2017, www.cassandra.co

---

Real metrics are used to emphasize points within the text through standalone data boxes that bring attention to the importance of metrics in marketing. **Data boxes** present tangible facts and numerical examples of elements discussed in the text, and serve as important examples of how metrics are used by the industry.

### Loblaw Community Giving in 2016

| | |
|---|---|
| Charitable donations | $65 million |
| President's Choice Children's Charity | 449,000 children received nutritious meals |
| Food drives | $2.8 million + 1.8 million pounds of food |
| B.C. Cancer Agency mobile mammography service | Assisted 19,815 women to receive a mammogram |

**Source:** *Our Purpose: Live Life Well: 2016 Corporate Social Responsibility Report*, Loblaw Companies Limited, accessed June 2017 at http://www.loblaw.ca/en/responsibility/reports.html.

**Marketing Tips** showcase valuable thoughts from real-world marketers that are relevant to the topics discussed in each chapter.

## marketing TIP

*"Ubiquitous and always-connected smart devices have rendered old-fashioned paper-based mail, and Canada Post's exclusive privilege to deliver it, far less meaningful."*

*– Deepak Chopra, president and CEO, Canada Post*

**Ask Yourself** checkpoints, found near the end of major sections in each chapter, allow students to test their comprehension of the chapter material before moving on.

## ask YOURSELF

1. What is the first stage in the consumer purchase decision process?
2. What is the name of the grouping of brands that a consumer considers buying out of the set of brands in a product class?
3. What is the term for post-purchase anxiety?

**Marketing NewsFlash boxes** provide exciting, current examples of marketing in action, making the material relevant and memorable. **Focus on Ethics boxes focus** on current topics of ethical and social concern. Discussion questions at the end of each box encourage students to apply marketing concepts and critically assess marketing situations.

## marketing NewsFlash

The McDonald's kiosk and other innovations may appeal to millennials.

### McMillennials

While enjoying a Big Mac™ for lunch in Squamish, British Columbia, a McDonald's customer may wonder if the experience she is enjoying is similar in other locations. Hopping on a plane and travelling to the East Coast, the customer will generally have a consistent experience at a McDonald's in Halifax.

Offering this level of consistency among all its locations is one of the strengths of McDonald's and why its brand is considered among the Top 10 global brands. Maintaining this consistency can pose a challenge with a company with over 1,400 stores in Canada. This can also get costly as innovation is needed to service future generations of customers.

According to *UCLA Magazine*, the millennial demographic is now larger than the baby boomer demographic. Marketers need to understand how to appeal to their desire for high-end brands and technology. Furthermore, millennials seem to be drawn to products from

companies that have similar social and political values. Millennials are comfortable testing new technology and enjoy receiving content in small chunks. Millennials seem to shy away from old business models and look to models that embrace digital technology.

## focus on Ethics

### Social Issues and Consumer Behaviour

One of the most powerful forms of marketing is a natural activity: talking. Telling others your opinion about products and brands. Word-of-mouth marketing is an extraordinary tool for marketers to use to promote their brands, and technology has enabled word-of-mouth promotions, allowing social media to create a forum with mass reach.

In a study involving cultural industries that create, produce, and commercialize anything from musical performances to video games, it was found that professional commentators had a more positive influence on buying decisions than the comments made by ordinary consumers. These opinion leaders have an influence in the future buying decisions of Canadians. When Canadians use online group-buying sites, Internet advertising and electronic word of mouth have a positive influence on consumers.

Being extremely impactful to the future economy as a generation, marketers need to better understand what drives the millennials to word of mouth and loyalty. One key driver to the purchases of millennials is social issues like the environment; millennials reward brands with this focus through word of mouth and loyalty.

Based in Regina, Saskatchewan, tentree International is a company that catches a millennial's attention. It commits to ten trees planted for every product purchased, whether that be directly from its online store, or from one of its over 300 retail partners. By planting millions of trees, tentree is providing employment, protecting wildlife, restoring eco-systems, and educating locals, as well as providing wood for fuel, cooking, and building in impoverished areas. tentree also has partnerships across

Used with permission of tentree International

the world to help identify areas that can benefit from planting trees. ●

#### Questions

1. How does the impact that tentree International makes to the environment and communities across the world influence your decision to purchase clothing from this company?
2. When you consider buying a large ticket item, how much do you consider social issues in your purchase decision?

**AdAlyze** features give students the opportunity to critically evaluate and dissect the message of an actual print advertisement, helping them understand real-world application.

At the end of each chapter, the **Summary** and list of **Key Terms** help students review the chapter's most important concepts. **Hands On…Apply Your Knowledge** assignments direct students back to the beginning of the chapter to solve a practical marketing scenario. **Chapter Vignette… Activity** challenges students to answer questions that the companies in the vignette will face, which test their understanding of chapter topics and their ability to apply them. **Infographic… Data Analysis** features focus students on relevant metrics and asks them to complete an exercise such as updating the data and analyzing changes.

# Superior Learning Solutions and Support

The McGraw-Hill Education team is ready to help instructors assess and integrate any of our products, technology, and services into your course for optimal teaching and learning performance. Whether it's helping your students improve their grades, or putting your entire course online, the McGraw-Hill Education team is here to help you do it. Contact your Learning Solutions Consultant today to learn how to maximize all of McGraw-Hill Education's resources.

For more information, please visit us online: http://www.mheducation.ca/he/solutions

# Acknowledgements

We appreciate the time and effort spent by individual marketers who shared their expertise, knowledge, examples, and videos to make this book real, practical, and a true reflection of marketing in Canada today. This content is spread across chapter-opening vignettes, Marketing NewsFlash and Focus on Ethics boxes, videos, and chapter content. It brings the content alive and makes a difference to marketing education in Canada. We specifically thank the following people for their contributions:

Erin Arthrell, *KAO Canada*
Sameera Banduk, *Thalmic Labs*
Tom Benson, *WildPlay Limited*
Jeff Brettell, *Luxor CRM*
Heather Carney, *KAO Canada*
Glenn Cressman, *Share of Marketing*
Mike Drake, *9Round*
Jason Easton, *General Motors Canada*
Mario Fleury, *Be Sweet Inc.*
Dave Freeman, *Maple Leaf Sports and Entertainment*
David Haggith, *Maple Leaf Sports and Entertainment*
Jon Hamilton, *Canada Post*
Shannon Hudson, *9Round*
Jay Klein, *The PUR Company*
Rob Linke, *Canada Post*
Larry Lubin, *BLUERUSH*
Susan O'Neill, *Delvinia*
Eric Russell, *Be Sweet Inc.*
Andre Samuels, *SeeWhy Learning*
Raffi Sarmazian, *Sarmazian Brothers Flooring*
Rupen Seoni, *Environics Analytics*
Anna Seymour, *Corby Spirit & Wine Ltd.*
Cory Snyder, *SeeWhy Learning*
Lukas Szczurowski, *Luxor CRM*
Allison Whiteside, *Environics Analytics*
Matt Wrobel, *BLUERUSH*

To all the companies who have provided us with images to include in the book, we thank you.

In addition, we extend our appreciation to the reviewers who helped steer the development of this new edition with their comments, feedback, and suggestions:

Marc Ford, *Durham College*
Malcolm Howe, *Niagara College*
Steve Janisse, *St. Clair College*
Deborah Lawton, *Thompson Rivers University*
Antonia Mantonakis, *Brock University*
Nicole Rourke, *St. Clair College*
Sheilagh Seaton, *Okanagan College*
Thomas Wolsey, *NAIT*

We also extend our gratitude to the people at McGraw-Hill Education for their professionalism, namely Sara Braithwaite (portfolio manager), Amy Rydzanicz (content developer), Stephanie Gibson and Janie Deneau (supervising editors), Derek Capitaine (permissions editor), and Mike Kelly (copy editor), who were invaluable in their attention to detail and moving the process forward.

Finally, we would like to thank our families for their enthusiasm and patient support.

**Arsenio Bonifacio and Carol Bureau**

# connect 2

## The Complete Course Solution

**We listened to educators from around the world, learned about their challenges, and created a whole new way to deliver a course.**

Connect2 is a collaborative teaching and learning platform that includes an instructionally designed complete course framework of learning materials that is flexible and open for instructors to easily personalize, add their own content, or integrate with other tools and platforms.

- Save time and resources building and managing a course.
- Gain confidence knowing that each course framework is pedagogically sound.
- Help students master course content.
- Make smarter decisions by using real-time data to guide course design, content changes, and remediation.

### MANAGE — Dynamic Curriculum Builder

Quickly and easily launch a complete course framework developed by instructional design experts. Each Connect2 course is a flexible foundation for instructors to build upon by adding their own content or drawing upon the wide repository of additional resources.

- Easily customize Connect2 by personalizing the course scope and sequence.
- Get access to a wide range of McGraw-Hill Education content within one powerful teaching and learning platform.
- Receive expert support and guidance on how best to utilize content to achieve a variety of teaching goals.

### MASTER — Student Experience

Improve student performance with instructional alignment and leverage Connect2's carefully curated learning resources. Deliver required reading through Connect2's award-winning adaptive learning system.

- Teach at a higher level in class by helping students retain core concepts.
- Tailor in-class instruction based on student progress and engagement.
- Help focus students on the content they don't know so they can prioritize their study time.

### MEASURE — Advanced Analytics

Collect, analyze and act upon class and individual student performance data. Make real-time course updates and teaching decisions backed by data.

- Visually explore class and student performance data.
- Easily identify key relationships between assignments and student performance.
- Maximize in-class time by using data to focus on areas where students need the most help.

### Course Map

The flexible and customizable course map provides instructors full control over the pre-designed courses within Connect2. Instructors can easily add, delete, or rearrange content to adjust the course scope and sequence to their personal preferences.

### Implementation Guide

Each Connect2 course includes a detailed implementation guide that provides guidance on what the course can do and how best to utilize course content based on individual teaching approaches.

### Instructor Resources

A comprehensive collection of instructor resources are available within Connect2. Instructor Support and Seminar Materials provide additional exercises and activities to use for in-class discussion and teamwork.

For more information, please visit www.mheconnect2.com

# Marketing Fundamentals

**M**arketing centres on understanding consumers—how they think, what drives purchases, how purchases are made, where purchases are made, and many other factors. Marketers need to be knowledgeable about the technological changes that impact the path-to-purchase, and understand what new communication options are surfacing. They also need to have insights into the new marketing trends and the ways consumers interact with brands and with companies.

Chapter 1 begins with an introduction to the fundamentals of marketing and an explanation of the building blocks and concepts used by marketers to reach consumers. It also touches on evolving areas to ensure that new approaches are top of mind with readers. We examine The PUR Company, a Canadian company focused on meeting the needs of its customers.

In 2010, Jay Klein noticed that friends and family often expressed their concerns about artificial ingredients in food products, and especially the use of chemical sweeteners. Being an entrepreneur, Jay immediately speculated that if this small "focus group" was looking for products without additives, perhaps a product without chemical sweeteners would have mass appeal. Shortly thereafter came the birth of an upstart, The PUR Company.

Typical of many product categories, chewing gum is at different stages of its life cycle globally. Worldwide, the chewing gum market is growing at 20 percent and is expected to continue this double-digit growth. This trend is not duplicated in North America. The chewing gum industry in Canada declined by 2 percent in 2015, and

**Our Mints take you there.**

Used with permission of The PUR Company

the decline has been even greater in the United States. With Wrigley's and Cadbury Adams holding 96 percent market share in Canada, how can a small company compete? Interestingly, one sub-segment of the chewing gum industry is continuing to grow at a significant pace—specialty gum.

PUR Gum is made in Switzerland where the company can ensure high quality and high standards with regard to the ingredients used and the manufacturing processes employed. PUR Gum's philosophy has been to make simple substitutions to ingredients without sacrificing taste or quality.

Jay Klein remembers the early days: "When I first started PUR, I would walk up and down the aisles of airplanes asking people's opinions about what they thought of the product. People were excited to hear that there was an alternative to chemical sweeteners such as aspartame and were pleasantly surprised that there was no compromise in taste or quality of the gum."

PUR Gum focuses on consumers who make active decisions toward living a healthier lifestyle. The marketing mix (product, price, place, and promotion) for PUR Gum is designed to meet the needs of these consumers and ultimately generate a strong, recurring revenue stream and profit for the company.

> **Product:** PUR Gum is available in eight flavours: Peppermint, Wintergreen, Spearmint, Coolmint, Pomegranate Mint, Bubblegum, Chocolate Mint, and Cinnamon. Each of PUR Gum's varieties offers the same unique benefits, which differentiate PUR from any other brand on the market. The initial concept was based on the elimination of chemical sweeteners, and as a result, PUR uses xylitol, which is an all-natural sweetener. But this is only the beginning of its unique profile. PUR is non-GMO, dairy-free, gluten-free, nut- and soy-free, and vegan.
>
> A new line of PUR Mints has been launched in some of the same minty flavours, as well as with more adventuresome flavours such as Mojito Lime Mint and Tangerine Tango. PUR Mints have the same branding and healthy profile as the chewing gum.
>
> **Price:** PUR Gum is definitely a premium product in the chewing gum category. With a focus on long-term customer loyalty and accessibility, the price of PUR Gum is comparable to the other chewing gum brands. PUR Gum blisters of 9 pieces sell for $1.49 and packages of 55 pieces sell for $4.99.
>
> **Place:** Initially, focus was placed on health food and specialty stores. PUR focused on educating these independent store owners about the benefits of the brand.

Over time, PUR penetrated the stores where its health-conscious consumers shopped. Expansion was done carefully. When PUR felt comfortable that it had market penetration in the independent stores, it pursued listings in larger conventional retailers such as Loblaws and Walgreens. In these stores, PUR is placed with conventional chewing gum. PUR Gum is currently available in 30,000 stores in over 30 countries.

Now, existing customers are familiar with the brand and have better access to it. New customers are exposed to the fresh and unique PUR brand as they contemplate which chewing gum to purchase. PUR Gum has even been sold on the Home Shopping Network in the U.S. PUR can also be purchased directly online from **thepurcompany.com**.

**Promotion:** Mass marketing doesn't match the profile for PUR Gum and its target audience. PUR takes a very targeted approach to its marketing communications.

**Sampling:** PUR lives by the motto "convert curiosity into consumption." In-store sampling has been a core tactic to ensure that potential customers can try PUR and, in an instant, be convinced of its great taste. While sampling the product, customers can be informed about PUR's ingredients and unique values.

**Word of mouth:** Loyal customers are PUR's best asset. Word-of-mouth recommendations by satisfied customers are common. The opinion of satisfied customers is powerful and is another way in which the word is spread about PUR. Take a quick look at PUR's Twitter feed (@ThePURCompany), and the love for PUR by its customers is obvious.

**Digital:** PUR has a focus on social media and creating media buzz. PUR makes use of Twitter, Facebook, Pinterest, Instagram, and LinkedIn to create an ongoing dialogue with customers. This communication can vary from brand-specific messaging to more general "healthy lifestyle" communication. Digital marketing keeps PUR close to its customers and encourages a two-way dialogue.

If you are interested in subscribing to PUR's newsletter, you will receive regular online purchase promotions and the opportunity to be entered into seasonal contests—great incentives for the loyal PUR customer!

**Media buzz:** PUR Gum was featured on *Dragons' Den* in October 2014. This appearance brought national exposure and additional consumer attention to the brand. The Dragons were impressed with PUR's business model, market success, and ability to expand the brand beyond confectionery products.

PUR has been able to focus on a specific *target market* of health-conscious individuals. PUR Gum offers customers a *product* with simple ingredient substitutions that don't compromise taste or quality. PUR is *priced* in line with its competitors and is *available* at a broad range of independent and chain stores. PUR *communicates* with its customers on a personal level and focuses on product trial and loyalty to sustain sales.

While PUR is a relatively small company, its innovation is breathing life into the stagnant chewing gum industry. Gum and mints are not the end of the road for PUR. Jay Klein envisions PUR to be "the #1 healthy lifestyle brand on the market." Stay tuned.[1]

---

## reality CHECK ⊘

As you read Chapter I, refer back to the PUR Gum vignette to answer the following questions:

- Describe the target market for PUR Gum?
- How does PUR Gum differentiate itself from the competition?
- What marketing tools does PUR use to create relationships with its customers?

revenue = έσοδα

# THE ROLE OF MARKETING

**LO 1**

The PUR Gum vignette illustrates the link between business success and carefully designed product, pricing, distribution, and promotional strategies that meet consumer needs, trends, and expectations. Brands need to be differentiated and marketers are challenged to stay current to ensure that their strategies and messages resonate with customers.

Often students believe marketing only consists of television commercials and advertising. In fact, marketers' ultimate objectives are to drive profits for a company, or if working in the non-profit sector, to generate revenue and support to fund programs and run operations. Only one aspect of marketing revolves around promotion, with all other elements—including product, price, and place—required to maximize profitability or generate revenue. Marketing is responsible for a large portion of organizational expenses and, conversely, its revenue. Because of this, marketers also need to be financially savvy, be able to create realistic forecasts, dissect a profit and loss statement, and discuss return on investment (ROI) strategies.

Marketing plays an integral function in any business. Figure 1–1 illustrates how a marketing department interacts with other departments in an organization and with society, as well as the impact that external environmental forces can have on marketing strategies. Marketing is intertwined with both internal and external stakeholders.

Within an organization, marketing needs to work cooperatively with other functional areas. Research and development is a main contributor to new product development. Manufacturing produces a company's products, ensuring quality and cost efficiency. Finance monitors sales and costs. Information systems coordinates e-commerce and digital marketing technologies. Human resources ensures that qualified and innovative people are filling roles within the organization. The success of an organization is dependent upon each of these functions cooperating and working collaboratively toward a common vision.

**Figure 1–1**
The role of the marketing function

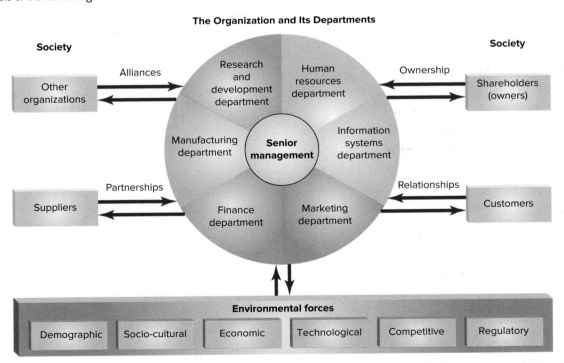

**The Organization and Its Departments**

A marketing department relates to many people, organizations, and forces. Note that the marketing department both *shapes* and *is shaped by* its relationships with these internal and external groups.

A marketing department relates to many external people and organizations. Often marketing is the interface between the customer and the organization. Marketing creates, communicates, and delivers value to potential and existing customers.

Marketing planning starts with a scan of the environment. External demographic, socio-cultural, economic, technological, competitive, and regulatory forces create opportunities that a company can maximize and threats that the company should minimize.

This chapter works to explain the fundamental principles that guide marketing, dispelling the myth that advertising and marketing are one and the same. In this introductory chapter, the basic marketing principles of meeting customer needs and providing customer value are emphasized; we also provide background on the evolution of business approaches. The marketing process and the concept of target markets are explained, as well as the importance of integrating each element of the marketing mix into programs that address consumer needs. Technological advances are resulting in new and evolving marketing approaches that impact current marketing practices in Canada. Time-tested offline marketing strategies are often supplemented by layers of online digital strategies to better reach consumers. Metrics, analytics, evolving marketing regulations, and ethical considerations are reviewed. Finally, there is a discussion on marketing careers.

## FOCUSING ON CUSTOMER NEEDS AND WANTS

Successful marketing is focused on customer needs and wants and developing programs that engage consumers and inspire customer loyalty. A **need** occurs when a person feels deprived of basic necessities such as food, clothing, and shelter. A **want** is a need that is shaped by a person's knowledge, culture, and personality. So if you feel hungry, you have a basic need to eat something. Let's say you then want to eat an apple or a frozen pizza snack because, based on your past experience, you know these will satisfy your hunger need. Effective marketing, in the form of creating an awareness of good products at convenient locations, can clearly shape a person's wants. A principal activity of an organization's marketing department is to research its consumers to understand what they need and want, and the forces that shape those needs and wants.

**need**
Occurs when a person feels deprived of basic necessities.

**want**
A need that is shaped by a person's knowledge, culture, and personality.

However, consumers do not always know what they want and may not want (or be able) to describe what they need or want. In certain categories, such as fragrances or luxury cars, choices are not entirely rational, but partly based on self-image and emotional attachment to a brand, which can be difficult to articulate. In other situations where children or professionals are the consumers, a child may be unable to express ideas while professionals may not have the time to participate in research. Sometimes, marketers may not be asking the right questions.

The digital world adds another level of complexity to market research. On the one hand, it facilitates the online gathering of information; on the other hand, it introduces new communication platforms that challenge marketers to understand the biases that may exist in this new environment.

There are some general insights about how consumers navigate the online environment that marketers need to consider when developing marketing programs. First, the initial point of contact for consumers with a brand is often online—for example, a corporate website, a promotional microsite, a company blog, one of its social media sites, perhaps a third-party product review site, or even a friend's Facebook page. Marketers must therefore understand the role of the online environment in the consumer path-to-purchase and the need to have a solid presence on all these online destinations with information that engages, informs, and motivates. Second, consumers have unlimited opportunities to become informed or distracted. Consumers average ten different touch points per purchase, most of these online. Therefore, consumers must be able to quickly find a company's online site through search engines such as Google or Safari. Websites must be written so that they are highly ranked by the search engines, and so consumers can find them quickly during online searches.[2]

Consider customers who want to purchase a new tablet. Their first stop might be a product review site such as **PCMag.com**. Customers might check out the top ten tablets as rated by the magazine and then narrow down based upon their needs. Customers may want to check out manufacturers' websites (such as **Apple.ca**, **Samsung.ca**, or **Microsoft.ca**) for more detailed specifications on each tablet. Pricing is a big factor, so customers will often check out several websites (such as **Bestbuy.ca** or **Amazon.ca**) to determine the average prices and also the least expensive option. Customers may then decide to go to the bricks-and-mortar store location to talk to a salesperson, and look at and try the tablets. In any case, the connected customer is a much more informed customer.

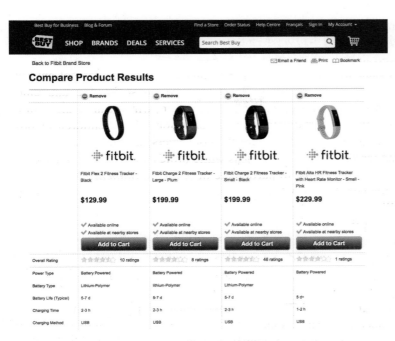

**Compare Product Results**

| | Fitbit Flex 2 Fitness Tracker - Black | Fitbit Charge 2 Fitness Tracker - Large - Plum | Fitbit Charge 2 Fitness Tracker - Small - Black | Fitbit Alta HR Fitness Tracker with Heart Rate Monitor - Small - Pink |
|---|---|---|---|---|
| Price | **$129.99** | **$199.99** | **$199.99** | **$229.99** |
| | Available online, Available at nearby stores | Available online, Available at nearby stores | Available online, Available at nearby stores | Available online, Available at nearby stores |
| | Add to Cart | Add to Cart | Add to Cart | Add to Cart |
| Overall Rating | 10 ratings | 8 ratings | 46 ratings | 1 ratings |
| Power Type | Battery Powered | Battery Powered | Battery Powered | Battery Powered |
| Battery Type | Lithium-Polymer | lithium-Polymer | Lithium-Polymer | |
| Battery Life (Typical) | 5-7 d | 5-7 d | 5-7 d | 5 d+ |
| Charging Time | 2-3 h | 2-3 h | 2-3 h | 1-2 h |
| Charging Method | USB | USB | USB | USB |

The Bestbuy.ca site allows customers to easily compare products.

Used with permission of Best Buy Canada. Prices as of June 26, 2017. Accessed at http://www.bestbuy.ca/

Best Buy understands this process and ensures that the customer's interaction with its site is seamless by providing reviews, price comparisons, and comprehensive product details. Best Buy also has a lowest price guarantee,[3] which accepts the possibility that customers will complete other research and so will match the price of any online or offline competitor.

> Successful marketing is focused on customer needs and wants and developing programs that engage consumers and inspire customer loyalty.

## CREATING CUSTOMER VALUE

Providing customer value can ensure that customers remain loyal over time. Companies must first create products and services that not only meet customer needs but also provide added value versus the competition. Repeat purchases should be encouraged through marketing programs and incentives that focus on generating repeat purchases.

Marketers must be able to communicate a clear, **customer value proposition,** which conveys the unique

combination of benefits received by targeted consumers that will satisfy their needs. These benefits could include quality, price, convenience, delivery, and both before-sale and after-sale service. Walmart's customer value proposition can be clearly described as "everyday low prices for a broad range of products that are always in stock in convenient locations." Marketers work diligently to deliver this value by carefully managing each element of the marketing mix (product, price, place, and promotion) so that this value is evident to consumers who in turn purchase or use the products.

Creating products with added value is often achieved through a combination of (1) product design, (2) pricing strategies, and (3) service elements. For example, Walmart focuses on the lowest price, Mountain Equipment Co-op focuses on providing the best products, PUR Gum highlights its natural

Naturally sweet, just like you.

The PUR Company very simply highlights customer benefits in this ad.

Used with permission of The PUR Company

ingredients and health benefits, and Pizza Pizza (with its award-winning app for mobile ordering) highlights its fast purchase and delivery service as added-value elements for its consumers. Let's examine Amazon to find out how it balances product design, pricing, and service levels to create meaningful products with added value.

Amazon is an online brand that presents customers with outstanding value through a searchable database of well-priced products that are peer-rated and reviewed. It also recommends related products and tracks delivery dates through timely e-mails—design, price, and service all rolled into one. Customized e-mails are sent out to its database of customers to encourage loyalty through special offers, featured products, and the announcement of new releases. Amazon's consistent value proposition continues to result in strong business metrics. It dominates online retailing, evidenced by its ranking as #7 on the National Retail Federation's top 100 list.[4] In 2015, Amazon became the fastest company ever to reach $100 billion in annual sales.[5] Amazon added further value to its brand in Canada with Amazon Prime membership, which for an annual $79 fee provides members with free shipping on hundreds of items, unlimited photo storage, and access to additional flash sales.[6]

## APPEALING TO TARGET MARKETS

In a competitive marketplace, companies cannot satisfy everyone's needs with a single product, and so products are designed to appeal to specific groups of consumers. Marketing follows the principle that, with limited funds, it is better to channel resources toward consumers who are most interested in purchasing a product, rather than target everyone and squander funds on those who have may have little interest. A **target market** can be formally defined as the specific group (or segment) of existing and potential consumers to which marketers direct their marketing efforts. Marketers ensure that each element of the marketing mix appeals to the characteristics of the target market.

**target market**
The specific group or segment(s) of existing and potential consumers to which marketers direct their marketing efforts.

**marketing mix**
The 4 Ps—product, price, place, and promotion.

**product**
Attributes that make up a good, a service, or an idea, including product design, features, colour, packaging, warranty, and service levels.

**price**
What is exchanged for a product, including the expected regular retail or sale price.

**place**
Distribution channels, retail formats, and merchandising used to sell a product.

**promotion**
Communication tools needed to inform consumers about a product, including advertising, public relations, sales promotion, direct response, event marketing, sponsorship, online approaches, and personal selling.

## COORDINATING THE MARKETING MIX

**LO 2** The elements of the **marketing mix**—known as the 4 Ps: product, price, place, and promotion—are all controllable factors that need to be carefully managed by marketers to ensure that they are well-coordinated and that each appeals to the distinct characteristics of the target market. There is no point in having an amazing product if consumers cannot find it at the retail stores they frequent or online through a search. If the product is priced too high for the target market, it will be unaffordable; if it's priced too low, it will simply portray the wrong image. If marketers promote a product on TV, but the target market rarely watches TV, instead spending time online, then the message will not be received. In all instances, marketers need to understand what makes their consumers tick, what they desire, and how best to communicate with them. This information is often clarified by market research on consumer behaviour to help determine how marketing efforts can be designed or modified to meet the needs of the target market. Marketers use this information to improve marketing programs and coordinate each element of the marketing mix. These elements are all included in a brand's annual marketing plan where details for each element of the marketing mix are outlined, together with the required budgets and profit and loss statements for the brand. Chapter 15 provides more details on this area.

The elements of the marketing mix can be simply described as follows:

1. **Product:** All the attributes that make up a good, a service, or an idea, to satisfy the customer need, including product design, features, colour, packaging, warranty, and service levels.

2. **Price:** What is exchanged for a product, including the expected regular retail or sale price.

3. **Place:** The way in which your product gets to the consumer, including the distribution channels, retail formats, and merchandising used to sell a product.

4. **Promotion:** The tools needed to communicate with consumers about a product, including advertising, public relations, sales promotion, direct response, event marketing, sponsorship, online approaches, and personal selling.

*Marketers need to understand what makes their consumers tick.*

*The digital reality has made the marketing mix __more complex.__*

Axe targets the young male segment.

Robcartorres/Shutterstock.com

Dove aims to improve self-esteem and body image for women.

©Phil Date | Dreamstime.com

We look at two Unilever products, Axe and Dove, to review how marketers at this company carefully craft each element of the marketing mix to appeal to two distinct target groups. Axe, targeting males aged 18 to 24, is a line of body washes, deodorants, and hair care products.[7] All Axe products come in black packaging with intriguing names such as Apollo, Black Chill, and Dark Temptation. Axe shampoo bottles are shaped like barbells—can't get much more masculine than that, right? The product line is relatively inexpensive, making it affordable for its young male target audience. It is merchandised at retail in superstores, drugstores, and grocery stores. Promotion has focused on how Axe could make a man confident and attractive to the opposite sex. This strategy catapulted Axe to the #1 men's fragrance brand in Canada.[8] Today, promotional efforts focus on expanding to a more inclusive view of masculinity, encouraging men to find their own definition of attractiveness.[9] What has been maintained in its messaging is that Axe is the one common element that makes all men masculine. Promotional elements include television commercials and print ads supplemented by a strong online and social media presence.

On the other hand, Dove targets everyday women of any age. The Dove brand was positioned as a soap for many years; now Dove is a beauty brand. Dove's products for women are packaged in white or pink bottles.[10] The products are sold at a premium price, reflecting its new positioning in the beauty category. Its "Real Beauty" campaign began in 2004 after a study was conducted by Unilever to help understand how women felt about their appearance. When the results showed that only 2 percent of women would describe themselves as beautiful, the iconic "Campaign for Real Beauty" was launched.[11] Dove has evolved this message of self-esteem and inspiration by partnering with associations such as Girl Guides/Girl Scouts and other community thought leaders to extend its messages worldwide.

With both Axe and Dove, Unilever aligned each element of the marketing mix to appeal to its specific target group. Neither product is geared to appeal to everyone. Instead, Axe targets young men and Dove targets women of all ages. It is important to note that, over time, marketers gather extensive information on their target markets, being able to identify purchase motivation that goes beyond age and gender into behavioural and psychological motivation, which are important determinants in many purchases. In this way, marketers define their target markets in more complex terms, including elements such as likes, dislikes, motivation, interests, and concerns.

The digital reality has made the marketing mix more complex. Marketers realize that each element now has many layers that need to be managed, no easy task in the online environment. A product, for example, now has many faces: offline in stores and online on corporate websites, on blogs, on promotional microsites, on apps, and on social media sites where marketers carefully monitor and join conversations to engage consumers. This is made even more complex by the different technical requirements needed for websites to render appropriately on different mobile devices.

## ask YOURSELF

1. *What is the role of marketing in an organization?*

2. *What is a target market?*

3. *What is the marketing mix?*

# THE MARKETING PROCESS

The **marketing process** involves (1) identifying consumer needs, (2) managing the marketing mix to meet these needs, and (3) realizing profits, or in the case of non-profits, securing revenue support or providing services to those in need (see Figure 1–2). The marketing process requires marketers to understand their customers and apply strategic, analytical, and creative-thinking skills. Throughout the cycle, marketers constantly evaluate program success, recommending and implementing changes to strengthen efforts. Let's consider Amazon Prime and how this process works.

Amazon Prime was created to offer regular Amazon customers the ability to have free two-day delivery on an unlimited number of products, with no minimum order size. Shoppers prefer to have free shipping when purchasing online, but many sites have minimum order sizes or longer shipping times. The price is for Amazon Prime is $79 CDN per year to provide value to the customer.[12] The average Canadian online shopper spends $1,151 annually, resulting in potentially high shipping charges.[13] Amazon offers a 30-day free trial, after which time the customer is charged the annual fee. The free trial eliminates barriers to trial and allows customers to see the value prior to spending any money. Although there is a charge for Amazon Prime, customers still feel as though they have free shipping, without any barriers.[14] Amazon Prime is available online, on the **Amazon.ca** site, where the customer is already shopping. Customers also receive an offer to purchase Amazon Prime at checkout, once they have seen their shipping charges for the order in their shopping cart.[15] Amazon Prime has been communicated using simple and clear messaging, through e-mail promotion (to existing Amazon customers), through online promotion (on its site), and through social media. While paying the shipping charges can be very costly to customers, it is estimated that there are between 3 and 10 million Amazon Prime subscribers, and that they spend more than three times what they would without the subscription.[16]

Marketers are ultimately responsible for generating company profits (or revenues and support for non-profit organizations), and marketing programs are designed with this end in mind. Formally, **marketing** is described as the process of planning and managing goods, services, or ideas to meet consumer needs and organizational objectives. It includes the development of these products and the pricing, distribution, and promotion designed to make a profit and generate revenue (or support) for an organization.[17]

**Exchange** is the trade of things of value between buyers and sellers so that each benefits. In simple terms, the trade is money for a product or service. However, there is more to exchange than just money—customers may provide referrals to a tutoring service or to a fitness club in return for discounts or additional services. A consumer may volunteer time with a non-profit organization such as the Heart and Stroke Foundation, which in return may satisfy the consumer's need to support the cause. In the online environment, exchange is often more complex. In many instances, websites may not be selling a product at all but instead providing free information or a service that drives traffic to their website, where advertising is used to help pay for the service. The numbers of page views

**marketing process**
The process of (1) identifying consumer needs, (2) managing the marketing mix to meet these needs, and (3) realizing profits.

**marketing**
The process of planning and managing goods, services, or ideas to meet consumer needs and organizational objectives. It includes the conception of these products and the pricing, promotion, and distribution programs designed to make a profit and generate revenue or support for an organization.

**exchange**
The trade of things of value between buyers and sellers so that each benefits.

## Figure 1–2
The marketing process

| 1 Identify consumer needs | 2 Manage the marketing mix to meet consumer needs | 3 Realize profits for a company (or objectives for non-profit organizations) |

A process that focuses on consumer needs.

*The marketing process requires marketers to understand their customers and apply strategic, analytical, and creative-thinking skills.*

to the website and data on its demographics are used to sell this advertising space and generate revenue for the website. Many news websites, such as **Macleans.ca**, and web portals, such as **Google.ca** and **Canada.com**, fall into this category.

## WHAT CAN BE MARKETED?

**LO 4** In marketing, the term *product* encompasses goods, services, and ideas. These products can all be marketed to encourage people to buy something or, as in the case of ideas, to encourage support.

A **good** is a product that is tangible—you can touch it and own it. Examples are a can of Red Bull or a pair of Adidas running shoes. Adidas running shoes are tangible products that are marketed in different styles and colours, sold at a premium price, merchandised in sporting goods and shoe stores, and promoted with ads and social media with a focus on performance and style. Adidas achieves publicity through the sponsorship of athletes and sporting events. Adidas repeats its message across all forms of social media and demonstrates the value of its shoes on its YouTube channel.

A **service** is an intangible product you cannot touch. It does not result in something you can own. A physiotherapy session, a vacation, or going to a movie are examples of services. When you watch a movie at Cineplex Entertainment, marketers have worked to ensure the experience encourages you to return. Movie selection, theatre layout, seating, loyalty programs, and concession items have all been carefully selected and designed with the comfort and needs of the target market in mind. The Cineplex-Scotiabank SCENE loyalty rewards program has

*Ideas can also be marketed.*

been created with rewards that encourage customers to return to Cineplex Entertainment theatres time after time to collect points and receive benefits such as discounted concession items, free movies, or discounted DVDs.[18]

Ideas can also be marketed. An **idea** is a concept that typically looks for support. An example is Mothers Against Drunk Driving (MADD) Canada. MADD Canada's mission is "to stop impaired driving and to support victims of this violent crime." Statistics show that on average, four Canadians are killed every day by impaired drivers and another 175 are injured. MADD increases the awareness of the impact of impaired driving through campaigns such as Project Red Ribbon, when millions of red ribbons are sold each year. It has been estimated that almost 37,000 lives have been saved through the efforts of MADD and its awareness campaigns.[19] Another example is the Movember Foundation campaign that asks men to grow moustaches in November to support men's health initiatives. For about this campaign, see the Marketing NewsFlash box, "Marketing the 'Mo.'"[20]

Many successful marketers today launch products with layers of goods, services, and ideas to connect with consumers. For example, you may decide to purchase a new smartphone. You select an iPhone from Apple. This smartphone comes with 16 GB of storage, weighing 130g, and is 7 mm thick and 4.7 inches long (*product*). Once you begin to use your phone, you download songs using iTunes. You also like to shop, so you sign up for Apple Pay so that you can use your iPhone to pay for purchases (*services*).

**good**
A product you can touch and own.

**service**
A product that is intangible; an activity, benefit, or satisfaction that you cannot touch.

**idea**
A concept that typically looks for support.

**market**
Potential consumers with both the willingness and the ability to buy.

### *ask* YOURSELF

1. What steps are involved in the marketing process?

2. What are the differences between goods, services, and ideas?

3. Are credit cards goods, services, or ideas?

## WHAT IS A MARKET?

The term **market** is used in marketing to describe potential consumers who have both the willingness and the ability to buy a product. Importantly, just being

# Marketing the "Mo"

As the seasons change to winter, it is inevitable that we see our male colleagues, friends, and family growing facial hair that lasts for a full month's time.

The Movember Foundation was started in Australia in 2004 by two friends. What started as an idea to bring the moustache back in fashion has dovetailed into a fundraising campaign for men's health. Those two friends were able to entice 30 of their friends to grow moustaches in 2003 for no money. They then thought about the potential power of this platform and subsequently formalized Movember. The Movember Foundation focuses on four specific issues: prostate cancer, inactivity, testicular cancer, and mental health.

It is a fairly simple idea: Men grow moustaches during the month of November and have friends and family sponsor their endeavour. What evolved from this simple idea has been historic!

In 2007, Movember was launched in Canada. Since its inception, the Movember campaign in Canada has raised approximately $700 million. In fact, the Movember Foundation is one of the largest investors in men's health in the world. Movember has created its own language and culture. "Mo," "Mo Bro," "Mo Sista," and "Mo Mentor" are just a few of the

terms that supporters are quite familiar with. Advice about how to grow a "Mo" and how to eat with a "Mo" is shared on the foundation's website.

Throughout the ten years it has been in existence in Canada, Movember has consistently managed to maintain its relevance without brand fatigue by diversifying the initiatives it creates, while maintaining the foundation of men's health.

To further the cause, Movember has partnered with corporations including Visa, the NHL, Harley-Davidson, and GoodLife Fitness to introduce MOVE. MOVE encourages donations for individuals who commit to MOVE-ing every day during the month of November. This expands participation beyond growing a moustache.

Wanting to extend its message beyond the month of November, Movember Canada has recognized April as Testicular Cancer Awareness Month, with a #knowthynuts campaign. This campaign is meant to encourage men to complete their own self-exams to ensure early detection of testicular cancer, a type of cancer most common in younger men.

Why does growing a moustache work? Setting up a very masculine competition aligns well with the platform of men's health. Pitting

Used with permission of Movember Foundation

men against each other to see who can grow the best "Mo" takes advantage of their competitive spirit. There is also a touch of humour around growing moustaches, not a current fashion trend.

Movember is a month-long opportunity for participants to outwardly show their support for men's health, generating conversation, exchange of knowledge, and ultimately donations to the Movember Foundation. ●

## Questions

1. How do not-for-profits stay relevant?

2. How do partnerships help spread a non-profit organization's message?

willing to buy a product does not constitute a market. For example, the Nintendo Wii is a gaming console that has been targeted to families. The Wii has a multitude of action games, such as those in its Super Mario/Luigi franchise, as well as interactive games that simulate bowling, golf, baseball, and boxing. Although the Wii is used by kids, kids are not considered to be the product's market because they do not have the money

or the physical means to buy the product. The market would consist of parents with children up to their teenage years.[21]

The Wii touches on an interesting marketing issue: Sometimes the market, target market, and consumers are different groups of people, and marketers need to decide on a balance of whom should be targeted with their programs. While the market for the Nintendo Wii is parents with children, the marketing also needs to focus on the children, who may exert some influence over their parents. Therefore, we see that the target market for the product includes both children and parents. Finally, the consumers of the product, in this case the users, are mainly the children, not the parents, and marketers need to ensure that the product is designed with their abilities and interests in mind, without overlooking the parents, who are the main decision-makers in the purchase process.

# THE EVOLUTION OF BUSINESS PHILOSOPHIES

**LO 5** Marketing was not always the driving force in business philosophy. Until the 1930s, businesses were in the **production orientation** stage. This stage focused on manufacturing, which until the Industrial Revolution, was not a widespread phenomenon. Manufactured goods tended to sell, regardless of their quality, because they were in short supply. Consumer needs were not a priority. It was during this era that the Ford Motor Company introduced the assembly line, manufacturing cars in a fast and efficient way. The second stage, from the 1930s to the 1960s, was the **sales orientation** stage. This stage focused on selling as many products as possible. The market had become more competitive, production had become more efficient, and products were in abundance. Companies started to hard-sell to make a profit, and consumer needs were still not a major consideration. As the marketplace became more competitive, businesses developed more-sophisticated approaches. In the 1960s, consumer needs became more important, and the marketing concept became the focus of businesses. The **marketing orientation** stage focuses on the idea that an organization should strive to satisfy the needs of consumers while also trying to achieve an organization's goals. An organization that has a marketing orientation focuses its efforts on continuously collecting information about customers' needs, sharing this information across departments, and using it to create customer value.

Marketing has evolved from a discipline with a short-term focus on transactions to one that now also focuses on building long-term customer relationships. This **relationship marketing** stage sees organizations considering the lifetime value of their customers and striving to offer better services, along with higher-quality products to encourage long-term relationships with customers. Over the last few years, relationship marketing has included a greater use of social media, and an increased focus on customer relationship management and corporate social responsibility to create meaningful relationships. These approaches emphasize customer retention and ongoing customer satisfaction rather than short-term transactions. Organizations carefully collect and use information on customer interests to develop relationships with customers and retain their loyalty. Businesses recognize that improved customer relationships can result in increased customer loyalty, improved customer retention levels, and greater profits for an organization. (Figure 1–3 summarizes this evolution of business philosophies.)

Database technology has surfaced as a tool that facilitates relationship marketing by putting a focus on **customer relationship management (CRM)** for the marketing industry. This approach is rooted in the knowledge that it is less expensive to service and maintain current customers than to constantly acquire new ones. CRM identifies a firm's most-valued customers and builds

**production orientation**
Focusing organizational efforts on the manufacture of goods.

**sales orientation**
Focusing organizational efforts on selling as many products as possible.

**marketing orientation**
Focusing organizational efforts to collect and use information about customers' needs to create customer value.

**relationship marketing**
When organizations create long-term links with customers, employees, suppliers, and other partners to increase loyalty and customer retention.

**customer relationship management (CRM)**
The overall process of building and maintaining profitable customer relationships by delivering superior customer value and satisfaction.

**Figure 1–3**
The evolution of business philosophies

*customer value proposition relates to the benefits customers receive*

| Production orientation | 1930s | Sales orientation | 1960s | Marketing orientation | 1990s | Relationship marketing orientation |

*Promotion is one aspect of marketing*

programs to appeal to their needs. It systematically identifies what will lead to customer satisfaction and profitable brand loyalty. It is often facilitated by CRM software and databases. Formally, CRM is defined as the process of building and developing long-term customer relationships by delivering customer value and satisfaction.[22]

We can look to the Canadian retail industry to better understand CRM and to find out how it is applied. In its simplest form, CRM involves the occasional customer e-mail about upcoming sales or advanced notice of new product launches. In a more advanced state, it includes sophisticated customer loyalty programs that reward continued purchases and usage. Air Miles is an example of a widely recognized and sophisticated CRM program that partners with brands to provide members with rewards.

Retailers use CRM loyalty programs to help secure a greater share of wallet from their customers. Share of wallet refers to the percentage of a customer's purchases that a company has in a specific product category. They use loyalty cards to track individual purchases and then correlate the data with offers and incentives to determine what works best. Offers are then customized to meet their purchase habits. Pioneers of CRM in Canada include Hudson's Bay with its HBC Rewards card and Shoppers Drug Mart with its Optimum card.

Advanced CRM considers customer lifetime value and what offers will keep customers loyal over their lifetime. Customer lifetime value refers to the potential sales that will be generated by a customer if that customer remains loyal to that company for a lifetime. Let's look at a simple example. If a pregnant woman buys prenatal vitamins at a store that uses CRM tracking software, such as through its loyalty cards, in time she may start receiving coupons for diapers, baby food, and tips on infant nutrition; her prenatal purchase has triggered sophisticated computer programs to recognize her eventual need for baby products. As this woman's needs evolve, and as the children get older, the offers may change to include over-the-counter medications for toddlers or school supplies for youths. This is one of the ways that companies can use CRM to encourage customer loyalty. CRM is covered in

more detail in Chapter 14.

Finally, corporate social responsibility (CSR) has become an important part of the relationship marketing stage, with companies realizing that consumers want to be associated with companies that share their values and interests. CSR is a concept where organizations voluntarily consider the well-being of society and the environment by taking responsibility for how their businesses impact consumers, customers, suppliers, employees, shareholders, communities, the environment, and society in general. In this manner, CSR programs become part of a brand's fabric and help to build long-term relationships and solidify brand connections with consumers. The apparel company, tentree, provides an excellent example of CSR being integrated into the brand itself (see the Marketing NewsFlash box, "tentree—Making CSR the Brand!").[23]

CSR initiatives can range from the simple to the complex, and typically include one of three approaches. In its simplest forms, CSR can involve (1) the sponsorship and/or spearheading of community programs, and (2) the sponsorship and/or involvement in fundraising initiatives for charitable organizations. In its most advanced form, CSR is used (3) as a business philosophy of an organization that implements socially responsible business practices to positively impact the community at large.

Loblaw Companies Limited provides an excellent example of a company that has demonstrated a commitment to give back to the community and operate in a responsible manner. Loblaw's CSR strategy has three pillars: sourcing, environment, and community. Responsible sourcing targets many components of the supply chain for Loblaw, from the working conditions of suppliers' employees, to the elimination of concerning ingredients from products, to a priority focus on informative labelling. The environmental pillar targets waste reduction by decreasing the use of plastic shopping bags (10 billion to date) and donating perishable food. With a focus on energy efficiency, Loblaw was able to reduce electricity consumption by 1.8 percent. Community giving at Loblaw includes the donation of $65 million to local charities and not-for-profits through the President's Choice Children's Charity and the Shoppers LOVE.YOU initiatives. Loblaw donated $5 million to the Canadian Red Cross to support residents affected by the Fort McMurray, Alberta wildfires. The addition of Shoppers Drug Mart to the Loblaw portfolio expanded its definition of community to include accessible health care. To this end, Loblaw has implemented in-store wellness programs, and has supported the expansion of the role of pharmacists in disease screening and awareness.[24]

**share of wallet**
The percentage of a customer's purchases that a company has in a specific product category.

**customer lifetime value**
The potential sales that will be generated by a customer if that customer remains loyal to that company for a lifetime.

**corporate social responsibility (CSR)**
When organizations voluntarily consider the well-being of society by taking responsibility for how their businesses impact consumers, customers, suppliers, employees, shareholders, communities, the environment, and society in general.

# tentree—Making CSR the Brand!

Corporate social responsibility (CSR) initiatives can often seem as though they were an afterthought or an add-on to corporate strategy. For tentree International, CSR is its brand!

The founders of tentree were inspired by TOMS, the shoe company best known for its promise to give a pair of shoes to a needy child for every pair of TOMS shoes purchased. TOMS' focus of giving has expanded beyond shoes to include programs to improve water quality, vision, safe birthing practices, and bullying. To date, these programs have impacted people in over 70 countries.

tentree was established in 2012 by three enterprising friends from Regina, Saskatchewan. They founded tentree on the belief that consumers were savvy enough to be concerned about the impact of their purchase decisions on the environment. It turns out they were right!

tentree's brand is a direct take on its promise, as tentree will plant ten trees for every item of apparel purchased. It doesn't stop there—tentree products are produced in factories that are socially and environmentally responsible and that also maintain fair labour practices. tentree utilizes locally sourced materials for use in its apparel, and it focuses on reducing pollution from manufacturing through to its shipping practices. This vision has proven to be a compelling message for consumers.

Each piece of tentree apparel comes with a code. Consumers can register the code and track where their trees are planted (out of ten countries worldwide that tentree is planting in). tentree has relied on social media and word of mouth to grow its business. With over 350,000 likes on Facebook, 2.1 million followers on Instagram, and 25,000 followers on Twitter, tentree engages in an active dialogue with its target audience.

The socially concerned consumer is alive and well across the globe. A recent Nielsen study showed that 55 percent of global online consumers were willing to pay more for products from companies that were socially responsible. The likelihood of embracing social responsibility is even greater in Asia Pacific, Latin America and the Middle East/Africa. Canada is only the launching pad for tentree's impactful strategy. ●

## Questions

1. What strategies do you believe that tentree should focus on to remain relevant?

2. Do you believe that tentree is a fad, or is it here to stay?

Responsible sourcing is a key pillar of Loblaw's CSR strategy.

Valentino Visentini/Alamy Stock Photo

# Infographic

## Corporate Citizenship: What Does The Research Say?

Andrea Donlan, President and CEO of Manifest Communications Inc.

Companies in the early stages of creating their corporate citizenship program, are always asking: "What does the research say about this so that I can convince my boss this is a good idea?"

Here are the 15 most important stats you can have at the ready to reinforce the idea that corporate citizenship can deliver both social and business benefits.

# CORPORATE GIVING IS GROWING

**MORE THAN HALF OF COMPANIES HAVE SIGNATURE CAUSES OR PROGRAMS** to guide their decision making processes and share their charitable giving story.[1]

**55%**

Canadian companies donate approximately **$2,295 billion** in cash each year.

That's up by more than **581%** since 1990.[1]

Giving is trending upward in Canada with companies contributing **1.1%** of pre-tax profits.[1]

## Society is increasingly expecting businesses to play a more active social role

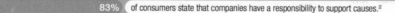

- **83%** of consumers state that companies have a responsibility to support causes.[2]
- **77%** of university graduates consider a company's commitment to society when determining where to work.[3]
- **72%** of employees wish their employers would do more to support a cause or social issue that they care about.[4]
- **55%** of consumers believe CEOs need to make a long-term commitment to address social issues.[5]
- **52%** of consumers believe CEOs need to motivate employees to take part in societal issues.[6]

### Customers expect you to make them aware of your charitable efforts

**80%** of Canadian consumers say that it is critical for companies to make consumers aware of their community investment efforts.[5]

**61%** of global consumers don't think that companies are giving them enough details about their efforts, including the amounts donated to charity.[6]

###  CUSTOMERS REWARD COMPANIES THAT GIVE BACK

- **92%** of Canadians have a more positive image of a company that supports a cause they care about.
- **91%** of consumers are likely to switch brands to one associated with a good cause (price and quality being equal).
- **41%** of Canadian consumers said they would be willing to pay extra for products that are committed to positive social and environmental impact.[7]
- **37%** of Millennials are attracted to cause marketing promotions where their purchase contributes to a charitable contribution.[8]
- **47%** of consumers have bought a brand at least monthly that supports a cause – this is up from 32% in 2010.[5]

SOURCES
1. Corporate Giving in Canada. Imagine Canada.
2. Do Well Do Good. 2010.
3. 2007 Cone Cause Evolution Survey.
4. 2006 Millennial Cause Study.
5. 2013 Cone Communications/Echo Global CSR Study.
6. 2010 Cone Cause Evolution Study.
7. Nielsen 2013 Consumers Who Care Study.
8. American Millennials: Deciphering the Enigma Generation.

Andrea Donlan is the President and CEO of Manifest Communications Inc. – a communications agency focused exclusively on social change.

@IfManifest ifmanifest.com

Used with permission of Manifest Communications

## Loblaw Community Giving in 2016

| | |
|---|---|
| Charitable donations | $65 million |
| President's Choice Children's Charity | 449,000 children received nutritious meals |
| Food drives | $2.8 million + 1.8 million pounds of food |
| B.C. Cancer Agency mobile mammography service | Assisted 19,815 women to receive a mammogram |

**Source:** *Our Purpose: Live Life Well: 2016 Corporate Social Responsibility Report*, Loblaw Companies Limited, accessed June 2017 at http://www.loblaw.ca/en/responsibility/reports.html.

Many organizations now include CSR components in their business plans, issuing annual CSR reports and CSR plans to ensure they live up to their directives. Loblaw has published an annual corporate social responsibility report every year since 2007. *Maclean's* magazine has partnered with Sustainalytics, a leading organization in sustainability analytics, to determine Canada's top 50 socially responsible companies by reviewing their environmental, social, and governance approaches to business. Its latest report points out that best-in-class organizations perceive CSR as fundamental to the fabric of their organizations. Among the organizations that rank highly on the *Maclean's* Top 50 Social Responsible Companies 2015 are Telus and Pepsico. Recognized in the telecom/electronics category. Telus's data centres consume 80 percent less

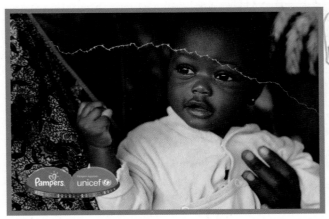

Procter & Gamble partners with UNICEF to support tetanus vaccinations in underprivileged areas.

Courtesy of Procter & Gamble Babycare Western Europe and Unicef/United Nations Children's Fund. Used with permission.

power than a typical data centre. Telus is also a major sponsor of We Day, and through its employee volunteer program called "Telus Days of Giving," over 337,000 volunteer hours have been invested in communities across Canada.[25] Pepsico was recognized in the food and beverage category for reducing water usage by 40 percent at its manufacturing plants and being the first in Canada to adopt all-electric, green-powered delivery trucks.[26]

Procter & Gamble provides another great example of CSR. Pampers has partnered with UNICEF since 2006 to battle maternal and neonatal tetanus (MNT) in underprivileged areas. This partnership has funded 300 million vaccines, protecting 100 million mothers and babies around the world.[27]

Unfortunately, a few companies have taken advantage of the environmental movement by deceptively positioning products as being green, when in fact they do little to help the environment. This has given rise to the term **greenwashing,** which refers to the deceptive use of marketing practices to imply that a good, service, or organization is environmentally friendly. Dawn dish soap has come under fire in the past due to its claims that "Dawn helps save wildlife." All the while, triclosan, an antibacterial agent declared toxic to aquatic life, is an ingredient in the dish soap. Procter & Gamble maintains that it is complying with current regulatory requirements in Canada.[28] The Canadian Marketing Association provides a number of resources on how to market environmentally friendly products to help reduce unethical business practices. Its website at **www.the-cma.org** includes green tips and information on best practices.

The marketing community is also putting an increased focus on the well-being of society and the environment in its marketing programs. It is commonplace to now see marketing initiatives that focus on the consumer and the well-being of society, an approach described as the **societal marketing concept.** One of the pioneers of societal marketing is The Body Shop. The Body Shop was started on the belief that only natural ingredients should be used in products and that those products should not be tested on animals. Back in 1976, this was a very original business strategy. Since that time, The Body Shop has supported a range of causes including human rights, environmental protection, and fair and ethical trade. In 2016, The Body Shop launched the Limited Edition "Change" Hemp Hand Protector. The

**greenwashing**
The deceptive use of marketing practices to give the impression that a good, service, or organization is environmentally friendly.

**societal marketing concept**
Marketing programs that focus on the consumer *and* the well-being of society.

**digital marketing**

Using digital technology to reach consumers through computers, gaming devices, out-of-home electronic screens, or mobile devices such as smartphones and tablets.

packaging was developed by a world-renowned street artist named Eine, and the product sports a strong message of CHANGE on the label. A portion of the revenue from each unit sold is donated to The Body Shop Foundation to support a range of projects dedicated to improving the planet, oceans, people, and animals.[29]

# NEW AND EVOLVING MARKETING PRACTICES

**LO 6** Marketing today focuses on meeting short-term consumer needs and generating immediate company profits, as well as the long-term viability and sustainability of a business through the transparent connections it makes with its business partners and by creating meaningful customer relationships and community initiatives. Many new tools are now available for marketers to communicate organizational approaches and product benefits. In this section, we review some of the latest new and evolving marketing practices.

Some of the recent marketing approaches include customer relationship management programs and corporate social responsibility (as already discussed), with newly evolving areas including (1) digital marketing, including content marketing, mobile marketing, and social media marketing; (2) real-time marketing; (3) experiential marketing; (4) partnership marketing; (5) metrics and analytics; and (6) new marketing regulations and ethical considerations.

## DIGITAL MARKETING

The backdrop to new and evolving marketing approaches is the rapid adoption of Internet technology by our society, with consumers and businesses having access to lower-priced computers, multiple mobile devices, high-speed Internet connections, and cloud computing. In addition, many free online services are available, such as e-mail, online search, cloud file storage, and social media platforms.

Digital technology has changed consumer behaviour, with many people using smartphones and tablets to

Digital marketing provides many online communication tools.

©3dm1983/Dreamstime.com/GetStock.com

### Internet Usage—Rankings by Country

Average monthly data per visitor

| Rank | Country | Website Visits/Month | Hours per Visitor/Month |
|------|---------|---------------------|------------------------|
| 1. | Canada | 90 | 36.7 |
| 2. | U.S. | 80 | 35.2 |
| 3. | U.K. | 75 | 33.0 |
| 4. | Italy | 74 | 33.5 |
| 5. | Russia | 73 | 32.5 |

**Source:** Paul Rich, Ben Martin, and Leah Jenkins, "2015 Canada Digital Future in Focus," comScore, March 27, 2015. https://www.comscore.com/Insights/Presentations-and-Whitepapers/2015/2015-Canada-Digital-Future-in-Focus.

stay connected with friends, family, and work throughout the day and to get media updates on their areas of interest. In 2016, there were over 30 million subscribers to mobile devices in Canada.[30] The number of people who use multiple platforms on a regular basis is approaching the majority. People in Canada are the most connected in the world, spending over 36 hours per month online. Online video viewing is particularly high, with Canadians logging an average of 25 hours per month watching online videos. Social networking is also very popular, with people increasingly accessing social networks on mobile devices.[31]

The widespread use of digital technology in Canada is the most important trend impacting how marketers do business. Digital technology has changed the path-to-purchase and drives how consumers gather information, connect with each other and businesses, and purchase products. The amount of time consumers spend on the Internet has changed significantly over the last few years, prompting marketers to increasingly use digital marketing approaches to reach consumers. **Digital marketing** is an approach that uses electronic means to reach consumers, whether this be through computers, gaming devices, out-of-home electronic screens, or mobile devices such as smartphones and tablets.

**Starbucks is serious about its customers' ideas!**

FotograFFF/Shutterstock.com

Digital marketing includes many stellar online tools, such as display advertising, affiliate marketing, search engine marketing, search engine optimization, pay-per-click advertising, mobile marketing, e-mail marketing, and social media marketing. An example of an integrated digital marketing campaign can be seen with Starbucks. Starbucks is heavily invested in social media with record-breaking engagement with its Facebook, Twitter, and Instagram platforms. Starbucks has tried to maximize its mobile interactions with customers by encouraging mobile payments, which decrease the time that a customer stands in line. With over 200,000 ideas submitted to the My Starbucks Idea website, Starbucks shows its customers that it values their suggestions.[32] When customers wanted molasses cookies back on the menu, they got it! When customers asked for more choices when they order a frappuccino, Starbucks offered them thousands of combinations with the However-You-Want-It Frappuccino! As Starbucks' digital presence has increased, it has seen a similar increase in its stock performance.[33]

## Content Marketing

Integral to the success of any digital marketing campaign is the concept of **content marketing,** when brands or companies reach out by creating and sharing expertise and/or brand information that is designed to inform and engage using tools such as research papers, e-books, infographics, videos, blogs, webinars, e-newsletters, case studies, podcasts, and events. This information can be readily found with search engines.[34] Many business-to-business marketers use this approach to attract new customers by providing valuable tools and expertise to help companies manage their businesses.

General Electric (GE) is a company known for its technological innovation across a broad range of industries including energy, health, finance, and transportation. GE uses a variety of platforms to engage customers. *GE Reports* started as a blog and evolved into a magazine that is a go-to source for industry information for marketers and innovators in the industries that GE serves. Storytelling is a key component of the reports, providing relevant information that includes the brand story. Content is also widely available on GE's multiple YouTube channels. The videos not only highlight GE's innovations but also allow customers to tell their stories and reinforce the success of their partnerships with GE. A series of videos reinforce key innovations and trends, and create another point of engagement with GE's customers.[35]

## Mobile Marketing

**Mobile marketing** occurs when organizations communicate and engage with their audience with any mobile device or network. The communication can occur using elements such as smartphones, tablets, or handheld gaming devices. Mobile marketing uses specific marketing tools that render appropriately on mobile devices; these tools include apps, mobile web, mobile advertising, and various mobile sales promotional tools that we discuss in detail in Chapter 13.[36]

Marketers understand the popularity of mobile devices in Canada and increasingly use mobile marketing approaches to reach consumers both in and out of the home or work environment. Common approaches include short-code messaging to donate to charities. Mobile apps are also created to facilitate interactions, such as the Swiss Chalet app that allows for easy ordering on a mobile device and the Weather Network app for weather updates.

Mobile marketing may also include branded games that can be played on mobile devices to encourage brand

**content marketing**
Creating and sharing expertise, information, or branded content that is designed to inform and engage with tools such as research papers, e-books, infographics, how-to videos, blogs, webinars, e-newsletters, case studies, and events that can readily be found with search engines.

**mobile marketing**
A set of practices that enables organizations to communicate and engage with their audiences in an interactive and relevant manner through any mobile device or network.

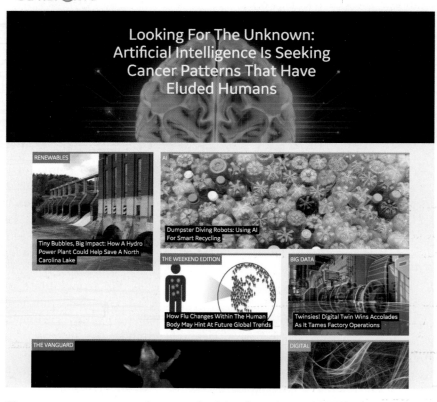

Looking For The Unknown:
Artificial Intelligence Is Seeking
Cancer Patterns That Have
Eluded Humans

RENEWABLES

AI

Dumpster Diving Robots: Using AI
For Smart Recycling

Tiny Bubbles, Big Impact: How A Hydro
Power Plant Could Help Save A North
Carolina Lake

THE WEEKEND EDITION

BIG DATA

How Flu Changes Within The Human
Body May Hint At Future Global Trends

Twinsies! Digital Twin Wins Accolades
As It Tames Factory Operations

THE VANGUARD

DIGITAL

**GE communicates emerging industry trends while telling a brand story.**
Used with permission of GE Reports. Accessed at http://www.gereports.com/

loyalty. The Scarecrow game by Chipotle Mexican Grill is such an example; it was created to connect users with the brand and to allow game winners to receive discount coupons off its products. Other mobile marketing tools include e-mail marketing approaches that render correctly on mobile devices; 2D barcodes, such as QR codes that can be scanned by a mobile device for further information; and local **proximity marketing** approaches, which allow consumers to opt in to receive marketing information in a restricted geo-location, such as a shopping mall, local business district, or event.

## Social Media Marketing

**Social media,** with its ability to interact with consumers, often in real time, through social networks such as Facebook, YouTube, Google+, Twitter, LinkedIn, Instagram, Tumblr, Pinterest, and blogs, has added a new dimension to relationship marketing, making it more immediate and interactive. Social media is formally defined as a form of online media that allows members to create their own network of friends and contacts to share comments, articles, opinions, videos, and images as a form of self-expression. Social media provides consumers with the ability to interact with marketing messages by posting comments that are visible to all. This open environment encourages companies to be more transparent and interactive in their communications.

**proximity marketing**
The distribution of marketing content to mobile devices that have opted in at a particular local geo-location to receive information.

**social media**
A form of online media that allows members to create their own network of friends and contacts to share comments, articles, opinions, videos, and images as a form of self-expression.

**Mobile marketing reaches people on their personal devices.**
©Marcel De Grijs | Dreamstime.com

**Social media marketing** is when brands reach out to consumers online through social media networks. Brands can take various approaches with social media. A brand can place ads on social networks that accept advertising to increase awareness and can hire social media community managers to deploy social media programs and to monitor, measure, and respond to questions, comments, and inquiries. While the popularity of social networks can rapidly change due to the ease with which consumers gravitate to different platforms, the most popular social networks in Canada today are Facebook, YouTube, Twitter, Pinterest, Google+, Instagram, and LinkedIn, among numerous other niche social networks.[37]

With more than 97 million fans on Facebook, Coca-Cola dominates as a leader in social media marketing. What is interesting is that Coca-Cola is not very active on its Facebook page, posting once per month and sometimes even less frequently. The company is able to do this because it has such a strong brand identity, and perhaps doesn't need the constant engagement with customers on social media. Very few brands have such strong brand equity that this lack of engagement wouldn't matter.[38]

Nike provides an excellent example of a very active brand on social media. While its numbers are not as high as Coca-Cola, Nike has fairly strong consumer engagement. With several Facebook pages, one for Nike Corporation and others focused on dedicated areas of business (for example, Nike Football and Nike Golf), their fan bases range from the lower millions on some pages to over 42 million on the Nike Football page. The dedicated sports pages are normally updated daily, while the corporate site is updated less often. Postings will typically attract a few thousand likes, thousands of shares, and a few hundred comments. Nike also benefits from athletes who tweet and post content about Nike, creating even more interest and offering Nike even more content.[39]

## REAL-TIME MARKETING

**Real-time marketing** is when brands make themselves relevant online during events or newsworthy occurrences by creating or joining conversations as they occur to create buzz that is shared by others on social media. Sophisticated approaches use large-scale media events such as the Super Bowl, the Olympic Games, or the Academy Awards as pivotal points, and real-time marketing experts creatively engage in online conversations related to the event to take advantage of the buzz and reach a wide audience. Real-time marketing is planned with teams of real-time marketing experts ready during

Oreo aligns its marketing with current events.
gmstockstudio/Shutterstock.com

the selected events to create and post engaging marketing messages. The teams often include brand specialists and advertising experts, as well as senior executives and lawyers that may be needed to approve messaging. On a smaller scale, real-time marketing is used by many companies on a daily basis through empowered front-line social media managers who continuously monitor social media conversations and respond to issues, questions, and conversations as they occur.[40]

Oreo made its way into the social media history books when the power went out during the 2013 Super Bowl. While the power was out, play was halted and millions of fans watching the game from home were left with nothing to do. Oreo did not produce a commercial to show at the game, but it did send out one very relevant tweet during this blackout: "Power out, no problem" with a picture of an Oreo in a darkened space. The caption on the picture was "You can still dunk in the dark." This tweet is now considered the birth of real-time marketing. The message was seen by tens of thousands of fans and re-tweeted over 16,000 times, generating over 20,000 Facebook likes. The Oreo team skillfully aligns the

**social media marketing**
Reaching out to consumers online through social media networks.

**real-time marketing**
A planned tactical approach where brands make themselves relevant online during events or newsworthy occurrences by diving into conversations as they occur with aligned short-term messaging that takes advantage of the current buzz.

Oreo brand with major events taking place worldwide. When the Mars Rover landed, a picture of an Oreo with red filling (to resemble the Mars surface) was released, with tire treads embedded in the filling. On Pride Day, Oreo releases pictures with rainbow-coloured filling. Using the #PlaywithOreo tag, customers are encouraged to post their own innovative picture of Oreos on Instagram. With this exciting, ever-changing, and current content, Oreo has over 42 million likes on Facebook, more than 820,000 followers on Twitter, and over 2.1 million followers on Instagram.[41]

## EXPERIENTIAL MARKETING

Marketers often embed experiential marketing approaches within their marketing programs to create buzz and in many cases, a focal point for social media programs. **Experiential marketing** is an approach where marketers create fun and memorable opportunities for consumers to directly interact with a brand.[42] The consumers (and the company) will spread the word about their experience through social media. This approach can build awareness and generate word-of-mouth buzz and other forms of publicity for the brand. The brand goes from being passive to actively interacting with the target market. A brand can follow a number of approaches with experiential marketing, often using a combination of public relations, event marketing, and promotions to break through the clutter of competing marketing messages.

In the future, experiential marketing is expected to evolve and become more sophisticated. The mainstream use of virtual reality creates an additional platform for customer interaction. Pop-ups are an effective tool to reach niche customers by setting up in very specific locations. Nike launched the SNKRS XPRESS, a remodelled streetcar, outfitted with its newest models of sport and running shoes. The streetcar travelled the streets of Toronto and other North American cities during the 2016 NBA All-Star Game. Customers could try on and ultimately buy the new shoe styles during the 25-minute trip around Toronto.[43] Inventive outdoor marketing will interact with customers in a more engaging way. Lego has been successful installing Instagram-ready bus stop

**experiential marketing**
Creating opportunities for consumers to directly interact with brands.

**partnership marketing**
The creation of formal associations between brands that will result in incremental business for both brands that could not have been achieved separately.

**strategic alliance**
Long-term arrangement between companies with similar values and marketing objectives that extends beyond short-term promotional offers into long-term formal business agreements.

displays, where customers can superimpose themselves into a Star Wars scene, choosing the "dark side" or the "light side" and posting to Instagram using the hashtag indicating their choice.[44] The integration of live streaming also adds another touch point. Companies such as Nestlé have utilized Periscope, a video-streaming service from Twitter, to stream real customer experiences with their products. Periscope will automatically post a link to the video from the customer's Twitter account, extending its reach. Nestlé was the first to use Periscope, focused on its Drumstick ice cream product, with its #FirstDayofSummer campaign. The campaign generated more than 5,000 views and more than 50,000 hearts (indicating approval) in just over 12 hours.[45]

*brand partnerships = cobranding*
*partner marking = affinity marketing*

## PARTNERSHIP MARKETING

Partnership marketing has gained momentum over the last few years with companies providing customers with added value through complementary promotional offers. The intent of **partnership marketing** is to create formal associations between brands that will result in incremental business for both brands that could not have been achieved separately. Partnership marketing, also referred to as *affinity marketing*, is rooted in the idea that brands with similar customers can combine marketing expertise and use each other's strengths to build brand awareness and incremental revenue streams among a larger audience. The challenge lies in finding appropriate partners, setting realistic goals, tracking results, and aligning partnership goals with business objectives.[46]

Brand partnerships (sometimes referred to as *co-branding*) can manifest themselves in many ways. Nutella has mastered the brand partnership by integrating its delicious hazelnut and chocolate spread as a key ingredient in the product offerings of its partners. Rather than being satisfied as a take-home spread from the grocery store, Nutella has partnered with Tim Hortons to offer a Nutella donut, as well as Nutella-filled pastries. Nutella has also partnered with Longo's grocery store chain in Ontario, with pop-up kitchens making crepes with Nutella filling.[47]

Another form of partnership marketing, with a longer-term focus, is the **strategic alliance.** This involves long-term arrangements between companies with similar values and objectives that extend beyond short-term promotional offers into long-term business agreements. An example of a strategic alliance exists with the SCENE loyalty movie rewards program where Cineplex Entertainment and Scotiabank formed a long-term

# The faster way to earn SCENE points

Get 5 FREE movies† when you open a bank account with a SCENE® debit card. Plus, earn SCENE points on all your everyday purchases.

Learn more at www.scotiabank.com/scene

You're richer than you think.® Scotiabank

A strategic alliance between Scotiabank and Cineplex Entertainment created the SCENE loyalty card.

Used with permission of Bank of Nova Scotia

arrangement to benefit both companies. SCENE members collect points when purchasing Cineplex Entertainment tickets or concession items. Points can be redeemed for free movies or snacks. Scotiabank Visa credit card holders earn additional points when paying with their Scotiabank Visa card. There are over 7 million SCENE members, many of them between the ages of 18 and 34, a much-desired demographic for the banking industry.[48]

## METRICS AND ANALYTICS

The Canadian business world is a performance-based culture that uses metrics and analytics to improve programs and deliver better results. A key role of the marketer is to collect and analyze metrics to make better brand decisions. Digital technology has resulted in a deluge of data that challenges marketers to interpret and manage. Easy-to-use software gathers the data, sorts it into actionable areas for increased focus and analysis, and flags elements that require immediate attention. Robust paid analytics platforms can be provided by companies such as IBM and Salesforce with their analytics platforms, or through free metrics platforms such as Google Analytics and Social Mention.

Metrics and analytics software can measure and track online sales and drill down into the origin of each sale. It can also measure website interactions such as unique visitors, time on site, page views, returning visitors, newsletter signups, and digital downloads. It can measure the effectiveness of online advertising campaigns, as well as the impact of social media programs. In the social media sphere, for example, analytics platforms can collect data that measure online buzz, identify positive and negative sentiment, and point to online brand advocates. It can flag online conversations about a brand, keep an eye on competitor sentiment, and track topics of interest, whether they are on blogs, social networks, video-sharing sites, photo-sharing sites, or the websites of mainstream media. Importantly, this data can be combined with a marketer's costing information so that financial insights can determine costs per click, costs per conversion, costs per interaction, and ultimately, the return on investment (ROI) of specific programs.

In the offline marketing world, metrics and analytics are also important, again pointing to performance. Routine metrics are measured against marketing plan targets and look at elements such as sales, market share, profit margins, and profit levels. Program-specific metrics analyze specific marketing programs and measure performance against benchmarks and targets. These metrics can include elements such as ROI, awareness levels, ad recall, sales conversions, coupon redemption rates, contest entries, or media mentions, depending on the task at hand.

**Metrics** refers to numeric data that is collected and grouped to track performance. It is often presented in spreadsheets and dashboards, so it is easy to

**metrics**
Numeric data that is collected and grouped to track performance, often presented in spreadsheets and dashboards.

Metrics and analytics provide important measures of performance.

triloks/iStock.com

understand and interpret. **Dashboards** visualize data using graphs, charts, and numbers so that the data is easy to use and understand. **Analytics** refers to the process of taking metrics data and applying smart thinking and technology to gain actionable insights that can help make better business decisions. An analytics platform helps answer questions and provides customer insights, and predicts patterns that can improve marketing performance. Analytics can help segment customers, plan and forecast, manage risk, and take corrective action.

Marketers are challenged to use metrics and analytics to better understand how to build better customer relationships. Metrics, analytics, and types of data are covered in more detail in Chapter 4.

## MARKETING REGULATIONS AND ETHICAL CONSIDERATIONS

In Canada, regulations are put in place to safeguard people, communities, and the environment from businesses that may not have their well-being in mind. These regulations can take many forms, such as pollution-emission thresholds, water safety guidelines, food and safety regulations, advertising standards, competitive guidelines, and telemarketing regulations, just to name a few. The Government of Canada sponsors a website that collects and distributes information on product recalls in Canada. It can be accessed at http:// healthycanadians.gc.ca/.

The evolution of digital technology has forced marketing associations and government bodies to revise and update legislation and implement new guidelines. New laws now protect consumers' rights to privacy and provide strict guidelines that marketers need to follow. Anti-spam legislation has also been put in place to regulate e-mail marketing practices, while do-not-track policies have been created for online behavioural advertisers to use. In addition, new industry associations and regulatory bodies have surfaced to control the wireless industry in Canada so that its marketing practices are ethical, legal, and transparent. Chapter 2 reviews in more detail the regulations that govern marketing in Canada, and the Focus on Ethics box, "The Ethics of Uber," offers a case study of one current ethical issue in marketing today.[49]

In addition to government regulations, many companies, industries, and professional associations have guidelines and codes of ethics that provide direction to employees and members on areas that are considered unacceptable. The Canadian Marketing Association (CMA) is the professional body for the marketing industry, and its guidelines, codes of ethics, and educational programs help shape marketing in Canada. The CMA provides input on legislative issues such as Canada's anti-spam legislation (CASL) and digital advertising do-not-track guidelines. The CMA has dealt with policy issues concerning telemarketing regulations, electronic commerce, and consumers' right to privacy. It has hundreds of corporate members, including major financial institutions, insurance companies, manufacturers, publishers, retailers, charitable organizations, agencies, relationship marketers, and those involved in e-business and digital marketing.

> " The CMA website also contains a wealth of information for marketers.

The CMA has a code of ethics by which all members must comply. Its purpose is to encourage high marketing standards that are honest, truthful, accurate, fair, and professional. The code of ethics covers topics such as accurate representations, truthfulness in marketing communications, price claims, fulfillment practices, privacy, marketing to children, and marketing to teenagers. It also provides direction on direct marketing practices, sales promotion, public relations, and media usage. Navigate to the CMA code of ethics on its website at **www.the-cma.org** to review the details in this important document.

The CMA website also contains a wealth of information for marketers with practical guides, best practices, white papers, case studies, news releases, job postings, and information on its educational courses

**CANADIAN MARKETING ASSOCIATION**

**CMA**

The Canadian Marketing Association provides excellent resources for marketers.

Used with permission of Canadian Marketing Association

# The Ethics of Uber

©Worawee Meepian | Dreamstime.com

It was the inability to hail a taxi in Paris while in the pouring rain that ignited Garrett Camp, the Canadian co-founder of Uber, to revolutionize the taxi industry. In 2009, Uber began as UberCab in San Francisco, eventually entering Canada in 2012.

Uber is a ride-sharing app that connects a person looking for a ride with a driver. This service is valuated at US$70 billion, yet it is still not profitable globally. Uber has entered many cities like a "bull in a china shop," enraging the taxi industry.

As with many ethical cases, the truth probably lies somewhere in between the two extremes. The taxi industry in Canada consists of approximately 30,000 taxis, and the introduction of an innovative technology such as Uber disrupts the existing industry. Those who oppose Uber insist that it is taking advantage of regulatory grey areas or loopholes and relying on weak enforcement of existing laws. Uber's competitive advantage lies in the fact that it has little overhead, which allows cheaper rates for customers. Uber has been accused of trying to dishonestly recruit drivers from other companies, conducting insufficient background checks of its drivers, a lack of safety for passengers, and unreasonable "surge" pricing policies.

Supporters of Uber believe that the taxi laws are in place simply to protect taxi drivers and to ensure that their income is kept as high as possible. The coexistence of Uber with the existing industry will be a long, painful process requiring appropriate regulatory changes.

It some ways, Uber has become mainstream—partnerships with Air Miles for first-time riders, Loblaw offering rides to customers ordering through its Click & Collect program, and Roots collecting second-hand clothing for delivery to Goodwill. In another context, Uber is represented as an unregulated, unmonitored, and unregistered danger to society that is taking jobs away from hard-working taxi drivers in each city that the company enters.

One strategy undertaken to improve the image of Uber to its customers is the Uber Safe program. Wireless kiosks armed with breathalyzers were set up in downtown areas. If a person blew over the legal limit, an Uber driver was dispatched to the location to offer the customer a free ride home.

With a focus on customer experience, Uber operates in 483 cities in more than 60 countries. With a 93 percent customer satisfaction rate, taxis, cities, and Uber may just need to learn to get along. ●

## Questions

1. What are the ethical considerations surrounding Uber?

2. Do you think that Uber will ultimately win?

---

and conferences. CMA student memberships are available at significantly discounted prices for students who are enrolled full-time in Canadian post-secondary education.

1. *What are the stages in the evolution of business philosophies?*

2. *What are the key components of a relationship marketing orientation?*

3. *In your own words, explain mobile marketing?*

4. *What is CSR?*

# MARKETING CAREERS

**LO 7** Getting a job is usually a lengthy process, and it is exactly that—a process that involves careful planning, implementation, and evaluation. The starting point is to get an education and, while studying, to create a network of business professionals to contact upon graduation. Creating this network can be done through summer jobs, co-op placements, and internships. Network with guest speakers who may visit your school, involve yourself in on-campus clubs, participate in volunteer opportunities. Have you created a promotional plan, a research report, or a marketing plan in your classes? Throughout your education, gather samples of your work as a demonstration of your knowledge and abilities. All of these methods provide opportunities to meet professionals in the marketing field and gain exposure to the marketing discipline. Despite these strengths, you still need to market yourself.

The process of getting a job involves the same activities that marketing managers use to develop and introduce products and brands into the marketplace. The only difference is that you are marketing yourself, not a product. Start by conducting a personal SWOT analysis. SWOT analyses are used by business to assess themselves and develop strategies. (See Chapter 15 for more information on SWOT analysis.) Ensure that you understand your strengths and what differentiates you from the competition. Conversely, what areas do you need to improve to increase your chances in the job market—these are your weaknesses. Consider how you are currently perceived and how you want to be perceived.

What opportunities exist in the marketing field? As in any field, it is somewhat dependent on the strength of the economy, but entry-level marketing jobs exist for college and university graduates. Entry-level positions exist in sales, marketing, and promotions in a variety of fields. Job titles vary from company to company, but typical jobs include marketing coordinators, marketing analysts, marketing assistants, sales representatives, and account coordinators. These entry-level jobs usually include on-the-job training, liaison with other departments within the company, exposure to marketing program development, and the potential to move up within the organization. Areas of growth are in promotions and digital marketing services. Opportunities exist in creating your own business, as well as working in small, medium, and large organizations in the private sector, in the non-profit sector, or in the government. In the private sector, marketers are required in consumer marketing and in the business-to-business market.[50]

What threats exist? Are there certain industries that are cutting back? Do other job candidates possess sought-after skills?

Once you have completed this research, create a game plan. Select a target market—those job opportunities that match your goals and strengths. Now, create the marketing mix or 4 Ps to position your personal brand to that target market. The product is you and the skills, experience, and competencies that you have to differentiate your personal brand. Price is the salary range you are seeking. Promotion is communicating with potential employers electronically, in writing, or in person. Place focuses on where you will interact with employers—online, career fairs, or through your career centre.

Be sure to also bookmark Canadian marketing job-search websites and to track job postings. Examples of sites that have job postings include www.iabcanada.com, www.strategyonline.ca, www.the-cma.org, www.mediajobsearchcanada.com, and more general job search sites such as www.workopolis.com and www.indeed.ca.

Students wanting to get into the marketing field need to be analytical, be able to work with others, be capable of working in teams, and have strong communication skills in both written and verbal contexts. They must be competent with technology, be able to problem-solve, and not hesitate to drill down into data analysis. As a marketer, you need to keep your finger on the pulse of the consumer. This requires you to stay current and to be intellectually curious. Marketers need to read online web portals, blogs, newspapers, and magazines; follow social media sites; attend conferences and webinars; surf the Internet, watch TV, and listen to the radio; and absorb the trends that are evolving in society and around the world. Publications such as *Strategy* magazine (**www.strategyonline.ca**), *Canadian Business* (**www.canadianbusiness.com**), and *Maclean's* magazine (**www.macleans.ca**) are highly recommended, as is subscribing to the *eMarketer* (**www.emarketer.com**) online newsletter. Daily newspapers such as the *Globe and Mail* (**www.globeandmail.com**) and *National Post* (**www.nationalpost.ca**) are good up-to-date sources of business and marketing news.

Marketing is an exciting area where change is the norm and being able to rise to the challenge is imperative. Learn the fundamentals through education and apply your knowledge by working in the industry.

**Job Seekers**

**Employers**

**Career Resources**

**Professional Development**

**Marketing Job Bank**

Your Canadian Marketing Career Resource Centre

The Canadian Marketing Association has a job bank that can be used by its members.

Used with permission of Canadian Marketing Association, https://www.the-cma.org/job-bank

1. Who is the target market for this product?

2. Why do you think this poster was so appealing to PUR Gum's target market?

**LO 1**
- The role of marketing is to focus on consumer needs and to generate revenue, profits, or support for an organization.
- Successful marketing focuses on customer needs and wants and developing programs that engage consumers and inspire customer loyalty.

**LO 2**
- The marketing mix, also known as the 4 Ps, consists of product, price, place, and promotion.
- Product refers to all the attributes that make up a good, a service, or an idea. Product elements include areas such as product design, product features, colour, packaging, warranty, and service levels.
- Price refers to what is exchanged for a product, including the expected regular retail or sale price.
- Place is the way in which your product gets to the consumer, including the distribution channels, retail formats, and merchandising used to sell a product.
- Promotion refers to the tools needed to communicate with consumers about a product, including advertising, public relations, sales promotion, direct response, event marketing, sponsorship, online approaches, and personal selling.

**LO 3**
- The marketing process follows three main steps: (1) identifying consumer needs, 2) managing the marketing mix to meet consumer needs, and (3) realizing revenues or profits.

**LO 4**
- A product in marketing can be a good, a service, or an idea. A good is a product you can touch and own. A service is a product that is intangible that you cannot touch. An idea is a concept that typically looks for support.

**LO 5**
- The evolution of marketing has progressed from a production orientation stage, to a sales orientation stage, to a marketing orientation stage, and finally to a relationship marketing stage.
- Important areas of the relationship marketing stage are customer relationship management (CRM) and corporate social responsibility (CSR).

**LO 6**
- New and evolving marketing practices have surfaced in the areas of (1) digital marketing, including content marketing, mobile marketing, and social media marketing; (2) real-time marketing; (3) experiential marketing; (4) partnership marketing; (5) metrics and analytics; and (6) new marketing regulations and ethical considerations.
- The Canadian Marketing Association (CMA), the professional body for the marketing industry, responds to legislative issues and sets guidelines on responsible marketing practices.

**LO 7**
- The starting point to a marketing career is to get an education and, while studying, to create a network of business professionals to contact upon graduation. Careers exist in sales, market research, advertising, promotions, marketing analytics, and brand management.
- The process of getting a job involves the same activities that marketing managers use to develop and introduce products and brands into the marketplace. The only difference is that you are marketing yourself, not a product.

analytics
content marketing
corporate social responsibility (CSR)
customer lifetime value
customer relationship management (CRM)
customer value proposition
dashboards
digital marketing
exchange
experiential marketing
good
greenwashing
idea

market
marketing
marketing mix
marketing orientation
marketing process
metrics
mobile marketing
need
partnership marketing
place
price
product
production orientation
promotion

proximity marketing
real-time marketing
relationship marketing
sales orientation
service
share of wallet
social media
social media marketing
societal marketing concept
strategic alliance
target market
want

**Marketing Mix Assignment** PUR Gum has experienced success focusing on the health-conscious customer and an integrated promotional strategy. Review the opening vignette on PUR Gum and then brainstorm on a new marketing mix for PUR Gum that includes new forms of content marketing, real-time marketing, social media marketing, mobile marketing, and partnership marketing. Outline the new marketing mix under the headings Product, Price, Place, and Promotion.

This chapter's opening vignette examines PUR Gum's approach to marketing. Brainstorm in groups, the idea of evolving the PUR Company into a "healthy lifestyle" company. What new products would you consider? Would CSR be part of your plan?

Review the Infographic that details information on corporate citizenship. What is your favourite brand or company? Does it participate in any corporate social responsibility (CSR) initiatives? Research your favourite brand or company and document its CSR investments. Are you surprised by this brand or company's significant support or perhaps lack of support for CSR initiatives? Does this make a difference to you?

# The Marketing Environment

The impact of the external environment is a key component of the strategic planning process for most companies. This chapter focuses on understanding the marketing environment and how it provides marketers with direction on the development and marketing of new products, as well as the successful marketing of current products. We start by looking at the very rapid change in the external business environment for Canada Post. Canada Post is a Crown corporation, responsible for the delivery of letter mail and parcels to Canadians.

Used with permission of Canada Post Corporation

Nothing has had more impact on Canada Post's business over the last five years than a monumental change in consumer behaviour, choice, and preferences. When was the last time you mailed a letter? Well, 50 percent of Canada Post's revenue still comes from letter mail delivery, but Canadians mailed 1.6 billion fewer pieces of mail in 2015 than they did in 2006. Annual volume declines of 5 or 6 percent are now common. What happens to a company when its major revenue stream is affected by such a significant external threat?

Let's look at the range of external factors that Canada Post needs to consider, now and going forward, to be successful:

**Demographic factors:** The number of homes in Canada continues to grow each year. From Canada Post's perspective, the number of postal addresses has grown by 1.5 million since 2006. That means more homes to deliver mail to.

Canada Post does not receive taxpayers' money, but it has an obligation to provide mail delivery to all postal addresses in Canada. The increase in the number of addresses puts a significant strain on the company's profitability. In response, in 2014, Canada Post began to convert the one-third of addresses with mail delivered to the door to delivery to a community mailbox, which would reduce costs. This initiative ended in late 2015, awaiting the outcome of a review of the postal service by the federal government.

**Socio-cultural factors:** Between 2007 and 2015, the volume of letter mail per address declined by 38.7 percent. This places significant pressure on Canada Post's finances. Less mail but more homes to deliver to means less revenue, but higher costs; this does not add up to a successful future.

However, the same Internet that is eroding the mail business is driving Canada Post's highest growth, which is in its parcels business. Consumers are gravitating toward online shopping. About 76 percent of Canadian households shop online. Every year, consumers are shopping online more often, and buying items of greater variety and higher value.

And when Canadians do spend money online, they want a sense of control over the delivery of purchases—they want accurate shipping costs provided at checkout, with precise shipping times, and they want to be able to track purchases throughout the delivery cycle so they always know where their order is.

**Economic factors:** Canadian spending levels are somewhat volatile, up one month and down the next. Consumers are still a bit nervous about spending too much. However, higher growth in spending has been seen on items such as clothing and shoes. By 2019, it is estimated that Canadians will spend $39 billion online.

Statistics Canada has estimated that only 13 percent of Canadian businesses are selling online. This number will grow rapidly in the short term. To avoid falling behind other markets, the push is on for Canadian companies to set up e-commerce platforms for their businesses.

**Technological factors:** Canadians are more likely to have access to the Internet than people in any other G20 country. In fact, 87 percent of Canadian households are connected to the Internet and the majority of Canadians have access to high-speed Internet. As a result, there has been a steady movement to e-billing and online

## CHAPTER FEATURES

**Canada Post Capitalizes on E-commerce Trend**
Changes in the external environment shape the future of Canada Post.

**Statistics Canada— Demographic Trends**
Canada's population is aging and being impacted by an ever-changing ethnic mosaic.

**Millennials versus Generation Z**
Marketers need to recognize the differences between generations.

**Ethnic Shoppers**
Canadian companies are focused on meeting the needs of ethnic consumers.

**Technology Is Evolving Rapidly**
Technological advances keep marketers on their toes.

**The Little Black Book of Scams**
The Competition Bureau helps consumers recognize and ultimately avoid scams.

## CHAPTER OUTLINE

- Canada Post
- Marketing environment
- Demographic and socio-cultural forces
- Economic and technological forces
- Competitive and regulatory forces
- Steps in an environmental scan

banking, which has drastically reduced the volume of mail.

The impact of the digital movement is evident in the advertising field as well. Over the last ten years, digital advertising has grown tenfold while physical direct mail has decreased.

In a digital world, Canada Post has a major challenge to remain relevant and profitable, given that half of its revenue comes from paper bills, statements, and letters, and another 19 percent comes from direct mail advertising.

**Competitive factors:** By law, Canada Post has a monopoly to deliver letters. But the parcel delivery business is another story. There, Canada Post faces stiff competition. Companies that are larger on a global scale, such as FedEx and UPS, are investing in Canada. Barriers to entry have historically been high in the national parcel delivery business since broad distribution networks and sophisticated tracking technology have been required, and brand recognition has been important to customers. Other Canadian companies are also competing for more business. There are also emerging or potential threats, such as Uber.

Finally, e-commerce retailers themselves are eager to reduce their delivery costs, using such initiatives as ship-from-store or promoting in-store pickup of online orders. In this tough business environment, Canada Post grew to become the country's number-one parcel company in 2015 (by revenue). It is also the majority owner of Purolator, the second-largest parcel company.

**Regulatory factors:** Mail delivery in Canada is regulated under the Canada Post Corporation Act. All other delivery is not regulated.

The Government of Canada has recognized the importance of keeping Canadians connected and has developed the Digital 150 plan, which includes investments in making high-speed Internet available in all areas of the country, and providing support to small businesses to help them integrate digital technology into their businesses.

## Canada Post's transformation

Canada Post considered all of these factors and the impact that they have on its business. With traditional mail volumes declining at a steady pace, it needed to reinvent its business for the digital age. Canada Post's growth strategy centres on two of its three business units: parcels and direct marketing.

With the current and future growth of e-commerce, Canada Post decided to focus on parcel delivery and improving the end-to-end customer experience. Two out of every three parcels that Canadians order online are delivered by Canada Post. Excellent customer service anchors this success. Canada Post works to integrate its services into retailers' websites to provide a seamless customer experience from purchase (providing accurate shipping rates), through sorting and shipping (providing tracking of the parcel), and finally to delivery (on time, secure, and convenient).

One benefit of having two-thirds of the online shopping delivery business is that Canada Post has amassed data about the purchasing behaviour of Canadians. While respecting privacy laws that protect individuals' information, the data can be used by direct mail customers to more accurately target their advertising dollars. One Canadian marketer calls Canada Post "the offline Google" because of its data prowess.

Altitude Sports in Montreal has integrated Canada Post into its online fulfillment, with pickup twice daily from its warehouse to ensure quick delivery. Altitude Sports had always relied on online marketing to its customers. The company decided to add print magazines to its promotional mix and with the help of Canada Post, it targeted two customer groups: those who purchased specific types of outerwear, and very active online buyers. Altitude Sports mailed targeted catalogues and tracked the promo codes on each catalogue. The integration of data with a traditional marketing approach improved on the results the company would have obtained using only digital. What an excellent example of e-commerce generating customer data, which triggers a personalized direct mail, which generates additional orders!

It seems as though Canada Post has e-commerce all wrapped up![1]

### reality CHECK ⊘

As you read Chapter 2, refer back to the Canada Post vignette to answer the following questions:

- Which major environmental changes have impacted Canada Post?
- What new services do you think that Canada Post should offer to continue to meet customer needs?

# THE MARKETING ENVIRONMENT

**LO 1** Marketers and consumers do not function in a vacuum, and marketers understand that successful marketing programs must reach out and address changes and new opportunities in the marketplace. In the Canada Post example highlighted in this chapter's opening vignette, the combination of a significant decline in the use of letter mail, but an increasing number of postal addresses to deliver to, created a big threat to the continued profitability of Canada Post. Simultaneously, an increase in e-commerce spending created an opportunity for increasing its parcel delivery business. However, with competitors such as UPS, FedEx, and other national parcel delivery companies providing excellent customer service, Canada Post needed to understand the customer's needs for rapid delivery, parcel tracking, and instant shipping charge quotations, This resulted in a remodelled parcel delivery service that met the needs of the online shopper.

Marketers constantly monitor the marketing environment with a view to capitalizing on new opportunities and curtailing potential threats that may challenge their businesses. In short, marketers scan the marketing environment in six key areas: (1) demographic forces, (2) socio-cultural forces, (3) economic forces, (4) technological forces, (5) competitive forces, and (6) regulatory forces. This chapter looks at developments in these areas, providing a variety of examples that demonstrate how noting and responding to these changes can result in more-effective marketing programs.

Canada Post has two-thirds of the online delivery business in Canada.

Used with permission of Canada Post Corporation

# AN ENVIRONMENTAL SCAN

**LO 2** An **environmental scan** is the process of continually acquiring information on events occurring outside an organization to identify external trends, that are opportunities or threats to a business. Marketers use this knowledge to ensure that goods, services, and ideas are relevant and meaningful, using an environmental scan to define the opportunities and threats to their existing business. An environmental scan is often the first step in developing a more extensive

**environmental scan**
The process of continually acquiring information on events occurring outside an organization to identify trends, opportunities, and threats to a business

*Successful marketing programs must reach out and address changes and new opportunities in the marketplace.*

**SWOT analysis**
The assessment of how well an organization or brand is servicing its businesses and target markets by evaluating its internal strengths and weaknesses, and its external opportunities and threats.

**demographics**
The statistical data on a population according to characteristics such as gender, age, ethnicity, income, education, and occupation.

**SWOT analysis.** A SWOT analysis (**S**trengths, **W**eaknesses, **O**pportunities, and **T**hreats) is discussed in more detail in Chapter 15, but in simple terms, it involves assessing how well a company is servicing its businesses and/or consumers by assessing an organization's internal strengths and weaknesses, as well as its external opportunities and threats (from an environmental scan). This information is then used to set the future direction for a business and to lay the groundwork for competitive marketing programs. An environmental scan looks at six key external areas, namely demographic forces, socio-cultural forces, economic forces, technological forces, competitive forces, and regulatory forces.

## DEMOGRAPHIC FORCES

**LO 3** The statistical study of populations is referred to as **demographics.** It looks at characteristics of a group of people, such as gender, age, ethnicity, income, education, and occupation. Marketers can access demographic information through Statistics Canada and through surveys and external databases. It is important for marketers to clearly understand changes that are occurring in the demographic arena to ensure that marketing efforts are well placed and opportunities are not overlooked.

Statistics Canada provides demographic data through its census information, which is collected every five years. The latest Census of Canada occurred in 2016 and shows that the Canadian population is aging, contains diverse generations, is settling in large cities,

and is ethnically mixed.[2] We look at these trends and identify their impact on marketing efforts.

**An Aging Population** The 2016 Census of Canada shows that Canada is populated by approximately 35.2 million people. There has been a significant growth in the population over the age of 65. For the first time in census history, the population over the age of 65 (5.9 million) outnumbers children under 14 (5.8 million). In addition, seniors represent 16.9 percent of the population, a 20 percent increase from 2011.[3] Although this representation of seniors is high, it is in fact among the lowest in the G7 countries; for example, Italy, Germany, and Japan all have senior populations that account for over 20 percent of their country's population (see Figure 2–1). The G7 countries are the world's most industrialized nations and consist of Canada, France, Germany, Italy, Japan, the United Kingdom, and the United States.

By 2035, it is estimated that there will be more than 10 million Canadians over the age of 65. This represents a growth of 75 percent over the 20-year period from 2015 to 2035 (see Figure 2–2).[4]

Government agencies and marketers are taking note of these demographic changes and determining the needs of the aging market. Hospitals, for example, are reviewing the need for more orthopedic surgeons to conduct joint replacement surgeries; the health care industry is reviewing its home support service policies; and marketers of personal care items are creating more products for an older population, such as face creams that reduce the signs of aging, medicines such as Tylenol Arthritis Pain to relieve painful joints, and a large variety of vitamins and herbal supplements to maintain health.

**Diverse Generations** A generation is a group of people who are bound together by similar events that they

### Figure 2–1
Percentage of people over 65 years, G7 countries

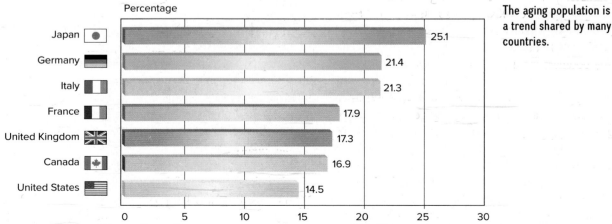

The aging population is a trend shared by many countries.

| Country | Percentage |
|---|---|
| Japan | 25.1 |
| Germany | 21.4 |
| Italy | 21.3 |
| France | 17.9 |
| United Kingdom | 17.3 |
| Canada | 16.9 |
| United States | 14.5 |

**Source:** Statistics Canada, "Age and sex, and type of dwelling data: Key results from the 2016 Census," The Daily, May 3, 2017, http://www.statcan.gc.ca/daily-quotidien/170503/dq170503a-eng.htm?HPA=1.

## Figure 2–2
Canada's aging population

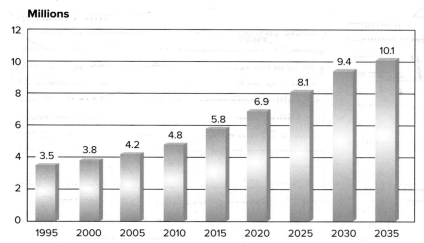

**Millions**

Canada's population over 65 years of age

*Generation Z = Net Generation* (handwritten)

Bar chart values:
- 1995: 3.5
- 2000: 3.8
- 2005: 4.2
- 2010: 4.8
- 2015: 5.8
- 2020: 6.9
- 2025: 8.1
- 2030: 9.4
- 2035: 10.1

**Source:** Statistics Canada, "Population aged 0 to 14 and 65 years and older, as of July 1, 1995 to 2035, Canada," CANSIM tables 051-0001 and 052-0005, accessed February 2017, http://www.statcan.gc.ca/daily-quotidien/150929/cg-b003-eng.htm.

experienced as they grew up. Marketers note four main generational groups of consumers: baby boomers, generation X, generation Y (or millennials), and generation Z. The definitions as to when these generations start and stop vary by publication and researcher. Keep in mind that although the specific birth dates are inconsistent depending on the source, the characteristics of each generational group are still consistent and relevant.

**Baby boomers** are the generation of people born between 1946 and 1965.[5] There are 9.6 million baby boomers in Canada, accounting for 27 percent of the population.[6]

Baby boomers are redefining the concept of aging with a keen interest in health and an active self-image. Many boomers act and feel many years younger. Baby boomers are generally well educated and culturally diverse. Boomers have been known to be brand-loyal customers.

There are many lifestyle decisions to be made for baby boomers: They will have more leisure time; they will probably downsize their homes; and they will have to deal with an increasing number of health issues over time. Marketers have noted these changes in lifestyle and are developing products that address these needs, such as larger smartphone screens, educational vacations, and luxury retirement homes.[7]

Baby boomers increasingly use digital technology to communicate with others and conduct research. A report conducted by Media Technology Monitor concludes that baby boomers in Canada are adopting new technology, although at a slower pace than younger Canadians: 61 percent of boomers use smartphones compared with 88 percent for younger Canadians. When it comes to connectivity, 75 percent of baby boomers connect to the Internet with their devices versus 92 percent of younger Canadians.[8]

**Generation X** is the group of people born after the baby boomers, between 1966 and 1980. In Canada, this generation numbers 7.2 million, accounting for 20 percent of the population.[9] This generational cohort is smaller than the baby boomers or generation Y cohorts. These consumers are highly educated, most of them have children, and most are employed (mainly full-time).[10] They often feel financial pressure with high levels of debt. As a result, they tend to be knowledgeable consumers, searching for good value in their purchases. They like to use the Internet to make purchases. They prefer to use the same brand rather than try new ones. Once you build a relationship with the generation X consumer, they remain loyal. They are less prone to materialism and extravagance than the baby boomers. Generation X is becoming a key influence in the market.[11]

**Generation Y** or **millennials** is the group of people born between 1981 and 2000. These are mostly children of baby boomers. They number 9.6 million and account for 27 percent of the Canadian population.[12] Music, video games, sports, and computer purchases are key products developed to meet the needs of this demographic group. In time, this generation is expected to become as influential as their baby boom parents. Generation Y is often casually referred to as the millennials. The millennials are highly influenced by Internet technology and are moulding society with their effortless integration of digital technology in all aspects of their lives.[13]

**Generation Z** is the group of people born in 2001 and beyond. They were born into an online world with social media, extensive connectivity, and multiple devices. They are discoverers and creators of content

**baby boomers**
Generation of people born between 1946 and 1965.

**generation X**
People born between 1966 and 1980.

**generation Y**
People born between 1981 and 2000. This generation is also referred to as *millennials*.

**millennials**
People born between 1981 and 2000. This generation is also referred to as *generation Y*.

**generation Z**
People born in 2001 and beyond.

# Infographic

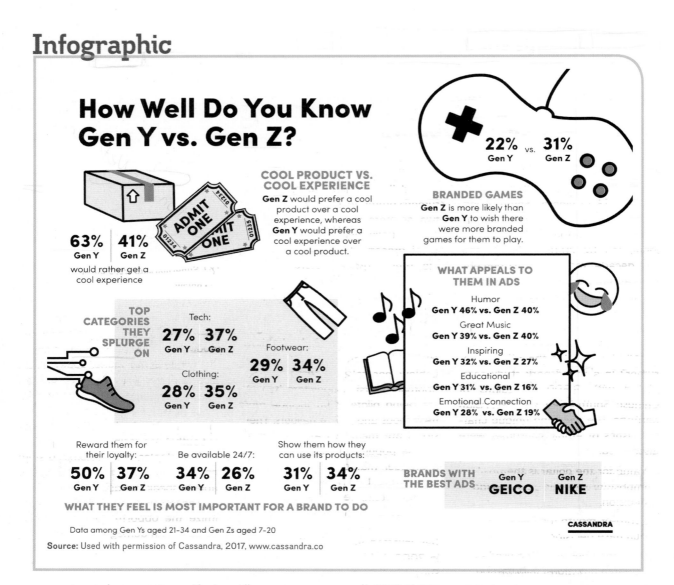

## How Well Do You Know Gen Y vs. Gen Z?

**22%** vs. **31%**
Gen Y    Gen Z

**63%** | **41%**
Gen Y | Gen Z

would rather get a cool experience

### COOL PRODUCT VS. COOL EXPERIENCE

**Gen Z** would prefer a cool product over a cool experience, whereas **Gen Y** would prefer a cool experience over a cool product.

### BRANDED GAMES

**Gen Z** is more likely than **Gen Y** to wish there were more branded games for them to play.

### TOP CATEGORIES THEY SPLURGE ON

Tech:
**27%** **37%**
Gen Y   Gen Z

Footwear:
**29%** **34%**
Gen Y   Gen Z

Clothing:
**28%** **35%**
Gen Y   Gen Z

### WHAT APPEALS TO THEM IN ADS

Humor
**Gen Y 46% vs. Gen Z 40%**

Great Music
**Gen Y 39% vs. Gen Z 40%**

Inspiring
**Gen Y 32% vs. Gen Z 27%**

Educational
**Gen Y 31% vs. Gen Z 16%**

Emotional Connection
**Gen Y 28% vs. Gen Z 19%**

Reward them for their loyalty:
**50%** **37%**
Gen Y   Gen Z

Be available 24/7:
**34%** **26%**
Gen Y   Gen Z

Show them how they can use its products:
**31%** **34%**
Gen Y   Gen Z

**BRANDS WITH THE BEST ADS**    Gen Y **GEICO**    Gen Z **NIKE**

**WHAT THEY FEEL IS MOST IMPORTANT FOR A BRAND TO DO**

Data among Gen Ys aged 21–34 and Gen Zs aged 7–20

**CASSANDRA**

**Source:** Used with permission of Cassandra, 2017, www.cassandra.co

---

that they readily critique and share with others. They are more comfortable communicating online than in person.[14] In Canada, they number 5.8 million and account for 16 percent of the population.[15]

Each of these four generations has very different tastes, consumption patterns, and attitudes. For each generation, marketers need to develop distinct marketing programs, products, and services. For example, each of these generations uses the media quite differently, and marketers have to carefully select which communication tools should be used. Canada Post is focusing on those consumers who purchase over the Internet, which means focusing on meeting the needs of the millennials and generation X consumers.

**③ Big-City Growth**   Looking at the 2016 census data, a population growth rate of 1 percent per year sets Canada as the fastest-growing country in the G7. Each province and territory, other than New Brunswick, experienced growth, with Nunavut leading the way at 12.7 percent, followed closely by Alberta at 11.6 percent.[16] Boosted by immigration,

big cities continue to grow faster than rural areas, with the cities in Western Canada growing more rapidly. Calgary grew by 14.6 percent, Edmonton increased 13.9 percent, and Saskatoon and Regina saw growth rates of 12.5 and 11.8 percent, respectively. There is a significant concentration of the Canadian population (three in five Canadians) living in Ontario and Quebec, two-thirds of the population live close to the Canadian border, and 35.5 percent of the population live in Toronto, Montreal, and Vancouver.[17]

**④ Ethnic Diversity**   Canada prides itself on being a multicultural country. The latest census shows that two-thirds of the nation's growth between 2011 and 2016 was due to immigration.[18] By 2036, the largest increase in immigration will be from Asia (from 44.8 percent of immigrants in 2011 to over 55 percent of immigrants in 2036), and a decrease in immigration will be seen from Europe (from 31.6 percent in 2011 to between 15.4 and 17.8 percent in 2036).[19]

The increase in immigration has reinforced the linguistic diversity of Canada. Immigrant languages

# Understanding the "Big 3"—Ethnic Shoppers

The largest ethnic consumer groups are called the "Big 3"—Chinese, South Asian, and Filipino shoppers will make up 7.3 million of the country's population by 2031, and over the next decade, more than 70 percent of retail sales growth will come from ethnic shoppers. Grocery store chains are clamouring to determine the needs of this large segment of the population and to meet those needs.

What motivates the ethnic consumer? In a Brandspark study completed with 8,800 Canadians of Chinese, South Asian, and East Asian heritage, the following unique characteristics of ethnic consumer were discovered:

- Value for the dollar is the most important factor in each buying decision.
- Word-of-mouth feedback drives purchase decisions.
- Web searches are often used to research nutritional information.
- These consumers are early adopters of tablets and smartphones.
- They are more likely to eat frozen or takeout food.

Of extreme interest to grocery store chains is where ethnic shoppers currently spend their grocery dollar. Ethnic consumers prefer to shop at two or more stores each week—usually one traditional grocery store and one ethnic grocery store—often topping up with one or two trips per month to a big box store such as Costco.

Loblaw has established strategies to entice shoppers to include a Loblaw-owned store in their shopping routine. Loblaw has taken a three-pronged approach. First, Superstore formats are being piloted that include more fresh foods and global flavours. These stores are meant to attract a more diverse population but also bring in a broader market that is becoming more adventurous with their food choices. Next, recognizing that the ethnic consumer prefers to visit ethnic food stores each week, Loblaw has invested in this market as well. In 2009, Loblaw purchased the T&T Supermarket grocery store chain, and in 2014, it expanded into Middle Eastern cuisine by purchasing Arz Fine Foods. The last strategy Loblaw has taken is boosting the amount of ethnic food choices in each of its traditional grocery stores; in fact, it has

T&T Supermarkets were purchased by Loblaw.

JHVEPhoto/Shutterstock.com

been able to expand T&T-branded products to its Superstore locations.

Loblaw is not alone. Sobey's has also launched FreshCo store formats focused on the South Asian population. These stores carry authentic Indian sweets, fresh produce popular in South Asian recipes, and large sizes of food staples. This customized store ensures that a portion of the staff is able to speak Punjabi and Hindi.

The lesson for marketers is to maximize the opportunities that evolve as Canadian demographics shift. ●

## Questions

1. What other strategies could grocery stores adopt to attract more ethnic shoppers?

2. What other industries do you believe should target ethnic consumers?

---

(those other than English, French, the Aboriginal languages, and sign languages) are spoken at home by 7.3 million Canadians. The main immigrant languages are Mandarin, Cantonese, Punjabi, Spanish, Tagalog, and Arabic.[20]

This multicultural mix creates an interesting array of opportunities for marketers. In fact, many companies in Canada have recognized the potential impact of multicultural marketing strategies. Specific ethnic groups have their own particular interests and habits, which can be addressed in unique ways. Pepsi launched its "Get Hyped for Cricket" campaign targeted to the South Asian community. Companies such as Rogers Communications have risen to this challenge, offering a diverse list of multicultural programming—Canadians can watch Polish, Korean, Arabic, and Cantonese programming, just to mention a few.[21] The Marketing NewsFlash box, "Understanding the 'Big 3'—Ethnic Shoppers," discusses how marketers are working to meet the needs of Canada's growing diversity.[22]

**World Markets** The world's population has reached over 7.4 billion people, with Africa and Asia accounting for over 75 percent of the population. China is home to almost 1.4 billion people, 18.7 percent of the world's population. India is home to 1.3 billion people,

*Canada prides itself on being a multicultural country.*

or 17.9 percent of the population.[23] Canada ranks number 38 on the list of most populous countries in the world. One of the major opportunities for future expansion is into foreign markets. The sheer size of these countries presents an enormous opportunity for growth.

**Changing Household Composition** In Canada, the composition of households has changed significantly. For the first time, the dominant household structure is the one-person household, surpassing couples with children. This shift has been driven by an aging population, an increase in the economic independence of Canadians, and an increase in separation/divorce rates. In addition, Canada has seen a growth in the number of couples living without children, the number of common-law relationships, the number of same-sex couples, and the number of multi-generational families.[24]

### Five Largest Countries (population in millions)

| | |
|---|---|
| China | 1,382.3 |
| India | 1,326.8 |
| United States | 324.1 |
| Indonesia | 260.6 |
| Brazil | 209.6 |

**Source:** World Population Review, "Country Population 2016," accessed May 2016, http://worldpopulationreview.com/.

## SOCIO-CULTURAL FORCES

**socio-cultural forces**
Cultural values, ideas, and attitudes, as well as society's morals and beliefs.

**showrooming**
Using mobile devices in-store to check online competitive product reviews and prices, which results in the online purchase of a cheaper product.

Socio-cultural trends are more difficult to pinpoint than demographic changes. It is not easy to identify societal and cultural shifts in attitudes, or to track newly evolving trends. Socio-cultural changes tend to be gradual, over a prolonged period of time, and are sometimes very subtle. Statistical data is not as readily available in these areas, but marketers observe changes in society and conduct research to identify evolving trends and opportunities. Sometimes, identifying these trends involves consumer research; other times, it involves a keen eye and good intuition.

When we discuss **socio-cultural forces,** we are referring to cultural values, ideas, and attitudes that are learned and shared among a group of people. It also includes society's morals and beliefs that are demonstrated through behaviour common among a socio-cultural group. Canadians are known to be fair and inclusive. Canadian society is diverse, and Canadians value a good quality of life, access to education, health care, clean air and water, work–life balance, and the availability of social programs. Marketers monitor changes in these areas in order to capitalize on new opportunities with their marketing programs. Most recently, marketers are responding to socio-cultural changes as they relate to communications, food, health, shopping, entertainment, and the environment.[25]

### Media

**DEVICE CONNECTIVITY** Consumers' widespread use of the Internet, and their ability and desire to access it numerous times throughout the day and on multiple devices, is changing the way marketers relate and communicate with consumers, and how people communicate and interact with each other—impacting socio-cultural norms within our society. In Canada today, we find a society that increasingly relies on electronic communication rather than face-to-face interaction.

Research from Internet analytics company comScore reveals that electronic devices play different roles throughout the day: A typical consumer starts the day at home checking messages and e-mails on a smartphone or tablet. At work, the consumer uses a desktop or laptop computer, and in the evening, tablets dominate.[26] In a survey by Media Technology Monitor, it was found that 51 percent of the time, people are watching television and accessing the Internet simultaneously.[27]

The proliferation of devices and connectivity means that many shoppers will access information about a product from social networks, product reviews, and online stores on mobile devices. This has coined the term **showrooming,** the practice of using mobile devices in store to check competitive online product reviews and prices and to then purchase the cheaper product online. Best Buy enacted a lowest price policy to combat showrooming. Best Buy guaranteed it would match the price of local and online retailers, so consumers would be encouraged to buy while in the store. Recently, reverse showrooming has become popular. Consumers tend to do a lot of research on a product before heading to the store and then armed with all the information they need, they prefer purchasing from the store.[28]

**SOCIAL MEDIA** Social media is no longer only a platform for people to stay in touch with friends. Social media sites allow consumers to express their opinions about products, conduct research before making a purchase, and communicate directly with companies. Marketers must use social media to speak to consumers. Brands need to have Facebook pages, Instagram accounts, Twitter feeds, and YouTube channels to build relationships with customers and manage their brand in an open communication forum. Facebook engages consumers with ads and offers, Twitter connects with newsworthy updates and by responding to customer questions, and YouTube is used for posting engaging videos, brand advertising, and how-to content.[29]

An Insights West study indicates that the social networks most used by Canadians are Facebook, YouTube, Twitter, and Pinterest (see Figure 2–3). Facebook usage continues to grow faster than other social networks. YouTube and Instagram are also increasing in usage, while Twitter, Google +, and Pinterest are declining. A study by Forum Research focused on the generational differences in social media usage. This study showed that the usage of Facebook is highest in the 18 to 34 age group and then decreases with age. LinkedIn is most popular with generation X, and its use is growing. Twitter is used most frequently by millennials.[30]

**TV AND VIDEO VIEWING** Canadians are highly engaged with TV and video viewing. While this data are changing rapidly, when it comes to TV, Canadians currently watch over 27 hours per week of television, though this number has been steadily declining over the last few years. The younger viewers are watching less than the average (19.7 hours), while older viewers are watching 42 hours per week.[31] This is at least partially due to online streaming of content. "Cord cutters" are people who decide to cancel TV cable or satellite and focus on online viewing. A recent study by the Convergence Consulting Group estimated that approximately 200,000 Canadians cancel their traditional TV service annually, and this number has been growing by about 80 percent each year.[32]

When it comes to online content, Canadians spend the majority of their time on television programming, news, music, and games.[33] Canadian Netflix subscriptions have now surpassed 5 million.[34] The video-streaming market has expanded to meet consumer demand: Bell has launched Crave TV; Apple TV is available; and many Canadians illegally access the Netflix U.S. content by using a VPN (virtual private network) blocker. The ability of streaming services to provide entire seasons for viewing on-demand

## Figure 2–3

Canadian social media usage statistics

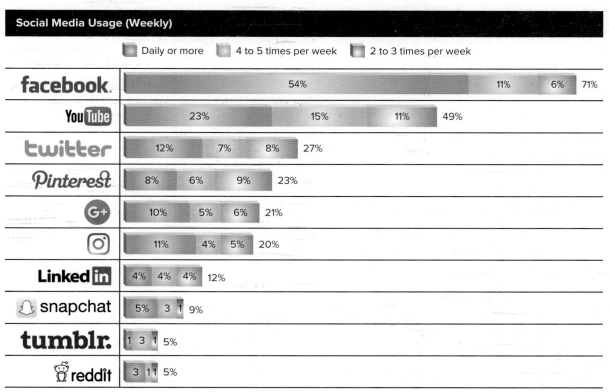

| Social Media Usage (Weekly) | | | |
|---|---|---|---|
| | Daily or more | 4 to 5 times per week | 2 to 3 times per week |
| facebook. | 54% | 11% | 6% — 71% |
| YouTube | 23% | 15% | 11% — 49% |
| twitter | 12% | 7% | 8% — 27% |
| Pinterest | 8% | 6% | 9% — 23% |
| G+ | 10% | 5% | 6% — 21% |
| Instagram | 11% | 4% | 5% — 20% |
| LinkedIn | 4% | 4% | 4% — 12% |
| snapchat | 5% | 3 | 1 — 9% |
| tumblr. | 1 | 3 | 1 — 5% |
| reddit | 3 | 1 | 1 — 5% |

**Source:** Ron Cann, "Key Trends in Canada's Social Media Landscape," Insights West 2016 Canadian Social Media Monitor, May 2016, http://www.insightswest .com/wp-content/uploads/2016/05/Rep_InsightsWest_CDNSocialMediaMonitor_2016.pdf.

**Logos:** (facebook): Craig Ruttle/AP Photo; (youtube): TP/Alamy Stock Photo; (twitter): Ingvar Björk/Alamy Stock Photo; (pinterest): © Pinterest 2017; (google+): © Google; (linkedin): PRNewsFoto/PwC/AP Images; (instagram): © Instagram, Inc.; (snapchat): © 2017 Snap Inc.; (tumblr): © Jeffrey Blackler/Alamy Stock Photo; (reddit): © PSL Images/Alamy Stock Photo

is promoting a new form of viewing, **binge viewing** (popular among the 18- to 34-year-old demographic). This is where consumers watch episodes of complete or partial seasons over a few days. **Social TV** is an industry term that refers to viewers watching live TV while adding comments on social networks. Social conversations about television are increasing with Canadians, with the majority using Facebook.[35]

## Food Consumption

Canadians are increasingly concerned with what they eat. The rise in chronic diseases in Canada has focused attention on the need for healthier food choices. As a result, there has been increased pressure put on food suppliers, the industry, and the government to ensure transparent labelling. Consumers want to have clarity around the definitions of food claims, such as "low-fat" and "fat-free," and they want to be aware of the health implications of the food they are purchasing.[36] Even Kraft Dinner has eliminated artificial preservatives and colours.[37]

Consumers are switching from processed fruits and vegetables to fresh products. This trend has caused a shift in the frozen food segment, with marketers focusing on the freshness and nutrient value of their frozen products.[38] In an effort to eat healthier and fresher food, Canadians are also buying local. A Business Development Bank of Canada study confirmed that two-thirds of Canadians are making an effort to buy local Canadian products.[39] There has been steady growth in the demand for products to meet specific dietary requirements, such as gluten-free, lactose-free, and sugar-free (diabetic) foods. This market is expected to be worth $645 million by 2020.[40] Thousands of products have been launched in the "food intolerance" segment. Companies such as Glutino focus only on gluten-free products, but even private brands, such as the Compliments label from Sobey's, carry a wide range of fresh and processed gluten-free options.

Ethnic foods will continue to be popular with Canadians and in fact have become mainstream. Most supermarket chains have ethnic food aisles with Asian, South American, European, and Caribbean products. When it comes to ethnic foods, consumers in Canada are exposed to a wide variety of international meals from friends, families, restaurants, and multicultural communities. This variety trickles down

Gluten-free foods have become mainstream.
Used with permission of Sobeys Capital Incorporated

to the foods people enjoy and wish to purchase. Marketers note these trends and develop products geared to evolving palates. Examples are Patak's, which markets a full line of Indian sauces in mainstream supermarkets, and Club House, with its blends of spices and seasonings that include Thai, Greek, Cajun, and Indian Masala varieties.

Consumers are demanding more prepared food and ready-to-eat meals. But they are not looking for frozen dinners or fast-food takeout; they want a variety of fresh and delicious meals. This trend is referred to as home meal replacement (HMR), and it is currently estimated to be a $2.4-billion business in Canada. Consumers look to grocery stores for a broad selection of healthier HMR options. Chains such as Loblaw have added hundreds of new, fresh dishes across its locations in Canada. The HMR segment is now the fastest-growing grocery segment, with customers choosing the convenient fresh meal options over fast-food restaurants.[41] We also see a recent influx of gourmet meal delivery services that deliver fresh ingredients and recipes to your door for you to cut, chop, and cook. These services can provide very specialized vegan, gluten-free, or otherwise customized meals, decreasing shopping time, while providing the healthy and fresh options that consumers want. Easy, fresh, convenient, and customized—that is what Canadians want!

## Healthy Living

With a large aging population, there is an ever-increasing consumer interest in maintaining and improving health. This interest includes healthy eating and exercise, as well as living an holistic lifestyle. This trend is particularly influential for baby boomers. Statistics Canada estimates that by 2036,

Fitbit monitors activity, eating, and sleep patterns.
Kelvin Wong/Shutterstock

> *There is an ever-increasing consumer interest in maintaining and improving health.*

25 percent of Canadians will be over 65, and so this trend is expected to continue for many years to come.[42]

Companies are responding to this shift in the socio-cultural environment by modifying their products to make them healthier and by creating new products and services that address concerns related to health, nutrition, obesity, and associated medical conditions. This interest in healthy living extends into a variety of sectors such as technology, food, pharmaceuticals, clothing, and travel. These sectors are developing products and applications that address these trends. One very successful example is the Fitbit, a wristband activity tracker that monitors your movements, sleeping patterns, and heart rate. The Fitbit app for your smartphone or tablet tracks your data on a dashboard, and its connectivity allows users to challenge friends to fitness competitions and to track performance. Apple offers 43,000 health care apps, with thousands also available for Android devices, resulting in a dilemma for doctors who are asked by patients to recommend apps to improve health.[43] Several companies, including Akira, Equinoxe, and Ask the Doctor, have launched virtual health care apps that allow you to consult with a Canadian doctor using mobile or Internet technology. For travellers, the opportunities for health and medical tourism are growing. Tourism can range from spas to health-focused cruises to "medical tourism." Medical tourism refers to Canadians travelling abroad for medical treatment.[44] More than 52,000 Canadians travel out

of the country annually to avoid long wait times for medical care and to have access to treatments not readily available in Canada.[45]

One of the most significant changes stemming from the socio-cultural interest in health, fitness, and nutrition is the Canadian Children's Food and Beverage Advertising Initiative (CAI). Introduced in 2007, this directive was voluntarily created by some of Canada's largest food and beverage companies to restrict children's advertising messages to healthy choices. Today, CAI consists of 17 members that promote healthier dietary choices for children under 12 years of age. The initiative is monitored by Advertising Standards Canada. Monitoring includes traditional TV, radio, Internet, and print advertising, as well as word-of-mouth promotions, company websites or microsites, and ads placed in elementary schools. Campbell Company, Danone, General Mills, Kellogg, McDonald's, Parmalat, and Post all focus on more nutritious choices in child-directed ads, while Coca-Cola, Kraft, Ferrero, Hershey, Nestlé, Mars, Mondelez, PepsiCo, Unilever, and Weston Bakeries have committed to not advertising their products to children under 12.[46]

**Ethical Consumption** Canadians show a keen interest in being less wasteful by making choices that do not negatively impact the environment and by supporting businesses that adhere to ethical business practices. Canadians are among the most likely to recycle, more likely to buy used or preowned goods, and more likely to use their own bags in a store than consumers in other countries.[47] Green consumers are those buyers who consider the environmental impact of every purchase they make. However, with a variety of environmental certifications, eco-labelling options and numerous products making green claims, Canadians are confused and skeptical at the point of purchase. Retailers have adopted "green" aisles

ECOLOGO, Canada Organic, and the Fairtrade Canada logos help consumers identify green/environmental/ethical products.

(left): ECOLOGO is a trademark of UL LLC. Used with permission; (centre right): Used with permission of Canadian Food Inspection Agency; (right): © Fairtrade Canada. This Mark appears on products which have been independently audited and adhere to international standards of Fairtrade.

**economy**
The collective income, expenditures, and resources that affect the cost of running a business or a household.

**macroeconomic forces**
The state of a country's economy as a whole as indicated by its growth rates, inflation rates, unemployment rates, and consumer confidence indexes.

**gross domestic product (GDP)**
The total dollar value of all goods and services produced in a country within a specified time period.

**inflation**
When the cost to produce and buy products and services gets higher as prices rise.

**recession**
A time of slow economic activity with two consecutive periods of negative growth.

in their stores to highlight their eco-friendly products and to capture green customers in a focused shopping environment.[48]

In order to avoid the green product confusion that currently exists, the industry is being advised to collaborate and standardize the claims being made. For companies without their own green certification program, there are several independent bodies that have created standards for green, environmental, and ethically produced claims. Once a product has been reviewed and meets the required standards, it can bear the logo of the certifying organization.[49]

As more information is accessible regarding a company's business practices, Canadians are willing to make decisions and support companies that adopt responsible and ethical practices. Sixty percent of Canadians consider themselves "ethical consumers," while 75 percent say they will pay more for products that are ethically produced.[50] Considering the amount of information that is readily available to consumers through social media and other sources, companies need to be fully transparent and aware of their ethical practices. Canadian companies such as Canadian Tire have put a framework in place to ensure a positive impact on the environment throughout their business operations.[51]

## *ask* YOURSELF

1. *What is meant by "cutting the cord"?*
2. *What are the marketing implications of ethnic diversity in Canada?*
3. *How are important values such as health, fitness, and environmental awareness reflected in the marketplace today?*

## ECONOMIC FORCES

**LO 4** The economy is another area in an environmental scan that marketers need to consider. The ability of a consumer to purchase a product is what interests marketers, and with the global economy being interconnected, this area has become even more difficult for businesses to forecast. When the economy experiences a significant downward turn, consumer confidence wanes, resulting in delayed or cancelled purchases of unnecessary or higher-priced items. An economic downturn can also result in lower household income, again negatively impacting consumers' ability and desire to purchase. If people become unemployed, for example, they will likely defer the purchase of a new car and concentrate purchases on life's necessities. Conversely, an upswing in the economy can result in greater confidence and an increase in spending power.

Canadian consumer confidence is starting to stabilize. However, Canadians are cautious in their spending, focusing on paying down debt. Canadians still like to splurge when they have a few extra dollars, resulting in an increase in spending on dining out, clothing, and home and garden.[52]

Marketers need to recognize how the economy affects the purchase behaviour of their target markets. Some products, such as camping gear, thrive in a poor economy, with consumers wanting to take less-expensive and close-to-home vacations. While new automobile sales will decline in a poor economy, services such as automobile repair thrive.[53]

The economy consists of macroeconomic forces and microeconomic forces. **Macroeconomic forces** refer to the state of a country's economy as a whole. Indicators of strength and weakness should be on marketers' radar screens so that they can react quickly to changes that affect their consumers. A country's key economic indicators are its economic growth rate (usually measured by the change in gross domestic product), its inflation rate, and its unemployment rate. Consumer confidence is also an important indicator of the economy's health, showing how people feel about their long-term economic prospects.

A country's **gross domestic product (GDP)** is the total dollar value of all goods and services produced in a country within a specified time period. GDP is normally a fairly accurate indicator of the economic health of a country.[54]

Another key economic indicator is **inflation**, a period when the cost to produce and buy products and services gets higher as prices rise. From a marketing standpoint, if prices rise faster than consumer income, consumer purchasing power decreases.

A **recession** is a time of slow economic activity with two consecutive periods of negative growth. During recessions, production levels decline, unemployment levels rise, and many consumers have less money to spend. At these times, consumers tend to focus their spending on life's necessities.

**Interest rates** can affect consumer spending. If interest rates are high, people may lean toward saving money and earning higher interest. Conversely, when interest rates are low, people may be more inclined to spend and borrow money.[55]

**Unemployment rate** measures the share of the labour force that is unemployed. When unemployment is high, spending can decline due to the uncertainty of future income.

A country's business cycle fluctuates between different levels of growth depending on the state of the economy, international economic factors, and global pressures. Marketers keep apprised of a country's key economic indicators—economic growth rate, inflation rate, and unemployment rate—to understand whether to expect a downturn or upswing in the economy. Based upon the projected economic climate, marketers may adjust marketing programs to maximize business results.

**Microeconomic forces** directly refer to the supply and demand of goods and services and how this is impacted by individual, household, and company decisions to purchase. A marketer needs to be alerted as to how these areas affect consumer buying power. Here are some terms you need to know (see Figure 2-4):

- **Gross income:** This is the total amount of money made in one year by a person, household, or family unit, including taxes.
- **Disposable income:** This is the after-tax income that consumers have left for spending and savings. Typical ongoing purchases are for rent, clothing, and transportation. If taxes rise at a faster rate than income, consumers have less disposable income with which to pay the bills.

- **Discretionary income:** This is the after-tax income a consumer has left after paying for necessities such as food, shelter, and clothing. This income is used for discretionary purchases that are not deemed a necessity. Examples include going to a movie, eating at a restaurant, or going on vacation.

## TECHNOLOGICAL FORCES

**LO 5** Changes in how consumers use technology must be understood by marketers. Marketers need to know not only what new inventions are coming on the scene but also how consumers are integrating technology into their lives.

**Technological forces** refer to inventions or innovations that stem from scientific or engineering research. Each new wave of technology can replace existing products, and companies need to be aware of technological changes to ensure that products do not become obsolete.

### Figure 2–4
Three levels of consumer income

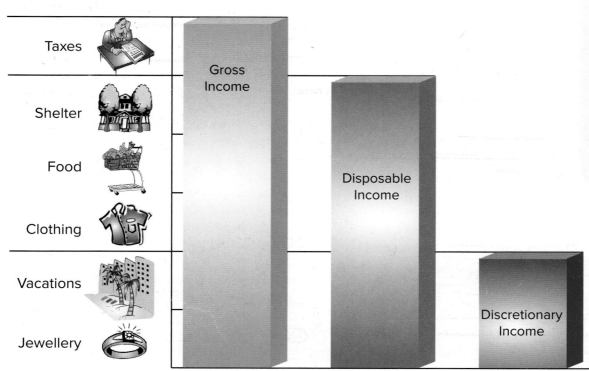

Marketers are challenged to keep up with technological advances.

manaemedia/iStock Editorial/Getty Images Plus

In recent years, with the influx of new devices, better functionality, and improved connectivity, it has become a multi-device landscape. Canadians seamlessly move from one device to another during the day, based upon their location and their needs.[56] Of their time spent online, Canadians spend half of their time on computers, 35 percent on smartphones, and 15 percent on tablets.[57] Marketers recognize this and must now create content that can be accessed across all devices. Consumers want consistent interactions with brands across devices, which means that content must be properly adapted and maximized for each device. Equally important is the need to understand online consumer behaviour.[58]

*Marketers need to know how consumers are integrating technology into their lives.*

Let's look at some of the latest data on Canadians' use of technology that marketers need to note:

- **Internet access:** Internet usage is high in Canada, with 87 percent of Canadian households having Internet access.[59]

- **E-commerce:** Online sales account for 6 percent of retail sales in Canada. E-tailing has not evolved as quickly in Canada as it has in the United States, due to established shopping habits, a limited number of online Canadian retailers, and high shipping costs because of a very large geographic base.

It is projected that with rapid growth over the next few years, Canada will catch up by 2019.[60] Currently, 76 percent of Canadians have purchased a product online, and at least a quarter of those shoppers are considered frequent purchasers, buying online four to ten times per year.[61]

- **Cloud-based services:** "The cloud" simply refers to web services and storage that takes place on the Internet, rather than on a local computer. Examples of cloud-based services are Google Apps (used for mail, documents, messaging), Blogger for blog creation, Dropbox for document storage, Google Analytics or Salesforce.com for online measurement, and Facebook, YouTube, Instagram, and Twitter to share videos, photos, or links.[62]

- **Privacy:** Canadians are concerned about privacy, with 70 percent worried about hackers and the potential loss of their personal information.[63]

- **Music:** In Canada, music streaming is becoming increasingly popular. Music-streaming apps such as Spotify and Apple Music have seen a volume increase of 94 percent, with an estimated 71 percent of Canadians streaming music.[64]

- **Online video:** Canadians increasingly watch online video. The most common areas of interest for online viewing are TV shows, news, entertainment, and games.[65] Close to 70 percent of Canadians adults watch YouTube at least once per month, making it the most popular choice for online viewing by far.[66]

- **Computers:** Despite the increased usage of new devices (smartphones and tablets), computers, including desktops and laptops, still account for 48 percent of Internet traffic, with this number skewing up to 61 percent in the older ages.[67]

- **Smartphones:** Ownership of smartphones is rapidly increasing in Canada, where smartphone penetration has reached 73 percent and continues to climb. Smartphones are used for everything on the go, with usage including taking photos, messaging, social networking, listening to music, conducting searches, using apps, and playing games.[68]

- **Tablets:** These have quickly become popular and are used by over 52 percent of Canadians.[69] They are used mainly during the evening hours at home.

- **Beacons/trackers:** Beacons are used by retailers to track shoppers' movements (with their permission) and send out location-based brand notifications through a brand's app. Uptake of beacon technology has been fairly low in Canada to date, with an estimated 12 percent of retailers using installed beacons, compared with 30 percent globally.[70]

- **Mobile payments:** Mobile payment technology (digital wallets, Apple Pay, Samsung Pay) has been fairly slow to catch on. Research has shown that 10 percent of Canadians use mobile payments. It is felt that the uptake of mobile payments will be slow in Canada due to the existing simplicity of widely available systems such as Interac Flash, which allows consumers to tap their debit or credit cards to make a payment.[71]

The last two decades have seen disruptive technological change that is altering our lives. The way we shop, communicate, pay, and entertain ourselves has evolved dramatically.

## marketing TIP

*"Ubiquitous and always-connected smart devices have rendered old-fashioned paper-based mail, and Canada Post's exclusive privilege to deliver it, far less meaningful."*

*– Deepak Chopra, president and CEO, Canada Post*

## COMPETITIVE FORCES

**LO 6** Another important element in an environmental scan is competition. This puts a focus on **competitive forces** that consumers can examine to satisfy a need. There are various types of competition, and each company must consider its present and potential competitors when designing its marketing strategy. Determining a product's main competitors can be done in a number of ways. Large organizations often purchase research data from companies such as the Nielsen Company or comScore to obtain competitive market share data and to identify general industry trends and market growth patterns. Smaller companies may prefer to reduce their expenditures in this area, instead relying on competitive information obtained from salespeople, suppliers, customers, and retailers.

One of a marketer's primary concerns is to monitor the competitive activity of products that compete head-to-head with its brands. Any changes made by a major competitor in areas of product, price, place, and promotion are routinely noted, and detailed analyses are conducted to determine the impact on business results. These head-to-head competitors are called **direct competitors** and refer to very similar products sold in the same category. Examples are Coke versus Pepsi in the cola category and Nike versus Adidas in the running shoe category.

Marketers also understand that consumers do not function in a vacuum and often make choices between products that do not directly compete in the same category. Marketers therefore also look (a little less intently) at **indirect competitors,** those products that compete for the same buying dollar but in a slightly different category. For example, while Pepsi may focus on Coke, they should not ignore Canada Dry ginger ale, A&W root beer, or San Pellegrino water because these indirect competitors also compete for consumers wanting to purchase carbonated beverages.

Marketers need to be intimately familiar with competitive products and try to anticipate competitive moves in the marketplace. When analyzing the competitive

**competitive forces**
Alternative products that can satisfy a specific market's needs.

**direct competitors**
Similar products sold in the same category.

**indirect competitors**
Products competing for the same buying dollar in a slightly different but related category.

Direct and indirect competitors must be considered in the soft drink category.

©McGraw-Hill Education/Jill Braaten

## Figure 2–5
Types of competitions

**Monopoly**
One firm
Example: regional
electricity companies

**Oligopoly**
Few firms
Example: airlines

**Monopolistic
Competition**
Many firms,
similar products
Example: running shoes

**Perfect
Competition**
Many firms,
identical products
Example: apple farmers

**monopoly**
When only one company sells in a particular market.

**oligopoly**
Type of competition that occurs when a few companies control a market.

**monopolistic competition**
Type of competition where a large number of sellers compete with each other, offering customers similar or substitute products

environment, a marketer needs to review all major competitors, present and future. More attention is given to those that can directly impact a marketer's business. Apart from understanding direct and indirect competitors, marketers need to have a clear understanding of the competitive nature of the industry in which they function and factor this into an environmental scan. If, for example, there are very few competitors, a marketer will consider changes among competitors to be significant, while in a situation where numerous competitors and undifferentiated products exist, changes may be viewed differently. Figure 2–5 shows the four basic types of competition as identified by economists.

At one end of the competition spectrum is a **monopoly.** A monopoly exists when there is only one company selling in the market. Monopolies are legal in Canada but they are carefully monitored by the Competition Bureau to ensure that consumers are not charged excessive prices. Examples of monopolies in Canada are regional electricity companies.

The second point in the continuum is an **oligopoly,** which occurs when a few companies control a market. In Canada, this situation exists with network providers that control the telecommunications industry. Companies such as Bell, Telus, and Rogers dominate the market. Because there is limited competition, it is thought that prices are usually higher because companies want to protect their profits. Marketers who function in an oligopoly need to be acutely aware of competitive moves and particularly changes in price.

The third type of competition is **monopolistic competition.** This is when a large number of sellers

What type of competition typifies the hotel industry—monopoly, oligopoly, monopolistic competition, or perfect competition?

Digital Vision/Alamy Stock Photo

compete with each other, offering customers similar or substitute products. Marketers need to know that in this instance, branding plays an important role, as does product differentiation and added-value activities to draw consumers to the product. Being in touch with consumer needs and adjusting the marketing mix to meet those needs is crucial for long-term survival. The market for running shoes is a good example. This market is dominated by major brands such as Nike, Adidas, New Balance, and Reebok, as well as many less-popular brands. The result is that when it comes to buying running shoes, consumers are presented with a wide array of options. Marketers in this category need to keep the competitive nature of this market top-of-mind when marketing products.

The fourth type of competition is **perfect competition,** when there are many sellers with nearly identical products and little differentiation. Companies that deal in commodities—that is, products such as grains, vegetables, or rice—often function in an environment where perfect competition exists. In this instance, marketers need to know that pricing plays a key role in securing business, and that the focus will be on cost reduction in every element of the business.

---

### ask YOURSELF

1. *What is the difference between a consumer's disposable and discretionary income?*

2. *What type of competition is found in the gasoline industry?*

3. *What are the indirect competitors to Monster energy drinks?*

---

## REGULATORY FORCES

The final area involved in an environmental scan relates to **regulations,** which are restrictions placed on marketing practices by government and industry associations. These regulations are put in place to protect consumers from unscrupulous business practices, to set acceptable standards of practice, and to encourage fair competition. Marketers need to clearly understand all the legal and ethical guidelines that affect their business practices and to retain legal guidance as needed to ensure that their practices are legal. Ethical business practices should also be followed to avoid consumer backlash and negative publicity.

Below we review the key regulatory groups and regulations that affect marketing practices in Canada. It is worth noting that regulations are updated and changed by these groups as needed to meet changing business practices. Marketers are strongly advised to check these associations regularly for updates and changes, and to consult with a marketing lawyer to ensure practices are both legal and ethical.

The key groups that regulate marketing practices in Canada are the Competition Bureau, Advertising Standards Canada (Ad Standards), the Canadian Radio-television and Telecommunications Commission (CRTC), the Canadian Marketing Association (CMA), and the Office of the Privacy Commissioner of Canada (OPC). In addition to these general regulatory bodies, the Canadian Wireless Telecommunications Association (CWTA) and the Mobile Marketing Association (MMA) provide specific guidance on mobile marketing practices, and the Digital Advertising Alliance of Canada (DAAC) oversees online behavioural advertising. Marketers also need to review other regulatory bodies and associations specific to their industry, as well as those that have jurisdiction in other countries, provinces, or states where they conduct business.

**Competition** The Competition Bureau is an independent law-enforcement agency tasked to ensure that the market in Canada is competitive and innovative. In this manner, people in Canada can benefit from fair prices, product choice, high-quality services, and a reduction in fraudulent business practices. It is responsible for the administration and enforcement of the *Competition Act,* the *Consumer Packaging and Labelling Act,* the *Textile Labelling Act,* and the *Precious Metals Marking Act,* just to name a few areas of responsibility.

The Canadian Anti-Fraud Centre (CAFC) is managed jointly by the RCMP, the Ontario Provincial Police (OPP), and the Competition Bureau to reduce marketing fraud. The CAFC maintains a website, **www.antifraudcentre.ca,** with up-to-date data on fraudulent marketing schemes and an area for consumers to report scams. These scams use various communication tools such as mail, e-mail, the Internet, and the telephone to take advantage of unsuspecting people. The Competition Bureau regularly updates its publication of "The Little Black Book of Scams," which highlights the wide range of scams that exist (see the Focus on Ethics box, "The Little Black Book of Scams").[72]

The Competition Bureau also reviews mergers and acquisitions and prohibits deceptive business practices that include, among others, price fixing

**perfect competition**
Type of competition where there are many sellers with nearly identical products and little differentiation.

**regulations**
Restrictions placed on marketing practices by government and industry associations.

**The Competition Bureau can levy hefty fines.**

Minister of Innovation, Science and Economic Development, *Fraud Prevention Month* poster, "Lotteries, Sweepstakes and Contest Scams." Reproduced with the permission of the Minister of Innovation, Science and Economic Development, 2017.

among competitors, predatory pricing by large competitors to run small companies out of business, and bid rigging among competitors to inflate prices on government contracts. Prohibited pricing practices to lure consumers include bait-and-switch advertising, fraudulent advertising claims, and misleading pricing practices such as double ticketing. Bait-and-switch advertising refers to the practice of advertising a low-priced product (bait) to lure consumers into a store and then, because the product is not made available in large quantities, selling these consumers higher-priced products (switch). In 2014, the *Competition Act* was amended to include new areas that relate to Canada's anti-spam legislation making it an offence to include false or misleading information in electronic messages.

Failure to abide by Competition Bureau rules can result in fines and jail time. False and/or misleading representations to sell products can result in orders by the Competition Bureau for companies to publish corrective notices, stop the prohibited practice, pay administrative costs, and pay restitution to purchasers. In addition, the Competition Bureau has the legal clout to levy hefty fines on individuals and/or companies. To find out more about the Competition Bureau, and to see a complete list of its regulations and recent rulings, visit its website at **www.competitionbureau.gc.ca**.

**Advertising** Advertising Standards Canada (Ad Standards) is a self-regulatory non-profit body supported by advertising, media, and marketing companies with the purpose of setting and regulating standards of professional practice in the advertising industry. The industry has agreed to abide by its leadership, code, process, and rulings. Ad Standards sets and regulates advertising guidelines, monitored through a consumer complaint process. A single complaint will trigger a review of advertising placed in the Canadian media, with the eventual withdrawal of the ad if changes are required and not made. Ad Standards also provides advice and pre-clearance services for advertisers.

Ad Standard's jurisdiction does not carry over into the legal arena. It does not levy fines or engage in legal proceedings. Instead, it relies on industry compliance to ensure that ads contravening its guidelines, the Canadian Code of Advertising Standards (or the Code), cease to air. Deceptive and fraudulent advertising, although covered under the Code, is also scrutinized by the Competition Bureau, which can levy fines and take legal action if necessary.

The Code has a comprehensive set of guidelines designed to encourage truthful, fair, and accurate marketing communications. It covers 14 areas, as shown in Figure 2–6, that address issues such as comparative advertising, accuracy, safety, decency, and advertising to children. These guidelines are updated as required with a detailed list of guidelines available at **www.adstandards.ca**.[73]

**Do Not Call List** The Canadian Radio-television and Telecommunications Commission (CRTC) is another government agency that sets guidelines and enforces a clear set of regulations on Canadian businesses. The areas most relevant to marketing are the *Broadcasting Act*, the *Telecommunications Act*, the *Wireless Code*, the *Do Not Call List*, and particular areas of Canada' anti-spam policy.

The *Broadcasting Act* and the *Telecommunications Act* set guidelines for broadcast standards, and in 2013, the CRTC created the Wireless Code, a mandatory code of conduct for all wireless service providers.

The CRTC adjudicates on the cross-media ownership of media companies to ensure that a single media

## focus on **Ethics**

# The Little Black Book of Scams

Scams are a big business. They can come to you in many different ways—mail, online, over the phone. It is estimated that in 2016, Canadians lost $90 million to scams. As technology infiltrates our lives, the ease of carrying out a scam also increases. The Competition Bureau of Canada is taking this seriously and is focused on ensuring Canadians are aware of these dangers. "The Little Black Book of Scams" was first published in 2012, and with the continual influx of new types of scams, the book is available online and is updated regularly. What type of cons should Canadians be aware of? Here are just a few:

1. Internet scams most commonly take the form of phishing e-mails. Have you ever received an e-mail from your bank asking you to click on a link to its website and re-enter your personal information? This is phishing! Phishers may send millions of copies of the same e-mail, and all they need is for a few to respond to make it worth their efforts.

2. Dating and romance scams netted almost $17 million from Canadians in one year. Online dating has become the norm for many singles. It is estimated that at least 20 percent of online dating profiles are fake. The scam begins when a person meets someone wonderful online and after ongoing communication, they ask for money and then disappear.

3. Lottery scams begin with an e-mail telling you that you have won an amazing prize. In order to claim the prize, you need to pay a fee or the taxes on the funds.

4. Investment scams, sometimes referred to as pyramid or Ponzi schemes, steal millions from Canadians every year. Investors are promised really high rates of return but never pay the money back.

Follow these tips to protect yourself:

- Protect your personal details and only give out personal information to people you know and trust.
- Don't send money to anyone that you don't know, and never pay fees to claim prizes or obtain a job.
- Never reply to spam e-mails or open attachments from any suspicious e-mails.
- Install security software on your computer.
- If you think you have been the victim of a scam, act immediately to limit your damages

Scams are big business.

karen roach/Shutterstock

and report it to the appropriate authority.

"The Little Black Book of Scams" can be downloaded from the Competition Bureau website at **www.competitionbureau.gc.ca**. ●

## Questions

1. Do you think the number of scams and cons will continue to rise in Canada? Why or why not?

2. Many consumers are unaware of the frequency of scamming in Canada. How can social media help increase awareness of these practices?

---

organization or conglomerate does not overpower local markets. It also approves broadcast licences for TV and radio stations and sets guidelines on the broadcast of Canadian content. In addition, the CRTC sets limits on the number of minutes of advertising permitted hourly on TV. While it does not directly regulate the content of ads, primarily an Ad Standards concern, it does oversee the advertising of alcohol beverages and works with Ad Standards on issues related to advertising to children.

The CRTC also has jurisdiction over the national **Do Not Call List (DNCL).** The DNCL gives consumers the ability to elect to not receive telemarketing calls on cellphones and landline phones by registering their phone numbers. Registration keeps these numbers in the DNCL for five years, after which consumers must re-register. Telemarketers are required by law to subscribe to the DNCL and to not call the numbers in its database.

There are five exemptions to the DNCL: registered charities, newspaper

**Do Not Call List (DNCL)**

Gives customers the ability to elect to not receive telemarketing calls on cellphones and landline phones by registering the numbers of their communication devices.

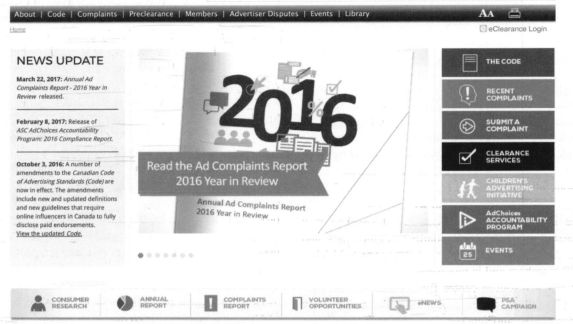

Through their support of ASC, these companies and organizations demonstrate their committment to responsible advertising regulation.

Navigate to adstandards.ca to review guidelines and reports on advertising in Canada.

Reprinted with permission from Advertising Standards Canada

## Figure 2–6

Advertising Standards Canada—The Code

Advertising Standards Canada (Ad Standards) encourages truth in advertising through a code that provides guidelines under these areas:

- Accuracy and clarity
- Disguised advertising techniques
- Price claims
- Bait and switch
- Guarantees
- Comparative advertising
- Testimonials
- Professional or scientific claims
- Imitation
- Safety
- Superstitions and fears
- Advertising to children
- Advertising to minors
- Unacceptable depictions and portrayals

Details can be found on the Ad Standards website at www.adstandards.ca.

Reprinted with permission from Advertising Standards Canada.

subscriptions, political parties/candidates, market research companies, and companies where business has been conducted in the last 18 months. Failure to comply with the DNCL can result in fines of up to $1,500 for an individual and up to $15,000 for a corporation for each violation. A major challenge for the CRTC is the onslaught of call centres located outside of Canada. The resolution of many of these cases required the cooperation of international regulators.[74] You can read more about the CRTC at www.crtc.gc.ca.

**Marketing** The Canadian Marketing Association (CMA) guides the practices of the marketing industry through its Code of Ethics and Standards of Practice. It is mandatory for all members to abide by these policies, which are clearly outlined on the CMA website at www.the-cma.org. This website provides marketers with numerous practical guides on topics such as native advertising, anti-spam legislation, digital marketing, privacy compliance, telemarketing, promotional contests, fundraising, marketing lists and data, and marketing to children and teenagers.[75]

**Mobile** The Canadian Wireless Telecommunications Association (CWTA) provides resources on the wireless industry in Canada. It deals with the government on issues related to cellular phones, personal communication devices, text messaging, and wireless and mobile satellite carriers, and represents companies working in that space. Its website provides useful statistics on the industry as well

> *The Canadian Marketing Association (CMA) guides the practices of the marketing industry.*

as regulations that control the sector.[76] The CWTA introduced common short code (CSC) guidelines to regulate the industry's use of text messaging. This includes outlining protocols to ensure that all messaging is permission-based, allowing customers to immediately opt-out by using the keyword STOP. To read more about mobile marketing regulations, go to Chapter 13. Updates on CSC regulations can be found at www.cwta.ca and www.txt.ca.[77]

The Mobile Marketing Association (MMA) is a global association that sets standards and guidelines, and shares best practices on mobile marketing. The MMA has over 800 members and is represented in nearly 50 countries. It has a resource centre for marketers; publishes a code of conduct, a best practices guide, and privacy policy templates; and sets standards for mobile messaging, mobile advertising, and mobile promotions. You can read more about the MMA at www.mmaglobal.com.[78]

**Privacy** The collection of personal data by private sector companies is governed by the *Personal Information Protection and Electronic Documents Act* (PIPEDA). Personal information includes age, name, social status, ID numbers, income, ethnicity, opinions, comments, evaluations, purchase habits and disputes, credit records, loans, medical information, employee files, and disciplinary actions. It does not include employee information such as name, title, address and telephone number. These acts are periodically updated, and guidelines and reports can be found on the Office of the Privacy Commissioner of Canada's website at www.priv.gc.ca.

Federal legislation for the private sector falls under PIPEDA and is reviewed by the government every five years to ensure that it remains current and actionable in the light of new technologies. Many provinces and territories have their own privacy legislation similar to PIPEDA and have specific requirements pertaining to health care as well as the banking and credit sectors.[79]

PIPEDA requires organizations to obtain consent from individuals for the collection, use, and disclosure of information, including video surveillance. It also stipulates that information must be safely stored and security breaches must be communicated to consumers.

PIPEDA and the Canadian Marketing Association require businesses to regularly review their privacy policies, to appoint a privacy policy officer, and to collect only necessary information. In the online environment, privacy policies must be clearly posted on all websites and detail the type of personal information that is collected, how it is collected, how it is used and protected, whether information is disclosed to outside parties, and whether the company complies with Canadian privacy legislation and anti-spam laws.

Individuals can table complaints on privacy issues directly to an organization's privacy officer as well as to the Office of the Privacy Commissioner of Canada. If the Office of the Privacy Commissioner of Canada finds an individual or organization knowingly contravened PIPEDA, this can be processed through the courts and result in penalties of up to $100,000. Due to the rapid changes in digital marketing practices, PIPEDA is under constant pressure to update its legislation, and therefore, marketers are strongly advised to be well-versed in the latest privacy regulations and fines, and to check the website of the Office of the Privacy Commissioner of Canada at www.priv.gc.ca, and the Canadian Marketing Association website at www.the-cma.org, for updates and guidelines. The most recent updates prohibit the use of automated computer programs in the unauthorized collection of e-mail addresses to comply with Canada's anti-spam policy. PIPEDA is constantly under pressure to include amendments that relate to evolving digital marketing practices.[80]

**Spam** Canada's anti-spam legislation (CASL) came into effect in July 2014 to protect consumers and businesses from unwanted commercial electronic messages (CEMs), including messages to e-mail addresses, social networking accounts, and text messages sent to a cellphone. In 2015, additional legislation was put in place to protect individuals from the installation of computer programs and mobile apps without their prior consent

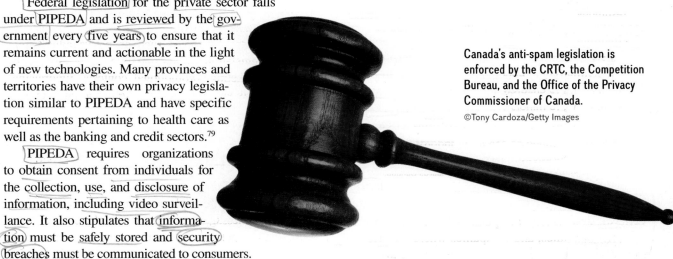

Canada's anti-spam legislation is enforced by the CRTC, the Competition Bureau, and the Office of the Privacy Commissioner of Canada.

©Tony Cardoza/Getty Images

**spam**

The dissemination of unsolicited electronic messages to recipients.

**online behavioural advertising (OBA)**

The use of web-based programs to track consumers' online activity so as to deliver ads that correspond to browsing interests.

and knowledge. **Spam** refers to the dissemination of unsolicited electronic messages to recipients.

CASL is enforced by the CRTC, the Competition Bureau, and the Office of the Privacy Commissioner of Canada. Contravening CASL can be costly. Administrative monetary penalties for businesses reach as high as $10 million per violation for businesses, with fines of up to $1 million per violation for individuals. An online spam-reporting centre is available at **fightspam.gc.ca** for businesses, organizations, and consumers to file complaints on unsolicited CEMs and those containing false and misleading information.[81]

CASL requires the following conduct with respect to electronic messaging:

- Must have opt-in consent.
- Must include accurate sender information, subject line information, and content.
- Must not be altered and sent to another destination without consent.
- Must include an unsubscribe mechanism.
- Online promotions must not be false or misleading.
- Restrictions on the unauthorized collection of email addresses through automated computer programs.
- Computer software cannot be installed on an electronic device without explicit consent.
- Personal information cannot be collected by unlawfully accessing a computer.

Nonetheless, various exemptions exist, such as those for registered charities that are conducting fundraising, political parties, immediate family members, and legitimate interactions between organizations and its employees. Exemptions also exist for legitimate business inquiries, quotes, applications, complaints, warranties, recalls, and safety or security issues. Since this legislation is relatively new and its legal interpretation is still evolving, marketers are strongly advised to become compliant with the anti-spam legislation, to obtain legal advice on their use of CEMs, and to check the CMA website for updates. The CMA advises marketers to obtain expressed opt-in consent from all business relationships so that they are in compliance with the new CASL law.[82]

## Online Behavioural Advertising

**Online behavioural advertising (OBA)** refers to the tracking of consumers' online browsing activities in order to deliver online ads that correspond to their browsing interests.[83] OBA works by storing a text file (called

This AdChoices logo is used by online behavioural advertisers that are compliant with the DAAC.

Used with permission of Digital Advertising Alliance of Canada

a cookie) in a computer's web browser to track which websites are visited by the browser. It then predicts interests and serves ads that meet these interests.

The Digital Advertising Alliance of Canada (DAAC) was formed to ensure that consumers were aware of OBA and could opt out of the collection and use of OBA data on their devices. In 2013, the DAAC announced its AdChoices program, a self-regulatory framework that guides online behavioural advertising in Canada, making it consistent with existing privacy laws in Canada and aligned with similar self-regulatory programs in the U.S., Europe, and Australia. AdChoices asks behavioural advertisers to follow a set of OBA principles and use a standardized triangular blue OBA icon next to OBA ads and websites where such data is begin collected. Viewers can click on the icon to learn more and opt out, if they so choose. Advertising Standards Canada monitors program participants for compliance and accepts consumer complaints about OBA as part of the Canadian AdChoices program.[84]

### ask YOURSELF

1. What role does the Canadian Radio-television and Telecommunications Commission (CRTC) play in Canadian marketing regulations?

2. What government body oversees privacy issues in Canada?

3. Does self-regulation work? Why or why not?

# STEPS IN AN ENVIRONMENTAL SCAN

**LO 7** Environmental scans are conducted routinely by marketers, often with the help of other departments in an organization to ensure that products and marketing approaches stay relevant and resonate with consumers. An environmental scan will often be conducted annually as part of the marketing planning process, but marketers should be monitoring changes and developments in each area on an ongoing basis.

Here is a quick checklist and a step-by-step guide:

### Step 1: Collect the facts and identify trends.

- **Gather data and information.**
  The starting point is to gather accurate and relevant information on all areas of an environmental scan (see Figure 2–7).

- **Conduct competitive reviews.**
  Delve deeper into the competition and conduct a rigorous review of the marketplace to determine competitive practices and new approaches in each area of the marketing mix (product, price, place, and promotion). Understand consumer triggers and their connectivity to a brand by putting on your consumer's hat and visiting stores to review competitive products and to speak to sales representatives. Read product reviews and industry research reports.

- **Cluster information into facts and trends.**
  Gather and sort the information you have gathered into facts and trends for each area of the marketing environment scan. Capture this information in a simple table that can be easily understood, such as that shown in Figure 2–8 for Canada Post.

  Note: Some information may fall into more than one area in a marketing environment scan. The information should be repeated as necessary to ensure adequate focus.

## Figure 2–7
Information sources for an environmental scan

| Factors in an Environmental Scan | Sources of Information |
|---|---|
| **Demographic**<br>• Shifts in age, gender, ethnicity, rural or urban populations, family status, home ownership, family life cycle, education, occupation | • Euromonitor reports (www.euromonitor.com)<br>• Statista (www.statista.com)<br>• Statistics Canada (www.statcan.gc.ca) |
| **Socio-cultural**<br>• Evolving attitudes, values, shopping habits, usage of technology, cultural norms, product consumption | • Alliance for Audited Media (www.auditedmedia.com)<br>• Blogs and social media<br>• Consumerology report (consumerology.ca)<br>• Euromonitor reports (www.euromonitor.com)<br>• Forrester Research (www.forrester.com)<br>• GFK Group (www.gfk.com)<br>• Interactive Advertising Bureau of Canada (iabcanada.com)<br>• Ipsos Canada (www.ipsos.ca)<br>• Leger (www.leger360.com.)<br>• News sources: use Google News (news.google.ca) or newspaper sites, for example, *Globe and Mail* (www.globeandmail.com), *National Post* (www.nationalpost.com), *New York Times* (www.nytimes.com)<br>• Numeris (numeris.ca)<br>• Pew Research Center (www.pewresearch.org)<br>• Solutions Research Group (www.srgnet.com)<br>• *Strategy* magazine (strategyonline.ca)<br>• Statista (www.statista.com) |
| **Economic**<br>• Changing discretionary and disposable income levels, economic growth, inflation, unemployment rates | • Bank of Canada (www.bankofcanada.ca)<br>• Euromonitor reports (www.euromonitor.com)<br>• Major banks publish reports on the Canadian economy<br>• News sources: use Google News (news.google.ca) or newspaper sites, for example, *Globe and Mail* (www.globeandmail.com), *National Post* (www.nationalpost.com), *New York Times* (www.nytimes.com)<br>• Organization for Economic Cooperation and Development (OECD) (www.oecd.org)<br>• Statistics Canada (www.statcan.gc.ca)<br>• Statista (www.statista.com) |

*(Continued)*

**Figure 2–7** (Continued)

| Factors in an Environmental Scan | Sources of Information |
|---|---|
| **Technological**<br>• Technological inventions and innovations that impact business | • Euromonitor reports (www.euromonitor.com)<br>• GFK Group (www.gfk.com)<br>• Industry Canada (www.ic.gc.ca)<br>• News sources: use Google News (news.google.ca) or newspaper sites, for example, *Globe and Mail* (www.globeandmail.com), *National Post* (www.nationalpost.com), *New York Times* (www.nytimes.com)<br>• Trade magazines |
| **Competitive**<br>• Change in the competition's marketing mix—product, price, place, and promotion—as well as changes in the structure of the industry | • Blogs and social media<br>• Competitors' websites<br>• comScore reports (www.comscore.com)<br>• *eMarketer* (www.emarketer.com)<br>• Industry association websites<br>• Industry Canada (www.ic.gc.ca)<br>• Nielsen Canada reports (www.ca.nielsen.com)<br>• News sources: use Google News (news.google.ca) or newspaper sites, for example, *Globe and Mail* (www.globeandmail.com), *National Post* (www.nationalpost.com), *New York Times* (www.nytimes.com)<br>• Product reviews and industry research reports<br>• SEDAR (www.sedar.com) or EDGAR (www.sec.gov/search/search.htm)<br>• *Strategy magazine* (strategyonline.ca)<br>• Statista (www.statista.com)<br>• Trade publications and industry articles<br>• Visit retailers and see what the competition is doing<br>• World Advertising Research Center (WARC) (www.warc.com) |
| **Regulatory**<br>• Evolving federal and provincial legislation and industry association guidelines | • Advertising Standards Canada (www.adstandards.ca)<br>• Canadian Marketing Association (www.the-cma.org)<br>• Canadian Radio-television and Telecommunications Commission (www.crtc.gc.ca)<br>• Competition Bureau (www.competitionbureau.gc.ca)<br>• Industry association websites<br>• Euromonitor reports (www.euromonitor.com)<br>• Government of Canada (www.canada.gc.ca)<br>• Law firms and consultants: Gowlings (www.gowlingwlg.com), Deloitte (www2.deloitte.com)<br>• Office of the Privacy Commissioner (www.priv.gc.ca) |

**Step 2: Determine the impact that this fact/trend will have on the business.**

● **Set business objectives.**
Based upon your analysis and the state of your current business, determine business objectives.

● **Analyze the external trends to determine their impact.**
Determine the impact (positive or negative) that each trend will have on the business.

**Step 3: Brainstorm, evaluate, and implement ideas to meet business objectives.**

● **Brainstorm.**
Brainstorm ideas that address the facts, trends, and business objectives. All reasonable ideas should be

considered at this point as they will be screened down to a few actionable elements in the subsequent step.

● **Evaluate and implement alternatives.**
Evaluate the realistic alternatives against the business objectives and select those that are worthwhile and can be implemented.

For greater clarification, review the marketing environmental scan for Canada Post (Figure 2–8). Canada Post monitors its external environment regularly, so it has been able to determine which external factors are changing and which will have an impact on its business.

Canada Post was discussed in this chapter's opening vignette. After gathering data and information on the market and competition, Canada Post identified potential opportunities and determined the approach it wanted to take.

## Figure 2–8
Impact of an environmental scan—Canada Post

| Factors in an Environmental Scan | STEP 1<br>Facts and Trends<br>Collect the facts and identify trends in each category. | STEP 2<br>Determine Impact<br>Analyze each external trend to determine its impact on the business. | STEP 3<br>Ideas for Implementation<br>Brainstorm, evaluate, and implement ideas to meet business objectives. |
|---|---|---|---|
| **Demographic factors** | • Significant increase in the number of postal addresses in Canada. | • Additional costs to deliver to more addresses. | • Grow the parcel business to increase revenue.<br>• Maximize automated sorting of letter mail to manage costs per address. |
| **Socio-cultural factors** | • People are mailing fewer letters.<br>• Online shopping has taken off with the majority of Canadians.<br>• When Canadians order products online, they want control over their purchases. | • Decrease in revenue from letter mail.<br>• An increase in online shopping means more available parcel delivery business. | • Ensure Canada Post delivery is an option upon online checkout.<br>• Offer an excellent customer experience—accurate shipping rates, delivery options, fast and efficient delivery, tracking of the package along its journey, and if necessary, easy returns.<br>• Open "parcel pick-up" stores with drive-thru parcel pickup and change rooms to allow the customer to try on clothes purchased online and return them immediately if needed. |
| **Economic factors** | • Canadians spend $39 billion online annually.<br>• Only 13 percent of Canadian businesses are currently selling online. | • Parcel business could grow even further if more Canadian businesses sold products online. | • Collect customer data from parcel delivery.<br>• Help retailers with bricks-and-mortar stores implement ship-from-store solutions.<br>• Increase the number of new retailers selling online by helping them with their e-commerce startup and integrate Canada Post's technology into their websites.<br>• Introduce Canada Post E-Commerce Innovation Awards to recognize retailer success and identify promising startups to nurture and grow to the next level. |
| **Technological factors** | • There is widespread access to high-speed Internet service in Canada.<br>• Increase in e-billing.<br>• Digital advertising is growing, and the use of physical direct mail advertising is declining. | • Potential decrease in revenue from direct mail promotions.<br>• Decrease in revenue from letter mail. | • *Smartmail*—help businesses better target their customers for direct mail promotion.<br>• Offer help with post-campaign analysis.<br>• Conduct "*Science of Activation*" research to reinforce the value of direct mail in the promotional mix.<br>• *Epost* for the management of online bill payments. |

(Continued)

**Figure 2–8** (*Continued*)

| Factors in an Environmental Scan | STEP 1<br>Facts and Trends<br>Collect the facts and identify trends in each category. | STEP 2<br>Determine Impact<br>Analyze each external trend to determine its impact on the business. | STEP 3<br>Ideas for Implementation<br>Brainstorm, evaluate, and implement ideas to meet business objectives. |
|---|---|---|---|
| **Competitive factors** | • Parcel delivery business is quite competitive with three key competitors: Purolator, FedEx, and UPS.<br>• Emerging competition from regional/local competitors for parcel delivery.<br>• Barriers to enter the national parcel delivery business are high due to the required infrastructure. | • Canada Post has a comprehensive delivery infrastructure in place to compete effectively in the parcel delivery market. | • Create a competitive e-commerce parcel shipping business by providing excellent customer experience for the retailer and customers. |
| **Regulatory factors** | • Letter mail monopoly in Canada falls under the *Canada Post Corporation Act*.<br>• Consumer prices for letter mail are determined by regulation.<br>• Government of Canada is investing in the expansion of digital connectivity and digital commerce. | • Canada Post is responsible for the delivery of mail to all Canadian addresses.<br>• Future increases in e-commerce and demand for parcel delivery. | • Working with government-appointed review panel to determine the best path forward to serve Canadians while keeping Canada Post financially self-sufficient. |

**LO 1**
- An environmental scan is the process of continually acquiring information on events occurring outside an organization to identify external trends that are opportunities or threats to a business.

**LO 2**
- Elements in an environmental scan include demographic factors, socio-cultural factors, economic factors, technological factors, competitive factors, and regulatory factors.

**LO 3**
- Demographics is the statistical data about a population according to characteristics such as gender, age, ethnicity, income, education, and occupation.

- Socio-cultural forces look at cultural values, ideas, and attitudes, as well as society's morals and beliefs.

**LO 4**
- Economic forces consider macro and micro environmental factors. These forces reflect the state of the overall economy as well as the ability of consumers to spend.

**LO 5**
- Technological forces relate to scientific inventions and innovations that may impact the running of a business and influence consumer behaviour and interactions.

**LO 6**
- Competitive forces refer to direct and indirect competitors as well as the competitive nature of the market in which they function.

- Regulatory forces are the restrictions placed on businesses, products, or services by the government or industry associations.

**LO 7**
- Steps in a marketing environment scan involve (1) collecting the facts and identifying trends, (2) determining the impact that these facts/trends will have on the business, and (3) brainstorming, evaluating, and implementing ideas.

## key terms and concepts... **A REFRESHER**

baby boomers
binge viewing
competitive forces
demographics
direct competitors
discretionary income
disposable income
Do Not Call List (DNCL)
economy
environmental scan
generation X
generation Y

generation Z
gross domestic product (GDP)
gross income
indirect competitors
inflation
interest rates
macroeconomic forces
microeconomic forces
millennials
monopolistic competition
monopoly
oligopoly

online behavioural advertising (OBA)
perfect competition
recession
regulations
showrooming
social TV
socio-cultural forces
spam
SWOT analysis
technological forces
unemployment rate

## hands-on... **APPLY YOUR KNOWLEDGE**

**Focus on demographic factors.** The Marketing NewsFlash box, "Understanding the 'Big 3'—Ethnic Shoppers," focused on the efforts of grocery chains to meet the needs of ethnic consumers. There are many articles that have been written on the topic of ethnic marketing. Do some research on the topic and choose a company that has adopted ethnic marketing strategies. Outline its strategies and tactics. Has it been successful? What should the company do next?

This chapter's opening vignette examines the massive changes made at Canada Post based upon the changes taking place in the external environment. Assume that you are a marketing manager for UPS or FedEx. How would you respond to these changes and better compete?

## infographic... **DATA ANALYSIS**

Research new products that have been introduced in the automotive industry. Use recent data from Canadian newspapers (*National Post*, *Globe and Mail*), as well as other reputable business sources such as *Canadian Business*, *Maclean's*, and the DesRosiers Automotive Consultants website **(www .desrosiers.ca)**.

Review the "How Well Do You Know Gen Y vs. Gen Z?" Infographic. If you were an automobile manufacturer, what impact would this information have on the following:

- The products that you develop to target each generational group
- The way that you communicate with each group

# Consumer Behaviour

**U**nderstanding how prospective customers behave is a key element to the success of a business. Prior to making a purchase decision, Canadians traditionally identify a need and then seek information. They use that information to determine and evaluate alternatives to address their need. Once they have made a decision on how to address their need, they proceed with their purchase and then reflect on that purchase. With technology advancing to exciting levels, the purchase decision process has accelerated, leaving Canadians with more ways to buy products and services and more challenges to manage their spending.

(top): © Georgejmclittle | Dreamstime.com; (bottom): Used with permission of BLUERUSH

Approximately 30 years ago, the Canadian banking industry designed services focused specifically on the future of Canada. By cultivating a youth market, banks began to reap the rewards from post-secondary graduates. The key to their strategy involved building a relationship at an early age that was difficult to break in future years. Education of Canadians at a young age is key to this strategy. In the competitive banking market, banks offer students access to loans to start early relationships for life. These strategies are intended to help win their long-term business; however, it is important for students to stay in control of debt.

Fast forward a number of years and the now middle-aged Canadians are among the many who face a challenge with growing household debt. Although challenging economies and high-risk lending products may contribute to this issue, certain trends have been identified with respect to demographic and geographic characteristics. Although warning signs were identified years ago, Canadians predilection to borrowing, a weak Canadian dollar, and an obvious gap in financial literacy have created an issue.

Why debt continues to grow could be due to the speed at which decisions for purchases are now being made. Consumer purchase decisions can already be made quickly, and consumers have access to many credit facilities that facilitate their growing debt. Furthermore, programs for individuals struggling with debt in Canada are few and far between, making it difficult for consumers to access the right advice. And the individuals most affected with debt are younger Canadians.

BLUERUSH president and CEO Larry Lubin is helping financial services organizations address the need to educate Canadians on debt management as well as all essential areas of financial planning. Larry believes that the ease at which purchase decisions are made has caused Canadians to take on more debt. Larry speculates that "the reason many Canadians are in over their heads is they don't spend a lot of time evaluating the alternatives on what they purchase." Ironically, he finds that Canadian consumers don't engage with financial services companies as readily as companies with consumer products. "Financial services is a low engagement category. It typically takes seven impressions versus four (for non-financial categories) for the average person to absorb and recall a branded communication." That's where marketing comes in! "To drive a change in consumer behaviour takes effort and skill, not blind luck."

In an ever-increasing time of digital customer engagement, BLUERUSH is a digital marketing and solutions company specializing in developing personalized digital customer experiences for clients in North America. With 30+ years of expertise in marketing and selling financial products and services, BLUERUSH is able to explain complex concepts and products, and drive consumers to take action to purchase. With longstanding relationships with Canada's top brands, BLUERUSH delivers against its value proposition to enable the sale of products within a personalized digital customer experience.

For example, when Manulife Bank was ready to launch a new mortgage product in Canada, it turned to BLUERUSH for help. Manulife Bank understood that it needed a

**consumer behaviour**
Actions a person takes when purchasing and using products and services.

new approach to launch this product, and BLUERUSH knew that it needed to be sold differently. BLUERUSH combined its INDIVIDEO™ technology with its expertise-building financial calculators. Through an award-winning campaign, BLUERUSH helped Manulife Bank invite prospects across Canada to get their Manulife One number. Prospects had access to two interactive tools—a mortgage and debt calculator (on its own), and a combined INDIVIDEO™ and debt-consolidation calculator to help them make a sound decision. In other words, BLUERUSH made the evaluation of alternatives step in the decision-making process more engaging. The results of the campaign credited Manulife One as the second-most successful launch of a financial product in Canada. Manulife Bank saw a year-on-year increase in revenue and an increase in online engagement!

BLUERUSH also lent its expertise to the home and auto insurance market. One of the greatest challenges for an insurance company is increasing its conversion rate online. Insurance quoting is a competitive business, and most consumers use two or even three quoting engines from competing brands to arrive at the right deal. Allstate Canada approached BLUERUSH and launched a challenge to the company using INDIVIDEO™—develop an online conversion program that works all year long. BLUERUSH analyzed the instance where the business is a risk and devised a creative solution to increase consumer conversion rate as part of a quote nurture program. The result of increased engagement led to tripling quote conversions.

When making purchasing decisions, consumers are influenced by a number of factors, including the marketing mix chosen by companies. Consumers are also influenced by psychological, socio-cultural, and situational influences. There is no easy sale in financial services, and most successes are short-lived. Marketers can focus their effort to enable the sale by removing the obstacles that impede that sale in the first place. This can be achieved by isolating the value proposition that matters most to the target audience and educating consumers with content that is personalized to their unique situation.[1]

Since an organization's resources are limited, deciding where to allocate them is an important decision. By understanding the habits of potential customers, organizations can direct their resources in the appropriate manner. The INDIVIDEO™ videos describe how BLUERUSH helps businesses build a brand and reach target consumers. The market segmentation process relies on **consumer behaviour**—the actions a person takes in purchasing and using products and services—and insight to group buyers that have common needs and similar habits.

### reality CHECK ⊘

As you read Chapter 3, refer back to the BLUERUSH vignette to answer the following questions:

- When considering a purchase at a retail outlet, how much time do you spend online versus in-store evaluating your alternatives?
- How can financial services organizations make the decision-making process more engaging for Canadians?
- How do you believe consumer debt impacts the consumer purchase decision process?

# CONSUMER PURCHASE DECISION PROCESS

**LO 1**

Whether you are purchasing toothpaste or a new laptop for school, behind the visible act of making a purchase lies an important decision process. The stages that a consumer passes through when making choices about which products and services to buy is the **purchase decision process**. This process has five stages, as shown in Figure 3–1: problem recognition, information search, evaluation of alternatives, purchase decision, and post-purchase behaviour. Although technology has not changed the core elements of the process, the introduction of online and mobile technology has allowed consumers to make faster and more informed decisions.

A consumer's involvement in the purchase decision process varies based on the complexity of the decision. The time spent in each stage will depend on various factors, including what is being purchased. Access to information makes decision making a lot easier for Canadians, and access to credit makes purchasing items

**Figure 3–1**

Purchase decision process

| Problem recognition: Perceiving a need | → | Information search: Seeking value | → | Evaluation of alternatives: Assessing value | → | Purchase decision: Buying value | → | Post-purchase behaviour: Value in consumption or use |

easier as well. This has put Canadians in a challenging situation where they are now laden with debt due to purchasing items they have no room to store.[2]

Furthermore, businesses make decisions that follow a similar purchase decision process when considering products and services from suppliers. Chapter 5 looks at marketing to organizations in detail, including the different approaches required due to the magnitude of the decisions needed.

## PROBLEM RECOGNITION: PERCEIVING A NEED

Problem recognition, the initial step in the purchase decision, occurs when a person realizes that the difference between what he or she has and what he or she would like to have is big enough to actually do something about it. The problem can be solved or the need can be met by purchasing a good or a service.[3] The process may be triggered by a situation as simple as finding no milk in the refrigerator. It could be more tenuous for a college or university student realizing his wardrobe is not in style with his classmates. Furthermore, problem recognition can be as complex as purchasing a new laptop computer to excel in studies. In marketing, advertisements, salespeople, or peers activate the consumer purchase decision process by highlighting the shortcomings of existing products and services. Consider smartphone advertisements that have stimulated problem recognition by emphasizing maximum use from one device.

## INFORMATION SEARCH: SEEKING VALUE

After recognizing a problem, consumers begin to search for information about what product or service might satisfy the newly discovered need. First, they may scan their memory for knowledge of or previous experiences with products or brands. This action is called *internal search*. For frequently purchased products such as shampoo and conditioner, an internal search may be all

a consumer needs. If the decision is more complex, however, a consumer may undertake an *external search* for information.[4] An external search is beneficial when a consumer lacks experience with or knowledge about a product, the risk of making a bad decision is high, and the cost of gathering information is low. The primary sources of external information are *personal sources,* such as relatives and friends who the consumer trusts; *public sources,* including various product-rating organizations such as Consumer Reports or government agencies; and *marketer-dominated sources,* such as information from sellers that includes advertising, company websites, salespeople, and point-of-purchase displays in stores.

During their daily lives, consumers engage with multiple screens, which adds additional content to their information search.[5] The Infographic, "The New Multi-Screen World," helps us understand how consumers use multiple platforms to access information when making purchase decisions.

When purchasing a smartphone, your information search may include friends and relatives, advertisements for smartphones, brand and company websites, and stores carrying smartphones (for demonstrations). You might also study comparable evaluations of various smartphones as found in Consumer Reports, either published in hard copy or found online.

Once you have your smartphone, you will experience how mobile technology has added new behaviours to the consumer purchase decision process. Showrooming is an example of how all organizations, not just retailers, must integrate online mechanisms to optimize the overall customer experience. Since consumers can now review products and prices online, organizations that do not seamlessly incorporate online tools and technologies into their marketing, sales, and customer service efforts will be at a distinct competitive disadvantage. Online marketing is critical to small and medium-size businesses as consumers in Asia and North America have a high tendency to exhibit this showrooming behaviour.[6]

> **purchase decision process**
> Stages that a buyer passes through when making choices about which products or services to buy.

# Infographic

## The New Multi-Screen World
### Understanding Cross-Platform Consumer Behaviour

**■ Majority of media consumption is screen-based**

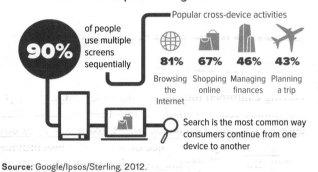

**90%** of all media interactions are screen-based

**38%** of our daily media interactions are on smartphones

**■ Television no longer commands our full attention**

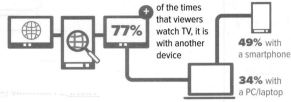

**77%** + of the times that viewers watch TV, it is with another device

**49%** with a smartphone

**34%** with a PC/laptop

**■ Consumers move between multiple devices to accomplish their goals**

**90%** of people use multiple screens sequentially

Popular cross-device activities

**81%** Browsing the Internet

**67%** Shopping online

**46%** Managing finances

**43%** Planning a trip

Search is the most common way consumers continue from one device to another

**■ Online shopping is a multi-screen activity**

Smartphones' accessibility enables spur-of-the-moment shopping

**67%** of people have used multiple devices sequentially to shop online

**19%** Planned

**81%** Spontaneous

**Source:** Google/Ipsos/Sterling, 2012.

# Infographic

## Consumers and Their Smartphones

### How are they using their phones?

**43%** of people use their phones to read reviews while in store

**31%** use their phones to compare price

**15%** use their phones to look up product information

**25%** use their phones to get advice from friends and family

**14%** use their phones to check availability at abother store

**23%** use their phones to take photographs of the product

**14%** use their phones to see if it's easier to order online

Used with permission of Kantar TNS

# ③ EVALUATION OF ALTERNATIVES: ASSESSING VALUE

The information-search stage clarifies the problem for the consumer by suggesting criteria, or points to consider, for the purchase; providing brand names that might meet the criteria; and developing consumer value perceptions. What selection criteria would you use in buying a smartphone? Would you use price, features, or some other combination?

Think about all the factors you may consider when evaluating smartphones. These factors are a consumer's *evaluative criteria,* which represent both the objective attributes of a brand (such as the number of applications available on the iPhone versus the Samsung Galaxy) and the subjective ones (such as the status of a business executive owning a iPhone) you use to compare different products and brands.[7] Firms try to identify and make the most of both types of evaluative criteria to create the best value for consumers. These criteria are often emphasized in advertisements.

For a product like a smartphone, the information-search process would probably involve visiting wireless providers such as Rogers and Telus, checking out these providers' websites, and talking to friends who own smartphones. Consumers often have several criteria for comparing products. For example, among the evaluative criteria you might think of, suppose that you focus on two that are crucial for you, namely pixel density and screen size. These criteria determine the brands in your *evoked*

Samsung continues to be a strong competitor in the smartphone market with offerings like the Galaxy S7.

Leszek Kobusinski/Shutterstock.com

*set*—the group of brands that a consumer would consider acceptable from among all the brands in the product class of which he or she is aware.[8] In this example, your two evaluative criteria may result in an evoked set of two brands (Samsung Galaxy and iPhone). For a further discussion about brands and their impact on consumer purchase behaviour, see the Marketing NewsFlash box, "Brands and Behaviour."[9]

# ④ PURCHASE DECISION: BUYING VALUE

Having examined the alternatives in the evoked set, you are almost ready to make a purchase decision. Three choices remain: the chosen brand, from whom to buy, and when to buy. The choice of which wireless provider to buy from will depend on such considerations as the provider's location, your past experience buying from the provider, and the return policy.

Deciding when to buy is frequently determined by a number of factors. For instance, you might buy sooner if one of your preferred brands is on sale or its manufacturer offers a rebate. Other factors, such as the store atmosphere, pleasantness of the shopping experience, salesperson persuasiveness, time pressure, and financial circumstances, could also affect whether a purchase decision is made or postponed.

If your decision is the latest Samsung Galaxy, you may decide to buy it from Telus because it offers unlimited local calling for six months as an added incentive.

Technology has enabled the process of gathering information, evaluating alternatives, and making buying decisions. The addition of this technological dimension to the consumer purchase decision process can accelerate the process because it puts information at consumers' fingertips.

Smartphones have become an integral part of our society and the consumer purchase decision process.

© Darrenbaker/Dreamstime.com/GetStock.com

# Brands and Behaviour

Consumer decisions are influenced by a number of factors. One of the psychological influences on decisions is the brand loyalty developed through learning. Corporate logos help consumers form strong perceptions of organizations. Consumers like to align themselves to brands that reflect their own self-concepts and self-images.

Along with learning, consumers are psychologically influenced by lifestyle. For example, it is suggested that millennials would rather rent than own. Unlike previous generations that look to home ownership as a milestone, millennials tend to put off purchasing homes and see home buying as an investment. The high cost of entry and the potential for a highly leveraged position are common reasons why millennials put this purchase off.

Understanding how brands drive consumer behaviour in consumer cohorts like millennials will help make marketers more effective. If millennials would rather not tie up their funds in huge purchases, it's no wonder why companies like Bose are winning millennials over. Millennials are independent and value quality. Bose has approached them with a strategy that emphasizes the firm's high-quality sound production, which millennials are willing to pay a premium for. Furthermore, confident in its technology, Bose took the time to understand millennials and partnered with Spotify, a digital music service frequented by millennials. Together, Bose and Spotify co-produced videos that educated the audience on sound and music production. These mini-documentaries are appealing to millennials, and the companies cross-marketed the series on their respective websites. ●

Bose and Spotify partnered on a project to engage millennials.

Mark Kelly/Alamy Stock Photo

## Questions

1. What associations come to mind with respect to Bose and Spotify?

2. As a consumer, give examples of brands that elicit positive associations with you and those that elicit negative associations with you.

**Effects of Mobile Technology on Purchase Behaviour** Mobile devices are not only popular consumer purchases, they are enablers of the consumer purchase decision. Mobile devices have allowed the purchase decision to evolve by making the information-search and purchase-decision stages easier. The younger and future consumer expects an online presence from companies and uses technology to research products, voice opinions, and express needs.[10]

Mobile devices have empowered consumers a great deal and caused companies to take notice. Best Buy uses a variety of strategies to successfully retain customers in its stores, even those that exhibit showrooming behaviour.[11] Cineplex Entertainment has leveraged mobile technology to enhance the consumer experience. When choosing a movie at the theatre, tickets can be purchased online at your home computer, at the box office, or at a kiosk on-site. Cineplex Mobile offers an easy-to-use service for moviegoers to purchase tickets online.

By using kiosks or purchasing tickets online, moviegoers can avoid the traditional lineups at the theatre.

Used with permission of Cineplex

## ⑤ POST-PURCHASE BEHAVIOUR: VALUE IN CONSUMPTION OR USE

After buying a product, the consumer compares it with his or her expectations and is either satisfied or dissatisfied. A company's sensitivity to a customer's consumption experience strongly affects the value a customer perceives after the purchase. Studies show that satisfaction or dissatisfaction affects consumer communications and repeat-purchase behaviour. Satisfied buyers tell three other people about their experience. Dissatisfied buyers complain to nine people![12] Furthermore, mobile technology allows buyers to share complaints and dissatisfaction in a more timely manner with even more reach.

In response, some companies are hiring employees to exclusively monitor sites such as Twitter and interact with unsatisfied customers right on the site. They are beginning to realize that the voice of the consumer on the web is very powerful. Consumers who are not finding satisfaction when a problem occurs may take matters into their own hands online. If a company were to Google its name followed by the word "sucks," it will find a large number of hits that consist of negative stories about consumers' experiences with its products. Other consumers are venting their frustrations on Twitter and Facebook. Progressive companies use this feedback as an opportunity to link up with these disgruntled customers and resolve the problems.

Often, a consumer is faced with two or more highly attractive alternatives, such as choosing between an iPhone and a Samsung Galaxy. If you choose the Samsung Galaxy, you may think, "Should I have purchased the iPhone?" This feeling of post-purchase psychological tension or anxiety is called *cognitive dissonance*. To alleviate it, consumers often attempt to applaud themselves for making the right choice. So, after purchase, you may seek information to confirm your choice by asking friends questions like, "What do you think of my new smartphone?" or by reading ads of the brand you chose. You might even look for negative features about the brand you didn't buy. Firms often use ads or follow-up calls from salespeople in this post-purchase stage to assure buyers that they made the right decision. It is important for firms to address consumer feelings of dissonance as it impacts their satisfaction and loyalty levels.[13]

# INVOLVEMENT AND PROBLEM-SOLVING VARIATIONS

**LO 2** Depending on the purchase decision, consumers may not engage in the five-step purchase decision process in the same manner. They may skip or minimize one or more steps depending on the level of **involvement** required. The level of involvement that a consumer has in a particular

Cognitive dissonance is the anxiety or tension felt after a purchase.

noppawan09/Shutterstock

purchase depends on the personal, social, and economic consequences of that purchase to the consumer.[14] Items such as soft drinks or toothpaste may have such a low level of involvement for consumers that they may skip or minimize one or more steps in the process. But consumers may do just the opposite for a high-involvement purchase like a computer or an automobile.

High-involvement purchase occasions typically have at least one of three characteristics: The item to be purchased is expensive; it is bought infrequently; or it could reflect on one's social image. For these occasions, consumers engage in extensive information search, consider many product attributes and brands, form attitudes, and participate in word-of-mouth communication. Marketers who sell high-involvement products such as cars, homes, and computers must understand the information-gathering and evaluation process of consumers. Researchers have identified three general variations in the consumer purchase process based on consumer involvement and product knowledge. Figure 3–2 summarizes some of the important differences between the three problem-solving variations.[15]

**Routine Problem-Solving** For products such as table salt and milk, consumers recognize a problem, make a decision, and spend little effort seeking external information and evaluating alternatives. The purchase process for such items is virtually a habit and typifies low-involvement decision-making. Routine problem-solving is typically the case for low-priced, frequently purchased products. An example is a consumer who stops by Tim Hortons on his way to work and purchases a coffee and a bagel. He doesn't ponder the potential benefits of going to a

**involvement**
Personal, social, and economic significance of a purchase to the consumer.

## Figure 3–2
Comparison of problem-solving variations

| Characteristics of Purchase Decision Process | Range of Consumer Involvement Low ←————————————→ High | | |
| --- | --- | --- | --- |
| | Routine Problem-Solving | Limited Problem-Solving | Extended Problem-Solving |
| Number of brands examined | One | Several | Many |
| Number of sellers considered | Few | Several | Many |
| Number of product attributes evaluated | One | Moderate | Many |
| Number of external information sources | None | Few | Many |
| Time spent searching | Minimal | Little | Considerable |

Second Cup or specialty coffee store even though they are all on his way to work. Marketers strive to attract and maintain habitual buying behaviour by creating strong brand relationships with the consumer.

### b) Limited Problem-Solving
Limited problem-solving is characterized by low consumer involvement but significant perceived differences among brands. For example, a consumer loves Activia yogourt but switches to BioBest yogourt, not out of dissatisfaction but just out of a desire to try something new. The consumer may have spent a moderate amount of time evaluating the available brands in the store before selecting BioBest. With limited problem-solving behaviour, consumers rely on past experience more than external information but they may pay attention to new varieties shown in advertising and point-of-purchase displays. Marketers of leading brands should focus on getting consumers to shift to routine problem-solving behaviour by dominating shelf space and running advertisements that remind consumers of the benefits of their brands. Consumers might use limited problem-solving when choosing a pair of jeans, deciding on a restaurant for dinner, and making other purchase situations in which they have little time or effort to spend researching options.

### c) Extended Problem-Solving
In extended problem-solving, each of the five stages of the consumer purchase decision process is used in the purchase, including considerable time and effort on external information search and identifying and evaluating alternatives. Several brands are in the evoked set, and these are evaluated on many attributes. Extended problem-solving exists in high-involvement purchase situations for items such as automobiles, houses, and financial investments.

Consumers might use limited problem-solving when choosing a restaurant for dinner.
© Iofoto/Dreamstime.com/GetStock.com

## CONSUMER PURCHASE DECISION PROCESS INFLUENCERS

Whether decisions require routine, limited or extended problem solving, a company's marketing mix influences the consumer purchase decision process. Figure 3–3 shows how the marketing mix and other influences play a role in decisions. The decision to buy a product can be impacted by important situational, psychological, and sociocultural influences. These influences are discussed throughout the remainder of this chapter.

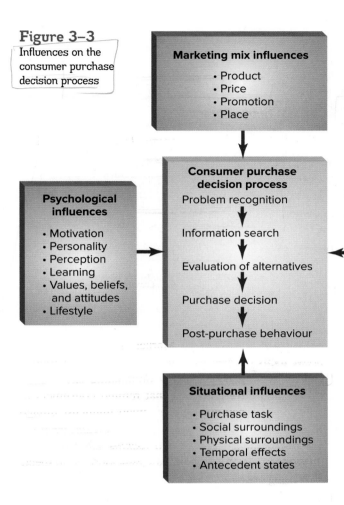

**Figure 3–3**
Influences on the
consumer purchase
decision process

**Marketing mix influences**

- Product
- Price
- Promotion
- Place

**Consumer purchase
decision process**

Problem recognition

↓

Information search

↓

Evaluation of alternatives

↓

Purchase decision

↓

Post-purchase behaviour

**Psychological
influences**

- Motivation
- Personality
- Perception
- Learning
- Values, beliefs,
  and attitudes
- Lifestyle

**Socio-cultural
influences**

- Personal
  influence
- Reference
  groups
- Family
- Culture
- Subculture

**Situational influences**

- Purchase task
- Social surroundings
- Physical surroundings
- Temporal effects
- Antecedent states

1. The *purchase task* is the reason for engaging in the decision in the first place. Information searching and evaluating alternatives may differ depending on whether the purchase is a gift, which often involves social visibility, or for the buyer's own use. For example, some consumers may be frugal shoppers when it comes to purchasing products for themselves, but may spend lavishly if the product is a gift for a friend.

2. *Social surroundings*, including the other people present when a purchase decision is made, may also affect what is purchased. For example, Paco Underhill, a behavioural research consultant, has shown that when two women shop together, they spend more time in the store shopping than they would if they were alone.[17]

3. *Physical surroundings* such as decor, music, and crowding in retail stores may alter how purchase decisions are made. Crowding, for example, is a two-edged sword. When consumers see a throng of people in the Apple Store, they may be eager to enter the store to be part of the experience. On the other hand, some people may be turned off because they don't like shopping in a crowded environment.

4. *Temporal effects*, such as time of day or the amount of time available, will influence where consumers have breakfast and lunch and what is ordered.

5. Finally, *antecedent states*, which include the consumer's mood or the amount of cash on hand, can influence purchase behaviour and choice. For example, a consumer who procrastinates buying a gift may choose one in an anxious state but may regret the purchase. If that consumer did not wait to the last moment, a more satisfying product may have been purchased instead.

# SITUATIONAL INFLUENCES ON CONSUMER DECISIONS

**LO 3** Often, the purchase situation will affect the purchase decision process. Five *situational influences* have an impact on your purchase decision process: the purchase task, social surroundings, physical surroundings, temporal effects, and antecedent states.[16]

# PSYCHOLOGICAL INFLUENCES ON CONSUMER BEHAVIOUR

**LO 4** Psychology helps marketers understand why and how consumers behave as they do. In particular, concepts such as motivation and personality; perception; learning; values, beliefs, and attitudes; and lifestyle are useful for interpreting buying processes and directing marketing efforts. Although every consumer is a unique individual, common factors can cause similar behaviours.

## MOTIVATION AND PERSONALITY

Motivation and personality are two familiar psychological concepts that have specific meanings and marketing implications. They are both used frequently to describe why people do some things and not others.

**Motivation** Motivation is the energizing force that stimulates behaviour to satisfy a need. Because consumer needs are the focus of the marketing concept, marketers try to arouse these needs.

An individual's needs are boundless. People have physiological needs for basics such as water, food, and shelter. They also have learned needs, including esteem, achievement, and affection. The late psychologist Abraham Maslow developed a theory that characterized needs and arranged them into a hierarchy. He argued that people take care of their lower-level needs first and then are motivated to satisfy their higher-level needs. Figure 3–4 shows Maslow's hierarchy of needs, which contains the following five need classes:[18]

**motivation**
Energizing force that stimulates behaviour to satisfy a need.

1. *Physiological needs* are basic to survival and must be satisfied first. A

Self-actualization needs: Fulfillment of ambitions and hopes

Esteem needs: Status, respect, prestige

Social needs: Friendship, belonging, love

Safety needs: Freedom from harm, financial security

Physiological needs: Food, water, shelter

**Figure 3–4**
Maslow's hierarchy of needs

fast-food advertisement featuring a juicy hamburger attempts to activate the need for food.

2. *Safety needs* involve self-preservation and physical well-being. Smoke detector and burglar alarm manufacturers focus on these needs. Michelin combines security with parental love to promote tire replacement for automobiles.

3. *Social needs* are concerned with love and friendship. Dating services such as eHarmony and fragrance companies try to arouse these needs.

4. *Esteem needs* are represented by the need for achievement, status, prestige, and self-respect. Using the TD Aeroplan Infinite card and shopping at Holt Renfrew appeal to these needs. Sometimes, firms try to arouse multiple needs to stimulate problem recognition.

Shopping malls like the West Edmonton Mall host various consumers with different purchase decision motivations.

© Fallsview | Dreamstime.com

1. *Self-actualization needs* involve personal fulfillment. For example, travel providers offer specialized educational and exotic trips to enhance a consumer's life experience.

While Maslow believed that needs were innate, studies have found that social culture contributes to our identification of these needs. Therefore, it is critical for marketers to first understand our consumer needs in order to satisfy them.[19]

## Personality

**Personality** refers to a person's character traits that influence behavioural responses. Although numerous personality theories exist, most identify key traits such as assertiveness, extroversion, compliance, dominance, and aggression, among others. Research suggests that compliant people prefer known brand names and use more mouthwash and toilet soaps. In contrast, aggressive types use razors, not electric shavers; apply more cologne and aftershave lotions; and purchase signature goods such as Gucci, Yves St. Laurent, and Donna Karan as an indicator of status.[20]

Personality characteristics are often revealed in a person's *self-concept,* which is the way people see themselves and the way they believe others see them. Marketers recognize that people have an actual self-concept and an ideal self-concept. The actual self refers to how people actually see themselves. The ideal self describes how people would like to see themselves. Marketers appeal to these two self-images in the products and brands a person buys, including automobiles, home appliances and furnishings, magazines, clothing, grooming products, and leisure products, and in the stores where a person shops. The use of attractive models in ads for grooming products appeals to a person's ideal self-concept. Men are becoming more concerned about their self-concept when it comes to body image and grooming. Unilever has responded to this trend by introducing a line of grooming products for men called Dove Men+Care.

Dove Men+Care products appeal to the trend of men concerned about body image and grooming.

Used by permission of Unilever Canada Inc.

> *Research suggests that compliant people prefer known brand names and use more mouthwash and toilet soaps.*

# PERCEPTION

One person sees a Porsche as a mark of achievement; another sees it as showing off. This is the result of **perception**—that is, the process by which an individual selects, organizes, and interprets information to create a meaningful picture of the world.

## Selective Perception

The average consumer operates in a complex, information-rich environment. The human brain organizes and interprets all this information with a process called *selective perception,* which filters the information so that only some of it is understood or remembered or even available to the conscious mind. *Selective exposure* occurs when people pay attention to messages that are consistent with their attitudes and beliefs and ignore messages that are inconsistent. Selective exposure often occurs in the post-purchase stage of the consumer decision process, when consumers read advertisements for the brand they just bought. It also occurs when a need exists—you are more likely to "see" a McDonald's advertisement when you are hungry rather than after you have eaten a pizza.

*Selective comprehension* involves interpreting information so that it is consistent with your attitudes and beliefs. A marketer's failure to understand this can have disastrous results. For example, Toro introduced a small, lightweight snow-blower called the Snow Pup. Even though the product worked, sales failed to meet expectations. Why? Toro later found out that consumers perceived the name to mean that Snow Pup was a toy or too light to do any serious snow removal. When the product was renamed Snow Master, sales increased sharply.[21] *Selective retention* means that consumers do not remember all the information they see, read, or hear, even minutes after exposure to it. This affects the internal and external information-search stage of the purchase decision process. This is why furniture and automobile retailers often give consumers product brochures to take home after they leave the showroom.

### Perceived Risk

Consumers' beliefs about the potential negative consequences of a product or service strongly affect their purchasing decisions. **Perceived risk** represents the anxieties felt because the consumer cannot anticipate the outcomes of a purchase but believes that there may be negative consequences. Examples of possible negative consequences concerning snowboarding are the price of the product (Can I afford $400 for a snowboard?) and the risk of physical harm (Is snowboarding more dangerous than alpine skiing?). Some products such as hair colouring lend themselves to perceived risk. There is always the fear that the hair colouring may not turn out to the consumer's satisfaction. Perceived risk affects the information-search step of the purchase decision process: The greater the perceived risk, the more extensive the external search is likely to be.

Recognizing the importance of perceived risk, smart marketers develop strategies to make consumers feel more at ease about their purchases. Strategies and examples of firms using them include the following:

- **Obtaining seals of approval:** The Good Housekeeping seal that appears on many brands.
- **Securing endorsements from influential people:** Nike's products endorsed by LeBron James.
- **Providing free trials of the product:** Samples of perfume offered at Hudson's Bay.
- **Providing illustrations:** Photos of different colours and hairstyles on Clairol Canada's website.
- **Providing warranties and guarantees:** BMW's four-year, 80,000-kilometre warranty.[22]

## LEARNING

Why do consumers behave in the marketplace as they do? Over consumers' lifetimes, they learn behaviours and they also learn responses to those behaviours—this learning is a continual process. Consumers learn which sources to use for information about products and services, which evaluative criteria to use when assessing alternatives, and how to make purchase decisions. **Learning** refers to those behaviours that result from repeated experience and reasoning.

### Behavioural Learning

*Behavioural learning* is the process of developing automatic responses to a type of situation built up through repeated exposure to it. Four variables are central to how one learns from repeated experience: drive, cue, response, and reinforcement. A *drive* is a need, such as hunger, that moves an individual to action. A *cue* is a stimulus or symbol that one perceives. A *response* is the action taken to satisfy the drive, and a *reinforcement* is the

In 2015, LeBron James signed a lifetime endorsement deal with Nike.

Jason Miller/AP Photo/The Canadian Press

**perceived risk**
Anxiety felt when a consumer cannot anticipate possible negative outcomes of a purchase.

**learning**
Behaviours that result from repeated experience or reasoning.

New BMW vehicles like this one have a four-year, 80,000-kilometre warranty.

Thampapon/Shutterstock.com

*Consumers familiar with one product will often transfer their feelings to others that seem similar—whether the similarity is in a brand name or in the shape and colour of the packaging.*

reward. Being hungry (a drive), a consumer sees a cue (a billboard), takes action (buys a hamburger), and receives a reward (it tastes great!). If what the consumer experiences upon responding to a stimulus is not pleasant (I feel sick now!), then *negative reinforcement* has occurred. Behavioural learning plays a major role in consumer decision-making—in this case, causing the consumer to avoid the behavioural response rather than repeat it.

Marketers use two concepts from behavioural learning theory. *Stimulus generalization* occurs when a response brought about by one stimulus (cue) is generalized to another stimulus. Using the same brand name to launch new products is one common application of this concept, as when the makers of Tylenol followed up their original pain reliever with Tylenol Cold, Tylenol Flu, Tylenol Sinus, and others. Consumers familiar with one product will often transfer their feelings to others that seem similar—whether the similarity is in a brand name or in the shape and colour of the packaging. Are you familiar with President's Choice Cola or Costco's Simply Soda? They use red cans, similar in colour to Coca-Cola cans—this is stimulus generalization in action!

*Stimulus discrimination* refers to one's ability to perceive differences among similar products. Consumers may do this easily with some groups of products, such as automobiles. But in many cases, such as low-involvement purchases, advertisers work to point out the differences. For example, consumers' tendency to perceive all light beers as being alike led to Budweiser Light commercials that distinguished between many types of lights and Bud Light.

### Cognitive Learning
Consumers also learn without direct experience—through thinking, reasoning, and mental problem solving. This type of learning, called *cognitive learning*, involves making connections between two or more ideas or simply observing the outcomes of others' behaviours and adjusting your own accordingly. Firms also influence this type of learning. Through repetition in advertising, messages such as "Advil is a headache remedy" attempt

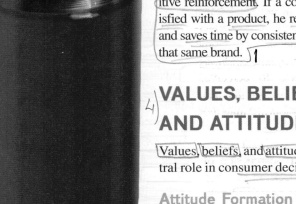

In the competitive soft drink market, companies may choose to package their colas in red cans similar to other brands.

© Akkaranant | Dreamstime.com

to link a brand (Advil) and an idea (headache remedy) by showing someone using the brand and finding relief.

### Brand Loyalty
Learning is also important to marketers because it relates to habit formation. Developing habits means that a consumer is solving problems (such as what to do when she's hungry) routinely and consistently, without much thought. Not surprisingly, there is a close link between habits and **brand loyalty**, which is a favourable attitude toward and consistent purchase of a single brand over time. Brand loyalty results from positive reinforcement. If a consumer is satisfied with a product, he reduces his risk and saves time by consistently purchasing that same brand.

## VALUES, BELIEFS, AND ATTITUDES

Values, beliefs, and attitudes play a central role in consumer decision-making.

### Attitude Formation
An **attitude** is a "learned predisposition to respond to an object or class of objects in a consistently favourable or unfavourable way."[23] Attitudes are shaped by our values and beliefs, which we develop in the process of growing up. For example, we speak of core values, including material well-being and humanitarianism. We also have personal values, such as thriftiness and ambition. Marketers are concerned with both, but focus mostly on personal values. Personal values affect attitudes by influencing the importance assigned to specific product attributes, or features. Suppose thriftiness is one of your personal values. When you evaluate cars, fuel economy (a product attribute) becomes important. If you believe a specific car has this attribute, you are likely to have a favourable attitude toward it.

**brand loyalty**
Favourable attitude toward and consistent purchase of a single brand over time; the degree of target market commitment toward a brand over time that results in varying levels of purchase commitment.

**attitude**
Tendency to respond to something in a consistently favourable or unfavourable way.

**beliefs**
Consumer's perceptions of how a product or brand performs.

Beliefs also play a part in attitude formation. In consumer terms, beliefs are one's perception of how a product or brand performs on different attributes. Beliefs are based on personal experience, advertising, and discussions with other people. Beliefs about product attributes are important because, along with personal values, they create the favourable or unfavourable attitude the consumer has toward certain products and services.

**Attitude Change**  Marketers use three approaches to try to change consumer attitudes toward products and brands, as shown in the following examples:[24]

1. *Changing beliefs about the extent to which a brand has certain attributes.* To reduce consumer concern that Aspirin use causes an upset stomach, Bayer Corporation successfully promoted the gentleness of its Extra Strength Bayer Plus Aspirin.

2. *Changing the perceived importance of attributes.* Consumers up to now were divided on the number of hours of sleep required for good health. Recent articles in the media are changing consumers' perceived importance of required hours. The Mayo Clinic, for example, recommends seven to nine hours of sleep for adults.[25] Sleep Country Canada emphasizes in its commercials the importance of getting a good night's rest and how Sleep Country can help the situation by providing a mattress that can improve the quality of sleep.

3. *Adding new attributes to the product.* Colgate-Palmolive included a new antibacterial ingredient, triclosan, in its Colgate Total Toothpaste and spent $100 million marketing the brand. The result? Colgate Total Toothpaste is now a billion-dollar-plus global brand.

## LIFESTYLE

Lifestyle is a way of living that reflects how people spend their time and resources (activities), what they consider important in their environment (interests), and how they think of themselves and the world around them (opinions). The analysis of consumer lifestyles, called *psychographics,* has produced many insights into consumer behaviour. For example, lifestyle analysis has proven useful in segmenting and targeting consumers for new and existing products and services. One of the most psychographic systems is the VALS system from Strategic Business Insights.[26] The VALS, which stands for "values and lifestyles," identifies eight interconnected categories of adult lifestyles based on a person's self-orientation and resources. *Self-orientation* describes the patterns of attitudes and activities that help a person reinforce his or her social self-image. Three patterns have been uncovered, which are oriented toward principles, status, and action. A person's resources range from minimal to abundant and include income, education, self-confidence, health, eagerness to buy, intelligence, and energy level. Each of these categories exhibits different buying behaviour and media preferences.

VALS is an American-based system, and the psychographics of Americans differ significantly from those of Canadians. When some market researchers have tried to use American values and lifestyles to describe Canadians, they have not succeeded. For Canadian insights, marketers can turn to one of the leading firms in marketing and analytical services: Environics Analytics. Through its PRIZM5 segmentation system, Environics Analytics has segmented the Canadian population into a variety of data points, including demographics, lifestyles, and values. Figure 3–5 provides an example of segments in the Canadian population that rank high on attending professional basketball games. Although these segments have unique characteristics, there are similar traits among them that create a larger target market for products and services related to basketball.

As part of the PRIZM5 system, Environics Analytics provides exceptional insight into 68 segments of the Canadian population. For example, it describes a

**Figure 3–5**

PRIZM5 segments that attend professional basketball games

**11 URBAN DIGERATI**
U3 URBAN YOUNG | SINGLES SCENE Y1
Younger, well-educated city singles

**15 HERITAGE HUBS**
S3 SUBURBAN UPSCALE DIVERSE | OLDER PARENTS, YOUNGER KIDS F3
Middle-aged, diverse suburban families

**27 DIVERSE CITY**
U2 URBAN UPSCALE DIVERSE | OLDER FAMILIES F9
Middle-income, diverse city dwellers

**43 NEWCOMERS RISING**
U4 URBAN YOUNGER DIVERSE | YOUNG DIVERSE FAMILIES F1
Downscale, younger and middle-aged city immigrants

**65 YOUNG & CONNECTED**
U6 URBAN DOWNSCALE | STARTER NESTS Y2
Low-income, diverse urban renters

**Source:** © 2017 Environics Analytics; PRIZM is a registered trademark of Claritas, LLC and used with permission.

*Psychographics clusters tie lifestyle traits to postal codes.*

specific segment of the population as Grads & Pads—number 38 on the 68-rung socio-economic ladder. These individuals are described as young, well-educated individuals living near post-secondary education institutions who like to stay active skiing and working out at health clubs. While this generalized description may not describe every individual in the segment, it provides an overall theme of the expected consumer behaviour of the individuals living in postal codes associated with that segment.[27]

Environics Analytics is one of the leaders in consumer segmentations. The sample segments described earlier fall into much broader socio-economic categories, and life-stage groups continue to change with every new Canadian census. Figure 3–6 provides examples of the broader socio-economic categories of the PRIZM5 segmentation system. By using the key drivers of demographics, lifestyles, and values, Environics Analytics creates added-value tools for marketers to understand consumer behaviour and markets anywhere in Canada.

## Figure 3–6
Examples of PRIZM5 cluster categories

| Segment Code | Cluster Category | Brief Description |
|---|---|---|
| U1 | Urban Elite | The most affluent Canadian households belong to Urban Elite, the social group that ranks at the top of several demographic measures: income, home value, and educational achievement. With their university degrees and positions as executives and professionals, these middle-aged and older residents tend to live in fashionable homes in big-city neighbourhoods and close-in suburbs. |
| S1 | Suburban Elite | The households in Suburban Elite represent the most upscale suburban social group, characterized by middle-aged and older families living in single-family homes. One socio-economic rung down from Urban Elite, these Canadians have university and college educations, and hold service-sector and white-collar jobs. |
| E1 | Exurban Elite | Exurban Elite consists of the wealthiest households outside the nation's metropolitan sprawl, beyond the suburbs but within reasonable commutes to city jobs. The residents in this exurban group tend to be married, middle-aged and older couples and families who live in comfortable homes and hold a mix of white-collar, blue-collar, and service-sector jobs. With their large families of school- and college-aged children, households here have high rates of enjoying team and winter sports, golfing, boating, community theatre, and all types of exhibitions: craft, cottage, fitness, gardening, pet, and home. |
| U2 | Urban Upscale Diverse | Generally found in Toronto, Vancouver, and Montreal, the Urban Upscale Diverse group consists of four mostly middle-income segments with high concentrations of immigrants, especially from Asia, Europe, Central America, and the Middle East. Their households are a mix of middle-aged and older couples and families, with children in their late teens and twenties. Many residents inhabit a bi-cultural world, with nearly a third speaking a language at home other than English or French. |
| S2 | Suburban Younger | The four Suburban Younger segments contain family-filled households where most maintainers are under 45 years old. Because the adults in this group have varying educational backgrounds—from high school to university degrees—and many having only recently entered the labour force, household income levels range from upscale to lower-middle, earned from a broad mix of jobs. But most families can afford to own their homes, typically recently built singles, semis, and row houses. |
| E2 | Exurban Middle-Aged | The Exurban Middle-Aged group represents the nation's middle-aged, mostly midscale couples and families living in Canada's growing exurban communities. In these mixed households—the families feature children of all ages—parents holding college diplomas or less work at a range of blue-collar, white-collar, and service-sector jobs; their average incomes allow them to own single-family homes built after 1980. With their neighbourhoods located outside the nation's big cities, the cost of living is lower than average, and residents pursue active, outdoorsy lifestyles. |
| U3 | Urban Young | Home to the nation's youngest residents, Urban Young consists of households with maintainers who are typically under 45 years old. With many just entering the workforce, these university-educated singles and couples earn a range of incomes—from upper-middle to lower-middle income—from their white-collar and service-sector jobs. Without the financial obligations of a family, they're able to rent decent apartments in older, downtown neighbourhoods and lead a hip, progressive lifestyle. |

**Source:** © 2017 Environics Analytics; PRIZM is a registered trademark of Claritas, LLC and used with permission.

1. The problem with the Toro Snow Pup was an example of selective _____.

2. What three attitude-change approaches are most common?

3. What does the concept of lifestyle mean?

# SOCIO-CULTURAL INFLUENCES ON CONSUMER BEHAVIOUR

**LO 5** Socio-cultural influences, which evolve from a consumer's formal and informal relationships with other people, also have an impact on consumer behaviour. These include personal influence, reference groups, family, culture, and subculture.

## PERSONAL INFLUENCE

A consumer's purchases are often influenced by the views, opinions, or behaviours of others. Two aspects of personal influence are important to marketing: opinion leadership and word-of-mouth activity.

**opinion leaders**
Individuals who have social influence over others.

**word of mouth**
People influencing each other in personal conversations.

**Opinion Leadership** Individuals who have social influence over others are called **opinion leaders**. Opinion leaders are more likely to be important for products that provide a form of self-expression. Automobiles, clothing, and club memberships are products affected by opinion leaders, but appliances usually are not.[28]

A small percentage of adults—from influential community leaders and business executives to movie stars—are opinion leaders. Identifying, reaching, and influencing opinion leaders is a major challenge for companies. Some firms use sports figures or celebrities as spokespersons to represent their products, such as NFL quarterback Eli Manning for Citizen watches.

**Word of Mouth** People influencing each other during conversations is called **word of mouth**. Word of mouth is perhaps the most powerful information source for consumers, because it typically involves friends or family who are viewed as trustworthy.

The power of personal influence has prompted firms to make efforts to increase positive and decrease negative word of mouth.[29] For instance, "teaser" advertising campaigns are run in advance of new-product introductions to stimulate conversations. Other techniques such as advertising slogans, music, and humour also heighten positive word of mouth. On the other hand, rumours about McDonald's (worms in hamburgers) and Corona Extra beer (contaminated beer) have resulted in negative word of mouth, none of which was based on fact. Overcoming negative

Companies like Citizen use celebrities as spokespeople to represent its products and influence consumer decision-making.

Courtesy Citizen Watch Company of America, Inc.

## focus on Ethics

# Social Issues and Consumer Behaviour

One of the most powerful forms of marketing is a natural activity: talking. Telling others your opinion about products and brands. Word-of-mouth marketing is an extraordinary tool for marketers to use to promote their brands, and technology has enabled word-of-mouth promotions, allowing social media to create a forum with mass reach.

In a study involving cultural industries that create, produce, and commercialize anything from musical performances to video games, it was found that professional commentators had a more positive influence on buying decisions than the comments made by ordinary consumers. These opinion leaders have an influence in the future buying decisions of Canadians. When Canadians use online group-buying sites, Internet advertising and electronic word of mouth have a positive influence on consumers.

Being extremely impactful to the future economy as a generation, marketers need to better understand what drives the millennials to word of mouth and loyalty. One key driver to the purchases of millennials is social issues like the environment; millennials reward brands with this focus through word of mouth and loyalty.

Based in Regina, Saskatchewan, tentree International is a company that catches a millennial's attention. It commits to ten trees planted for every product purchased, whether that be directly from its online store, or from one of its over 300 retail partners. By planting millions of trees, tentree is providing employment, protecting wildlife, restoring eco-systems, and educating locals, as well as providing wood for fuel, cooking, and building in impoverished areas. tentree also has partnerships across

Used with permission of tentree International

the world to help identify areas that can benefit from planting trees. ●

### Questions

1. How does the impact that tentree International makes to the environment and communities across the world influence your decision to purchase clothing from this company?

2. When you consider buying a large ticket item, how much do you consider social issues in your purchase decision?

---

word of mouth is difficult and costly. Firms have found that supplying factual information, providing toll-free numbers for consumers to call the company, and giving appropriate product demonstrations also have been helpful.

The term buzz marketing refers to a brand becoming popular as a result of people talking about it to friends and neighbours. Another way that a company can create buzz is by hiring an outside agency. Word-of-mouth agencies such as Matchstick specialize in product-seeding programs. Product seeding consists of hiring people to talk up a brand to others. The Word of Mouth Marketing Association (WOMMA) has issued ethical guidelines on product seeding, including the guideline that brand representatives must always disclose their relationship to the brand when promoting it to others.

> *Product seeding consists of hiring people to talk up a brand to others.*

The power of word of mouth has been magnified through online marketing. The online version of word of mouth is called viral marketing. This includes the use of messages that consumers pass along to others through online forums, social networks such as Facebook and Twitter, chat rooms, bulletin boards, blogs, and e-mails. These messages can be positive or negative. Companies are now recognizing the value of social media platforms such as Twitter and Facebook, and are monitoring messages so that they can respond to consumers quickly. The Focus on Ethics box, "Social Issues and Consumer Behaviour," considers the impact of social issues for some consumers' purchasing habits.[30]

## REFERENCE GROUPS

A **reference group** is a group of people who influence a person's attitudes, values, and behaviours. For example, you might consider your family or the other students in your school as a reference group. Other examples of reference groups are movie stars and sports celebrities. Reference groups affect consumer purchases because they influence the information, attitudes, and aspiration levels that help set a consumer's standards. Reference groups have an important influence on the purchase of luxury products but not of necessities—reference groups exert a strong influence on the brand chosen when its use or consumption is highly visible to others.[31]

Consumers have many reference groups, but three groups have clear marketing implications:

**reference group**
A group of people who influence a person's attitudes, values, and behaviour.

**family life cycle**
A family's progression from formation to retirement, with each phase bringing distinct needs and purchasing behaviours.

- **Membership group:** One to which a person actually belongs, including fraternities and sororities, social clubs, and family. Such groups are easily identifiable and are targeted by firms selling insurance, insignia products, and vacation packages.
- **Aspiration group:** One that a person wishes to be a member of or wishes to be identified with. An example is a person whose dream it is to play in the NHL. Brands such as Gatorade and Nike frequently rely on spokespeople or settings associated with their target market's aspiration group in their advertising.
- **Dissociative group:** One that a person wishes to maintain a distance from because of differences in values or behaviours.

## FAMILY INFLUENCE

Family influences on consumer behaviour result from three sources: consumer socialization, passage through the family life cycle, and decision making within the family or household.

**Consumer Socialization** The process by which people acquire the skills, knowledge, and attitudes necessary to function as consumers is *consumer socialization*.[32] Children learn how to purchase by interacting with adults in purchase situations and through their own purchasing and product usage experiences. Research demonstrates that children show signs of brand preferences as early as age 2, and these preferences often last a lifetime. This knowledge prompted Time Inc. to launch *Sports Illustrated for Kids*. The brand of toothpaste, laundry detergent, or soft drink used in your home will very likely influence your brand choice when you purchase these items for yourself.

**Family Life Cycle** Consumers act and purchase differently as they go through life. The **family life cycle** concept describes the distinct phases that a family

The late Steve Jobs co-founded Apple, built it into the world's leading tech company, and led a mobile computing revolution with wildly popular deices such as the iPod, iPhone, and iPad that connected different generations of a family.

**left:** © Aflo Foto Agency/Alamy Stock Photo; **right:** © Paul Sakuma, File/AP Photo/The Canadian Press

progresses through from formation to retirement, each phase bringing with it identifiable purchasing behaviours.[33] Today, the traditional family—married couples with children—constitute just over 26 percent of all Canadian households. Nearly 30 percent are households without children.[34]

Young single consumers' buying preferences are for nondurable items, including prepared foods, clothing, personal care products, and entertainment. They represent a significant target market for recreational travel, automobile, and consumer electronics firms. Young married couples without children are typically more affluent than young singles because usually both spouses are employed. These couples exhibit preferences for furniture, housewares, and gift items for each other. Young marrieds with children are driven by the needs of their children. These families make up a sizable market for life insurance, various children's products, and home furnishings. Single parents with children are the least financially secure type of households. Their buying preferences are usually affected by a limited economic status and tend toward convenience foods, child care services, and personal care items.

Middle-aged married couples with children are typically better off financially than their younger counterparts. They are a significant market for leisure products and home improvement items. Middle-aged couples without children typically have a large amount of discretionary income. These couples buy better home furnishings, status automobiles, and financial services. Persons in the last two phases—older married and older unmarried—make up a sizable market for prescription drugs, medical services, vacation trips, and gifts for younger relatives.

**Family Decision-Making** A third family-based influence on consumer decision-making occurs in the context of the relationship dynamics of the household. Two decision-making styles exist: spouse-dominant and joint decision-making. With a joint decision-making style, most decisions are made by both husband and wife. Spouse-dominant decisions are those for which either the husband or the wife has more influence in the purchase decision. Research indicates that wives tend to have the most say when purchasing groceries, children's toys, clothing, and medicines. Husbands tend to be more influential in home and car maintenance purchases. Joint decision-making is common for cars, vacations, houses, home appliances and

electronics, medical care, and long-distance telephone services. As a rule, joint decision-making increases with the education of the spouses.[35]

> *Even though women are often the grocery decision makers, they are not necessarily the purchaser. Husbands do about one-half of food shopping.*

Roles of individual family members in the purchase process are another element of family decision-making. Five roles exist: information gatherer, influencer, decision maker, purchaser, and user. Family members assume different roles for different products and services.[36]

Furthermore, since 70 to 80 percent of consumer purchasing is done by the buying power of influence of women, men's clothing stores may choose to advertise in women's magazines such as *Chatelaine* and *Redbook*. Even though women are often the grocery decision makers, they are not necessarily the purchaser. Husbands do about one-half of food shopping. Increasingly, preteens and teenagers are the information gatherers, influencers, decision makers, and purchasers of products and services items for the family, given the prevalence of working parents and single-parent households. Children

Families may influence the decisions made by their family members.
gilaxia/iStock/Getty Images Plus

and teenagers directly influence billions of dollars in annual family purchases. These figures help explain why, for example, Johnson & Johnson, Apple, Kellogg, P&G, Sony, and Oscar Mayer, among countless other companies, spend billions annually in media that reach preteens and teens.[37]

# CULTURE AND SUBCULTURE

**LO 6**

**Culture** refers to the set of values, ideas, and attitudes that are learned and shared among the members of a group. Thus, we often refer to Canadian culture, American culture, or Japanese culture. Describing Canadian culture may be difficult due to the diversity in the nation, but many could agree that Canadians are individuals who are polite and fair. Canadians value politeness and feel uncomfortable in situations of conflict. It is a balance of pride and humility. This generalization does not stem to all Canadians, and inaccurate perceptions of Canada were addressed by Molson through its "rant ad" beer commercials in 2000.[38]

Subgroups within the larger, or national, culture with unique values, ideas, and attitudes are referred to as **subcultures**. Subcultures can be defined by regions, by demographic groups, or by values. The most prominent types of subcultures are racial and ethnic, and many of these exist within the Canadian mosaic of people. French, German, Italian, Chinese, and Ukrainian subcultures are the ones we see most in Canada, and they make up nearly 40 percent of the Canadian population. Each one exhibits unique buying patterns and socio-cultural behaviours.

Canada's outlook on ethnicity is that cultural and ethnic groups are welcome to continue with their traditions, languages, and values. Canada is a nation of many faces, and people have been immigrating here continually over many decades. A person may regard herself as Italian, yet never have been to Italy—her grandparents may have immigrated here many years ago. If Italian customs have been maintained by the family, she may behave much like a recently arrived Italian. Some countries encourage immigrants to join the mainstream national culture, while diversity is encouraged in Canada.

Our ethnic composition, and the philosophy that we take toward it, has led to the creation of many ethnic neighbourhoods in our cities. As our population becomes more diverse, people immigrating here bring foods from their native lands. Canadians do not have a lot of native food and preparation styles, so the country has been particularly welcoming of cuisine from around the world. Immigration has had a major influence on Canada's food market, both in the many restaurants and in food items available from all corners of the globe. Not only food consumption is affected by immigration but also many cultural events have become mainstream, and many local happenings are the result of a tradition or celebration brought here by some new Canadians.

## Examples of Canadian Subcultures

There are almost 10 million French-speaking Canadians in this country, about 30 percent of the population.[39] By far, the largest majority of them live in the province of Quebec. Research shows that French-speaking Quebecers do exhibit different consumption behaviour than the rest of Canada.[40] For example, when asked what is important to them, Quebecers are more likely than other Canadians to say "enjoying life" and "seeking happiness." French Canadians, more so than English Canadians, are more likely to believe that everybody should be free to do their own thing. Quebecers are also more willing to pay higher prices for convenience and premium brands. Some people feel that French Quebec can be characterized by a set of values that are traditional, consistent, and relatively static, but changes are evident. While values are still strong regarding family life and having children in a marriage, the use of birth control is rising, and the marriage rate is below the national average.

**culture**
A set of values, ideas, and attitudes that are learned and shared among the members of a group.

**subcultures**
Subgroups within a larger culture that have unique values, ideas, and attitudes.

## Canada's Diverse Consumers

**Identifiable Ethnic Group**

| Identifiable Ethnic Group | |
|---|---|
| English | 20% |
| French | 16% |
| Scottish | 14% |
| Irish | 14% |
| German | 10% |
| Italian | 4% |
| Chinese | 4% |
| North American Indian | 4% |
| Other | 51% |

**Note:** Respondents identified with more than one ethnic group, so percentages add up higher than 100 percent.
**Source:** "Canada," Central Intelligence Agency, The World Factbook website, accessed March 2017 at https://www.cia.gov/library/publications/resources/the-world-factbook/geos/ca.html.

French Quebecers are members of a Canadian subculture who are cautious about new products and often postpone trying something new until they see that the product has proven itself. They exhibit brand loyalty, but they will switch brands if offered a special. French Quebecers are less likely to buy grocery items on impulse, and are increasingly calculating in their food purchases. Some grocery chains have responded to this characteristic by offering more discount coupons, weekly specials, and money-saving tips. Quebecers like things that please the senses. For example, they like fine restaurants and fine wines. Quebecois women are also very fashion-conscious, and upscale brands such as Prada and Lancome sell well in Quebec. This desire for beauty helps explain why campaigns for anti-wrinkle products are even more successful in Quebec than in the rest of Canada.[41]

While the province of Quebec has the highest percentage of alcohol drinkers and the most-relaxed drinking laws in Canada, it also has the lowest percentage of excessive drinkers and the fewest alcohol-related problems. French Quebecers are big buyers of lottery tickets and more likely to subscribe to book clubs, but they make fewer long-distance phone calls. They travel less, whether for business or pleasure. More French Quebec adults hold life insurance policies, but they are less likely to have a credit card. They also tend to use the services of credit unions (*caisses populaires*) rather than banks. Marketers must realize that certain products and other elements of the marketing mix may have to be modified in order to be successful in French Quebec. In addition to cultural differences, there are other issues that marketers must address. Commercial advertising to children is prohibited, and greater restrictions exist for alcohol advertising. Provincial regulations also require that labels and packages must be both English and French, while storefront signage must be in French, not English. Good investigation and analysis of this market is a requirement for all companies wishing to do business in this province.

Another Canadian subculture and one of the largest and fastest-growing visible minorities in Canada's population is Chinese, with 40 percent residing in Toronto and 31 percent in Vancouver. The average Chinese household spends $63,500 each year, slightly higher than the Canadian average of $58,500. In general, these consumers are relatively young, educated, and affluent. They tend to spend their money on home furnishings, automobiles, kids' education, high-tech gadgets, travelling, and gifts. They like to do business within their own communities and prefer media in their own languages. They have strong allegiance to brands and are very family-oriented. Because they live in close-knit communities, word of mouth is very important to them.[42]

Chinese-Canadians have a preference for luxury vehicles, and many car dealerships see them as good potential

Chinese New Year celebrations take place in Vancouver each year and have become an integral part of the city's cultural fabric.
© Richard Lam/The Canadian Press

customers for new cars. In general, they tend to eat out at restaurants more than the average Canadian, and there has been significant growth in the number of Chinese restaurants in Canada, and particularly in Vancouver and Toronto, over the past ten years. For these, and a number of other factors, many marketers cater to the Chinese market as they see them as being good prospective customers.

## GLOBAL CULTURAL DIVERSITY

Canada has become increasingly multiethnic and multicultural, making it one of the most diverse countries in the world. Different countries take different approaches to admitting immigrants and integrating them into society. Canada's approach is often referred to as a mosaic, meaning that people who come to the country from another are welcome to maintain their cultural identities and customs—the belief is that this will create a situation where all Canadians can learn from the rich variety of over 200 cultures that make up the citizenry of the country. This environment works to increase Canadian companies' sensitivity and orientation toward other cultures, so the transition to global activities and relationships is facilitated.

Just as marketers must be sensitive to subcultures in Canada, they must appreciate the cultural differences of people in other countries if they want to market products and services to them. A necessary step in this process is **cross-cultural analysis**, which involves the study of similarities and differences among consumers in two or more nations or societies.[43] A thorough cross-cultural analysis involves an understanding of and an appreciation for the values, customs, symbols, and language of other societies.

### Values

A society's values represent socially preferable modes of conduct or states of existence that tend to persist over time. Understanding and working with these aspects of a society are important factors in global marketing. For example, consider the following:[44]

- McDonald's does not sell hamburgers in its restaurants in India because the cow is considered sacred by almost 85 percent of the population. Instead, McDonald's sells the McMaharajah: two all-mutton patties, special sauce, lettuce, cheese, pickles, onions on a sesame-seed bun.

- Germans have not been overly receptive to the use of credit cards such as Visa or MasterCard, nor to the idea of borrowing to purchase goods and services. The German word for "debt," *Schuld*, is the same as the German word for "guilt."

### Customs

Customs are what is considered normal and expected about the way people do things in a specific country or culture. Clearly, customs can vary significantly from country to country. Some customs may seem unusual to Canadians. Consider, for example, that in France, men wear more than twice the number of cosmetics that women do, and that the Japanese consider slurping their food to be a sign of approval and appreciation to the chef.

The custom of giving token business gifts is popular in many countries where they are expected and accepted. However, bribes, kickbacks, and payoffs offered to entice someone to commit an illegal or improper act on behalf of the giver for economic gain is considered corrupt in most cultures. The widespread use of bribery in global marketing has led to an agreement among the world's major exporting nations to make bribery of foreign government officials a criminal offence.

**cross-cultural analysis**
Study of similarities and differences among consumers in two or more societies.

**customs**
Norms and expectations about the way people do things in a specific country or culture.

Coca-Cola executives learned valuable lessons when they used the Eiffel Tower and the Parthenon in global advertising campaigns.
**(left)** ©Wam1975/Dreamstime.com/GetStock.com; **(right)** ©Bcbounders/ Dreamstime.com/GetStock.com

The Organisation for Economic Co-operation and Development (OECD) is an international body whose goal is to foster democratic government and a market-driven economy. With its global reach, OECD addresses issues of general interest to its members and affiliates. Corruption has become an issue of major importance in the past decade, and the OECD has taken action to set guidelines and procedures for preventing international bribery and corruption. Canada has adopted the OECD's anti-corruption convention and has made bribery of foreign public officials a criminal offence.[45]

Bribery paid to foreign companies is another matter. In France and Greece, bribes paid to foreign companies are a tax-deductible expense!

The Nestlé Kit Kat bar influences teens in Japan through its translated meaning.
Courtesy of Nestlé

## Cultural Symbols

**Cultural symbols** are objects, ideas, or processes that represent a particular group of people or society. Symbols and symbolism play an important role in cross-cultural analysis because different cultures attach different meanings to things. By cleverly using cultural symbols, global marketers can tie positive symbolism to their products and services to enhance their attractiveness to consumers. However, improper use of symbols can spell disaster. A culturally sensitive global marketer will know the following:[46]

- North Americans are superstitious about the number 13, and Japanese feel the same way about the number 4. *Shi*, the Japanese word for "four," is also the word for "death." Knowing this, Tiffany & Company sells its fine glassware and china in sets of five, not four, in Japan.

- "Thumbs-up" is a positive sign in Canada. However, in Russia and Poland, this gesture has an offensive meaning when the palm of the hand is shown, as AT&T learned. The company reversed the gesture depicted in ads, showing the back of the hand, not the palm.

Cultural symbols stir up deep feelings. Consider how executives at Coca-Cola's Italian office learned this lesson. In a series of advertisements directed at Italian vacationers, the Eiffel Tower, Empire State Building, and the Tower of Pisa were turned into the familiar Coca-Cola bottle. However, when the white marble columns in the Parthenon that crown Athens's Acropolis were turned into Coca-Cola bottles, the Greeks were outraged. Greeks refer to the Acropolis as the "holy rock," and a government official said the Parthenon is an "international symbol of excellence" and that "whoever insults the Parthenon insults international culture." Coca-Cola apologized for the ad.[47]

## Language

Global marketers should know not only the basics of the native tongues of countries in which they market their products and services but also the subtleties and unique expressions of the language. For example, Pepsi found that Spanish-speaking people in Argentina tend to pronounce the soft drink as Pecsi rather than Pepsi. Pepsi responded by launching a successful marketing campaign that temporarily used the spelling Pecsi rather than Pepsi on billboards in Argentina. The brand name Pepsi was never really legally changed, but humorously altered for the period of the campaign.[48]

About 100 official languages exist in the world, but anthropologists estimate that at least 3,000 different languages are actually spoken. There are 11 official languages spoken in the European Union, and Canada has two official languages (English and French). Seventeen major languages are spoken in India alone.

English, French, and Spanish are the principal languages used in global diplomacy and commerce. However, the best language with which to communicate with consumers is their own, as any seasoned global marketer will agree. Language usage and translation can present challenges. Unintended meanings of brand names and messages have ranged from the absurd to the obscene, as in the following examples:

- When the advertising agency responsible for launching Procter & Gamble's successful Pert shampoo in Canada realized that the name means "lost" in French, it substituted the brand name Pret, which means "ready."

- The Vicks brand name common in North America is German slang for sexual intimacy; therefore, Vicks is called Wicks in Germany.

Experienced global marketers use **back translation**, where a translated word or phrase is retranslated back into

**cultural symbols**
Objects, ideas, or processes that represent a particular group of people or society.

**back translation**
Retranslating a word or phrase back into the original language by a different interpreter to catch errors.

# marketing NewsFlash

## McMillennials

The McDonald's kiosk and other innovations may appeal to millennials.

Tribune Content Agency LLC/Alamy Stock Photo

**W**hile enjoying a Big Mac™ for lunch in Squamish, British Columbia, a McDonald's customer may wonder if the experience she is enjoying is similar in other locations. Hopping on a plane and travelling to the East Coast, the customer will generally have a consistent experience at a McDonald's in Halifax.

Offering this level of consistency among all its locations is one of the strengths of McDonald's and why its brand is considered among the Top 10 global brands. Maintaining this consistency can pose a challenge with a company with over 1,400 stores in Canada. This can also get costly as innovation is needed to service future generations of customers.

According to UCLA Magazine, the millennial demographic is now larger than the baby boomer demographic. Marketers need to understand how to appeal to their desire for high-end brands and technology. Furthermore, millennials seem to be drawn to products from companies that have similar social and political values. Millennials are comfortable testing new technology and enjoy receiving content in small chunks. Millennials seem to shy away from old business models and look to models that embrace digital technology. Moreover, millennials view shopping as a sport, leading retailers to adopt a more experienced-based marketing strategy.

Interpreting what future generations need and want is a challenge. However, making bold moves to change the way traditional business is done is something McDonald's is a pioneer for across the world. For Canadians, McDonald's Canada has introduced a solution that will appeal to millennials who embrace utility. Self-service kiosks and table delivery is now available for individuals who choose not to stand and wait for their food. Furthermore, additions to the menu will allow for custom-made burgers. The 1,400 stores in Canada receiving this innovation will cost approximately $200,000 each to refit. By marketing to millennials who embrace digital technology, this can attract a new generation of brand-loyal consumers who value a consistent experience as well as a consistent product. ●

### Questions

1. How are your consumer behaviours similar to the generalizations describing millennials?

2. How will McDonald's kiosks impact your decision to go to McDonald's?

---

the original language by a different interpreter to catch errors.[49] IBM's first Japanese translation of its "Solution for a small planet" advertising message yielded "Answers that make people smaller." The error was caught by back translation and corrected. Sometimes, unintended translations can produce favourable results. Consider Kit Kat bars marketed by Nestlé worldwide. Kit Kat is pronounced "kitto katsu" in Japanese, which roughly translates to "I will win." Japanese teens eat Kit Kat bars for good luck, particularly when taking crucial school exams.[50]

Successful marketers understand the differences and similarities in consumers. They draw together commonalities and segment their audience into groups that will find their products and services appealing. By keeping current with the changing trends in consumer values and attitudes, marketers can stay in sync with their audiences. See, for example, the Marketing NewsFlash box, "McMillennials."[51]

Courtesy of Lufthansa USA

1. *What type of consumer involvement is required when choosing an airline ticket?*

2. *Describe the consumer purchase decision process as it relates to purchasing an airline ticket.*

**LO 1** • The first stage of the purchase decision process is problem recognition where the consumer perceives a need.

- The second stage is the information search where the consumer seeks value in the potential purchase options.

- The third stage is the evaluation of alternatives where the consumer assesses the value of each option.

- In the fourth stage, the consumer executes the purchase decision.

- In the fifth stage, the consumer determines the value of the purchase in post-purchase behaviour.

**LO 2** • Consumer purchase decisions range in complexity. This creates three variations of the consumer purchase decisions.

- Routine problem-solving, such as purchasing tissues when you have a cold, requires little effort.

- Limited problem-solving may occur when consumers compare and decide upon different brands, such as for refreshments.

- Extended problem-solving routinely involves time and consideration in each of the five distinct stages of the consumer purchase decision process. Purchasing electronics usually requires extended problem-solving.

**LO 3** • There are five situational influences that impact the consumer purchase decision process.

- The reason for engaging in the decision in the first place is called the purchase task. Why you are making the purchase may determine how much you plan on spending.

- Social surroundings, including who else is present in the process, also have an impact on the decision process.

- Another situational influence is the physical surroundings during the process. A store that is busy may have a positive or negative effect on the consumer.

- When the purchase is being made is a temporal effect, and the momentary mood or antecedent state of the consumer also affects the process.

**LO 4** • The main psychological influences affecting consumer behaviour are motivation and personality; perception; learning; values, beliefs and attitudes; and lifestyle.

- Motivation is the energizing force that causes consumers to satisfy a need, while personality and character traits influence behavioural responses.

- Perception is important to marketers because of the selectivity of what a consumer sees or hears, comprehends, and retains.

- Consumers learn from repeated experience, and brand loyalty is a result of learning.

- The values and beliefs of a consumer create their learned predisposition or attitudes toward a product.

- The consumers' lifestyle identifies how they plan to spend their time and resources.

**LO 5** • The consumer purchase-decision process can be affected by personal influence, reference groups, and family influences.

- Personal influence can be seen in opinion leadership and word-of-mouth activity. These are normally created by individuals with social influence. Personal influence can also take the form of reference groups.

- Family influences on consumer behaviour include where the family is in its family life cycle and how decisions are made within the household.

**LO 6** • Culture is the set of values, ideas, and attitudes that are learned and shared among the members of a group.

- There are subgroups within larger cultures that have unique values, ideas, and attitudes. These subgroups are called subcultures.

- Both culture and subculture influence consumer behaviour as these values permeate through situational, psychological, and socio-cultural influences.

| | | |
|---|---|---|
| attitude | culture | perceived risk |
| back translation | customs | perception |
| beliefs | family life cycle | personality |
| brand loyalty | involvement | purchase decision process |
| consumer behaviour | learning | reference group |
| cross-cultural analysis | motivation | subcultures |
| cultural symbols | opinion leaders | word of mouth |

**Changing Technology and Consumer Purchase Behaviour Assignment**   BLUERUSH helps financial services organizations engage consumers through online marketing. BLUERUSH has adapted as the needs of consumers have adapted over the years. Reflecting on how technology has evolved in your lifetime and on new technology products on the rise, provide a prediction of how consumers will be searching for information in the next 5, 10, and 15 years.

*chapter vignette...* **ACTIVITY**

The vignette at the beginning of the chapter stresses the importance of engaging consumers, especially when it comes to financial services products. The chapter also discusses the various influences affecting whether a consumer purchases a particular product. In your class, work individually or within a group to list how opening a new bank account would fall within each of the stages of the consumer purchase decision process. After listing the steps, identify which situational, psychological, and socio-cultural influences might affect your decision.

*infographic...* **DATA ANALYSIS**

The Infographic entitled "The New Multi-Screen World" discusses the integrated access to information that consumers use to make purchase decisions. Reviewing recent articles in the *Toronto Star,* the *Globe and Mail,* and other reputable business sources, add one more section to the Infographic specifically about purchasing a laptop.

The Infographic entitled "Consumers and Their Smartphones?" illustrates how consumer habits with their smartphones. Try to find the most recent information online and update this Infographic.

# Market Research, Metrics, and Analytics

**M**arket research, metrics, and analytics are tools used by marketers to gather data and obtain insights to make fact-based decisions easier and more accurate. Today, forward-thinking organizations use these tools and foster a culture of measurement, analytics, and continuous improvement by investing in technology, partnerships, and people. The goal is to manage data and to discern patterns, correlations, and insights that are actionable and provide a competitive edge. This chapter focuses on these tools, explaining their purpose and how they are used in this era of big data.

Used with permission of Delvinia

The market research industry is being driven by the needs of its clients. And clients are demanding insights faster than ever before, often with reduced budgets and a multitude of different research objectives all to be delivered by one research study. Delvinia recognized these changes early on and felt that it could take advantage of this opportunity by delivering digital tools and platforms that provide faster, lower-cost alternatives to traditional market research.

Delvinia has been on the cutting edge of the technology race with its AskingCanadians online research panel and, most recently, Methodify. Delvinia has partnered with national brands and loyalty programs including HBC Rewards, Aeroplan, Walmart, Petro-Points, and VIA Préférence, to reward panellists for their participation in surveys.

The alcoholic drink industry has experienced modest growth over the past few years. Companies are searching out opportunities for growth. Historically, Canadians have sought out premium products—higher-priced wines and ultra-premium spirits.

But rising prices and diminishing disposable incomes have created increased competition among key industry players.

Corby Spirit and Wine, a leader in the wine and spirits industry in Canada, was interested in a cost-effective way to gather customer insights quickly. Corby's portfolio of owned brands includes some of the most renowned brands in Canada, including J.P. Wiser's® Canadian whisky, Lamb's® rum, Polar Ice® vodka, and McGuinness® liqueurs. For Corby, managing its own in-house customer panel would be difficult and costly. This is where Delvinia was able to step in and partner with Corby to create a targeted customer research community with over a million AskingCanadians panel members. From this large panel, 30,000 people above the legal drinking age were opted in to be part of the panel. Using Corby's proprietary consumer segmentation tool, this group of 30,000 was further classified into various consumer types based on values, attitudes, socializing patterns, and socio-demographic lifestyle variables.

This was the beginning of the Corby Panel. What are the advantages to Corby? Using the same panel over time provides consistency and efficiency in results. And the process is fast: A survey can be initiated today, and results can be available within days, rather than weeks. This fast turnaround allows Corby to tap into the minds of its customers to obtain insights regarding specific brands, flavours, advertising concepts, and packaging on a regular basis.

To date, over 80 separate research projects have been initiated using the Corby Panel. What have been the results for Corby?

- Optimization of elements of the marketing mix through pre-testing of packaging, flavours, new products, taglines, and promotional campaigns
- Enhancing partnerships with business customers, including bars, restaurants, and liquor stores, by sharing customer insights and implementing programs to enhance sales
- Exploratory research to determine the best customer segments for each brand and/or new product

Corby has used the panel to better understand the impact of the Corby Safe Rides campaign on the corporate brand. The campaign started in 2013 and is a partnership with the Toronto Transit Commission (TTC), providing complimentary TTC rides on New Year's Eve. Beginning at 7 p.m. on New Year's Eve until 7 a.m. on New Year's Day, the initiative is in support of "responsible consumption and safe transportation options on one of the busiest nights of the year."

The objectives of the Corby Safe Rides study were the following:

- Track awareness of the Corby Spirit and Wine brand.
- Understand brand associations and consumer perceptions on key images, as well as changes since the Corby Safe Rides program began.

Used with permission of Delvinia

● Assess the ongoing impact of the Corby Safe Rides program, and look for new ways to optimize the program.

Based on the results of the Corby Panel research, the Corby Safe Rides initiative has become even more impactful. In 2015, Corby encouraged the public to take a pledge not to drink and drive on New Year's Eve. Those who made the commitment were entered in a contest for a year of free TTC passes. Riders were encouraged to take the pledge by using the Shazam app on their smartphones to scan specially marked posters appearing in buses, in streetcars, and on token boxes attached to bottles of Corby's liqueur brands available at 65 LCBO stores across Toronto. Corby also attached 11,000 complimentary tokens to bottles to provide safe, free rides to Torontonians over the holiday season.

In December 2015, Corby announced it was extending its partnership with the TTC into 2019.

The Corby Panel enables Corby to be a responsive business, being able to act in real time. The Corby Panel is "always on" and ensures that customer issues do not remain unknown or unaddressed. Patrick O'Driscoll, Corby CEO agrees: "The Corby Panel is an invaluable tool used by multiple teams for diverse projects, and it empowers us to keep our finger on the pulse of Canadians. Our customers provide us with crucial feedback that allows us to offer some of the most innovative, successful, and unique products on the market today." Delvinia and Corby were awarded

a Confirmit Achievement in Customer Excellence Award in recognition of the work done with the Corby Panel to achieve a direct dialogue with customers.

Based upon the success of the AskingCanadians panel, Delvinia launched Methodify, an online platform that allows marketers to gain customer insights within 48 hours—now those are fast results!

And what better way to ensure that customer needs are being met, than by involving the customer in the development of the service. This is what Delvinia did by partnering with the Royal Bank of Canada (RBC), a longtime client, to participate in beta testing during the research and development (R&D) phase.

The Methodify platform is ideal for concept and ad testing. However, the platform can also be used to gauge everything from the optimal price for a product, to finding out what customers really think of your brand. Methodify empowers marketers to bring the customer into the conversation. With three easy steps, and from any device, marketers can select the research method they would like to use, upload their ad or creative concept, launch a study, and see real-time results.

The future of market research will be driven by technology. While the informational needs of marketers have changed drastically, the methods of collecting and analyzing that information are also changing. This has resulted in the ability to understand customers at a much deeper level, on an as-needed basis. What an exciting time in the market research field—48-hour turnaround, new research-automation platforms, and ready access to a demographically and psychographically segmented customer panel. There is no doubt that no matter what the future holds, Delvinia will be at the forefront of the innovation. You can obtain more information on Delvinia at **www.delvinia.com**.[1]

# MARKET RESEARCH AND METRICS

**LO 1** Organizations require data to evaluate performance and to analyze its customers, competitors, products, and services. It needs to collect this information (metrics), analyze it, and interpret the data using analytics. Based upon the results, an organization may need to conduct further market research studies and analysis to strengthen its business and improve its return on investment (ROI). **Market research** is formally defined as the process of planning, collecting, and analyzing information in order to recommend actions to improve marketing activities.[2] Although market research is not perfect at explaining consumer behaviour, it can reduce the risk and uncertainty of making poor business choices. It provides managers with insights to help make sound decisions. Solid marketing assessments are often the result of managers using vision, knowledge, and experience, together with clear market research insights.

Many companies have a **marketing information system (MIS)**, a set of procedures and processes for collecting, sorting, analyzing, and summarizing marketing information on an ongoing basis to help manage the data. This data can become an important competitive advantage and a key marketing input for program development and assessment. It can help marketers understand how elements impact its business, anticipate competitive moves, and predict consumer behaviour and preferences.

levels, brand loyalty, retention rates, and a brand development index. Metrics data can point to return on investment, customer lifetime value, brand advocates, and sales conversion rates. Figure 4–1 describes a few rules that marketers can use to ensure that the metrics selected are relevant, measurable, and actionable.

Figure 4–2 provides a snapshot of key metrics that marketers often use to analyze performance. Importantly, companies frequently identify their specific metrics requirements and their key performance indicators to track and evaluate business results. Metrics are selected based on company protocols, normally based on the results needed to achieve business objectives. Marketers are often advised to use no more than five to seven key metrics to make the data focused, clear, and actionable.

Let's look at brand health metrics as an example of how metrics are used. Two key drivers are market share and brand development index. **Market share** is the percentage of sales volume for a product, relative to the entire sales volume of the category in which it competes. A car brand sold in Canada, for example, may have a market share of 17 percent, meaning that 17 percent of all car sales in Canada are

**market research**
The process of planning, collecting, and analyzing information in order to recommend actions to improve marketing activities.

**marketing information system (MIS)**
A set of procedures and processes for collecting, sorting, analyzing, and summarizing information on an ongoing basis.

**key performance indicators (KPIs)**
Types of metric that are used to evaluate performance.

**market share**
The percentage of sales volume for a product, relative to the entire sales volume of the category in which it competes; ratio of a firm's sales to the total sales of all firms in the industry.

## METRICS

**LO 2** As introduced in Chapter 1, *metrics* refers to numeric data that is collected and grouped to track performance. Metrics are often presented in spreadsheets and dashboards to make the data easy to understand and interpret. *Dashboards* visualize data and **key performance indicators (KPIs)**, using graphs, charts, and numbers, so numerical information tells a story that is insightful, easy to use, and understand.

Metrics data can come from a variety of sources, such as tracking data from websites, social media pages, call centre interactions, online ads, app downloads, webinars, and subscribers, as well as sales, costs, profits, and competitive and market growth data. Metrics data can measure elements such as revenue, market share, profit margins, buzz, sentiment, engagement, response rates, awareness

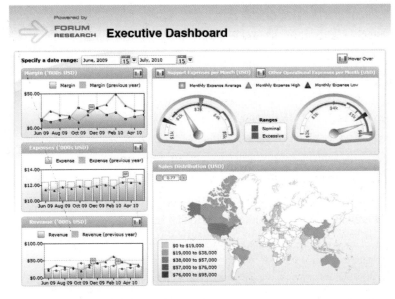

Dashboards help marketers visualize metrics.

**Source:** "Dashboards and Reporting," Forum Research, accessed June 2016 at http://www.forumresearch.com/solutions-dashboards-and-reporting.asp. Used with permission of Forum Research.

## Figure 4–1
Rules of marketing metrics

| | |
|---|---|
| **Metrics should be easy to understand.** | The metrics you are monitoring should make sense to those collecting the data and those using the data. They should also be understood across the organization. |
| **Metrics should be available on a regular basis.** | Marketers should focus on data that is available regularly and can be tracked from one time period to the next. |
| **Metrics should be actionable and impact the business.** | Seeing a metric decrease by 10 percent is important information to have and tells you that something is impacting your business. However, if you can't determine why this decrease happened or take any action to improve that metric, then the metric alone is not valuable. |

**Source:** Linda J. Popky, "Identify the Marketing Metrics That Actually Matter," *Harvard Business Review*, July 14, 2015, https://hbr.org/2015/07/identify-the-marketing-metrics-that-actually-matter.

**brand development index (BDI)**

An index that shows how well a brand's sales are developed in a region relative to the region's population size.

attributed to this brand. This is a useful metric when tracked over time and compared to competitive market share levels.

**Brand development index (BDI)** shows how well a brand's sales are developed in a region relative to the region's population size. It is the percentage of total brand sales in a particular region relative to the percentage of the country's population in

that region. This is a useful metric when trying to determine regional growth opportunities for a brand. For example, let's assume that the same car brand has 30 percent of its sales in Ontario. However, 38.5 percent of Canada's population is in Ontario.[3] The BDI is calculated by dividing 30 percent by 38.5 percent to achieve a BDI of 77.9. Regions with a BDI below 100 may have an opportunity for growth, while regions with a BDI greater than 100 could be seen as doing very well, with less opportunity for significant future growth.

## Figure 4–2
Key marketing metrics

| Website | E-commerce | Online Ad Campaigns | Social Media | E-mail Programs |
|---|---|---|---|---|
| Visits | Purchases | Reach | Demographics | Sent and delivery rates |
| Unique visitors | Purchase frequency | Impressions | Followers | Open rates |
| Returning visitors | Average order value | Engagement | Views | Forward rates |
| Page views | Returns | Dwell time | Comments | Click-through rates |
| Time on site | Churn rates | Search/display overlap | Likes/unlikes | Bounce rates |
| Traffic sources | Complaints | Conversions | Post reach | Subscribe rates |
| Referrals | Customer satisfaction | Cost per click (CPC) | Shares | Unsubscribe rates |
| Bounce rates | Customer acquisition costs | Cost per thousand views (CPM) | Sentiment | Complaints |
| Return on investment (ROI) | Conversion rates | Click-through rates (CTR) | Engagement | E-mail revenue |
| | Customer lifetime value (CLV) | Cost per conversion (CPC) | Conversion rates | Lead generation |
| | Shopping cart abandonment | Keywords | Churn rate | Return on investment (ROI) |
| | Customer service calls | Return on investment (ROI) | Visitor frequency | |
| | Product reviews | | Return on investment (ROI) | |
| | Return on investment (ROI) | | | |

| Brand Health | Financial | Customer Relationship Management (CRM) | Offline Ad Campaigns | Public Relations |
|---|---|---|---|---|
| Sales | Sales/revenue | Prospects and leads | Awareness | Interviews |
| Growth rates | Cost of goods sold | Conversion rates | Recall (aided and unaided) | Press releases |
| Market share | Gross margins | Retention rates | Share of voice | Journalist inquiries |
| Awareness levels | Profit margins | Churn rates | Clarity of communication | Events and conferences |
| Brand loyalty | Marketing expenditures | Engagement | Memorable elements | Share of voice |
| Brand trial rates | Earnings before income and taxes (EBITA) | Cost per acquisition (CPA) | Reach | Impressions |
| Repeat purchase rates | Return on investment (ROI) | Cost per interaction | Frequency | Audience |
| Brand development index (BDI) | | Share of wallet | Gross rating points (GRP) | Reach |
| Category development index (CDI) | | Customer lifetime value (CLV) | Impressions | Coverage |
| Profitability trends | | Return on investment (ROI) | Cost per impression (CPI) | Message impact |
| Return on investment (ROI) | | | Cost per thousand (CPM) | Mentions |
| | | | Return on investment (ROI) | Advertising value equivalency (AVE) |
| | | | | Return on investment (ROI) |

*By 2020, 2.3 zettabytes of data will be transmitted annually.*

# BIG DATA AND ANALYTICS

**LO 3**

**Big data** refers to the massive amounts of data from traditional and online sources that are used for ongoing analysis.[4] Big data is broken into four dimensions, referred to as the 4 Vs of big data—volume, velocity, variety, and veracity (see Figure 4–3).[5] Big data can come from a variety of sources such as promotions, financial records, distribution partners, social media interactions, e-mail programs, customer service communications, mobile downloads, e-commerce purchases, and website metrics, just to name a few. This huge

volume of data is constantly changing, often in real time, making it difficult for marketers to manage and use.

Today, there is so much information available to companies. Customer touch points have increased, generating much more data. Cisco, a major player in the data management industry, estimates that by 2020, 2.3 zettabytes (yes, zettabytes) of data will be transmitted annually.[6] While this may seem hard to believe, there are 3.2 billion Internet users, with 2.3 billion active users of social media. That is a lot of communication and data exchanging hands.[7]

Marketers and information technology professionals are flooded with a deluge of big data, and challenged to determine which information is reliable, accurate, and relevant. People are drowning in data, and many companies, unprepared for the onslaught of big data, find it difficult to manage data and determine actionable insights. Data is

**big data**
Massive amounts of data from traditional and online sources that are used for ongoing analysis.

**Figure 4–3**
The 4 Vs of big data

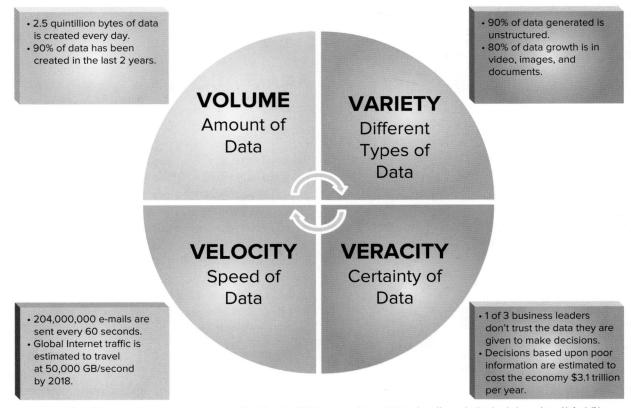

**Source:** Adapted from "Extracting business value from the 4 Vs of big data," IBM, accessed June 2016 at http://www.ibmbigdatahub.com/sites/default/files/infographic_file/4Vs_Infographic_final.pdf.

> ## Many companies find it difficult to manage data.

now seen as one of an organization's most valuable assets, showing how customers behave on the path-to-purchase.

Combining data sources can reveal new insights that allow marketers to ask important questions, discover opportunities, segment the market, review program performance, and make recommendations that improve return on investment. Marketers establish key performance indicators (KPIs) and then analyze data to help provide insights. With internal company data, this analysis can be completed in a fairly efficient way with internal systems and resources. However, with the extensive data that can be collected from external sources, it can be much more complicated. Many companies use analytics software that is capable of delivering automated visual dashboards of graphs and key metrics that flag important issues and opportunities for marketers. These insights can be used in various ways such as improving loyalty programs, finding cross-promotional partners, identifying profitable customers, recognizing product advocates, measuring program performance, and improving return on investment.

While companies organize for big data in different ways, it is important to remember that regardless of data collection practices and approaches, big data will not automatically deliver results and is not a substitute for creative ideas and smart thinking. Managing big data takes time and perseverance, and it is the insights that count.

**structured data**

Data that can be easily tagged, stored, and searched in a database using consistently identifiable terms that are systematically organized into columns, rows, and tables.

**unstructured data**

Data that comes from word-processed documents, presentations, audio files, images, video, and e-mail or social media messages that cannot be easily categorized and tagged in a database using fixed terms and definitions.

**descriptive analytics**

A type of analytics that focuses on *what has happened*

**Big data presents marketers with many challenges.**

Used with permission of Delvinia

## TYPES OF DATA

Various types of data add to the complexity of big data. There is **structured data** that can be easily tagged, stored, and searched in a database using consistently identifiable terms that can be systematically organized into columns, rows, and tables. Examples are numbers, statistics, and dates related to purchase data, inventory levels, financial information, age, fixed survey responses, and website analytics. The majority of data in an organization is unstructured data, with a hybrid of semi-structured data also surfacing. **Unstructured data** comes from word-processed documents, presentations, audio files, images, video, and e-mail or social media messages that cannot be easily categorized and tagged in a database using fixed terms and definitions.

Today, organizations are challenged to manage unstructured and structured data in real time so that it is easily accessible and actionable. This has led to an increased demand for data scientists and analysts who are well versed in computer programming and statistics and use mathematical modelling and visualizations to analyze structured and unstructured data.

> ## Organizations are challenged to manage unstructured and structured data in real time.

## ANALYTICS

 **LO 4** *Analytics* refers to the process of taking metrics data and applying smart thinking and technology to gain actionable insights that can help make better business decisions. An analytics platform helps give a picture as to where the company is today, answers questions, provides customer insights, and predicts patterns that can improve marketing performance. Analytics can help segment customers, plan and forecast, manage risk, and take corrective action. It may start by mining data, analyzing the information, modelling the data to predict outcomes, and visualizing data with dashboards that appear in reports.

Let's look at two of the main categories of big data analytics: descriptive and predictive.

**Descriptive Analytics** **Descriptive analytics** focus on *what has happened*. It is the simplest and most common form of analytics. Web analytics, social analytics, and RFM (recency, frequency, and monetary value) analysis are descriptive.

# Image Mining with "Selfies"

In a world where many people's lives are readily on display through social media, selfies have become a new and relevant source of consumer insights. With the majority of the population carrying smartphones (61 percent of boomers and 88 percent of millennials), marketers are interested in discovering what they can learn about their customers and their products.

Generally, marketers are using selfies in two ways:

## Mining for Brand Mentions and Pictures

Marketers are mining social media to find spontaneous mentions and/or pictures of their brand. How are their products being used? What are customers happy about? What aren't customers happy about? What products or services are used together? Selfies can answer these questions and a lot more. Selfies are becoming part of the data collected on a regular basis, as part of a company's marketing information system. Image mining and data mining are both important tasks for social analysis.

Social networks such as Instagram and Pinterest are the territory of marketers who are searching for visual mentions of their brands. Due to the more frequent use of privacy settings with Facebook, it is not normally used for image mining.

Companies monitor social media sites for publicly shared pictures of their products—this could be a pair of running shoes being worn in the picture, a bottle of water being held, or a customer shopping at a particular retail store. Kraft is a believer in image mining. The company can readily see the type of customers who are eating

KD, what they are eating or drinking with it, who they are with when eating KD, and whether they are smiling. Having this data allows Kraft to think about potential product co-promotions or consider a new target market for its products.

Of course, this type of image mining has to be done very methodically, taking into account privacy regulations and the policies of each social media platform, but the results can provide valuable information that consumers don't regularly articulate with the use of other research methods. And when combined with more traditional data mining of social media sites, the results can be powerful.

## Offering Selfie Compilations

Market research providers are quickly picking up on the selfie trend and are providing specialized services focused on the compilation of selfies for specific products. Procter & Gamble has used the selfie format to understand more about how and when their customers are using Crest toothpaste. Freshii, the Canadian healthy food chain, also buys into the format. Using a company called Pay Your Selfie, both companies have gained insights regarding the use of their products and the mindset of their customers. This pay-for-selfie format of market research offers a fee of $0.20 to $1.00 per selfie. It has been found that people are willing to be very authentic and open with their pictures when they are not made public.

Freshii wanted a better understanding of the types of "on-the-go"

Selfies can tell researchers when and where products are used.

Cultura/Image Source

snacks that people were eating, so it commissioned Pay Your Selfie to have people submit selfies while they were having their favourite on-the-go snacks. While Freshii had targeted the uber-healthy consumer, it found that some of the selfies featured less healthy snacks, such as chocolate bars. This was an eye-opener for Freshii, which decided that it needed to adjust its focus to ensure that it wasn't alienating the broader market. Freshii also paid attention to where people were located in their selfies. For example, more pictures in an office setting might mean an opportunity to locate stores in business districts.

Traditional research studies are limited by what people want to tell us. Selfies may provide a more authentic view of what the consumer actually does. ●

## Questions

1. Why would image mining be a good market research activity?

2. What ethical issues do market researchers need to be concerned about when image mining?

**Web analytics** is the measurement and analysis of website data, looking at elements such as visits, unique visitors, page views, time on site, traffic sources, referrals, and bounce rate. Google Analytics is an example of an excellent, free web analytics tool.

**Social analytics** gains insights from social media interaction and social listening. Social media interactions, such as followers, views, comments, likes/unlikes, reach, shares, engagement, sentiment, conversion rates, and churn rate, are analyzed to determine the level of interaction with customers and the success of marketing programs on social platforms. **Social listening** pays attention to real-time public conversations on social networks to discover trends as well as common themes, attitudes, topics, and areas of interest. Social analytics can measure social media campaign performance, assess message resonation and amplification, determine a brand's buzz level, and gauge sentiment toward a brand through words or images. It can identify key influencers, brand advocates, and opinion leaders, and it can interact in real time with consumers. See the Marketing NewsFlash, "Image Mining with 'Selfies'" for more detail about how marketers are collecting and analyzing data from publicly available selfies.[8]

There are many free and paid social analytics tools. Examples include Hootsuite, which provides a basic, free social analytics tool, as well as a more-robust paid platform for businesses, and Salesforce Marketing Cloud, which is a paid social media analytics platform. Visit **www.hootsuite.com** and **www.salesforce.com/marketingcloud** to see details about these services.

An example of how big data analytics is used can be seen with **RFM analysis** (recency, frequency, and monetary value analysis). This approach can use automated software to classify customers on the basis of how recently products were purchased (recency), how often products were purchased (frequency), and the dollar value of the transactions (monetary value). Customers are scored using these attributes and then automatically ranked so that organizations can segment the market and tailor offers to different categories of consumers. Let's think about how strategies can be created for specific segments. For customers who have purchased recently, who purchase frequently, and who spend at a high level, a company will want to create offers for these customers that will keep them coming back

**web analytics**
The measurement and analysis of website data, looking at elements such as page views, time on site, bounce rate, new visitors, returning visitors, and referral traffic.

**social analytics**
The real-time measurement, interaction, and analysis of social media to assess social media campaign performance, message resonation and amplification, consumer sentiment, and common themes.

**social listening**
Research that monitors public online consumer conversations on social media sites such as social networks, blogs, and forums.

**RFM analysis**
The rating of customers on the basis of how recently products were purchased (recency), how often products were purchased (frequency), and the dollar value of the transactions (monetary value)

# Infographic

and keep them loyal. For customers who have purchased recently, who purchase frequently, but who spend at a low level, a company will want to keep them coming back but to increase the value of their purchases.

Non-profit organizations often use RFM analyses to target people most likely to make donations. Customer relationship management (CRM) loyalty programs use these analyses to segment customers. Loyalty programs such as those from Shoppers Drug Mart and Loblaw use loyalty cards to collect ongoing customer purchase data, and then use data-mining techniques to customize offers based on past purchases. In this way, RFM analysis can be descriptive in that it captures data and then categorizes customers based on that data; it can also be predictive by determining the factors that drive purchases and link these factors to future behaviour, which allows offers to be made based upon past behaviour.[9]

**Predictive Analytics** **Predictive analytics** combines data from varied sources to reveal patterns that are modelled to predict *what might happen* in the future. For example, data can be combined from CRM databases, social media analytics, marketing program metrics, customer service databases, and purchased data to reveal groupings of customers with common attitudes and purchase patterns. This information can then be used to predict future consumer behaviour and to customize offers for specific groupings. **Data mining** refers to the processing of large amounts of data using software to find insightful correlations and patterns that lead to better business decisions.

Various companies provide data management and analytics services. Salesforce.com and IBM are examples, providing top-quality services that help transform data into actionable insights. Salesforce.com uses cloud-based platforms to help companies manage and use data from e-mail, mobile, social media, customer service, sales, and CRM interactions. IBM has business intelligence products that allow users to collaborate, analyze, model, plan, and create reports. It has predictive analytics products that use statistical algorithms and data-mining techniques to predict outcomes, and it has performance management products that create integrated systems to increase performance. Leading-edge data management and analytics companies deal with these areas to help improve an organization's performance.[10]

# TYPES OF MARKET RESEARCH

**LO 5** Companies often require market research to answer questions that cannot be answered through regular metrics and analytics. They turn to market research studies and field market research projects to gather accurate and reliable information that helps answer these questions. Market research studies and projects can help identify consumer trends, assess future business opportunities, evaluate new product ideas, and determine purchase intent. Market research can also assess marketing tactics and highlight any potential problems. A methodical approach is normally followed to increase efficiency, to ensure that the results are accurate, and to help contain costs.

Market research is not an easy undertaking, as obtaining accurate information from consumers can be difficult. If a researcher asks the wrong questions, or fails to investigate an important insight, the research will be inaccurate. For example, sometimes, the topic being researched is personal, which can result in reluctant respondents and

**predictive analytics**
The combination of data from varied sources to reveal patterns that are modelled to predict *what might happen* in the future.

**data mining**
The processing of large amounts of data using sophisticated software to find insightful correlations and patterns that lead to better business decisions.

Market research helps provide clarity on marketing issues and opportunities.
Stuart Kinlough/Getty Images

> *Market research is not an easy undertaking.*

untruthful responses; other times, a market researcher may ask respondents about pricing options, and inevitably, respondents will suggest a lower price; in other situations, respondents may be asked about new product concepts they have never seen, and they will find it difficult to respond.

The task of a market researcher is to overcome these challenges and to reveal actionable and accurate insights for marketers. Methodical approaches are used to plan the research, and marketers and researchers work together to carefully plan areas of inquiry and to script questions. This all occurs within mathematical frameworks to certify that the data is accurate and reliable.

Market research can be classified into three basic areas: (1) exploratory research, (2) descriptive research, and (3) causal research. Each area serves a different function and uses different techniques.

## EXPLORATORY RESEARCH

Preliminary research that clarifies the scope and nature of a marketing problem or opportunity is referred to as **exploratory research**. It generally provides researchers with a better understanding of the dimensions of the marketing problem or opportunity before focusing on areas that require further research. Marketers who are well versed in their businesses may be quick to assume general conclusions about their research needs and prone to avoiding the exploratory research step. However, exploratory research provides research projects with direction and identifies where business problems and opportunities may lie. Marketers understand that avoiding exploratory research comes with the risk of heading down the wrong path and missing potential opportunities or issues.

Exploratory research is often conducted with the expectation that subsequent and more-conclusive research will follow. For example, Danone markets Oikos Greek yogurt (see the Marketing NewsFlash box, "Danone—Oikos Greek Yogurt"). Danone reviewed secondary market data from Nielsen on the Greek yogurt market to help understand the brand position in the market. The company also gathered general data on different population segments, such as "late millennials," to determine if there were specific market segments that might be interested in Greek yogurt.

## DESCRIPTIVE RESEARCH

Research designed to describe the basic characteristics of a given population or to clarify its usage and attitudes is known as **descriptive research**. Unlike exploratory research, with descriptive research the researcher has a general understanding of the marketing problem and is seeking more-conclusive data that answers particular questions. Examples of descriptive research include providing more-detailed profiles of product purchasers (e.g., the characteristics of the Canadian health food shopper), describing the size and characteristics of markets (e.g., the types of products sold in Canadian pizza restaurants), detailing product usage patterns (e.g., how frequently people use bank machines), or outlining consumer attitudes toward particular brands (e.g., Canadian attitudes toward store brands). Magazines, radio stations, and television stations almost always conduct descriptive research to identify the characteristics of their audiences in order to present it to prospective advertisers. As a follow-up to its exploratory research, Danone conducted descriptive research to determine the values and attitudes of the "late millennials," as well as attitudes toward Oikos and the competition.

## CAUSAL RESEARCH

Research designed to identify cause-and-effect relationships among variables is termed **causal research**. In general, exploratory and descriptive research precede causal research. With causal research, there is usually an expectation about the relationship to be explained, such as predicting the influence of a price change on product demand.

Typical causal research studies examine elements such as the effect of advertising on sales, the relationship between price and perceived product quality, and the impact of package design on sales.

# THE SIX-STEP MARKET RESEARCH APPROACH

**LO 6** Effective market research is not left to chance. A systematic approach ensures that market research is done thoroughly, that all elements are considered, and that results are accurate. Danone is the manufacturer of Oikos Greek yogurt.

**exploratory research**
Preliminary research conducted to clarify the scope and nature of the marketing problem or opportunity.

**descriptive research**
Research designed to describe basic characteristics of a given population or to clarify its usage and attitudes.

**causal research**
Research designed to identify cause-and-effect relationships among variables.

# Danone—Oikos Greek Yogurt

**W**ith the Greek yogurt market growing at an exponential rate in Canada, Danone was focused on determining how it could differentiate Oikos from all other Greek yogurts on the market. Greek yogurt has been available in Canada since the 1980s. However, it remained a fairly low-key product for decades, and uptake was slow. By 2014, there were a vast array of national, private-label, and niche brands in the market. Danone's main competitors were iÖGO and Liberté. The price of Greek yogurt was higher than traditional yogurt due to the more complex manufacturing process, creating an even more competitive environment.

All brands of Greek yogurt made three claims: thicker texture, high in protein, and low in fat. Therefore, differentiating a product in this competitive market needed to go beyond product features. Let's examine how Danone utilized market research to address this issue.

## Step 1: Define the Problem/Issue/Opportunity

- Danone focused on the following research question: How can Danone differentiate itself and be perceived as superior to the competition?

## Step 2: Design the Research Plan

- **Sample:** Danone's target market had been older Canadians with high disposable income. However, as the market for Greek yogurt grew, the "late millennial" segment became interesting as a growth segment. Danone focused its research on males and females between the ages of 29 and 39, with a household income of

≥$100,000. The key markets for the research were Toronto, Montreal, and Vancouver.

- **Information requirements:** Danone's information needs were twofold: 1) Develop a psychographic profile of the "late millennial" customer, and 2) determine the perceptions and points of differentiation of Greek yogurt brands in the minds of consumers.

- **Collection methods:** Danone decided to utilize secondary and primary qualitative data sources.

## Step 3: Conduct Exploratory and Qualitative Research

- **Exploratory research with Ipsos:** An initial profile of the "late millennials" indicated that they valued their health, that experiences and knowledge were important to them, and that they were connected.

- **Primary qualitative (customer profile):** In order to further understand the "late millennial" segment, Danone talked to them about their values and attitudes. Building on the knowledge from the exploratory research, Danone was able to confirm that "late millennials" loved to indulge, especially in food; they have little time; they don't want to compromise on quality; they value authenticity; they are confident; and they feel privileged.

- **Primary qualitative (Greek yogurt brands):** Danone needed to understand the competitive landscape. Both Oikos and Liberté were seen as high-quality brands, and choices seemed to

OIKOS® of The Danone Company, Inc., used under license.

be made based on flavour and texture preference. However, Oikos was differentiated in the eyes of the consumer in two ways: 1) Its name and packaging reflected Greek heritage and so it was seen as being more authentic than the competition; and 2) Oikos was seen as having a better variety of interesting flavours. Snacking was highlighted as a major opportunity. Not only were consumers snacking more often, but this is how/when Greek yogurt was usually eaten.

## Step 4: Collect Quantitative Primary Research

Quantitative research was not conducted.

## Step 5: Compile, Analyze, and Interpret Data

The main consumer insight obtained from the qualitative research was summarized as follows: "For me, eating is one of the best pleasures in life. Whether consuming a big meal or a small snack, it has to be an experience every time."

A second insight was that there was no strong point of differentiation among the brands of Greek yogurt based upon the product attributes.

## Step 6: Generate Reports and Recommendations

- **Recommendations:** Referring back to the research problem, *"How can Danone differentiate itself and be perceived as superior to the competition?"* and the customer insights gathered in the research, the team came up with its recommendations. It was recommended that the marketing team *differentiate Oikos on an emotional level* and *align Oikos with the trend of snacking.*

- **Implementation:** The following changes were made to the Oikos strategy, based upon the research results:

  1. Oikos positioning statement was updated to "Oikos, THE dream snack, inspired by the authentic Greek art of living well."

  2. A promotional campaign spanned television and social media (since the "late millennials" are connected). The social media platforms engaged customers with contests.

  3. Wanting to make an emotional connection with the customer, brand messaging focused on the ability of Oikos to help you escape reality for a few moments while enjoying its taste. The "escape" or "dream" included reference to Greek history and mythology, reinforcing the authenticity of the brand. The variety of flavours was highlighted, as this was still a key driver for consumers.

Was the campaign a success? Did the research point Danone in the right direction? While the campaign itself reached 3.1 million unique visitors, with over 12.7 million impressions, the real test of success was the impact on sales. In the first quarter of the campaign, Oikos had a 21 percent increase in sales versus the previous year and a 7 percent gain in market share. Due to its success, Danone is continuing the dream–escape story with the launch of its Oikos Creations line. ●

## Questions

1. Why did Danone decide to conduct further research with "late millennials"?

2. What key performance indicators (KPIs) did Danone use to measure the success of its marketing campaign?

---

### Figure 4–4
The basic market research process

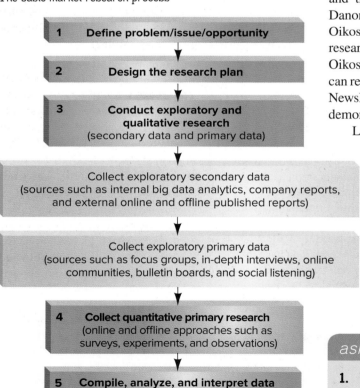

| 1 | Define problem/issue/opportunity |
| 2 | Design the research plan |
| 3 | Conduct exploratory and qualitative research (secondary data and primary data) |

Collect exploratory secondary data
(sources such as internal big data analytics, company reports, and external online and offline published reports)

Collect exploratory primary data
(sources such as focus groups, in-depth interviews, online communities, bulletin boards, and social listening)

| 4 | Collect quantitative primary research (online and offline approaches such as surveys, experiments, and observations) |
| 5 | Compile, analyze, and interpret data |
| 6 | Generate reports and recommendations |

The Canadian Greek yogurt market was growing quickly and there was a lot of competition for market share. Danone needed to understand how consumers perceived Oikos, as well as its competitors. Danone utilized market research to help determine how it could differentiate Oikos from all other Greek yogurts on the market. You can read more about this research project in the Marketing NewsFlash box, "Danone—Oikos Greek Yogurt," which demonstrates market research in practice.[11]

Let's look at the basic six-step approach that is commonly used to conduct market research studies. It is worth noting that not all research projects require qualitative and quantitative studies (steps 3 and 4). In many instances, qualitative research can suffice, while in others, quantitative studies are required for greater certainty.

Figure 4–4 shows this sequence of steps, and in the next few pages, we will discuss these steps in detail.

### ask YOURSELF

1. *What are the three types of market research?*

2. *What steps are included in the six-step market research process?*

# STEP 1: DEFINE THE PROBLEM/ISSUE/OPPORTUNITY

The first step in the market research process is to clearly define the problem, issue, or opportunity, and to clarify the research objectives. This is often posed as a question that needs to be answered. Most market researchers would agree with the saying that "a problem well-defined is half-solved," but defining a problem is a difficult task. Most market research issues stem from poorly defined problems and objectives that are vague and unclear: If objectives are too broad, the problem may not be tangible; if the objectives are too narrow, the value of the research may be questionable. Market researchers spend considerable time precisely defining marketing problems and clarifying research objectives in formal proposals that clearly describe the research task and its approach. **Objectives** are specific, measurable, and achievable goals that the decision maker seeks to achieve. Common research objectives are to discover consumer needs and wants, and to determine why a product is not selling.

Using the Danone scenario as an example, the Greek yogurt market was growing and very competitive. Danone needed to be able to differentiate Oikos and connect with its target audience. This was the basis of the problem and its research objectives.

# STEP 2: DESIGN THE RESEARCH PLAN

The second step in the market research process is to identify which approach will be taken to complete the project. This includes identifying what information is needed, how it will be collected, and whether a sampling plan is needed. Let's look at these three areas.

**Information Requirements** Often, market research studies collect data that is interesting but not relevant to the task at hand. Marketers need to avoid this situation because it is time-consuming, confusing, and costly. In Danone's situation, the researchers may have been curious about which packaging size of yogurt was desired by customers, but this information was probably not that relevant to the research objective—determining how to differentiate Oikos.

**Collection Methods** When determining the way in which data will be collected, methodology, cost, efficiency, and accuracy of results are important considerations. As a result, it is important to have a data collection plan. There are mathematical considerations and operational issues that the researcher must consider. Determining how to collect the data is often as important as actually collecting the data. Researchers can consider whether available pre-existing data is sufficient to answer the research question or whether they need to conduct their own research using a variety of data collection methods such as in-depth personal interviews, focus groups, telephone surveys, personal questionnaires, or mail surveys. The Internet also provides numerous online tools that facilitate the gathering of information. Surveys can be easily completed online, and online communities and online bulletin boards can also be used to provide additional data.

To ensure that accurate answers are obtained, researchers carefully select research methodologies that encourage honesty. The method chosen is critical to obtaining accurate results. In the case of Danone, since the company wanted to understand the attitudes and values of "late millennials," it might have been more useful to conduct focus groups or personal interviews, rather than online surveys where the responses cannot be easily articulated and probed for more detail.

Canadian market researchers rely on their training, expertise, and judgment to make appropriate methodology decisions. They can also turn to their professional association, the Marketing Research and Intelligence Association, for resources and training.

**Sampling** Sampling is another important factor in research design. A researcher's sampling plan identifies who is to be sampled, how large the sample should be, and how the sample will be selected. Rarely does a research project involve a complete census of every person in the research population, because this is time-consuming and costly. Therefore, market researchers use smaller samples that are representative of the population being surveyed. **Sampling** is the process of gathering data from a subset of the total population, rather than from all members of that particular group.

**objectives**
Specific, measurable, and achievable goals.

**sampling**
The process of gathering data from a subset of the total population rather than from all members of that particular group.

*Rarely does a research project involve a complete census of every person in the research population, because this is time-consuming and costly.*

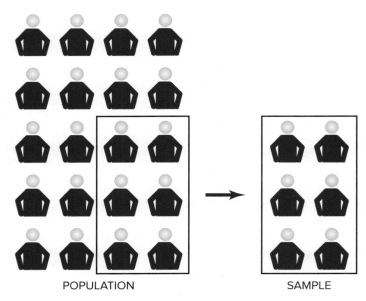

A properly selected sample should be representative of the population being studied.

**probability sampling**

Selecting a sample so that each element of a population has a specific known chance of being selected.

**non-probability sampling**

Selecting a sample so that the chance of selecting a particular element of a population is either unknown or zero.

A properly selected sample should be representative of the population being researched; however, unless the entire population can be included, sampling errors can occur. Increasing the sample size can help decrease sampling error, but the larger the sample size, the higher the cost.

Other factors that may impact research design are the timelines for the research to be completed and the budget. Currently, a number of market researchers are debating the validity of online market research studies, questioning whether online samples are valid because they exclude respondents who are not online. In reality, all research methodologies have advantages and disadvantages. Market researchers always need to understand the limitations of the methodology they select.

There are two basic sampling techniques: probability and non-probability sampling. **Probability sampling** involves precise rules to select the sample so that each element of the population has a specific known chance

of being selected. For example, if your university wants to know how last year's 1,000 graduates are doing, it can put their names into a bowl and randomly select 100 names to contact. The chance of being selected (100 out of 1,000, or 1 in 10) is known in advance, and all graduates have an equal chance of being contacted. This procedure helps to select a sample (100 graduates) that should be representative of the entire population (the 1,000 graduates), and allows conclusions to be drawn about the population being researched.

**Non-probability sampling** involves the use of arbitrary judgment by the market researcher to select a sample so that the chance of selecting a particular element of the population is either unknown or zero. If your university decided to talk to 100 of last year's graduates, but only selected those who lived closest, many graduates would be excluded. This would introduce a bias, tainting the representativeness of the sample and its ability to draw accurate conclusions.

It is worth noting that the researcher may decide to follow non-probability sampling when time and budgets are limited, or for exploratory research purposes when conclusions are mostly directional and may require further research. In general, market researchers use data from such non-probability samples with caution. The data can provide valuable information, but the results need to be viewed carefully as they may not accurately represent the population being researched.

# STEP 3: CONDUCT EXPLORATORY AND QUALITATIVE RESEARCH

Exploratory research is preliminary research conducted to clarify the scope and nature of a marketing problem. It is done to ensure that researchers have not overlooked key insights that are important to the study. Exploratory research is often conducted with the expectation that subsequent and more-conclusive quantitative research may follow.

If researchers decide to conduct exploratory research, they have two avenues from which to obtain data. The first avenue is to collect exploratory *secondary data,* which is already available through big data analytics, company reports, or external online and offline published reports. A second avenue involves researchers creating their own data, exploratory *primary data,* through options such as focus groups, in-depth interviews, online communities, online bulletin boards, and social listening research. Let's look at these approaches in more detail.

Focus group research, in-depth interviews, online communities, observational studies, online bulletin boards, and social listening are forms of research called **qualitative research**. This research provides insightful and directional information to the researcher with the understanding that although the data is not obtained from a large consumer base, it provides useful direction to the research study and may in fact thoroughly answer the questions at hand. In this manner, it may allow marketers to avoid costly quantitative research studies. In other instances, qualitative research may not be enough to draw firm conclusions and will be used instead to provide insights and direction for a more detailed quantitative research study.

## marketing TIP

*"In today's data-driven economy, market research is about speed more than it ever has been before. The need for faster, cheaper, and better research is changing the marketing landscape."*

*– Raj Manocha, EVP, Delvinia*

Let's consider Danone and its initial exploratory research, which involved the use of secondary Nielsen data on the Greek yogurt market. From this research, Danone understood that the market was undergoing significant growth and that although it was the market leader, its share of the market had been slowly declining. Danone also gathered preliminary data on the "late millennial" population, learning enough to know that this population was promising as a target audience for Oikos.

Exploratory research may be followed up by focus groups or research with online communities and bulletin boards to further probe attitudes and opportunities.

**Quantitative research**, discussed later in this chapter, is statistically reliable information that uses observational techniques and/or questioning methods such as surveys or experiments with large samples to deliver statistically significant results.

**Secondary Data** Exploratory research can include the gathering of **secondary data**. An overview of information sources can be seen in Figure 4–5. This data comes in two forms: external data and internal data. *Internal data* exists within a company and can include data derived from data analytics, or simpler approaches that review basic sales reports, profitability data, and costing information. *External data* comes from published sources outside the organization.

As a form of self-promotion, many research companies, service experts, and media companies now publish top-line research data on their websites free for public viewing, with full report access requiring either a subscription or payment. Such companies include Leger, The Research Intelligence Group; Ipsos Canada; Nielsen; Solutions Research Group; comScore; Euromonitor International; Forrester Research;

**qualitative research**
A form of research that uses approaches such as focus groups, in-depth interviews, online communities, online bulletin boards, and social listening to provide insightful and directional information.

**quantitative research**
Statistically reliable information that uses observational and/or questioning techniques such as observations, surveys, and experiments.

**secondary data**
Facts and figures that have already been recorded by a third party.

## Figure 4–5
Sources of information

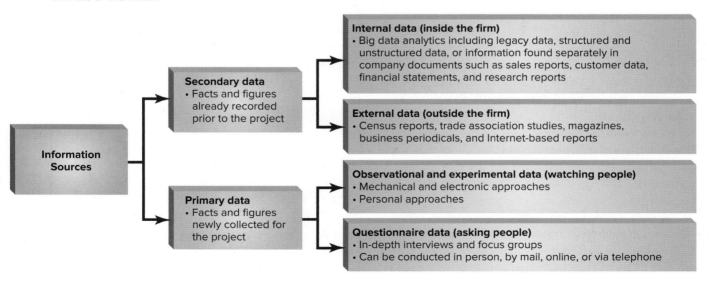

## Figure 4–6

A selection of market research sources for online secondary data

| | |
|---|---|
| Alliance for Audited Media | www.auditedmedia.com |
| Bank of Canada | www.bankofcanada.ca |
| Canadian Marketing Association | www.the-cma.org |
| comScore | www.comscore.com |
| eMarketer | www.emarketer.com |
| Euromonitor International | www.euromonitor.com |
| Forrester Research | www.forrester.com |
| GFK Group | www.gfk.com |
| Government of Canada | www.canada.gc.ca |
| Innovation, Science and Economic Development Canada (formerly Industry Canada) | www.ic.gc.ca |
| Interactive Advertising Bureau of Canada | www.iabcanada.com |
| Ipsos Canada | www.ipsos.ca |
| Leger, The Research Intelligence Group | www.leger360.com |
| Nielsen Canada | www.ca.nielsen.com |
| Numeris | www.numeris.ca |
| Organisation for Economic Co-operation and Development (OECD) | www.oecd.org |
| Pew Research Center | www.pewresearch.org |
| SEDAR | www.sedar.com |
| Solutions Research Group | www.srgnet.com |
| Statista | www.statista.com |
| Statistics Canada | www.statcan.gc.ca |
| World Advertising Research Center | www.warc.com |

**Worth Noting**

Your library may have access to various online databases that can assist with research projects. Examples of these databases are Business Source Complete, CBCA Business, Canadian Newsstand, Conference Board of Canada, Factiva, LexisNexis Academic, Mergent Online, Proquest, Scott's Canadian Business Directory, and ThompsonOne.

and the Interactive Advertising Bureau of Canada (IAB Canada). In addition, industry associations often conduct research on behalf of their members regarding industry trends and then publish this information. Leger posts research data on demographic trends and voting intentions; Ipsos Canada posts research highlights on economic, social, lifestyle, and political studies; Nielsen posts research updates on Canadian consumer insights; Solutions Research Group focuses on digital consumer behaviour; comScore provides updates on digital marketing trends; Forrester Research specializes in business and technology; and IAB Canada routinely publishes reliable research reports on digital marketing.

Statistics Canada, the federal government's statistical agency, publishes a wide variety of useful reports, such as census data that includes information on the number of people per household and their age, gender,

ethnic background, income, occupation, and education. Statistics Canada also publishes a wide range of other statistical reports that are used by businesses across the country. These reports include information on the following:

- Economic indicators
- International trade
- Culture and leisure
- Agriculture
- Tourism and travel
- Manufacturing
- Government
- Environment
- Justice and crime
- Health

A list of online secondary research sources is detailed in Figure 4–6. These sources are often posted online. Marketers can read interesting articles, view snapshots of research projects, download full reports, or read synopses of research studies. Examples include third-party organizations that audit magazine and newspaper circulation or the popularity of TV shows. Similarly, competitive market share data is available for marketers to purchase to help track competitive activity.

**LO 7** **Primary Data** In a research project, a general rule is to first obtain secondary data followed by detailed, proprietary primary data. This sequencing is because secondary data is lower in cost and easier to obtain than primary data. Secondary data can also help illuminate further data requirements. These advantages of secondary data must be weighed against its

### ask YOURSELF

1. *Why do researchers use exploratory research?*

2. *What are some of the online tools available to market researchers?*

3. *What are the advantages and disadvantages of secondary data?*

What form of research is a focus group?

Marmaduke St. John/Alamy Stock Photo

disadvantages, namely that (1) the secondary data may be out of date, (2) the definitions or categories may not be right for the project, and (3) the data may not be accurate or specific enough for the study. **Primary data** is data that is original and specifically collected for the project at hand. Let's review the primary sources of information.

FOCUS GROUPS   A popular qualitative research technique is the focus group. A **focus group** is an informal interview session in which six to ten people are brought together in a room with a moderator to discuss topics surrounding the market research problem. The moderator poses open-ended questions and encourages individuals to discuss the issues. Often, focus group sessions are watched by observers and are videotaped. Participants are always informed that they are being observed and/or taped and asked for permission to do so.

*A popular qualitative research technique is the focus group.*

IN-DEPTH INTERVIEWS   Another qualitative research technique used to obtain primary data involves the use of in-depth interviews. **In-depth interviews** are detailed individual interviews where a researcher discusses topics with an individual at length in a free-flowing conversation in order to discover information that may help solve a marketing problem. Sometimes, these interviews can take a few hours, and they are often recorded with respondents' consent.

ONLINE RESEARCH COMMUNITIES   A relatively new qualitative research tool used by marketers to gain feedback on marketing approaches is the online research community. **Online research communities** involve the use of consumer groups, brought together privately in an online environment, to answer questions, respond to ideas, and collaborate with researchers in real time. This approach uses vocal consumers, often in high-involvement categories, such as sports and entertainment, or other areas where consumers are passionate about their products, such as chocolate and baby food. These consumers provide feedback to researchers in a private online environment where only the marketers, researchers, and respondents are privy to the conversations. Typically, this approach invites consumers to join an online community on a specific topic in return for interesting and lively debate, thought-provoking ideas, and a small stipend for their time. An online community is managed by a research company to ensure that the community is engaged and continues to be interested in the topic. Participants can be gathered from a variety of sources such as website visitors, consumer lists, or company databases. The community involves regular two-way communication visible to all within the community, is managed by a researcher, and can involve 200 to 300 people depending on the need. Multinational brands often maintain large global communities to help answer their marketing questions.

ONLINE RESEARCH BULLETIN BOARDS   Another new research tool available to researchers is the online research bulletin board. **Online research bulletin boards** are private online forums where respondents can post their responses to questions. They are static website locations where questions are posted online, and respondents are asked to comment on ideas. Only those with access to the bulletin board are privy to the posted questions and responses. While online bulletin boards may not provide researchers with the depth of information available through an online community, they are easier to manage and administer.

SOCIAL LISTENING   The growth in social media and its ability to influence consumers has given rise to a new

**primary data**
Data that is original and specifically collected for a project.

**focus group**
A qualitative research technique where a small group of people (usually six to ten) meet for a few hours with a trained moderator to discuss predetermined areas.

**in-depth interviews**
Detailed interviews where a researcher questions an individual at length in a free-flowing conversational style in order to discover information that may help solve a marketing problem.

**online research communities**
The use of consumer groups, brought together privately in an online environment, to answer questions, respond to ideas, and collaborate with researchers in real time.

**online research bulletin boards**
Private online static forums, without real-time dialogue, where respondents can post their responses to questions posed by researchers.

exploratory research technique, *social listening*, which monitors public online consumer conversations and images on social media sites such as social networks, blogs, and public forums. The metrics derived from social listening can measure positive and negative sentiments, popularity scores, and message reach, the levels of conversation, and buzz and crisis monitoring. Social listening research can take the form of qualitative or quantitative information depending on the parameters of the study.[12]

Pizza Hut Canada has used social listening extensively and has been able to make product strategy decisions based on the results. In the past, Pizza Hut has used social media to post different product images and then track the response and conversation around each image. The one that received the largest response was used in its ads. In another case, Pizza Hut was monitoring social media in the U.K. and noted that customers believed that the new "Triple Treat" box was too big for one person. Using this information, when the "Triple Treat" was launched in Canada, Pizza Hut emphasized sharing the pizza with friends and family, thereby avoiding the negative feedback seen in the U.K.[13]

Social listening raises an important ethical issue: While participants in social networks realize many of their comments and pictures are publicly posted, they may not be aware that their conversations may be monitored and used for research purposes. Social networks are required to have privacy policies that protect consumer data from being kept and misused by third parties, and marketers need to abide by these laws.

Pizza Hut uses social listening to make product strategy decisions.

simon evans/Alamy Stock Photo

*Social listening raises an important ethical issue.*

## STEP 4: COLLECT QUANTITATIVE PRIMARY RESEARCH

Further research can be conducted using quantitative research through observational and/or questioning techniques. The main advantage of quantitative research is that it is designed to be statistically accurate and it is less open to interpretation. The main disadvantage of quantitative research is that it is far more costly and time-consuming to collect than qualitative or secondary research. The primary quantitative research techniques include (1) observational research, (2) surveys/questionnaires, and (3) experiments (see Figure 4–7).

**Observational Research** **Observational research** is obtained by watching how people behave, either in person or by using a machine to record events. While observational research can be qualitative if small sample numbers are recorded, large samples are used for reports such as those provided by Nielsen with its Homescan program. With Homescan, panellists scan the barcodes on products that they purchase each week.[14] Other examples of observational research can be in the form of the social listening research mentioned earlier, as well as web-tracking software such as Google Analytics, which measures website traffic, unique visitors, page views, time on site, and referring sites. Observational research can also be done in person, with researchers observing elements such as consumer interaction with a salesperson. Observational research tools are both useful and flexible, but they can be costly and unreliable when dependent upon human observation, which can at times report different conclusions after watching the same event.

**Surveys** Surveys are used to gather quantitative information. Survey questions can be standardized in the form of a **questionnaire** and asked to a large representative sample to obtain accurate data. These surveys can be conducted in person, on the telephone, by mail, or through the Internet, with each method having limitations.

*Market researchers have to make important trade-offs to balance costs against the expected quality of information.*

## Figure 4–7
Quantitative research: Comparing techniques

| Technique | Examples | Advantages | Disadvantages |
|---|---|---|---|
| **Observational research** | • Homescan<br>• Google Analytics<br>• Personal observations of consumer interactions<br>• Social listening | • Reflect actual behaviour<br>• Highly accurate when collected by machines<br>• Mechanical observations reduce interviewer bias<br>• Appropriate when respondents cannot clearly articulate opinions | • Do not indicate why consumers behave as they do<br>• Do not provide data on attitudes and opinions<br>• Different researchers may interpret behaviour differently<br>• May require further explanation<br>• Ethical questions exist around privacy issues |
| **Surveys/ Questionnaires** | • Personal interviews<br>• Central location interviews such as mall-intercepts<br>• Mail questionnaires<br>• Telephone interviews<br>• Internet surveys | • Can ask numerous questions<br>• Questions are standardized<br>• Questions can be administered via mail, telephone, the Internet, or in person<br>• Personal interviewers can often probe for more in-depth answers | • Results can be biased by the methodology<br>• Results can be influenced by the interviewer<br>• Can be expensive and time-consuming |
| **Experiments** | • Test markets<br>• Simulated test markets<br>• Lab experiments | • Researchers can change key variables and measure results in a controlled setting<br>• Can avoid costly failures by allowing marketers to modify marketing programs prior to full launch<br>• Can provide a more accurate reflection and predictor of consumer behaviour since people are behaving more naturally | • Can be expensive and time-consuming<br>• Results can be difficult to interpret<br>• Actual test markets may be visible to the competition<br>• Difficult to find a representative sample |

In choosing from these alternatives, market researchers have to make important trade-offs to balance costs against the expected quality of information. Personal interviews have the major advantage of enabling interviewers to ask probing questions and get reactions to visual materials. However, this approach is very costly.

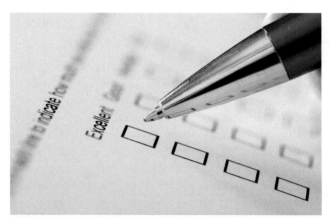

Surveys can gather data from a large number of consumers.

©Andreypopov/Dreamstime.com/GetStock.com

Mail surveys are not used very often anymore. They are less costly but have low response rates and are usually biased because those most likely to respond have had positive or negative experiences. Telephone interviews allow respondents to be probed but they are increasingly difficult to complete due to call-display features and respondents' reluctance to participate. Internet surveys are restricted to respondents that have the technology, but this approach is becoming an increasingly popular method of gathering information. Figure 4–8 summarizes the advantages and disadvantages of different survey approaches.

Also, time needs to be taken to ensure that survey questions are well-written so that answers will properly address research questions. Check out Figure 4–9 for hints on how to write better survey questions.

Researchers can reduce the costs of proprietary questionnaires by joining established syndicated studies that are conducted by well-respected research conglomerates. **Syndicated studies** are

**syndicated studies**

A hybrid of primary and secondary research whereby the cost of a research study is shared among clients and made available at a price to interested parties.

## Figure 4–8

Advantages and disadvantages of survey techniques

| Survey Technique | Advantages | Disadvantages |
|---|---|---|
| Personal interview | • Can probe for detailed responses<br>• Can demonstrate marketing programs<br>• Can result in high levels of accuracy | • Time-consuming<br>• Expensive<br>• Interviewers can bias responses |
| Telephone survey | • Can be conducted quickly and cheaply<br>• Computerized techniques allow for randomized calling<br>• Appropriate when data is needed quickly | • People are reluctant to participate<br>• Low response rates<br>• Call-display features screen-out calls<br>• Increasing number of people with no home phone<br>• Interviews are limited to 5 to 10 minutes<br>• Interviewers can bias responses<br>• Questionable representativeness of samples |
| Mail survey | • No interviewer bias<br>• Useful for national surveys<br>• If using a panel, can track changes over time<br>• Can be affordable if part of a syndicated or omnibus survey | • Lengthy time-lag for data collection<br>• Low response rates<br>• Questionable data accuracy<br>• Inability to probe respondents |
| Internet survey | • No interviewer bias<br>• Can be conducted quickly and cheaply<br>• Efficient for electronic data collection<br>• High Internet penetration can lead to good sampling<br>• Can easily target customer databases<br>• Useful for national surveys<br>• If using a panel, can track changes over time<br>• Can be affordable if part of a syndicated or omnibus survey | • Difficult to verify respondents' identity<br>• Questionable data accuracy due to anonymity<br>• Inability to probe respondents<br>• Some debate over sample representativeness |

**panel**
A large sample of respondents that voluntarily complete questionnaires on a regular basis so that researchers can assess changes in behaviour and attitudes.

**omnibus survey**
The voluntary participation of respondents in routine research surveys that allow marketers to add a small number of questions to an existing survey to receive cost-effective data.

**experiment**
In marketing, changing a variable involved in a customer purchase to find out what happens.

a hybrid of primary and secondary research conducted by a research company, spreading the cost across many clients to reduce the price. These studies are routinely conducted with extensive panels of consumers to determine trends.

Formally, a survey **panel** includes a large sample of respondents that voluntarily complete questionnaires on a regular basis so that researchers can assess changes in behaviour and attitudes. An **omnibus survey** also includes the voluntary participation of respondents in routine surveys, allowing individual marketers to add a small number of questions to an existing survey to receive cost-effective data in response to their questions.

Ipsos conducts omnibus surveys with homeowners, parents, teens, and separate provincial online omnibus surveys, even providing an overnight omnibus survey for next-day results.

### marketing TIP

*"With automation, and access to consumer panels, brands can now gather customer opinions in a matter of hours, giving them the ability to react in real time and implement the feedback they receive."*

– Raj Manocha, EVP, Delvinia

**Experiments** Experiments are the third quantitative research approach used in market research. It involves measuring changes in consumer behaviour over time to determine reactions to new product introductions or new promotional offers. A marketing **experiment** involves changing a variable involved in a purchase to find out what happens. Ideally, the researcher changes just one element, usually one of the factors in the marketing mix, and keeps the other variables constant.

Experiments can be conducted either in contrived environments that mimic real-life situations, known as *simulated* test markets, or *in-market* through real-time

**Figure 4–9**
Mistakes to avoid when writing survey questions

**1. Leading or loaded questions**
Questions designed to make a person think in a specific way.
**Avoid:** Some people say that the food at XYZ restaurant is fantastic, what do you think? (You have already put a positive impression in the mind of the respondent.)
**Better:** What do you think about the food at XYZ restaurant?

**2. Non-specific questions**
Questions that cannot be clearly understood.
**Avoid:** Do you watch Netflix regularly? (What is regularly? This term can have different meanings to different people.)
**Better:** How often do you watch Netflix?

**3. Missing options**
Potential answers are missing.
**Solutions:**
o Conduct a pre-test to determine potential responses.
o Include "Other (please specify)" as an option.

**4. Asking two questions at one time**
Questions that ask two things but the respondent can only provide one answer.
**Avoid:** What is the fastest and least expensive Internet provider?
**Better:** What is the least expensive Internet provider? What is the fastest Internet provider?

**5. Confusing wording**
Questions that include acronyms, industry jargon, or any other language that may be unfamiliar to the respondent.
**Avoid:** Do you own an iOS smartphone?
**Better:** Do you own an iPhone?

**Source:** Sam Lloyd, "The 10 Commandments for Writing Outstanding Survey Questions," Qualtrics, January 28, 2013, https://www.qualtrics.com/blog/good-survey-questions/; Tara Wildt, "Marketing Research 101: Six Common Mistakes in Survey Questionnaire Design," Lightspeed GMI, September 21, 2015, http://blog.lightspeedgmi.com/marketing-research-101-six-commons-mistakes-in-survey-questionnaire-design.

in-field tests where the product/promotion is actually sold in a limited location and monitored for success during a specific time period. Contrived, simulated experiments use computer simulations to predict consumer behaviour. Marketers typically input marketing mix variables and rely on complex forecasting programs to determine potential success levels. Formally, a **test market** is an in-market localized approach, or short-term online destination, used to test the success of promotional offers, new services, or new product launches.

Test markets can provide a more realistic evaluation of product or promotional success than other research options. However, test markets are time-consuming, costly, and visible to the competition. In terms of promotional offers, Internet marketers routinely test pay-per-click advertising campaigns, alternative online consumer offers, and the design of various website landing pages. For new products, large companies often use test markets to determine whether consumers will buy new products or brands, or shop at a new store concept. There are several cities in Canada that are used regularly as test markets for a variety of different products/services. McDonald's Chicken McNuggets and Tim Hortons Dark Roast coffee were tested in London, Ontario. Test cities tend to be under 1 million in population and need to be similar culturally to the rest of the country, with a variety of socio-economic backgrounds represented. Other frequent test markets in Canada are Edmonton, Alberta, and Barrie, Ontario.[15]

# STEP 5: COMPILE, ANALYZE, AND INTERPRET DATA

After data has been collected, it has to be compiled, analyzed, and summarized so that it can be turned into actionable information. The researcher must know how to analyze the data and what tools to use. There are many statistical packages that can make this task easier. Market researchers face the challenge of synthesizing and simplifying pages of data into dashboards as well as individual charts with relevant observations and conclusions that can help

**test market**
An in-market localized approach, or short-term online destination, used to test the success of promotional offers, new services, or new product launches.

marketers address business problems, challenges, and opportunities.

In the Danone Oikos example, results of the qualitative research were compiled and analyzed. This resulted in two main customer insights: 1) The target group felt that eating was key source of pleasure, and that each meal/snack should be an experience; and 2) there was no strong point of differentiation among the brands of Greek yogurt.

## STEP 6: GENERATE REPORTS AND RECOMMENDATIONS

Once the data has been analyzed, the researcher will discuss the results with a marketing manager and prepare a report to communicate the research findings. The report will include recommendations that address the marketing problem and research objectives. It is important to understand that marketing data and information have little value unless translated into findings and recommendations that lead to marketing action. Managers generally prefer clear, concise reports where key findings are highlighted within dashboards and individual charts, graphs, and tables of data.

In the Oikos example, the recommendations were to focus on differentiating Oikos on an emotional level and aligning Oikos with snacking. These recommendations were actionable in marketing messages and promotions.

*The future of market research sees a continued growth in online market research approaches as well as the increased use of analytics platforms to help manage big data and obtain insights.*

### ask YOURSELF

1. *Which survey approach provides the greatest flexibility for asking probing questions: mail, telephone, Internet, or personal interview?*

2. *In the field of research, what is the difference between an online community and social listening?*

# THE FUTURE OF MARKET RESEARCH

In today's world of big data, marketers have extensive information on consumers, the competition, and the market. This information can come from secondary sources or primary sources and is used to help marketers make fact-based decisions. Technology is facilitating the gathering and sifting of this information, using analytics platforms to flag issues and highlight opportunities for marketers. Market research projects are sometimes needed to reveal

further insights, and these projects increasingly use the Internet to discern attitudes and opinions.

The future of market research sees a continued growth in online market research approaches as well as the increased use of analytics platforms to help manage big data and obtain insights. Organizations are expected to increasingly invest in technology and training programs that will help marketers to focus on meaningful, actionable data. Organizations will come to realize that actionable data and data-savvy employees are among their most valuable assets and will invest in these areas.

Ethically and legally, marketers and market research practitioners will need to keep consumers' privacy top-of-mind. Privacy laws in Canada require businesses to comply with the *Personal Information Protection and Electronic Documents Act* (PIPEDA) as well as Canada's anti-spam legislation (CASL). You can read more about these areas in Chapter 2 where marketing regulations are discussed in detail. Marketers are well advised to check the latest privacy legislation and anti-spam laws in Canada at the Canadian Marketing Association's (CMA) website at **www.the-cma.org**, the CASL website at **http://fightspam.gc.ca**, and the Office of the Privacy Commissioner of Canada at **www.priv.gc.ca**. Legal marketing experts should be consulted to ensure that market research practices are legal.

Market researchers are also well advised to visit the website of the Marketing Research and Intelligence Association (MRIA) of Canada at **http://mria-arim.ca**, a not-for-profit association that represents all aspects of the market intelligence and survey research industries, including social research, competitive intelligence, data mining, insight, and knowledge management. It provides education for market researchers, publishes a market research magazine, and provides a wealth of information to its members.

**LO 1** • Market research, metrics, and analytics are used by marketers to help gather data and obtain insights. Metrics use numeric data to track performance. Analytics applies smart thinking and technology to metrics data to gain actionable insights.

**LO 2** • The main types of metrics are website performance, e-commerce interactions, e-mail program performance, online/offline ad campaigns results, social media interactions, brand health, financial performance, customer relationship management (CRM), and public relations impact.

**LO 3** • Big data is the massive amounts of data characterized as high-volume, high-velocity, high-variety, and high-veracity information. The challenge is to gain valuable insight.

• Data can be categorized as structured data and unstructured data.

**LO 4** • There are numerous types of analytics. Two of the main types are descriptive analytics and predictive analytics.

**LO 5** • Market research can be classified as exploratory, descriptive, or causal research.

• Exploratory research is preliminary research that clarifies the scope and nature of a marketing problem. Descriptive research clarifies usage and attitudes toward a product or theme. Causal research identifies cause-and-effect relationships.

**LO 6** • The market research process follows six steps: (1) describe the problem, issue, or opportunity and establish the research objectives; (2) design the research plan and identify the methodology required to gather the information; (3) conduct exploratory and qualitative research; (4) collect quantitative research; (5) analyze and interpret the data; and (6) create research reports and recommendations.

**LO 7** • Primary research data consists of qualitative or quantitative studies.

• Qualitative studies include focus groups, in-depth interviews, online communities/bulletin boards, and social listening.

• Quantitative studies include surveys, observations, and experiments.

## key terms and concepts... **A REFRESHER**

| | | |
|---|---|---|
| big data | marketing information system (MIS) | questionnaire |
| brand development index (BDI) | non-probability sampling | RFM analysis |
| causal research | objectives | sampling |
| data mining | observational research | secondary data |
| descriptive analytics | omnibus survey | social analytics |
| descriptive research | online research bulletin boards | social listening |
| experiment | online research communities | structured data |
| exploratory research | panel | syndicated studies |
| focus group | predictive analytics | test market |
| in-depth interviews | primary data | unstructured data |
| key performance indicators (KPIs) | probability sampling | web analytics |
| market research | qualitative research | |
| market share | quantitative research | |

**Market Research Assignment**    The course you are completing may require you to submit a report on the marketing of a product. Navigate your way to the online research sources identified in Figure 4–6 to review and collect secondary data on your product, the industry it competes in, and its target market. Summarize and source your findings with bullet points for future reference.

This chapter's opening vignette examines how the research firm Delvinia provides customers with the ability to obtain customer insights fast. The Corby Panel was used to gain insights into the Corby Safe Rides program. Answer the Reality Check questions at the end of the vignette by reviewing Figure 4–2 on key marketing metrics and researching more information on Delvinia at **www.delvinia.com** and Corby Spirit and Wine Limited at **www.corby.ca**.

Review the Infographic "The next level of customer experience" from SAS. This infographic summarizes how retailers can gather data about their customers and turn that data into a customer-centric strategy using analytics. Think about your favourite retail store (online or bricks and mortar). What do wish your retailer would provide you with? Which services? What products? What promotional offers? How should they communicate with you? Make recommendations. How could your favourite retailer obtain this information about your preferences to provide you with more value as a shopper?

# B2B Marketing

**B**eing able to provide consumers with what they need, when they need it, is critical for customer satisfaction. Many retail businesses rely on intermediaries in their supply chains and marketing channels to ensure they have the inventory required to deliver to their consumers on time.

Used with permission of Sarmazian Brothers Flooring.

When you enter into a home, one important consideration is the presence or absence of hardwood flooring. Consumer preference determines how important this feature of a home is, and Raffi Sarmazian, one of the owners of Sarmazian Brothers Flooring, believes more and more Canadians prefer this option.

Regardless of whether you rent or buy, having a place to call home is a primary need of Canadian consumers. Living spaces have basic amenities as well as distinct differences that make a home more personal to the owner. Carpet, hardwood, laminate, tile, and stone have various benefits and considerations. Since the process of building a home is involved, consultants like Sarmazian Brothers need good partners in their supply chain in order to be successful.

For over 45 years, Sarmazian Brothers has helped turn houses into homes. Started by four brothers as a carpet installation company, this business has offered a second generation of ten cousins the opportunity to run a thriving business as co-owners. Focusing on quality workmanship, product selection, and customer service, the company has gathered numerous awards in the flooring industry. Raffi Sarmazian has this insight to share on marketing his businesses to consumers: "As retailers, we need to meet the needs of our consumers." Sarmazian Brothers does not manufacture its own product. It relies on intermediaries in its supply chain to get the right products to the consumers.

Under the North American Industry Classification System (NAICS), Sarmazian Brothers would be classified under 238330 – Flooring Contractors. Raffi explains that the personal selling approach of companies that prospect him is extremely important. "We have built a business based on quality and workmanship. We can expect no less from businesses that sell us raw materials, supplies, and business services that support our business."

Sarmazian Brothers is a small Canadian business with two locations. Each location has an established gatekeeper to ensure the executives can manage their time effectively. "Being a small business, there are many opportunities for us to consider," shares Raffi. "It can be an all-consuming job reviewing proposals from companies. We need a gatekeeper to ensure that the people we are meeting with will have something to offer our business."

Generally speaking, when Raffi and his executive team make purchases, they are much larger than the typical consumer. That allows them to use economies of scale to reduce their costs and potentially pass the savings on to their customers.

Even though the company is relatively small, there are a number of individuals to consider when making purchase decisions. Similar to how consumers go through the consumer purchase decision process, business like Sarmazian Brothers recognize a problem, search for information, evaluate the options, make the purchase, and then evaluate the decision. "The process of making a business purchase decision has similarities to the consumer decision making process," states Raffi. "Scale plays a factor though as my partners and I are generally making larger-dollar-value purchases. This means we need to be collaborative in our decision-making." Ultimately, Raffi is a key decision-maker, but he relies on his sales consultants to influence his decision. Furthermore, the users of the flooring product have a large say in future decisions. "Customers don't join us for our decision-making meetings; however, their feedback is always considered. We want to ensure that the products on our shelves are going to meet their needs in the future, so we take their feedback very seriously."

One of the companies that Raffi trusts to supply his company with flooring product is Melmart Distributors Inc. When choosing a supplier, Raffi ensures that

## CHAPTER FEATURES

**Suppliers and Success**
How suppliers help a family business extend its commitment to quality.

**Volatile Is the New Up**
The opportunities Canadian businesses have to export to the United States.

**Just out of the Top 10**
Canada is 11th in the list of top global exporters.

**Xerox Contently Rebranding**
Learn about Xerox Company's thought leadership in content marketing.

**Leading by Example**
The Government of Canada sets high standards for its suppliers.

**We Are the World**
How does Canada's largest company fare on the global stage?

**Marketing Mishaps in the Global Economy**
Explore the perception of different cultures on marketing plans.

## CHAPTER OUTLINE

- Suppliers and success
- The nature and size of organizational markets
- Measuring industrial, reseller, government, and non-profit markets
- Characteristics of organizational buying
- The organizational buying process and the buying centre
- Business market segmentation
- Online buying in organizational markets

all of his company's partners focus on relationship and service.

"The flooring market is extremely competitive," explains Raffi. "We have overhead and expenses to maintain and can't cover all options efficiently. Fortunately, we have partners like Melmart to rely on." Melmart Distributors was founded by Melvin William Martin around the same time Sarmazian Brothers was formed. As a flooring distributor, Melmart carries a wide range of options and dedicates one representative for each product. Melmart thrives on providing its flooring to a number of retail businesses. To do this, the company identifies a contact within a prospective target company. With a smaller organization like Sarmazian Brothers, the relationship is directly with the owners. In larger organizations, it may involve an entire department dedicated to purchasing.

Being a small business that purchases from suppliers helps Sarmazian Brothers understand the buying process of a business that require its services. Not only does Sarmazian Brothers sell directly to consumers, it also work with builders as contractors. It responds to requests for proposals and works with the decision-makers to agree upon pricing for large orders of flooring. "The scale on a builder sale can be 100 times more than a single retail customer purchase," explains Raffi. "Having business-to-business opportunities as well as our business-to-consumer sales diversifies our company's revenue stream." Although margins are smaller in business-to-business, profits can be made through volume.

Sarmazian Brothers is in a very competitive industry with low barriers to entry, and Raffi knows there is still a great deal of opportunity to help home buyers. "Choosing the right flooring not only creates a great living atmosphere for the owner, it also improves the resale value of the home when it is time to move on." So long as consumers continue to invest in their homes, Sarmazian Brothers will continue to invest in their business.[1]

> ## reality CHECK ⊘
>
> As you read Chapter 5, refer back to the Sarmazian Brothers Flooring vignette to answer the following questions:
>
> - As a retailer, choosing the right suppliers is critical to meeting your customers' needs. What individuals at Sarmazian Brothers Flooring would be involved in choosing a supplier?
> - Considering the makeup of the buying centre in this small business, how would you approach Sarmazian Brothers Flooring if you wanted them as a customer?

# THE NATURE AND SIZE OF ORGANIZATIONAL MARKETS

**business marketing**
Marketing to firms, governments, or non-profit organizations.

**organizational buyers**
Manufacturers, wholesalers, retailers, and government agencies that buy goods and services for their own use or for resale.

**LO 1** Effective marketers have a clear understanding of buying behaviour. Effective business marketers also have an understanding of organizational markets. Also referred to as business-to-business (B2B) marketing, **business marketing** is the marketing of products to companies, governments, or non-profit organizations for use in the creation of goods and services that they then produce and market to others.[2] Many firms engage in business marketing, so it is important to understand the buying behaviour of organizational buyers, as it differs from consumer buying behaviour. Marketing plans are important as road maps for firms selling industrial products, just as they are for companies that sell consumer products. Chapter 15 describes marketing plans in greater detail.

**Organizational buyers** are those manufacturers, wholesalers, retailers, and government agencies that buy goods and services for their own use or for resale. For example, these organizations buy computers and smartphones such as the BlackBerry for their own use. Manufacturers buy raw materials and parts that they reprocess into the finished goods they sell, and wholesalers and retailers resell the goods they buy without reprocessing them. Organizational buyers include all buyers in a nation except ultimate consumers. These organizational buyers purchase and lease large volumes of equipment, raw materials, manufactured parts, supplies, and business services. They often buy raw materials and parts, process them, and sell them. This upgraded product may pass through several different organizations (as it is bought and resold by different levels of manufacturers, distributors, wholesalers, and retailers) before it is purchased by the final organizational buyer or final consumer. So the total purchases of organizational buyers in a year are far greater than those of ultimate consumers.

According to Industry Canada, there are a variety of industries that a business can sell to, including construction, manufacturing, wholesale trade, retail trade, and public administration. Organizational buyers are divided into three different markets: industrial, reseller, and government markets.[3]

## INDUSTRIAL MARKETS

Industry Canada also notes there are over 2.4 million business locations in Canada. These *industrial firms* in some way reprocess a product or service they buy before selling it again to the next buyer. For example, there are many suppliers that sell to car companies. Although the consumer purchases one consumer product (i.e., the car), the automobile company purchases parts from many suppliers just to make that one car. There are suppliers for such parts as steering wheels, brakes, doors,

Organizational buyers make purchases on a larger scale than consumers.

©Auremar/Dreamstime.com/
GetStock.com

tires, seats, and so on. The business market involves more purchases and dollars than the consumer market.

The importance of services in Canada today is emphasized by the composition of the industrial markets. Primary industries (agriculture, fishing, mining, and forestry), utilities, manufacturers, and construction firms sell physical products. The service market sells diverse services such as legal advice, auto repair, and dry cleaning, and includes organizations such as finance, insurance, and real estate businesses; transportation, communication, and public utility firms; and non-profit associations. Furthermore, there are over 1 million small businesses in Canada. Small businesses are defined as having fewer than 100 employees.[4]

## RESELLER MARKETS

Wholesalers and retailers that buy physical products and sell them again without any reprocessing are *resellers*. In Canada, there are over 200,000 retailers and over 65,000 wholesalers. Some of the largest Canadian-owned retailers in Canada include Loblaw, Alimentation Couche-Tard, Empire Company Limited (Sobeys), Metro, Shoppers Drug Mart, and Canadian Tire. This chapter focuses on how resellers act as organizational buyers and make decisions on which products they choose to carry.

## GOVERNMENT MARKETS

*Government units* are the federal, provincial, regional, and municipal agencies that buy goods and services for the constituents that they serve. With a spending budget of over $280 billion in 2013, the federal government is a major customer, possibly the largest in Canada. To hold itself accountable, it created an online database to explain where taxpayer dollars are going.[5] In addition to specialized purchases for the military, government agencies also buy almost everything that regular consumers buy, from toilet paper to chewing gum to cars for federal prisons, hospitals, and schools. At the federal government level, the bulk of the purchasing is done by Public Works and Procurement Canada. Provincial and municipal governments typically have government departments that do the buying for them. In addition, hundreds of government departments, agencies, and Crown corporations (owned by the government on behalf of the people of Canada) such as CBC, VIA Rail, and the Royal Canadian Mint purchase supplies and services to operate. An example of a very successful Canadian company is Bombardier. Over the years, it has produced regional aircraft, business jets, mass transportation

# Infographic

**VOLATILE IS THE NEW UP**
Global Export Forecast: Fall 2015

THE GLOBAL ECONOMY IS RETURNING TO GROWTH, LED BY THE U.S.

GLOBAL GROWTH IN 2015: **3.0%**
GLOBAL GROWTH IN 2016: **3.6%**

2016 EXPORTS: **+7%**

U.S. GROWTH: (GDP)
2.2% 1.5% 2.4% 2.5% 2.9%
2012 2013 2014 2015 2016

THERE'S NEVER BEEN A BETTER TIME FOR
**CANADIAN COMPANIES**
TO EXPORT TO THE UNITED STATES

**CANADIAN DOLLAR DOWN** $ **18%**
AGAINST U.S. DOLLAR SINCE MID-2014

CONSUMER SPENDING GROWING

HOUSING MARKET RISING

BUSINESS CAPACITY CONSTRAINTS

**BUT DON'T OVERLOOK CHINA**

FORECAST GROWTH 2015: **6.9%**
FORECAST GROWTH 2016: **6.8%**

CHINA'S SHARE OF CANADA'S EXPORTS
**3.8%**

FOR BRITISH COLUMBIA **17.7%**  FOR SASKATCHEWAN **8.0%**  FOR MANITOBA **7.5%**

**ALL PROVINCES AND SECTORS**
WILL SEE EXPORT GROWTH IN 2016

TOP PERFORMERS
SECTORS

ENERGY **+18%**  AEROSPACE **+17%**  METALS & ORES **+7%**  CHEMICALS & PLASTICS **+7%**

PROVINCES

ALBERTA **+15%**  NEWFOUNDLAND & LABRADOR **+11%**  QUEBEC **+8%**  ONTARIO **+6%**

Learn more about EDC's Global Export Forecast at www.edc.ca/gef

Canada  ✦EDC
Realize a World of Opportunity

Used with permission of Export Development Canada, www.edc.ca.

---

equipment such as subways and passenger rail vehicles, and recreational equipment. Many of its sales are to governments. Furthermore, as seen in the Infographic, "Volatile Is the New Up," government organizations like Export Development Canada promote the importance of business-to-business sales outside of Canada, such as Canadian company Invoice Delivery Services to health care organizations in the United States.

## NON-PROFIT ORGANIZATIONS

Organizations that operate without having financial profit as a goal, and which seek to provide goods and services for the good of society, are called *non-profit organizations*. They are also known as charitable organizations, and some 83,000 of them are registered with the Canada Revenue Agency.[6] Tax advantages make it beneficial for this type of organization to register with the federal government.

You are probably familiar with many non-profit organizations. Were you a member of the Boy Scouts or Girl Guides? Have you participated in a Canadian Cancer Society run or marathon? Have you been asked for a donation to the United Way? Hospitals, arts organizations, cultural groups, and some research institutes can be classified as non-profit organizations. In your school, you may have a foundation office that raises money for student awards and aid; this too is a non-profit organization. In the past, marketing in these organizations has been limited, but increasingly they are adopting the same types of marketing techniques that other business firms employ, and with good success. As purchasers, this sector of business buys a wide array of goods and services to conduct their operations.

---

## Just out of the Top 10

Canada is the 11th largest exporter in world merchandise trade.

| | |
|---|---|
| 1. China | 6. Republic of Korea |
| 2. United States | 7. Hong Kong, China |
| 3. Germany | 8. France |
| 4. Japan | 9. United Kingdom |
| 5. Netherlands | 10. Italy |
| | 11. Canada |

**Source:** "World Trade Statistical Review: 2016," *World Trade Organization*. Retrieved from https://www.wto.org/english/res_e /statis_e/wts2016_e/wts2016_e.pdf.

Car manufacturers are part of the industrial market.
©Bill Pugliano/Stringer/Getty Images

# MEASURING INDUSTRIAL, RESELLER, GOVERNMENT, AND NON-PROFIT MARKETS

The measurement of industrial, reseller, government, and non-profit markets is an important first step for a firm interested in determining the size of one, two, or all of these markets in Canada and around the world. This task has been made easier with the **North American Industry Classification System (NAICS).**[7] The NAICS provides common industry definitions for Canada, Mexico, and the United States, which facilitate the measurement of economic activity in the three member countries of the North American Free Trade Agreement (NAFTA). The NAICS replaced the Standard Industrial Classification (SIC) system, a version of which had been in place for more than 50 years in the three NAFTA member countries. The SIC neither permitted comparability across countries nor accurately measured new or emerging industries. Furthermore, the NAICS is consistent with the *International Standard Industrial Classification of All Economic Activities,* published by the United Nations, to help measure global economic activity.

The North American Industry Classification System (NAICS) provides common industry definitions for Canada, Mexico, and the United States.
U.S. Department of Commerce

The NAICS groups economic activity to permit studies of market share, demand for goods and services, competition from imports in domestic markets, and similar studies. The NAICS designates industries with a numerical code in a defined structure. A six-digit coding system is used. The first two digits designate a sector of the economy, the third digit designates a subsector, and the fourth digit represents an industry group. The fifth digit designates a specific industry and is the most detailed level at which comparable data is available for Canada, Mexico, and the United States. The sixth digit designates individual country-level national industries. Figure 5–1 presents an abbreviated breakdown within the Arts, Entertainment, and Recreation sector (code 71) to illustrate the classification scheme.

> **North American Industry Classification System (NAICS)**
> Provides common industry definitions for Canada, Mexico, and the United States.

## CONTENT MARKETING

**LO 2** Because of the lengthy process for making decisions, as well as the extensive research required by businesses before decisions are made, companies like Sarmazian Brothers Flooring in the opening vignette need to adopt effective content marketing strategies. Content marketing keeps potential customers engaged by ensuring that relevant and valuable content is available at various touch points.

## Figure 5–1
NAICS breakdown for the Arts, Entertainment, and Recreation sector: NAICS code 71 (abbreviated)

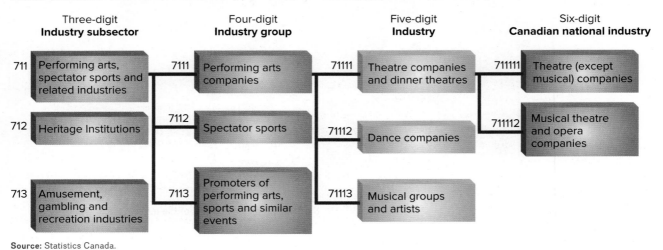

Source: Statistics Canada.

**derived demand**

Demand for industrial products and services driven by demand for consumer products and services.

Although content marketing has been a part of marketing strategy for hundreds of years, as technology has evolved, the importance of content marketing has increased. In fact, nine out of ten B2B marketers use content marketing tactics; that is, they will choose various ways to reach their target audience, including social media, e-newsletters, videos, and research reports, as discussed in the Marketing NewsFlash, "Xerox Contently Rebranding."[8] B2B marketers can engage audiences to act by implementing an effective content marketing strategy, so companies may now spend approximately a quarter of their marketing budgets on getting content marketing right for their audience. Since technology and talent are now readily available to most organizations, there is tremendous value to a company to get its message right and keep it relevant.

Not only has technology allowed businesses to reach other businesses through a variety of channels, it has provided the opportunity for regular feedback. By tracking usage and views, B2B marketers can adjust content accordingly to make information for clients more and more relevant.[9]

# CHARACTERISTICS OF ORGANIZATIONAL BUYING

**LO 3** Organizations are different from individuals in the way they purchase goods and services, so buying for an organization is different from buying for yourself and your family. In both cases, the objective in making the purchase is to solve the buyer's problem—to satisfy a need or want. Unique objectives and policies of an organization put special constraints on how it makes buying decisions. Understanding the characteristics of organizational buying is essential in designing effective marketing programs to reach these buyers. Key characteristics of organizational buying are listed in Figure 5–2 and discussed next.[10]

## DERIVED DEMAND

Consumer demand for products and services is affected by their price and availability and by consumers' personal tastes and discretionary income. By comparison, industrial demand is derived. **Derived demand** means that the demand for industrial products and services is driven by, or derived from, demand for consumer products and services, as demonstrated in Figure 5–3. For example, the demand for Weyerhaeuser's pulp and paper products is based on consumer demand for newspapers, Domino's "keep warm" pizza-to-go boxes, FedEx packages, and disposable diapers. Derived demand is often based on expectations of future consumer demand. For instance, Whirlpool purchases parts for its washers and dryers in anticipation of consumer demand, which is affected by the replacement cycle for these products and by consumer income. Another example of derived demand is the car industry. Demand for auto parts is driven by new car sales. Magna International Inc., a Canadian company based in Aurora, Ontario, is Canada's largest automobile parts manufacturer, and one of the country's largest companies.

# Xerox Contently Rebranding

## Contently

**W**eb communities have emerged as business enablers for B2B marketing. By creating interactive and collaborative environments, social media has become the go-to resource for B2B customers, not only to share feedback about companies they are doing business with but also to monitor discussions about products and services they are considering. The control of a B2B company's brand is rapidly changing from corporate marketing departments to the customer-to-customer conversations taking place on social media networks.

Not surprisingly, customers recognize their growing influence and realize the impact of their praise or, more importantly, their criticism on a company. Businesses of all sizes are learning the importance of listening, rather than preaching, in order to acquire and retain their customers. Customers using social media are not interested in vague and impersonalized advertising and sales pitches.

This new environment creates big challenges but also incredible opportunities for B2B sales. Sales professionals can no longer completely rely on traditional e-mail and cold-calling campaigns. Companies like Contently offer companies content marketing solutions to help keep business customers engaged.

Working with Contently allows business sales professionals to gain timely and relevant insights about their customers as well as engage at a very deep and personal level—two huge boons to the B2B sales process. Thanks to social media monitoring and conversation, individuals within the organization have the ability to champion the identity of their corporate brand.

Social media is just one tactic in content marketing. In 2013, Xerox was recognized for its content marketing thought leadership as it expanded into the health care industry. The HealthBiz Decoded website was launched by Xerox and filled with articles from Xerox subject matter experts and other freelance journalists. The end result is a digital magazine that hosts videos and infographics to enhance the content. It is a subtle but effective strategy for Xerox to show it is not just a copier company; it is a company that is an effective service provider. Recently, Xerox has worked with the technology solutions company Contently to help rebrand itself. ●

## Questions

1. If you are a new, small B2B company with limited resources, how could content marketing enable your business?

2. How has content marketing levelled the playing field between business marketers and their customers?

## Figure 5–2
Key characteristics of organizational buying behaviour

| Characteristics | Dimensions |
|---|---|
| Market characteristics | • Demand for industrial products is derived.<br>• The number of business customers is typically small, and their purchase orders are typically large. |
| Product or service characteristics | • Products or services are technical in nature and purchased on the basis of specifications.<br>• Many goods purchased are raw or semi-finished.<br>• Heavy emphasis is placed on delivery time, technical assistance, and postsale service. |
| Buying process characteristics | • Technically qualified and professional buyers follow established purchasing policies and procedures.<br>• Buying objectives and criteria are typically spelled out, as are procedures for evaluating sellers and their products or services.<br>• There are multiple buying influences, and multiple parties participate in purchase decisions.<br>• There are reciprocal arrangements, and negotiation between buyers and sellers is commonplace.<br>• Online buying over the Internet is widespread. |
| Marketing mix characteristics | • Personal selling to organizational buyers is used extensively, and distribution is very important.<br>• Advertising and other forms of promotion are technical in nature.<br>• Price is often negotiated, evaluated as part of broader seller and product or service qualities, and frequently affected by quantity discounts. |

## Figure 5–3
Direct versus derived demand

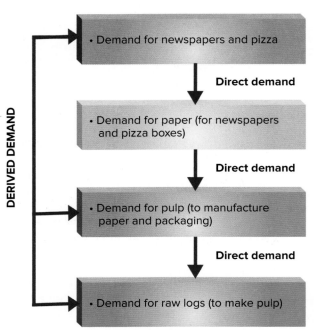

**DERIVED DEMAND**

- Demand for newspapers and pizza

↓ **Direct demand**

- Demand for paper (for newspapers and pizza boxes)

↓ **Direct demand**

- Demand for pulp (to manufacture paper and packaging)

↓ **Direct demand**

- Demand for raw logs (to make pulp)

up, a car manufacturer will still order the same quantity. A single business product, such as a brake pad, is only one of many parts that go into making the final product, and is only a minor portion of the price of the car.

## FLUCTUATING DEMAND

Small changes in demand for consumer products can result in large increases or decreases in demand for the facilities and equipment needed to make the consumer product. This is referred to as **fluctuating demand**. A product's life expectancy also has a bearing on this type of demand. For example, business products such as large machinery are purchased infrequently. Demand for such products can be high one year when they are wearing out but low in the following year if the old machinery is operating satisfactorily.

## SIZE OF THE ORDER OR PURCHASE

The size of the purchase involved in organizational buying is typically much larger than that in consumer buying. The dollar value of a single purchase made by an organization often runs into the millions of dollars. For example, in 2009, the Toronto Transit Commission (TTC) received approval to spend $1.2 billion to purchase 204 new streetcars from Bombardier. The

## INELASTIC DEMAND

**inelastic demand**
Demand for products does not change because of increases or decreases in price.

**Inelastic demand** means that regardless of whether there is an increase or decrease of the price of a B2B product, customers will buy the same quantity. For example, if the price of brake pads goes

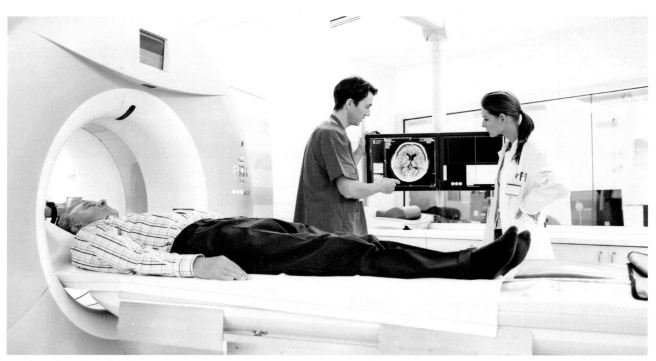

The number of potential buyers of magnetic resonance imaging (MRI) scanners is limited.

alvarez/Vetta/Getty Images

Bombardier markets to organizational buyers such as the Toronto Transit Commission (TTC). In 2010, Bombardier sold 186 new subway cars to the Toronto Transit Commission (TTC) for a value of $390 million.

(left): ©Peter Power/The Globe and Mail/The Canadian Press; (right): njene/Shutterstock.com

following year, Bombardier sold 186 new subway cars to the Toronto Transit Commission (TTC) for a value of $390 million.[11]

With so much money at stake, most organizations place constraints on their buyers in the form of purchasing policies or procedures. Buyers must often get competitive bids from at least three prospective suppliers when the order is above a specific amount, such as $5,000. When the order is above an even higher amount, such as $50,000, it may require the review and approval of a vice president or even the president of the company. Knowing how the size of the order affects buying practices is important in determining who participates in the purchase decision and makes the final decision, as well as the length of time required to arrive at a purchase agreement.

## NUMBER OF POTENTIAL BUYERS

Firms selling consumer products or services often try to reach thousands or millions of individuals or households. For example, your local supermarket or bank probably serves thousands of people, and Kellogg tries to reach millions of Canadian households with its breakfast cereals and probably succeeds in selling to a third or half of these in any given year. In contrast, firms selling to organizations are often restricted to far fewer buyers. Bombardier Aerospace can sell its Challenger business jets to a few thousand organizations throughout the world, and B. F. Goodrich sells its original equipment tires to fewer than ten car manufacturers.

**fluctuating demand**
Demand for business products and services fluctuates more than demand for consumer products and services.

## ORGANIZATIONAL BUYING OBJECTIVES

Organizations buy products and services for one main reason: to help them achieve their objectives. For business firms, the buying objective is usually to increase profits through reducing costs or increasing sales. 7-Eleven buys automated inventory systems to increase the number of products that can be sold through its convenience stores and to keep those products fresh. Nissan Motor Company switched its advertising agency because it expects the new agency to devise a more effective ad campaign to help it sell more cars and increase sales. To improve executive decision-making, many firms buy advanced computer systems to process data.

The objectives of non-profit firms and government agencies are usually to meet the needs of the groups they serve. Thus, a hospital buys a high-technology diagnostic device to serve its patients better. Understanding buying objectives is a necessary first step in marketing to organizations.

*Understanding buying objectives is a necessary first step in marketing to organizations.*

# ORGANIZATIONAL BUYING CRITERIA

Consumers use criteria when purchasing a product. Businesses also use criteria in their purchasing: They specify *organizational buying criteria,* which are detailed specifications for the products and services they want to buy and the characteristics of the suppliers that will supply them. When suppliers are selected, their products and their firm's characteristics are evaluated using these criteria. The following lists some of the most commonly used criteria:

- Price
- Ability to meet the quality specifications required
- Ability to meet the required delivery schedules
- Technical capability
- Warranties and claims policies
- Past performance on previous contracts
- Production facilities and capacity

Many organizational buyers today are transforming their buying criteria into specific requirements that are communicated to suppliers. This practice, called *reverse marketing,* means that organizational buyers are attempting to work with suppliers to make their products, services, and capabilities fit the buyer's needs. Working closely and collaboratively like this with suppliers also helps build buyer–seller relationships and leads to supply partnerships. Companies such as Tim Hortons will work with external partners to build stores and host events.

# FEAR IN ORGANIZATIONAL BUYING BEHAVIOUR

It's important at this point to examine the role of emotion in the organizational buying process. Emotions drive human behaviour and are the engines that propel people forward to reach their goals.

According to one author, B2B buying decisions are usually driven by one emotion—fear. Specifically, B2B buying is all about minimizing fear by eliminating risk. There are two distinct types of risk. There is organizational risk, typically formalized and dealt with in the buying process, and then there is personal risk, which is unstated but remains a huge influencing factor in organizational buying. For example, a buyer who chooses to deal with the same trusted supplier for many years is minimizing fear by eliminating organizational risk. Personal risk is explained by the buyer who chooses not to work with a new supplier even if that potential supplier's products offer better value. The buyer may fear that the latter may not produce a quality product, for example, and the buyer fears being reprimanded and thus may fear working with new suppliers to avert any risk. Humans do not always make rational decisions. In fact, some decisions are made irrationally. People use shortcuts, gut feel, emotions, beliefs, instincts, and habits to reach decisions. Consumer research found this out long ago, but for some reason, many people refuse to accept that the same mechanisms are at play in the business world.[12]

# BUYER–SELLER RELATIONSHIPS AND SUPPLY PARTNERSHIPS

Another distinction between organizational and consumer buying behaviour lies in the nature of the relationship between organizational buyers and suppliers. Specifically, organizational buying is more likely to involve complex and lengthy negotiations concerning delivery schedules, price, technical specifications, warranties, and claims policies. These negotiations can last for more than a year.

Reciprocal arrangements also exist in organizational buying. Reciprocity is an industrial buying practice in which two organizations agree to purchase each other's products and services. Governments frown on reciprocal buying because it restricts the normal operation of the free market. However, the practice exists and can limit the flexibility of organizational buyers in choosing alternative suppliers. The Focus on Ethics box, "Leading by Example," has more about government buying practices.[13]

Fear may cause organizational buyers to make irrational decisions they will regret.

© Tetra Images/Alamy Stock Photo

# Leading by Example

As of December 2012, there were over 1.1 million businesses in Canada. With over 98 percent of these organizations having less than 100 employees, businesses cannot overlook the opportunity to work with small businesses as either buyers or sellers.

The Government of Canada purchases over $16 billion worth of goods and services from various businesses each year. These purchases are made on behalf of the various federal agencies and departments that help run our country. Given the size of the Canadian government, leveraging its purchasing power allows the Government of Canada to receive great value from its purchases. Furthermore, contracts flow through Public Services and Procurement Canada once costs for goods and services exceed $25,000. This makes the organizational buying process more fair and structured.

In fact, the Government of Canada has made it easier for businesses to sell to it by breaking down its buying procedure. It clearly articulates its organizational buying behaviour and prepares businesses for future bidding opportunities. The Government of Canada strives to makes its process accessible and fair while promoting competition among the different businesses it interacts with.

Being one of the largest purchasers in Canada, the Government of Canada is also practising green procurement; that is, federal departments and agencies consider environmentally responsible procurements by identifying green goods and services as well as the companies that supply them. These programs include the ECOLOGO® Certification program, which outlines criteria and life cycle–based standards, and EnerGuide, which promotes energy efficiency. ●

ECOLOGO is a trademark of UL LLC. Used with permission.

## Questions

1. As a small business in Canada, what do you believe would be the pros and cons of selling products and services to the Government of Canada?

2. Knowing the green procurement practices of the Government of Canada, what steps do you believe small businesses need to take with respect to the production of their goods and services?

---

Because of the need to ensure that both buyer and seller perspectives are understood and addressed, buyer–seller relationships develop into supply partnerships in some cases. These partnerships are long-term relationships built on transparency and understanding.[14] A **supply partnership** exists when a buyer and its supplier adopt mutually beneficial objectives, policies, and procedures for the purpose of lowering the cost or increasing the value of products and services delivered to the ultimate consumer. For example, Sarmazian Brothers, featured in the opening vignette, partners with companies that are market leaders in flooring to enhance its offering.

### ask YOURSELF

1. *What is derived demand?*
2. *A supply partnership exists when.*

# THE ORGANIZATIONAL BUYING PROCESS AND THE BUYING CENTRE

**LO 4** Organizational buyers, like consumers, engage in a decision process when selecting products and services. **Organizational buying behaviour** is the decision-making process that organizations use (1) to establish the need for products and services, and (2) to identify, evaluate, and choose among alternative brands and suppliers. There are important similarities and differences between

**supply partnership**
Relationship between a buyer and supplier that adopt mutually beneficial objectives, policies, and procedures.

**organizational buying behaviour**
Process by which organizations determine the need for goods and then choose among alternative suppliers.

the two decision-making processes. To better understand the nature of organizational buying behaviour, we first compare it with consumer buying behaviour. We then describe a unique feature of organizational buying: the buying centre.

## STAGES IN THE ORGANIZATIONAL BUYING PROCESS

As shown in Figure 5–4, the five stages that a student might use in buying a smartphone also apply to organizational purchases. However, comparing the two right-hand columns in Figure 5–4 reveals some key differences. For example, when a smartphone manufacturer buys digital cameras for its smartphones, more individuals are involved, supplier capability becomes more important, and the post-purchase evaluation behaviour is more formal. The buying decision process of an organization purchasing cameras for smartphones is typical of the steps made by organizational buyers.

## THE BUYING CENTRE: A CROSS-FUNCTIONAL GROUP

For routine purchases with a small dollar value, a single buyer or purchasing manager often makes the purchase decision alone. In many instances, however, several people in the organization participate in the buying process. The individuals in this group, called a **buying centre**, share common goals, risks, and knowledge important to purchase decisions. For most large multi-store chain resellers, such as 7-Eleven convenience stores or Safeway, the buying centre is very formal and is called a *buying committee*. However, most industrial firms or government units use informal groups of people or call meetings to arrive at buying decisions.

A firm marketing to industrial firms and government units must understand the structure, technical, and business functions represented, and the behaviour of the buying centre. One researcher has suggested four questions to provide guidance in understanding the buying centre in these organizations:[15]

- Which individuals are in the buying centre for the product or service?
- What is the relative influence of each member of the group?

**buying centre**
Group of people in an organization who participate in the buying process.

- What are the buying criteria of each member?
- How does each member of the group perceive the potential supplier, its products and services, and its salespeople?

**People in the Buying Centre**   Who makes up the buying centre in a given organization depends on the specific item being bought. Although a buyer or purchasing manager is almost always a member of the buying centre, individuals from other functional areas are included, depending on what is to be purchased.[16]

In buying a million-dollar machine tool, the president (because of the size of the purchase) and the production vice president would probably be members. For key components to be included in a final manufactured product, a cross-functional group of individuals from research and development (R&D), engineering, and quality control are likely to be added. For new word-processing software, experienced office staff who will use the equipment would be members. Still, a major question in understanding the buying centre is finding and reaching the people who will initiate, influence, and actually make the buying decision.

*A major question in understanding the buying centre is finding and reaching the people who will initiate, influence, and actually make the buying decision.*

Formal presentations to buying centres are part of the organizational buying process.

© PhotoAlto sas/Alamy Stock Photo

## Figure 5–4

Comparing the stages in a consumer and organizational purchase decision process reveals subtle differences

| Stage in the Buying Decision Process | Consumer Purchase: Smartphone for a Student | Organizational Purchase: Camera for a Smartphone |
|---|---|---|
| **Problem recognition** | Student doesn't like the features of the cellphone now owned as compared to the features of a smartphone and desires to purchase one. | Marketing research and sales departments observe that competitors are improving the quality of cameras on their new models, which will be purchased from an outside supplier. |
| **Information search** | Student uses past experience and that of friends, ads, the Internet, and magazines to collect information and uncover alternatives. | Design and production engineers draft specifications for the camera. The purchasing department identifies suppliers of cameras. |
| **Evaluation of alternatives** | Alternative smartphones are evaluated on the basis of important attributes desired in a smartphone, and several stores are visited. | Purchasing and engineering personnel visit with suppliers and assess facilities, capacity, quality control, and financial status. They drop any suppliers not satisfactory on these factors. |
| **Purchase decision** | A specific brand of smartphone is selected, the price is paid, and the student leaves the store. | They use quality, price, delivery, and technical capability as key buying criteria to select a supplier. Then they negotiate terms and award a contract. |
| **Post-purchase behaviour** | Student re-evaluates the purchase decision, and may return the smartphone to the store if it is unsatisfactory. | They evaluate the supplier using a formal vendor-rating system and notify the supplier if the camera does not meet their quality standard. If the problem is not corrected, they drop the firm as a future supplier. |

## Figure 5–5

Roles in the buying centre

*Users* are the people in the organization who actually use the product or service, such as office staff who will use new word-processing software.

*Influencers* affect the buying decision, usually by helping define the specifications for what is bought. They usually have specialized knowledge. The information systems manager would be a key influencer in the purchase of a new computer network.

*Buyers* have formal authority and responsibility to select the supplier and negotiate the terms of the contract. The purchasing manager probably would perform this role in the purchase of a computer network.

*Deciders* have the formal or informal power to select or approve the supplier that receives the contract. Whereas in routine orders the decider is usually the buyer or purchasing manager, in important technical purchases it is more likely to be someone from R&D, engineering, or quality control. The decider for a key component being included in a final manufactured product might be any of these three people.

*Gatekeepers* control the flow of information in the buying centre. Purchasing personnel, technical experts, and office staff can all help or prevent salespeople (or information) from reaching people performing the other four roles.

**Roles in the Buying Centre**  Researchers have identified five specific roles that an individual in a buying centre can play (see Figure 5–5).[17] In some purchases, the same person may perform two or more of these roles.

## Buying Situations and the Buying Centre

The number of people in the buying centre largely depends on the specific buying situation. Researchers who have studied organizational buying identify three types of buying situations, called **buy classes**. These buy classes vary from the routine reorder, or *straight rebuy*, to the completely new purchase, termed *new buy*. In between these extremes is the *modified rebuy*.[18]

- **Straight rebuy:** Here the buyer or purchasing manager reorders an existing product or service from the list of acceptable suppliers, probably without even checking with users or influencers from the engineering, production, or quality control departments. Office supplies and maintenance services are usually obtained as straight rebuys.

- **Modified rebuy:** In this buying situation, the company is purchasing a product that it has experience purchasing, such as new laptops for salespeople, but it wants to change the

**buy classes**
Three types of organizational buying situations: straight rebuy, modified rebuy, or new buy.

## Figure 5–6
How the buying situation affects buying centre behaviour

| Buying Centre Dimension | Buy-Class Situation | | |
| --- | --- | --- | --- |
| | Straight Rebuy | Modified Rebuy | New Buy |
| People involved | I | 2–3 | Many |
| Decision time | Short | Short | Long |
| Problem definition | Well-defined | Minor modifications | Uncertain |
| Buying objective | Low-priced supplier | Low-priced supplier | Good solution |
| Suppliers considered | Present | Present | New/present |
| Buying influence | Purchasing agent | Purchasing agent and others | Technical/operating personnel |

product specifications, price, delivery schedule, or supplier. The changes usually mean involving users, influencers, and/or deciders in the buying decision—more input than would be necessary for a straight rebuy.

- **New buy:** In this situation, the company is buying the product or service for the first time. This purchase involves greater potential risk and is more complex than other buying situations. The buying centre is larger, comprising people representing those parts of the organization having a stake in the new buy. In 2013, the Government of Canada awarded a $15 million contract to ARUP Canada Inc. for a new St. Lawrence Bridge in Montreal. ARUP Canada Inc. will provide engineering and coordination services for the new bridge.[19]

Figure 5–6 summarizes how buy classes affect buying centre tendencies in different ways.[20]

# B2B MARKET SEGMENTATION

**LO 5** Chapter 6, "Segmentation, Targeting, and Positioning," focuses primarily on the consumer market. Here we focus on the business market. Consumer market segmentation groups consumers into groups that have common needs and respond similarly to marketing programs. The process of segmenting business markets divides markets based on type of customer, size, buying situation, customer location, and benefits sought. By applying market segmentation concepts to groups of business customers, a marketer can develop a strategy that best suits a particular segment's needs.

## TYPE OF CUSTOMER

The NAICS codes discussed earlier provide a useful tool for identifying business target markets. For example, Steelcase, a major producer of office furniture, segments its customers into ten industries, including banking, higher education, hospitality, and health care.

## SIZE OF CUSTOMER

Many B2B marketers divide their potential market into large and small accounts, using separate distribution channels to reach each segment. For example, marketers may develop one strategy to reach Fortune 500 corporations, which have complex purchasing procedures, and another strategy for small firms where decisions are made by one or two people. American Express provides information and assistance for small business owners with its Small Business Services unit, which is dedicated exclusively to the success of small business owners and their companies.

## TYPE OF BUYING SITUATION

B2B marketers can divide their potential market by the three types of buy classes: new buy, modified rebuy, and straight rebuy. We recognized in the buy-class discussion above that a new buy is significantly different from a straight rebuy in several important respects. Consequently, a business seller might well segment its market into the three buy-class categories.

## CUSTOMER LOCATION

The product manager might segment on the basis of region or actual location of the potential customer. Firms located in a metropolitan area might receive a personal sales call, whereas those outside this area might be contacted by telephone.

## BENEFITS SOUGHT

The market may also be segmented on the basis of benefits sought. Xerox may decide to focus on firms looking for quality products and good customer service as opposed to those looking simply for lower prices.

### ask YOURSELF

1. What one department is almost always represented by a person in the buying centre?
2. What are the three types of buying situations or buy classes?

# ONLINE BUYING IN ORGANIZATIONAL MARKETS

**LO 6** Organizational buying behaviour and business marketing continue to change with the use of the Internet and e-commerce. Due to the rising competition, organizations are learning from their successes and adapting to their failures. Scale allows organizations to vastly outnumber consumers in terms of both online transactions made and purchase volume.[21] In fact, organizational buyers account for about 80 percent of the total worldwide dollar value of all online transactions. Online organizational buyers around the world purchased between $8 and $10 trillion worth of products in 2010. Organizational buyers in North America will account for about 60 percent of these purchases.

## PROMINENCE OF ONLINE BUYING IN ORGANIZATIONAL MARKETS

Online buying in organizational markets is prominent for three major reasons.[22] First, organizational buyers depend heavily on timely supplier information that describes product availability, technical specifications, application uses, price, and delivery schedules.

This information can be conveyed quickly online. The Internet has altered one aspect of B2B purchasing: Buyers have much more knowledge at their fingertips about the seller's product than in the past. Second, web-based technology has been shown to substantially reduce buyer order-processing costs. At General Electric, online buying has cut the cost of a transaction from $50 to $100 per purchase to about $5. Third, business marketers have found that web-based technology can reduce marketing costs, particularly sales and advertising expenses, and broaden their potential customer base for many types of products and services. For these reasons, online buying is popular in all three kinds of organizational markets. For example, airlines order over $400 million in spare parts from the Boeing Company website each year.

*At General Electric, online buying has cut the cost of a transaction from $50 to $100 per purchase to about $5.*

Online buying can assume many forms. Organizational buyers can purchase directly from suppliers. For instance, a buyer might acquire a dozen desktop photocopiers from Xerox.ca. This same buyer might purchase office furniture and supplies online through a reseller, such as Staples at staples.ca. Increasingly, organizational buyers and business marketers are using e-marketplaces and online auctions to purchase and sell products and services.

## E-MARKETPLACES: VIRTUAL ORGANIZATIONAL MARKETS

A significant development in organizational buying has been the creation and growth of online trading communities, called **e-marketplaces**, that bring together buyers and supplier organizations.[23] These online communities go by a variety of names, including portals, exchanges, and e-hubs, and make possible the real-time exchange of information, money, products, and services. Globally, the number of e-marketplaces for businesses is extensive.

E-marketplaces can be independent trading communities or private exchanges. Independent e-marketplaces typically focus on a specific product or

**e-marketplaces**
Online trading communities that bring together buyers and supplier organizations.

service, or serve a particular industry. They act as a neutral third party and provide an online trading platform and a centralized market that enable exchanges between buyers and sellers. Independent e-marketplaces charge a fee for their services and exist in settings that have one or more of the following features:

- Thousands of geographically dispersed buyers and sellers
- Frequently changing prices caused by demand and supply fluctuations
- Time sensitivity due to perishable offerings and changing technologies
- Easily comparable offerings between a variety of suppliers

Well-known independent e-marketplaces include PaperExchange (paper products), PlasticsNet (plastics), Altra Energy (electricity, natural gas, and crude oil), and FarmTrade (agricultural products). Small business buyers and sellers, in particular, benefit from independent e-marketplaces. These e-marketplaces offer suppliers an economical way to expand their customer base and reduce the cost of purchased products and services.

Large companies tend to favour private exchanges that link them with their network of qualified suppliers and customers. Private exchanges focus on streamlining a company's purchase transactions with its suppliers and customers. Like independent e-marketplaces, they provide a technology trading platform and central market for buyer–seller interactions.

Large firms such as IBM, General Motors, and Toyota have formed private exchanges. Some, such as IBM and GE, have mandated that their suppliers must deal with them primarily through online exchanges. These private exchanges provide tremendous cost savings through the elimination of periodic negotiations and routine paperwork.

Ariba is an e-marketplace that connects one million businesses. Ariba's global membership includes buyers and suppliers from a variety of industries. It was originally set up as a one-stop solution to specifically meet the e-procurement needs of the natural resource industry.[24]

The growth of virtual B2B interactions has not limited face-to-face interactions, however, particularly in the global business community. The Marketing NewsFlash box, "Marketing Mishaps in the Global Economy," looks at some common mishaps to avoid when working with international business partners.[25]

**traditional auction**

Occurs when a seller puts an item up for sale and would-be buyers bid in competition with each other.

**reverse auction**

Occurs when a buyer communicates a need for something and would-be suppliers bid in competition with each other.

# ONLINE AUCTIONS IN ORGANIZATIONAL MARKETS

Online auctions have grown in popularity among organizational buyers and business marketers. Many e-marketplaces offer this service. Two general types of auctions are common: a traditional auction and a reverse auction.[26] Figure 5–7 shows how buyer and seller participants and price behaviour differ by type of auction. Let's look at each auction type more closely to understand the implications of each for buyers and sellers.

In a **traditional auction**, a seller puts an item up for sale and would-be buyers are invited to bid in competition with each other. As more would-be buyers become involved, there is an upward pressure on bid prices. Why? Bidding is sequential—that is, bidders bid in order, one at a time. Prospective buyers observe the bids of others and decide whether to increase the bid price. The auction ends when a single bidder remains and "wins" the item with its highest price. Traditional auctions are frequently used to dispose of excess merchandise. For example, Dell Computer sells surplus, refurbished, or closeout computer merchandise at its dellauction.com website.

A reverse auction works in the opposite direction from a traditional auction. In a **reverse auction**, a buyer communicates a need for a product or service and would-be suppliers are invited to bid in competition with each other. As more would-be suppliers become involved,

# Marketing Mishaps in the Global Economy

There is a heightened sense of formality in Japanese interaction. When doing business in Japan, your suitability with respect to conducting business will be assessed during a first meeting. It is important to maintain a sense of professionalism and be aware of the host country's customs. Offending a professional from another country could affect your business relationship.

In Japanese society, the bow is used when meeting, when getting attention, to show gratitude, to express sympathy, or as an apology. When doing business in Japan as a Westerner, you would not be expected to bow. You will most likely be greeted with a handshake combined with a slight nod of the head. Introduce yourself with your full name followed by your company name. It is important to use proper titles when addressing someone, so

always establish the position of the other person.

The diversity of our world offers interesting challenges in business. What some cultures deem as humorous may be quite offensive to others. Marketers blunder if the differences between cultures are not taken seriously.

When doing business in Japan, the exchanging of business cards involves a degree of ceremony. The card is seen to represent the individual, so it should be treated with respect. Before travelling to Japan, ensure that you have ample cards and have one side translated into Japanese. Include your position within the company on it. Invest in a carrying case to store cards and keep this in an easy-to-access location. When exchanging cards, offer your card, with the Japanese side up, with both hands. Ensure that there is no barrier between you and

the recipient, such as a table, chair, or plant. When accepting a card, always use two hands as this shows deference.

The Japanese like dealing with quiet, sincere, and compromising individuals. Extroverts are seen as brash and arrogant. Early on in negotiations, remain humble, indirect, and non-threatening. Silence is considered a virtue. If things go quiet when doing business in a meeting, don't panic. Reflection is taking place. Silence may be also be accompanied by the closing of the eyes. Never interrupt or break the silence.

Some marketing mistakes that have happened in the past include Nike's release of women's leggings in New Zealand that had a pattern that resembled a Samoan tattoo. The international company did not realize that the tattoo was reserved for men. Nike was made aware of its error and pulled the product.

North Americans are comfortable with slang phrases. So comfortable that Coors launched a cool campaign entitled, "Turn It Loose." Unfortunately, the phrase, which was intended to infer releasing inhibitions and having fun, did not translate that way in Spanish-speaking markets as the translation was "suffer from diarrhea." ●

Presenting business cards with two hands is normal business practice in Japan.
©Phillip Jarrell/Getty Images

## Questions

1. Can you think of other customs that a businessperson should be aware of in doing business in other countries?

2. What are some ways you can prepare for meetings or discussions with business people from other countries?

## Figure 5–7

How buyer and seller participants and price behaviour differ by type of online auction

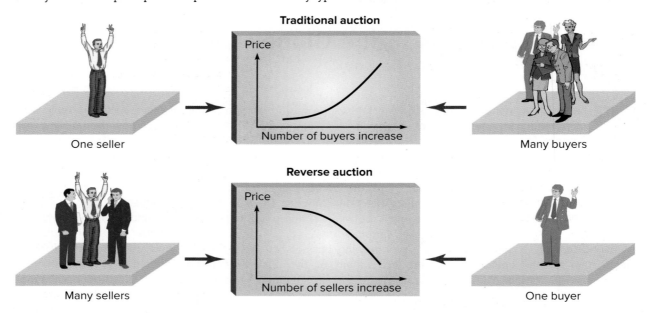

there is a downward pressure on bid prices for the buyer's business. Why? Like traditional auctions, bidding is sequential and prospective suppliers observe the bids of others and decide whether to decrease the bid price. The auction ends when a single bidder remains and "wins" the business with its lowest price. Reverse auctions benefit organizational buyers by reducing the cost of their purchases. As an example, General Electric, one of the world's largest companies, has its own Global eXchange Services unit, which runs online reverse auctions for the company. It claims that it saved $780 million on the purchase of $6 billion worth of products and services.[27]

Clearly, buyers welcome the lower prices generated by reverse auctions. Some suppliers also favour the reverse auction process because it gives them a chance to capture business that they might not have otherwise had because of a longstanding purchase relationship between the buyer and another supplier. On the other hand, suppliers argue that reverse auctions put too much emphasis on prices, discourage consideration of other important buying criteria, and threaten supply partnership opportunities.[28]

### ask YOURSELF

1. *What are e-marketplaces?*

2. *How do traditional auctions and reverse auctions affect bid prices?*

**LO 1**
- Organizational buyers are divided into four different markets:
  - Industrial firms reprocess a product or service and then sell it.
  - Resellers buy physical products and sell them without reprocessing them.
  - Government units at the federal, provincial, regional, and municipal levels purchase goods and services to help serve their constituents.
  - Non-profit organizations purchase products and services to help their organizations serve the good of society as opposed to a financial goal.
- The North American Industry Classification System (NAICS) is a convenient starting point to begin the process of measuring business markets.

**LO 2**
- Content marketing keeps potential customers engaged by ensuring that relevant and valuable content is available at various touch points.

**LO 3**
- Key differences between the business and consumer buying processes include demand characteristics, number of potential buyers, buying objectives, buying criteria, size of the order or purchase, buyer–seller relationships and partnerships, and multiple buying influences within companies.

**LO 4**
- The buying centre is a group of people in an organization that participate in the buying process.

- The buying centre usually includes a person from the purchasing department and possibly representatives from R&D, engineering, and production, depending on what is being purchased. These people can play one or more of five roles in a purchase decision: user, influencer, buyer, decider, or gatekeeper.
- The organizational purchasing process is influenced by the extent of the buying situation:
  - A straight rebuy is a routine purchase that may not involve any users or influencers.
  - A modified rebuy would involve users and influencers since there is a change to the specifications of the original purchase.
  - A new buy will be more complex and involve more people in the buying centre.

**LO 5**
- The process of segmenting business markets divides markets based on type of customer, size, buying situation, customer location, and benefits sought.
- By applying market segmentation concepts to groups of business customers, a marketer can develop a strategy that best suits a particular segment's needs.

**LO 6**
- Online buying is prevalent in industrial, reseller, and government markets.
- Globally, the number of e-marketplaces for businesses is extensive, and online auctions are commonly used by organizational buyers and business marketers.

business marketing
buy classes
buying centre
derived demand
e-marketplaces

fluctuating demand
inelastic demand
North American Industry Classification
    System (NAICS)
organizational buyers

organizational buying behaviour
reverse auction
supply partnership
traditional auction

**B2B Marketing Differences** In the opening vignette, Raffi Sarmazian discusses the importance of finding good suppliers. In particular, for larger purchases and key partnerships, decisions need to be made by a committee as opposed to an individual. Review the opening vignette and identify other differences in the organizational-buying purchase decision process that need to be considered in B2B marketing.

Strategic partnerships are critical to the success of many businesses. This chapter's opening vignette describes how B2B marketing helped build a partnership between Melmart Canada and Sarmazian Brothers. At the end of the vignette, consider the question about the individuals involved when businesses rely on their suppliers to meet the needs of their customers. Relate this to the concept of the buying centre and the different roles of individuals outlined in this chapter.

The Infographic in this chapter, "Volatile Is the New Up," suggests that although there is uncertainty in economies, growth seems to persevere. Reviewing recent articles and reflecting on your knowledge of Canada and other countries, suggest what you think will happen to Canadian exports over the next five years. Explain your rationale.

# Segmentation, Targeting, and Positioning

Market segmentation, target markets, and product positioning are the foundations of marketing practices. We turn to Jason Easton, director of sales, service, and marketing for Toronto and the Greater Toronto Area (GTA) for General Motors of Canada. We asked Jason to describe how proper customer segmentation, targeting, and messaging can drive business in the automobile industry. We then explore these concepts in more detail throughout the chapter.

Darren Brode/Shutterstock.com

More than 3.8 million Chevy Cruzes have been sold worldwide since its launch. It made quite an impact in the Canadian marketplace at launch and was named Canadian Car of the Year. Close to 32,000 Cruzes were sold in 2015. Jason Easton struggled with the challenge of keeping the Cruze relevant and growing sales in an extremely competitive marketplace.

When it came to developing a marketing plan for the Greater Toronto Area (GTA), Jason was interested in leveraging the strengths Chevrolet had with its customers nationally. Jason approached Environics Analytics to determine where these same customer types could be found in the GTA. Environics Analytics is one of the most respected and utilized data-analysis companies in North America. Environics has created the PRIZM5 customer segmentation system, which allows companies to target their marketing programs to specific customers who have been grouped into 68 lifestyle segments based on their demographics, psychographics, and media preferences.

In the course of this analysis, Environics and GM came to the realization that the typical national Chevrolet buyer does not really exist in the GTA, with its broad range of consumer types (young/old, urban/suburban, and mix of ethnicities). Nationally, Chevrolet's customer base is mainly blue-collar homeowners, not culturally diverse, who live outside of urban centres and who were buying the Cruze as a second vehicle. Historically, Chevrolet sales and market share in the GTA had been declining since the mid-90s. As a result, the national marketing messages being delivered for Chevrolet and the Cruze were not reaching, or resonating, with the GTA consumer.

From existing data on registrations in the GTA, Environics used the PRIZM5 clusters as a foundation for defining the customers most likely to purchase Chevrolet. They concluded that there were seven main customer target groups that GM should focus on:

| Targets | Description |
|---|---|
| City Renters | • Multicultural, urban dwellers, employed in blue-collar and service-sector positions, single/married<br>• Average family income $69,000 |
| Older Urban Families | • Low cultural diversity, urban dwellers, blue- and white-collar employment, families<br>• Average family income $117,000 |
| Multicultural Suburbanites | • Multicultural, suburban dwellers, mix of employment types, families<br>• Average family income $98,000 |
| Single Retirees | • Low ethnic diversity, urban dwellers, retired, empty nesters<br>• Average family income $61,000 |
| Busy Diverse Families | • Very multicultural, suburban dwellers, mix of employment types, families<br>• Average family income $106,000 |
| Wealthy Older Families | • Low cultural diversity, urban dwellers, white-collar employment, families<br>• Average family income $232,000 |
| Urban Asian Conquest | • Very multicultural, urban dwellers, white-collar employment, families<br>• Average family income $108,000 |

What does the Cruze have to offer these target groups? For the younger demographic and smaller families, the Cruze provides great value. It is an affordable vehicle to purchase but it has enough room to accommodate a small family and its belongings. It could be the only car purchased for these segments, but it could also be a second vehicle in the household. For the older, wealthier segments, the Cruze provides a great vehicle to drive around the city.

## CHAPTER OUTLINE

What were the overall implications of this new GTA segmentation to the marketing plan for the Cruze? Chevrolet implemented the following programs, focused on meeting the needs of its GTA targeted groups:

**Switch to urban-focused imagery:** Generally, a key insight for GTA consumers is that they do not have a high level of attraction to advertising images of nature and the environment, which is a bit counter-intuitive for some. They are much more receptive to urban-focused imagery. A car driving in a downtown centre was more interesting to the GTA target segments than a car driving through a mountain range or by a lake. The brand messaging continues to evolve, driven by ongoing customer insights.

**Personalized experience:** The most relevant GTA consumer insight was that consumers wanted a personalized experience. This insight was utilized for the development of a customized approach to a test drive.

**"Best Cruze Ever" test drive program:** This program was aimed at the younger target groups and budget-conscious young families. Jason Easton explains, "The 'big idea' was tapping into the customer need for a personalized experience, making a test drive much more than a retail sales tactic." After signing up for a test drive on BestCruze.ca, the customer was able to customize the test drive by specifying a pick-up location, preferred snacks, and music preferences. The test driver could even bring along a couple friends. Those who took a test drive were rewarded with gift cards not only for the Cruze but also for local trendy restaurants, once again integrating local interests into the campaign. The program surpassed all benchmarks with website visits exceeding benchmarks by almost 300 percent, leads and test drives achieved 103 percent of the benchmark, and media impressions were at 172 percent of benchmark.

**GTA Chevrolet dealers marketing programs:** Dealers played a critical role in the success of this initiative. They were involved in the process and were provided with insights relevant to their individual market areas. With this information, they could then select the best media and messages to use to reach the target groups in their specific areas.

**YouTube partnership with local relevant influencers:** Gunnarolla is one of the top-ten influencers in Toronto and popular amongst millennials. Gunnarolla was videotaped test-driving the Cruze and invited others to do the same.

**New Cruze model introduced in 2016:** The next-generation Cruze was introduced in 2016. This Cruze focuses on offering improved value for its target customers. At a retail price starting at between $15,995 and $23,895 (depending on the model purchased), the Cruze offers many customizations for a very reasonable price. A focus has been placed on making the driving experience enjoyable. Chevrolet has included features such as Chevrolet MyLink radio, digital touchscreen, and Apple CarPlay connectivity.

The GTA segmentation has been a resounding success for GM and the Chevy Cruze. Cruze sales have increased 13 percent year on year (2015–2016) in the Toronto area versus a 2 percent decline nationally over the same period. The feedback and learning from this program was utilized for the Chevy Cruze hatchback launch in fall 2016.

In the future, GM intends to apply this same approach to other major markets in Canada, including Vancouver, Calgary, and Montreal. Jason Easton offers the following advice to marketers, "Don't be afraid to ask questions, engage the right partners, and be open to surprising results!"[1]

> ## reality CHECK ⊘
>
> As you read Chapter 6, refer back to the Chevy Cruze vignette to answer the following questions:
>
> - What market segmentation strategy is General Motors using: mass marketing, segment marketing, niche marketing, or individualized marketing?
> - What is the demographic profile of GM's targeted segments in the GTA?
> - How did the national target market for the Chevy Cruze differ from the customers in the GTA?

# SEGMENTATION, TARGETING, AND POSITIONING

Segmentation, targeting, and product positioning are fundamental concepts that are central to how marketers run their businesses and market their products. These concepts are intertwined and work together to create and reinforce a product's image to its consumers and to the market in general.

A market segmentation analysis allows marketers to identify which segments could be a focus, where gaps in the market exist, and where future opportunities may lie. Having a clear position in the market allows more focused and consistent communication with customers in a meaningful way. Marketers are careful to consistently reinforce a product's image by ensuring that all elements of the marketing mix are well-coordinated to reflect the product's positioning and target market needs and wants.

General Motors Canada uses these approaches to ensure that its product features and marketing programs are relevant and focused to meet the needs of its target audience. In such a competitive marketplace, this approach helps GM maintain a competitive edge.

> *Segmentation, targeting, and product positioning are fundamental concepts that are central to how marketers run their businesses and market their products.*

## MARKET SEGMENTATION

**LO 1** The concepts of market segmentation, target markets, and product positioning are based on three important facts. First, consumers have a range of different needs, and a single product cannot satisfy everyone. Second, companies have limited amounts of money, and it needs to be spent efficiently and effectively on consumers who are most likely to purchase the product. Third, marketers need to

have clear consumer insights on their target markets in terms of product needs, price expectations, purchase habits, and the communication tools most used.

In simple terms, a market segment is a piece of the market. In the marketing world, there are two main market segments: the consumer market and the business market. The **consumer market** consists of goods, services, and ideas that a person can purchase or support for his or her own personal use. The **business market** involves products that are purchased either to run a business or to be used as a component in another good or service. How a product is classified depends on its usage. Let's look at an example to clarify this point. A person buys an iPad in order to connect on social networks, surf the Internet, stream music, upload photos, and watch movies for entertainment. A company buys its salespeople iPads so that they can make better customer presentations and more easily access head-office files. The products are exactly the same. In the first instance, the iPad is a consumer product for personal use; in the second instance, the iPad is a business product for assisting salespeople. There are many other similar examples, but it is important to understand that many products are tailored specifically for one market or the other, and not necessarily both. Heavy machinery used for landscaping is not a consumer product, and a comic book is not a business product.

Formally, **market segmentation** involves aggregating prospective buyers into groups that have common needs and respond similarly to marketing programs. These groups are relatively homogeneous and consist of people who are fairly similar in terms of their consumption behaviour, attitudes, and profiles.

There is normally more than one firm vying for the attention of prospective buyers in a market. This results in marketers following a strategy of **product differentiation** to position their products apart from the competition in the eyes of consumers so that they appear distinct from competitive offerings. It is important to note that product differentiation does not mean a product has to be better than the competition. Marketers position their products as best they can to meet the needs of their target consumers. Sometimes, this may mean adding a unique feature; other times, it may mean creating a unique image or a better price.

**consumer market**
Goods, services, and ideas that a person can purchase, use, or support for personal use.

**business market**
Products that are purchased either to run a business or to be used as a component in another product or service.

**market segmentation**
The aggregation of prospective buyers into groups that have common needs and respond similarly to marketing programs.

**product differentiation**
Positioning a product to a target group so that it appears distinct from competitive offerings.

# FORMS OF MARKET SEGMENTATION

**LO 2** There are a number of different approaches companies can take to segment the market. Whether a company is in the business-to-business market or the consumer market, it can follow one of these four strategies: a mass marketing strategy, a segment marketing strategy, a niche marketing strategy, or an individualized marketing strategy (see Figure 6–1).

**Mass Marketing** This approach exists in a limited capacity today due to the competitiveness of the market and the need for marketers to specifically address consumer needs with their offerings. A **mass marketing strategy** is when a product with broad appeal is widely marketed to the entire market with no product or marketing differentiation at all. Examples can be found in the utilities area, with items such as natural gas being marketed to all consumer groups with no variation from either a product or marketing perspective. Other examples can be found in the fruits and vegetables market with products such as broccoli, radishes, and spring onions also being sold indiscriminately to all target groups. Today, there are few products that ascribe to a mass marketing approach. With the influx of data and the range of technology to communicate with consumers, it makes it more practical for a brand to better profile consumers and engage them through more-focused messaging.

**Segment Marketing** This form of market segmentation is the most common form of segmentation, followed by companies such as General Motors Canada, discussed in this chapter's opening vignette. Segment marketing involves the marketing of a wide range of different products and brands to specifically meet the needs of an organization's varied target markets. Examples of this approach can be seen in

**What segmentation strategy is used to market these products?**
filmfoto/Getty Images

competitive industries that are dominated by large organizations, such as the food business, car industry, and smartphone market, just to name a few. For example, in the car industry, companies such as General Motors market cars, trucks, sport utility vehicles, crossovers, and minivans under a wide range of brands and models. Well-known General Motors brands include Cruze, Camaro, Yukon, Sierra, Equinox, and Corvette, as well as its premium Cadillac brand with its luxury vehicles such as the Escalade. These brands are created and marketed to appeal to different market segments in the automobile market—all owned and marketed by General Motors.

Let's look at the laundry detergent category for additional clarity and examine Procter & Gamble's (P&G) brand approach to market segmentation. If we look at laundry detergent in general, there are products that appeal to different demographic and behaviouristic groups. For example, there are detergents that are superior at cleaning your clothes, detergents that are gentle on clothing, and detergents that make your clothing smell great. When P&G started making laundry detergent, it was a "one size fits all" product. Tide was the first "heavy-duty synthetic detergent" available on the market. Mass marketing approaches were used to promote and sell the original Tide. Using the slogan "oceans of suds," Tide became the top-selling laundry detergent. Over time, this strategy shifted to a segmented approach, with P&G launching multiple laundry detergent brands with an assortment of product offerings under each brand. Tide focuses on consumers who want

**mass marketing**
Marketing a product with broad appeal to the entire market without any product or marketing differentiation.

## Figure 6–1
Companies can take different approaches to market segmentation

| Mass Marketing | Segment Marketing | Niche Marketing | Individualized Marketing |

Broad ———— Target Market ———— Narrow

> *A segment marketing strategy is also followed by companies in the business-to-business market.*

superior cleaning; Ivory Snow focuses on families who want a gentle detergent for their children's clothing; and Gain focuses on consumers who want their clothes to smell great. Through the development of innovative new products, P&G has expanded into even more targeted segments, including products for consumers who are energy conscious, consumers who want whiter clothes, and consumers who want products without added fragrance, just to name a few.

Each product not only caters to the specific product needs of distinct target markets but also has its own marketing program to ensure that each target group's needs are properly met. If you look at the packages for these products, they reflect different target market interests and needs. Ivory Snow, for example, has soft pink packaging with images of hearts to reflect its gentle formulation. Tide has bright packaging featuring a bull's-eye and bright orange colour to boldly stand out on the shelf. Gain is packaged in a bright green package with whimsical images of flowers, reflecting the focus on product fragrance.[2]

As discussed in Chapter 5, a segment marketing strategy is also followed by companies in the business-to-business market, using variables such as the type of customer, size of customer, location of customer, type of buying situation, or benefits sought. An example can be seen in the food-service industry. French's ketchup and mustard are well-known in the Canadian consumer market, but French's also has an ingredient business, selling its products to food manufacturers and restaurants. Many fast-food restaurants provide small, individual 9g ketchup packages to customers with their meal. A fast-food chain may order the ketchup from its head office to supply to its many restaurants. The head office may order pallets of 40 boxes with 1,500 ketchup packages in each box, and then distribute the boxes to its restaurants. French's may also have a poultry processor as a customer. This poultry processor uses ketchup in the seasoning for its chicken wings that it sells to customers in the frozen-food section at grocery stores. This poultry processor's specification would take into account the volume of ketchup it requires, the taste of the ketchup, how it is used in the manufacturing process, and packaging. Since this customer requires hundreds of gallons of ketchup annually, and all processing is done in one location, it orders 330-gallon stackable totes of the ketchup. These totes provide the volume needed by the poultry processor, and the totes can be easily stacked and stored at the plant. In these two examples, French's is segmenting its customers by the type of customer (restaurant versus food manufacturer). Another key segmentation variable is benefits sought. The fast-food chain requires individual packets that can be easily distributed to its individual restaurants, while the poultry processor requires large volumes that can been easily stored.[3]

**Niche Marketing** The market segmentation strategy where a company restricts its efforts to marketing a limited product line to a narrow but profitable single segment of the market that is of marginal interest to

Brands such as Heinz and French's follow a segment marketing strategy in their food-service businesses.

(left/middle): Used with permission of The French's Food Company LLC; (right) Rosenfeld Images Ltd/Science Photo Library

**niche marketing**

Marketing a limited product line to a narrow but profitable segment of the market that is of marginal interest to major competitors.

**individualized marketing**

One-to-one marketing that involves customizing offers and, in some cases, products to fit individual needs.

major competitors is called **niche marketing**.[4] Staying within the car industry and laundry detergent market, we look at the Tesla Motors car brand and Eco-Max laundry detergent to see niche marketing approaches. Tesla Motors is an independent car company headquartered in California that manufactures and markets electric vehicles only. Its first car, a Roadster, was launched in 2008; today, it also markets a Model S sedan and a Model X sport utility vehicle that compete with high-end car manufacturers such as BMW and Mercedes, but it restricts its offerings to only the niche electric-vehicle category. Tesla products are not sold through dealerships, but instead through a small number of exclusive Tesla stores, some located in upscale shopping malls.[5]

Eco-Max laundry detergent is an example of a product that started out using a niche marketing approach. Eco-Max was initially launched to consumers in 2007 by Prism Care Corporation, a company focused on replacing toxic cleaning products with natural non-toxic and effective formulations. Its products are made from "100% plant-based ingredients that are biodegradable, renewable and sustainable." Eco-Max has focused on consumers who are eco-conscious and want products that are safer to use, as well as being safe for the environment.[6]

**What segmentation strategy is used by Eco-Max with its laundry detergent?**

Used with permission of Prism Care Corporation

**mi adidas allows customization of shoes and apparel to meet individual customer needs.**

Sandi Gorkic/Shutterstock.com

Let's now consider the world of entertainment. Rogers Communications offers a variety of very specialized channels for its customers. These pay and specialty channels cater to very niche groups of sports enthusiasts (World Fishing Network, ATN Cricket Plus), ethnic groups (Telelatino, Mediaset Italia, Aboriginal Peoples Television Network), the religious (Hope Channel), and SciFi fans (SPACE). Many of these channels can be selected independently as pick-and-play options or for online streaming. The growth of specialty-channel profits in Canada has outpaced that of the larger broadcasters such as CBC.[7]

## Individualized Marketing

New technology has boosted individualized marketing as a segmentation option for marketers. **Individualized marketing** can also be called one-to-one marketing with "segments of one," and it involves customizing products to fit individual needs.[8] It is important to differentiate between individualized segmentation and individualized marketing communication. With the wide-scale use of technology and collection of customer data, messages and offers are regularly being customized for target audiences. But with individualized market segmentation, product and service offerings are also customized to meet individual needs.

Marketers are rediscovering today what previous generations knew running a general store a century ago. Every customer is unique, has particular wants and needs, and requires special care from the seller. Efficiencies in manufacturing and marketing during the past century made mass-produced goods so affordable that most customers were willing to compromise their individual tastes and settle for standardized products. Today's Internet ordering and flexible manufacturing and database marketing techniques have facilitated individualized market segmentation by making it easier to tailor goods and services to suit individual customer needs.

Consider adidas with its "mi adidas" online functionality that allows individuals to customize their shoe order by selecting their preferred colours and designs, as well as an option to include personal embroidery or logos on the shoe.[9]

Another example is the Coke Freestyle machine. This drink dispenser, available at thousands of locations worldwide, offers hundreds of customized drink combinations to meet the tastes of individual customers. With

*Every customer is unique, has particular wants and needs, and requires special care from the seller.*

a handy app downloaded to a smartphone, a consumer can locate a Coca-Cola Freestyle dispenser near them.[10]

Let's revisit the car industry and the Mini "build and price" functionality. Once a customer has selected the car model he or she is interested in, the customization begins. Customized choices allow the customer to book a test drive, estimate payments, and send the order to a local dealer, without leaving home.[11]

The key to successful product differentiation and market segmentation strategies lies in finding the ideal balance between satisfying a customer's individual wants and being able to do this profitably.

# TARGET MARKET PROFILES AND PERSONAS

## SEGMENTATION VARIABLES IN CONSUMER MARKETS

**LO 3** Marketers need to understand what makes their consumers tick, what they desire, and how best to communicate with them. A *target market* is the specific group or segment(s) of existing and potential consumers to which marketers direct their marketing efforts.

Developing an accurate **target market profile** is crucial to the success of all marketing initiatives as it drives decisions about the product's marketing mix and the product's positioning in the market. Markets are segmented using four variables: (1) geographics, (2) demographics, (3) psychographics, and (4) behaviouristics. Figure 6–2 clearly outlines these four variables.

Often, students wonder why it is important to identify all these variables when describing a target market. If consumers are buying chewing gum, what is the relevance of their income level or where they live? In fact, usually only a few elements in a target market profile are the main determinants in why a consumer purchases a product. Nonetheless, all variables need to be included in the target market profile as this profile is used in other marketing areas. If elements are missing, crucial errors can be made. For example, a target market profile is used extensively when creating advertising programs. The consumer insights are used to help develop campaigns that speak to the target group, and media is bought against the specific target market data such as age, income, location, interests, and media habits.

**Geographics** A **geographics** descriptor of a target market looks at where a target market lives, using variables such as country, region, province, city size, and population density, such as urban, suburban, or rural. Marketers often find that Canadians differ in terms of needs or preferences based on where they live. An example is a product such as the Smart car, which is small and compact and geared toward urban

**target market profile**
A description of the target market that contains specific information about the target group in four areas: geographics, demographics, psychographics, and behaviouristics.

**geographics**
Where a target market lives, using variables such as country, region, province, city size, and population density, such as urban, suburban, or rural.

Who is the target market for the car2go?
© Howesjwe/Dreamstime.com/GetStock.com

dwellers. The target market for this car mainly resides in city centres. Daimler, the maker of the Smart car, focuses its car2go car-sharing business in Canada to an even more focused target market. In Canada, car2go currently operates only in the city centres of Vancouver, Montreal, Toronto, and Calgary, where its cars, located at numerous local city parking lots, can be located through a smartphone app and accessed with a

## Figure 6–2

Examples of typical target market variables in Canadian consumer markets

| Target Market Profiles | | |
|---|---|---|
| **Categories** | **Variables** | **Typical Breakdowns** |
| **Geographics** (Where does the target market live and work?) | Region | Atlantic; Quebec; Ontario; Prairies; British Columbia |
| | City or census metropolitan area (CMA) size | Under 5,000; 5,000–19,999; 20,000–49,999; 50,000–99,999; 100,000–249,999; 250,000–499,999; 500,000–999,999; 1,000,000–3,999,999; 4,000,000+ |
| | Density | Urban; suburban; rural |
| **Demographics** (What is the basic census-type information on the target market as a whole?) | Age and family composition | Infant; under 6; 6–11; 12–17; 18–24; 25–34; 35–49; 50–64; 65+ |
| | Gender | Male; female |
| | Marital status | Single or equivalent; married or equivalent |
| | Income | Under $24,999; $25,000–$34,999; $35,000–$49,999; $50,000–$74,999; $75,000–$99,999; $100,000–$149,999; $150,000+ |
| | Occupation | Professional; managerial; clerical; sales; blue collar; white collar; student; retired; housewife; unemployed |
| | Education | Some high school; high school graduate; completed college or university; completed post-graduate studies |
| | Ethnic background | Country of origin |
| | Home ownership | Own home; rent home |
| **Psychographics** (What are the prevailing attitudes, values, interests, habits, and approaches to life that this target market shares?) | Personality traits | Social; compulsive; extroverted; introverted; intuitive; analytical; judgmental |
| | Lifestyle values and approaches | Rigid; disciplined; discontented; fearful; confident; positive; optimistic; energetic; resentful; dependent; negative; caring; materialistic; conformist; adventurous; independent; sharing |
| | Leisure activities, hobbies, and interests | Politics; music; sports; the arts; entertaining; fashion; gaming; health and fitness; travel; food; gardening; cars; movies; arts and crafts; the environment |
| | Media habits | Internet; newspaper; magazine; TV; radio; out-of-home |
| | Technology usage | Desktop computer; laptop; tablet; smartphone; TV; tech-savvy; tech-naive |
| **Behaviouristics** (How does this target market use and interact with the product?) | Main occasion for product use | Leisure; recreation and socializing with friends; professional and work situations; medical and personal care, home care, family care, etc. |
| | Main product benefit sought | Entertainment; self-improvement; fashion; fun; personal status; performance; specific product features such as taste, nutritional value, speed, etc. |
| | Primary and secondary product usage | Specific main usage and secondary usage of the product. (For example, the main usage of a cereal may be as a nutritious start to the day, but its secondary usage may be as a baking ingredient.) |
| | Frequency of use | Multiple times throughout the day; daily; weekly; monthly; every few months; biannually; annually |
| | Frequency of purchase | Daily; weekly; monthly; every few months; biannually; annually |
| | Product usage rate | Light user; medium user; heavy user |
| | Product usage status | Non-user; ex-user; prospect; first-time user; regular user |
| | Product loyalty status | None; some; medium; strong |

one-time registration that allow members to rent cars by the minute, the hour, or the day. The car drop-off is at any of its parking lot locations and does not require the user to return the car to its original pick-up spot. Car2go has over 280,000 members currently using its Canadian car-sharing service.[12]

### Demographics

One of the easiest factors to determine is the *demographics* profile of a target market. This includes identifying ranges for age, gender, family composition, income, occupation, education, ethnic background, and home ownership for the main target market. This information can be identified through a company's market research information and other secondary data sources, such as Statistics Canada. An example of where demographics plays a leading role in a target market profile is with the Centrum vitamin brand. Centrum formulates and markets many of its products based on age and gender requirements. Centrum Men 50+ is formulated for men over 50 years of age; Centrum Women 50+ is formulated specifically to meet the needs of women over 50 years of age. There are also formulations for women and men under 50. Centrum Junior is focused on children between the ages of 4 and 12 and Centrum Prenatal is for women who are pregnant.[13]

### Psychographics

**Psychographics** is one of the most difficult variables to identify for marketers. It involves understanding consumers' attitudes to life, values, personalities, general interests, opinions, media usage, technology preferences, and activities. This information is generally based on the primary research that marketers conduct to gather insights on their consumers. Image-based products gear much of their marketing efforts around these psychographic variables. The fragrance industry, for example, relies heavily on psychographics, as do many soft drink companies. Reflect for a minute on Coca-Cola, positioned as a traditional, refreshing soft drink rooted in old-fashioned Americana. Now think of Pepsi-Cola, marketed as the energetic cola for those with a youthful attitude to life. The products may vary only slightly in taste, but their target markets differ considerably in attitudes, interests, and opinions. Coca-Cola and Pepsi-Cola use psychographics as main variables in their marketing efforts.

### Behaviouristics

**Behaviouristics** directly refers to how and why consumers buy and use products. It is one of the most important target market variables as it can direct the product's positioning in the market and can drive the main marketing communication messages of the brand, as well as promotional ideas and areas for new product development.

Behaviouristics looks at why consumers buy a product, the expected product benefits, how a product is used, how frequently they buy, where they buy, and whether consumers are brand loyal in their purchase behaviour. Database marketing analytics can collect data on consumer purchases and over time identify what triggers consumer purchases as well as how loyal customers are. Primary research can help uncover why consumers purchase a product, what products benefits are most important, and how the product is used. Secondary data such as Nielsen data can provide industry data regarding where products are most frequently purchased.

Companies in the telecommunications industry often use behaviouristics to market to different customer groups with completely separate companies and brands. Rogers Communications, for example, owns Fido, which is used to market cheaper plans with no contracts to younger consumers who want basic talk, text, and

How do the target markets for Rogers Communications and Fido differ?

™Trademarks of Rogers Communications Inc. or an affiliate, used with permission.

**psychographics**
Understanding consumers' attitudes to life, values, personalities, general interests, opinions, and activities.

**behaviouristics**
How and why consumers buy and use a product, including the desired product benefits, how frequently they buy, where they buy, and whether consumers are brand loyal in their purchase behaviour.

---

## Demographic and Geographic Profile: *Canadian Living* Magazine

| | | |
|---|---|---|
| Gender | Men/women | 22%/78% |
| Age | Principal target | 25–54 years |
| Income | Average annual household income | $83,062 |
| Geography | Ontario | 50.8% |
| | Prairies | 20.7% |
| | B.C. | 15.3% |

**Source:** "Canadian Living Media Kit 2016," Quebecor Media Sales, accessed July 2016 at http://quebecormediasales.ca/content/media/pdf/2016/CanadianLiving-MediaKit2016.pdf.

social media access. Similarly, Bell owns Virgin Mobile to market to a hip, younger, budget-conscious crowd. How and why these consumers use their phones and the benefits they desire are key drivers in these marketing efforts. *Brand loyalty* refers to the favourable attitudes that a consumer has over time toward a brand that result in varying levels of purchase commitment to the brand. Marketers strive toward having highly committed, brand-loyal consumers as this helps insulate their brands from competitive marketing practices and a rapidly changing marketing environment.

### ask YOURSELF

1. *Market segmentation involves aggregating prospective buyers into groups that have two key characteristics. What are they?*

2. *What is the difference between psychographics and behaviouristics?*

## PERSONAS

**Personas** are character descriptions of a brand's typical customers. Personas bring target market data alive by creating fictional character narratives, complete with images, in one-page descriptions or snapshots that capture the personalities, values, attitudes, beliefs, demographics, and expected interactions of a typical user with a brand. Personas take target market research data and simplify and synthesize it, adding a few fictional details, such as name and image, so that human traits and characteristics become memorable for marketers. Well-defined personas usually include information on gender, age, interests, hobbies, education, goals, jobs, influencers, media usage, technology preferences, fears, concerns, drivers, and delights and interactions with a brand. They may capture a "day in the life of" a typical user. A branded product may have more than one persona; a primary persona on the typical main consumer, and a secondary persona that captures the profile of other, less important groups who should not be overlooked. Let's think about the possible personas for a Red Bull customer. Based upon an analysis of Red Bull and its marketing communications, two possible personas for Red Bull can be developed, as displayed in the images below.

**personas**

Character descriptions of a typical customer in the form of fictional character narratives, complete with images that capture the personalities, values, attitudes, beliefs, demographics, and expected interactions with a brand.

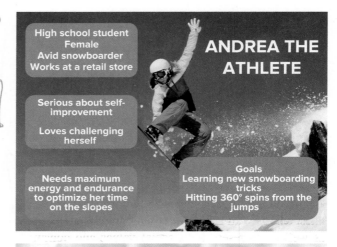

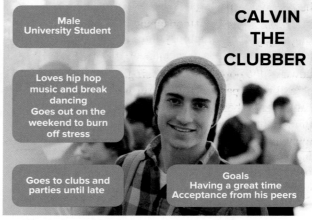

Possible personas for Red Bull.

**Source:** Kayla Hrynk, "Content Marketing: Red Bull's Secret Ingredient for Success," Bright Inbound Marketing, December 22, 2012, http://www.brightinbound.com.au/inbound-marketing-blog/bid/90632/Content-Marketing-Red-Bull-s-Secret-Ingredient-for-Success; Photos: (left) Adie Bush/Cultura/Getty Images; (right) David Schaffer/Caiaimage/Getty Images

## SEGMENTATION ANALYTICS

**LO 4** Marketers need to be aware that research companies can provide general data on the size and growth of markets, as well as general consumer and lifestyle trends, to assist in segmentation analysis. Data can be purchased from companies such as Nielsen or Euromonitor, which shows trends, market size, competitive products, market share, and future prospects for industries. Euromonitor, for example, provides data on over 200 product categories in over 200 countries.[14]

Other segmentation analytics companies provide segmentation data on a more granular basis to pinpoint information on population clusters that assists marketers. These companies, such as Environics Analytics, Pitney Bowes, and SuperDemographics, analyze populations and create market segments and detailed data to help marketers target specific groups with high levels of accuracy.

Environics Analytics is a highly respected marketing and analytical services company. It helps Canadian companies turn demographic, lifestyle, and behavioural data into customer insights, strategy, and results. Its PRIZM5 segmentation system slices the Canadian population into 68 lifestyle segments, such as Cosmopolitan Elite, Electric Avenues, Les Chics, and Lunch at Tim's, based on common demographics, lifestyles, interests, and values. Its data synthesizes information from the latest census with Environics' demographic projections, as well as its research on social values and consumer behaviour. This data gives users the ability to review information on what consumers are purchasing, what they enjoy doing, and their attitudes to life. Data funnels down to the granular postal code level where a breakdown of the population for a single postal walk is available. This is particularly useful for database marketing campaigns where postal code information triggers a host of data that assists companies in their targeting and segmentation efforts. This information helps guide marketing campaigns and media strategies.[15]

The Infographic, "In Search of the Perfect Barbecue: A Tale of Two PRIZM5 Segments," illustrates the differences in consumer behaviour seen by two different PRIZM5 segments ("Lunch at Tim's" and "Pets & PCs") in how they approach purchasing a barbecue. The "Lunch at Tim's" segment is characterized as "urban, downscale singles and families." This group is more likely to rely on flyers or attending home shows for information on barbecues. They are also much less likely to buy home and garden goods online. In contrast, the "Pets & PCs" segment is characterized as "younger, upscale, suburban families." They are more likely to research products on websites and look for consumer reviews on social media. They are much more likely to purchase their home-and-garden products online. This information can be very powerful for businesses and can provide information that can be used to better target customer segments through the communication vehicles that are most impactful to them, with the messages that are most likely to motivate purchase.[16]

Pitney Bowes PSYTE HD also provides granular segmentation data through its segmentation system, which results in 57 unique lifestyle clusters. Postal code detail helps marketers discover untapped markets, finesse

# Infographic

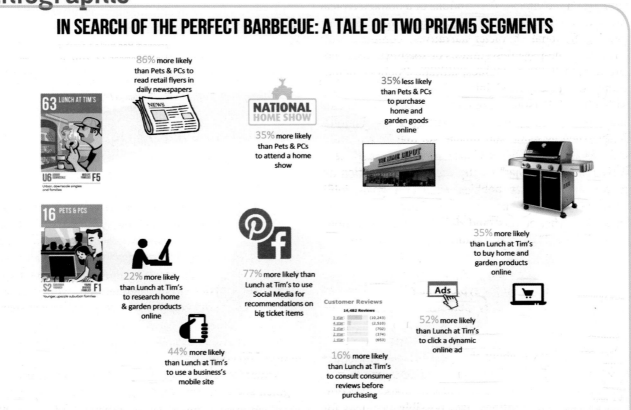

## IN SEARCH OF THE PERFECT BARBECUE: A TALE OF TWO PRIZM5 SEGMENTS

**63 LUNCH AT TIM'S**
U6 · F5
Urban, downscale singles and families

**16 PETS & PCS**
S2 · F1
Younger, upscale suburban families

86% more likely than Pets & PCs to read retail flyers in daily newspapers

NATIONAL HOME SHOW
35% more likely than Pets & PCs to attend a home show

35% less likely than Pets & PCs to purchase home and garden goods online

22% more likely than Lunch at Tim's to research home & garden products online

77% more likely than Lunch at Tim's to use Social Media for recommendations on big ticket items

35% more likely than Lunch at Tim's to buy home and garden products online

44% more likely than Lunch at Tim's to use a business's mobile site

Customer Reviews
14,482 Reviews
5 star: (10,243)
4 star: (2,510)
3 star: (702)
2 star: (374)
1 star: (653)

16% more likely than Lunch at Tim's to consult consumer reviews before purchasing

Ads
52% more likely than Lunch at Tim's to click a dynamic online ad

**Source:** Vito Di Filippis, "Omni-Channel Marketing: Not Your Father's Customer Journey," June 10, 2016, http://www.environicsanalytics.ca/blog-details/ea-blog /2016/06/10/omni-channel-marketing-not-your-fathers-customer-journey. © 2016 Environics Analytics. Used with permission.

# marketing NewsFlash

## Prince Sports Segments Tennis

**P**rince Sports is a racquet sports company whose portfolio of brands includes more than 150 racquet models and countless types of bags, apparel, and other accessories. Prince prides itself on its history of innovation in tennis—including inventing the first "oversize" and "longbody" racquets, the first "synthetic gut" tennis string, and the first "Natural Foot Shape" tennis shoe. Its challenge today is to continue to innovate to meet the needs of all levels of tennis players.

A recent study concluded that tennis participation in Canada is up by 32 percent. The global tennis market is also expected to continue to grow through 2019. The factors driving this growth are the success of Canadians in international tennis as well as the strong tennis programs that are run nationally. Much of this growth is due to the increased interest from younger players. As a result, many racquet manufacturers are interested in gaining a share of this growing market.

Prince is keenly aware that all tennis players have the desire to play better. As a result, it has dedicated itself to the development of tennis racquets that improve performance and control with a comfortable feel. Prince has conducted a lot of research with its customers and determined that there are three key segments that make up the tennis market: the performance segment, the recreational segment, and the

Thomas Northcut/Getty Images

junior segment. Prince uses these distinct segments to guide the development and evolution of its racquet designs. The following chart outlines the three segments that Prince focuses on and their subsegments:

| Major Segment | Subsegments | Characteristics |
|---|---|---|
| **Performance** | *Precision* | • Touring professional players<br>• Want great feel<br>• Want control<br>• Want spin |
| | *Thunder* | • Competitive players<br>• Want bigger "sweet spot"<br>• Want added power |
| **Recreational** | *Small head size* | • Recreational players<br>• Want added control<br>• Want forgiving racquet |
| | *Large head size* | • Recreational players<br>• Want added power<br>• Want larger "sweet spot" |
| **Junior** | *More experienced* | • 8 to 15 years of age<br>• Want lighter racquet<br>• Want shorter racquet |
| | *Beginner* | • 5 to 11 years of age<br>• Want much lighter racquet<br>• Want much shorter racquet |

Successful market segmentation means that Prince can ensure that the 4 Ps meet the needs of each segment:

- **Product:** Design racquets whose features match the needs of the segment.
- **Price:** An overall premium-pricing strategy can be adjusted to reflect the innovative technology utilized in specific racquets.
- **Place:** Mass merchandisers can be used to distribute a limited product line for the less experienced junior and recreational segments. Specialty tennis stores can carry a wider selection of racquets for all segments, especially the more experienced players.

- **Promotion:** Prince can tailor its promotional plan to specifically communicate with each segment. For example, to reach juniors, Prince can sponsor tennis clinics for younger players, and actively communicate with juniors on social media.

In order to be successful in this market, Prince needs to have a hand in growing all segments of the market. But where Prince can shine is by listening to its customers, focusing on their specific needs, and continuing to drive innovation. ●

## Questions

1. What environmental forces (social, economic, technological, competitive, and regulatory) impact the success of Prince Sports in the tennis racquet market?

2. What promotional tactics could Prince use to reach the performance player segment?

---

the targeting of their marketing campaigns, launch new products in appropriate markets, design cost-effective mailing and sampling programs, streamline retail offerings, and select the most profitable locations for new stores, restaurants, and retail developments.[17]

SuperDemographics from Manifold Data Mining is another reputable service provider in the segmentation analytics area. It too provides data down to the postal code level. It uses census data as well as statistics from Citizenship and Immigration Canada, Health Canada, Industry Canada, Bank of Canada, real estate boards and companies, provincial ministries of health, Numeris Canada, and Manifold proprietary databases.[18] The Marketing NewsFlash box, "Prince Sports Segments Tennis," examines how one company takes advantage of segmentation analytics.[19]

Students are advised to visit the websites of these three analytics companies to review samples of the rich data that is available for marketers. While Internet sites can change, the following websites currently provide a solid understanding of what data is available from these companies:

- Navigate to the PRIZM5 section of the Environics website at **www.environicsanalytics.ca/prizm5** and enter a postal code to review an overview of the cluster information.

- Navigate to the PSYTE HD Neighbourhood Segmentation Cluster Handbook under the PSYTE HD Canada Product Documentation link at **www.pbinsight.com/support/product-documentation/details/canadian-segmentation-and-survey-data** and read through the details about each cluster. Use the maps provided to find specific geographic areas that you might be interested in.

- Navigate to the SuperDemographics website at **www.superdemographics.com** and try to create a free trade report. Follow the steps and fill in the postal code to view the clusters within the area and its demographic breakdown.

## STEPS IN MARKET SEGMENTATION

**LO 5**  Segmenting a market and selecting target markets is an integral part of the overall marketing planning process (see the section on the planning phase of the marketing plan in Chapter 15). This section focuses on the process of market segmentation and target market selection. As part of the marketing plan, target market decisions and actions will be evaluated as part of the objective setting and evaluation phases.

A marketer needs to combine strong analytical skills, sound strategic thinking, an understanding of the consumer, a vision on where the market is heading, and how this all fits with the company's direction. The process of segmenting a market for both the consumer market and business-to-business market is divided into six steps, which can be seen in Figure 6–3.

1. *Identify consumer/customer needs and common characteristics in the market.* This should be done from a consumer/customer perspective, looking at what drives the category and what future trends are evolving. Marketers should be able to easily identify common interests and evolving trends by analyzing what products currently exist in the category, which areas of the market are expanding and shrinking, and where consumer/customer interests lie. Looking to other countries sometimes provides interesting ideas on where potential future interests may lie. At this point, marketers will turn to market research studies and analytics data to see what the facts reveal. Database analyses may reveal some interesting facts about purchase patterns and point to segments that had not been considered. Sometimes, marketers may need to conduct further market research to clarify questions.

## Figure 6–3

The six-step process for segmenting a market

**Steps in Market Segmentation**

1. Identify consumer/customer needs and common characteristics in the market.
2. Cluster common consumer/customer variables to create meaningful market segments.
3. Estimate the size and feasibility of each segment.
4. Identify the segment(s) to be targeted.
5. Take actions with marketing programs to reach the segment(s).
6. Monitor and evaluate the success of these programs compared with objectives.

2. *Cluster common consumer/customer variables to create meaningful market segments.* A marketer needs to stand back from the market and look for clusters of products and gaps in the market that point to common consumer/customer interests, usage patterns, and prevailing attitudes. New areas of interest should not be overlooked as these may point to evolving segments. These clusters will identify the segments that exist in the market. Sometimes there is overlap between segments, and other times the segments are not well-defined, but this is generally a reflection of the consumers/customers, who can be fickle and non-committal.

Segmentation analytics companies, as noted earlier, can provide marketers with data on market clusters, which, combined with marketing analytics, can help reveal profitable new approaches and opportunities. Companies may use its own data from customer relationship management (CRM) databases that group consumers by purchase behaviour and monetary value to a company. Software can run an *RFM analysis* (recency, frequency, and monetary value) to rate customers on how *recently* products were purchased (recency), how *often* products were purchased (frequency), and the *dollar value* of the transactions (monetary value). Customers are then scored and rated to create segments that organizations use to tailor offers and marketing messages. Non-profit organizations frequently use RFM analyses to target those most likely to make donations, while CRM loyalty programs use loyalty cards to collect customer purchase data to then customize offers.

It is very important during this step to review the market from a consumer/customer perspective and not from a product perspective. For example, if we continue to review the laundry detergent market, we may group products into those that contain bleach and establish this as a segment. The segment is in fact better defined, and more meaningful to marketers, when identified as appealing to adults who want to fight tough stains.

Laundry detergent customers can be grouped into potential segments based upon their attitudes, needs, and demographic profile. Three possible market segments are shown in Figure 6–4.

3. *Estimate the size and feasibility of each segment.* Based on external data analysis and/or the use of segmentation analytics data, the size of the segment needs to be estimated. The marketer is then tasked with forecasting the sales potential for this segment, which should also consider anticipated competitive reactions.

4. *Identify the segment(s) to be targeted.* A target market segment must be selected carefully. Marketers should use the following criteria select a target market:

- **Market size:** The estimated size of the segment is an important factor in deciding whether it's worth going after. Is the segment large enough to generate expected sales levels? Is the segment manageable so that the marketing budget is sufficient to support marketing initiatives?

## Figure 6–4

Identifying consumer clusters

| Consumer Clusters Example: Laundry Detergents | | |
|---|---|---|
| **Consumer Cluster** | **Cluster Attributes** | **Product Examples** |
| Clean Fanatics | Adults with families<br>Want clothes to continue to look like new<br>Stain removal is important<br>Family-oriented | Tide |
| Scent Lovers | Want fresh-smelling clothes<br>Cleaning is important | Gain |
| Gentle and Purists | Family-oriented<br>Prefer gentle and pure products<br>Want soft clothes<br>Focused on baby clothes and other fine washables | Ivory Snow |

**Source:** Amira El Deeb, "Class 5/1 Segmentation, Targeting, Differentiation & Positioning," Marketers' Magazine [blog], July 14, 2010, http://mmauc.blogspot.ca/2010/07/class51-segmentation-targeting.html.

Marketers segment the market to more effectively and more efficiently reach their target markets.

mstanley/Shutterstock

a marketing plan needs to be developed and implemented. Essential decisions need to be made regarding the marketing mix (product, price, place, and promotion) that are consistent with the needs and wants of the target market. Specific objectives should be set to define success for the programs. Objectives should be evaluated regularly, and plans should be adapted accordingly.

6. *Monitor and evaluate the success of these programs compared with objectives.* Marketers often work with financial analysts to determine the sales forecasts, costs, and profits realized in comparison with the cost and sales projections outlined in Steps 3 and 5 of the segmentation process. Chapter 9 reviews budgeting and profit-and-loss statements.

- **Expected growth:** Although the size of the market in the segment may be small now, perhaps it is growing significantly or is expected to grow in the future. For example, the market for environmentally friendly laundry detergents was very small a decade ago, but has grown significantly. Tide Coldwater was launched to meet the needs of this segment, far before the market potential had been reached.

- **Competitive position:** Is there a lot of competition in the segment now, or is there likely to be in the future? The less the competition, the more attractive the segment is.

- **Compatibility with the organization's objectives and resources:** Will targeting this segment be consistent with overall company objectives, including sales and profit objectives, market share targets, as well as corporate social responsibility initiatives and new business focus.

- **Cost of reaching the segment:** A segment that is inaccessible to a firm's marketing actions or if the cost of reaching that segment is too great, it should not be pursued.

5. *Take actions with marketing programs to reach the segment(s).* Once a target market has been selected,

## POSITIONING

**LO 6** One of the central elements in marketing is product positioning. Marketers position products in the market to appeal to certain target groups and to present a particular impression relative to the competition. **Product positioning** refers to the impression of the branded product you want to establish in consumers' minds relative to their needs and also in contrast to the competition. Companies generally use a combination of factors to position their products, always leading with the elements that are real; to differentiate the product; and to create long-term, memorable impressions with consumers. In this way, there are three basic factors, or combinations of factors, that tend to surface in product positioning:

1. **Image:** Products are often positioned as leaders, contenders, or rebels in the market, also taking on characteristics such as trusted, prestigious, or thrifty. TSN, for instance, positions itself with the "Champions Live Here" image to solidify its place as the leader in sports broadcasting.[20]

**product positioning**
The impression of the product you want to establish in consumers' minds relative to their needs and the competition.

2. **Product attribute:** Products with features that differentiate them from the competition are often positioned on this platform, bringing product claims to the forefront. The fast-food restaurant Subway, for example, positions itself as having healthy and fresh sandwiches.

3. **Price:** Products with brand parity and little product differentiation may position themselves on a price platform. Retailers such as Walmart position themselves as offering the lowest retail prices ("Everyday low prices") to support its image in the market.

How is Volvo positioned in the automobile market?

Paceman/Shutterstock.com

Marketers create positioning statements to clearly and simply outline the positioning of a product in the market. These statements are used to crystallize the image for marketers so that they can design a marketing mix that aligns with the product's positioning. This is very important; otherwise, the product may present a confusing image to consumers who will refrain from buying it. A **positioning statement** is a formalized statement that identifies the image a branded product represents in the market and what sets it apart from the competition. A positioning statement is generally included in a brand's annual marketing plan and its relevant strategic documents. It is important for all functional areas in a company to understand a product's positioning, as it drives activities throughout the organization.

Positioning statements are simple, clear, and focused. They average a short paragraph and identify four elements: (1) the target market and need, (2) the branded product name, (3) the category in which the product competes, and (4) the brand's unique attributes and benefits (what sets the product apart from the competition and meets customer needs). Positioning statements should take the following format:

*For (target market) who desire (target market need), (brand) is the (product category) that offers (product benefits).*

The positioning statement for Volvo could be:

> *Positioning statements are simple, clear, and focused.*

*For upscale families who desire a carefree driving experience, Volvo is a premium-priced automobile that offers the utmost in safety and dependability.*

This positioning statement directs Volvo's marketing strategy and focuses its product development efforts, such as the inclusion of side door airbags in its automobiles. The statement also directs Volvo's marketing communications message. Volvo advertising stresses safety and dependability—the two benefits that are the basis of its "Volvo for life" slogan.

## REPOSITIONING

Companies rarely change a product's positioning but do so when long-term changes in consumer attitudes or opinions of the brand require a shift in the brand's image to more accurately meet consumer needs and to reflect how it fits their lifestyle and needs. Repositioning is often implemented in stages over time with a refresh of a brand and the elements of its marketing mix. Many recent examples can be found in the fast-food industry, as restaurant chains struggle to

**positioning statement**
A formalized statement that identifies the image a branded product represents in the market and what sets it apart from the competition.

**repositioning**
Changing the place a product occupies in consumers' minds relative to competitive products to more accurately meet consumer needs.

keep up with changing tastes and emerging competitive threats.

McDonald's is a good example of a repositioning effort that included restaurant redesigns, menu updates, and a focus on the McCafé concept. Redesigns included free WiFi, comfortable seating areas with fireplaces and TVs, and the addition of in-store ordering kiosks. McDonald's has also launched several smaller McCafé locations and kiosks. This repositioning flowed into McDonald's menu choices where healthier food items were added, such as oatmeal, apple slices, yogurt, veggie wraps, and salads, with other products reformulated to contain less sodium and no trans fats. McDonald's has rolled out its McCafé brand with high-quality teas, coffees, and fruit smoothies, along with all-day breakfast (at some locations) competing with other coffee establishments such as Starbucks and Tim Hortons and fitting with its new restaurant redesigns. McDonald's has also focused on a range of customizable and premium burger selections to provide a quick-service option to gourmet burger restaurants. McDonald's is listening to its customers, and its goal is to be Canada's favourite place to eat and drink. It is working to gain a greater share of the food-service beverage market.[21]

Increased competition in the burger/fast-food restaurant business has resulted in a change in positioning for A&W. The restaurant needed to expand its target audience to a younger customer base. Based on customer insights from the 25- to 44-year-old target market, A&W has differentiated itself with the quality of its ingredients. It was the first fast-food restaurant to only serve beef raised without the use of hormones and steroids. Menu changes also included using only chicken that was antibiotic-free and hens that were only vegetarian-fed to produce quality eggs. This repositioning based on changing customer needs,

A&W has repositioned itself based on the use of better ingredients.

Used with permission of A&W Food Services of Canada Inc.

has created a unique and differentiated place in the fast-food restaurant market that has resulted in sales and market share.[22] For another examples of repositioning, see the Marketing NewsFlash box, "Interac's 'Debit Is Better' Positioning."[23]

## POSITIONING MAPS

Positioning maps, also known as *perceptual maps*, are visual representations of how products or product groups are positioned within a category to consumers/customers. Positioning maps can visually represent categories within a market, or more specifically, product and brand offerings within a category. Positioning maps are useful tools for marketers as they can reveal gaps in the market where consumers may be under-served, while also highlighting the competitive nature of the category.

A key to positioning a product or brand effectively is discovering the perceptions in the minds of potential customers by taking three steps:

1. *Identify the important attributes for a product or brand class.* One might rush to immediately identify price as a key variable, but often this is a less important feature, evaluated by consumers once a short list of attributes on which they initially evaluate a purchase are identified. Let's make this clear with two examples. First, in the laundry detergent market, scent and strength might be key attributes used by families evaluating different product offerings (price would come into play later in the purchase decision). In the second example, we can look at beverages. Research reveals the key attributes adults use to judge various drinks are nutrition and children's drinks versus adult drinks, as shown by the two axes in Figure 6–5.

2. *Discover how target customers rate competing products or brands with respect to these attributes.* Continuing with the beverage example, the factors of nutrition and adult/child–focused drink can be used objectively to evaluate products in the category. Figure 6–5 shows where beverages are placed on the positioning map and how one is positioned against another. It plots milk, tea, sports drinks, fruit juices, and soft drinks relative to each based on nutritional value and whether they are appropriate for adults or children. For these key elements, we can see diet drinks are geared to adults, while milkshakes appeal to children.

# Interac's "Debit Is Better" Positioning

Interac helps customers "Be in the Black."
LDprod/Shutterstock

How many times a day do you tap your debit card to pay for a coffee or a slice of pizza? All bank cards in Canada come with Interac functionality, and Canadians have widely accepted Interac Debit and Interac Flash as an important form of payment. In fact, the Interac network processes 54 percent of all card payment transactions (that includes all credit cards combined). This equates to an average of 12 million transactions daily across Canada.

Unlike the debit network used in other countries, Interac in Canada is a not-for-profit association, created through a partnership between the five major banks in Canada that strove to create a network to give people more extensive access to their money.

Even though everyone uses it, consumers are at a loss to explain Interac or its benefits. Competitive threats as well as changes in consumer attitudes to spending compelled Interac to better define its position in the minds of consumers and create a meaningful point of differentiation.

● **Competition:** The number of players in the card-payments market was increasing. There were more specialized services such as PayPal and Square, prepaid credit cards from Visa and MasterCard, and the launch of VISA debit. All of these new players created confusion in the minds of consumers.

● **Customer attitudes:** Consumers were more inclined to use credit cards for everyday essentials such as groceries in order to earn points or cash back. While collecting points, consumers are also collecting increasing levels of debt with household debt levels in Canada reaching record levels.

The resulting positioning for Interac was based upon image as well as product attributes and resulted in the following differentiator: *"Life feels better when you use your own money."* Interac's unique product attribute is that you are accessing your own money for payment rather than using credit. In addition, Interac is creating an emotional connection with the consumer as the card that puts the consumer in control and confident of their finances.

Interac anchored this positioning in a key slogan, "Be in the Black," which has become a memorable phrase that speaks directly to Canadians to be financially responsible. ●

## Questions

1. How did consumer attitudes about spending help Interac reposition its brand?

2. How can a financial service such as Interac create an emotional connection with the customer?

| Credit Cards | Interac |
|---|---|
| • Bills and interest<br>• Go into debt with every purchase<br>• Heavy use and debt creates anxiety | • Easiest and most familiar payment method<br>• No bill<br>• No interest<br>• Consumers feel "on top" of their money when using Interac |

## Figure 6–5

A positioning map to suggest a strategy for positioning beverages

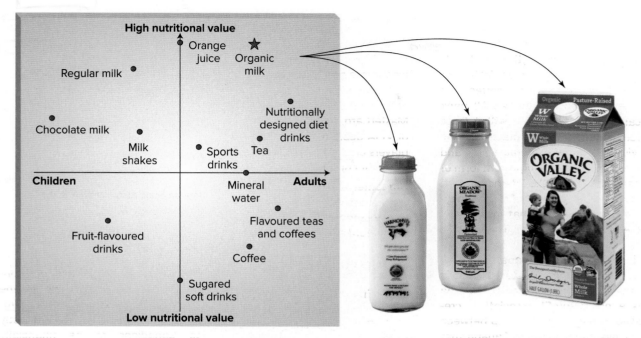

(left): Used with permission from Harmony Organic Milk; (middle): Used with permission from Organic Meadow; (right): Used with permission from Organic Valley

**3.** *Discover where the company's product or brand is on these attributes in the minds of potential customers.* With a focus on chocolate milk, Figure 6–5 shows that it is viewed as mainly a children's drink with moderate nutritional value. The makers of chocolate milk could consider repositioning themselves as an adult drink to expand their business.

### ask YOURSELF

1. *What is product positioning and what is the purpose of a positioning statement?*

2. *Why do marketers use positioning maps?*

Used with permission of A&W Food Services of Canada Inc.

1. *What psychographic interests can you determine about the target market from this ad?*

2. *What behavioural insights can you determine about the target market from this ad?*

**LO 1**
- Market segmentation involves aggregating prospective buyers into groups that have common needs and respond similarly to marketing programs.
- In the marketing world, there are two main market segments: (1) the consumer market and (2) the business market.

**LO 2**
- There are four different market segmentation strategies: mass marketing, segment marketing, niche marketing, and individualized marketing.

**LO 3**
- Marketers define their target markets by looking at four main variables: (1) geographics, (2) demographics, (3) psychographics, and (4) behaviouristics.
- Geographics looks at where a target market lives, such as a country, region, province, city size, and population density, such as urban, suburban, or rural.
- Demographics includes identifying ranges for age, gender, family composition, income, occupation, education, ethnic background, and home ownership.
- Psychographics involves understanding consumer attitudes to life, values, personalities, general interests, opinions, and activities.
- Behaviouristics looks at why consumers buy a product, the product benefit, how and when the product is used, and whether consumers are brand loyal in their purchase behaviour. Usage rate also plays a role in this information.
- Personas are character descriptions of a product's typical customers in the form of fictional character narratives, complete with images that capture the personalities, values, attitudes, beliefs, demographics, and expected interactions of a typical user with a brand.

**LO 4**
- Segmentation analytics analyzes market segments and provides data to help target specific groups with high levels of accuracy.
- Segmentation analytics data clusters consumers into lifestyle segments and provides information that details geographics, demographics, psychographic, and behaviouristic data by postal code, defined shopping areas, or neighbourhood.

**LO 5**
- Segmenting the market involves six steps that require strong analytical skills, sound strategic thinking, an understanding of the consumer, a vision on where the market is heading, and how this all fits with the company's direction.
- The six market segmentation steps start with identifying customer needs and common characteristics in the market, and continues by clustering consumer variables to create meaningful segments, estimating the size and feasibility of each segment, and finally identifying the target segment(s), taking marketing actions to reach the segment(s), and monitoring and evaluating the success of these programs compared with objectives.

**LO 6**
- Product positioning refers to the image of a branded product in the consumers' minds relative to the competition.
- Marketers create positioning statements to clearly and simply outline the positioning of a product.
- Repositioning includes a shifting of the product image and adjusting its marketing mix to more accurately meet consumer needs.
- Positioning maps are otherwise known as perceptual maps. They visually represent how products or product groups are positioned within a category to consumers.

## key terms and concepts... A REFRESHER

behaviouristics
business market
consumer market
geographics
individualized marketing
market segmentation

mass marketing
niche marketing
personas
positioning maps
positioning statement
product differentiation

product positioning
psychographics
repositioning
target market profile

**Target Market and Personas Assignment**   Go to one of the segmentation analytics websites outlined in the text. Enter in your postal code to come up with a profile of the consumer who lives in your neighbourhood or select a consumer profile you find interesting. Create a persona for this consumer including an image of the consumer and a description, including gender, age, interests, hobbies, education, goals, jobs, influencers, media usage, technology preferences, fears, and concerns.

This chapter's opening vignette examines how General Motors Canada segments its target audience for the Chevrolet Cruze in the Greater Toronto Area, as well as the rest of Canada. Using the information in the vignette, as well as your own research, create a positioning map similar to Figure 6–5 for the Chevrolet Cruze.

Review the Infographic that compares the purchasing behaviour of two Environics Analytics PRIZM5 clusters. Navigate to the PRIZM5 website at **www.environicsanalytics.ca/prizm5** and compare two other clusters (by using the postal code search) to create a new infographic in Microsoft PowerPoint. Write a short analysis of the differences that exist between the two new clusters that you have selected.

# Products and Brands

**M**anaging the marketing mix is no easy task, and this chapter explores the areas that marketers consider when managing products and brands. We speak with Dave Freeman, the former head of brand marketing at Maple Leaf Sports & Entertainment (MLSE), who was responsible for the marketing strategy of the NBA's Toronto Raptors. He took us through the history of the franchise that led to the ultimate rebranding, with the "We The North" mantra.

Mark Blinch/The Canadian Press

No one is sure what your brand is all about. Connection with the brand is low. Your brand has little brand equity and is losing customer loyalty. What do you do? Well, this is exactly the position that the Toronto Raptors found themselves in. The year is 2014.

Professional basketball was brought to Canada in 1995 with the launch of the Toronto Raptors and the Vancouver Grizzlies National Basketball Association

(NBA) teams. The Grizzlies were relocated to Memphis in 2001, leaving the Raptors as the only Canadian NBA team. The Raptors got off to a rough start, finding it difficult to engage Canadians in the sport. After acquiring Vince Carter in 1998, the excitement for the franchise grew, and in 2000, the Raptors made it to the playoffs for the first time, the first of three consecutive playoff appearances, further igniting the support of Canadian fans.

But over time, the team had long periods without great success and without a stronghold in Canadian sports culture, and fan support started to weaken. Although the Raptors are the only Canada-based NBA team, basketball just didn't resonate with Canadians in the same way that hockey or baseball did. The Blue Jays and Maple Leafs were outperforming the Raptors. Players were leaving the team, and the Raptors brand was becoming irrelevant. In a Decima poll conducted in 2014, 30 percent of Canadians did not believe that the Raptors brand displayed *any* of the main attributes that typically lead to sports team success.

The Raptors are part of the much larger Maple Leaf Sports & Entertainment (MLSE) organization, whose franchises include the Toronto Maple Leafs of the National Hockey League (NHL), the Toronto FC of Major League Soccer (MLS), and the Toronto Raptors of the National Basketball Association (NBA). Winning championships is the highest priority in the organization, and MLSE strives to ensure that each of its teams is set up for success.

David Freeman, the former head of brand marketing for MLSE, embarked on a four-year plan to rebrand the Raptors. Nothing was sacred; this rebrand would shake up the brand strategy, brand positioning, brand image, brand logo, and brand messaging. The overarching objective was to create a brand story that all Canadians would respond to. The foundation of this rebrand was building upon Canadian pride and embracing being the "outsider" in the NBA. As the only Canadian team, fans could bond together with a strong and bold brand personality that would ultimately unite Canadian fans around the Raptors. "We The North" was the rallying cry behind this rebrand.

Rather than focusing on the 8 million people in the GTA. The Raptors wanted to speak to the 35 million people across Canada. The Raptors were Canada's basketball team. We The North resonated with Canadians. It was short, patriotic, and inclusive.

The Raptors set out to re-establish the brand, and one of the first tasks was to rework the team logo, which historically had included a dinosaur in the image. Fans did like the dinosaur, but it really had no meaning or connection to Canadians or the Canadian culture. The new logo introduced in 2015, includes a claw image on a basketball as a nod to the dinosaur, and the words "Toronto Raptors" in bold letters.

Fan engagement is a huge priority for sports franchises. Connecting with fans to grow and mobilize a fan base must span mobile, broadcast, experiential, and digital platforms. The Raptors did just that, using an integrated approach to the campaign. With an annual media budget between $1 and $2 million, the marketing team established the following promotional platforms:

**Merchandise:** The merchandise design (including hats, flags, scarves, shirts) was simple, clearly articulating the We The North mantra. We The North merchandise sales topped the $1.2 million mark in 2016, only two years post-launch, and overall Raptors merchandise sales increased by 78 percent over the same time period.

**YouTube:** The Raptors enjoyed a strong YouTube presence with teaser ads leading up to one-minute vignettes telling the story of We The North. Videos were promoted through Raptors social media, including Facebook, Instagram, and Twitter.

**Experiential activities:** Activities such as the interactive Hotline Bling box were created to get fans engaged. The Hotline Bling box, similar to the one used in Drake's video of the same name, was installed at the Air Canada Centre, allowing fans to dance and have an even better time at the game.

**TV commercials:** One-minute vignettes were aired on sports channels on a regular basis to get the new messaging out to the target audience.

**Social media:** With 1.2 million followers on Twitter, 2.2 million likes on Facebook, and 851,000 followers on Instagram, the Raptors can keep their fans involved, informed, and excited about the team. On average, interactions across social media platforms after the launch of We The North were four times greater than before the launch.

**Global brand ambassador:** Drake has taken on the role of global brand ambassador for the Raptors. He has taken the Raptors from being only a sports team into the larger entertainment realm. He is engaging to a broad audience because of his love for the sport, Toronto, and the Raptors. This partnership extends to a clothing collaboration, marketing initiatives (such as the Hotline Bling box mentioned earlier), and a role in the planning for the 2016 NBA All Star game.

The overall results of the rebranding were remarkable. Measurements of brand equity showed an increase of 8 points from April 2014 to April 2016. Since the 2012–2013 season, the Raptors have experienced a massive 72 percent growth in season-ticket sales, and a 7.5 percent growth in the percentage of tickets sold came as a result of team performance and the brand awareness gained from the rebrand.

The branding has been hijacked by others. The Montreal Canadiens adopted "Oui the North," and golfers used "Weir the North" to support Canadian Mike Weir. The meaning behind We The North resonates with Canadian sports fans. The Raptors have learned that to build a brand, you must consistently present an authentic message. We The North is not just a slogan, it is a mentality and in many ways has become a brand on its own.[1]

---

## reality CHECK ⊘

As you read Chapter 7, refer back to this vignette on the Toronto Raptors to answer the following questions:

- Describe the Toronto Raptors in terms of its core, actual, and augmented product offerings.
- Review the elements of a good brand name and discuss the strength of the Toronto Raptors and its We the North branding in the sports and entertainment industry.

# TYPES OF PRODUCTS

**LO 1** One of the key functions of marketing lies in managing and developing products and brands that meet the needs of their target markets. As discussed in Chapter 1, in marketing, a *product* is a good, a service, or an idea, consisting of a bundle of tangible and intangible attributes. Tangible attributes include physical characteristics such as colour or sweetness, and intangible attributes include those aspects of a product that can't be "touched," such as how watching a Toronto Raptors game makes you feel.

Products are available in both the online and offline environment. In the offline environment, examples of products are laundry detergents, cars, or the services provided by a hairdresser. In the online world, examples are search engines such as Google, online gaming websites, and music stores such as iTunes. It is important to realize that with the widespread use of the Internet today, most offline products develop a strong web presence. The first point of contact for consumers with a brand is often online at a company website or on its Facebook page. The Toronto Raptors have both a strong offline and a strong online presence, using pages on the official NBA website to integrate information about players and games, and to even sell merchandise.

Products are divided into three main categories: (1) non-durable goods, (2) durable goods, and (3) services. A **non-durable good** is an item that does not last and that is consumed only once, or for a limited number of times. Examples of non-durable goods are food products and fuel. A **durable good** is a product that lasts for an extended period of time and encompasses items such as appliances, automobiles, and computers. A *service* is an intangible activity, benefit, or satisfaction, such as banking, conducting an online search, using cloud-based software to create websites or blogs, visiting a doctor, taking a vacation, going to a movie, or taking a course. Canada has a strong service-based economy with services accounting for approximately 71 percent of its gross domestic product (GDP).[2]

In the service industry, it is useful to distinguish between a company's primary service and its supplementary services. An airline's primary service may be providing flights from one location to another, but it also offers supplementary services such as food and drink, magazines, airport lounges, and in-flight entertainment. Supplementary services often allow products to differentiate their offerings from the competition while also adding value to consumers. Common supplementary services for products can include product updates, free delivery, and payment terms as well as complimentary consultations, order-taking, and sales assistance.

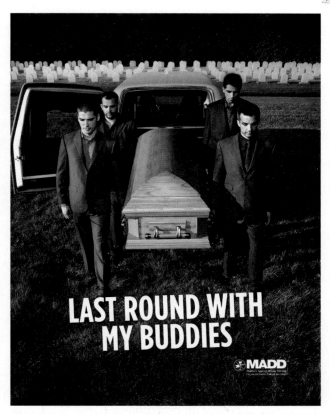

**LAST ROUND WITH MY BUDDIES**

MADD

What type of product is being marketed by MADD?

Used with permission of MADD Canada

Companies also offer free trials, online support services, complimentary webinars, and elements such as free subscriptions as added-value services to its customers. The Toronto Raptors organization offers a free newsletter and podcasts so that fans can keep up with the team.

Many products cannot be defined as "pure goods" or "pure services" but are in fact hybrids—a combination of goods and services to offer a more competitive product to consumers. Many goods are augmented with intangible services such as warranties, websites, and online support. Services also use goods to ensure a more complete offering to consumers. For example, a theatre provides an entertainment experience, but it also provides the customer with a booklet about the show; a travel agency that books travel also provides glossy catalogues of potential destinations. Importantly, the online environment is giving rise to new **virtual services** that exist only online and have no form of physical person-to-person interaction or tangible component. Travel sites, online gaming sites, and online analytics are examples of virtual services.

**non-durable good**
An item that does not last and is consumed only once, or for a limited number of times.

**durable good**
An item that lasts over an extended number of uses.

**virtual services**
Services that exist only online and have no person-to-person interaction.

**Figure 7–1**
The service continuum

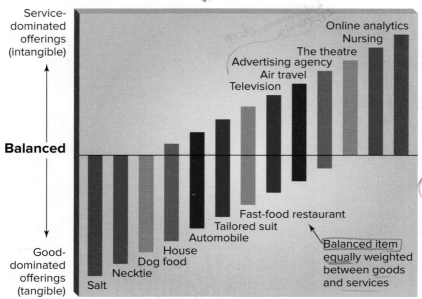

As companies look at what they bring to market, there is a range from the tangible to the intangible, or goods-dominant to service-dominant. This is defined as the **service continuum** and is demonstrated in Figure 7–1 where the services continuum for a number of products is shown. Online analytics, nursing, and going to the theatre are examples of intangible, service-dominated offerings, while salt, neckties, and dog food are goods-dominated offerings. Fast-food restaurants are in the middle of the service continuum, offering a combination of both tangible and intangible goods and services; the food is the tangible good, while the courtesy, cleanliness, speed, and convenience are the intangible services they provide.

## THE UNIQUENESS OF SERVICES

There are four unique elements to services: intangibility, inconsistency, inseparability, and inventory. These four elements are referred to as the *four Is of services.*

**Intangibility** ┃ Services are intangible; that is, for the most part, they cannot be held, touched, or seen before a purchase. In contrast, before purchasing a physical good, a consumer can touch a box of laundry detergent, kick a car tire, or sample a new beverage. Services tend to be more performance-oriented and, as experiences, cannot generally be tried before purchase. Free trials are often provided to overcome

this drawback. To help consumers assess and compare services, it is important for marketers to demonstrate the benefits of using the service. A spa may highlight a virtual tour of its facilities as well as include testimonials from customers to help the consumer evaluate the service. Online services often provide potential customers with free limited online trials or time-sensitive downloads as a means of testing out the service.

**Inconsistency** ┃ Delivering services is challenging because the quality of a service is dependent on the people who provide it, and it can therefore differ in consistency. Quality can vary with each person's capabilities, experience, motivation, and even personality. One day, the Toronto Raptors basketball team may have a great game, and then the next day, it may have a very disappointing showing. Similarly, you may have a very enjoyable stay at one location of a Hilton hotel, but then have a terrible experience at another due to the varying standards of the staff at its locations. Companies try to overcome the inconsistent delivery of services by training employees on how to deliver a consistent quality experience.

Online products are often able to overcome issues of inconsistency through standardized software, consistent website interfaces, and reliable Internet servers that limit service disruptions.

**Inseparability** ┃ A third difference between services and goods, and related to problems of consistency, is inseparability. In most cases, the consumer cannot (and does not) separate the deliverer of the service from the service itself. For example, the quality of a spa and its facilities might be excellent, but if you are not satisfied with the massage that you received or if it took too long to be registered and brought into the facility, this immediately reflects poorly on the spa.

**Inventory** ┃ In many instances, the inventory of services is more complex than that of goods due to the nature of services. Inventory problems exist because services cannot necessarily be stored and accessed when in demand. For example, in the instance of sporting events, unsold tickets cannot be stored and sold at a later date; therefore, they represent lost revenue. Online services can often be stored and accessed

**service continuum**

A range from tangible goods to intangible services.

# Infographic

**Source:** "The Good, The Bad and the Ugly: The Impact of Customer Service," Zendesk, 2013, accessed July 2016 at https://www.zendesk.com/blog/impact-of-good-customer-service-2013/. Copyright Zendesk, Inc. Used by McGraw-Hill Education under license.

at a later date, as evident with online virus scans that can be run as needed. Similarly, online movies are often configured to be conveniently viewed on-demand to suit viewers.

*Many products cannot be defined as 'pure goods' or 'pure services' but are in fact hybrids—a combination of goods and services to offer a more competitive product to consumers.*

In the service industry, issues arise due to fluctuating demand throughout the day and the difficulty in assessing the requirements needed to service customers at peak times. **Idle production capacity** is expensive and arises when a service is available when there is little demand. Idle production capacity is formally defined as a situation when the supply of a service exceeds its demand. To deal with this issue, the service industry often uses part-time employees who are paid an hourly wage and are scheduled to work shifts. This is clearly demonstrated in a grocery store setting where the number of cashiers varies depending on the time of day and day of the week. The number of cashiers at 2:30 p.m. during the week will be far fewer than the number of cashiers available at noon on a Saturday due to the number of people shopping at these times.

**idle production capacity**
When the supply of a service exceeds its demand.

### ask YOURSELF

1. *Explain the difference between non-durable goods, durable goods, and services.*

2. *What elements make services unique?*

# PRODUCT ELEMENTS

## THE TOTAL PRODUCT CONCEPT

**LO 2** Marketers view products as having three different layers: the core product layer, the actual product layer, and the augmented product layer. The more complex and expensive the product, the more intricate the layers used to differentiate the product from the competition. Figure 7–2 shows how these layers work together.

**Figure 7–2**
The total product concept applied to a bicycle

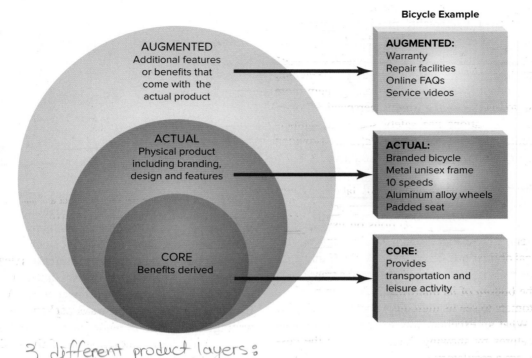

**Bicycle Example**

AUGMENTED
Additional features
or benefits that
come with the
actual product

**AUGMENTED:**
Warranty
Repair facilities
Online FAQs
Service videos

ACTUAL
Physical product
including branding,
design and features

**ACTUAL:**
Branded bicycle
Metal unisex frame
10 speeds
Aluminum alloy wheels
Padded seat

CORE
Benefits derived

**CORE:**
Provides
transportation and
leisure activity

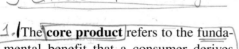

**core product**
The fundamental benefit that a consumer derives from having the product.

**actual product**
The physical good or the services that a consumer purchases.

**augmented product**
The additional features and attributes that accompany a product.

1. The **core product** refers to the fundamental benefit that a consumer derives from having the product. In the case of a bicycle, the core benefit may be the transportation it provides, or the pleasure of participating in a leisurely sport. For a service such as a massage, the core benefit may be the relaxation it provides.

2. The **actual product** is the physical good or the service that a consumer purchases when buying a product. It includes the product's branding, design, and features. With a bicycle, a consumer purchases a piece of equipment, directly associated with a brand name, design, and features. With a massage, the actual product is the massage itself and the time spent having a trained and expert massage therapist relax a client's muscles. In this instance, one may think that branding has no role to play. On the contrary, in the case of a massage, the brand becomes either the name of the massage therapist or the organization providing massage services.

3. Finally, the **augmented product** refers to the additional features and attributes that accompany a product. For a bicycle this may be a warranty, service facilities, delivery options, or videos on a website to help with small mechanical issues. Generally, augmented product layers exist for more expensive purchases such as cars, computers, or TVs, and are not part of a simple purchase such as a chocolate bar or a newspaper.

## PACKAGING AND LABELLING

Marketers need to pay close attention to a product's packaging and labelling, as well as the logos it uses to communicate its brand positioning to consumers. For many products, the packaging and labels are an integral part of the product; for other products (such as online products), there may be no packaging at all and their websites become a form of packaging, central to communicating the brand elements to consumers. Packaging can be a key source of competitive advantage since along with providing functional benefits, packaging can communicate information about the product and reinforce the brand image.

> Marketers view products as having three different layers: the core product layer, the actual product layer, and the augmented product layer.

**Function** First and foremost, packaging has functional benefits. It allows a product to be conveniently used, allows for better storage, protects a product that is fragile, improves product quality, provides a safety function, makes a product easier to use, and makes a product more efficient to transport. Take, for example, the influx of squeeze bottles for condiments such as ketchup, mayonnaise, relish, and even jams, making them more convenient to use. From a safety perspective, over-the-counter medications use safety seals and tamper-resistant containers, and best-before dates are provided for meat, dairy, and other perishable food products.

**Communication** Packaging and labelling also serve as platforms from which to communicate detailed product information, offers, directions on usage, nutritional content, and other packaging requirements needed to meet legal obligations. Take, for example, Campbell's Chunky soup. Campbell's recently adopted a transparent stripe at the bottom of its microwaveable soup bowls to allow customers to see its ingredients before purchasing the soup. What an excellent way to communicate your product features by showing them directly to the customers![3] From a regulatory standpoint, all pre-packaged food needs to include a nutritional label, defined and regulated by Health Canada. Any health claims made on a label, also need to follow guidelines set out in the *Food and Drugs Act*.[4]

**Brand Image** Packaging and labelling decisions are of paramount importance to a product's success, and

Campbell's incorporated a transparent stripe at the bottom of its packaging so that consumers can see what they are buying.

Used with permission of Campbell's Soup Company

Brand names, logos, and packaging reflect a brand's image.

Used with permission of Boxed Water Is Better LLC

marketers work hard to ensure that designs clearly reflect a product's positioning, its brand equity, and its image, which have all been nurtured over time. For example, Boxed Water is a brand of water packaged in a box. The writing on the simple white box states "Boxed Water is Better," a clear representation of the positioning of the brand versus its competition as having more pure water, more sustainable packaging, and a lower carbon footprint. In this case, the packaging is a key component of the brand itself.

Another example is the craft beer industry, where competition is increasing and the awareness of individual brands is quite low. The number of breweries in Canada has grown to over 500, driven by an influx of very small, low-volume producers. In this industry, branding plays an important role in getting customers to choose a specific brand of craft beer. Customers tend to sample a variety of craft beers, and since cans and bottles are usually sold separately, this is quite easy to do. However, this is not the only challenge, as customers generally do not remember the names of the beers. These facts are driving many craft breweries to focus on creating distinctive packaging and impactful brand names to catch people's attention and be remembered. Cameron's Brewing, located in Oakville, Ontario, made significant updates to its packaging, incorporating more colourful and modern images. There was an immediate impact on sales, with monthly sales increasing close to 300 percent after the update.[5]

Companies are constantly reviewing the competitive landscape and making adjustments to ensure that their connections with consumers remain strong. Marketers must consider the balance between making a customer connection, and other challenges including handling environmental concerns, managing health and safety issues, and monitoring packaging costs. The Marketing

# Packaging the Brand

As customers walk down the aisle in a local grocery store, they see a multitude of product options to select from. As a marketer, how do you ensure that your product is noticed? How do you ensure your product is considered for purchase? How do you ensure that customers understand enough about your product to make an informed decision?

Packaging provides the marketer with the opportunity to catch the attention of the consumer, and to convey the image and positioning of the brand. Packaging has come under the spotlight as a key component and communicator of a brand message, in addition to being a driver of brand loyalty and equity. Some interesting trends have been driving packaging innovation, including the following:

- *Personalization:* The success of Coca-Cola's "Share a Coke" campaign has put a focus on the capability of digital printing technology to more easily produce customized packaging. Coke's campaign alone is credited for increasing its sales by 2 percent in a declining market. As a follow-up, Coke launched the "One of a Kind" program, spotlighting millions of unique images on Diet Coke bottles. Canadians can find that one design that reflects who they are. Recent studies have shown that 61 percent of consumers feel more positive about a brand when its messages are personalized. In addition, 20 percent of millennials seek out personalized packaging, and this number is even higher in China. Many companies are following suit, with Oreo introducing its "Colourfilled" campaign that allows customers to design their own packaging. Bud Light and Corona have both customized their

bottles, with Bud Light focusing on NFL-themed cans and Corona highlighting boxers on its bottles.

- *Flexibility and right-sizing:* Larger family sizes, smaller trial sizes, resealable packages, pouches and bags—all are in great demand by consumers. There has been a 56 percent growth in the use of flexible packaging (such as bags, pouches, zip seals, and spouts). Soups and sauces have increasingly become available in pouches with resealable spouts. Not only does this mean that consumers can use only what they need, but the packaging is also more environmentally friendly and convenient. Simultaneously, marketers are busy trying to determine the right package size for their consumers. With snacks, health-conscious consumers would like to have smaller-pack sizes, and with family-oriented products such as cereal and milk, consumers are demanding larger-value containers.

- *Clarity:* Consumers don't want too much information on packaging, but they want important information clearly communicated so that purchasing decisions can be easily made. Product transparency is a necessity for the 58 percent of consumers who check ingredient information on labels before purchasing. Providing clear information on packaging builds trust in a brand.

- *More green:* The demand for environmentally friendly packaging has not diminished, and many consumers are quite frustrated that packaging hasn't evolved more quickly.

Mobile-connected packaging engages the consumer with the brand.

Patrick Bernard/AFP/Getty Images

Consumers want greener packaging, but are not always willing to pay more.

- *Mobile engagement:* QR codes are a thing of the past; new technology (using Bluetooth and near-field communication) can be integrated into packaging design with little infringement on branding or creative components. Consumers can locate the product in a store, and obtain ingredient information, usage instructions, allergy warnings, and a plethora of other information through company websites, apps, and even customer service lines. The near-field communication (NFC) technology is already being used by Diageo on its liquor bottles, allowing the product to communicate with the consumer via smartphone. This technology takes brand engagement to a whole new level.

Marketers must not forget that packaging is a key component of the product/brand and can play an integral role in driving not only sales but also loyalty. ●

## Questions

1. Which packaging trend do you believe will have the most lasting influence?

2. Give an example of how packaging can encourage brand loyalty.

NewsFlash box, "Packaging the Brand," describes some of the latest packaging trends that are driving product sales by listening to customer needs and wants.[6]

# PRODUCT LINES AND PRODUCT MIXES

**LO 3** Marketers often manage groups of products that are closely related under an umbrella product line and brand name. A **product line** is a group of similar products that are closely related because they satisfy a similar need and are directed at the same general target market. Examples of a product line can be seen by examining Coca-Cola's product offerings. Coca-Cola Canada offers six product lines: sparkling soft drinks, water, juices/mixers, sports drinks, energy drinks, and iced teas. Its sparkling soft drink line for example, includes Coca-Cola (and its different varieties), Sprite, Barq's, Fresca, Fanta, and Pibb.[7]

Looking to the service industry, online and offline products in this sector can also be grouped into product lines. The services offered by the Hospital for Sick Children, for example, can be grouped into three main product lines based on usage: in-patient hospital care, out-patient physician services, and medical research. Looking to the digital arena, the product lines for a digital brand such as Google can also be grouped into product lines based on usage. For example, one of Google's product lines consists of advertising services for businesses that wish to reach consumers through online ads. This product line currently includes Google Search/Display Ads, YouTube Ads, Adword Express, Shopping Ads, and App Campaigns.[8]

Most organizations offer a **product mix**, which consists of all the product lines marketed by a company.

While one can slice and analyze a company's product mix in many different ways depending on the depth of analysis required, it is often helpful to drill down into the product mix by looking at product lines and the products within each line.

A more in-depth analysis can then be conducted to pinpoint the specific products within each line, as shown in Figure 7–3. The **product mix width** refers to the number of different product lines offered by the company. For P&G the product mix width is four. The **product line length** refers to the number of product or brands in the product line. Using Figure 7–3, we can see that there are eight products listed in the beauty product line. Therefore, P&G Canada's beauty product line length is eight. The **product line depth** refers to the number of different versions of each product sold within its product lines. For example, Dawn dish detergent has approximately 18 different versions offered. Visit the Procter & Gamble website at **www.pg.ca** and examine its product mix width, product line length, and product line depth.[9]

## ask YOURSELF

1. What is included in the total product concept?
2. What benefits can be derived from a brand's packaging and labelling?

The product mix for Procter & Gamble consists of baby, feminine, and family care; beauty; fabric and home care; and health and grooming product lines.

(Always): Keith Homan/Shutterstock.com; (Bounce): Keith Homan/Shutterstock.com; (Tide): Roman Tiraspolsky/Shutterstock.com; (Head & Shoulders): Robson90/Shutterstock.com; (Old Spice): Keith Homan/Shutterstock.com

## Figure 7–3
Reviewing the Procter & Gamble Canada product mix

### PRODUCT MIX FOR PROCTER & GAMBLE

Width of Product Mix →

Product Line Length →

| Beauty | Baby, Feminine, and Family Care | Fabric and Home Care | Health and Grooming |
|---|---|---|---|
| • Aussie<br>• Head & Shoulders<br>• Herbal Essence<br>• Ivory<br>• Olay<br>• Old Spice<br>• Pantene<br>• Secret | • Always<br>• Bounty<br>• Charmin<br>• Pampers<br>• Puffs<br>• Tampax | • Bounce<br>• Cascade<br>• Cheer<br>• Dawn<br>• Downy<br>• Febreze<br>• Gain<br>• Ivory Snow<br>• Mr. Clean<br>• Swiffer<br>• Tide | • Align<br>• Braun<br>• Clearblue<br>• Crest<br>• Fixodent<br>• Gillette<br>• Metamucil<br>• Oral-B<br>• Pepto-Bismol<br>• Scope<br>• Venus<br>• Vicks |

**Source:** "All Brands," Procter & Gamble website, accessed July 2017 at http://www.pg.ca/en-CA/our-brands.

**consumer products**
Products purchased for their personal use by the ultimate consumer.

**business products**
Products that are purchased either to run a business or to be used as a component in another product or service.

**convenience products**
Items purchased frequently that are inexpensive and require minimum risk and shopping effort.

**shopping products**
Items that require comparison-shopping between different brands and an investment of shopping time.

**specialty products**
Items for special occasions that require a specific product or brand and require considerable time and effort to purchase.

# CONSUMER AND BUSINESS PRODUCTS

**LO 4** Products are classified as either consumer or business products depending on their usage. **Consumer products** are purchased by the ultimate consumer for their personal use, while **business products** (also called *industrial goods* or *organizational products*) are purchased either to run a business or to be used as a component in another product or service. In many instances, the differences are obvious: Monster Energy drinks and the Ontario Science Centre are examples of consumer products, while a cement mixing truck is primarily a business product. Some products, however, are both consumer and business products depending on their usage. A Canon printer can be classified as a consumer product when purchased as a final product for personal use, or it can be classified as a business product when purchased by an organization to help run a business. Consumer and business products consist of numerous types of products, as explained below.

## CONSUMER PRODUCTS

The consumer market consists of four different categories of products: convenience, shopping, specialty, and unsought. These items differ in terms of the amount of effort that a consumer puts into making a purchase, and how often the items are purchased.

**Convenience products** are inexpensive items that a consumer purchases frequently with minimal shopping effort. If the product does not meet expectations, there is little risk because the product is inexpensive and easy to purchase. Examples of convenience products are bread, gum, or items purchased from a vending machine. **Shopping products** are items for which the consumer comparison-shops, assessing the attributes and prices of different products and brands. These types of products require a greater investment of shopping time, are more expensive than convenience products, and require a greater assurance of purchase satisfaction. Examples are jeans, airline tickets, and electronic items such as smartphones or tablets. **Specialty products** are items that require

Rolex watches are specialty products.

**Figure 7–4**
Classification of consumer products

| | Type of Consumer Product | | | |
| --- | --- | --- | --- | --- |
| | **Convenience** | **Shopping** | **Specialty** | **Unsought** |
| **Purchase behaviour of consumers** | • Frequent purchases<br>• Little time and effort spent shopping | • Occasional purchases<br>• Needs to comparison-shop | • Infrequent purchases<br>• Needs time to search and purchase | • Very infrequent purchases<br>• Some comparison-shopping |
| **Brand loyalty of consumers** | • Aware of brand, but will accept substitutes | • Prefers specific brands, but will accept substitutes | • Very brand loyal<br>• Will not accept substitutes | • Will accept substitutes |
| **Product examples** | • Newspapers, chocolate bars, soft drinks, and bread | • Cameras, TVs, briefcases, and clothing | • Wedding dresses, luxury items such as Rolex watches | • Insurance products, such as life and disability insurance |
| **Price** | • Inexpensive | • Fairly expensive | • Usually very expensive | • Varies |
| **Place (distribution)** | • Widespread; many outlets | • Large number of outlets | • Very limited distribution | • Often limited distribution |
| **Promotion (communication)** | • Emphasis on price, availability, and awareness | • Emphasis on differentiation from competitors | • Emphasis on uniqueness of brand and status | • Emphasis on awareness |

considerable time and effort to purchase. They tend to be more expensive branded products in a category that are needed for special occasions. They include specialty brands and require high purchase satisfaction. Examples of specialty products include a Rolex watch, or taking a cruise with Norwegian Cruise Lines. **Unsought products** are items that the consumer either does not know about or is not interested in purchasing.

The manner in which a consumer product is classified depends on the individual. One person may view a camera as a shopping product and quickly visit a couple of stores before deciding on a brand to purchase. A friend, however, may view a camera as a specialty product, looking for a high-end camera for her photography hobby. This may result in extensive shopping at high-end camera shops for a specific type of camera. It is important to understand that although many products are clearly separated into one category or another, people in varying stages of life will classify products differently. Figure 7–4 generally

> *Products are classified as either consumer or business products depending on their usage.*

compares the different types of consumer products and how their marketing mixes may vary depending on the type of product.

# BUSINESS PRODUCTS

A major characteristic of business products is that their sales are often the result of **derived demand**; that is, sales of business products frequently result (or are derived) from the sale of consumer products. For example, as consumer demand for Ford cars (a consumer product) increases, Ford may increase its demand for paint-spraying equipment (a business product). Business products may be classified as production goods and services, or support goods and services.

## Production Goods and Services

Items used in the manufacturing process that become part of the final product are production goods and services. These can include raw materials, such as grain or lumber, or component parts, such as door hinges used by Ford in its car doors.

## Support Goods and Services

The second class of business products is support goods and services, which are items used to assist in

**unsought products**
Unknown items or those of no interest to the purchaser.

**derived demand**
Demand for industrial products and services driven by demand for consumer products and services.

producing other goods and services. These include the following:

- *Installations* such as buildings and fixed equipment.
- *Accessory equipment* such as tools and office equipment and is usually purchased in small-order sizes by buyers.
- *Supplies* such as stationery, paper clips, and brooms.
- *Services* are intangible activities needed to assist a business in its operations and in producing its goods and services. This category can include transportation services, maintenance and repair services, and advisory services such as tax or legal counsel. This may also include online analytics to monitor website traffic, the creation of a website to support a business, or the use of an e-mail database to send out newsletters.

## ask YOURSELF

1. What are the differences between consumer products and business products?

2. What are the four main types of consumer products?

3. What are the classifications of business products?

# BRANDING

**LO 5** A **brand** is a name, phrase, symbol, or design uniquely given by a company to identify its product(s) and to distinguish the product(s) from the competition. Brand names and logos are often created in tandem, designed to visually represent the brand to consumers and to build brand recognition. Over the long term, the support that goes into marketing a brand results in strong brand associations and a certain degree of consumer loyalty. This creates **brand equity**, which is formally described as the value of a brand that results from the favourable exposure, interactions, associations, and experiences that consumers have with a brand over time.

Developing and nurturing a brand is an important factor in the marketing of a product. This involves creating a new brand name or selecting a name that already exists in a company's arsenal. A brand also needs to be supported with marketing activity, starting with creating its logo and designing its packaging (if relevant) and

**brand**
A name, phrase, symbol, or design uniquely given by a company to a product to distinguish it from the competition.

**brand equity**
The value of a brand that results from the favourable exposure, interactions, associations, and experiences that consumers have with a brand over time.

website, as well as developing new products and promotions to engage users and bring revenues and profits into the company. Research needs to be conducted periodically to help determine trends and requirements, while metrics and analytics are needed to determine success and areas of improvement.

Ipsos Reid annually conducts its Most Influential Brands study, which looks at "key dimensions that define and determine the most influential brands in Canada," including leading edge, trustworthy, presence, corporate citizenship, and engagement.[10] Ipsos conducts its own research and, with input from advertising agencies and associations as well as consumers, determines this annual influential brand study and rankings.

Let's look at these brand elements in more detail:

- **Trustworthiness:** This is considered the most important element for a brand. It encompasses the consistently dependable image that consumers have for a brand and fosters their ongoing confidence in recommending it to others.

- **Engagement:** Brands that engage consumers encourage brand loyalty by creating interactions, so consumers can learn more about a brand and ultimately share it with others.

- **Leading edge:** Brands that stand out are often unique, innovative, and forward-thinking. Their approach tends to be edgy and somewhat different, and stands as a benchmark for other brands.

- **Corporate citizenship:** Brands that are caring have the ability to connect with consumers by instilling pride.

- **Presence:** Brands need to have a high profile with consumers and stand out from the crowd. These brands make a statement about themselves and the people that use them. Often these brands have many advocates that support them.

The top ten most influential brands in Canada in 2016 were as follows:

1. Google
2. Facebook
3. Microsoft
4. Apple
5. Amazon
6. YouTube
7. Walmart
8. Visa
9. Tim Hortons
10. CBC

> Brand equity is the result of considerable marketing investment and needs to be protected.

Eight of these brands are U.S. brands, with Google topping the list for five consecutive years. From this report, Ipsos confirmed that Google is considered an innovative brand that has transformed the way we look for information and is a leader in the exploration for innovative new technology. Google is a brand that focuses on users and their needs, which has resulted in strong scores across the influence, leading edge, and trustworthiness indices. Tim Hortons topped the list of Canadian brands in Ipsos' Most Influential Brands study at number nine.

Brands influence generations differently. Boomers take more of a traditional view of brands and like the brands that they grew up with, rating brands such as the CBC, Visa, and Canadian Tire higher. Gen X'ers gravitate toward both online and offline brands with a mix of preferences, including Apple and Microsoft as well as Walmart and President's Choice. Millennials love the technology and online environment and rank social platforms higher.[11]

Many large, well-entrenched brands are often marketed around the world and have become global brands. **Global brands** tend to enjoy strong brand equity due to their hefty marketing budgets and well-recognized trademarks. Starting in 2000, Interbrand has conducted an annual study on global brands with publicly available financial records. To be included in this brand study, a brand needs to meet certain criteria: 30 percent of its revenues need to be from outside its home country; it must be present in Asia, Europe, North America, and emerging markets; it must have publicly available financial records; it must have future profit growth expectations; and it must have a public profile and awareness levels outside its own marketplace. Interbrand's Best Global Brands 2016 identified Apple, Google, Coca-Cola, Microsoft, and Toyota as the top five global brands in the world. Its ratings look specifically at a brand's competitive strength, the role it plays in the purchase decision, and its financial performance.[12]

## BRAND STRATEGIES

Brands are classified as either individual brands or family brands, depending on whether the name has been extended to cover more than one product category. An **individual brand** is when a company uses a brand name solely for a specific product category. Two examples are the Tide brand name, used by Procter & Gamble only for laundry detergent, and Twitter, used solely for the micro-blogging social networking site.

A **family brand** is when a company uses a brand name to cover a number of different product categories. The brand name Crest, although initially used only for toothpaste, is now used by Procter & Gamble for toothpaste, dental floss, mouthwash, and teeth-whitening products. Crest extended

### global brands
Brands that are sold in a variety of international markets and that enjoy wide recognition in these markets.

### individual brand
When a company uses a brand name solely for a specific product category.

### family brand
When a company uses a brand name to cover a number of different product categories.

### Interbrand's Top 10 Global Brands

| Ranking | Brand | Brand Value ($ million) |
|---------|-------|-------------------------|
| 1 | Apple | 178,119 |
| 2 | Google | 133,252 |
| 3 | Coca-Cola | 73,102 |
| 4 | Microsoft | 72,795 |
| 5 | Toyota | 53,580 |
| 6 | IBM | 52,500 |
| 7 | Samsung | 51,808 |
| 8 | Amazon | 50,338 |
| 9 | Mercedes-Benz | 43,490 |
| 10 | GE | 43,130 |

**Source:** "Best Global Brands 2016," Interbrand website, accessed March 2017 at http://interbrand.com/best-brands/best-global-brands/2016/.

Kimberly-Clark has used a family branding approach to leverage the brand equity of Huggies with mothers across a range of baby products.

© Mike Hruby

**brand extension**
When new goods or services are introduced under an existing flagship brand name.

**sub-brand**
A brand that uses the family brand name as well as its own brand name and identity so that it can take on the strengths of the parent brand but also differentiate itself.

**patents**
Used to legally protect new technologies, unique processes, or formulations from usage by other companies.

**copyrights**
Used to legally protect original written works, sound recordings, or forms of communication from being copied by others.

**trademarks**
Used by people or organizations to protect brand images, names, slogans, and designs from usage by others.

the use of the brand name and used it to market other products; we call this a **brand extension**. Sony, Nike, and Microsoft are also examples of a family brand, where the company name is also the brand name, and all product categories launched by the company are using the corporate name. A **sub-brand** uses both the family brand name and its own brand name. This is a common strategy in the automobile industry. For example, Porsche successfully markets its higher-end Porsche Carrera and its lower-end Porsche Boxster, with both products benefiting from the quality and performance associated with the Porsche name.

The advantage of using an established family brand name for new goods or services is that brand equity is quickly transferred from the flagship brand to the new product, thus saving the company the marketing funds needed to build up this brand equity from scratch. A disadvantage of using a family branding approach is that if the new product does not live up to the image of the flagship brand, or does not share in its values, then the brand equity built up over time can be eroded for all products under this family brand name.

Scrabble protected its trademark from online knock-offs.

© The McGraw-Hill Companies, Inc./Jill Braaten, photographer

## PROTECTING BRANDS— PATENTS, TRADEMARKS, AND COPYRIGHT

Brand equity is the result of considerable marketing investment and needs to be protected. Patents, copyrights, and trademarks are used to protect products, brands, and processes from unethical infringement and illegal use. **Patents** are used to legally protect new technologies, unique processes, or specific formulations from other companies that may wish to benefit from their use. A patent is a right, granted by government, to exclude others from making, using, or selling an invention.[13] In Canada, patents currently protect owners for a period of 20 years after the patent is filed, providing that maintenance fees are paid during this time. After 20 years, this patent then becomes available to the market.

**Copyrights** are used to legally protect original written works, sound recordings, or forms of communication from being copied by others. It covers music, literature, and performances. In Canada, a copyright is protected for a lifetime plus 50 years.[14]

**Trademarks** are used by people or organizations to protect brand images, names, slogans, and designs from usage by others.[15] Trademarks are limited to a period of 15 years from the date of registration, but can be renewed by their owners to maintain their investment. A trademark legally protects a brand name and its related logo, colours, fonts, and various combinations that exist for use in a particular category and in a part of the world. If trademarks are to be used in foreign countries, the owner is wise to register an international application. Companies hold separate trademarks for each version of a brand name and its associated graphics and logo. For a brand to be trademarked, a company first conducts a trademark search to ensure that the trademark is not already owned by another company. If the trademark is available and not challenged, then the brand and its associated design and logos can be legally registered in the company name. Care must be taken to renew these trademarks as required to ensure that they do not expire. Information on trademarks in Canada can be found at the Canadian Intellectual Property Office website at **www.cipo.ic.gc.ca**. Here you can easily conduct a search of the trademark database and its registered trademarks. The Canadian Intellectual Property Office provides information on which trademarks are registered, when they were registered, and who owns the trademark.

Protecting your brand trademark has become even more important and more challenging in an increasingly online environment. Read the Focus on Ethics box, "#Protectyourbrand," for more details and examples of how companies are struggling to keep up with their brands on social media.[16]

## BRAND LOYALTY

Just how much do consumers like and insist on a particular brand? Will they choose another if their first choice is not available, or will they insist on finding their brand?

# focus on **Ethics**

## #Protectyourbrand

Reckitt Benckiser has registered a hashtag for its Mucinex brand of cough and cold products.

Mucinex and the Mr. Mucus character are trademarks of Reckitt Benckiser LLC. Used with permission.

With the rapid uptake in social media usage and the subsequent popularity of digital marketing tools, brands need to be even more vigilant about protecting their intellectual property and ultimately protecting brand equity. With over 1.65 billion monthly users of Facebook, 310 million active Twitter users, and 330 million domain names registered globally, the world of social media and the Internet can be challenging for marketers. Dell, for example, currently manages 26 pages/groups on Facebook and 34 Twitter feeds. In the past, the protection of trademarks and copyrights was fairly straightforward, but with companies supporting dozens of different social media sites, websites, and tweets throughout any given day, there are many questions to be asked:

- Does my company have rights to the social media usernames, hashtags, and domain names that are needed to promote the company's products?

- How can my company monitor social media for trademark infringement?

- Are trademark policies clearly outlined on the social media sites my company uses?

*Cybersquatting* is the registering of an Internet name with the intent of profiting on another company's name. Domain names using a trademark are protected in Canada by the Canadian Internet Registration Authority (CIRA), and complaints are resolved through the CIRA Domain Name Dispute Resolution Policy (CDRP) for .ca domain names. Using this process, Papa John's gained the rights to the domain name papajohns.ca. Someone had registered the domain name that

did not have any rights to the trademarked name, and so the rights to the domain name reverted back to the company that owned the trademark.

Companies are more frequently focusing on the value of a branded hashtag in their social media marketing campaigns. Hashtags can quickly spread globally, and since hashtags can be used by anyone, including competitors, they can create positive or negative viral discussions about a brand. Marketers are now including hashtags in their brand strategy, which begs the question: Can hashtags be protected so that marketers can manage their brand messages? Well, companies are certainly attempting to register their hashtags as close to 2,900 trademark applications for hashtags have been made globally since 2010. Coca-Cola is a leader in trademark protection, and the social media platform is no different. It has begun to trademark its hashtags, including #smilewithacoke and #cokecanpics. PepsiCo has registered #SayItWithPepsi; Reckitt Benckiser has registered #blamemucus for its Mucinex brand of cough and cold products; and Procter & Gamble has registered #LikeAGirl for its Always line of products. Only a small number of decisions on hashtag trademarks have been resolved to date.

On social media sites such as Twitter, Instagram, and Facebook, usernames are assigned on a first-come, first-served basis and cannot be reserved. Therefore, someone could take your trademark as a username, and unless they are misleading people to believe that they are affiliated with your business, nothing can be done. For example, if someone other than Coca-Cola registers cocacola as a username and then posts information about competitive

products, which is then confusing to viewers and may be harmful to the Coca-Cola brand, Coke may have the grounds to submit a trademark infringement claim.

In the case of trademark protection on social media, prevention is the best policy. It is also recommended that companies develop clear policies on how to deal with each potential source of infringement. Here are some tips to protect your brand in social media:

1. Protect company names, logos, slogans, and brand names using trademarks.

2. Consult a professional regarding the need for and use of trademarks and copyright in social media.

3. Use defensive registration by registering all trademark domain names and usernames (including common misspellings) up front.

4. Create trademark use guidelines to ensure that the company is consistent in its use of trademarks, preventing confusion.

5. Regularly conduct searches (or hire a professional watching service), not only to detect potential trademark infringement, but to monitor potential defamation and to be aware of how your brand is being perceived.

6. Claim your trademarks as usernames as soon as possible.

Marketers must include social media in their intellectual property strategy to maximize as well as protect their brand messaging and brand equity. ●

## Questions

1. It is important for companies to monitor social media for trademark infringement. Can you suggest how this could be done?

2. While companies and brands have faced issues with cybersquatting, celebrities have as well. What is the main motivator for cybersquatters?

These are brand loyalty decisions. The degree of attachment that consumers have to a particular brand tells a marketer about their brand loyalty. Brand loyalty refers to the favourable attitudes that a consumer has over time toward a brand that result in varying levels of purchase insistence and commitment to the brand. Brand loyalty varies by product and from person to person. Marketers strive to have highly committed, brand-loyal consumers as this helps insulate their brand from competitive marketing practices.

Consumers that readily switch brands depending on price generally have very little brand loyalty. Consumers with a stronger brand attachment may have some brand loyalty but may easily brand-switch if the brand is not available. A brand's most loyal consumers will insist on purchasing their brand of choice and will postpone a purchase if the brand is not available. Most people have different degrees of brand loyalty depending on the product, brand, or category. Consider the products you purchase, and determine where you have strong brand loyalty and where you have very little.

**brand personality**
A set of human characteristics associated with a brand.

> The degree of attachment that consumers have to a particular brand tells a marketer about their brand loyalty.

## BRAND PERSONALITY

Marketers recognize that brands offer more than product recognition and identification. Successful brands take on a **brand personality** of their own—a set of human characteristics associated with the brand.[17] Research shows that consumers often associate particular human personality traits with certain brands and prefer those whose personalities are most appealing. For example, Pepsi-Cola is seen as being youthful in spirit and exciting, while Dr Pepper is viewed as being unique and non-conformist. The traits often linked to Harley-Davidson are masculinity, defiance, and rugged individualism. Millward-Brown conducted a study of 500,000 people globally to determine how brands were aligned with personality traits. There were some cultural and regional differences that were noted. The most successful brands in Canada were seen described as "creative" and "in control." Brand personalities described as "different" were not as successful in Canada.[18] Through marketing and promotion, marketers work to associate brands with specific personality traits and to help consumers make emotional connections with their brands.

## 50%
One-half of Canadians anticipate buying the same brand of vehicle the next time they are in the market.

## 50%
One-half plan to abandon their current automotive brand for a new one when they buy next.

**Automobile manufacturers need to work hard to create brand loyalty. Only 50 percent of Canadians plan to purchase the same brand of automobile.**

**Source:** "The Canadian Automotive Brand Telemetry Report," Bond Brand Loyalty, 2016, accessed July 2017 at http://info.bondbrandloyalty.com/automotive-brand-telemetry-report.

## BRAND NAMES

When we say Xbox, iPad, Duracell, Porsche, Coke, or Nike, we typically do not think about how companies determined these brand names. Selecting a successful brand name can be a long and sometimes expensive process. Companies can spend thousands of dollars developing and testing a new brand name. Companies can spend between $25,000 and $100,000 to identify and test a new brand name. Here are some key points to consider when determining a good brand name:

- *The name should suggest the product benefits.* This is demonstrated by brand names such as Easy-Off (oven cleaner) and Chevrolet Spark (electric car), both of which clearly describe the product's benefits. Care should be taken to review how the brand name translates into other languages to avoid future pitfalls.

- *The name should be memorable, distinctive, and positive.* A number of new brands have been introduced over the last few years with distinctive brand names such as iPad, Xbox, Twitter, and Google. All these names are very distinctive and were entirely unique and unknown when first introduced. Today, these brand names have high awareness in Canada and enjoy very strong brand recognition.

- *The name should fit the company or product image.* Brand names such as Duracell or Eveready clearly suggest that these products provide reliable and long battery life. Twitter expresses the short conversations (tweeting) that can occur on this platform of 140 characters.

- *The name should have the ability to be legally protected.* A brand name must be "trademarkable" to protect a company's investment. If the brand name is too generic, or the trademark is owned by another company, the proposed brand name cannot be trademarked. Increasingly, brand names also need a corresponding website address, which can complicate name selection, as there are close to 330 million domain names registered globally.[19] An example that made international headlines was that of MikeRoweSoft.com. A 17-year-old teenager in Victoria, British Columbia, named Mike Rowe, set up this website for his graphic design business. He thought that since his name was Mike Rowe, it would be humorous to add Soft to the end and have an interesting play on words. Once Microsoft became aware of the site, it quickly sent a letter to Mike Rowe demanding that the website be shut down immediately due to trademark infringement. In what has now become a page in Internet history, Mike Rowe eventually settled the lawsuit for an Xbox and a few games.[20] This case was a pioneer in the cybersquatting (registering an Internet name with the intent of profiting on another company's name) world, and on average, 3,400 cybersquatting cases are filed annually, although this number has been declining in the last few years.[21]

- *The name should be simple.* The brand names iPad, Xbox, Twitter, and Google are all simple names to spell and remember. This makes them more memorable and helps build brand equity.

## TYPES OF BRANDS

**LO 6** There are three types of brands: (1) manufacturer's brands, (2) private-label brands, and (3) generic brands.

A **manufacturer's brand** is one that is owned and produced by the manufacturer. Gravol (dimenhydrinate is the name of the drug) is the manufacturer's brand created by Church & Dwight and sold to drugstores throughout Canada. Church & Dwight invested considerable resources, time, and money into the development and marketing of the brand. When Gravol was launched in Canada, it was protected by a patent, but as mentioned earlier, a patent is restricted to a limited number of years, currently 20 years in Canada. Once a patent expires, other manufacturers can produce a similar product. Church & Dwight has subsequently launched brand extensions with naturally sourced ingredients, as well as additional formats to extend the life of Gravol as a manufacturer's brand.

A **private-label brand**, otherwise known as a store brand, is owned by a retailer that contracts its manufacturing out to major suppliers and then sells the product at its own retail stores, under its own store-brand name. Often these products are manufactured in the same factories as the manufacturer's brand. Private-label products are very popular in Canada, with 18 percent of shopping dollars spent on private-label products. This is higher than the global average. Canadian customers believe that private-label products are good alternatives to manufacturer's brands, offering good quality and good value.[22] A private-label brand provides a retailer with the opportunity to offer its customers a less expensive alternative to a manufacturer's brand. Private-label products are generally sold at prices

**manufacturer's brand**
A brand owned and produced by the manufacturer.

**private-label brand**
Otherwise known as a store brand, a brand owned by a retailer that contracts its manufacturing to major suppliers, and then sells the product at its own retail stores, under its own store-brand name.

**What type of brand is Mastercraft?**

Used with permission of Canadian Tire Corporation

*A private-label brand provides a retailer with the opportunity to offer its customers a less expensive alternative to a manufacturer's brand.*

25 to 30 percent lower than manufacturer's brands. Because these store brands do not have to pay high listing fees and they have lower marketing costs, retailers often make more profit on private-label brands. This is an incentive to invest in the development of more private-label products.[23]

Examples of private-label products are Life brand, available at Shoppers Drug Mart; Selections and Irresistibles brands at Metro; and Mastercraft at Canadian Tire.

A **generic brand** has no branding at all and is sometimes produced as a cheap alternative to a manufacturer's brand and to a private-label branded product. A generic brand is typically named using the main product ingredient, with its main point of difference being price. Generic products most commonly found in the pharmaceutical industry. Once the patent has expired for a prescription medication, many generic versions are created and sold to pharmacies by generic drug manufacturers such as Apotex Inc. or Novopharm. Once a generic is available,

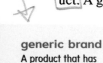

**generic brand**
A product that has no branding and is produced as a cheap alternative to a manufacturer's brand and to branded private-label products.

these cheaper versions are often substituted by pharmacists for the branded medicines when a prescription is filled. This can save governments, insurance companies, and consumers substantial sums of money. Although a less expensive alternative to other branded products, a generic product lacks the brand equity and product recognition that is enjoyed by both a manufacturer's brand and branded private-label products.

Outside of the pharmaceutical industry, generic products can often be found at various retail outlets such as dollar stores where select products with no associated brand names are sold. Dollarama stores, for instance, sell plastic clogs for $2 per pair that are direct knock-offs of Crocs but have absolutely no branding at all.

## ask YOURSELF

1. *What are the advantages and disadvantages of using a family brand rather than an individual brand to launch a new product?*

2. *Explain the difference between a private-label brand and a generic brand.*

3. *What type of price differences would you expect to see for a manufacturer's brand, a private-label brand, and a generic brand for products within the same category?*

**LO 1**
- A product is a term used in marketing to designate non-durable goods, durable goods, and services that are marketed. Some products are a combination of both goods and services.
- There are four unique elements to services: intangibility, inconsistency, inseparability, and inventory. These four elements are referred to as the four Is of services.

**LO 2**
- The total product concept includes the core product, the actual product, and the augmented product.

**LO 3**
- Product mix is the combination of product lines managed by a company. The product mix width refers to the number of different product lines offered by the company. The product line length refers to the number of product or brands in the product line. The product line depth refers to the number of different versions of each product sold within its product lines.

**LO 4**
- Consumer products are classified into convenience products, shopping products, specialty products, and unsought products.

- Business products are classified into production or support goods. Production goods include raw materials and components parts, while support goods include installations, accessory equipment, supplies, and services.

**LO 5**
- A brand is a name or phrase used to identify a product and to distinguish it from the competition. Brand equity is the result of the positive experiences consumers have with the brand over time and results in brand loyalty.
- Trademarks are used to legally protect brands, patents are used to protect unique processes, and copyrights are used to protect the written or spoken word.

**LO 6**
- Companies may restrict a brand name for use with a single product line, thus using an individual brand, or may extend a brand name to encompass a number of different product categories, resulting in the creation of a family brand and, in some instances, sub-brands.
- Brands are categorized as manufacturer's brands, private-label brands, and generic brands.

---

actual product
augmented product
brand
brand equity
brand extension
brand personality
business products
consumer products
convenience products
copyrights
core product
derived demand

durable good
family brand
generic brand
global brands
idle production capacity
individual brand
manufacturer's brand
non-durable good
patents
private-label brand
product line
product line depth

product line length
product mix
product mix width
service continuum
shopping products
specialty products
sub-brand
trademarks
unsought products
virtual services

---

**Branding Assignment** In groups, pick a favourite company. Gather information on that company and its brands from the Internet, including the company's website and social media. Describe the product mix width as well as the product line length and depth. Choose one of the company's brands. Brainstorm with your group ways in which the company could improve brand equity and increase brand loyalty.

The Toronto Raptors adapted its brand to appeal to a larger audience using the "We The North" branding. Carefully review the opening vignette and conduct your own research. Outline the strengths and weaknesses of the Toronto Raptors brand.

List the external factors that are currently impacting the Raptors. What external opportunities and threats should the Raptors be most concerned about in the future?

Review the Infographic, "The Good, the Bad, & the Ugly: The Impact of Customer Service," that details the customer service report from Zendesk and Dimensional Research. Write a short analysis of your findings.

# New Product Development

This chapter looks at new products and how they are developed, launched, and managed over time. Sameera Banduk, marketing director at Thalmic Labs, an innovative Canadian technology company, describes the development of the Myo armband, a significant step forward in wearable technology.

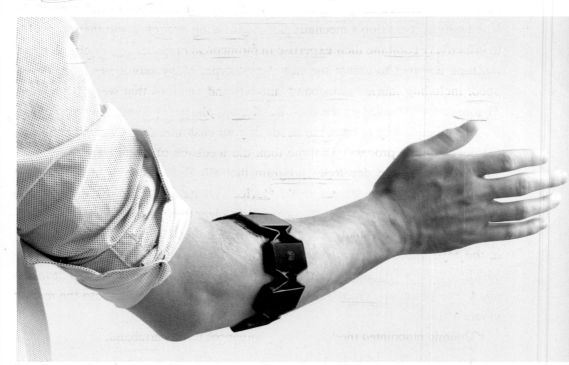

Used with permission of Thalmic Labs

Blurring the lines between the real and the digital worlds, Thalmic Labs is the mastermind behind the innovative Myo armband technology. Through the creative brainstorming of co-founders Stephen Lake, Matthew Bailey, and Aaron Grant, a device was created that can interpret the electrical activity in muscle movements and allow the user to wirelessly control devices.

With products such as Google Glass being introduced and the pervasiveness of wearable technology, the founders wondered if they could take an active role in driving the way in which people interact with technology of the future. Their fundamental question was, "How do we connect the real and the digital worlds as we move towards wearable and ubiquitous computing?"

Imagine watching your favourite episode of *Suits* on Netflix and, by spreading your fingers, the show starts to play. Do you want to fast forward? Simply wave your hand. Do you want to turn up the volume? Make a fist. All thanks to the Myo armband.

The Myo armband works in two ways. First, it uses patented electromyography sensors to detect the electrical activity taking place in your muscles when you make a gesture or a movement with your hand. Second, it has a highly sensitive motion sensor that measures all the motions and rotations of your hand and forearm. It communicates this information over a Bluetooth connection to whatever device you are using. With over 100 applications (spanning gaming, device control, presentation management, digital tools, and multimedia players) available at the Myo Market app store (https://market.myo.com/), potential uses appear endless.

It took quite a bit of work to come up with the final product. The initial concept was developed in spring 2012. The three co-founders are graduates of the University of Waterloo's mechatronics engineering program, and they were able to effectively combine their expertise in biomedical engineering, electronics, and machine learning to create the initial prototype. Many prototypes were developed, including fabric "sweatband" models and versions that were 3D-printed. Thalmic finally landed on the one-size-fits-all, plastic-moulded, flexible device.

What better way to meet the needs of your customer than to involve them in the development process? Thalmic took the feedback of its audience very seriously and created a developer program that allowed accepted developers and partners to have early access to the device and its software. With over 1,000 partners and developers using the device, it is clear that the final design was well-informed by this test-audience feedback. Based on the rapid uptake in interest in the Myo armband from tech experts worldwide, Thalmic was able to secure $14.5 million in financing in 2013 to help fuel continued innovation and development. The consumer version of the Myo armband was launched into the market in late 2014.

Thalmic pinpointed three key target audiences for the armband:

**Presenters:** Myo reads the muscle activity of the presenter so that presentations can be controlled with gestures and motion.

**Cable cutters:** Myo lets you browse the web from a distance "with the flick of a wrist."

**Remote/radio-control (RC) hobbyists:** RC toys (like drones) can be controlled "like you have superpowers."

How did Thalmic get the word out to its target audiences? A combination of comprehensive social media promotion, online advertising, PR, and partnership marketing did the trick. A viral YouTube video was the game-changer in launching the Myo armband to the world. Myo caught the eye of many techies, and so the PR generated by the device was significant, crossing boundaries from the traditional press (*New York Times*, *Time* magazine, *Business Insider*) to technical journals (*TechCrunch*, *Wareable*) to blogs.

Aware that its target audiences were extremely active on social media sites, Thalmic ensured that its visibility was high on Facebook, Twitter, Google Plus, YouTube, and Instagram. For additional impressions, Thalmic purchased online ad space and paid social media opportunities, while actively optimizing for organic search.

Prior to launch, Myo was pre-ordered by consumers. Although they did not actually have to put money down until their order was ready to ship, at a price of US$149, 10,000 pre-orders were placed within 48 hours of the release of a product video. Orders were received from nearly 150 countries. What a great way to validate the interest in the product and validate the sales potential!

Currently, Myo can be purchased at a variety of retail outlets including Best Buy Canada and Amazon.com, as well as directly from Myo.com. The device is available for US$199 or CDN$249. Thalmic Labs also has distribution of the Myo armband in Europe and Asia.

With its extensive pre-orders, Myo quickly moved through its introductory stage and sales began to grow. Although Microsoft Kinect and Leap Motion existed prior to the Myo armband, both used camera-based technology and limited the user to a specific physical space. The Myo armband was the first gesture-control technology that would actually move with the user. More recently, other input devices have hit the market, including smart rings.

It is of utmost importance for Thalmic to continue research and development activities for the device to extend its life cycle. Priority areas of focus are prosthetics and the use of Myo for education—to help students learn how to code. In fact, Thalmic launched a program called "Myo for Education," which provides educators with all the tools they need (including lesson plans) to utilize the Myo in the classroom to teach programming concepts.

Innovation is at the heart of the corporate culture at Thalmic. They are obsessed with being leaders in the future of consumer electronics and wearables. Employees are encouraged to interact and brainstorm in an open-concept office environment. In the longer term, Thalmic Labs is focused on continuing to invent technology that will take the human experience to a whole level by further blurring the lines between the real and digital worlds. The Myo armband is a just the beginning![1]

---

### reality CHECK ⊘

As you read Chapter 8, refer back to the Myo armband opening vignette to answer the following questions:

- What type of innovation is the Myo armband: a minor innovation, a continuous innovation, or a radical innovation?
- What stage in the product life cycle is the Myo armband: introductory, growth, maturity, or decline?
- Considering the adoption curve (Figure 8-6), which group of consumers is Thalmic targeting with its Myo armband: innovators, early adopters, or the early majority?

# THE PRODUCT LIFE CYCLE

**LO 1** The concept of the **product life cycle** describes the stages that a new product goes through, starting with its initial introduction into the marketplace and moving through to the stages of growth, maturity, and decline. The concept of the product life cycle is used by many marketers to help manage a product from its initial launch through to its eventual decline. Marketers try to manage products so that they extend the time until the decline stage or, perhaps, so they don't reach the decline stage at all. This is done by changing, updating, and repositioning products to meet evolving consumer needs and competitive challenges.

While all products follow this same product life cycle, products in the online and technology areas often experience shorter cycles that require frequent product updates to stay competitive. We see this frequently with social media sites such as Facebook, Pinterest, and Twitter, which frequently add new features for its users, as well as new tools for marketers.

Figure 8–1 traces the curve of a product life cycle by plotting a product's sales and profits over time. The curves change in response to the competitive environment and to consumers' demand for the innovation.

Initially, during the introduction stage, a product experiences minimal sales that are growing slowly, minimal or nonexistent profits, and very few competitors. Over time, propelled by marketing programs and product demand, a product moves into a period of rapid growth, and profit increases. As the competition becomes more severe, consumers are presented with competitive products, which cause a product's sales and profits to flatten out and eventually, if not addressed by a marketer, decline. The length of each stage in the product life cycle depends on the product, the category, and how it is being marketed.

A more detailed example of how products are marketed through their life cycles can be seen in the smartphone category. Apple launched the original iPhone in 2007, and it has changed the product's features, services, pricing, and marketing over time to stay relevant and competitive against Samsung and the variety of other smartphone manufacturers that have entered the market (see Figure 8–2). In 2007, the original iPhone was revolutionary. At that time, the smartphone market was focused mainly on the corporate market, and features focused on e-mail and work-related functions. The iPhone changed all that. While the typical smartphone functions were still available, the iPhone had a large colourful screen and touch features that eliminated the external keyboard. Apple targeted the consumer market rather than only the corporate segment. Initially, the Apple operating system was fairly basic and features were limited. Over time, the market became more competitive, with companies like Samsung introducing new models and features at a rapid pace. Throughout its

> **product life cycle**
> The stages that a new product goes through, starting with introduction and evolving into growth, maturity, and decline.

Apple's iPhone continuously introduces new features and models to keep it relevant and competitive.

© Apple

**Figure 8–1**
Product life cycle

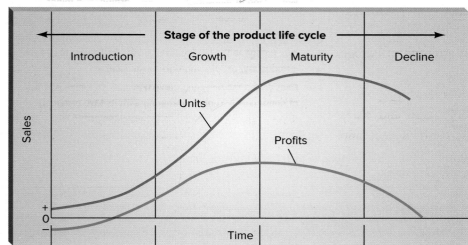

## Figure 8–2
Apple iPhone product life cycle

| Apple's iPhone—Managing the Product Life Cycle (PLC) | | | |
|---|---|---|---|
| **Product** | **Product Description** | **Stage in PLC** | **Price (US$)** |
| **2007: Original iPhone** | • One model<br>• 4, 8, 16 GB<br>• 3.5" multi-touch screen<br>• 2 megapixel camera<br>• iOS 3<br>• No apps | Introduction | $499–$599 |
| **2008/2009: iPhone 3**<br>• iPhone 3G<br>• iPhone 3GS | • Two models<br>• 8, 16, 32 GB<br>• 3.5" multi-touch screen<br>• 2–3 megapixel camera<br>• iOS 3<br>• Grew from 500 to 50,000 apps<br>• NEW: App Store; faster; less battery usage, ability to cut, copy, and paste text; visual voicemail; parental controls; photo geo-tagging; voice dialing; landscape keyboard | Introduction, entering growth | $199–$299 |
| **2010/2011: iPhone 4**<br>• iPhone 4<br>• iPhone 4S | • Two models<br>• 8, 16, 32, 64 GB<br>• 3.5" multi-touch screen<br>• 5–8 megapixel camera<br>• iOS 4/5<br>• Grew from 225,000 to 360,000 apps<br>• NEW: Stainless steel design, dual-core processor, location-based systems, iCloud, Facetime, iBooks, HD video, and iMessage | Growth, approaching maturity | $199–$399 |
| **2012/2013: iPhone 5**<br>• iPhone 5<br>• iPhone 5S<br>• iPhone 5C | • Three models<br>• 8, 16, 32, 64 GB<br>• 8 megapixel camera<br>• 4" multi-touch screen<br>• iOS 6/7<br>• Grew from 700,000 to 900,000 apps<br>• NEW: Passbook, improved Maps app, A7 chip provides two-times faster performance, fingerprint sensor, larger screen | Growth/early maturity | $199–$399 |
| **2014/2015: iPhone 6**<br>• iPhone 6<br>• iPhone 6 Plus<br>• iPhone 6S<br>• iPhone 6S Plus | • Four models<br>• 32, 64, 128 GB<br>• 8–12 megapixel camera<br>• 4.7"–5.5" multi-touch screen<br>• 1.3 million apps<br>• NEW: Faster A8/9 processing chips, HD 4K video (6S), 3D touch (6S), improved iSight camera, Apple Pay, near-field communication | Maturity | $199–$499 |
| **2016:**<br>• iPhone 7<br>• iPhone 7 Plus | • Two models<br>• 32, 128, 256 GB<br>• 12 megapixel camera<br>• 4.7" screen<br>• iOS 10<br>• NEW: Water resistant, no headphone jack (new EarPods headphones), stereo speakers | Maturity | $649 |

**Source:** "How Apple's iPhone has evolved since launch," *USA Today*, March 21, 2016, http://www.usatoday.com/story/tech/news/2016/03/21/how-apples-iphone-has-evolved-since-launch/82071340/; "Compare iPhone models," Apple website, accessed July 2016 at http://www.apple.com/ca/iphone/compare/; "Compare [Apple iPhones], GSM Arena website, accessed July 2016 at http://www.gsmarena.com/compare.php3?idPhone1=4910&sSearch2=iphone+5s&idPhone2=5685&idPhone3=5690; Matt Rosoff, "The end of iPhone's amazing eight-year run," *Business Insider*, April 25, 2016, http://www.businessinsider.com/apple-iphone-sales-by-year-2016-4; Scott Stein, "Jet-black Apple iPhone 7 is here," *CNET*, September 7, 2016, http://www.cnet.com/products/apple-iphone-7/preview/.

**Figure 8–3**
Managing the stages of the product life cycle

| Stage in Product Life Cycle | Introduction | Growth | Maturity | Decline |
|---|---|---|---|---|
| Competition | Few competitors exist | More competitors enter the market | Many competitors in the market | Reduced competition, with some competitors leaving the market |
| General marketing objective | Awareness | Product differentiation | Brand loyalty | Product rationalization |
| Product | Focus on a new product or brand | Introduce more features | Ensure full product line is available and innovative with new ideas | Retain only best sellers or discontinue |
| Price | Use a skimming or penetration strategy | Prices are slowly reduced | Price discounts are used frequently | Very low prices |
| Place (distribution) | Limited distribution | Distribution is increased | Full distribution is achieved | Distribution is reduced |
| Promotion (communication) | Focus on building awareness with advertising | Emphasize points of difference versus the competition | Focus on pricing and sales promotion | Only minimal promotion, if any |
| Profit | Minimal profits, if any | Increased profits that reach their maximum | Maximized profits that level off | Decreasing and minimal profits |

growth phase. Apple continued to improve its features, such as camera quality, memory, screen size, faster performance, and touch sensors. In addition, Apple placed a significant focus on the development of exclusive apps and services to increase the functionality of its devices. The number of apps available for the iPhone has exceeded 2 million, and Apple has provided services such as iCloud, iBooks, Apple Pay, iMessages, and location-based services.

At launch, Apple focused on generating awareness and demand for the iPhone. Advertising showcased the elegance of the iPhone, which was so different from the existing genre of smartphones. As the functionality of the iPhone improved during the growth phase, Apple used advertising to highlight its unique features and the evolution of the Apple App Store. Up to this point, Apple wanted to convince customers that they needed an iPhone. As the iPhone settles in to the maturity phase, ads now focus on confirming that the iPhone is an integral part of life, reinforcing to consumers that they have made the right decision by selecting the iPhone. This message is validated by the continuing evolution of differentiating features such as the touch ID and the excellent 4K video quality.[2]

In the following sections, we look at each stage of the product life cycle in more detail to appreciate how marketers use this concept to manage their products profitably (see Figure 8–3). The product life cycle concept is used by marketers in many different ways. It is most often used to help manage products or brands and in some instances, to analyze an industry in general.

# INTRODUCTION STAGE

The introduction stage of the product life cycle occurs when a product is first introduced to its intended target market. During this period, profits are minimal typically due to three things: (1) slow sales growth, (2) high product development costs, and (3) high levels of marketing spending needed to launch the new product. The key marketing objective during this stage is to create consumer awareness and to stimulate trial (or the first purchase) of the new product.

This stage is characterized by little competition and a lack of consumer awareness about the product. Radical new categories or technological innovations also come with the added challenge of having to educate consumers on the existence and relevancy of the category itself. In many cases, the money spent on advertising and promotion, is focused on developing demand for the product class rather than just the brand, since there are few competitors established in the market. The other elements of the marketing mix are also carefully crafted to ensure that they are in step with the product launch and its consumers.

During the introduction stage, pricing can be high or low. A high initial price is called a price skimming strategy and is used by companies to help recover research and development costs. This approach takes advantage of the price insensitivity of innovators and early adopters. The price skimming strategy is very common in the electronics market, with products such as 4K TVs and smartphones being launched at high prices to recover costs and then lowering their price to attract a larger more

*Distribution can often be a challenge during the introduction stage of the product life cycle because channel members may be hesitant to carry a new product that is unproven.*

price-sensitive market. If a company uses a low price to enter the market, this is referred to as a penetration pricing strategy and is used to encourage rapid acceptance of an innovation or to combat a competitive threat. Pricing strategies are discussed in greater detail in Chapter 9.

Distribution can often be a challenge during the introduction stage of the product life cycle because channel members may be hesitant to carry a new product that is unproven. Listing fees may also present themselves as an expensive proposition for marketers, who often experience retailers charging to recover the costs and risks of listing, shelving, and merchandising a new product in stores.

Looking at the iPhone during its introductory stage, it was launched at a high price, and Apple has focused on continuous innovation to protect its brand value and pricing.[3]

## GROWTH STAGE

The growth stage of the product life cycle sees an increase in competition and a rapid rise in sales and profits. The market is flooded with competing brands that thrust a category and its products into the forefront. This results in new consumers being enticed into the category and a resultant increase in sales.

In this competitive arena, marketers focus their programs on differentiating products from competitive offerings. New features are added to original designs, and product proliferation often occurs. Pricing levels are generally lowered to become more competitive and distribution increases. Promotion at this stage becomes more product-specific, with advertising playing a key role in focusing consumers toward particular brands. Profits often reach their peak at this stage due to more focused promotion and a decline in development and production costs. Marketing objectives focus on product differentiation.

Let's look at the Apple Watch as an example of a product that moved through the introductory stage and then struggled with the growth stage of the life cycle. The Apple Watch was launched in April 2015 with 1 million pre-orders in place. People pre-ordered an average of 1.3 watches

each, with average order sales value of $503.83 U.S. per watch. Apple was able to take over market leadership of the smartwatch market in its first year, albeit a very small market. Many of the pre-orders were placed by early adopters and true Apple fans. At launch, demand far exceeded supply.[4] One year later, the broader market for smartwatches appears to be waiting for the next generation of technology to appear and for a lower price point to be offered to consumers. With an increasing number of competitors on the market, Apple is struggling with the next innovation for the Apple Watch. It is expected that with an increase in available applications, updates to their functionality, improvements in their look, and connectivity improvements, the smartwatch market will recover and experience significant growth.[5]

## MATURITY STAGE

The maturity stage of the product life cycle is characterized by a slowdown of sales growth and profit. Competitors are well-established and fewer new consumers enter the market. Marketing focuses on holding or gaining market share by continuing to differentiate the product and building on existing customer loyalty. Profits level off at this stage, often due to price competition. A major consideration in a company's strategy in this stage is to control overall marketing costs by improving promotional and distribution efficiency.

The maturity stage is generally the longest stage in the product life cycle, with marketers focusing efforts to ensure that the product does not go into decline. Marketers use short-term promotional tactics such as consumer promotions to encourage consumers to purchase the product. Product innovation can also become a priority as marketers try to reposition products in the market and revamp product lines to be more competitive and relevant to consumers' needs. The purpose of this renewed focus on innovation is to try to take the product back into the growth or early maturity stages of the product life cycle, as we have seen with products such as the iPhone.

Numerous well-established products are in the maturity stage of their product life cycles; examples include Heinz Ketchup, Hellmann's Mayonnaise, and Kraft Dinner (KD). What do marketers of these products do to maintain product relevancy in these categories and to stop them from going into decline? Packaging

*The maturity stage of the product life cycle is characterized by a slowdown of sales growth and profit.*

Kraft has changed the name of Kraft Dinner to KD and launched several additional varieties and formats.

Used with permission of Kraft Heinz Foods Company

changes, product modifications, and extended-usage approaches are often used to keep them relevant.

## DECLINE STAGE

The decline stage of the product life cycle occurs when sales and profits steadily decline over time. Frequently, a product enters this stage when products become obsolete due to technological innovation or changes in consumer needs. Downloadable music files are replacing CDs, video streaming is replacing DVDs, and laptops/tablets have replaced desktop computers.

Products in the decline stage tend to take a disproportionate share of management and financial resources relative to their future value. As a result, a company follows one of two strategies to deal with a declining product. It will either **delete** the product, or **harvest** the product. Deletion is when a product is discontinued. Normally, decisions to discontinue a product are not taken lightly as there can be residual customers who still use this product. Harvesting is when a company keeps the product but reduces marketing support in an attempt to reap some minor profits at this stage in the life cycle.

## LENGTH OF THE PRODUCT LIFE CYCLE

The length of a product life cycle varies according to the industry, the competition, technological innovation, and approaches to marketing the product. There is no set timeframe for a product to move through its life cycle. Generally, consumer products have shorter life cycles than business products. For example, some new consumer food products such as FritoLay's Baked Lay's potato chips move from the introduction stage to maturity quickly. The availability of mass communication

vehicles informs consumers quickly and shortens life cycles. Technological change shortens product life cycles as product innovation replaces existing products. For example, smartphones have largely replaced digital cameras in the amateur photography market. Other products, such as Heinz ketchup, have extended product life cycles that have continued for years, driven by marketing approaches that keep the product relevant.

## SHAPE OF THE PRODUCT LIFE CYCLE

The generalized life cycle shown in Figure 8–1, does not always apply to all products. Figure 8–4 shows four product life cycle curves that apply to different types of products. These products and their life cycles can be categorized into four main areas: high-learning products, low-learning products, fashion products, and fad products.

A **high-learning product** is one where there is an extended introductory period due to the significant efforts required to educate customers on the usage and benefits of the product. Movie-streaming services are an example of such a product. A switch to online movie streaming from DVD or blu-ray was a real shift in thinking for many consumers who were a bit slow to understand the advantages of the new technology, how to use it, and what to do with their old DVDs and video rental memberships. It also required consumers to overcome issues of insufficient bandwidth, the necessity to use a computer or other device (prior to the introduction of SMART TVs), and the fact that few movie titles were initially offered for streaming. It

**delete**
When a company discontinues a product.

**harvest**
When a company keeps a product but reduces marketing support in an attempt to reap some minor profits.

**high-learning product**
Significant consumer education is required for these products, which have an extended introductory period.

**low-learning product**

Little consumer education is required, resulting in a short introductory stage for the product.

**fashion product**

The life cycle for fashion is relatively short and cyclical, going from introduction to decline within two to three years, only to resurface again a few years later.

**fad**

Novelty products with very short product life cycles that experience immediate rapid growth, followed by an equally rapid decline.

took considerable time for consumers and the industry to fully adopt this technology, resulting in an extended introductory period for movie streaming services.

② In contrast, a **low-learning product** has a short introductory stage in the product life cycle. In these instances, the benefits of purchasing these products are self-evident and very little learning is required. An example of a successful low-learning product is the Apple Watch, which required little education on behalf of consumers. Consumers trusted the Apple brand, and were familiar with its touch technology from use of the Apple iPhone.

③ The product life cycle for a **fashion product** is cyclical. The length of the cycle will vary, but it is relatively short, going from introduction to decline, generally within a two- to three-year period, only to resurface again a few years later. Life cycles for fashion products most often appear in men's and women's footwear and apparel. Whether we like it or not, fashion trends such as bell bottom pants, crop tops, and parachute pants have gone away only to come back again years later.

④ A **fad** refers to a product with a very short product life cycle. It typically experiences immediate rapid

**Figure 8–4**
Alternate product life cycles

**A. High-learning products**

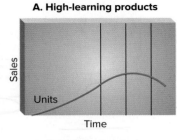

**B. Low-learning products**

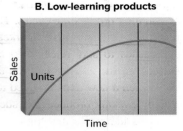

**C. Fashion products**

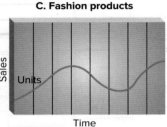

**D. Fad products**

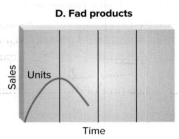

growth, followed by an equally rapid decline, with no real maturity stage at all. These products tend to be novelties, such as the Pet Rock craze and Pokémon Go. Children's toys often fall into this category.

# PRODUCT LIFE CYCLE STRATEGIES

**LO 2** It is important for a firm to manage its products through their life cycles, profitably extending and prolonging their relevance in the market. Product life cycles can be extended in a number of ways, namely by (1) modifying the product, (2) modifying the market, (3) repositioning a product, and (4) introducing a new product. It is important to realize that a combination of these approaches is most often used to keep products fresh and relevant.

## MODIFYING THE PRODUCT

Product improvements and line extensions are often used by marketers to ensure that products remain competitive and address new trends in the market.

**Product Improvements** Examples can be seen in the food industry, where marketers are addressing consumers' demand healthier foods. For example, Kraft eliminated the yellow colouring from its line of Kraft Dinner products, and General Mills is using non-GMO corn in its original Cheerios cereal.[6]

## ask YOURSELF

1. What are the four stages in the product life cycle? How do they differ in terms of sales and profits?

2. How do high-learning and low-learning products differ?

3. What is the shape of the product life cycle for a smartphone in today's marketplace?

**Line Extensions** Some of the most successful and long-lasting brands use line extensions to extend their product life cycles. They also include innovative marketing approaches to stay relevant to consumers. A **line extension** is the term used when a new item is added to an already existing product line, such as Cheerios adding Banana Nut Cheerios and Chocolate Cheerios to its already well-established Cheerios product line. To capitalize on the green trend, Procter & Gamble introduced Tide Coldwater (for cold-water washing) and Tide Free & Gentle (free of dyes and perfumes).[7]

## MODIFYING THE MARKET

There are three key market modification strategies. Companies may decide that their current product is under-represented with certain consumer groups and may see an opportunity to target these consumers. In addition, marketers may try to increase a product's use within its existing customer group, which is an especially useful strategy where there is strong brand loyalty. Lastly, a company may develop new uses for a product, extending its utility to the customer.

**Finding New Customers** Marketers are often cautious and somewhat reluctant to follow this approach as it can be an expensive proposition that yields few results. Harley-Davidson has tailored a marketing program to encourage women to take up biking, thus doubling the number of potential customers for its motorcycles.

A *Canadian Business* special report, Canada's Best Brands 2017, highlighted the results of the Rogers Consumer Insights Team survey of Canadians and how they rate their brands. The survey of 1,500 Canadians ranks brands based on reputation (defined as the quality of its products), its customer service, its innovation, its level of community involvement, and the person's overall opinion of the brand. The top three Canadian brands were identified as (1) Mountain Equipment Co-op, re-branded as MEC; (2) Home Hardware; and (3) WestJet. MEC did a phenomenal job of expanding its existing customer base from a very small niche market of mountain climbers and kayakers, to a more urban, educated, fitness-oriented consumer. To accomplish this, MEC expanded its original limited product line to include products for walking, running, cycling, yoga, and fitness.[8]

**Increasing a Product's Use** This approach encourages more frequent usage of a product by existing customers. It is typically used by products with a strong and loyal customer base. It has been a strategy of Campbell Soup Company. Because soup consumption rises in the winter and declines during the summer, the company now advertises more heavily in warm months to encourage consumers to think of soup as more than a cold-weather food. Similarly, the Florida Orange Growers Association advocates drinking orange juice throughout the day rather than for breakfast only.

Kraft keeps its product lines fresh with new items and marketing campaigns.

Used with permission of Kraft Heinz Foods Company

Procter & Gamble utilizes a line-extension strategy for Tide laundry detergent.

RosalreneBetancourt 6/Alamy Stock Photo

MEC has expanded its customer base to address the needs of a larger range of active consumers.

Used with permission of Mountain Equipment Co-op (MEC)

# Pokémon Go Creates a New Augmented-Reality Craze

Pokémon Go had many people wondering what all the hype is about. But for many of the 75 million people who downloaded the app, it became an obsession. Pokémon Go is an augmented-reality app based on the Pokémon characters originally launched in the mid-1990s as a children's trading-card game, and then eventually the concept was released as a video game by Nintendo. The same children that played Pokémon in the 1990s are now older and have smartphones and disposable income.

And this app does not disappoint. It takes the action to a whole other level. Pokémon Go is an augmented-reality game that incorporates GPS technology into the action. Players are challenged to search for and capture different Pokémon characters. This requires a person to walk or drive around to find them and ultimately capture them. Although the app is free to download, players can purchase coins and objects that help enhance their game. This phenomenon has created a community of gamers interacting not only in the game but also outside the game by exchanging hints and locations.

The app was developed (and is owned) by Niantic Labs and The Pokémon Company. Niantic, previously owned by Google, is a small online-gaming company that developed Pokémon Go. This app is an excellent example of product development built upon a foundation of the online-gaming and location-based technology expertise derived from Niantic. Pokémon Go was unleashed to the market in July 2016. Early numbers gathered post-launch showed that on average, people were on Pokémon Go for 43 minutes per day, compared to 30 minutes per day for the next highest app, WhatsApp.

Pokémon Go quickly rose to the top of the app downloads and surpassed every standard set by other apps. But as with many product launches, this one also had its problems. Crashing apps, overloaded servers, the necessity to provide full Google account information, and other issues were quickly resolved by Niantic. Canadians were quick to jump on the bandwagon, with thousands downloading the game before it was even officially available in Canada.

New product launches can have a significant impact on a company's value. In the case of Pokémon Go, investors initially believed that the app was owned by Nintendo, causing Nintendo share value to double. About one month after the app launched, Nintendo clarified its minimal stake in the app (32 percent of voting power in The Pokémon Company). This announcement caused an immediate 20 percent drop in share price as investors realized that Nintendo

**Niantic Labs created the new augmented-reality version of the Pokémon game.**
dennizn/Shutterstock.com

would see very little of the profits from the new app.

Niantic had gone through two rounds of financing and was able to raise $25 million prior to the launch of Pokémon Go. In the month post-launch, the app was generating close to $1 million per day in revenue. It has been estimated that based on the success of Pokémon Go, Niantic is worth close to $4 billion.

As can be seen with Pokémon Go, new product development can be integral to the success or failure of a company. Niantic has certainly been taken from start-up to a fast-growing, revenue-generating organization in a fairly short period of time. What's next? ●

## Questions

1. What product life cycle strategy is Pokémon Go an example of?

2. Why do you think Pokémon Go was so successful?

3. Where is Pokémon Go in its product life cycle?

---

**Creating a New Use Situation** Finding new uses for an existing product is not a simple task, because many products do not lend themselves to this approach. This has been a strategy used by Rice Krispies cereal by promoting its use as a baking ingredient for Rice Krispie Squares. Follow the links at **www.kelloggs.ca** to see the extended usage recipes used to market Rice Krispies.

Another example is Arm & Hammer baking soda, which is sold as a baking ingredient but is also marketed as a product that eliminates odours, unblocks sinks, and cleans various household items. The Marketing NewsFlash box, "Pokémon Go Creates a New Augmented-Reality Craze," looks at a new use for a 1990s fad.[9]

## 3. REPOSITIONING A PRODUCT

Once a product has reached its maturity stage, it often needs an injection of newness to focus the market on the product and to provide it with a renewed competitive advantage. This can be achieved through repositioning the product to meet changing consumer needs, to react to a competitor's move, or to improve the value offered to the consumer.

Based on consumer interest in healthy and fresh products, McDonald's is focused on repositioning its brand image from processed and unhealthy to fresh and premium. McDonald's began this repositioning by focusing on its McCafé business, offering fresh coffee made from Arabica beans and a selection of fresh pastries. This has expanded to include offering premium sirloin burgers and Signature McWraps. The "Create Your Taste" option allows customers to customize their burger selection with a choice of 30 premium ingredients and toppings such as guacamole, blue cheese, and caramelized onions. McDonald's intends to compete with restaurants such as Chipotle Mexican Grill and Panera Bread, which are experiencing growth in this segment.[10]

## 4. INTRODUCING A NEW PRODUCT

Adding a new product to a line can provide the focus that a mature product needs, bringing it back in the product life cycle to either the growth or early maturity stage. Apple has done this successfully by regularly introducing new versions of its iPhones, iPads, and computers with updates to its technology and design. Regardless of the type of product, new products have a greater chance of success if they provide meaningful benefits to its target market.

**Drivers of Product Success** When it comes to new products, the 2016 BrandSpark Canadian Shopper Study reviewed the opinions and attitudes of over 48,000 respondents in Canada. The study tells us that consumers want value for their money. Convenience plays a lesser role in shopping decisions. Shoppers like trying new products and are willing to pay more if the new product is better than what is currently available.[11]

The BrandSpark Best New Products Awards of 2017 echo the drivers for product success. These annual

McDonald's "Create Your Taste" option helps reposition McDonald's in a more premium space.

Fir Mamat/Alamy Stock Photo

### Best New Product Award Winners

| Product | Category |
|---|---|
| Jergens Moisturizer for Wet Skin (body moisturizer/lotion) | Health and beauty products |
| Jamieson Omega with No Fishy Aftertaste (vitamin/supplement) | |
| Pantene Airspray Hairspray (hairspray) | |
| Old Spice Odor Blocker Antiperspirant (men's antiperspirant) | |
| Country Harvest Canadian Rustic Bean (bread/wrap) | Food and beverage products |
| Black Diamond Natural Cheese Sticks - Marble (cheese) | |
| Twistos Garden Dill and Cream Cheese Baked Snack Crackers (crackers) | |
| Chapman's Yukon Moose Sandwich (frozen dessert) | |
| Milk-Bone Good Morning Daily Vitamin Treats (dog food/treat) | Household products |
| Sponge Towels Ultra Strong Minis (household paper) | |
| Vim Power & Shine Bathroom Spray (bathroom cleaning) | |
| Purex OXI Plus (liquid laundry detergent) | |

Source: "Winners of BrandSpark International's 2017 Best New Product Awards announced from a survey of 20,000 Canadians," BrandSpark International [news release], March 20, 2017, http://www.bestnewproductawards.biz/canada/pdf/2017/2017-BNPA-News-Release-FINAL.pdf.

1. *What approaches can be used to extend a product's life cycle?*

2. *Niantic developed Pokémon Go as a new augmented-reality app using the characters from Nintendo's Pokémon franchise. What strategy was used to extend the product life cycle for Pokémon?*

awards include the opinions of over 20,000 consumers on new products in the consumer packaged-goods industry (health and beauty, food and beverage, and household care). The winning products all provide good value and are seen as innovative in their categories. In the health and beauty segment, Colgate Max Fresh KnockOut won in the toothpaste category for combining the benefits of a whitening toothpaste with odour-neutralizing capabilities. In the food and beverage segment, Catelli SuperGreens Pasta was recognized in the pasta category for its healthier pasta packed with vegetables.[12]

**minor innovations**

Minor product modifications that require no adjustments on behalf of the consumer.

**continuous innovations**
New products with more than just a minor product improvement, but that do not require radical changes by the consumer.

**radical innovations**
New products that involve the introduction of a product that is entirely new and innovative to the market.

# NEW PRODUCTS

## TYPES OF NEW PRODUCTS

**LO 3** New products are the lifeblood of a company, helping to make products relevant and to bring future revenues into the company. There are many types of new products, ranging from a slight product modification to a more radical innovation.

How new products are categorized depends on the degree of newness involved, and how much time a consumer needs to learn to use the product. Based on these factors, we classify innovations as (1) minor innovations, (2) continuous innovations, and (3) radical innovations (see Figure 8–5).

**Minor innovations** refer to minor product modifications that require no adjustments on behalf of the consumer. Consumers do not need to be educated on how to use the product. Colgate Max Fresh KnockOut is an example of a minor innovation. The extra features in the new toothpaste do not require buyers to learn new behaviours, so effective marketing for a product like this is focused on generating awareness for the new innovation.

**Continuous innovations** refer to new products that include more than just a minor product improvement but do not require radical changes in consumer behaviour. Continuous innovations are not as common and require extensive product development by a company. Marketers must invest in marketing communication programs to launch these innovative products and to communicate their benefits to consumers. Electric cars are an example of a continuous innovation. While consumers drive an electric car in a similar manner to gasoline-powered vehicles, there are some points of difference that require education and communication, such as shorter driving ranges, the availability of charging stations, and the uncertainty around the cost of operating an electric vehicle.[13]

**Radical innovations** are the least common form of innovation. They involve the introduction of a product

 *New products are the lifeblood of a company, helping to make products relevant and to bring future revenues into the company.*

## Figure 8–5
Degree of product innovation

|  | Minor Innovation | Continuous Innovation | Radical Innovation |
|---|---|---|---|
| Definition | Requires no new learning by consumers | Changes consumer's normal routine but does not require totally new learning | Requires new learning and consumption patterns by consumers |
| Examples | New and improved detergents or diapers | Electric toothbrushes or digital cameras | Drones or wearables |
| Marketing emphasis | Gain consumer awareness and wide distribution | Advertise points of difference and benefits to consumers | Educate consumers through advertising, product trial, and personal selling; public relations can play a major role |

Drones, which are unmanned aircraft, are an example of radical innovation.

Doxieone Photography/Getty Images

that is entirely new to the market. The success of these products is often dependent on the education of the consumer, usually through advertising and/or public relations efforts.

Drones are an example of radical innovation. Drones are unmanned aircraft that were originally developed for use in war, to surprise and attack the enemy. Unlike the remote control aircraft that came before them, drones can operate somewhat autonomously. Drones combine technology such as GPS, cameras, controllers, computer programming, and radio-frequency or WiFi communication. Now, drones are disrupting the way business is done in many industries. The commercial use of drones has evolved for package delivery, agriculture monitoring, real estate development, news coverage, law enforcement, and simply for entertainment. Drones represent an exciting convergence of several cutting-edge technologies. Regulators are struggling to keep pace. The significant potential dangers of flying drones, as well as privacy concerns, are creating an urgent need for the development of rules to govern drone use.[14]

## THE ADOPTION CURVE

**LO 4** The success of a new product and how quickly it is adopted by consumers is demonstrated in Figure 8–6, which shows the adoption curve. The **adoption curve** takes the point of view that some consumers are more ready than others to buy a product innovation. North American research (statistics vary across the world) shows that 2.5 percent of the population are innovators who are the first to purchase new products; 13.5 percent are considered early adopters, another group that will accept a

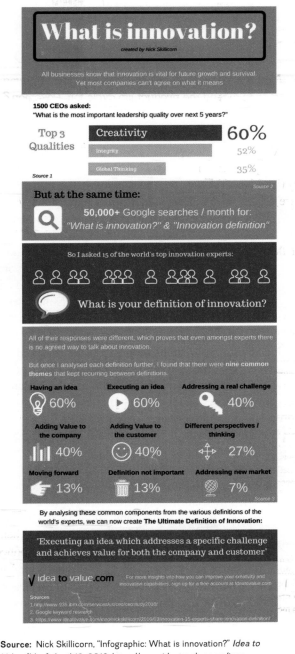

**Source:** Nick Skillicorn, "Infographic: What is innovation?" *Idea to Value* [blog]. April 19, 2016, https://www.ideatovalue.com/inno/nickskillicorn/2016/04/infographic-what-is-innovation/.

new offering sooner rather than later. In the middle of the pack are the early and late majority, each comprising approximately 34 percent of the population. Once accepted by the innovators and early adopters, the adoption of new products moves on to the early majority and late majority, who respond to the

> **adoption curve**
> The sequential diffusion and acceptance of an innovation into the market by consumers.

## Figure 8–6
The adoption curve

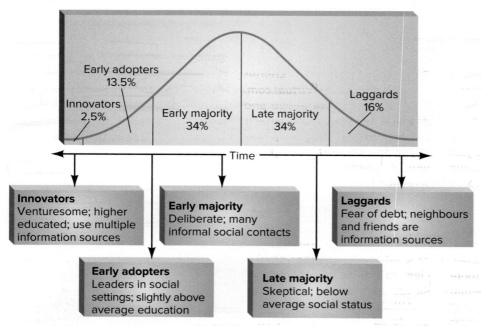

**Innovators**
Venturesome; higher educated; use multiple information sources

**Early majority**
Deliberate; many informal social contacts

**Laggards**
Fear of debt; neighbours and friends are information sources

**Early adopters**
Leaders in social settings; slightly above average education

**Late majority**
Skeptical; below average social status

Early adopters 13.5%
Innovators 2.5%
Early majority 34%
Late majority 34%
Laggards 16%

Time

---

product being well-established in the market and are influenced by the purchase habits of their peers. Another 16 percent of the population are the laggards, who are either reluctant or late purchasers of the innovation and may in fact never purchase it.[15]

For any product to be successful it must be purchased by innovators and early adopters. Often, marketers spend a lot of effort involving innovators and early adopters with their new product prior to launch. These consumers are the opinion leaders in a particular product category, and so their experiences can play an integral role in future demand for the product. Marketers then try to move the product from the innovators and early adopters through to the early majority so as to quickly reap the benefits of increased sales and profits as soon as possible. In this manner, marketers design marketing programs to target these specific groups in different ways, and separately focus their marketing programs on the demographic and psychographic needs and interests of these target groups. There are several types of barriers that can deter a consumer from adopting a new product. Common reasons are usage barriers (the product is not consistent with existing usage habits), value barriers (there is no incentive to change), risk barriers (the existence of physical, economic, or social risks if the product is purchased), and psychological barriers (cultural or image differences).[16]

A new product currently struggling to move along the adoption curve is the electric car. Electric cars have earned less than 1 percent of global automobile sales. A usage barrier exists because prospective buyers believe these cars are not compatible with existing driving habits. Contributing to this belief is the lack of charging stations across Canada and the perception that electric cars have very short travelling ranges. Second, there is also a value barrier. Consumers have not recognized the superiority of electric cars over vehicles with internal combustion engines. Third, a risk barrier exists due to buyer uncertainty about the actual cost of owning an electric-powered car. This has been an even greater issue since gasoline prices have stabilized.[17]

Another industry that is that is looking for rapid uptake and adoption is virtual health care. Read about the experience of Equinoxe in the Marketing NewsFlash box "Equinoxe Virtual Health Care Clinic."[18]

---

### ask YOURSELF

1. Describe the three types of product innovation and explain which ones are most common.

2. What type of innovation are electric cars?

3. How does the adoption curve apply to the diffusion of new products in the marketplace?

# Equinoxe Virtual Health Care Clinic

It's 5 p.m. on a Monday evening and your throat is scratchy. You know that a virus has been going around your school. Do you line up at the nearest walk-in clinic to see a doctor? Do you just ignore the symptoms and continue doing your school work? Imagine if those weren't your only two choices.

People are busy and don't always have time to visit a doctor, wait times to see physicians have increased, and people are becoming more health-conscious. Environmental changes such as these have created the opportunity for easy-to-access virtual health care services. There has been a proliferation of health care apps, with Apple listing more than 43,000 health care apps, and thousands also available for Android devices.

An even more significant development has been the real-time virtual clinic. With the click of a mouse, you are able to access a doctor in virtual clinics anywhere in Canada. Equinoxe LifeCare has been around for 25 years, providing health care services ranging from home care to specialized care for individuals or organizations. Adding technology-based health care to its mix was a natural for Equinoxe. Equinoxe was clearly able to build upon its strengths—knowledge and experience in the health care sector in Canada—to launch this excellent example of continuous innovation.

EQ Virtual Clinic turns the traditional doctor visit around. Rather than the patient going to the doctor, the doctor comes to the patient through the patient's computer, tablet, or smartphone.

Once a new patient creates an account at EQVirtual.com, he or she can move ahead and describe symptoms and attach any photos that may help the physician diagnose the problem. All patients are initially screened by a care manager and then connected to a doctor. Doctors are able to not only consult with the patient but also provide a prescription or a referral to another physician, as well as provide orders for lab work or other testing.

Although Equinoxe is headquartered in Montreal, its technology-based services do not have geographic boundaries. EQ Virtual's services are covered by some provincial health plans (except Ontario, where there is a fee for each visit). Some organizations offer the service as part of their employee benefit plan, and in other cases, individuals pay directly for the service. Over 30,000 people have received care through EQ Virtual since it was established.

Equinoxe is not the only company that has jumped into the virtual clinic business in Canada. Akira and Ask the Doctor are two other companies that have decided that virtual health care is a trend that is here to stay. These companies have chosen either a subscription-based model or a fee-for-service concept. In either case, the patient receives an "instant" consultation.

Virtual health care clinics were created to meet the needs of Canadians who are extremely busy, yet interested in staying healthy. Virtual clinics also minimize patient wait times and ensure continuity of

Equinoxe connects patients with a doctor in a virtual clinic.

Anja Schaefer/Alamy Stock Photo

care. Dr. Ed Brown, the CEO of Ontario Telemedicine Network, believes that "by 2020, 25 percent of health will be delivered virtually." Marketers should take a lesson from Equinoxe: Marketers need to be on top of external trends and need to ensure that new product concepts not only consider those external opportunities but also exploit internal company strengths. Whether it is through e-mail, text, an app, or FaceTime, next time you don't feel well, the solution may only be a only click away. ●

## Questions

1. What value does a virtual clinic bring for the patient?

2. Do you think the concept of virtual clinics will be a success? Why or why not?

# NEW PRODUCT DEVELOPMENT

Developing and launching new products is an expensive undertaking with a high risk of failure. Research costs are high, as is the time and effort spent on developing prototypes and marketing materials. We are familiar with successful new products and brands such as Google, Xbox, Twitter, and iPad, yet research has shown that only 15 to 50 percent of new products are successful. Success rates vary between industries, with consumer products experiencing the highest failure rates.[19]

Product failure can result in expensive product write-offs and a lack of future credibility in the market. Hundreds of thousands of dollars are often at stake. It is important at this point to remember that new products become successful over time and that marketers work to finesse these new products with upgrades and improvements that better meet consumer needs and expectations. However, many product launches also fail for reasons spanning an insignificant point of difference to an inadequate market distribution strategy (see Figure 8–7). There are many examples of product failure, even from very large companies. New Coke is the textbook example of a new product launch gone wrong. Introduced in April 1985 and rapidly removed from the market in July 1985, Coke failed to understand the intense loyalty of its customers for the original Coke brand.[20]

In 2014, Burger King launched Satisfries. Satisfries were a lower-calorie french fry, developed to meet the needs of the health-conscious consumer.

Burger King's Satisfries did not meet the needs of consumers.
Saul Loeb/AFP/Getty Images

Touted by Burger King as "one of the biggest fast food launches," Satisfries did not satisfy its customers and were on the market for less than one year. In the fast-food market, many customers view products as indulgences, and so tinkering with them is often not well-received. McDonald's had a similar issue when it switched to a trans fat–free oil. Customers complained about the flavour of the fries made with this new oil.[21]

In order to avoid expensive product failures, companies can use a number of different approaches when developing new products. These range from providing clear strategic direction, to creating particular company structures, to instituting rigorous product development processes. We look at these areas in more detail in the sections that follow.

## Figure 8–7
Avoiding new product failure

| Why New Products and Services Fail | |
|---|---|
| **Issue** | **Potential Solution** |
| **Insignificant point of difference** | • Determine a distinctive and meaningful point of difference for the target audience.<br>• Conduct research with consumers and monitor competitors' products/activities. |
| **Incomplete new concept definition** | • Identify consumer insights and clearly define the product's features and benefits.<br>• Develop a clear positioning. |
| **Insufficient market attractiveness** | • Identify a target market (with a need) that is large enough and has growth potential to support the product. |
| **Poor execution of the marketing mix** | • Ensure the 4 Ps—product (including brand name and package), price, promotion, distribution—are aligned and attractive to consumers.<br>• Focus on gaining sufficient distribution to access consumers. |
| **Bad timing** | • Launch products when consumers are eager to purchase.<br>• Monitor market conditions and competitor actions. |

**Sources:** Barbara Thau, "The Five Biggest Reasons Why Consumer Products Fail," *Forbes*, June 3, 2014, http://www.forbes.com/sites/barbarathau/2014/06/03/the-five-biggest-reasons-why-consumer-products-fail-according-to-a-retail-insider/print/; Joan Schneider and Julie Hall, "Why Most Product Launches Fail," *Harvard Business Review*, April 2011, https://hbr.org/2011/04/why-most-product-launches-fail.

## Figure 8–8
Strategic approaches to growth

| Markets | Products | |
| --- | --- | --- |
| | **Current** | **New** |
| **Current** | **Market Penetration** | **Product Development** |
| | Finding ways to make current products appeal to current customers | Reaching current customers with a new product |
| **New** | **Market Development** | **Diversification** |
| | Reaching new customers with a current product | Reaching new customers with a new product |

# APPROACHES TO NEW PRODUCT DEVELOPMENT

1. **Strategic Direction** | From a strategic point of view, companies can follow different approaches to growth (see Figure 8–8). It is somewhat dependent on the degree of risk and investment that companies are willing to take. The most common forms of growth take either a market penetration or product development slant, focusing on current consumers with promotional tactics (market penetration), or looking to develop a new product for these current consumers (product development). Higher-risk considerations include either a market development or diversification strategy, taking the more expensive approach of either targeting new markets with current products (market development), or moving into new arenas with totally new products (diversification). More information about these strategies is included in Chapter 15.

2. **Company Structure** | Companies use different structures to encourage innovation. Some companies, such as Thalmic Labs, use internal teams and external customers to help get successful new products to consumers. Many companies use a cross-functional team-based approach that includes representation from many departments across an organization including marketers, regulatory experts, product developers, quality assurance specialists, and sales.

> 99 *New product development success ultimately requires the expertise of people with different specializations.*

Other companies may follow a more focused approach by centralizing product development responsibilities with one person (new product development manager) or to a full department. In other organizations, new product development is included in the role of the general marketer. In some instances, new venture teams are used to concentrate on all innovation projects for the company, which could include new products, new processes, or new business ventures.

Regardless of the formal structure, new product development success ultimately requires the expertise of people with different specializations and from varied backgrounds to ensure that the best product ideas are developed. These experts are either fully involved in the process from the start, or brought in along the way to contribute to the journey.

# THE NEW PRODUCT DEVELOPMENT PROCESS

**LO 5** In order to avoid expensive product failures, companies will use rigorous product development processes to minimize the risk. The **new product development process** includes the seven steps shown in Figure 8–9 and summarized in Figure 8–10, Today, many organizations use a formal Stage-Gate® process that focuses on the collection of data and analysis at each step in the process to determine whether the

> **new product development process**
> Sequence of steps that a firm takes to develop a new product idea and take it to market.

Cross-functional teams reduce new product development time.
Rawpixel.com/Shutterstock

## Figure 8–9

Steps in the new product development process

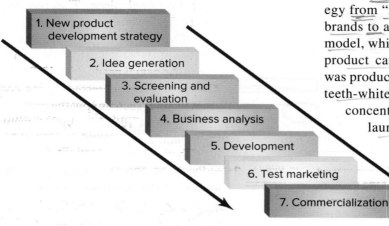

1. New product development strategy
2. Idea generation
3. Screening and evaluation
4. Business analysis
5. Development
6. Test marketing
7. Commercialization

results are successful enough to justify proceeding to the next stage. If results cannot be improved, the project doesn't proceed to the next step, and product development is halted.[22]

### Step 1: New Product Development Strategy

Having a clear definition and understanding of what you are trying to achieve with product innovation is one of the most important building blocks in the new product development process. A **new product development strategy** involves setting the new product strategic direction for the company as a whole, as well as the precise objectives for the innovation at hand. There must be consistency between the two.

An example can be seen with Procter & Gamble, which refocused its new product development strategy from "new-to-the-world" product categories and brands to a "transformational sustaining" innovation model, which focuses on evolving current brands and product categories with new initiatives. The result was products, such as Crest 3D White, with advanced teeth-whitening properties, and Tide Pods, a more concentrated and convenient format for Tide laundry detergent. As a result, P&G has been able to triple its new product success rate from 15 to 50 percent.[23]

Thalmic Labs is a company built on a foundation of innovation, and its goal is to concentrate on the ongoing development of wearables that will "change the way we interact with computers." This is a focused approach, guiding product development efforts to more radical innovation.[24]

### Step 2: Idea Generation

Once the purpose and direction for the product development project is clarified, the second step of **idea generation** comes into play. Ideas can be generated from a number of sources and in a number of different ways. Ideas can come from inside or outside the company, depending on the organization's approach to new product development. Brainstorming sessions can be utilized, which focus on participants coming up with new ideas for the project at hand. It is important for these brainstorming sessions to include individuals who are creative, have varied experiences, and have differing areas of expertise. This should stimulate a more varied and interesting pool of ideas.

## Figure 8–10

Elements in each stage of the new product development process

| Stage of Process | Purpose of Stage | Marketing Information and Methods Used |
|---|---|---|
| New product development strategy | Identify new-product development focus that meets company objectives | Company objectives; SWOT analysis of company/product/brand |
| Idea generation | Brainstorm new ideas | Ideas from employees, co-workers, and consumers |
| Screening and evaluation | Evaluate product ideas and develop concepts | Internal evaluation of technical requirements, external concept tests |
| Business analysis | Identify the product's features and its marketing strategy, and make financial projections | Product's key features and anticipated marketing mix; assessment of production, legal, and profitability issues |
| Test marketing | Test the product and marketing strategy in the marketplace on a limited scale (if necessary) | Test marketing in defined areas |
| Commercialization | Launch and fully market the product in the marketplace | Implement all areas of the marketing mix; possible regional rollout |

Brainstorming sessions can result in a host of interesting ideas, but for this approach to work, participants must be willing to share their most ridiculous or boring ideas with the group. Participants need to be open-minded, energetic, flexible, and willing to build on each other's ideas. Often, companies hire an outside moderator, skilled in these types of sessions, to promote creativity sessions that render results. Brainstorming is a key technique used by the founders of Thalmic Labs to generate ideas aligned with their innovation strategy. This is how the idea for the Myo armband was created.[25]

Valuable input can be obtained from customers and suppliers. Sales or purchasing personnel can talk to their customers to pinpoint unmet needs. Customers also feed their suggestions into companies through customer service and social media channels. Many companies invest in consumer research, focused on coming up with new product ideas. This input should be considered for future product development. Customers are the ones using a company's product, and they have a good understanding of potential improvements.

P&G spends billions of dollars each year on product research and development. A significant additional investment is made in consumer research, with an eye to generating ideas for product innovation. In 2012, with a $150-million marketing budget, P&G launched Tide Pods. Tide Pods are a revolutionary three-chamber liquid dose of Tide that cleans, fights stains, and brightens. Following its successful launch, P&G redesigned its packaging after discovering that some children thought the pods were candy and tried to eat them.[26]

## Step 3: Screening and Evaluation

The third stage of the new product development process, **screening and evaluation**, attempts to reduce the array of product ideas down to a manageable list of promising concepts. Ideas are initially screened internally by the new product development team, which eliminates ideas that do not meet the objectives, as well as those that are clearly not technically feasible. The short list of ideas is then further developed by the product development team into concepts. A concept is a more detailed idea, written in consumer terms, with enough detail for consumers to fully understand. Consumers are presented with a short descriptive

The ongoing development of Tide Pods came from consumer feedback.

mikeledray/Shutterstock.com

paragraph and an accompanying visual, which could be a sketch, mock-up, or promotional piece. They are then asked for feedback.

**Concept tests** are external evaluations of the new product idea, rather than the actual product itself. Several key issues are addressed during concept testing, such as how the customer perceives the product, who would use it, and how it would be used. The purpose of these evaluations is to get feedback on the strengths and weaknesses of the concepts and to understand what further modifications are required. Concept tests will result in some concepts being eliminated and others surfacing as more-promising opportunities that require further investigation.

## Step 4: Business Analysis

After the concept tests have determined which product, or line of products, are strong new product candidates, the **business analysis** step is necessary. This involves determining financial projections on bringing the new product to market and selling it in the future. Typical financial projections for a new product cover a three-year period and often look five years into the future.

At this point in the new product development process, marketers are checking the commercial viability of the new product. This requires strong analytical skills and the ability to understand the dynamics of the market. Marketers need to initially establish the positioning of the product in the market and what marketing elements are needed for a successful launch. The new product is also studied to determine whether it can, and should, be protected with a patent, trademark, or copyright. A marketer must also be able to anticipate competitive reactions and foresee target market needs.

The business analysis step requires marketers to determine market share projections, price points, cost parameters, special discounts, distribution requirements, research needs, and all the marketing communication programs needed to ensure product success. Marketers also need to understand whether a product will require an investment in infrastructure,

**screening and evaluation**
Reduces the list of ideas down to a list of promising concepts.

**concept tests**
External evaluations of a new product idea, rather than the actual product itself.

**business analysis**
Financial projections on the impact of bringing the new product to market and selling it in the future.

> ## The business analysis stage results in profit projections.

software, machinery, people, or training programs, and whether it will cannibalize the sales of existing products. The business analysis stage results in profit projections. Marketers review these projections, taking a realistic view of the product and the market to decide whether the concept has real financial merit. It is important for marketers to be as realistic as possible at this stage.

If the product can meet sales, profit, and market share targets, then the new product development process will continue to the next step. If not, marketers may reassess the concept, going back to consumers to conduct further research. This is usually the last checkpoint before significant resources are invested in creating a prototype, a full-scale operating model of the product.

Thalmic Labs decided to launch a pre-order campaign at this stage to ensure that it had a very realistic view of the sales demand. From that starting point, costs and resource requirements could be more accurately forecasted.[27]

## Step 5: Development

New product ideas that survive the business analysis step proceed to actual **development**, turning the idea into a prototype for further consumer research and manufacturing tests. This step is considerably complex, involving laboratory and consumer tests to ensure that the product consistently meets legal and quality control requirements. Manufacturing trials are also conducted to eliminate manufacturing problems and to reduce costs.

This step can be time-consuming, with some products requiring extensive testing before they can be safely brought to market. Pharmaceutical products, children's toys, cars, and food products are examples that fall into this category.

Thalmic went through several iterations of its armband concept before landing on the flexible one-size-fits-all Myo armband model. Developers

**development**
The new product idea is turned into a prototype for further consumer research and manufacturing tests.

**test marketing**
Offering a new product for sale on a limited basis in a defined geographic area to assess its success.

were engaged in the process to work with the prototype and the software, and most importantly, to provide feedback to Thalmic.[28]

The advantage of the development step is that it allows marketers to take actual product prototypes into consumer research or show them to potential buyers. This provides a platform to probe preliminary sales strategies with key accounts or marketing ideas with consumers.

## Step 6: Test Marketing

**Test marketing** involves offering a product for sale on a limited basis in a defined geographic area. This test is done to determine whether consumers will actually buy the product, and to what extent. Marketers may use this opportunity to test different marketing approaches to support the product.

There are several cities in Canada that are used regularly as test markets for a variety of different products/services. Test-marketing is often conducted in cities such as London, Ontario; Edmonton, Alberta; and Barrie, Ontario. Test cities tend to be under 1 million in population and need to be similar culturally to the rest of the country, with a variety of socio-economic backgrounds represented, making them representative of Canada in general. Using tracking systems by firms such as Nielsen, marketers can try to correlate local advertising campaigns to in-store purchases by

**McDonald's Chicken McNuggets and Tim Hortons® Dark Roast coffee were tested in London, Ontario.**

All Tim Hortons® trademarks and copyrights referenced herein are owned by Tim Hortons®. Used with permission.

*To minimize the risk of financial failure, many companies use regional rollouts.*

using data from store scanners. McDonald's Chicken McNuggets and Tim Hortons® Dark Roast coffee were tested in London, Ontario, before being launched throughout Canada.[29]

The main drawbacks of test markets are that they are expensive to conduct, and they immediately alert the competition. Competitors can easily sabotage test markets by altering their own pricing and marketing support to render the test market unsuccessful. These issues are so real that many marketers do not embark on test markets, relying instead on research to provide good direction for a full product launch.

In the business analysis stage, Thalmic launched a pre-order campaign, which generated thousands of orders. In the test marketing phase, Thalmic fulfilled these pre-orders and continued to sell the Myo armband directly to consumers from its website only.[30]

Technology is assisting marketers by creating simulated test markets through a number of software programs. An emerging trend uses virtual reality testing to allow marketers to present consumers with a range of experiences such as simulated store environments. Ipsos is an example of a reputable market research firm that conducts simulated test marketing services for its clients.

## Step 7: Commercialization

Commercialization is the step when the new product is brought to market with full-scale production, sales, and marketing support. Companies proceed very carefully at the commercialization stage because this is the most expensive stage for most new products. To minimize the risk of financial failure, many companies use regional rollouts, introducing the product sequentially into geographic areas of the country to allow production levels and marketing activities to build gradually. Grocery product manufacturers and some telecommunication service providers are examples of firms that use this strategy.

Marketing plays a crucial role in the success of a new product, and marketers need to intimately understand their consumers and what is important to their purchase decisions. Each element of the marketing mix needs to be carefully crafted to help make a new product successful.

After successfully fulfilling pre-orders in early 2015, Myo was launched online at Amazon and BestBuy. Thalmic continues to expand its global retail partnerships.[31]

**commercialization**
When the new product is brought to market with full-scale production, sales, and marketing support.

### ask YOURSELF

1. What are the main reasons that new products fail?

2. What occurs in the screening and evaluation step of the new product development process?

3. What is the purpose of the business analysis step in the new product development process?

4. What are the advantages and disadvantages of a test market?

**LO 1**
- Product life cycles are the stages that a new product goes through from its initial introduction through to growth, maturity, and decline.
- The shape of a product life cycle varies depending on the industry, the competition, technological innovation, and the marketing of the product.

**LO 2**
- Product life cycles can be extended through various marketing techniques that encourage new and current users to keep purchasing the product and to use it in new ways.
- Extending a product life cycle can be done by following one or a combination of these approaches: (1) modifying the product, (2) modifying the market, (3) repositioning a product, and (4) introducing a new product.

**LO 3**
- There are many types of new products, ranging from slight product modifications, to more innovative changes, to the more radical innovations that we see in the market. We term these minor innovations, continuous innovations, and radical innovations.

**LO 4**
- The adoption curve shows the sequential diffusion and acceptance of an innovation into the market by consumers. It categorizes people into five groupings: innovators, early adopters, early majority, late majority, and laggards.

**LO 5**
- The new product development process follows seven steps: (1) new product development strategy, (2) idea generation, (3) screening and evaluation, (4) business analysis, (5) development, (6) test marketing, and (7) commercialization.

key terms and concepts... **A REFRESHER**

adoption curve
business analysis
commercialization
concept tests
continuous innovations
delete
development

fad
fashion product
harvest
high-learning product
idea generation
line extension
low-learning product

minor innovations
new product development process
new product development strategy
product life cycle
radical innovations
screening and evaluation
test marketing

hands-on... **APPLY YOUR KNOWLEDGE**

**New Product Development Assignment** Thalmic's Myo armband was created as an innovative way to allow users to wirelessly control devices in a hands-off way, completely changing the way people interact with technology. Review this chapter's opening vignette on the Myo armband and gather additional information about this and other products in this category by going online to visit brand websites and social media sites. Also review the latest news in this category. Present your ideas on how the online environment can be used to market the Myo armband to consumers.

This chapter's opening vignette explains the development and launch of the Myo armband from Thalmic Labs. Thalmic used brainstorming as an important technique to come up with some of the initial ideas for Myo. Conduct a brainstorming session with a group of fellow students and come up with a list of at least 15 different ideas for future uses for the Myo armband.

Review the Infographic titled "What Is Innovation?" Pick an industry that you are interested in. Research some of the latest innovations impacting that industry. What specific consumer need/challenge do you believe is addressed by this innovation? Why do you believe this product/service is innovative? Review the definitions of innovation provided by the experts (in the infographic). Compare your response to their definitions. Do you agree with their perspectives? Explain.

# Pricing

In order to generate an appropriate return on investment, organizations require effective pricing strategies for their goods and services. Costs in the manufacturing of food in Canada increase year-over-year. This requires marketers to be creative with respect to managing the costs of production. This chapter discusses different pricing strategies and constraints that companies consider before determining final prices for their products and services. Companies generally use approaches based on demand, costs, profit, and competition.

Lotus_studio/Shutterstock

The palate of Canadians has broadened through immigration. What may traditionally been associated with English and French cuisine has expanded with immigration from Europe, Asia, and the Caribbean. Different ethnicities lead to different opportunities for food. It is a growing industry with the costs of production continuing to rise.

According to Agriculture and Agri-Food Canada, Canada supplies honey to 27 countries worldwide. The cost of honey has doubled over the past ten years, requiring companies that mass produce gulab jamun, baklava, and other honey-based foods to consider raising prices or cutting costs in other ways.

Understanding that food companies are cost-conscious, Mario Fleury of Be Sweet Inc., with his business partner Eric Russell, has uncovered an opportunity. An experienced food chemist, Mario developed a honey substitute that companies can use as a lower-cost alternative. "We were inspired by the Quaker Oats Company," explains Mario. "In 1966, Quaker Oats developed a pancake syrup under the Aunt Jemima brand." This lower-cost syrup was introduced under the campaign, "Aunt Jemima, what took you so long?"

Mario's formula contains a strategic amount of honey, allowing him to significantly reduce the costs of ingredients compared to using 100 percent honey. The Be Sweet formula allows industrial customers to include honey on their labels high on their ingredients list since ingredients are listed in order of quantity in their respective formulas. The final product offers an excellent match to the taste and functionality of raw honey. "Essentially, we are using science to overcome pricing challenges," shares Mario. "Climate and pesticides are decimating the bee population. This will lead to less production of honey and therefore an increase in demand and price." Mario's Be Sweet honey spread can offer consumers and businesses the same taste at half the price. Furthermore, flexibility with costs allows Be Sweet to be more competitive, allowing opportunities for business that may not be available otherwise.

Companies that use standard markup pricing or cost-plus pricing will benefit greatly from having less expensive ingredients to develop their products. If a honey-alternative is available, the Be Sweet solution allows food companies requiring honey in their recipes to be flexible with their costs. "Companies can replace a portion of the honey required in their recipes based on the functionality, taste, or ingredient restrictions required," says Mario. "And, they can still enjoy significant savings for themselves or pass them on to the consumer!"

In order to provide his product to intermediaries at a reasonable price, Mario leverages his many years of experience in the food ingredients industry. The formula for its honey substitute is a liquid blend of sweeteners and other ingredients. "The key is to minimize the fixed costs associated with your business," Mario claims. "By keeping your overhead low, your product sales can start contributing to your profits once you cross your break-even threshold." To achieve low fixed costs and reduce risk as a business owner, Mario minimizes what Be Sweet Inc. owns. He went to the largest industrial sweetener blender in the country so that he can not only create his product more efficiently but also access the sweeteners with significant buying power. Similarly, Mario went to another company that already bottles honey very efficiently and has strong buying power for the actual bottles and lids necessary to create his product. There are often very large minimum order requirements that would be difficult to achieve as a small business. "We own the trademark names and the formula, but leverage intermediaries to produce and distribute the product." Essentially, Be Sweet Inc. has the product idea and uses industrial third parties to manufacture, package, and distribute its products across North America.

Prior to starting Be Sweet Inc., Mario worked for a larger food ingredients company. "We spent hundred of thousands of dollars on sales and marketing with two simple goals: get a sample request or a price request." When constructing a pricing proposal, Mario put a great deal of thought and considered various factors, including the business, its cash flow, the ownership structure, annual volume, order quantity, competitors, and future business. "All these factors and more need to be considered when constructing a price that maximizes margins while maintaining high probability of winning business."

The costs of goods in Canada will continue to rise. Companies like Be Sweet Inc., through innovation, can help consumers find relief. By controlling costs and offering consumers less expensive alternatives, marketers can use financial savvy to help make their products a success. Lower costing gives smaller companies the opportunity to participate in larger pieces of businesses.[1]

# NATURE AND IMPORTANCE OF PRICE

**LO 1** The price paid for goods and services goes by many names. You pay *tuition* for your education, *rent* for an apartment, *interest* on a bank credit card, and a *premium* for car insurance. Your dentist or physician charges you a *fee*, a professional or social organization charges *dues*, and airlines charge a *fare*. And what you pay for clothes or a haircut is termed a *price*.

Price has many implications for marketing. Beyond it being a key element of the 4 Ps of the marketing mix, marketers need to know how pricing impacts their target markets and competitors.

## WHAT IS A PRICE?

From a marketing viewpoint, *price* is the money or other considerations, including other goods and services, exchanged for the ownership or use of a product. For example, Wilkinson Sword could exchange some of its knives for advertising that promotes its razor blades. This practice of exchanging goods and services for other goods and services rather than for money is called *barter*. In fact, barter transactions account for billions of dollars annually in domestic and international trade.

For most products, money is exchanged. Generally, consumers focus on purchasing necessities first. Prices for necessities increase with inflation. As seen in the Infographic, "Rising Canadian Food Prices," certain foods can increase drastically over time. When prices of necessities rise, consumers have less to spend on other products. Furthermore, how much money is paid is not always consistent with the list, or quoted, price because of discounts, allowances, and extra fees. While discounts, allowances, and rebates make the effective price lower, other marketing tactics raise the real price. One pricing tactic is to use "special fees" and "surcharges." This practice is driven by consumers' zeal for low prices combined with the ease of making price comparisons online. Buyers are more willing to pay extra fees than a higher list price, so sellers use add-on charges as a way of having the consumer pay more without raising the list price. Consider this when you purchase a cellphone. Examples of such special fees may include a "system licensing charge" or "911 emergency service access charge" that increase the monthly cellphone bill. You may also encounter an environmental surcharge on new tires and batteries for cars in some provinces.

The different factors that increase or decrease the price are put together in a *price equation,* which is shown for several different products in Figure 9–1.

Suppose that you decide you want to buy a Bugatti Veyron, the world's fastest production car, which can move

# Infographic

**Rising food prices have an impact to the Canadian consumer.**

Used with permission of Calgary Food Bank.

## Figure 9–1

The price of three different purchases

| Price Equation | | | | |
|---|---|---|---|---|
| **Item Purchased** | **Price** | **= List Price** | **– Incentives and Allowances** | **+ Extra Fees** |
| New car bought by an individual | Final price | = List price | – Rebate<br>– Cash discount<br>– Old car trade-in | + Financing charges<br>+ Special accessories<br>+ Destination charges |
| Term in university bought by a student | Tuition | = Published tuition | – Scholarship<br>– Other financial aid | + Special activity fees |
| Merchandise bought from a wholesaler by a retailer | Invoice price | = List price | – Quantity discount<br>– Cash discount<br>– Seasonal discount<br>– Functional or trade discount | + Penalty for late payment |

**value**
The ratio of perceived benefits to price.

you from 0 to 100 km/h in 2.5 seconds, with a top speed of 422 km/h. The Veyron has a list price of $2.5 million, but you want the clear-coat paint option, so it will cost an extra $430,000. An extended warranty will add an additional $70,000 to the cost. However, if you put $500,000 down now and finance the balance over the next year, you will receive a rebate of $50,000 off the list price. For your 2013 Honda Civic DX 4-door sedan that has 100,000 kilometres and is in fair condition, you are given a trade-in allowance of $5,000. Assume another $300,000 for additional taxes and charges. Finally, your total finance charge at an annual interest rate of 5 percent over a five-year period is $378,640.[2]

Applying the price equation (as shown in Figure 9–1) to your purchase, your final price is as follows:

Final price = List price − (Incentives + Allowances) + Extra fees

$$= \$2,500,000 - (\$500,000 + \$50,000 + \$5,000) + (\$430,000 + \$70,000 + \$300,000 + \$378,640)$$

$$= \$3,173,640$$

Are you still interested in buying this car? If so, put yourself on the waiting list.

## PRICE AS AN INDICATOR OF VALUE

From a consumer's standpoint, price is often used to indicate value when it is compared with the perceived

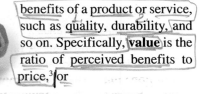

McDonald's increases value to consumers by reducing the overall price of food items purchased in a combo.
© Steve Stock/Alamy Stock Photo

benefits of a product or service, such as quality, durability, and so on. Specifically, **value** is the ratio of perceived benefits to price,[3] or

$$Value = \frac{Perceived\ benefits}{Price}$$

This relationship shows that for a given price, as perceived benefits increase, value increases. If you can purchase a medium or a large pizza for $13.99, which pizza would you choose? Would having more pizza to eat be more valuable? Many marketers often engage in the practice of *value pricing*—increasing product or service benefits while maintaining or decreasing price. McDonald's understands the importance of price to consumers and launched its McValue® Menu which has evolved into Value Picks®. McDonald's Extra Value Meal combinations show how lowering prices can increase the value of to a consumer.

Marketers must be careful when using price as an indicator of value. For example, for many consumers, a low price would imply poor quality, and ultimately, poor perceived value. This is particularly true for services. For example, what would be your perception of a dentist who charges only $25 for a checkup and cleaning, when the average dentist charges between $150 and $200? Consumers make comparative value assessments, so it is important for marketers to know what their competitors are charging.

Consider all the costs when purchasing items like the Bugatti Veyron.
© culture-images GmbH/Alamy

## Highlighting the Value of Services

The value of professional services and advice is difficult to quantify. A financial professional's recommendation may save consumers money; however, the knowledge, conversation, and expertise involved in that recommendation may be difficult for a consumer to value. H&R Block's unique pricing strategy with its online tax software helps it showcase the value of its tax experts.

Historically, there are numerous quotations and discussions about the certainty, dread, or complexity of taxation. In Canada, taxpayers search for options and evaluate alternatives for filing their personal and business taxes by their respective April deadlines. Whether they are students, professors, business professionals, or retired, Canadians who seek help for tax preparation services have a number of different options. After careful evaluation of their alternatives, Canadians remain loyal to only a few of them. Tax preparers who have discovered the correct strategy for effective pricing have realized the lifetime value of their clients.

Value involves a relationship with perceived benefits and price, and effective marketers use this to their advantage. In H&R Block's case, the value of the company's tax experts is seen through the exceptional services they provide their clients. H&R Block manages tax preparations services across more than 1,200 offices across Canada. The company's headquarters is in Calgary, Alberta, and it has had experience with Canadian tax returns for over 50 years.

What makes the organization successful and sustainable is its ability to see trends in its industry and act on them. There are approximately 11 million do-it-yourself tax filers among the 28 million Canadians tax filers. As technology helps enable the process of tax filing, it is important for H&R Block to provide services that offer perceived benefits in a technology-rich environment.

Todd McCallum, vice president, digital and business development, encapsulates the strategy. "Our 100% free guarantee is now available to users of our online and download tax software. We believe if Canadians want to file their own taxes—whether doing them online or with downloadable desktop software—they should be able to do so for free. And while there are other programs that claim to be free, we believe we are the only provider in Canada whose free is 100 percent guaranteed across all provinces, in English and French."

By providing free online tax software, H&R Block provides a service to do-it-yourselfers who believe they can complete their taxes on their own. In addition to the free service

H&R Block helps Canadian tax filers through over 1,200 offices across the country.
Used by permission of H&R Block

are options for do-it-yourselfers that include having H&R Block tax experts review the returns prior to filing. H&R Block has thus enhanced the value of tax experts by showcasing the perceived benefits for Canadians that include the benefit of potential for more accurate and better returns. ●

### Questions

1. Given your experience with taxes and your stage in life, would you choose H&R Block's free online software or tax preparation service? Why?

2. Can you think of a product in a different industry that may offer a service for free in order to increase the value of the product?

---

In a survey of home-furnishing buyers, 84 percent agreed with the statement, "The higher the price, the higher the quality." In turn, firms may use high prices to signify high quality.[4] For example, Kohler introduced a walk-in bathtub that is safer for children and the elderly. Although priced higher than conventional step-in bathtubs, it has proven very successful because buyers are willing to pay more for what they perceive as the benefit of extra safety. The Marketing NewsFlash box, "Highlighting the Value of Services," discusses how H&R Block quantifies the services it provides to Canadian tax filers.[5]

## PRICE IN THE MARKETING MIX

Pricing is a critical decision made by a marketing executive because price has a direct effect on a firm's

> *Pricing decisions influence both total revenue (sales) and total cost, which makes pricing one of the most important decisions marketing executives face.*

**profit equation**
Profit = total revenue − total cost.

profits. This is apparent from a firm's **profit equation:**

Profit = Total revenue − Total cost
= (Unit price × Quality sold)
− Total cost

What makes this relationship even more complicated is that price affects the quantity sold, as illustrated with demand curves later in this chapter, because the quantity sold sometimes affects a firm's costs because of efficiency of production, price also indirectly affects costs. Thus, pricing decisions influence both total revenue (sales) and total cost, which makes pricing one of the most important decisions marketing executives face.

# GENERAL PRICING APPROACHES

**LO 2**  A key to a marketing manager's setting a final price for a product is to find an "approximate price level" to use as a reasonable starting point. Four common approaches to helping find this approximate price level are demand-oriented, cost-oriented, profit-oriented, and competition-oriented approaches (see Figure 9–2). Although

these approaches are discussed separately below, some of them overlap, and an effective marketing manager will consider several in searching for an approximate price level.

# DEMAND-ORIENTED APPROACHES

Demand-oriented approaches emphasize factors underlying expected customer tastes and preferences more than such factors as cost, profit, and competition when selecting a price level.

**Skimming Pricing**  A firm introducing a new product can use *skimming pricing,* setting the highest initial price that those customers really desiring the product are willing to pay. These customers are not very price-sensitive because they weigh the new product's price, quality, and ability to satisfy their needs against the same characteristics of substitutes. As the demand of these customers is satisfied, the firm lowers the price to attract a more price-sensitive segment. Thus, skimming pricing gets its name from skimming successive layers of "cream," or customer segments, as prices are lowered in a series of steps.

In early 2003, many manufacturers of flat-screen TVs were pricing them at about $5,000 and using skimming pricing because many prospective customers were willing to buy the product immediately at the high price. Generally, prices of flat-screen TVs have dropped over time; however, retailers of TVs featuring new technology or larger screens continue to use skimming pricing.

**Penetration Pricing**  Setting a lower, more affordable, initial price on a new product to appeal immediately to the mass market is *penetration pricing,* the exact opposite of skimming pricing. This

### Figure 9–2
Four approaches for selecting an approximate price level

| Demand-oriented approaches | Cost-oriented approaches | Profit-oriented approaches | Competition-oriented approaches |
|---|---|---|---|
| • Skimming | • Standard markup | • Target profit | • Customary |
| • Penetration | • Cost-plus | • Target return on sales | • Above, at, or below market |
| • Prestige | | • Target return on investment | • Loss leader |
| • Odd-even | | | |
| • Target | | | |
| • Bundle | | | |
| • Yield management | | | |

strategy makes sense when consumers are price-sensitive; Nintendo consciously chose a penetration strategy when it introduced the Nintendo Wii, its popular video game console. It continues to use the strategy with Nintendo Wii U.

In addition to offering the potential to build sales, market share, and profits, penetration pricing discourages competitors from entering the market because the profit margin is relatively low. Furthermore, if the costs to produce drop because of the accumulated volume, competitors that enter the market will face higher unit costs, at least until their volume catches up with the early entrant. Walmart comes to mind when one thinks about penetration pricing. The same holds true for the very successful chain Dollarama, which is constantly increasing its number of stores in Canada.

In some situations, penetration pricing may follow skimming pricing. A company might price a product high in the early stages of the product life cycle to attract price-insensitive consumers. After the company has earned back the money spent on research and development and introductory promotions, it uses penetration pricing in the later stages of the product life cycle to appeal to a broader segment of the population and increase market share.[6]

**Prestige Pricing** Although consumers tend to buy more of a product when the price is lower, sometimes the reverse is true. If consumers are using price as a measure of the quality of an item, a company runs the risk of appearing to offer a low-quality product if it sets the price below a certain point. *Prestige pricing* involves setting a high price so that quality- or

Nintendo used penetration-pricing strategy to introduce its Wii video game console and its Wii U home console (shown here), and its Nintendo Switch.

Kazuhiro Nogi/AFP/Getty Images

status-conscious consumers are attracted to the product and buy it. Rolls-Royce cars, Chanel perfume, and Cartier jewellery have an element of prestige pricing in them and may not sell as well at lower prices than at higher ones.[7]

The higher the price of a prestige product, the greater the status associated with it and the greater its exclusivity, because fewer people can afford to buy it. Unlike products such as flat-panel TVs, which have decreased in price over the product life cycle, prices of prestige products remain high throughout the product life cycle.

An example of prestige pricing is the All Day Heels® collection of women's high-heeled shoes developed by Canadian retailer Ron White. This fashionable line of women's shoes combines elegance as well as comfort. The All Day Heels collection is set at a high price that matches its superior quality. The shoes provide arch support, built-in cushioning materials, and thin lightweight insoles made of Poron, a flexible high-tech elastic polymer developed by NASA.

**Price Lining** Often, a firm that is selling not just a single product but a line of products may price them at a number of different specific pricing points, which is called *price lining*. For example, a discount department store manager may price a line of women's dresses at $59, $79, and $99. In some instances, all the items may be purchased at the same cost and then marked up to different percentages to achieve these price points, based on colour, style, and expected demand. In other instances, manufacturers design products for different price points, and retailers apply approximately the same markup percentages to achieve the three price points offered to consumers.

**Odd-Even Pricing** If you are in hardware store, you may see a mitre saw for $399.99. In a grocery store, you may find Windex glass cleaner for $2.97. These firms are using *odd-even pricing*, which involves setting prices a few dollars or cents under an even number. The presumption is that consumers see the mitre saw as priced at "something over $300" rather than "about $400." The effect this strategy has is psychological: $399.99 *feels* significantly lower than $400—even though there is only one cent difference. There is some evidence to suggest this does work. However, research suggests that overuse of odd-ending prices tends to mute its effect on demand.[8]

**Target Pricing** Manufacturers will sometimes estimate the price that the ultimate consumer would be willing to pay for a product. They then work backward through markups taken by retailers and wholesalers to determine what price they can charge for the product. This practice, called *target pricing*, results in the manufacturer deliberately adjusting the composition and features of a product to achieve the target price to consumers.

### Bundle Pricing
A frequently used demand-oriented pricing practice is *bundle pricing*, which is the marketing of two or more products in a single "package" price. For example, Air Canada offers vacation packages that include airfare, car rental, and hotel. Bundle pricing is based on the idea that consumers value the package more than the individual items. This is due to benefits received from not having to make separate purchases as well as increased satisfaction from one item in the presence of another. Bundle pricing often provides a lower total cost to buyers and lower marketing costs to sellers.[9]

### Yield Management Pricing
Have you ever been on an airplane and discovered the person next to you paid a lower price for her ticket than you paid? Annoying, isn't it? But what you observed is *yield management pricing,* the charging of different prices to maximize revenue for a set amount of capacity at any given time.[10] Airlines, hotels, and car rental firms engage in capacity management by varying prices based on time, day, week, or season to match demand and supply.

## ② COST-ORIENTED APPROACHES

With cost-oriented approaches, a price is more affected by the cost side of the pricing problem than the demand side. Price is set by looking at the production and marketing costs and then adding enough to cover direct expenses, overhead, and profit. The chapter-opening vignette about Be Sweet Inc. highlights the importance of managing production and marketing costs.

### Standard Markup Pricing
In order to make a profit, firms sell their products at a price that exceeds their costs of producing or sourcing the items and the costs of marketing them. Conventionally, the difference between the selling price of an item and its cost is referred to as the **markup**, and this is normally expressed as a percentage. Markup is also often referred to as gross margin.

**markup**
The difference between selling price and cost, usually expressed as a percentage of cost.

Airlines use yield management pricing to help fill empty seats.

© AFP/Getty Images

Manufacturers commonly express markup as a percentage of cost, which is the difference between selling price and cost, divided by cost. This is also referred to as *standard markup.* Manufacturers use this approach because they are concerned most of the time with costs.

Parties who buy and resell products—for example, wholesalers and retailers—are nearly always dealing with selling prices. They often express markup as a percentage of price, which is the difference between selling price and cost, divided by the selling price. Using the same markup percentage for both of the above approaches will result in a different selling price (see the example in Figure 9–3).

Consider the example of a product that is produced by a manufacturer and sold to a wholesaler, who in turn

### Figure 9–3
Markup examples

| Markup Table Based on Selling Price | | |
|---|---|---|
| | **$** | **%** |
| Selling price | $75.00 | 100%* |
| − (minus) Cost | $60.00 | 80% |
| = (equals) Markup | $15.00 | 20% |

\* Price is always 100 percent when markup is relative to price.

| Markup Table Based on Cost | | |
|---|---|---|
| | **$** | **%** |
| Selling price | $72.00 | 120% |
| − (minus) Cost | $60.00 | 100%** |
| = (equals) Markup | $12.00 | 20% |

\*\* Cost is always 100 percent when markup is relative to cost.

sells it to a retailer, who then sells it to a consumer. The product will be subjected to a series of markups as shown below:

| | |
|---|---|
| **Manufacturer's cost:** | **$50.00** |
| Markup % (based on manufacturer's cost): | 40% |
| Markup $: | $20.00 |
| **Selling price to wholesaler:** | **$70.00** |
| **Wholesaler cost:** | **$70.00** |
| Markup % (based on selling price to retailer): | 15% |
| Markup $: | $12.35 |
| **Selling price to retailer:** | **$82.35** |
| **Retailer cost:** | **$82.35** |
| Markup % (based on retailer selling price): | 35% |
| Markup $: | $44.34 |
| **Retailer selling price:** | **$126.69** |

This may surprise you to find out that a product costing $50 to produce can end up costing a consumer more than twice that much when bought at a retailer, but this is not unusual. It is important to remember that markup is necessary at each stage so that companies involved can cover their costs of purchasing the item, can pay to market it to the next stage in the distribution channel, and can generate some profit. The markups shown would be representative of some items such as designer furniture.

This percentage markup varies depending on the type of retail store (such as furniture, clothing, or grocery) and on the product involved. High-volume products usually have smaller markups than do low-volume products. Supermarkets such as Loblaws and Sobeys mark up staple items such as sugar, flour, and dairy products 10 to 25 percent, whereas they mark up discretionary items such as snack foods and candy 25 to 47 percent. These markups must cover all expenses of the store, pay for overhead costs, and contribute something to profits. For supermarkets, these markups, which may appear very large, can result in only a 1 percent profit on sales revenue.

**Cost-Plus Pricing** Many manufacturers, professional services, and construction firms use a variation of standard markup pricing. *Cost-plus pricing* involves summing the total unit cost of providing a product or service and adding a specific amount to the cost to arrive at a price. Cost-plus pricing is the most commonly used method to set prices for business products.[11] Increasingly, however, this method is finding favour among business-to-business marketers in the service sector. For example, the rising cost of legal fees has prompted some law firms to adopt

a cost-plus pricing approach. Rather than billing business clients on an hourly basis, lawyers and their clients agree on a fixed fee based on expected costs plus a profit for the law firm. Many advertising agencies now use this approach. Here, the client agrees to pay the agency a fee based on the cost of its work plus some agreed-on profit.[12]

# PROFIT-ORIENTED APPROACHES

A company may choose to balance both revenues and costs to set price using profit-oriented approaches. These might involve either setting a target of a specific dollar volume of profit or expressing this target profit as a percentage of sales or investment.

**Target Profit Pricing** When a firm sets an annual target of a specific dollar amount of profit, this is called *target profit pricing.* For example, if you owned a picture frame store and wanted to achieve a target profit of $7,000 in the coming year, how much would you need to charge for each frame? Because profit depends on revenues and costs, you would have to know your costs and then estimate how many frames you would sell. Let's assume, based on sales in previous years, you expect to frame 1,000 pictures next year. The cost of your time and materials to frame an average picture is $22, while your overhead expenses (rent, manager salaries, and so on) are $26,000. Finally, your goal is to achieve a profit of $7,000. How do you calculate your price per picture?

$$\text{Profit} = \text{Total revenue} - \text{Total costs}$$
$$= (\text{Pictures sold} \times \text{Price/picture})$$
$$- [(\text{Cost/picture} \times \text{Pictures sold})$$
$$+ \text{overhead cost}]$$

Solving for price per picture, the equation becomes:

$$\text{Price/picture} = \frac{\text{Profit} + [(\text{Cost/picture} \times \text{Pictures sold}) + \text{overhead costs}]}{\text{Pictures sold}}$$

$$= \frac{\$7,000 + [(\$22 \times 1,000) + \$26,000]}{1,000}$$

$$= \frac{\$7,000 + \$48,000}{1,000}$$

$$= \$55 \text{ per picture}$$

Clearly, this pricing method depends on an accurate estimate of demand. Because demand is often difficult to predict, this method has the potential for disaster if the estimate is too high. Generally, a target profit pricing strategy is best for firms offering new or unique products, without a lot of competition. What if other frame stores in your area were charging $40 per framed picture? As a marketing manager, you'd have to offer increased customer value with your more expensive frames, lower your costs, or settle for less profit.

### Target Return-on-Sales Pricing

Firms such as supermarkets often use *target return-on-sales pricing* to set prices that will give them a profit that is a specified percentage—say, 1 percent—of the sales volume. This pricing method is often used because of the difficulty in establishing a benchmark of sales or investment to show how much of a firm's effort is needed to achieve the target.

### Target Return-on-Investment Pricing

Firms such as General Motors and many public utilities use *target return-on-investment pricing* to set prices to achieve a return-on-investment (ROI) target, such as a percentage that is mandated by its board of directors or regulators. For example, a hydro utility may decide to seek 10 percent ROI. If its investment in plant and equipment is $50 million, it would need to set the price of hydro to its customers at a level that results in $5 million a year in profits. The importance of achieving ROI estimates will be explored later in this chapter.

## 4 COMPETITION-ORIENTED APPROACHES

Rather than emphasize demand, cost, or profit factors, a company's approach may be based on an analysis of what competitors are doing.

> *Among watch manufacturers, Rolex takes pride in emphasizing that it makes one of the most expensive watches you can buy—a clear example of above-market pricing.*

### Customary Pricing

For some products where tradition, a standardized channel of distribution, or other competitive factors dictate the price, *customary pricing* is used. Candy bars offered through standard vending machines have a customary price of a few dollars, and a significant departure from this price may result in a loss of sales for the manufacturer. Hershey typically has changed the amount of chocolate in its candy bars depending on the price of raw chocolate, rather than vary its customary retail price so that it can continue selling through vending machines.

### Above-, at-, or below-Market Pricing

The "market price" of a product is what customers are generally willing to pay, not necessarily the price that the firm sets. For most products, it is difficult to identify a specific market price for a product or product class. Still, marketing managers often have a subjective feel for the competitors' price or the market price. Using this benchmark, they then may deliberately choose a strategy of *above-, at-, or below-market pricing*. The Focus on Ethics box, "Uber Controversial" discusses the impact of Uber's below-market pricing strategy.[13]

Among watch manufacturers, Rolex takes pride in emphasizing that it makes one of the most expensive watches you can buy—a clear example of above-market pricing. Manufacturers of national brands of clothing such as Christian Dior and retailers such as Holt Renfrew deliberately set higher prices for their products than those seen at The Bay.

**Items on a supermarket shelf may be priced using target return-on-sales pricing.**
MBI/Alamy Stock Photos

## Uber Controversial

Uber has been the target of protests and legal actions.

Michael Peake/Toronto Sun

When Travis Kalanick and Garrett Camp had trouble hailing a cab in 2008, their experience led to an idea that evolved into a transportation network company. Today, Uber offers a number of services that challenge the taxi industry. One of its services, UberX, offers low-cost options for reaching destinations. By linking individuals that need a ride with individuals that can offer a ride, Uber created an opportunity to avoid the issues Kalanick and Camp had years ago.

Uber fills a need and creates an experience in our busy, overscheduled lives. In order to help, consumers find a ride at the touch of an app, Uber requires satisfactory background checks as well as other criteria for its drivers. Uber imposes specific requirements on the vehicles in its fleet, but does not own any of the vehicles. This model allows Uber to offer rides to consumers at significantly competitive prices to taxi drivers.

Uber is available in Ontario, Quebec, and Alberta, and has been a target for protests and legal actions around the world. In Toronto, the UberX was legally able to operate in early 2016. This decision followed a controversial debate that lasted for months. Toronto City Council reduced regulations for taxis while asking Uber to raise its base fare.

The ability to operate a taxi cab is limited to individuals that own licences. Taxi licences are so coveted that they are passed on from generation to generation. However, when UberX was introduced in Toronto, the price competition that arose created concerns. Taxi licences in Toronto fell from $360,000 to below $100,000 in 2014.

Because of the disparity between what Uber charged and what Toronto taxi drivers traditionally charged, Toronto City Council had to pass certain rules to create a more fair, competitive landscape. The rules included compensation for taxi-plate owners who were impacted in a negative way by Uber. ●

### Questions

1. What competition-oriented approach pricing strategy did Uber employ to win market share in the Toronto market?

2. Is Uber's pricing approach fair in your opinion? Why or why not?

3. Predatory pricing is a key concern for the Competition Bureau. Figure 9–10 highlights four deceptive pricing practices. Which of the four do you feel is the most unethical and unlawful? Give reasons.

---

Large mass-merchandise chains such as Hudson's Bay generally use at-market pricing. These chains are often seen as establishing the going market price in the minds of their competitors. They also provide a reference price for competitors that use above- and below-market pricing.

In contrast, a number of firms use below-market pricing. Walmart positions itself this way. Manufacturers of generic products and retailers that offer their own private brands of products ranging from peanut butter to shampoo deliberately set prices for these products about 8 to 10 percent below the prices of nationally branded competitive products such as Skippy peanut butter or Pantene Pro-V shampoo.

**Loss-Leader Pricing** Retailers sometimes deliberately sell commonly used products, such as paper towels, soft drinks, and facial tissues, at very low prices to attract consumers who, the retailer hopes, will also buy other, regularly priced merchandise. The downside to loss-leader pricing is that some consumers move from store to store, making purchases only on those products that are loss leaders. This purchasing pattern, called

Rolex watches are priced above market.

© Lertsnim/Dreamstime.com/GetStock.com

Some video game consoles may be sold at a loss in order to create profit from the video games.

charnsitr/Shutterstock.com

cherry-picking, effectively foils the strategy underlying loss-leader pricing—to attract customers who will also buy products with healthier profit margins. For example, video game consoles may be sold at a loss to create the opportunity to profit from high-margin video games.

### ask YOURSELF

1. What products and brands would consider prestige pricing?
2. What is the difference between skimming and penetration pricing?
3. What is odd-even pricing?

# ESTIMATING DEMAND AND REVENUE

**LO 3** Creating the correct price for a product begins the process of forecasting. With the product's price known, marketers try to determine the extent of customer demand for it given their marketing efforts and the efforts of their competitors. Once an estimate for demand is known, marketing executives must translate this information to an estimate of revenues the firm expects to receive.

## THE IMPORTANCE OF ACCURATE FORECASTING

The forecasts created by the marketing department impact decisions made in other areas of an organization, including production and finance. Inaccurate information and poor estimates can be detrimental to the profitability of a marketing campaign. Similar to market research, both quantitative and qualitative analysis are used to make projections for an organization. Still, a forecast is still an estimate, so given the importance of the estimate, research continues to identify methodologies that can help marketers forecast more accurately.[14]

**Forecasting Methods** There are various methods that can be used to forecast. For our introductory purposes, consider the four broad categories of qualitative methods, regression methods, multiple equation methods, and time-series methods. Qualitative methods involve market experts coming to consensus using non-quantitative means to achieve projections. Regression methods link the forecast to a number of other variables through an equation. Multiple equations related to one another can also be used to forecast. Finally, time-series methods assume that the variable being forecast is affected by time.[15]

**Profit and Loss** Accurate profit and loss statements help organizations measure financial performance. The statement summarizes the revenues, costs, and expenditures outlined in a particular time frame and helps organizations project their ability for achieving future cash flow. For marketers, it is one of the best tools to gauge the success of a given marketing campaign or initiative.[16]

**Return on Investment (ROI)** With profit and loss capturing the performance of a given campaign, return on investment (ROI), or return on marketing investment (ROMI), evaluates the dollars invested in the initiative. When investing in a marketing campaign, marketers are essentially "risking" capital to achieve a desired result. The profit achieved from their initiatives in comparison to what was invested results in the return on marketing investment. Since this model assumes that an infinite number of customers are available to the firm, additional measures such as return on customer (ROC) are being explored to help marketing departments measure campaigns more accurately.[17]

$$\text{return on investment (\%)} = \frac{(\text{gain attributable to investment} - \text{cost of investment})}{\text{cost of investment}}$$

If a marketing investment of $10,000 in additional advertising and promotion was directly related to an increase in profits of $20,000, then the return on investment would be 100 percent.

$$\text{return on investment} = \frac{(\$20,000 - \$10,000)}{(\$10,000)} = 100\%$$

# FUNDAMENTALS OF ESTIMATING DEMAND

Demand for a product or service can be estimated in different ways. An organization can study the marketplace by reviewing historical results from its sales and its competitors' sales. An organization can also conduct tests to gauge the demand of its product. In 1986, *Newsweek* decided to conduct a pricing experiment at newsstands in 11 cities. In one city, newsstand buyers paid $2.25. In five other cities, newsstand buyers paid the regular $2.00 price. In another city, the price was $1.50, and in the remaining four cities it was only $1.00. By comparison, the regular newsstand price for a competing magazine, *Time,* was $1.95. Why did *Newsweek* conduct the experiment? According to a *Newsweek* executive, "We wanted to figure out what the demand curve for our magazine at the newsstand is."[18]

Unfortunately, forecasting is challenging as the marketplace for different products and services continues to change. In December 2012, *Newsweek* published its last print edition and is now under new management with goals to grow the brand in the digital age.[19]

## The Demand Curve

A **demand curve** shows the number of products that will be sold at a given price. Demand curve D1 in Figure 9–4A shows the newsstand demand for *Newsweek* under the pricing conditions when it still offered a print version. Note that as price falls, more people decide to buy and unit sales increase. But price is not the complete story in estimating demand. Economists emphasize three other key factors:

The last print issue of *Newsweek* was due to laws of demand.
© Kristoffer Tripplaar/Alamy Stock Photo

1. *Consumer tastes:* These depend on many factors, such as demographics, culture, and technology. Because consumer tastes can change quickly, up-to-date marketing research is essential. For example, although older readers prefer paper books, research finds it is easier for them to read from electronic tablets.[20]

2. *Price and availability of similar products:* The laws of demand work for one's competitors, too. Consider *Newsweek* in its print format again. If the price of *Time* magazine falls, more people will buy it. Fewer people will buy *Newsweek* since *Time*

> **demand curve**
> Graph relating quantity sold and price, which shows how many units will be sold at a given price.

## Figure 9–4
Illustrative demand curves for *Newsweek*

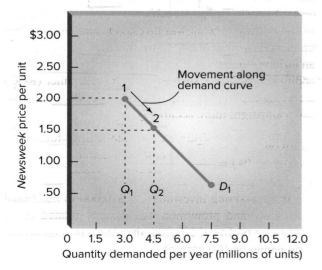

**A** Demand curve under initial conditions

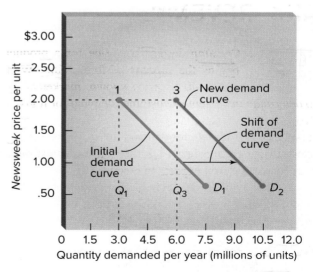

**B** Shift in the demand curve with different conditions

## marketing NewsFlash

# Zipping Wallets through Car Sharing

As gasoline prices and traffic volumes continue to rise, a number of Canadians have become members of Zipcar and other car-sharing services such as Turo. Car sharing has enjoyed rapid growth in recent years, and this trend has received attention from top automakers such as General Motors, which predicts 30 million people will use car sharing over the next ten years.

In an interview in 2010, David Zhao, an automotive research analyst with Frost & Sullivan, said it was a wake-up call for the automakers. "Once that population of shared vehicles gets bigger, the impact on the car market will become more serious," said Zhao, who published a report on car sharing. As of January 2015, Canada had 20 car-sharing services with more than 336,000 members and more than 5,200 vehicles. "It's a trend that will happen and vehicle manufacturers need to carefully gauge the potential impact on their total sales," Zhao concluded.

GM looked at car sharing as an opportunity rather than a threat and launched its car-sharing service, Maven, in 2016. After launching in Ann Arbor, Michigan, Maven is targeting Chicago, Boston, and Washington, D.C. for its additional cities.

Kevin McLaughlin, founder and president of AutoShare, suggested

as big cities improve public transit, as the cost of car ownership rises, and as young people rely more on technologies to connect and socialize, buying a car is becoming less of a priority. McLaughlin predicted that the number of Torontonians using car-sharing services would increase to over 20,000. In 2014, AutoShare, which operated only in Toronto, with 10,000 members and a fleet of about 210 cars representing 13 different models, from minivans to Mini Coopers to hybrids, was purchased by Enterprise Rent-A-Car Canada. The new company, Enterprise Car Share, expanded beyond Toronto.

Promoting car sharing also reduces air pollution and greenhouse-gas emissions. It is estimated that car-share members drive 31 percent less than they would if they owned their own vehicle. A consumer who owns a car wants to get as much use out of it as possible. Faced with the option of driving a few blocks, walking, or taking transit, most people hop in the car. Paying by the hour from a car-sharing company means that a consumer makes every trip a financial calculation and forces consideration of other options. The pay-as-you-go model encourages conservation every time, whether it's applied to mobile phone minutes, hydro use, or water consumption.

Another player in the car-sharing market is Shelby Clark, a former

Zipcar memberships help price-conscious consumers save money.
© Ulana Switucha/Alamy Stock Photo

Zipcar member. The Harvard MBA grad launched his own company, which recently rebranded as Turo. A pioneer in "peer-to-peer" car sharing, Turo appeals to a person who owns a car but doesn't use it very often. The individual signs up to Turo and offers to let other members drive his or her car for an hourly fee. Essentially, members rent out their cars. The Boston-based Turo maintains an online reservation system, provides the insurance, does the background checks, confirms that a safety inspection has been done, and acts as a payment clearinghouse. In return, it takes a 15 percent cut of the action. ●

## Questions

1. What do you see as the main benefits in a car-sharing service?

2. Do you feel car-sharing popularity will continue to increase or start to decrease in the next few years? Give reasons.

---

is considered by economists to be a substitute for *Newsweek*. In 2012, other online magazines were considered substitutes, so if their prices fell or their availability increased, the demand for a product (*Newsweek* magazine, in this case) would fall. The result was *Newsweek* magazine moving online.

3. *Consumer income:* In general, as real consumer income (allowing for inflation) increases, demand for a product also increases. More disposable income allows for additional purchases that are not

necessarily necessities. In 2015, Canada's inflation rate was 1.5 percent.

## marketing TIP

*"The key is to minimize the fixed costs associated with your business. By keeping your overhead low, your product sales can start contributing to your profits once you cross your break-even threshold."*

– Mario Fleury, co-founder, Be Sweet Inc.

The first of these two factors influences what consumers *want* to buy, and the third affects what they can buy. Along with price, these are often called *demand factors*, or factors that determine consumers' willingness and ability to pay for goods and services. It is often very difficult to estimate demand for new products, especially because consumer likes and dislikes are often so difficult to read clearly. (See the Marketing NewsFlash box, "Zipping Wallets through Car Sharing," to find out how these factors are impacting demand for owning a car.)[21]

### Movement along versus Shift of a Demand Curve

Demand curve D1 in Figure 9–4A shows that as the price is lowered from $2.00 to $1.50, the quantity demanded increases from 3 million (Q1) to 4.5 million (Q2) units per year. This is an example of a *movement along a demand curve* and assumes that other factors (consumer tastes, price and availability of substitutes, and consumer income) remain unchanged.

What if some of these factors change? For example, if advertising causes more people to want *Newsweek*, newsstand distribution is increased, or if consumer incomes rise, then the demand increases. Now the original curve, D1 (the blue line in Figure 9–4B), no longer represents the demand; a new curve must be drawn (D2). Economists call this a *shift in the demand curve*—in this case, a shift to the right, from D1 to D2. This increased demand means that more *Newsweek* magazines are wanted for a given price: At a price of $2, the demand is 6 million units per year (Q3) on D2 rather than 3 million units per year (Q1) on D1.

While print magazine were still in demand, what price did *Newsweek* select after conducting its experiment? It kept the price at $2.00. However, through expanded newsstand distribution and more aggressive advertising, *Newsweek* was later able to shift its demand curve to the right and charge a price of $2.50 without affecting its newsstand volume.

### Price Elasticity of Demand

Marketing managers must also pay attention to *price elasticity*, a key consideration related to the product's demand curve. Price elasticity refers to how sensitive consumer demand and the firm's revenues are to changes in the product's price.

A product with *elastic demand* is one in which a slight decrease in price results in a relatively large increase in demand, or units sold. The reverse is also true: With elastic demand, a slight increase in price results in a relatively large decrease in demand. Marketing experiments on products that are price-sensitive, such as cola, coffee, and snack foods, show them often to have elastic demand. So marketing managers may cut prices to increase the demand, the units sold, and total revenue for one of these products, depending on what competitors' prices are. The demand for many consumer products is elastic—think jeans, DVDs, and car stereos.

One major factor influencing the elasticity of demand is the availability of substitute products. If consumers can easily find close substitutes for a good or service, the product's demand tends to be elastic.

In contrast, a product with *inelastic demand* means that slight increases or decreases in price will not significantly affect the demand, or units sold, for the product. Products and services considered as necessities, such as hydro or going to the dentist, usually have inelastic demand. What about gasoline for your car? Will an increase of a few cents per litre cause you to drive fewer kilometres and buy less gasoline? No? Then you're like millions of other consumers, which is why gasoline has inelastic demand. This means that an increase of a few cents per litre may have a relatively minor impact on the number of litres sold, and may actually increase the total revenue of the gasoline producer. Inelastic demand is usually a relatively short-term phenomenon. Consumers, when they are faced with high prices for something they have to have, will seek out an alternative, and/or producers will see an opportunity to develop a new product. A hybrid car is, in some ways, a producer's response to high gas prices. Or maybe you could learn to love the bus!

Another example of inelastic demand is when buyers are less price-sensitive when the product they are buying is unique or is high in quality and prestige. In this case, consumers perceive that the high price means more quality and the demand for that product will not suffer very much. In some cases, a higher price may result in higher sales, which results in the demand curve actually sloping upwards.

---

## Tipping Etiquette

| Restaurants | 15% on the total bill before tax 20% for exceptional service |
|---|---|
| Hairdressers, manicurists, aestheticians, and taxi drivers | 10% minimum is common |

**Source:** "Canada: Tipping & Etiquette," Trip Advisor, accessed at http://www.tripadvisor.com/Travel-g153339-s606/Canada:Tipping.And.Etiquette.html.

**total revenue**
Total money received from the sale of a product.

**total cost**
Total expenses incurred by a firm in producing and marketing a product; total cost is the sum of fixed cost and variable costs.

**fixed cost**
Firm's expenses that are stable and do not change with the quantity of product that is produced and sold.

**variable cost**
Sum of the expenses of the firm that vary directly with the quantity of products that is produced and sold.

The ability to access product information online has changed the elasticity of demand for some products. In the past, a consumer's choice when considering buying a product was limited to the number of bricks-and-mortar stores available. Now, there are many more choices of suppliers to choose from. The large number of suppliers competing with each other has led to lower prices on products that were once available only in stores. The availability of different suppliers online combines to create more products with elastic demand.

## FUNDAMENTALS OF ESTIMATING REVENUE

While economists may talk about "demand curves," marketing executives are more likely to speak in terms of "revenues generated." Demand curves lead directly to an essential revenue concept critical to pricing decisions: **total revenue**. As summarized in Figure 9–5, total revenue (*TR*) equals the unit price (*P*) times the quantity sold (*Q*). Using this equation, let's recall our picture frame shop and assume our annual demand has improved so that we can set a price of $100 per picture and sell 400 pictures per year. So,

$$TR = P \times Q$$
$$= \$100 \times 400$$
$$= \$40,000$$

This combination of price and quantity sold annually will give us a total revenue of $40,000 per year. Is that good? Are you making money, making a profit? Total revenue is only part of the profit equation that we saw earlier:

Total profit = Total revenue − Total cost

The next section covers the other part of the profit equation: cost.

### Figure 9–5
Total revenue concept

Total revenue (TR) is the total money received from the sale of a product. If

    TR = Total revenue
    P  = Unit price of the product
    Q  = Quantity of the product sold
Then
    TR = P × Q

### ask YOURSELF

1. What is loss leader pricing?

2. What are three demand factors other than price that are used in estimating demand?

3. What is the difference between movement along a demand curve and a shift in a demand curve?

## DETERMINING COST, VOLUME, AND PROFIT RELATIONSHIPS

**LO 4** While revenues are the monies received by the firm from selling its products or services to customers, costs or expenses are the monies the firm pays out to its employees and suppliers. Marketing managers often use break-even analysis to relate revenues and costs, topics covered in this section.

## THE IMPORTANCE OF CONTROLLING COSTS

Understanding the role and behaviour of costs is critical for all marketing decisions, particularly pricing decisions. Many firms go bankrupt because their costs get out of control, causing their total costs to exceed their total revenues over an extended period of time. This is why sophisticated marketing managers make pricing decisions that balance both their revenues and costs. Three cost concepts are important in pricing decisions: **total cost**, **fixed cost**, and **variable cost** (Figure 9–6).

### Figure 9–6
Total cost concept

Fixed cost (FC) is the sum of the expenses of the firm that are stable and do not change with the quantity of product that is produced and sold. Examples of fixed costs are rent on the building, executive salaries, and insurance.

Variable cost (VC) is the sum of the expenses of the firm that vary directly with the quantity of product that is produced and sold. Examples are the direct labour and direct materials used in producing the product. Variable cost expressed on a per unit basis is called unit variable cost (UVC).

TC = FC + VC

Total cost (TC) is the total expense incurred by a firm in producing and marketing the product. Total cost is the sum of fixed cost and variable cost.

# BREAK-EVEN ANALYSIS

**LO 5** Marketing managers often employ an approach that considers cost, volume, and profit relationships, based on the profit equation. **Break-even analysis** is a technique that analyzes the relationship between total revenue and total cost to determine profitability at various levels of output. The *break-even point (BEP)* is the quantity at which total revenue and total cost are equal. Profit comes from any units sold after the BEP has been reached. In terms of the definitions in Figure 9–6,

$$BEP_{Quantity} = \frac{Fixed\ cost}{Unit\ price - Unit\ variable\ cost}$$

**Calculating a Break-Even Point** Consider again your picture frame store. Suppose that you wish to identify how many pictures you must sell to cover your fixed cost at a given price. Let's assume demand for your framed pictures has increased, so the average price customers are willing to pay for each picture is $100. Also, suppose your fixed cost (*FC*) has grown to $28,000 (for real estate taxes, interest on a bank loan, and other fixed expenses) and unit variable cost (*UVC*) for a picture is now $30 (for labour, glass, frame, and matting). Your break-even quantity (BEP$_{Quantity}$) is 400 pictures, as follows:

$$BEP_{Quantity} = \frac{Fixed\ cost}{Unit\ price - Unit\ variable\ cost}$$

$$= \frac{\$28,000}{\$100 - \$30}$$

$$= 400\ pictures$$

The bolded row in Figure 9–7 shows that your break-even quantity at a price of $100 per picture is 400 pictures. At less than 400 pictures, your picture frame store incurs a loss, and at more than 400 pictures it makes a profit. Figure 9–7 also shows that if you could double your annual picture sales to 800, your store would make a profit of $28,000—the row shaded in brown in the figure.

Figure 9–8 shows a graphic presentation of the break-even analysis, called a *break-even chart.* It shows that total revenue and total cost intersect and are equal at a quantity of 400 pictures sold, which is the break-even point at which profit is exactly $0. You want to do better? If your frame store could double the quantity sold annually to 800 pictures, the graph in Figure 9–8 shows that you can earn an annual profit of $28,000, as shown by the row shaded in brown in Figure 9–7.

**break-even analysis**
Examines the relationship between total revenue and total cost to determine profitability at different levels of output.

# APPLICATIONS OF BREAK-EVEN ANALYSIS

Because of its simplicity, break-even analysis is used extensively in marketing, most frequently to study the impact on profit of changes in price, fixed cost, and variable cost. The mechanics of break-even analysis are the basis of the widely used electronic spreadsheets such as Microsoft Excel that permit managers to answer hypothetical "what if" questions about the effect of changes in price and cost on their profit.

## Figure 9–7
Calculating a break-even point for a picture frame store

| Quantity of pictures sold (Q) | Price per picture (P) | Total revenue (TR) = (P × Q) | Unit variable cost (UVC) | Total variable cost (TVC) = (UVC × Q) | Fixed cost (FC) | Total cost (TC) = (FC + TVC) | Profit = (TR − TC) |
|---|---|---|---|---|---|---|---|
| 0 | $100 | $0 | $30 | $0 | $28,000 | $28,000 | −$28,000 |
| 200 | 100 | 20,000 | 30 | 6,000 | 28,000 | 34,000 | −14,000 |
| 400 | 100 | 40,000 | 30 | 12,000 | 28,000 | 40,000 | 0 |
| 600 | 100 | 60,000 | 30 | 18,000 | 28,000 | 46,000 | 14,000 |
| 800 | 100 | 80,000 | 30 | 24,000 | 28,000 | 52,000 | 28,000 |
| 1,000 | 100 | 100,000 | 30 | 30,000 | 28,000 | 58,000 | 42,000 |
| 1,200 | 100 | 120,000 | 30 | 36,000 | 28,000 | 64,000 | 56,000 |

## Figure 9–8
Break-even analysis for a picture frame store

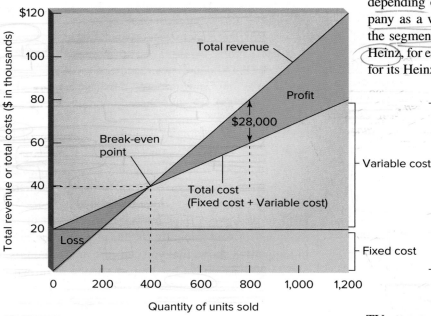

in setting objectives for marketing managers responsible for an individual brand. These objectives may change, depending on the financial position of the company as a whole, the success of its products, or the segments in which it is doing business. H. J. Heinz, for example, has specific pricing objectives for its Heinz ketchup brand that vary by country.

**Profit** Three different objectives relate to a firm's profit, which is often measured in terms of return on investment (ROI). These objectives have different implications for pricing strategy. One objective is *managing for long-run profits,* in which a company—such as many Japanese car or TV set manufacturers—gives up immediate profit in exchange for achieving a higher market share. Products are priced relatively low compared to their cost to develop, but the firm expects to make greater profits later because of its high market share.

A *maximizing current profit* objective, such as for a quarter or year, is common in many firms because the targets can be set and performance measured quickly. North American firms are sometimes criticized for this short-run orientation.

A third profit objective is a *target return* objective that occurs when a firm sets its price to achieve a profit goal (such as 20 percent for return on investment), usually determined by its board of directors. These three profit objectives have different implications for a firm's pricing objectives.

Another profit consideration for firms such as movie studios and manufacturers is to ensure that those firms in their channels of distribution make adequate profits. For example, Figure 9–9 shows where each dollar of your movie ticket goes. The 51 cents the movie studio gets must cover its profit plus the cost of making and marketing the movie. Although the studio would like more than 51 cents of your dollar, it settles for this amount to make sure theatres and distributors are satisfied and willing to handle its movies.

**Sales** As long as a firm's profit is high enough for it to remain in business, an objective may be to increase sales revenue, which will in turn lead to increases in market share and profit. Cutting the price on one product in a firm's line may increase its sales revenue but

### ask YOURSELF

1. **What is the difference between fixed costs and variable costs?**

2. **What is a break-even point?**

# PRICING OBJECTIVES AND CONSTRAINTS

**LO 6** With such a variety of alternative pricing strategies available, marketing managers must consider the pricing objectives and constraints that will impact their decisions. While pricing objectives frequently reflect corporate goals, pricing constraints often relate to conditions existing in the marketplace.

## IDENTIFYING PRICING OBJECTIVES

**pricing objectives**
Expectations that specify the role of price in an organization's marketing and strategic plans.

**Pricing objectives** specify the role of price in an organization's marketing and strategic plans. To the extent possible, these pricing objectives are carried to lower levels in the organization, such as

## Figure 9–9
Where each dollar of your movie ticket goes

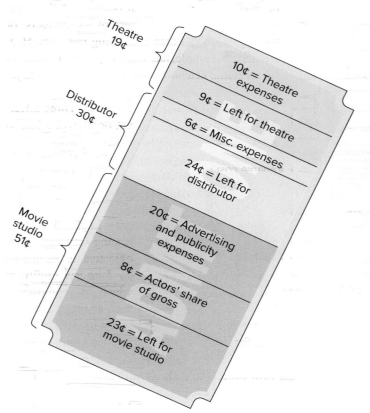

- 10¢ = Theatre expenses
- 9¢ = Left for theatre
- 6¢ = Misc. expenses
- 24¢ = Left for distributor
- 20¢ = Advertising and publicity expenses
- 8¢ = Actors' share of gross
- 23¢ = Left for movie studio

Theatre 19¢
Distributor 30¢
Movie studio 51¢

Francis Vachon/The Canadian Press

reduce those of related products. Objectives related to sales revenue or unit sales have the advantage of being translated easily into meaningful targets for marketing managers responsible for a product line or brand.

### Market Share
Market share is the ratio of the firm's sales to those of the industry (competitors plus the firm itself). Companies often pursue a market share objective when industry sales are relatively flat or declining. For example, the cola market is declining, but Coke wants to keep its market share by retaining its piece of a dwindling pie. Although increased market share is a primary goal of some firms, others see it as a means to increasing sales and profits.

Adopting a market share objective does not always imply low price. The lowest-priced brand rarely has the highest market share. Tropicana orange juice, French's mustard, and Heinz ketchup are market share leaders and are all premium-priced. Brands such as these retain their market share positions because they offer value to consumers.

### Volume
Many firms use volume, the quantity produced or sold, as a pricing objective. These firms often sell the same product at several different prices, at different times, or in different places in an attempt to match customer demand with the company's production capacity. Using volume as an objective can sometimes be misleading from a profit standpoint. Volume can be increased by using sales incentives (lowering prices, giving rebates, or offering lower interest rates). By doing this, the company chooses to lower profits in the short run to sell its product quickly. For example, a new health club might focus on getting a certain number of people to join by lowering its membership prices and accepting less profit, at first.

### Survival
In some instances, profits, sales, and market share are less important objectives of the firm than mere survival. Air Canada has struggled to attract passengers with low fares and aggressive promotions to improve the firm's cash flow. This pricing objective has helped Air Canada to stay alive in the competitive airline industry.

### Social Responsibility
A firm may forgo higher profit on sales and follow a pricing objective that recognizes its obligations to customers and society in general. Gerber supplies a specially formulated product free of charge to children who cannot tolerate foods based on cow's milk.

# IDENTIFYING PRICING CONSTRAINTS

Factors that limit the range of price a firm may set are **pricing constraints**. Consumer demand for the product clearly affects the price that can be charged. Other constraints on price vary from factors within the organization to competitive factors outside it.

## Demand for the Product Class, Product, and Brand

The number of potential buyers for a product class (cars), product (sports cars), and brand (Bugatti Veyron) clearly affects the price a seller can charge. So does whether the item is a luxury, like a Bugatti Veyron, or a necessity, like bread and a roof over your head.

## Newness of the Product: Stage in the Product Life Cycle

The newer the product and the earlier it is in its life cycle, the higher the price that can usually be charged. Consider the launch of the Apple iPad. With its new technology, Apple had no other direct competition at first, so it was possible to ask consumers to pay a high initial price for this innovative product.

Sometimes, such as when nostalgia or fad factors are present, prices may rise later in the product's life cycle. The legendary hockey jersey worn by Paul Henderson in the 1972 Summit Series was sold for over $1 million at an auction. Henderson was wearing the jersey when he scored the winning goal in Team Canada's emotional win over the Soviets.[22]

## Cost of Producing and Marketing the Product

In the long run, a firm's price must cover all the costs of producing and marketing a product. If the price doesn't cover these costs, the firm will fail; so in the long run, a firm's costs set a floor under its price.

## Competitors' Prices

When a firm sets its prices, an important consideration is the prices being charged by the competition. As we talked about previously, a firm has three choices. It can charge a higher price, the same price, or a lower price than its competitors. Each choice conveys a message

Canadian hockey legend Paul Henderson, who scored the game-winning goal during the 1972 Summit Series against the Soviet Union, holds his original 1972 Team Canada sweater.

Nathan Denette/The Canadian Press

to customers. For example, e-readers such as Amazon's Kindle and the Sony Reader were developed as single-function devices, meant solely for use as a reader. The iPad, on the other hand, is a multi-function appliance that allows the user to surf the Internet as well as use it as a reader. Because the e-readers made by Sony and Amazon have a limited use, they were forced to drop their prices dramatically when the iPad came on the scene.[23] Amazon has gone on to develop its own multi-function device, introducing the Kindle Fire in November 2011, which includes Internet, video, app, and gaming functionality to go along with its reader. Amazon's price for its Kindle Fire is significantly lower than the iPad, a strategy to reach consumers who are price-sensitive.

A high price signifies that the firm believes its offering represents a higher value in comparison to competing products—value being quality, brand image, benefits and unique features offering extra benefits, or something as simple as instant availability. Sony is known as a firm that typically prices higher than most of its competitors. Consumers wanting quality will pay a higher price.

Charging the same price as the competition means that the firm is relying on some aspect other than price to position and differentiate its products in the minds of customers—that differentiation may be a unique attribute, widespread availability, or an intensive marketing campaign. Thinking again of consumer electronics, Panasonic, JVC, and Sharp are examples of manufacturers whose prices are close for similar products. Consumers typically buy these brands on the basis of some unique attribute of the product, or because they prefer to deal with a specific retailer.

Lower prices can be a challenge, but many firms rely on this strategy. From the company standpoint, lower prices can mean lower profits on each sale, which may need to be offset by larger volume sales. In addition, larger volumes can result in production efficiencies and lower costs. Less well-known brands and some of the larger manufacturers such as RCA use this strategy. For consumers, the lower prices often mean forgoing some aspect such as quality or brand image.

The decision to charge a certain price is impacted by marketing and pricing objectives. If winning market share is an objective, lower prices may be the solution. If being perceived as the "best brand" is an objective, higher prices may be part of the answer. Being known as a *market leader* based on pricing is a title that could be ascribed to firms using either strategy.

Charging prices in line with the competition earns firms the title of *market follower*. This is a conscious choice of many smaller firms manufacturing and selling similar or often the same products. Emphasis is shifted away from price to some other aspect of the marketing mix.

There are occasions where other objectives override any consideration of competitor pricing, such as selling off discontinued models or time-sensitive items (summer-vacation packages, for example).

# LEGAL AND ETHICAL CONSIDERATIONS

Deciding on a final price is a complex process. In addition to the considerations we have just presented, there are laws and regulations that also play a role in the price decision. We will look at four of the most prominent considerations.

## Price Fixing
When competitors collaborate and conspire to set prices, they agree to increase, decrease, or stabilize a price for their benefit. This is called *price fixing*, and it is illegal—the *Competition Act* prohibits this practice. The *Competition Act* consists of federal regulations governing most business conduct in Canada.

Price fixing usually occurs where price is the most important factor in the marketing mix. Twelve global airlines that ran a cargo price-fixing cartel for years were hit with fines totalling $1.1 billion by European Union regulators. The European Commission slapped Air Canada with the third-smallest fine at $29.2 million. In Canada, Hershey Canada was fined $4 million in its role in a price-fixing chocolate cartel.[24]

## Price Discrimination
If different prices are charged to different customers for the same or very similar goods and the same terms, *price discrimination* has occurred. The *Competition Act* prohibits this, but in order for a firm to be charged with the offence, there has to be evidence of a "practice" of price discrimination—that is, that it is not just a one-time or occasional event.

## Deceptive Pricing
Price offers that mislead the consumer are considered *deceptive pricing*, and this is prohibited under the *Competition Act*. Figure 9–10 shows the most common deceptive pricing practices. Many companies across the country have been accused of deceptive pricing, but it can be difficult to police and the laws are hard to enforce. Often, regulators rely on the ethical standards of those making and publicizing pricing decisions. The Canadian Code of Advertising Standards provides guidelines for various aspects of promotion, and pricing is one of these; advertising industry members are expected to follow this Code and to self-regulate (ensure that they and their colleagues adhere to the Code).

## Figure 9–10
Most common deceptive pricing practices

| Deceptive Practice | Description |
| --- | --- |
| Bait and switch | A firm offers a very low price for a product (the bait), and when consumers come to purchase it, they are persuaded to buy a more expensive product (the switch). Uses techniques such as downgrading the advertised item or not having it in stock. |
| Bargains conditional on other purchases | A firm advertises "buy one, get one free" or "get two for the price of one." If the first items are sold at the regular price, this is legal. If the price for the first items is inflated for the offer, it is not. |
| Price comparisons | Advertising "retail value $100—our price $85" is deceptive if a substantial number of stores in the area are not using the $100 price—in other words, if it is not the "going price." Advertising "below manufacturer's suggested list price" is deceptive if no sales occur at the manufacturer's list price. Advertising that the price is reduced 50 percent is deceptive if the item was not offered for sale at the higher price for a substantial previous period of time. |
| Double ticketing | When more than one price tag is placed on an item, it must be sold at the lower price; this practice is not illegal, but the law requires that the lower price be charged. |

An example of deceptive pricing is menswear retailer Grafton-Fraser Inc. The retailer agreed to pay a $1.2 million penalty to settle an advertising case regarding misleading sale prices. The Competition Bureau found that Grafton-Fraser had significantly inflated the regular price of certain garments sold in its stores, resulting in an overstatement of the savings to consumers when these garments were on sale. The retailer joins other merchants, including Suzy Shier, Sears Canada Ltd., and Forzani Group Ltd., that the Competition Bureau found were inflating an item's regular price and thereby overstating the savings of the sale price. Grafton-Fraser, the bureau found, was tagging garments with both a regular and a sale price; however, the items did not sell "in any significant quantity or for any reasonable period of time at the regular price," the Bureau said. Grafton-Fraser runs stores across the country that operate under several names, among them Tip Top Tailors, George Richards Big & Tall, and Grafton & Co.[25]

**Predatory Pricing** Charging a very low price for a product with the intent of undercutting competitors and possibly driving them out of the market is called *predatory pricing*. After the competitors have been driven out, the offending firm raises its prices. If a company can genuinely operate more efficiently than others, and this lets them offer its products at a lower price, should this be classified as predatory pricing? No! It's not easy to prove that the intent of the lower price is to eliminate a competitor, and that the prices set are unreasonably and artificially low, so there are many more charges of predatory pricing than there are convictions.

## GLOBAL PRICING STRATEGY

Global companies face many challenges in determining a pricing strategy as part of their worldwide marketing effort. Individual countries, even those with free trade agreements, may place considerable competitive, political, and legal constraints on the pricing flexibility of global companies. For example, Walmart was told by German antitrust authorities that the prices in its stores were too low, relative to competitors, and faced a fine for violating the country's trade if the prices weren't raised![26]

Pricing too low or too high can have dire consequences. When prices appear too low in one country, companies can be charged with dumping, a practice subject to severe penalties and fines. Dumping occurs when a firm sells a product in a foreign country below its domestic price or below its actual cost. A recent trade dispute

involving U.S. apple growers and Mexico is a case in point. Mexican trade officials claimed that U.S. growers were selling their red and golden delicious apples in Mexico below the actual cost of production. They imposed a 101 percent tariff on U.S. apples, and a severe drop in U.S. apple exports to Mexico resulted. Later negotiations set a price floor on the price of U.S. apples sold to Mexico.[27]

When companies price their products very high in some countries but competitively in others, they face a grey market problem. A **grey market**, also called *parallel importing*, is a situation where products are sold through unauthorized channels of distribution. A grey market comes about when individuals buy products in a lower-priced country from a manufacturer's authorized retailer, ship them to higher-priced countries, and then sell them below the manufacturer's suggested retail price through unauthorized retailers. Many well-known products have been sold through grey markets, including Olympus cameras, Seiko watches, and Mercedes-Benz cars. Parallel channels are not strictly illegal in Canada, but there are mounting legal challenges to them. Parallel importing is legal in the United States. It is illegal in the European Union.[28]

### *ask* YOURSELF

1. *What is the difference between pricing objectives and pricing constraints?*

2. *Explain what bait and switch is and why it is an example of deceptive pricing.*

# SETTING A FINAL PRICE

**LO 7** The final price set by the marketing manager serves many functions. It must be high enough to cover the cost of providing the product *and* meet the objectives of the company. Yet it must be low enough that customers are willing to pay it. But not too low, or customers may think they're purchasing an inferior product. Confused? Setting price is one of the most difficult tasks the marketing manager faces, but four generalized steps are useful to follow.

## STEP 1: SELECT AN APPROXIMATE PRICE LEVEL

Before setting a final price, the marketing manager must understand the market environment, the features and

**dumping**
Occurs when a firm sells a product in a foreign country below its domestic prices or below its actual cost.

**grey market**
Situations where products are sold through unauthorized channels of distribution.

customer benefits of the particular product, and the goals of the firm. A balance must be struck between factors that might drive a price higher (such as a profit-oriented approach) and other forces (such as increased competition from substitutes) that may drive a price down. Marketing managers consider pricing objectives and constraints first, and then choose among the general pricing approaches—demand-, cost-, profit-, or competition-oriented—to arrive at an approximate price level. This price is then analyzed in terms of cost, volume, and profit relationships. Break-even analyses may be run at this point, and finally, if this approximate price level "works," it is time to take the next step: setting a specific list or quoted price.

## STEP 2: SET THE LIST OR QUOTED PRICE

A seller must decide whether to follow a one-price or flexible-price policy.

**One-Price Policy** A *one-price policy* involves setting one price for all buyers of a product or service. For example, when you buy a product at Walmart, you are offered the product at a single price. You can decide to buy it or not, but there is no variation of the price under the seller's one-price policy. Some retailers such as Dollarama married this policy with a below-market approach and used to sell mostly everything in their stores for $1! Dollarama has added more products at prices ranging from $1.25 to $4.

**Flexible-Price Policy** In contrast, a *flexible-price policy* involves setting different prices for products and services depending on individual buyers and purchase situations in light of demand, cost, and competitive factors.

Dollarama previously used a one-price policy.

Paul Chiasson/The Canadian Press

> *Is it any wonder that 60 percent of prospective car buyers dread negotiating the price?*

Dell Computer adopted flexible pricing as it continually adjusts prices in response to changes in its own costs, competitive pressures, and demand from its various personal computer segments (home, small business, corporate, and so on). "Our flexibility allows us to be [priced] different even within a day," says a Dell spokesperson.[29]

Flexible pricing is not without its critics because of its discriminatory potential. For example, car dealers have traditionally used flexible pricing on the basis of buyer-seller negotiations to agree on a final price. Is it any wonder that 60 percent of prospective car buyers dread negotiating the price?

## STEP 3: MAKE SPECIAL ADJUSTMENTS TO THE LIST OR QUOTED PRICE

**LO 8** When you pay $2 for a bag of M&Ms in a vending machine or receive a quoted price of $15,000 from a contractor to renovate a kitchen, the pricing sequence ends with the last step just described: setting the list or quoted price. But when you are a manufacturer of M&M candies and sell your product to dozens or hundreds of wholesalers and retailers in your channel of distribution, you may need to make a variety of special adjustments to the list or quoted price. Wholesalers also must adjust list or quoted prices they set for retailers. Three special adjustments to the list or quoted price are discounts, allowances, and geographical adjustments.

**Discounts** *Discounts* are reductions from list price that a seller gives a buyer as a reward for some activity of the buyer that is favourable to the seller. Four kinds of discounts are especially important in marketing strategy: quantity, seasonal, trade (functional), and cash.[30]

*Quantity discounts.* To encourage customers to buy larger quantities of a product, firms at all levels in the channel of distribution offer quantity discounts, which are reductions in unit costs for a larger order. For example, an instant photocopying service might set a price of 10 cents a copy for 1 to 24 copies, 9 cents a copy for 25 to 99, and 8 cents a copy for 100 or more. Because the photocopying service gets more of the buyer's business and has longer production runs that reduce its order-handling costs, it is willing to pass on some of the cost savings in the form of quantity discounts to the buyer.

- *Seasonal discounts:* To encourage buyers to stock inventory earlier than their normal demand would require, manufacturers often use seasonal discounts. A firm such as Toro that manufactures lawn mowers and snow blowers offers seasonal discounts to encourage wholesalers and retailers to stock up on lawn mowers in January and February and on snow blowers in July and August—months before the seasonal demand by ultimate consumers. This enables Toro to smooth out seasonal manufacturing peaks and troughs, thereby contributing to more-efficient production. It also rewards wholesalers and retailers for the risk they accept in assuming increased inventory carrying costs and gives them the benefit of having supplies in stock at the time they are wanted by customers.

- *Trade (functional) discounts:* To reward wholesalers and retailers for marketing functions they will perform in the future, a manufacturer often gives trade, or functional, discounts. These reductions off the list or base price are offered to resellers in the channel of distribution on the basis of where they are in the channel and the marketing activities they are expected to perform in the future.

  Traditional trade discounts have been established in various product lines such as hardware, food, and pharmaceutical items. Although the manufacturer may suggest trade discounts, the sellers are free to alter the discount schedule depending on their competitive situation. Suppose that a manufacturer quotes prices in the following form:

  List price − $100, less 30/10/5

  The first number in the percentage sequence (in this example, 30/10/5) always refers to the retail end of the channel, and the last number always refers to the wholesaler or jobber closest to the manufacturer

Toro uses seasonal discounts to stimulate consumer demand and smooth out seasonal manufacturing peaks and troughs.

Daniel Acker/Bloomberg via Getty Images

in the channel. The trade discounts are simply subtracted one at a time. This price quote shows that $100 is the manufacturer's suggested retail price:

- For the retailer, 30 percent of the suggested retail price ($100 × 0.3 = $30) is available to cover costs and provide a profit;

- Wholesalers closest to the retailer in the channel get 10 percent of their selling price ($70 × 0.1 = $7); and

- The final group of wholesalers in the channel (probably jobbers) that are closest to the manufacturer get 5 percent of their selling price ($63 × 0.05 = $3.15).

Thus, starting with the manufacturer's retail price and subtracting the three trade discounts shows that the manufacturer's selling price to the wholesaler or jobber closest to the manufacturer is $59.85 (see Figure 9–11).

- *Cash discounts:* To encourage retailers to pay their bills quickly, manufacturers offer them cash discounts. Suppose that a retailer receives a bill quoted at $1,000, 2/10 net 30. This means that the bill for the product is $1,000, but the retailer can take a two percent discount ($1,000 × 0.02 = $20) if payment is made within 10 days and send a cheque for $980. If the payment cannot be made within 10 days, the total amount of $1,000 is due within 30 days. It is usually understood by the buyer that an interest charge will be added after the first 30 days of free credit.

  Retailers provide cash discounts to consumers as well, to eliminate the cost of credit granted to consumers. These discounts take the form of discount-for-cash policies.

> Although the manufacturer may suggest trade discounts, the sellers are free to alter the discount schedule depending on their competitive situation.

**Figure 9–11**

How trade discounts work

**Allowances** Allowances—like discounts—are reductions from list or quoted prices to buyers for performing some activity.

- *Trade-in allowances:* A new car dealer can offset the list price of that new Toyota Camry by offering you a trade-in allowance of $500 for your old Honda. A trade-in allowance is a price reduction given when a used product is part of the payment on a new product. Trade-ins are an effective way to lower the price a buyer has to pay without formally reducing the list price.

- *Promotional allowances:* Sellers in the channel of distribution can qualify for promotional allowances for undertaking certain advertising or selling activities to promote a product. Various types of allowances include an actual cash payment or an extra amount of "free goods" (as with a free case of pizzas to a retailer for every dozen cases purchased). Frequently, a portion of these savings is passed on to the consumer by retailers.

**Geographical Adjustments** Geographical adjustments are made by manufacturers or even wholesalers to list or quoted prices to reflect the cost of transportation of the products from seller to buyer. The two general methods for quoting prices related to transportation costs are FOB origin pricing and uniform delivered pricing.

- *FOB origin pricing:* FOB means "free on board" some vehicle at some location, which means the seller pays the cost of loading the product onto the vehicle that is used (such as a barge, railroad car, or truck). FOB origin pricing usually involves the seller's naming the location of this loading as the seller's factory or warehouse (such as "FOB Montreal" or "FOB factory"). The title and ownership to the goods passes to the buyer at the point of loading, so the buyer becomes responsible for picking the specific mode of transportation, for all the transportation costs, and for subsequent handling of the product. Buyers furthest from the seller face the big disadvantage of paying the higher transportation costs.

- *Uniform delivered pricing:* When a uniform delivered pricing method is used, the price the seller quotes includes all transportation costs. It is quoted in a contract as "FOB buyer's location," and the seller selects the mode of transportation, pays the freight charges, and is responsible for any damage that may occur because the seller retains title to the goods until delivered to the buyer.

# STEP 4: MONITOR AND ADJUST PRICES

Rarely can a firm set a price and leave it at that. As you have learned, there are many constraints that affect setting prices, and the firm has objectives that it also takes into account. Things change both in the external business environment and within the firm itself; as a result, prices need to be reviewed and revised if necessary. A key activity is the monitoring of competitor activity, legislative changes, economic conditions, and—the ultimate measure—consumer demand! These factors, and their potential impact on the firm's ability to achieve its marketing goals, have to be examined and action taken when necessary.

**ask YOURSELF**

1. Why would a seller choose a flexible-price policy over a one-price policy?

2. What is the purpose of (a) quantity discounts and (b) promotional allowances?

# $29.95* student pricing.

## Keep more money in your pocket.

When you file with your taxes with H&R Block, you keep more money in your pocket. You'll also get great pricing, the best refund possible and a free SPC† card.

**For more information, speak to an H&R Block Tax Professional today.**

12345 Your Street
Enter City Name, Province
Office Phone: (123) 456-7890
Email: hrblock.12345@hrblock.ca

© H&R Block Canada, Inc.
* $29.95 valid for student tax preparation only. To qualify, student must present either (i) a T2202a documenting 4 or more months of full-time attendance at a college or university during the applicable tax year or (ii) a valid high school id card. Students pay $79.99 for Complex/Premier return. Expires 12/31/14. Valid only at participating locations.
†SPC Card available at participating locations in Canada only. Offers may vary, restrictions may apply. For full terms see www.spccard.ca

## H&R BLOCK®

hrblock.ca | 800-HRBLOCK (472-5625)

Used with permission of H&R Block

1. *What pricing strategies has H&R Block used in this advertisement?*

2. *How does the ad make you feel about working for or with this company?*

**LO 1** • Price is the money or other considerations exchanged for the ownership or use of a product or service.

• Price typically involves money and the amount exchanged can be different from the list or quoted price because of allowances and extra fees.

• When reviewing the perceived benefits of a good or service, price is used as an indicator of value by consumers.

**LO 2** • Four general approaches for finding an approximate price level for a product or service:

– Demand-oriented pricing approaches stress consumer demand and revenue implications of pricing and include eight types: skimming, penetration, prestige, price lining, odd-even, target, bundle, and yield management.

– Cost-oriented pricing approaches emphasize the cost aspects of pricing and include two types: standard and cost-plus pricing.

– Profit-oriented pricing approaches focus on a balance between revenues and costs to set a price and include three types: target profit, target return-on-sales, and target return-on-investment pricing.

– Competition-oriented pricing approaches emphasize what competitors or the marketplace are doing and include three types: customary; above-, at-, or below-market; and loss-leader pricing.

**LO 3** • A demand curve shows the maximum number of products consumers will buy at a given price and for a given set of (a) consumer tastes, (b) price and availability of other products, and (c) consumer income.

• The price elasticity of demand relates to the reaction of consumer demand and a firm's revenue when a price changes.

**LO 4** • Marketers need to understand the total revenue and total costs when considering pricing decisions as they will determine their ability to generate an appropriate profit.

**LO 5** • Break-even analysis shows the relationship between total revenue and total cost at various quantities of output for given conditions of price, fixed cost, and variable cost.

• The break-even point is where total revenue and total cost are equal.

**LO 6** • Pricing objectives, which specify the role of price in a firm's marketing strategy, may include pricing for profit, sales revenue, market share, unit sales, survival, or some socially responsible price level.

• Pricing constraints such as demand, product newness, costs, competitors, other products sold by the firm, and the type of competitive market restrict a firm's pricing range.

**LO 7** • In setting a final price, Step 1 is to set an approximate price level.

• Setting the list or quoted price is Step 2.

• Step 3 involves making special adjustments to prices through discounts and allowances.

• Finally, Step 4 requires marketers to monitor and adjust prices.

**LO 8** • Geographical adjustments to price reflect the cost of transportation.

• Organizations can reward buyers by offering discounts such as quantity discounts or seasonal discounts that also work in favour of the seller.

• When buyers perform an activity, they can sometimes receive allowances or reductions to listed or quoted prices.

*key terms and concepts...* **A REFRESHER**

break-even analysis
demand curve
dumping
fixed cost
grey market

markup
pricing constraints
pricing objectives
profit equation
total cost

total revenue
value
variable cost

**Pricing Your Services**   Review the Marketing NewsFlash box about H&R Block. Consider that you are the individual offering similar professional services and review the textbook section on break-even analysis. Determine how many hours you would have to work in order to break even if your annual fixed costs for your professional practice were $12,000 annually and variable costs for an hour of work were $25 dollars on average.

Effective marketing requires individuals with a variety of skill sets. Although creativity is an important skill in this discipline, the ability to analyze figures and data is critical in developing marketing strategy. Review this chapter's vignette about Be Sweet Inc. and the importance of key marketing calculations for developing an appropriate pricing strategy. In your class, work with a group to estimate the price of a Be Sweet honey-alternative product. Complete break-even analyses and return-on-investment calculations to see the impact of lowering the cost of ingredients from regular honey to Be Sweet Inc. to the manufacturing of baked goods requiring honey as an ingredient.

The Infographic from the Calgary Food Bank illustrates rising food prices. Consider other foods or products you have recently purchased and determine by what percentage their price has increased over the past 5, 10, and 20 years.

# Marketing Channels and Supply Chain

Consumers purchase goods and services at both bricks-and-mortar stores and via online e-commerce websites. Fulfillment of purchases—delivery to consumers—takes place through supply chain systems and marketing channels, which include logistics that are often unseen by the customer and sometimes taken for granted. However, efficient distribution is critical. Consumers satisfied in the delivery of their purchase offer directly influence a business's marketing and sales results.

© WildPlay Element Parks

Customer satisfaction comes from providing shoppers with what they need when they need it. Marketers are interested in ensuring that their distribution networks are organized and efficient, and in many cases, they want to strengthen long-term consumer value by optimizing their fulfillment experience.

Sometimes, meeting or exceeding customer needs isn't a straightforward process. Unique products and services often require marketers to consider extraordinary ways to execute and elevate their consumer experience. WildPlay Element Parks faces this challenge.

WildPlay is an expanding network of aerial challenge adventure parks with a mix of outdoor activity experiences (termed "Elements") that include aerial adventure courses, a bungy jump, primal swings, ziplines, and something called a "What's To Fear Jump." Founders Tom Benson and Gord Ross created the parks to share their 15 years of professional mountain-guiding experience with as wide a variety of people as possible. Their mission is to challenge people to push themselves beyond their self-imposed boundaries via thrilling aerial recreation activities located in areas that highlight and care for Mother Nature. The nature-based activities are delivered in a variety of environments in British Columbia and Ontario (and upcoming locations in the U.S.) that feature canyons and rocky terrain, grassy valleys, rivers and gorges, forests, animal habitats, public spaces, and more site-specific vegetation.

WildPlay's guests can purchase experiences online, by phone, and in person at a park; however, fulfillment of experiences requires people to visit the park location (currently in Kelowna, Maple Ridge, Victoria, and Nanaimo, British Columbia; and Niagara Falls, Ontario) and carries on after the visit has completed.

With great diversity in product and location, WildPlay focuses on optimizing six areas of distribution. The company's goals are to deliver the following:

1. Fast and simple customer booking and check-in
2. Consistent service and brand experience
3. Engagement and completion of elements that meet and exceed expectations
4. Accessible and protected park environments
5. Post-visit customer engagement
6. Expanded experience opportunities (via additional locations and activities)

These goals cover the entire consumer journey, during which there are multiple points of fulfillment. Customers require WildPlay to provide information, instructions, encouragement, care, and the tangible and intangible products and services they purchase.

To achieve its goals, WildPlay places the customer experience at the core of the business. Business units are focused on how to best deliver each stage of the customer journey. The company optimizes via practices and systems in areas of communication (internally and with consumers), advance and on-site employee and leadership training, brand definition, product innovation, park structure and health, and launch of new locations.

Growth of the park network represents the most significant challenges and opportunities to WildPlay's distribution strategy. Each new location must carry-forward

## CHAPTER FEATURES

**Wild about Canada**
WildPlay's distribution strategy allows it to bring exceptional experiences to its customers across Canada.

**Should Someone Stop Pokémon Go?**
Augmented reality and its potential to engage consumers.

**Top 100 Franchises**
Find out where the top franchises originated from.

**Maxed Out on McDonald's**
Discover the benefits and challenges of McDonald's franchises in Canada.

**Where Do You Go for Coffee?**
Compare the number of points of distribution for some of Canada's popular cafés.

**The SmartWay**
Developing supply chain strategies that reduce greenhouse emissions.

## CHAPTER OUTLINE

- Wild about Canada
- Nature and importance of marketing channels
- Channel structure and organization
- Vertical marketing systems
- Channel choice and management
- Logistics and supply chain management

the company's brand and best practices, as well as contend with distinct site-specific market situations and requirements. For example, WildPlay's recent expansion into Niagara Falls, Ontario, made the experience more accessible for consumers in central and eastern Canada and U.S.; however, the unique weather, terrain, and habitats surrounding WildPlay's MistRider Zipline to the Falls requires the company to alter its operating schedule to the environment. As well, the great volume of tourists in the area spurred WildPlay to develop new methods of managing the customer experience, from product and pricing strategies through check-in and completion of the experience.

"We rely on sharing our experience and standards across our park network, and we learn as we grow." says Tom Benson, co-founder and CEO of WildPlay. "By seeking feedback from customers and our front-line employees, and being nimble about change, we are able to tweak and perfect the ways in which we deliver our products and services to satisfy—and usually thrill—those who visit our parks."

The Niagara Falls park both tested and proved WildPlay's methods of distribution. The company's communication and sales systems were adopted and/or adapted to efficiently serve new customers. A high level of service was achieved via intensive employee training in standards and practices. The brand defined a consistent and accurate customer experience. Creative product and park design heightened the thrill of adventure in a valuable, nature-based space.

As WildPlay continues to expand, it will encounter more challenges. At each new location, the needs and wishes of its consumers will be as unique as the element activities it builds and the environment that surrounds its parks. "We'll always grow from our roots," says Benson, "and adapt for what the future has in store."[1]

> ## reality CHECK ⊘
>
> As you read Chapter 10, refer back to the WildPlay vignette to answer the following questions:
> - Why do you believe that the challenging logistics of marketing channels are sometimes taken for granted?
> - What skills are required for the individuals that plan the logistics of a supply chain?

# NATURE AND IMPORTANCE OF MARKETING CHANNELS

 **LO 1**

**marketing channel**
The set of individuals or firms involved in the process of making a product available.

**intermediaries**
Individuals or firms performing a role in the marketing channel, involved in making a product available.

Reaching potential buyers is obviously a critical part of successful marketing. Buyers benefit from well-structured and efficient distribution systems. The route to do this is direct in some cases and indirect in others.

Getting the product to the consumer is another key component of the marketing mix. In order to ensure an established place for consumers to acquire the product or service, marketers need to understand the distribution and supply chain aspects of bringing a product to market. Good marketers understand the value of the supply chain to perform the activities required to deliver a good or service to customers.

# WHAT IS A MARKETING CHANNEL?

You see the results of distribution every day. You may have purchased Lay's potato chips at Mac's convenience store, a book through chapters.indigo.ca, or Levi's jeans at Hudson's Bay. Each of these items was brought to you by a marketing channel of distribution, or simply a marketing channel. A **marketing channel** consists of individuals and firms involved in the process of making a product or service available.

Marketing channels can be compared with a pipeline through which water flows from a source to an endpoint. Marketing channels make possible the flow of goods from a producer, through **intermediaries**, to a buyer. There are several types of intermediaries, as shown in Figure 10–1. Intermediaries go by various names and perform various functions. Some intermediaries actually purchase items from the producer, store them, and resell them to buyers. For example, Nestlé Canada produces

**Figure 10–1**

Terms used for marketing intermediaries

| Term | Description |
|------|-------------|
| **Middleman** | Another name for intermediary |
| **Agent or broker** | Any intermediary with legal authority to act on behalf of another channel member (for example, a manufacturer) |
| **Wholesaler** | Any intermediary who sells to other intermediaries, usually to retailers—this term usually applies to intermediaries who deal in consumer goods |
| **Retailer** | An intermediary who sells to consumers |
| **Distributor** | A general term used to describe intermediaries who perform a variety of functions, including selling, maintaining inventories, extending credit, and others—usually used for those in business markets |
| **Dealer** | A general term that can mean the same as a distributor, a retailer, or a wholesaler |

Aero chocolate bars and sells them to wholesalers. The wholesalers then sell the bars to independent convenience and grocery stores, which in turn sell them to consumers. Other intermediaries, such as brokers and agents, represent sellers but do not actually ever own the products; their role is to bring a seller and buyer together. Real estate agents are examples of this type of intermediary.

# VALUE IS CREATED BY INTERMEDIARIES

Few consumers appreciate the value created by intermediaries; however, producers recognize that intermediaries make selling goods and services more efficient because the intermediaries minimize the number of sales contacts necessary to reach a target market. Figure 10–2

shows a simple example of how this comes about in the flat-panel TV market. Without a retail intermediary (such as Best Buy), LG, Toshiba, Sharp, and Samsung would each have to make four contacts to reach the four consumers shown, who are in the target market. When Best Buy acts as an intermediary, each producer has to make only one contact, reducing the number of industry transactions from 16 to 8, which reduces producer costs.

## Functions Performed by Intermediaries

Intermediaries make possible the flow of products from producers to ultimate consumers by performing three basic functions (see Figure 10–3).

- *Transactional function:* Intermediaries perform a transactional function when they buy and sell goods or services. But an intermediary such as a wholesaler

**Figure 10–2**

How intermediaries minimize transactions

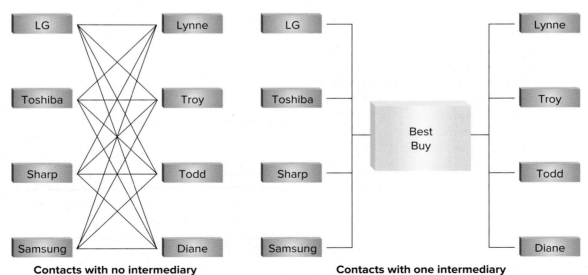

**Contacts with no intermediary**
4 producers × 4 buyers = 16 contacts

**Contacts with one intermediary**
4 producers + 4 buyers = 8 contacts

## Figure 10–3

Marketing channel functions performed by intermediaries

| Type of Function | Activities Related to Function |
|---|---|
| Transactional function | • *Buying:* Purchasing products for resale<br>• *Selling:* Contacting potential customers, promoting products, and seeking orders<br>• *Risk-taking:* Assuming business risks in the ownership of inventory |
| Logistical function | • *Selection:* Putting together a selection of products from several different sources<br>• *Storing:* Assembling and protecting products at a convenient location<br>• *Sorting:* Purchasing in large quantities and dividing into smaller amounts<br>• *Transporting:* Physically moving a product to customers |
| Facilitating function | • *Financing:* Extending credit to customers<br>• *Marketing information and research:* Providing information to customers and suppliers, including competitive conditions and trends |

also performs the function of sharing risk with the producer when it stocks merchandise in anticipation of sales. If the stock is unsold for any reason, the intermediary—not the producer—suffers the loss.

• *Logistical function:* The logistics of a transaction involve the details of preparing and getting a product to buyers. Gathering, sorting, and dispersing products are some of the logistical functions of the intermediary. Consider the critical role intermediaries played in the WildPlay Element Parks opening vignette.

• *Facilitating function:* Finally, intermediaries perform facilitating functions that, by definition, make a transaction *easier* for buyers. For example, Hudson's Bay issues credit cards to consumers so that they can buy now and pay later.

All three groups of functions must be performed in a marketing channel, even though each channel member may not participate in all three. Channel members often negotiate which specific functions they will perform. Sometimes disagreements result, and a breakdown in relationships among channel members occurs. This happened when Pepsi-Cola's bottler in Venezuela switched to Coca-Cola. Given the intermediary's logistical role—storing and transporting Pepsi to Venezuelan customers, in this case—Pepsi-Cola either had to set up its own bottling operation to perform these marketing channel functions, or find another bottler, which it did. Since then, Pepsi has continued to improve its bottling procedures to control costs in difficult years and a challenging market.[2]

## Consumer Benefits from Intermediaries

Consumers also benefit from the actions of intermediaries. Having the goods and services you want, when you want them, where you want them, and in the form you want them is the ideal result of marketing channels. In more specific terms, marketing channels help create value for consumers through these five utilities: time, place, form, information, and possession.

• *Time utility* refers to having a product or service when you want it. For example, Purolator provides next-morning delivery.

• *Place utility* means having a product or service available where consumers want it, such as having a Petro-Canada gas station located on a long stretch of a provincial highway.

• *Form utility* involves enhancing a product or service to make it more appealing to buyers. For example, retail stores such as Harry Rosen and Roots provide appealing displays of their products and an environment that caters to their customers.

Purolator adds value by offering time utility to customers.

Ron Bull/Toronto Star via Getty Images

- *Information utility* means providing consumers with the information they need to make an informed choice; information-packed websites and user manuals provide this type of utility.
- *Possession utility* involves efforts by intermediaries to help buyers take possession of a product or service, such as providing various ways for payment to be made for a product—by credit card, debit card, cash, or cheque.

# CHANNEL STRUCTURE AND ORGANIZATION

**LO 2** A product can take many routes on its journey from producer to buyer, and marketers search for the most efficient route from the many alternatives available. As you'll see, there are some important differences between the marketing channels for consumer goods and those for business goods.

## MARKETING CHANNELS FOR CONSUMER GOODS AND SERVICES

Figure 10–4 shows the four most common marketing channel configurations for consumer goods and services. It also shows the number of levels in each marketing channel—that is, the number of intermediaries between a producer and ultimate buyers. As the number of intermediaries between a producer and buyer increases, the channel is viewed as increasing in length. The producer → wholesaler → retailer → consumer channel is longer than the producer → consumer channel.

Channel A in Figure 10–4 represents a *direct channel* because a producer and ultimate consumers deal directly with each other. Many products and services are distributed this way. A number of insurance companies

sell their financial services using a direct channel and branch sales offices. The online store **justwhiteshirts .com** designs and produces high-quality men's shirts that are sold online and by catalogue to consumers around the world. Because there are no intermediaries with a direct channel, the producer must perform all channel functions.

The remaining three channel forms are *indirect channels* because intermediaries are inserted between the producer and consumers and perform numerous channel functions. Channel B, with a retailer added, is most common when the retailer is large and can buy in large quantities from a producer. Packaged goods companies such as Procter & Gamble use this channel with large retailers such as Loblaws and Sobeys. These retailers buy in sufficient quantities to make it cost-effective for a producer to deal with only a retail intermediary. Adding a wholesaler in channel C is most common when the wholesaler sells to small retailers, such as independent convenience stores and small grocery stores that do not buy enough to warrant a producer selling to these retailers directly. Channel C is most common for low-cost, low-unit value items that are frequently purchased by consumers, such as candy, confectionary items, and magazines. For example, Mars sells its line of candies to wholesalers in case quantities; wholesalers can then break down (sort) the cases so that individual small retailers can order in boxes of much smaller quantities.

Channel D, the most indirect channel, is employed when there are many small manufacturers and many small retailers and an agent is used to help coordinate a large

**Figure 10–4**
Common marketing channels for consumer goods and services

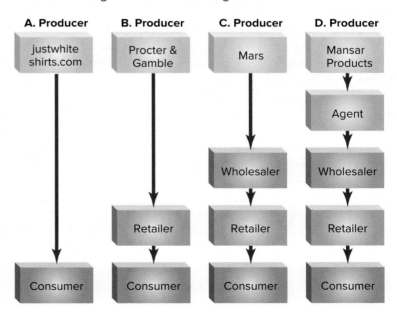

supply of the product. Mansar Products, Ltd., is a Belgian producer of specialty jewellery that uses agents to sell to wholesalers, which then sell to many small retailers.

# MARKETING CHANNELS FOR BUSINESS GOODS AND SERVICES

The four most common channels for business goods and services are shown in Figure 10–5. In contrast with channels for consumer products, business channels typically are shorter and rely on one intermediary or none at all because business users are fewer in number, tend to be more concentrated geographically, and buy in larger quantities. For these reasons, business channels can be served directly or by a limited number of intermediaries.

Channel A, represented by IBM's large, mainframe computer business, is a direct channel. Firms using this kind of channel maintain their own sales force and perform all channel functions. This channel is employed when buyers are large and well-defined, the sales effort requires extensive negotiations, and the products are of high unit value and require hands-on expertise in terms of installation or use. Bombardier and Airbus Industries would be other examples.

Channels B, C, and D are indirect channels with one or more intermediaries to reach industrial users. In channel B, an *industrial distributor* performs a variety of marketing channel functions, including selling, stocking, and delivering a full product assortment and financing. In many ways, industrial distributors are like wholesalers in consumer channels. Caterpillar relies on industrial distributors to sell and service its construction and mining equipment in almost 200 countries.

Channel C introduces another intermediary, an agent, who serves primarily as the independent selling arm of producers and represents a producer to industrial users. For example, Stake Fastener Company, a producer of industrial fasteners, has an agent call on industrial users rather than employing its own sales force.

Channel D is the longest channel and includes both agents and distributors. For instance, Culligan, a producer of water treatment equipment, uses agents to call on distributors who sell to industrial users.

# ELECTRONIC MARKETING CHANNELS

The marketing channels that we have just discussed for consumer and business goods and services are not the only routes to the marketplace. Advances in electronic commerce have opened new avenues for reaching buyers and creating customer value.

Interactive electronic technology has made possible **electronic marketing channels**, which employ the Internet to make goods and services available to consumers or business buyers. A unique feature of these channels is that they can combine electronic and traditional intermediaries to create time, place, form, information, and possession utility for buyers.[3]

Figure 10–6 shows the electronic marketing channels for books (Amazon.ca), travel reservation services (Travelocity.ca), and personal computers (Dell.ca). Are you surprised that they look a lot like common marketing channels? An important reason for the similarity resides in the channel functions detailed in Figure 10–3. Electronic intermediaries can and do perform transactional and facilitating functions effectively and at a relatively lower cost than traditional intermediaries because of efficiencies made possible by information technology. However, electronic intermediaries are incapable of performing elements of the logistical function, particularly for products such as books and automobiles. This function remains with traditional intermediaries or with the producer, as seen with Dell and its direct channel.

Many services are distributed through electronic marketing channels, such as travel services marketed by Travelocity.ca, financial securities by Royal Bank, and insurance

**electronic marketing channels**
Channels that use the Internet to make goods and services available to consumers or business buyers.

## Figure 10–5
Common marketing channels for business goods and service

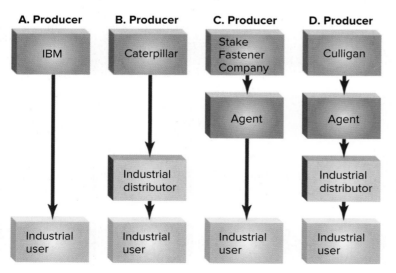

## Figure 10–6
Examples of electronic marketing channels

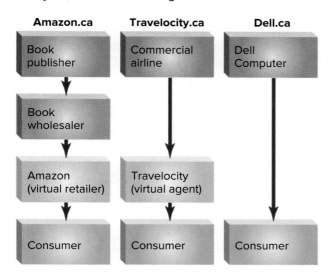

**Amazon.ca**
- Book publisher
- Book wholesaler
- Amazon (virtual retailer)
- Consumer

**Travelocity.ca**
- Commercial airline
- Travelocity (virtual agent)
- Consumer

**Dell.ca**
- Dell Computer
- Consumer

by Metropolitan Life. Software, too, can be marketed this way. However, many other services, such as health care and auto repair, still involve traditional intermediaries.

## MULTIPLE CHANNELS AND STRATEGIC ALLIANCES

In some situations, producers use **dual distribution**, an arrangement whereby a firm reaches different buyers by employing two or more different types of channels for the same basic product. For instance, GE sells its large appliances directly to home and apartment builders but uses retail stores, including Walmart, to sell to consumers. In some instances, firms pair multiple channels with a multibrand strategy. This is done to minimize

Coke distributes Canada Dry soft drinks to stores in Canada.

© Bradcalkins/Dreamstime.com/GetStock.com

cannibalization of the firm's family brand and to differentiate the channels. For example, Hallmark sells its Hallmark greeting cards through Hallmark stores and select department stores, and its Ambassador brand of cards through discount and drugstore chains.

A recent development in marketing channels is the use of *strategic channel alliances,* whereby one firm's marketing channel is used to sell another firm's products.[4] An alliance between Canada Dry and Coke is a case in point. Coke distributes Canada Dry soft drinks to stores in Canada. Strategic alliances are popular in global marketing, where the creation of marketing channel relationships is expensive and time-consuming. For example, General Mills and Nestlé have an extensive alliance that spans 70 international markets from Brazil to Poland to Thailand.

## MULTICHANNEL MARKETING TO THE ONLINE CONSUMER

Consumers and companies populate two market environments today. One is the traditional marketplace, where buyers and sellers engage in face-to-face exchange relationships in an environment characterized by physical facilities (stores and offices) and mostly tangible objects. The other is the *marketspace,* an Internet/web-enabled digital environment characterized by "face-to-screen" exchange relationships and electronic images and offerings.

The existence of multiple market environments has benefited consumers tremendously. Today, consumers can shop for and purchase a wide variety of products and services in either market environment. Many consumers now browse and buy in multiple environments, and more are expected to do so in the future. With so many consumers browsing and buying in different environments, few companies limit their marketing programs exclusively to the traditional marketplace or to the online marketspace.

Today, it is commonplace for companies to maintain a presence in both market environments. This dual presence is called *multichannel marketing.*

### Integrating Multiple Channels with Multichannel Marketing
Companies often employ multiple marketing channels for their products and services. Multichannel marketing bears some resemblance to dual distribution. For example, different communication and delivery channels are used, such as catalogues, kiosks, retail stores, and websites. However, the resemblance ends at this point. **Multichannel marketing** is the

---

**dual distribution**
Arrangement whereby a firm reaches buyers by using two or more different types of channels for the same basic product.

**multichannel marketing**
Blending of different communication and delivery channels that are mutually reinforcing in attracting, retaining, and building relationships with customers.

*blending* of different communication and delivery channels that are *mutually reinforcing* in attracting, retaining, and building relationships with consumers who shop and buy in the traditional marketplace and in the online marketspace. Multichannel marketing seeks to integrate a firm's communication and delivery channels, not differentiate them. In doing so, consumers can browse and buy any time, anywhere, any way, expecting that the experience will be similar regardless of channel.

Multichannel marketing is essential to success. Allowing business to measure results and make changes rapidly is one benefit, while ensuring a seamless customer experience is another benefit. At Eddie Bauer, for example, every effort is made to make the apparel shopping and purchase process for its customers the same in its retail stores, through its catalogues, and at its website. According to an Eddie Bauer marketing manager, "We don't distinguish between channels because it's all Eddie Bauer to our customers."[5]

Multichannel marketing can also leverage the value-adding capabilities of different channels. For example, retail stores leverage their physical presence by allowing customers to pick up their online orders at a nearby store, or return or exchange non-store purchases at the store if they wish. For instance, a consumer can purchase a laptop computer on the Staples website and pick up the computer at any Staples store.

Another example of multichannel marketing is the **cross-channel shopper**, who researches products online and then purchases them at a retail store. These shoppers represent both genders equally. Cross-channel shoppers want the right product at the best price, and they don't want to wait several days for delivery. The top reasons these shoppers look online before buying in stores include (1) the desire to compare products among different retailers, (2) the need for more information than is available in stores, and (3) the ease of comparing options without having to trek to multiple retail locations.

The evolution of how individuals make purchases leads us to the trend of omni-channel retailing. Omni-channel retailing creates a seamless experience among all available shopping channels. Since technology has made it difficult to distinguish between online and physical retail opportunities, the next step for retailers is to make the process seamless and potentially more engaging; see, for example, the Marketing NewsFlash box, "Should Someone Stop Pokémon Go?"[6] Both online and offline retailers need to be ready for the changes in the competitive landscape. It will become an expectation for them to invest resources toward omni-channel retailing to meet the demand of consumers.[7]

**Implementing Multichannel Marketing** It should not be surprising to you that not all companies use websites for multichannel marketing the same way. Different companies apply the value-creation capabilities of Internet/web technology differently depending on their overall marketing program. Websites can play multiple roles in multichannel marketing because they can serve as either a communication or delivery channel, or as both. There are two general types of websites, classified based on their intended purpose: transactional websites and promotional websites.

*Transactional websites* are essentially electronic storefronts. They focus mainly on converting an online browser into an online, catalogue, or in-store buyer using website design elements. Transactional websites are most common among store and catalogue retailers such as Lee Valley. The Gap, for instance, generates more sales volume from its website than from any one of its stores, except for one. The company has built on its online success and prepared for the future by forming an innovation and digital strategy group to take advantage of growing e-tailing in Canada.[8]

The Gap generates more sales volume from its website than any one of its stores, except for one.

© McGraw-Hill Education/Andrew Resek

## marketing NewsFlash

## Should Someone Stop Pokémon Go?

The first video game for entertainment dates back to the 1950s. Finding another way consumers can seek entertainment has blossomed over the decades.

In 2016, a smartphone game called Pokémon Go was launched in North America, New Zealand, Australia, and Europe. The augmented-reality game allows players to search for virtual Pokémon characters that appear in places across the world. The Pokémon creatures can be found when users hold up their smartphones in certain places at certain times of the day. Individuals had been seen flocking to the CN Tower in Toronto as well as restaurants, retail stores, and other places that are engaged in the game. This augmented reality is newer technology that marketers can use to engage with potential consumers.

A few months after the successful launch in Canada, two teenagers from Alberta were so engrossed in the game that they accidentally crossed the U.S. border in Montana. In fact, players across the world get so engrossed in the gameplay that Pokémon Go has been blamed for car accidents and other issues that stem from distracted players.

Pokémon Go has been a success across the world, increasing the profile of Nintendo, which is a part owner of the Pokémon copyright. Unfortunately, negative publicity regarding the game caused the Nintendo stock to fall. Although it is the responsibility of players to be aware of their surroundings, the addictive nature of the game and the dangers that can be created cause concerns. ●

Pokémon Go is an augmented-reality game.
xuanhuongho/Shutterstock.com

### Questions

1. What is the benefit to marketers of using augmented-reality technology like that used in Pokémon Go?

2. What other companies could implement this type of technology to engage potential consumers?

Transactional websites are used less frequently by manufacturers of consumer products, but a recurring issue for manufacturers is the threat of channel conflict by harming their relationships with their retailing intermediaries. Hudson's Bay, for instance, would not be very happy if a brand of jeans it carries is being sold online directly from the manufacturer to the consumer; however, Ethan Allen, the furniture manufacturer, markets its product line at **www.ethanallen.com** whenever feasible. Ethan Allen has attempted to address channel conflict by having retailers fill online orders and receive 25 percent of the sales price. For items shipped directly from the Ethan Allen factory, the store nearest the customer receives 10 percent of the sales price.[9]

*Promotional websites* have a different purpose than transactional sites: No actual selling takes place on them, but they showcase products and services and provide information.

## GLOBAL CHANNEL STRATEGY

Distribution is of critical importance in global marketing. The availability and quality of retailers and wholesalers as well as transportation, communication, and warehousing facilities are often determined by a country's economic infrastructure. Figure 10–7 outlines the channel through which a product manufactured in one country must travel to reach its destination in another country. The first step involves the seller; its headquarters is responsible for the successful distribution to the ultimate consumer.

The next step is the channel between two nations, moving the product from one country to another. Intermediaries that can handle this responsibility include resident buyers in a foreign country, independent merchant wholesalers who buy and sell the product, and agents who bring buyers and sellers together.

Once the product is in the foreign nation, that country's distribution channels take over. These channels can

## Figure 10–7
Channels of distribution in global marketing

Seller → Seller's international marketing headquarters → Channels between nations → Channels within foreign nations → Final consumer

**vertical marketing systems**

Professionally managed and centrally coordinated marketing channels designed to achieve channel economies and maximum marketing impact.

be very long or surprisingly short, depending on the product line. In Japan, fresh fish can go through three intermediaries before getting to a retail outlet. Conversely, shoes go through only one intermediary. The sophistication of a country's distribution channels increases as its economic infrastructure develops. Supermarkets are helpful in selling products in many nations, but they are not popular or available in many others where culture and a lack of refrigeration dictate shopping on a daily rather than a weekly basis. For example, when Coke and Pepsi entered China, both had to create direct distribution channels, investing in refrigerator units for small retailers.

## VERTICAL MARKETING SYSTEMS

**LO 3** The traditional marketing channels described so far represent a network of independent producers and intermediaries

brought together to distribute goods and services. However, channel arrangements have emerged for the purpose of improving efficiency in performing channel functions and achieving greater marketing effectiveness. These arrangements are called vertical marketing systems. **Vertical marketing systems** are professionally managed and centrally coordinated marketing channels designed to achieve channel economies and maximum marketing impact. They encourage collaboration, shared responsibility, and partnership between the manufacturers and retailers in a system.[10] Figure 10–8 depicts the major types of vertical marketing systems: corporate, contractual, and administered.

**Corporate Systems** Under a *corporate vertical marketing system,* a firm at one level of a channel owns the firm at the next level or owns the entire channel. For example, a producer might own the intermediary at the next level down in the channel. This practice, called *forward integration,* is exemplified by Polo/Ralph Lauren, which manufactures clothing and also owns

## Figure 10–8
Types of vertical marketing systems

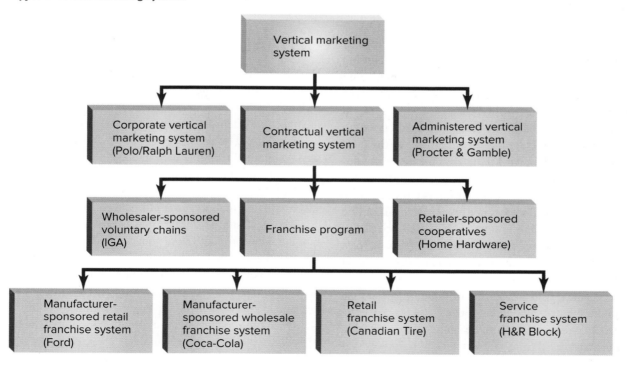

Vertical marketing system
- Corporate vertical marketing system (Polo/Ralph Lauren)
- Contractual vertical marketing system
  - Wholesaler-sponsored voluntary chains (IGA)
  - Franchise program
    - Manufacturer-sponsored retail franchise system (Ford)
    - Manufacturer-sponsored wholesale franchise system (Coca-Cola)
    - Retail franchise system (Canadian Tire)
    - Service franchise system (H&R Block)
  - Retailer-sponsored cooperatives (Home Hardware)
- Administered vertical marketing system (Procter & Gamble)

Tiffany & Co. and H&R Block represent two different types of vertical marketing systems.

(left) © Allstar Picture Library/Alamy Stock Photo; (right) Used with permission of H&R Block

apparel shops. Another example of forward integration is Goodyear, which distributes its tires not only through preferred stores but also through its own retail stores. Alternatively, a retailer might own a manufacturing operation, a practice called *backward integration*. For example, Tiffany & Co., the exclusive jewellery retailer, manufactures about half of the fine jewellery items for sale through its 150 stores and boutiques worldwide.

Companies seeking to reduce distribution costs and gain greater control over supply sources or resale of their products pursue forward and backward integration. Many companies favour contractual vertical marketing systems to achieve channel efficiencies and marketing effectiveness.

**Contractual Systems** Under a *contractual vertical marketing system,* independent production and distribution firms combine their efforts on a contractual basis to obtain greater functional economies and marketing impact than they could achieve alone. Contractual systems are the most popular among the three types of vertical marketing systems. They account for about 40 percent of all retail sales.

Three variations of contractual systems exist. The first contractual system, *wholesaler-sponsored voluntary chains,* involves a wholesaler that develops a contractual relationship with small, independent retailers to standardize and coordinate buying practices, merchandising programs, and inventory management efforts. With the organization of a large number of independent retailers, economies of scale and volume discounts can be achieved to compete with chain stores. Independent Grocers Alliance (IGA) was the largest group of independent grocers in Canada and pursued this strategy. The

# Maxed Out on McDonald's

McDonald's has more than 1,400 restaurants with over 80,000 employees in Canada—a fraction of its 33,000 restaurants and 1.7 million employees worldwide. With franchising being a key to its success, McDonald's has expanded over six continents into almost 120 countries.

Franchising is a popular method for businesses to expand internationally, and Canada has historically been the most popular country for U.S. companies to expand into. More recently, with changing markets and ever-evolving opportunities, franchise growth has expanded to South America, Asia, and Mexico.

Franchising has many benefits to a business as it facilitates the entry into consumer segments where there is demand. As a franchisee, the key to success is to follow direction from the corporate offices and leverage support of their resources and the company brand. For Canadian McDonald's franchises, a great example of leveraging resources was the national launch of the Signature McWrap in 2013. This new menu item was specifically designed for Canadian tastes, but modified the recipe of a similar, successful global menu item in McDonald's Europe.

Keeping in mind that business-model benefits are usually balanced with challenges, McDonald's U.S. franchisees faced increased store fees and raised concerns with their corporate parent. Franchisees were impacted by rent, training fees, and software. The concern among franchisees is that the business model is no longer as profitable as it has been in the past. To help address this rising channel conflict, McDonald's spokespeople have commented, "We are continuing to work together with McDonald's owner/operators and our supplier partners to ensure that our restaurants are providing a great experience to our customers, which involves investments in training and technology."

Being part of the marketing channels and supply chains, a number of

Innovative menu items help franchisees attract and retain consumers.

© Michael Neelon(misc)/Alamy Stock Photo

Canadian companies have a vested interest in the success of McDonald's in Canada. McDonald's is considered a channel captain in Canada with the ability to influence the behaviour of its partners and support success for all parties concerned. ●

## Questions

1. What are some of the challenges McDonald's franchisees face in their contractual vertical marketing system?

2. What are some of the key benefits of being part of a franchising arrangement?

---

group garnered the interest of Sobeys, which purchased the stores and incorporated a different business model.

*Retailer-sponsored cooperatives* exist when small, independent retailers form an organization that operates a wholesale facility cooperatively. Member retailers then concentrate their buying power through the wholesaler and plan collaborative promotional and pricing activities. Home Hardware is an example of a retailer-sponsored cooperative. The most visible variation of contractual systems is **franchising**, a contractual arrangement between a parent company (a franchiser) and an individual or firm (a franchisee) that allows the franchisee to operate a certain type of business under

an established name and according to specific rules set by the franchiser.

Four types of franchise arrangements are most popular. *Manufacturer-sponsored retail franchise systems* are prominent in the automobile industry, where a manufacturer such as Ford licenses dealers to sell its cars subject to various sales and service conditions. *Manufacturer-sponsored wholesale franchise systems* appear in the soft-drink industry, where Pepsi-Cola licenses wholesalers (bottlers) that purchase concentrate from Pepsi-Cola and then carbonate, bottle, promote, and distribute its products to supermarkets and restaurants. *Retail franchise systems* are provided by firms that have designed a unique approach for selling merchandise to consumers. Canadian Tire and McDonald's represent this franchising approach (see the Marketing NewsFlash box, "Maxed Out on McDonald's").[11]

**franchising**
Contractual arrangement in which a parent company (the franchiser) allows an individual or firm (the franchisee) to operate a certain type of business under an established name and according to specific rules set by the franchiser.

Service franchise systems exist when franchisers license individuals or firms to dispense a service under a trade name and specific guidelines. An example is H&R Block tax services. Service franchise arrangements are the fastest-growing type of franchise.

**Administered Systems** Ownership of a marketing system is not always necessary to achieve desired results. *Administered vertical marketing systems* achieve coordination at successive stages of production and distribution by the size and influence of one channel member. Procter & Gamble, given its broad product assortment ranging from disposable diapers to detergents, is able to obtain cooperation from supermarkets in displaying, promoting, and pricing its products. Given its position as the world's largest retailer, Walmart can obtain cooperation from manufacturers in terms of product specifications, price levels, and promotional support.

## ask **YOURSELF**

1. What is the difference between a direct and an indirect channel?

2. What is the major distinction between a corporate vertical marketing system and an administered vertical marketing system?

# CHANNEL CHOICE AND MANAGEMENT

**LO 4** Marketing channels not only link a producer to its buyers but also provide the means through which a firm executes various elements of its marketing strategy. Therefore, choosing a marketing channel is a critical decision.

## FACTORS AFFECTING CHANNEL CHOICE

The final choice of a marketing channel by a producer depends on a number of market, product, and company factors.

### Where Do You Go for Coffee?

Canadians have plenty of options when choosing their morning brew.

| | |
|---|---|
| McDonald's | Over 1,400 locations |
| Second Cup | Over 300 locations |
| Starbucks | Over 600 locations |
| Tim Hortons | Over 3,600 locations |

**Source:** "Fresh Facts," Tim Hortons corporate website, accessed at https://www.timhortons.com/ca/en/corporate/fresh-facts.php#!open_flyout; "Our History," Second Cup corporate website, accessed at http://www.secondcup.com/our-story;jsessionid=B8EB02561075E87B516B57B6A8869977; "Our Canadian Story," Starbucks website, accessed at https://www.starbucks.ca/careers/our-canadian-story; "Corporate Info," McDonald's Canada corporate website, accessed at http://www.mcdonalds.ca/ca/en/our_story/corporate_info.html.

## Market Factors

- *Geographic concentration of the market:* When most of a firm's customers are concentrated in a few geographic areas, a direct sale to customers is practical. When customers are geographically dispersed, a direct sale is likely to be impractical due to high travel costs. Sellers may establish sales branches in densely populated markets and use intermediaries in less-concentrated markets.

- *Number of potential customers:* A manufacturer with few potential customers may use its own sales force to sell directly to ultimate consumers or business users. Bombardier uses this approach in selling its jet aircrafts and subway cars. For a large number of customers, the manufacturer would probably use intermediaries. For example, Tim Hortons relies on numerous franchisee outlets to reach the large number of consumers buying coffee.

- *Type of market:* Consumer products are made available through retailers, while business products are sold either direct to customers or through intermediaries.

- *Order size:* Direct distribution makes sense when an order size is large. For example, Campbell's delivers its soups directly to large grocery chains. On the other hand, Campbell's uses wholesalers to reach small independent grocery and convenience stores, whose orders are usually too small to justify a direct sale.

 *It would not make sense for Hershey Canada to call on households to sell an Oh Henry! chocolate bar.*

Tim Hortons is an example of a retail franchise system.
© eye35.pix/Alamy Stock Photo

## Product Factors

- *Technical factors:* In general, highly sophisticated products, such as custom-built machinery and scientific computers, are distributed direct to buyers. The producer's sales force must provide considerable pre-purchase and post-purchase service for these types of products, and typically, wholesalers do not do these tasks.

- *Perishability:* Some goods, such as milk and bread, deteriorate fairly quickly. As a result, these types of products go directly from the producer to the retailer, no matter the size of the order.

- *Unit value:* The price attached to each unit of a product affects the amount of funds available for distribution. For example, a company like Bombardier can afford to use its own employees to sell aircraft costing millions of dollars. But it would not make sense for Hershey Canada to call on households to sell an Oh Henry! chocolate bar. That's why intermediaries such as convenience stores, vending machines, and gasoline service stations carry low unit-value products.

- *Product life cycle:* Over time, some products, such as the Apple iPad, become very popular, easy to operate, and available in more mainstream channels such as Walmart and Best Buy.

## Company Factors

- *Financial resources and ability of management:* A business with limited financial resources may be unable to employ its own salespeople, and thus resorts to using intermediaries such as selling agents or manufacturer's agents to reach customers. Also, businesses that have limited or no marketing know-how may elect to use intermediaries.

  A manufacturer of jams and marmalades may face limited markets for its products because it cannot afford the listing fees that supermarkets demand for the privilege of carrying the product. The manufacturer chooses instead to sell to small fruit and vegetable markets, who do not demand a listing fee and whose clientele enjoys buying products that are not available everywhere. The retailer may command a premium price for the jam because of its perceived quality and limited distribution.

- *Desire for channel control:* Some producers establish direct channels because they want to control their product's distribution, even though a direct channel may be more costly than an indirect channel. For example, Gap Inc. employs designers to come up with the styles that consumers want. Instead of selling Gap products to independent retailers, Gap Inc. assures distribution with its more than 3,000 Gap stores. Having its own stores assures Gap that its products are marketed properly and merchandised prominently.

# CHANNEL DESIGN CONSIDERATIONS

Marketing executives consider three questions when choosing a marketing channel and intermediaries:

1. Which channel and intermediaries will best reach the target market?

2. Which channel and intermediaries will best serve the needs of the target market?

3. Which channel and intermediaries will lead to the most cost-efficient and profitable results?

**Target Market Coverage** Achieving the best coverage of the target market requires attention to the density—that is, the number of stores in a given geographical area—and type of intermediaries to be used at the retail level of distribution. Three degrees of distribution intensity exist: intensive, exclusive, and selective.

**Intensive distribution** means that a firm tries to place its products and services in as many outlets as possible. Intensive distribution is usually chosen for convenience products or services, such as candy, newspapers, and soft drinks. For example, Coca-Cola's retail distribution objective is to place its products "within an arm's reach of desire."

**Exclusive distribution** is the extreme opposite of intensive distribution because only one retail outlet in a specified geographical area carries the firm's products. Exclusive distribution is typically chosen for specialty products or services such as specialty automobiles, some women's fragrances, men's and women's apparel and accessories, and yachts. Sometimes, retailers sign exclusive distribution agreements with manufacturers and suppliers.

**Selective distribution** lies between these two extremes and means that a firm selects a few retail outlets in a specific geographical area to carry its products. Selective distribution combines some of the market coverage benefits of intensive distribution with the control measures possible with exclusive distribution. For this reason, selective distribution is the most common form of distribution intensity. It is usually associated with products such as Rolex watches, Levi's jeans, and Samsung flat-panel TVs.

## Satisfying Buyer Requirements

A second objective in channel design is gaining access to channels and intermediaries that satisfy at least some of the interests buyers might have when they purchase a firm's products or services. These requirements fall into four categories: information, convenience, variety, and pre- or post-sale services.

Information is an important requirement when buyers have limited knowledge or desire specific data about a product or service. Properly chosen intermediaries communicate with buyers through in-store displays, demonstrations, and personal selling. Electronics manufacturers such as Apple and Sony have opened their own retail outlets, with highly trained personnel to inform buyers about their products and how they can meet the buyers' needs.

Convenience has multiple meanings for buyers, such as proximity or driving time to a retail outlet or hours of operation. For example, Mac's convenience stores, with outlets nationwide, many of which are open 24 hours a day, satisfy this interest for buyers. Candy and snack food firms benefit by gaining display space in these stores.

For other consumers, convenience means a minimum of time and hassle. Jiffy Lube and Mr. Lube,

**intensive distribution**
A firm tries to place its products or services in as many outlets as possible.

**exclusive distribution**
Only one retail outlet in a specific geographical area carries the firm's products.

**selective distribution**
A firm selects a few retail outlets in a specific geographical area to carry its products.

Tim Hortons® has added convenient locations to Esso service stations across Canada.
JHVEPhoto/Shutterstock.com

which promise to change engine oil and filters quickly, appeal to this aspect of convenience. Another example of convenience is Tim Hortons®, which has locations in Esso service stations across Canada.

Variety reflects buyers' interest in having numerous competing and complementary items from which to choose. Variety is seen in both the breadth and depth of products carried by intermediaries, which enhances their attractiveness to buyers. Thus, manufacturers of pet food and supplies seek distribution through pet stores such as PetSmart and PJ's Pets.

Services provided by intermediaries are an important buying requirement for products such as large household appliances that require delivery, installation, and credit. Therefore, Whirlpool seeks dealers that provide such services.

The late Steve Jobs, formerly Apple's CEO, was one person who believed that computer retailers have failed to satisfy the buying requirements of today's consumer. Believing that "buying a car is no longer the worst purchasing experience; buying a computer is number one," he launched Apple Stores.[12]

Profitability The third consideration in designing a channel is profitability, which is determined by the revenues earned minus cost for each channel member and for the channel as a whole. Cost is the critical factor of channel profitability. These costs include distribution, advertising, and selling expenses. The extent to which channel members share these costs determines the profitability of each member and of the channel as a whole.

# CHANNEL RELATIONSHIPS: CONFLICT AND COOPERATION

Unfortunately, because channels consist of independent individuals and firms, there is always potential for disagreements concerning who performs which channel functions, how profits are distributed, which products and services will be provided by whom, and who makes critical channel-related decisions. These channel conflicts necessitate measures for dealing with them.

Vertical conflict occurred between Coke and Costco.

© John Lee/Aurora Photos/Getstock.com

Conflict in Marketing Channels **Channel conflict** arises when one channel member believes another channel member is engaged in behaviour that prevents it from achieving its goals. Two types of conflict occur in marketing channels: vertical conflict and horizontal conflict. Although channel conflict may have a negative effect on channel performance, it can also encourage channels to find better efficiencies to deliver results.[13]

*Vertical conflict* occurs between different levels in a marketing channel—for example, between a manufacturer and a wholesaler or between a manufacturer and a retailer. An example of vertical conflict was when Coke and Costco had a disagreement on price. Costco claimed that Coke's selling price to Costco was too high. As a result, Costco stopped carrying Coke products. It took a month for the two channel members to resolve their differences before Coke once again was made available at Costco.[14]

Another type of vertical conflict arises when a channel member bypasses another member and sells directly to consumers, a practice called **disintermediation**. Apple is an excellent example of how disintermediation works. Before Apple Stores existed, Apple products were sold through independent retailers. When Apple started opening its own stores, its retailers began to complain. In 2005, independent Apple retailers filed a lawsuit against Apple, accusing the company of giving preferential treatment to its own stores and harming their sales. The lawsuit claimed that Apple had favoured Apple Stores by providing significant discounts that were unavailable to independent retailers. It also claimed that Apple was holding back product from the independent retailers.

*Horizontal conflict* occurs between intermediaries at the same level in a marketing channel, such as between two or more retailers or two or more wholesalers that handle the same manufacturer's brands. For instance, one Toyota dealer might complain to Toyota that another Toyota dealer has located too close to its dealership and is affecting its business.

*Conflict can have disruptive effects on the workings of a marketing channel.*

## Cooperation in Marketing Channels

Conflict can have disruptive effects on the workings of a marketing channel, so it is necessary to secure cooperation among channel members. One means is through a *channel captain,* a dominant channel member that coordinates, directs, and supports other channel members. Channel captains can be producers, wholesalers, or retailers. Procter & Gamble assumes this role because it has a strong consumer following in brands such as Crest, Tide, and Pampers. Therefore, it can set policies or terms that supermarkets will follow. Walmart and Home Depot are retail channel captains because of their strong consumer image, number of outlets, and purchasing volume.

A firm becomes a channel captain because it is the channel member with the ability to influence the behaviour of other members.[15] Influence can take four forms. First, economic influence arises from the ability of a firm to reward other members because of its strong financial position. Microsoft Corporation and Toys "R" Us have such influence. Expertise is a second source of influence. Third, identification with a particular channel member creates influence for that channel member. For example, retailers may compete to carry the Ralph Lauren line, or clothing manufacturers may compete to be carried by Hudson's Bay or Holt Renfrew. In both instances, the desire to be associated with a channel member gives that firm influence over others. Finally, influence can arise from the legitimate right of one channel member to direct the behaviour of other members. This situation occurs under contractual vertical marketing systems where a franchiser can legitimately direct how a franchisee behaves.

# LOGISTICS AND SUPPLY CHAIN MANAGEMENT

**LO 5** A marketing channel relies on logistics to make products available to consumers and industrial users. **Logistics** involves those activities that focus on getting the right amount of the right products to the right place at the right time at the lowest possible cost. The performance of these activities is *logistics management,* the practice of organizing the cost-effective flow of raw materials, in-process inventory, finished goods, and related information from point of origin to point of consumption to satisfy *customer requirements.* Although logistics primarily provide distribution services, there is underlying value to the supply chain.[16]

**logistics**
Activities that focus on getting the right amount of the right products to the right place at the right time at the lowest possible cost.

Three elements of this definition deserve emphasis. First, logistics deals with decisions from the source of raw materials to consumption of the final product—that is, the *flow* of the product. Second, those decisions have to be *cost-effective.* Third, while it is important to drive down logistics costs, there is a limit: A firm needs to drive down logistics costs as long as it can deliver expected *customer service,* while satisfying customer requirements. The role of management is to see that customer needs are satisfied in the most cost-effective manner. When properly done, the results can be spectacular. Procter & Gamble is a case in point. Beginning in the 1990s, the company set out to meet the needs of consumers more effectively by collaborating and partnering with its suppliers and retailers to ensure that the right products reached store shelves at the right time and at a lower cost. The effort was judged a success when, during an 18-month period, Procter & Gamble's retailers recorded a US$65-million savings in logistics costs while customer service increased.[17]

The Procter & Gamble experience is not an isolated incident. Companies now recognize that getting the right items needed for consumption or production to the right place at the right time in the right condition at the right cost is often beyond their individual capabilities and control. Instead, collaboration, coordination, and information sharing among manufacturers, suppliers, and distributors are necessary to create a seamless flow of goods and services to customers. This perspective is represented in the concept of a supply chain and the practice of supply chain management.

**supply chain**

Sequence of firms that perform activities required to create and deliver a product to consumers or industrial users.

**supply chain management**

Integration and organization of information and logistics activities across firms in a supply chain for the purpose of creating and delivering goods and services that provide value to consumers.

# SUPPLY CHAINS VERSUS MARKETING CHANNELS

A **supply chain** is a series of firms that perform activities required to create and deliver a good or service to consumers or industrial users. It differs from a marketing channel in terms of the firms involved. A supply chain is longer and includes suppliers that provide raw material inputs to a manufacturer as well as the wholesalers and retailers that deliver finished goods to you. The management process is also different. **Supply chain management** is the integration and organization of information and logistics activities across firms in a supply chain for the purpose of creating and delivering goods and services that provide value to consumers. The relation among marketing channels, logistics management, and supply chain management is shown in Figure 10–9. An important feature of supply chain management is its use of sophisticated information technology that allows companies to share and operate systems for order processing, transportation scheduling, and inventory and facility management.

# SOURCING, ASSEMBLING, AND DELIVERING A NEW CAR: THE AUTOMOTIVE SUPPLY CHAIN

All companies are members of one or more supply chains. A supply chain is essentially a series of linked suppliers and customers in which every customer is, in turn, a supplier to another customer until a finished product reaches the ultimate consumer. Even a simplified supply chain diagram for carmakers shown in Figure 10–10 illustrates how complex a supply chain can be.[18] A carmaker's supplier network includes thousands of firms that provide the 5,000 or so parts in a typical automobile. They provide items ranging from raw materials such as steel and rubber to components, including transmissions, tires, brakes, and seats, to complex sub-assemblies and assemblies such as in chassis and suspension systems that make for a smooth, stable ride. Coordinating and scheduling material and component flows for their assembly into actual automobiles by carmakers is heavily dependent on logistical activities, including

**Figure 10–9**

How distribution channels work: the relationships between supplier networks, marketing channels, logistics management, and supply chain management

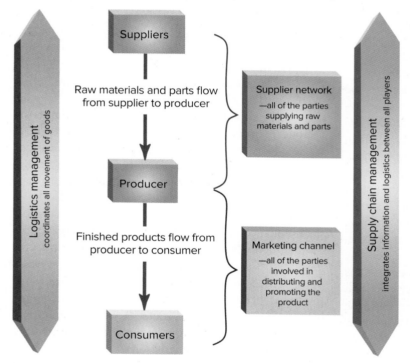

**Figure 10–10**

The automotive supply chain

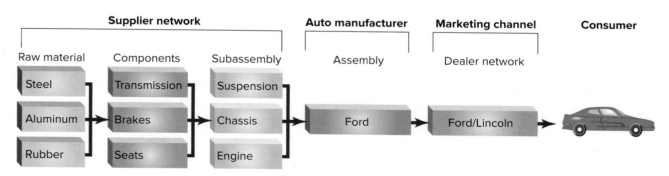

transportation, order processing, inventory control, materials handling, and information technology. A central link is the carmaker supply chain manager, who is responsible for translating customer requirements into actual orders and arranging for delivery dates and financial arrangements for automobile dealers.

Logistical aspects of the automobile marketing channel are also an important part of the supply chain. Major responsibilities include transportation (which involves the selection and management of external carriers—trucking, airline, railroad, and shipping companies—for cars and parts to dealers), the operation of distribution centres, the management of finished goods inventories, and order processing for sales. Supply chain managers also play an important role in the marketing channel. They work with extensive car dealer networks to ensure that the right mix of automobiles is delivered to each location. In addition, they make sure that spare and service parts are available so that dealers can meet the car maintenance and repair needs of consumers. All of this is done with the help of information technology that links the entire automotive supply chain. What does all of this cost? It is estimated that logistics costs represent 25 to 30 percent of the retail price of a typical new car.

# SUPPLY CHAIN MANAGEMENT AND MARKETING STRATEGY

The automotive supply chain illustration shows how logistics activities are interrelated and organized across firms to create and deliver a car for you. What's missing from this illustration is the linkage between a specific company's supply chain and its marketing strategy. Just as companies have different marketing strategies, they also manage supply chains differently. The goals to be achieved by a firm's marketing strategy determine whether its supply chain needs to focus on being more responsive or more efficient in meeting customer requirements.

### Aligning a Supply Chain with Marketing Strategy
There are a variety of supply chain configurations, each of which is designed to perform different tasks well. Marketers today recognize that the choice of a supply chain follows from a clearly defined marketing strategy. With the globalization of the world economy and increased competition, see the importance of

integrating supply chain management with their marketing strategy through the following three steps:[19]

1. *Understand the customer.* To understand the customer, a company must identify the needs of the customer segment being served. These needs, such as a desire for a low price or convenience of purchase, help a company define the relative importance of efficiency and responsiveness in meeting customer requirements.

2. *Understand the supply chain.* A company must understand what a supply chain is designed to do well. Supply chains range from those that emphasize being responsive to customer requirements and demand to those that emphasize efficiency with a goal of supplying products at the lowest possible delivered cost.

3. *Harmonize the supply chain with the marketing strategy.* A company needs to ensure that what the supply chain is capable of doing well is consistent with the targeted customer's needs and its marketing strategy. If a mismatch exists between what the supply chain does particularly well and a company's marketing strategy, the company will either need to redesign the supply chain to support the marketing strategy or change the marketing strategy. The bottom line is that a poorly designed supply chain can do serious damage to an otherwise brilliant marketing strategy.

How are these steps applied and how are efficiency and response considerations built into a supply chain? Let's briefly look at how two market leaders—Dell Computer Corporation and Walmart, Inc.—have harmonized their supply chain and marketing strategy.

### Dell Computer Corporation: A Responsive Supply Chain
The Dell marketing strategy targets customers who want to have the most up-to-date personal computer equipment customized to their needs. These customers are also willing to wait to have their customized personal computer delivered in a few days, rather than picking out a pre-packaged model at a retail store, and they pay a reasonable, though not the lowest, price in the marketplace. Given Dell's market segments, the company has the option of choosing either an efficient or a responsive supply chain.

Dell has a responsive supply chain.

© The McGraw-Hill Companies, Inc./Jill Braaten, photographer

An efficient supply chain may use inexpensive but slower modes of transportation, emphasize economies of scale in its production process by reducing the variety of PC configurations offered, and limit its assembly and inventory storage facilities to a single location, say Austin, Texas, where the company is headquartered. If Dell opted only for efficiency in its supply chain, it would be difficult if not impossible to satisfy its target customer's desire for rapid delivery and a wide variety of customizable products. Dell instead has opted for a responsive supply chain. It relies on more expensive express transportation for receipt of components from suppliers and delivery of finished products to customers. The company achieves product variety and manufacturing efficiency by designing common platforms across several products and using common components. Dell also has invested heavily in information technology to link itself with suppliers and customers.

### Walmart Stores Inc.: An Efficient Supply Chain

Walmart's marketing strategy is to be a reliable, lower-price retailer for a wide variety of mass-consumption consumer goods. This strategy favours an efficient supply chain designed to deliver products to consumers at the lowest possible cost. By competing on price, Canadians are considering Walmart for some of their grocery needs.

Walmart's efficient supply chain allows it to keep relatively low inventory levels. That is, most inventory is stocked in stores available for sale, not in warehouses gathering dust. The low inventory arises from Walmart's use of *cross-docking*—a practice that involves unloading products from suppliers, sorting products for individual stores, and quickly reloading products onto its trucks for a particular store. No warehousing or storing of products occurs, except for a few hours or, at most, a day. Cross-docking allows Walmart to operate only a small number of distribution centres to service its vast network of stores and supercentres, which contributes to efficiency. It also uses fleet-management software to enhance operations.

This does increase cost and investment, but the benefits in terms of responsiveness justify the cost in Walmart's case. Walmart has invested significantly more than its competitors in information technology to operate its supply chain. The company feeds information about customer requirements and demand from its stores back to its suppliers, which manufacture only what is being demanded. This large investment has improved the efficiency of Walmart's supply chain and made it responsive to customer needs.

Walmart's strategy allows for availability of product. When renovating stores, Walmart ensures any construction is performed during off-hours. When reviewing its supply chain, Walmart continues to enhance its program by diligently assessing associated risks; that is, it reviews the countries it sources from, and assesses the compliance of its potential suppliers.

In the United States, Walmart uses technology to efficiently run its supply chain. *RFID,* which stands for

Walmart operates with an efficient supply chain.
Niloo/Shutterstock.com

# The SmartWay

For decades, the impact of vehicle emissions on our environment has been a concern. Many businesses have used the reduction of greenhouse emissions in their business as a key focus of their corporate social responsibility. In 2013, the SmartWay program was introduced in Canada. Natural Resources Canada and the Supply Chain Management Association partnered to bring this program across the border from the U.S. The U.S. Environmental Protection Agency originally launched the program, which shares industry best practices on supply chain transportation with its members.

The SmartWay program boasts a tool that allows its members to benchmark supply chain fleets. It then measures its progress with respect to various emissions categories. This year-over-year analysis provides feedback to transportation companies and elicits accountability of each company's carbon footprint. Now, program members that can potentially have a negative impact on our environment can work together to create a greener process within the supply chain.

The SmartWay Transport Partnership helps improve environmental performance each year. The tools offered help truck carriers to benchmark operations and track fuel consumption. SmartWay helps its partners to find SmartWay shippers, reduce operating costs, and reduce their companies' carbon footprint. By joining SmartWay as a SmartWay Partner, organizations send a message to stakeholders that

Rouzes/E+/Getty Images

their company is committed to clean freight. ●

## Questions

1. What are the main benefits that organizations receive from being members of SmartWay?

2. What Canadian companies do you believe need to join SmartWay if they have not already?

---

*radio frequency identification,* is a tag that is incorporated in a product for tracking purposes. RFID improves the efficiency of inventory tracking and management. Walmart has already asked its suppliers to use RFID. Walmart says that RFID will result in a 30 percent reduction of out-of-stock items and less excess inventory in the supply chain.[20] Some suppliers have complied, but many to date have not. The cost of using this new technology is the reason for them not going ahead.

Three lessons can be learned from these two examples. First, there is no one best supply chain for every company. Second, the best supply chain is the one that is consistent with the needs of the customer segment being served and complements a company's marketing strategy. And finally, supply chain managers are often called upon to make trade-offs between efficiency and responsiveness on various elements of a company's supply chain.

For a discussion of linking supply chain management with corporate social responsibility, review the Focus on Ethics box, "The SmartWay."[21]

> *Walmart keeps relatively low inventory levels, and most inventory is stocked in stores available for sale, not in warehouses gathering dust.*

# KEY LOGISTICS FUNCTIONS IN A SUPPLY CHAIN

The four key logistics functions in a supply chain are transportation, order processing, inventory management, and warehousing. These functions have become so complex that many companies are outsourcing them to third-party logistics providers. Ultimately, successful logistics management minimize the total costs to logistics while delivering the appropriate level of customer service factors of time, dependability, communication, and convenience.

## TRANSPORTATION

There are five basic modes of transportation—railroads, motor carriers, air carriers, water carriers, and pipelines—as combinations involving two or more modes, such as highway trailers on a rail flatcar. Although many manufacturers pay transportation expenses, some retailers negotiate with their vendors to absorb this expense. The transportation modes can be evaluated on six basic service criteria:

- *Cost:* Charges for transportation
- *Time:* Speed of transit
- *Capability:* What can be realistically carried with this mode, such as controlled temperatures and humidity levels
- *Dependability:* Reliability of service regarding time, loss, and damage
- *Accessibility:* Ability to move products over a specific route or network; for example, some destinations, such as remote areas in northern parts of Canada, may be unavailable by truck or water
- *Frequency:* Refers to how often a marketer can ship products by a specific transportation mode. Pipelines provide continuous shipments whereas railways and water carriers follow specific schedules for moving products from one location to another.

## ORDER PROCESSING

Order processing is much more sophisticated these days with the use of **electronic data interchange (EDI)**. EDI is the computer-to-computer exchange of business documents from a retailer to a supplier and back. Purchase orders and invoices can be transmitted back and forth electronically, replacing manual processing. Walmart is a pioneer in using EDI. Now, many other retailers also use this system. The use of EDI increases the speed, accuracy, and streamlining of operations between retailer and supplier.

## INVENTORY MANAGEMENT

Inventory management entails maintaining the delicate balance between keeping too little and too much inventory. For example, a retailer that carries too much inventory ends up with a lot of capital tied up in storing products in a warehouse. Too little inventory means that there is an increased risk for being out of stock and having unhappy customers.

A solution to this problem is the **just-in-time (JIT) inventory system**, which is designed to deliver less merchandise on a more frequent basis than traditional inventory systems. This system requires fast on-time delivery. The firm gets the merchandise "just-in-time" for it to be used in production of another product, or for sale when the customer wants it, in the case of consumer products.

Although firms achieve great benefits from a just-in-time system, it is not without its costs. The logistics function becomes more complicated with more frequent deliveries. Greater order frequencies result in smaller orders, which are more expensive to transport and more difficult to coordinate.

## WAREHOUSING

There are two types of warehouses: a public warehouse offering storage for small companies or individuals, and a private warehouse is used usually by

Inventory management helps companies maintain optimal levels of inventory.
© Cultura Creative (RF)/Alamy Stock Photo

large firms. Most storage warehouses are located in the outskirts of the city where rail and truck transportation are easily available. Warehouses are places to store products, whereas distribution centres described below receive, store, and redistribute goods to customers.

Distribution centres can be divided into three types: traditional, cross-docking, and combination. In a traditional distribution centre, merchandise is unloaded from trucks and placed on shelves for storage. When the merchandise is required in stores, a worker goes to the shelf, picks up the item, and places it in a bin. A conveyer transports the merchandise to a staging area, where it is consolidated and made ready for shipment to stores.

The second type of distribution centre is called cross-docking. For example, Heinz ships ketchup pre-packaged in the quantity required for each Walmart store. It is then sent to a staging area rather than into storage. When all the merchandise going to a particular Walmart store has arrived in the staging area, it is loaded onto a Walmart truck that goes directly to the store.

The third type of distribution centre consists of a combination of the two types explained above. Most modern distribution centres are comprised of the third type. It is difficult for a company to operate without some storage facilities, even if merchandise is stored for only a few days.

## ask YOURSELF

1. *Explain the concept of cross-docking.*

2. *Describe a just-in-time inventory system.*

**LO 1**
• A marketing channel consists of individuals and firms involved in the process of making a product or service available for use by consumers or business users.

• Intermediaries make possible the flow of products and services from producers to buyers by performing transactional, logistical, and facilitating functions, thereby creating time, place, form, information, and possession utility.

**LO 2**
• Multichannel marketing is the blending of different communication and delivery channels that are mutually reinforcing in attracting, retaining, and building relationships with consumers.

• When consumers shop and buy in the traditional marketplace as well as in the online marketspace, marketers reinforce the consumer benefits of time, place, form, information, and possession utility.

**LO 3**
• Vertical marketing systems are channels designed to achieve channel function economies and marketing impact. A vertical marketing system may be one of three types: corporate, contractual, or administered.

• Corporate systems display ownership of the next level or the entire channel.

• Contractual systems benefit from functional economies and marketing impact by combining efforts on a contractual basis.

• Administered systems achieve coordination through size and influence rather than ownership.

**LO 4**
• The final choice of a marketing channel by a producer depends on a number of factors. They are market factors, product factors, and company factors.

• Channel design considerations are based on the target market coverage sought by producers, the buyer requirements to be satisfied, and the profitability of the channel.

• Target market coverage comes about through one of three levels of distribution density: intensive, exclusive, or selective distribution.

• Buyer requirements are evident in the amount of information, convenience, variety, and service sought by consumers.

• Profitability—of each channel member and the channel as a whole—is largely affected by costs and whether or not costs can be shared by members.

**LO 5**
• A supply chain is a sequence of firms that perform activities required to create and deliver a good or service to consumers or industrial users.

• Supply chain management is the integration and organization of information and logistics across firms for the purpose of creating value for consumers.

• The goals to be achieved by a firm's marketing strategy determine whether its supply chain needs to be more responsive or efficient in meeting customer requirements. Marketers today recognize that the choice of a supply chain involves three steps: (1) understand the customer; (2) understand the supply chain, and (3) harmonize the supply chain with the marketing strategy.

## key terms and concepts... **A REFRESHER**

channel conflict
cross-channel shopper
disintermediation
dual distribution
electronic data interchange (EDI)
electronic marketing channels

exclusive distribution
franchising
intensive distribution
intermediaries
just-in-time (JIT) inventory system
logistics

marketing channel
multichannel marketing
selective distribution
supply chain
supply chain management
vertical marketing systems

## hands-on... **APPLY YOUR KNOWLEDGE**

**The Importance of Supply Chain in Marketing** The opening vignette describes the reliance companies have on intermediaries performing a logistical function. Review Figures 10–1 and 10–3 and create a list of companies that could potentially work with WildPlay Element Parks to perform the transactional and facilitating function of the marketing channel.

chapter vignette... **ACTIVITY**

In the opening vignette, a WildPlay executive describes the role of the company's supply chain to produce exceptional experiences across Canada. Considering the comments in the vignette, as well as the figures describing intermediaries and the marketing function channels they perform, brainstorm other locations for future WildPlay Parks and outline what would be required from the intermediaries in its supply chains and marketing channels.

infographic... **DATA ANALYSIS**

The Infographic in this chapter that breaks down Canada's top 100 franchises illustrates that more than 4 in 10 of the top 100 franchises are food franchises. Consider the number of individuals directly employed by the industry. Now consider the different components of the restaurant supply chain. How many other jobs do you think are reliant on the success of the Canadian restaurant industry?

# Retailing and Wholesaling

**A**ccording to Statistics Canada, almost 98 percent of the 1.17 million businesses in Canada in 2015 were classified as small businesses. Small businesses employ less than 100 people and are essential to the Canadian economy; however, tens of thousands of small businesses disappear each year. Fortunately, there are various measures individuals with an entrepreneurial spirit can employ to make their small businesses successful.

Used with permission of 9Round.com Fitness & Kickboxing

Many Canadians work in retail as part of a corporate chain where decision-making and purchasing is centralized. Other Canadians venture independently, taking on all the risks and rewards of their business venture. Finally, contractual systems allow for a more-shared risk model for individuals wanting to start a business. Franchising is a type of contractual system.

Franchising offers franchisees a proven business concept along with a support network to make their business successful. Success in one franchise location leads to success in the entire franchise system, making all individuals involved vested in the success of one another. Furthermore, by having a support network and systems that have been successful in the past, a franchise model helps reduce the risks of business failure.

According to the Canadian Franchise Association, the decision to choose this type of contractual system is an important one for both the franchisee and the franchisor. The franchisee will become a small business owner assuming leadership in his or her business, while the franchisor will invest resources and support in the franchisee while assuming some reputational risk in the actions of the individual.

With locations in British Columbia, Alberta, Saskatchewan, and Ontario, 9Round offers a proven business model for a successful fitness business. Potential franchisees need to apply for consideration to join the 9Round team. "We are looking for individuals that a driven to succeed and had a strong work ethic," shares Shannon Hudson, 9Round's chief executive officer. "Starting a business is not easy, but our business model works for the right individual with an entrepreneurial spirit."

Upon mutual consent, franchisees pay a $24,000 franchise fee and then work with a development agent to begin their site selection process and 9Round gym construction. Plus, franchisees complete a four-day intensive training program at the 9Round corporate headquarters before opening their own gym.

9Round promises to deliver the ultimate body transformation program for all fitness levels. It is a specialized fitness centre dedicated to serving clients who want a unique, fun, and proven workout that guarantees results. 9Round offers a kick-boxing-theme fitness program that incorporates functional, interval, cardiovascular, and circuit training regimens within 1,000 to 1,500 square feet of retail space. The programs consist of a proprietary system of nine challenging workout stations developed by a professional fighter. Locations are primarily for workouts with some space allocated to retail specialized products.

Truly an international organization with locations in the United States, Mexico, Australia, New Zealand, Saudi Arabia, Jordan, and the United Kingdom as well as Canada, 9Round's business model is well-tested in multiple markets.

"Being a franchisee allows you to leverage other business owners in our franchise system," says Shannon. "9Round provides its franchisees with the business

## CHAPTER FEATURES

**Rounding Up Franchisees**
International franchisee 9Round finds success in Canada and across the globe.

**Trending**
The top retail trends in Canada.

**Convenient Consumption**
The breadth of line found in stores makes it more convenient for consumers to fulfill their needs.

**It's Not Easy Going Green**
Greentailing in Canada is led by Roots.

**Canadian Influencers**
Do the top five Canadian brands influence you?

**Kiosks in Good Taste**
McDonald's uses kiosks to create a customized experience.

**Online Presents**
Discover the top ten sites where Canadians shop.

## CHAPTER OUTLINE

- Rounding up franchisees
- The value of retailing
- Classifying retail outlets
- Target market selection and positioning
- Retailing mix
- Non-store retailing
- Online retailing
- Retailer's usage of the mobile channel
- Wholesaling

trends, marketing, and research required to make them successful. We have economies of scale when making purchases, and we have a trusted brand that is growing internationally." With all these benefits at their disposal, it is still necessary for franchisees to have a strong work ethic and a disciplined approach to building their business.

"Having a proven business model and plan of action gave me the confidence to start my own business," explains 9Round franchisee, Mike Drake. "I found an industry I was passionate about and an organization with a great strategy!" The marketing materials and strategies that 9Round provides its franchisees helps set franchisees up for success. "I believe my journey has been successful because I have ensured consistency with my retail business by following the 9Round standards and techniques."

Although there may be some flexibility to running the business, Mike finds it is much more effective to stick with the program.

"Clients come to my location to help me improve their level of fitness," reflects Mike. "They look to me as an expert in fitness. I look to 9Round as a franchisor as an expert in building a successful retail fitness business.[1]

### reality CHECK ⊘

As you read Chapter II, refer back to the 9Round vignette to answer the following questions:

- Why do you think so many small businesses disappear each year?
- How can becoming a franchisee reduce the risks of business ownership?

# THE VALUE OF RETAILING

**LO 1** **Retailing** includes all activities involved in selling, renting, and providing goods and services to ultimate customers for personal, family, or household use. Distribution involves creating a place where the customer can access a product. It is a key and evolving component of the marketing mix. As technology enables customers to access multiple channels of distribution, the challenge of retailers becomes anticipating customer needs and providing them with favourable purchasing options.

Retailing is an important marketing activity that engages consumers by offering a place for showcasing products that creates interest and excitement. Shopping is not only a way to acquire necessities but also a social activity and often an adventure—retailing makes this possible. Producers and consumers are brought together through retailing actions, and retailing also creates customer value and has a significant impact on the economy. Retailing's economic value is represented by the number of people employed in retailing as well as by the total amount of money exchanged in retail sales. Notwithstanding, trends in retailing do evolve, as shown in the Infographic titled "Canada's Top Retail Trends for 2015."

**retailing**
All activities involved in selling, renting, and providing goods and services to ultimate consumers for personal, family, or household use.

# CONSUMER UTILITIES OFFERED BY RETAILING

The utilities provided by retailers create value for consumers. Time, place, form, information, and possession utilities are offered by most retailers in varying degrees, but one utility is often emphasized more than others. Look at Figure 11–1 to find out how well you can match the retailer with the utility being emphasized in the description.

Placing minibanks in supermarkets puts the bank's products and services close to the consumer, providing place utility. Retail kiosks continue to grow in supermarkets and drugstores as this self-source technology is meant to improve service.[2] Hudson's Bay makes the purchase easier by offering different ways to pay for the purchase, providing possession utility. Form utility—production or alteration of a product—is offered by Ralph Lauren through its online "Create Your Own" program, which offers shirts that meet each customer's specifications. Finding toy shelves well-stocked year-round is the time utility dreamed about by every child (and many parents) who enters Toys "R" Us. Many retailers offer a combination of the four basic utilities. Some supermarkets, for example, offer convenient locations (place utility) and are open 24 hours (time utility). In addition, consumers may seek additional utilities such as entertainment, recreation, or information.

# Infographic

Used with permission of Linkett

## Figure 11–1

Which company best represents which utilities?

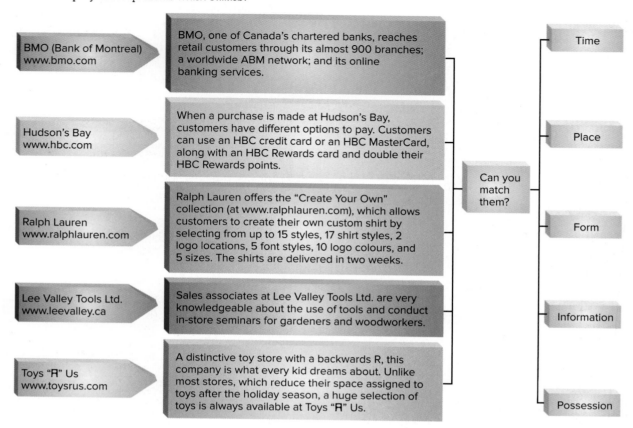

| | | |
|---|---|---|
| BMO (Bank of Montreal) www.bmo.com | BMO, one of Canada's chartered banks, reaches retail customers through its almost 900 branches; a worldwide ABM network; and its online banking services. | Time |
| Hudson's Bay www.hbc.com | When a purchase is made at Hudson's Bay, customers have different options to pay. Customers can use an HBC credit card or an HBC MasterCard, along with an HBC Rewards card and double their HBC Rewards points. | Place |
| Ralph Lauren www.ralphlauren.com | Ralph Lauren offers the "Create Your Own" collection (at www.ralphlauren.com), which allows customers to create their own custom shirt by selecting from up to 15 styles, 17 shirt styles, 2 logo locations, 5 font styles, 10 logo colours, and 5 sizes. The shirts are delivered in two weeks. | Form |
| Lee Valley Tools Ltd. www.leevalley.ca | Sales associates at Lee Valley Tools Ltd. are very knowledgeable about the use of tools and conduct in-store seminars for gardeners and woodworkers. | Information |
| Toys "Я" Us www.toysrus.com | A distinctive toy store with a backwards R, this company is what every kid dreams about. Unlike most stores, which reduce their space assigned to toys after the holiday season, a huge selection of toys is always available at Toys "Я" Us. | Possession |

Can you match them?

## THE CANADIAN RETAIL SCENE

Retail is a vibrant and important part of the Canadian economy as retailers develop strong ties with Canadians throughout their everyday lives.

In 2016, Canadian retailers had revenues of over $532 billion.[3] In Canada, Loblaw Companies Limited, Empire Company Limited, and Metro Inc. are the top three in terms of sales, while Wal-Mart Stores Inc., Costco Wholesale Corporation, and The Kroger Co. are the top three globally.[4]

Figure 11–2 tells us that $115 billion was spent on food and drink in 2016. Supermarkets make up the majority of that retail spend, so it follows logically that the three largest retailers in Canada in terms of sales are predominantly in the food business.

There is a growing trend for American retailers to open locations in Canada. However, entering the Canadian retail scene is not easy. HBC sold the bulk of its weakest chain Zellers Inc. to the U.S. retail giant Target. The chain assumed control of up to 220 Zellers stores. The move, which came after years of rumours and discussion about Target's desire to acquire space in Canada, dramatically reshaped the domestic retail landscape. It underscored the growing demand by foreign retailers for Canadian locations to take advantage of the country's relatively healthy economy as well as the importance of Canadian retailers to be competitive to keep Canadians shopping at home. Unfortunately, two years after it opened its first stores in Canada, Target closed down its Canadian retail operations.[5]

## THE GLOBAL RETAIL PICTURE

Retailing is also a very important factor in the global economy, and it is a difficult retail climate for store owners. In the past few years, the worldwide economy has been challenged by issues such as terrorism, economic downturn, reduced tourism, political crises, and low consumer confidence. All of these issues translate into lower sales for retail. At the same time, consumers are empowered, and it is more difficult to gain and maintain their loyalty. Profits have to be worked at very diligently. Technology is making the industry more sophisticated and streamlined, and consolidation makes some competitors large and very powerful. It is a demanding and thorny business.

Not all countries have experienced the soft demand and market challenges that have characterized the major industrialized nations. Some of the developing countries

## Figure 11–2

Retail sales ($ millions) for 2016 in Canada by industry

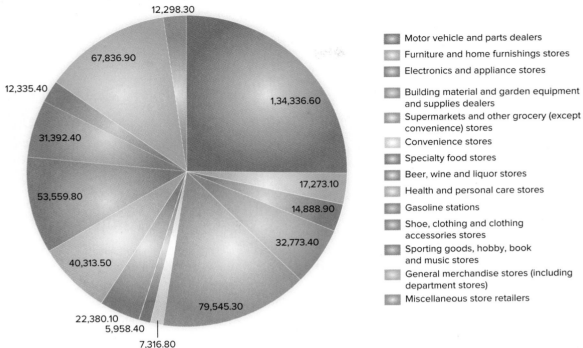

- 12,298.30
- 67,836.90
- 12,335.40
- 31,392.40
- 53,559.80
- 40,313.50
- 22,380.10
- 5,958.40
- 7,316.80
- 79,545.30
- 32,773.40
- 14,888.90
- 17,273.10
- 1,34,336.60

Legend:
- Motor vehicle and parts dealers
- Furniture and home furnishings stores
- Electronics and appliance stores
- Building material and garden equipment and supplies dealers
- Supermarkets and other grocery (except convenience) stores
- Convenience stores
- Specialty food stores
- Beer, wine and liquor stores
- Health and personal care stores
- Gasoline stations
- Shoe, clothing and clothing accessories stores
- Sporting goods, hobby, book and music stores
- General merchandise stores (including department stores)
- Miscellaneous store retailers

**Source:** Statistics Canada, CANSIM, table 080-0020, February 22, 2017, accessed at http://www.statcan.gc.ca/tables-tableaux/sum-som/l01/cst01/trad15a-eng.htm.

or emerging markets in Asia and Eastern Europe are experiencing solid growth and are developing modern types of retailing. China, India, and Russia are seen as some of the biggest growth opportunities for retail in the next few years.

A study of the top 250 global retailers by Deloitte ranks the world's biggest retailers. The chart accompanying Figure 11–3 shows that most of the top ten global retailers have sought opportunities to serve consumers outside their country of origin.

### ask YOURSELF

1. When Ralph Lauren makes shirts to a customer's exact preferences, what utility is provided?

2. The customer has different ways to pay for a purchase at Hudson's Bay. What utility is provided?

## Figure 11–3

Where do we find the top retailers in the world? Who are they?

| Rank | Country of Origin | Name of Company | 2015 Retail Revenue (US$ Millions) |
|---|---|---|---|
| 1 | US | Wal-Mart Stores, Inc. | $482,130 |
| 2 | US | Costco Wholesale Corporation | $116,199 |
| 3 | US | The Kroger Co. | $109,830 |
| 4 | Germany | Schwarz Unternehmenstreuhand KG | $94,448 |
| 5 | US | Walgreens Boots Alliance, Inc. | $89,631 |
| 6 | US | The Home Depot, Inc. | $88,519 |
| 7 | France | Carrefour S.A. | $84,856 |
| 8 | Germany | Aldi Einkauf GmbH & Co. oHG | $82,164 |
| 9 | UK | Tesco PLC | $81,109 |
| 10 | US | Amazon.com, Inc. | $79,268 |

**Source:** Deloitte Touche Tohmatsu Limited, *Global Powers of Retailing 2017: The art and science of customers,* accessed at http://www2.deloitte.com/global/en/pages/consumer-business/articles/global-powers-of-retailing.html.

# FORMS OF OWNERSHIP

**LO 2** For manufacturers, consumers, and the economy, retailing is an important component of marketing that has several variations. Because of the large number of alternative forms of retailing, it is easier to understand the differences among retail institutions by recognizing that outlets can be classified by ownership. **Form of ownership** distinguishes retail outlets on the basis of whether individuals, corporate chains, or contractual systems own or control the outlet. Each form has its own benefits and challenges.

## INDEPENDENT RETAILER

One of the most common forms of retail ownership is the independent business, owned by an individual. Small independent retailers account for more than 60 percent of the total retail trade in Canada. They tend to be retailers such as bakeries, sporting goods stores, jewellery stores, or gift stores. Other types of small independent retailers include restaurants, automotive supply stores, bookstores, paint stores, flower shops, and women's accessories outlets. The advantage of this form of ownership for the owner is that he or she can be his or her own boss. For customers, the independent store can offer convenience, quality personal service, and lifestyle compatibility. This is mainly due to the smaller organization being able to adapt and to be more efficient than its larger competitors.[6]

## CORPORATE CHAIN

A second form of ownership, the corporate chain, involves multiple outlets under common ownership. If you've ever shopped at Hudson's Bay, Sears, or Real Canadian Superstore, you've shopped at a chain outlet.

In a chain operation, centralization of decision-making and purchasing is common. Chain stores have advantages in dealing with manufacturers, particularly as the size of the chain grows. A large chain can bargain with a manufacturer to obtain good service or volume discounts on orders. Loblaw's large volume makes it a strong negotiator with manufacturers of most products. The buying power of chains is obvious to consumers who compare prices at chain stores with other types of stores. Consumers also benefit in dealing with chains because there are multiple outlets with similar merchandise and consistent management policies.

Retailing has become a high-tech business for many large chains. Walmart, for example, has developed a sophisticated inventory-management and cost-control system that

**form of ownership**
Distinguishes retail outlets on the basis of whether individuals, corporate chains, or contractual systems own the outlet.

McDonald's offers franchising opportunities.

David Cooper/Toronto Star via Getty Images

allows rapid price changes for each product in every store. In addition, stores such as Walmart are implementing pioneering new technologies such as radio frequency identification (RFID) tags to improve the quality of information available about products. RFID is a tag that is incorporated in a product for tracking purposes, which improves the efficiency of inventory tracking and management.

## CONTRACTUAL SYSTEM

Contractual systems involve independently owned stores that use leverage to act like a chain. Contractual systems include retailer-sponsored cooperatives, wholesaler-sponsored voluntary chains, and franchises. One retailer-sponsored cooperative is Home Hardware, which is a collection of independent hardware and home-renovation stores across Canada. Home Hardware actually created its own wholesale operation to take full advantage of dealings with manufacturers and suppliers. As a cooperative, members can take advantage of volume discounts commonly available to chains and also give the impression of being a large chain, which may be viewed more favourably by some consumers. Wholesaler-sponsored voluntary chains such as Independent Grocers' Association (IGA) try to achieve similar benefits.

In a franchise system, an individual or firm (the franchisee) contracts with a parent company (the franchisor) to set up a business or retail outlet. McDonald's, Holiday Inn, and Subway all offer franchising opportunities. The franchisor usually assists in selecting the store location, setting up the store, advertising, and training personnel. In addition, the franchisor provides step-by-step procedures for major aspects of the business and guidelines for the

Harry Rosen, a high-end men's clothing retailer, provides a good example of retail positioning.
Used by permission of Harry Rosen Inc.

most likely decisions a franchisee will confront. The franchisee pays a one-time franchise fee and an annual royalty, usually tied to the store's sales. By selling franchises, an organization reduces the cost of expansion, although they lose some control. To ensure mutual benefits to all parties involved, a good franchisor concentrates on enhancing the image and reputation of the franchise name.[7] Review the chapter-opening vignette, "Rounding Up Franchisees," to better understand franchises.[8]

# TARGET MARKET SELECTION AND POSITIONING

**LO 3** Retailing involves many decisions and considerations. In this section, we look at the issues in selecting a target market and the concept of retail positioning.

## SELECTING A TARGET MARKET

The first task in developing a retail strategy is to define a target market, describing it in detail. Without customers, even the best-conceived retail concept is nothing, so focusing on customers is the guiding principle of successful retail businesses. This focus involves understanding wants and needs, knowing customer preferences, analyzing behaviour, and deciding how to craft all of the dimensions of the retail concept to appeal to the targeted customer. Look at any mall or shopping district, and you will see the varied selection of retail offerings the customer has to choose from. This provides a challenge to retailers. It is no longer enough to

> *McDonald's and Subway look at demographics— population, family, and age characteristics—to determine where new restaurants should be located and what formats to offer.*

appeal to customers; now the retailer has to interest, engage, and delight customers in order to foster loyalty.

How do we define target markets? The most common descriptors are geographic, demographic, psychographic, and behaviouristic. Retailers study these factors and adjust their retail mix accordingly. McDonald's and Subway look at demographics—population, family, and age characteristics—to determine where new restaurants should be located and what formats to offer. Retailers such as Canadian Tire look at consumers' trends and tastes and adjust their product offerings and store composition to match customer preferences. Staples and Shoppers Drug Mart have adjusted their store hours to respond to the behaviour of consumers; many now prefer to shop and do errands in the evening after working during the day. In fact, some retailers are open 24 hours a day.

## RETAIL POSITIONING

Just as marketers of packaged goods position their products to differentiate themselves from competitors, so do retailers. For example, Harry Rosen is a high-end men's clothing retailer. It would be a mistake in times of recession for Harry Rosen to start carrying lower-quality, low-priced suits. Larry Rosen, CEO and chairman of Harry Rosen Inc., and son of founder Harry Rosen, says, "The customer who is used to the quality and calibre of our product is not looking for a cheaper product. Maybe he'll buy slightly less this year but it's not about reducing quality. It's about sticking to your guns, to who you are." The confidence to be able to do so comes from a deep understanding of your customers and their buying habits.[9]

---

### marketing **TIP**

*"Being a franchisee allows you to leverage other business owners in our franchise system."*

*–Shannon Hudson, chief executive officer, 9Round*

---

## SHOPPER MARKETING

Shopper marketing is a hot trend in marketing today. It is a discipline designed to understand how consumers behave as shoppers in different channels and formats. Consequently, shopper-marketing practices extend well outside of the store, to the place and time when a consumer first thinks about purchasing a product. That might be on a treadmill at the gym, at home reading a magazine, or in the car while driving to work. That means that shopper marketing is by necessity a multichannel practice that makes use of traditional media, new media, direct marketing, loyalty, trade promotion, and innumerable other marketing techniques.

Underneath it all is one area that is largely alien to traditional marketers, whose focus has been almost exclusively on understanding *consumers*—that is, the consumption of goods and services. What's been ignored is understanding *shoppers*—that is, consumers when they are in the shopping mode. Shopper marketing is new to Canada, but the distinction in understanding shoppers is important.[10]

## RETAILING MIX

**LO 4** The marketing mix, or the 4 Ps (product, price, place, and promotion), is used in retail just as it is in other businesses, but with some unique considerations. In this section, we look at the retailing mix, which includes product and service considerations, retail pricing, physical location factors, and communications, as shown in Figure 11–4. All of these

**retailing mix**
The goods and services, pricing, physical distribution, and communications tactics chosen by a store.

**level of service**
The degree of service provided to the customer by self-, limited-, and full-service retailers.

---

### Figure 11–4
The retailing mix

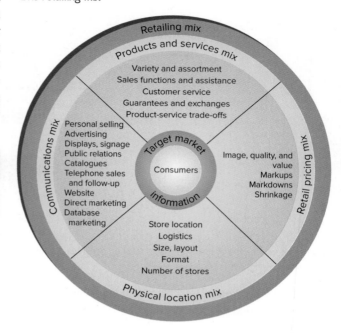

---

components of the mix focus on the consumer. In retail, it is often said that the consumer is king, and treating consumers that way is a winning idea for successful retailing.

The positioning of a retail store must be consistent with the store's **retailing mix**. The four elements must be coordinated so that they portray a clear position to consumers. For example, Winners is positioned as a store providing upscale designer clothing at a discount price. If prices suddenly rose and consumers came to the conclusion that they were not getting a bargain, Winners' positioning would not be effective.

## PRODUCTS AND SERVICES

One of the first decisions that retailers make is what they are going to sell. Usually, both services and products are offered. McDonald's offers a hamburger, which is the tangible product, but the smiles, thank yous, and clean washrooms make up some of the service components. A department store such as Hudson's Bay sells many products—from clothing to housewares—and also provides services such as bridal registries. First Choice Hair Cutters provides services such as haircuts, colouring, and styling, but also sells hair care products. The balance between products and services involves a trade-off between costs and customer satisfaction.

**Level of Service**   Most customers perceive little variation in retail outlets by form of ownership. Rather, differences among retailers are more obvious in terms of level of service. **Level of service** is used to describe the

## Figure 11–5

Breadth versus depth of merchandise lines

Breadth: Number of different product lines

| Shoes | Appliances | CDs | Men's clothing |
|---|---|---|---|

Depth: Number of items within each product line

| Nike running shoes<br>Florsheim dress shoes<br>Top Sider deck shoes<br>Adidas tennis shoes | Sony TV sets<br>JVC DVD players<br>General Electric dishwashers<br>Sharp microwave ovens | Classical<br>Rock<br>Jazz<br>Country western | Suits<br>Ties<br>Jackets<br>Overcoats<br>Socks<br>Shirts |
|---|---|---|---|

degree of service provided to the customer. Three levels of service include self-, limited-, and full-service retailers. Stores such as Costco do not offer bags, while outlets such as Holt Renfrew provide a wide range of customer services from gift wrapping to wardrobe consultation.

**SELF-SERVICE** Self-service is at the extreme end of the level-of-service continuum because the customer performs many functions and little is provided by the outlet. Home building-supply outlets and gas stations are often self-service. Warehouse stores such as Costco, usually in buildings several times larger than a conventional store, are self-service, with all non-essential customer services eliminated. Several new forms of self-service include FedEx's placement of self-service package shipping stations in retail stores and office buildings, and self-service scanning systems currently in use in Loblaw stores, Home Depot, Walmart, and other retailers.

**LIMITED SERVICE** Limited-service outlets provide some services, such as credit and merchandise return, but not others, such as alterations to clothes. General merchandise stores such as Shoppers Drug Mart and Ikea are usually considered limited-service outlets. Customers are responsible for most shopping activities, although salespeople are available in departments such as cosmetics at Shoppers Drug Mart.

**FULL SERVICE** Full-service retailers, which include most specialty stores and department stores, provide many services to their customers. Holt Renfrew, a Canadian specialty fashion retailer with nine stores across the country, is very committed to exemplary customer service. Its stores feature more salespeople on the floor than other similarly sized stores, and Holt Renfrew offers a national concierge service, as well as personal shopping in each store. Employees are trained in customer follow-up, and many call their clients to advise them of new merchandise and send thank-you notes after purchase. With an eye kept fixed on customers and

their evolving needs, Holt Renfrew is a leader in merchandise assortments and in innovations in customer services demonstrated by its previous successes and future expansion plans.[11]

**Merchandise Mix** Merchandise selection is one of the major attracting factors for customers, so choices and combinations must be made carefully and continually updated to reflect current trends and tastes. This involves finding sources of supply of the products, or having them manufactured, as well as managing inventory and warehousing. The **merchandise mix** describes how many different types of products a store carries and in what assortment. The Focus on Ethics box, "It's Not Easy Going Green," suggests that the move to carrying eco-friendly products is another factor in retailers' merchandise mix decisions.[12]

Retail outlets vary by their merchandise mix, the key distinction being the breadth and depth of the items offered to customers (see Figure 11–5). **Depth of product line** means the assortment of products within each product line, such as a shoe store that offers running shoes, dress shoes, and children's shoes. **Breadth of product line** refers to the variety of different lines a store carries, such as women's clothing, men's clothing, children's clothing, cosmetics, and housewares.

**DEPTH OF LINE** Stores that carry a large assortment (depth) of a related line of items are limited-line stores. Sport Chek sporting goods stores carry considerable depth in sports equipment, ranging from golf accessories to running shoes. Stores that carry tremendous depth in one primary line of merchandise are single-line stores. Victoria's Secret, a nationwide chain, carries great

**merchandise mix**
How many different types of products a store carries and in what assortment.

**depth of product line**
The assortment of products within each product line.

**breadth of product line**
The variety of different items a store carries.

# It's Not Easy Going Green

According to the Environmental Careers Organization (ECO) Canada, the green economy includes "inputs, activities, outputs, and outcomes as they relate to the production of green products and services." In essence, by "reducing resource consumption, harmful emissions, and minimizing all forms of environment impact," a new economy is created that can not only save money and our world but also create career opportunities. ECO Canada is a non-profit organization whose vision is to build the world's leading environmental workforce. It does this by creating online resources for careers and training.

Since consumers are becoming more and more aware of the impact of their purchases on the environment, green products have become increasingly available, and more emphasis is being placed on marketing these strategies. For example, apparel companies have begun to produce environmentally friendly clothing. For example, Roots employs sustainable practices through using eco-friendly materials and manufacturing clothes out of organic or recycled cottons. The company continues to develop more eco-friendly products each year.

Roots has made protecting the environment a core value. It believes the environment is one of the most critical issues of our time. Along with some of the world's leading environmentalists, Roots demonstrates its commitment through its actions and financial support of environmental organizations. A partial list of environmental organizations that Roots works with includes the David Suzuki Foundation, the Canadian Wildlife Federation, and the Jane Goodall Institute of Canada.

The larger strategy being considered in Canadian retailing and business is corporate social responsibility (CSR), where companies voluntarily conduct business in a manner that is sustainable from an economic, social, and environmental standpoint. Not only is CSR important locally, but Canadian companies see the value of incorporating their practices on an international scale. Considering what Roots is doing with

Jill Morgan/Alamy Stock Photo

its stores and apparel, it is surprising not to see them recognized in lists like *Maclean's* Top 50 Socially Responsible Companies. Furthermore, seeing Roots' competitors, such as Adidas, Nike, and Gap, get recognized helps confirm the importance of CSR in Canadian retailing. ●

## Questions

1. Describe the target market that retailers such as Roots are trying to reach by adopting green practices.

2. Considering a retailer you have made a purchase from, identify three changes it can make to its practices that would support a green economy.

---

depth in women's lingerie. Both limited- and single-line stores are often referred to as *specialty outlets*.

Specialty outlets focus on one type of product, such as electronics (Best Buy), office supplies (Staples), or books (Indigo Books & Music) at very competitive prices. These outlets are referred to in the trade as category killers because they often dominate the market. Indigo Books & Music, for example, controls a large percentage of the retail book market in Canada.

BREADTH OF LINE    Stores that carry a variety of product lines, with limited depth, are referred to as *general merchandise stores*. For example, large department stores such as Hudson's Bay, Sears, and Target carry a wide range of different lines of products but not unusual sizes. The breadth and depth of merchandise lines are important decisions for a retailer. Traditionally, outlets carried

## Canadian Influencers

Our top five most influential brands in Canada:

| Rank | Brand |
|------|-------|
| 1 | MEC |
| 2 | Home Hardware |
| 3 | WestJet |
| 4 | Tim Hortons |
| 5 | Cirque du Soleil |

**Source:** Bruce Philip and CB Staff, "Canada's Best Brands 2017: The Top 25," *Canadian Business*, October 11, 2016, accessed at http://www.canadianbusiness.com/lists-and-rankings/best-brands/canadas-best-brands-2017-the-top-25/image/3/.

## marketing NewsFlash

# Convenient Consumption

Icatnews/Shutterstock.com

**W**hen retail stores offer products unrelated to one another, it is considered to use a scrambled merchandising strategy. What used to be considered odd is now a common practice as retailers realize the importance of gaining the attention of consumers who are pressed for time.

Consider Dollarama, the largest dollar-store chain in Canada. With well over 800 stores across the country, it offers customers with compelling value in convenient locations, and a broad assortment of everyday consumer products, general merchandise, and seasonal items.

All stores are corporate-owned and provide customers with a consistent shopping experience. Dollarama's uncomplicated approach to its business involves operating clean stores, maintaining a consistent inventory of name brands and house brands, and dealing directly with suppliers. A leader in the industry, Dollarama knows the importance of investing in technology as it invested heavily in this area to increase efficiency during its

growth. In Canada, there is a dollar store for every 32,000 people, far less than the one per 15,500 people in the United States. Dollarama's current plans call for opening an additional 70 to 80 stores per year across the country.

An estimated 4,000 items line Dollarama's shelves year-round, and an additional 700 or so are seasonal products. This ability to capitalize on seasonal demand is widely admired.

To follow this eclectic trend set by Dollarama, retailers look to partnerships and other strategies to draw shoppers in to one convenient location and develop synergies. For example, in 2014 Loblaw purchased Shoppers Drug Mart for $12.4 billion in cash and stock. The synergies created by the two organization helped increase profitability and strengthened Loblaw in its pharmacy presence, which was already available in its superstores.

In 2016, Loblaw joined a number of different grocery stores and began offering beer in Ontario. Loblaw began with 19 stores across the province. The vision is to have 450 of Ontario's 1,500 supermarkets licensed

to sell beer and cider. Historically, Brewers Retail, rebranded The Beer Store, was the only retailer permitted to sell beer for off-site consumption in Ontario. Provincially owned, the Liquor Control Board of Ontario was another option for consumers.

Although Loblaw maybe a pioneer in selling beer through its grocery stores in Ontario, Ontario is not a pioneer of having beer sold through alternate channels. Quebec and New Brunswick have sold beer through their grocery stores for years. ●

## Questions

1. What are the benefits and challenges of adopting a scrambled merchandising strategy?

2. Do you believe consumers will demand more scrambled merchandising from its retailers? Why or why not?

---

related lines of goods. Today, however, **scrambled merchandising**, offering several unrelated product lines in a single store, is common. The modern drugstore carries food, cosmetics, camera equipment, magazines, paper products, toys, small hardware items, and pharmaceuticals. Supermarkets rent carpet-cleaning equipment, operate pharmacy departments, and sell flowers.

Scrambled merchandising makes it convenient for consumers because it eliminates the number of stops required in a shopping trip. However, for the retailer, this merchandising policy means that there is competition between very dissimilar types of retail outlets, or **intertype competition**. A local bakery may compete with a department store, discount outlet, or even a local gas station. Scrambled merchandising and intertype competition make retailing more challenging. The Marketing NewsFlash box, "Convenient Consumption," details

the scrambled merchandising strategy Canadian retailers are adopting.[13]

**PLANOGRAMS** A planogram is a visual diagram or drawing of fixtures and products that illustrates how and where retail products should be placed on a store shelf. It also illustrates how many facings should be allocated for each stock-keeping unit (SKU). The planogram is arranged so that the fastest-moving high-margin products get the most space on the shelf. For example, Procter & Gamble works closely with Walmart by providing the retailer with planograms, which lead to higher profits than if products were placed indiscriminately on the shelf.

**scrambled merchandising**
Offering several unrelated product lines in a single retail store.

**intertype competition**
Competition between very dissimilar types of retail outlets.

# !ndigo
## Enrich your life

Indigo Books & Music is the largest book retailer in Canada and is a category killer.

As competition increases, we're seeing suppliers and retailers becoming more aware of the importance of correctly merchandising their products. Some retailers produce their own planograms while others, such as Walmart, receive planograms from suppliers such as Procter & Gamble.

**Store Atmosphere** Store atmosphere is related to the positioning of a store. For example, Costco has a warehouse appearance that is consistent with the low prices that it offers. Store atmosphere refers to the physical characteristics of a store that provide an overall impression to the consumer. These characteristics consist of the exterior and interior appearance and physical layout of the store. The Apple Store's customer-friendly layout encourages consumers to mingle and sample the products. Apple successfully trademarked its store design, and

**shrinkage**
Breakage and theft of merchandise by customers and employees.

Apple offers a store atmosphere allowing consumers to engage with Apple products.

© Piero Cruciatti/Alamy Stock Photo

continues to trademark the distinctive design and layout of its retail store in Canada. It filed an application with the Canadian Intellectual Property Office and received a trademark for its distinctive design and layout.[14]

The Apple Store is usually quite crowded. This frenetic atmosphere draws in even more people who want to be part of the "event." Every Apple Store offers a range of services designed to help customers get the most out of their Apple products, including face-to-face support and advice at the Genius Bar, hands-on workshops, and special programs for kids.

## RETAIL PRICING

In setting prices for merchandise, retailers must decide on the markup. The markup refers to how much should be added to the cost the retailer paid for a product to reach the final selling price. We discussed the calculation of markup in Chapter 9. The difference between the final selling price and retailer cost is called the gross margin.

Discounting a product, or taking a *markdown*, occurs when the product does not sell at the original price and an adjustment is necessary. Often, new models or styles force the price of existing models to be marked down. Discounts may also be used to increase demand for related products.[15] For example, retailers might take a markdown on DVD players to increase sales of DVDs or reduce the price of cake mix to generate frosting purchases. The *timing* of a markdown can be important. Many retailers take a markdown as soon as sales fall off, to free up valuable selling space and obtain cash. However, other stores delay markdowns to discourage bargain hunters and maintain an image of quality. There is no clear answer, but retailers must consider how the timing might affect future sales.

Although most retailers plan markdowns, many retailers use price discounts as a part of their regular merchandising policy. In Canada, retailers such as Walmart and Bed, Bath & Beyond emphasize consistently low prices and eliminate most markdowns with a strategy often called *everyday low pricing*.[16] Consumers often use price as an indicator of product quality; however, the brand name of the product and the image of the store become important decision factors in these situations.[17]

A special issue for retailers trying to keep prices low is **shrinkage**, or breakage and theft of merchandise

> *What is surprising is that more than 50 percent of thefts are made not by consumers but by employees.*

by customers and employees. What is surprising is that more than 50 percent of thefts are made not by consumers but by employees.

Off-price retailing is a retail pricing practice that is used by retailers such as Winners. **Off-price retailing** involves selling brand-name merchandise at lower than regular prices. The difference between the off-price retailer and a discount store is that off-price merchandise is bought by the retailer from manufacturers with excess inventory at prices below wholesale prices, whereas the discounter buys at full wholesale price but takes less of a markup than do traditional department stores. Because of this difference in the way merchandise is purchased by the retailer, selection at an off-price retailer is unpredictable, and searching for bargains has become a popular activity for many consumers. Savings to the consumer at off-price retailers are reported as high as 70 percent off the prices of a traditional department store.

### ask YOURSELF

1. *What are the four components of the retailing mix?*

2. *What are some examples of stores with scrambled merchandising?*

3. *Would a shop for big men's clothes carrying pants in sizes 40 to 60 have a broad or deep product line?*

## PHYSICAL LOCATION

Another aspect of the retailing mix involves deciding where to locate the store and how many stores to have. Department stores, which started downtown in most cities, have followed customers to the suburbs, and in recent years, more stores have been opened in large regional malls. Most stores today are near several others in one of five settings: the central business district, the regional centre, the community shopping centre, the strip, or the power centre.

The **central business district** is the oldest retail setting, the community's downtown area. Until the regional outflow to suburbs, it was the major shopping area, but the suburban population has grown at the expense of the downtown shopping area.

**Regional shopping centres** consist of 50 to 150 stores that typically attract customers who live or work within a 5- to 15-km range. These large shopping areas often contain two or three anchor stores, which are well-known national or regional stores such as Sears and Hudson's Bay. One of the largest variations of a regional centre is the West Edmonton Mall in Alberta. The shopping centre is a conglomerate of over 800 stores, 7 amusement centres, 110 restaurants, and a 355-room Fantasyland hotel.[18]

A more limited approach to retail location is the **community shopping centre**, which typically has one primary store (usually a department store branch) and often about 20 to 40 smaller outlets. Generally, these centres serve a population of consumers who are within a 2- to 5-km drive.

Not every suburban store is located in a shopping mall. Many neighbourhoods have clusters of stores, referred to as a **strip location**, to serve people who are within a 5- to 10-minute drive. Gas station, hardware, laundry, grocery, and pharmacy outlets are commonly found in a strip location. Unlike the larger shopping centres, the composition of these stores is usually unplanned. A variation of the strip shopping location is called the **power centre**, which is a large shopping strip with many national stores. Power centres are seen as having the convenient location found in many strip centres and the added power of national stores. These large strips often have two to five anchor stores plus a supermarket, which brings the shopper to the power centre on a weekly basis.[19]

## COMMUNICATIONS

The elements of the retailing communication mix described in Figure 11–4 represent an exciting menu of choices for creating customer value

**off-price retailing**
Selling brand-name merchandise at lower than regular prices.

**central business district**
The oldest retail setting, the community's downtown area.

**regional shopping centres**
Consist of 50 to 150 stores that typically attract customers who live within a 5- to 15-km range; often containing two or three anchor stores.

**community shopping centre**
Retail location that typically has one primary store and 20 to 40 smaller outlets, serving a population of consumers within a 2- to 5-km drive.

**strip location**
A cluster of stores serving people who live within a 5- to 10-minute drive.

**power centre**
Large shopping strip with multiple anchor stores, a convenient location, and a supermarket.

**Power centres are unenclosed shopping centres.**
David Cooper/Toronto Star via Getty Images

in the marketplace. Each format allows retailers to offer unique benefits and meet particular needs of various customer groups. Today, retailers combine many of the formats to offer a broader spectrum of benefits and experiences. These **multichannel retailers** utilize and integrate a combination of traditional store and non-store formats such as catalogues and online retailing. Indigo Books & Music, for example, created chapters.indigo.ca to compete with Amazon.

Integrated channels can make shopping simpler and more convenient. A consumer can research choices online or in a catalogue and then make a purchase online, over the telephone, or at the closest store. In addition, the use of multiple channels allows retailers to reach a broader profile of customers. While online retailing may cannibalize catalogue business to some degree, a web transaction costs about half as much to process as a catalogue order. Multichannel retailers also benefit from the synergy of sharing information among the different channel operations.

## ask YOURSELF

1. *Explain how shrinkage impacts retailers.*

2. *A large shopping strip with multiple anchor stores is a _____ centre.*

3. *How do multichannel retailers make shopping simpler and more convenient?*

# NON-STORE RETAILING

**LO 5** Most of the retailing examples discussed earlier in the chapter, such as corporate chains, department stores, and limited- and single-line specialty stores, involve the consumer physically being in the store. Many retailing activities today, however, are not limited to sales in a store. Non-store retailing occurs outside a retail outlet through activities that involve varying levels of customer and retailer involvement. Forms of non-store retailing include automatic vending, television home shopping, and direct marketing (direct mail and catalogue retailing, telemarketing, direct selling, and online buying). Many traditional bricks-and-mortar stores are involved in non-store retailing, making them "click and mortar" concepts; for example, Indigo Books & Music has developed **chapters.indigo.ca**, its online store. Dell Computers, in contrast, relies mainly on non-store retailing for its consumer sales.

# AUTOMATIC VENDING AND KIOSKS

Non-store retailing includes vending machines, which make it possible to serve customers when and where stores cannot. Maintaining and operating vending machines is expensive, so product prices in vending machines tend to be higher than those in stores. Typically, small convenience products are available in vending machines. In Japan, products available in vending machines include dried squid, hair tonic, boxers, green tea, beer, CDs, books, clothing, and even music downloaded from a satellite transmission system. Best Buy uses automated vending kiosks in select airports across Canada. Furthermore, the Marketing NewsFlash box, "Kiosks in Good Taste," discusses how McDonald's uses kiosk technology to help enhance its customer experience.[20]

Improved technology will soon make vending machines easier to use by reducing the need for cash. In Europe, for example, Marconi Online Systems has installed 6,000 vending machines that allow consumers to pay for products using a cellphone. Similarly, the world's largest vending machine company, Canteen Services Inc., is testing a cashless system called FreedomPay, which allows consumers to wave a small wand in front of a sensor to make a purchase.

Another improvement in vending machines—the use of wireless technology to notify retailers when their machines are empty—is one reason automatic merchandising sales are expected to increase in the future.[21]

## TELEVISION HOME SHOPPING

Television home shopping is possible when consumers watch a shopping channel on which products are displayed; orders are then placed over the telephone or the Internet. One popular network is The Shopping Channel, which has 24-hour programming and calls itself a broadcast retailer. A limitation of TV shopping has been the lack of buyer-seller interaction. New Internet technologies, however, now allow consumers to explore different possibilities.

## DIRECT MARKETING FROM A RETAILING PERSPECTIVE

We talk in detail about direct marketing in Chapter 12; here we introduce the idea, as it is an important form of retailing. In its simplest terms, direct marketing is an interactive process of marketing that uses advertising media or direct consumer contact to offer products or services. When a direct communication to a consumer or a business market is intended to generate a response from the recipient, direct marketing is the tactic being used.

# Kiosks in Good Taste

The Canadian restaurant industry has a number of home-grown chains, including St-Hubert, Tim Hortons, and Pizza Pizza. Restaurants such as Harvey's, Wimpy's and The Works are established hamburger chains that are creating more competition for U.S.-based firms such as McDonald's.

For an organization that has built its brand on consistency, McDonald's is also an innovator. In 2016, McDonald's Canada ventured into customized burgers to enhance the retail experience of its customers. Some customers described the experience as upscale and personalized.

Following Australia and the U.K., the in-restaurant experience involves a kiosk, a 100 percent Canadian angus beef patty, and the choice of 30 quality ingredients. Individuals are different, and although many

enjoy a Big Mac®, many Canadians would rather make their own burger.

McDonald's Canada plans to install electronic ordering kiosks in its restaurants by the end of 2017. According to John Betts, chief executive of McDonald's Restaurants of Canada Ltd., there is a lot of interest from Canadians in personalizing a premium burger order. McDonald's Canada has developed the customization strategy because its customers want it and the market is demanding it.

The key to McDonald's Canada's strategy is to enhance the retail experience, not replace roles or automate it. In fact, it plans to hire 15,000 new restaurant employees to assist customers with the ordering kiosks. Furthermore, the company will invest $280 million to establish the kiosks across its 1,400 Canadian locations. ●

## Questions

1. How do you feel the customization strategy will affect McDonald's Canada's brand perception?

2. What other changes could McDonald's Canada make in order to address the personalization and customization that the marketplace is asking for?

---

**Direct Mail and Catalogues** Direct mail and catalogue retailing is attractive because it eliminates the cost of a store and clerks. It costs a traditional retail store more than twice the amount to acquire a new customer than it costs a catalogue retailer. Why? Because catalogues improve marketing efficiency through segmentation and targeting. In addition, they create customer value by providing a fast and convenient means of making a purchase. In Canada, the amount spent on direct mail catalogue merchandise continues to increase; internationally, spending is also increasing. IKEA delivers over 210 million copies of its catalogue to 48 countries in 28 languages, including over 7 million in Canada.[22]

One reason for the growth in catalogue sales is that traditional retailers are adding catalogue operations. Another reason is that many Internet retailers, such as Amazon, have also added catalogues. As consumers' direct mail purchases have increased, the number of catalogues and the number of products sold through catalogues have increased. A typical Canadian household now receives dozens of catalogues every year, and there are billions circulated around the world. The competition and recent increases in postal rates, however,

IKEA delivers over 210 million copies of its catalogue.
© Inter IKEA Systems B.V. 2017.

have combined to cause catalogue retailers to focus on proven customers rather than "prospects." Another successful new approach used by many catalogue retailers is to send specialty catalogues to market niches identified in their databases. L.L. Bean, a longstanding catalogue retailer, has developed an individual catalogue for fly-fishing enthusiasts. Lee Valley Tools Ltd. sends out specialized catalogues for hardware, woodworking, gardening, and Christmas.

**Telemarketing** Another form of non-store retailing, called **telemarketing**, involves using the telephone to interact with and sell directly to consumers. Compared with direct mail, telemarketing is often viewed as a more efficient means of targeting consumers, although the two techniques are often used together. Sears Canada utilizes telemarketing to increase sales of extended warranty programs and other services. Communications companies such as Bell Mobility telemarket new potential customers, and financial institutions such as HSBC and MBNA use telemarketing for customer follow-up and cross-selling. Telemarketing has grown in popularity as companies search for ways to cut costs but still provide convenient access to their customers. Twenty-five years ago, the telemarketing industry generated $3.1 billion in sales and planned to employ one million Canadians by the year 2000. By 2007, there were approximately 250,000 Canadians employed by the industry, and it generated $17 billion in sales annually.[23]

As the use of telemarketing grows, consumer privacy has become a topic of discussion among consumers, governments, and businesses. Issues such as industry standards, ethical guidelines, and new privacy laws are evolving

*IKEA delivers over 210 million copies of its catalogue to 48 countries in 28 languages, including over 7 million in Canada.*

to provide a balance between the varying perspectives. The Canadian Radio-television and Telecommunications Commission (CRTC) instituted a national Do Not Call List (DNCL), which was created to enable Canadian consumers to reduce the number of unsolicited telemarketing calls they receive. Every year, thousands of Canadians raise concerns about receiving unwanted telemarketing calls, despite being on the DNCL list.

**Direct Selling** Direct selling, sometimes called door-to-door retailing, involves direct sales of goods and services to consumers through personal interactions and demonstrations in their home or office. A variety of companies, including familiar names such as Avon, Tupperware, and Mary Kay Cosmetics, have created an industry with billions in sales by providing consumers with personalized service and convenience. However, sales have been declining as retail chains begin to carry similar products at discount prices and as the increasing number of dual-career households reduces the number of potential buyers who can be found at home.

**bestbuy.ca and ebay.ca are two examples of online retailers.**

(left): Used with permission of Best Buy Canada. (right): Used by permission of eBay Inc. The eBay logo is a trademark of eBay Inc. Used with permission. *Prices are as of July 31, 2017.

In response to change, many direct-selling retailers are expanding online and into other markets. Avon, for example, already has over six million sales representatives in over 100 countries, with over 10,000 reps trained to sell online. In Canada, the Avon sales force is 65,000 strong.[24] Direct selling is likely to continue to grow in markets where the lack of effective distribution channels increases the importance of door-to-door convenience and where the lack of consumer knowledge about products and brands will increase the need for a person-to-person approach. Furthermore, it will help maximize growth and customer loyalty.[25]

### ask YOURSELF

1. *Why are catalogue sales growing?*
2. *Where are direct-selling retail sales growing? Why?*

# ONLINE RETAILING

**LO 6** Online retailing allows customers to search for, evaluate, and order products through the Internet. For many consumers, the advantages of this form of retailing are the 24-hour access, the ability to comparison-shop, and the in-home privacy. Four in ten Canadians aged 16 and over use the Internet to purchase products and services. This is a space that can no longer be ignored by Canadian retailers, as reported by a Forrester Research study. Canadians may begin foregoing their loyalty to Canadian retailers if prices are cheaper online from non-Canadian retailers. Furthermore, Forrester Research believes that the online retail sales market will increase from $20 billion to $34 billion by 2018, creating a huge opportunity cost for Canadian retailers who have not ventured into an online retailing strategy.[26]

Studies of online shoppers indicated that men were initially more likely than women to buy something online. As the number of online households increased to more than 50 percent, however, the profile of online shoppers changed to include all shoppers. In addition, the number of online retailers grew rapidly for several years but then declined as many stand-alone, Internet-only businesses failed or consolidated. Today, there has been a melding of traditional and online retailers—"bricks and clicks"—that are using experiences from both approaches to create better value and experiences for customers.

Online buying is getting a boost from the comments that consumers are leaving on social media sites such as Facebook and Twitter. These sites are having an influence on what consumers are buying online. Research shows that Facebook and Twitter influences online buying decisions.[27]

## MOBILE BANKING AND CASHLESS FUTURE

One of the biggest problems that online retailers face is that nearly two-thirds of online shoppers make it to "checkout" and then leave the website to compare shipping costs and prices on other sites. Of the shoppers who leave, 70 percent do not return. One way online retailers are addressing this issue is to offer consumers a comparison of competitors' offerings. Online retailers are also trying to improve the online retailing experience by adding experiential, or interactive, activities to their websites. Montreal-based My Virtual Model Inc. develops software for apparel stores so that consumers can create models of themselves online to assist with the purchase process and help with product selection.[28] Car manufacturers such as BMW and Toyota encourage website visitors to build a vehicle by selecting interior and exterior colours, packages, and options and then view the customized virtual car.

## WHY CONSUMERS SHOP AND BUY ONLINE

Consumers typically offer six reasons why they shop and buy online: convenience, choice, communication, customization, cost, and control (see Figure 11–6).

- *Convenience:* Online shopping and buying is *convenient,* so websites must be easy to locate and navigate, and image downloads must be fast.

**Figure 11–6**
Why do consumers shop and buy online?

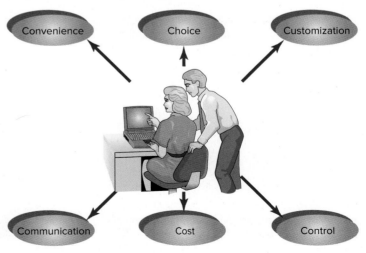

Convenience, choice, communication, customization, cost, and control result in a favourable customer experience.

- *Choice:* There are two dimensions to choice: *selection*—numerous websites for almost anything consumers want—and *assistance*—interactive capabilities of Internet/web-enabled technologies assist customers to make informed choices.

- *Communication:* Communication can take three forms: marketer-to-consumer e-mail notification, consumer-to-marketer buying and service requests, and consumer-to-consumer chat rooms and instant messaging.[29]

- *Customization:* Internet/web-enabled capabilities make possible a highly interactive and individualized information and exchange environment for shoppers and buyers. Consumers get what they want and feel good about the experience. An example is Dell, which allows consumers to choose the components of their computer rather than purchase a computer off the shelf at a bricks-and-mortar retailer.

- *Cost:* Many popular items bought online can be purchased at the same price or cheaper than in retail stores. Lower prices also result from Internet/web-enabled software that permits *dynamic pricing,* the practice of changing prices for products and services in real time in response to supply and demand conditions.

- *Control:* Online shoppers and buyers are empowered consumers. They readily use Internet/web-enabled technology to seek information, evaluate alternatives, and make purchase decisions on their own time, terms, and conditions.

## WHEN AND WHERE ONLINE CONSUMERS SHOP AND BUY

Shopping and buying also happen at different times in the online marketspace than in the traditional marketplace. Though most online retail sales occur Monday through Friday, the busiest shopping day is Monday. Canadians are the world's heaviest Internet users, spending on average 34 hours online monthly. However, Canadians are not the heaviest online consumers, with one in five stating they have never purchased anything online.[30]

## DESCRIBING THE ONLINE CONSUMER

Research indicates that more than 80 percent of Canadians over the age of 16 are now connected to the Internet. Ninety-four percent of Canadians say they use the Internet to compare prices, and 60 percent go online to read or

### Online Presents
### The Top 10 Online Shopping Sites in Canada

| Rank | Retailer |
|------|----------|
| 1 | Shop.ca |
| 2 | Murale.ca |
| 3 | iStoreworld.com |
| 4 | HoltRenfrew.com |
| 5 | TheBay.com |
| 6 | TheSeptember.com |
| 7 | Chapters.Indigo.ca |
| 8 | SHOEme.ca |
| 9 | TheChicCanuck.com |
| 10 | SSENSE.com |

**Source:** Madelyn Chung, "Online Shopping Canada: Our Fave Digital Stores," *Huffington Post Canada,* December 7, 2015, accessed at http://www.huffingtonpost.ca/2015/12/07/online-shopping-sites-canada_n_8742138.html.

write reviews. As a result, consumers are becoming smarter, increasingly informed, and more demanding. This trend will continue as more and more Canadians are now embracing mobile technologies from smartphones to iPads.[31]

Many consumers are spending online time at social media sites such as Facebook and Twitter as well as purchasing products and services on company websites. The following points describe the effects of social media on the online consumer:

- Research suggests that social media recommendations tend to increase the chances of people buying products or services. For instance, a study found that 50 percent of people under 35 followed the recommendations of

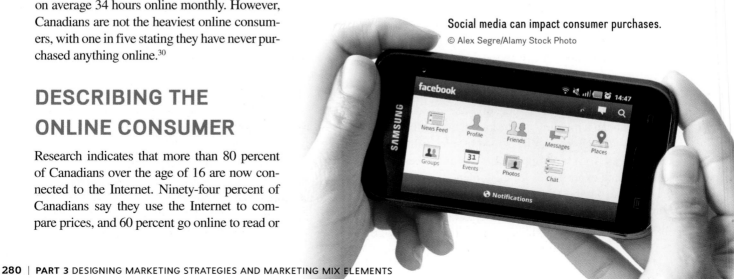

**Social media can impact consumer purchases.**
© Alex Segre/Alamy Stock Photo

*The influence of word of mouth on consumer purchases is still strong, be it face to face or on social media sites.*

their social media friends, compared to only 17 percent who bought because of celebrity endorsements.

- Another study reveals that while, on average, 7 percent of visitors to an online store make a purchase, if directed to the retailer via a social media site, the percentage of visitors who will make a purchase goes up to 71 percent. This means that people accessing an online retailer via social media are ten times more likely to buy something than other users.[32]

- Research has also shown that becoming a follower of a brand on Twitter or a fan on Facebook has a positive impact on the possibility of buying and recommending a product or service.

Recommendations from personal acquaintances or opinions posted by consumers online are the most trusted forms of advertising, according to a Nielsen global online consumer survey of over 25,000 Internet consumers from 50 countries. Ninety percent of consumers surveyed noted that they trust recommendations from people they know, while 70 percent trusted consumer opinions posted online. The influence of word of mouth on consumer purchases is still strong, be it face to face or on social media sites.[33]

## WHAT ONLINE CONSUMERS BUY

There is a lot marketers have to learn about online consumer purchase behaviour. Although research has documented the most frequently purchased products and services bought online, marketers also need to know why these items are popular in the digital marketplace.

## RETAILER USAGE OF THE MOBILE CHANNEL

**LO 7** Retailers are becoming increasingly aware of the value of smartphone-equipped customers. Like they did with the emergence of the Internet, many retailers initially

approached the mobile channel with a bit of trepidation. Today, retailers are looking at mobile as another important customer touch point. Cellphones, smartphones, and other handheld devices are a convenient way for customers to gather more information about a retailer's products or even conduct transactions on a mobile basis. In-store shoppers can research products and prices on their handsets using cameras, barcode scanners, QR codes, and other mobile applications. QR (quick response) codes are two-dimensional images that look like blobs of black on a white background. They are similar to standard barcodes but have much more functionality. QR codes are encoded with information ranging from text to photos to website addresses and are scanned by smartphones. They can be used to send consumers who scan the codes to places online and are very effective marketing tools.[34]

Retailers can provide immediate incentives by knowing the specific in-store location of the shopper via GPS technology. The customer can make the purchase in-store or over a mobile cellphone or smartphone. The key is to provide methods to retain customer interest and loyalty via a consistent shopping and branding experience across channels. Smartphones are being used to engage consumers and help them make better shopping choices.

The following scenarios demonstrate how mobile can be used:[35]

- Riding the chairlift of a major western ski resort, a customer of a ski apparel retailer pulls out a smartphone and clicks on the retailer's specialty application. The mobile software uses GPS technology to determine the skier's location, and the customer sees feedback on this specific mountain's terrain and recommendations on how to approach its trails.

- Walking through the pet food section of a major discount chain, a customer receives a text message with a digital coupon good for 20 percent off Iams dog food. The store has detected the shopper's presence in the pet food aisle, and knows that this particular shopper generally purchases the competitor's product, Purina. For the retailer's suppliers, this provides a chance to encourage a brand switch. For the retailer, it enhances loyalty from a customer who has opted in to participate in the mobile program.

- Two teenage girls rifle through the racks of tops in a major department store chain's juniors section. Stopping on one she likes, one girl takes out her phone and scans a QR

Smartphones are being integrated into the shopping experience.

© Jeffrey Blackler/Alamy Stock Photo

code on the shelf next to the shirt. On the screen of her phone, she sees product reviews from other shoppers, and also gets a special offer on a pair of shoes to complete the outfit.

- As he jockeys to make his flight at Calgary International Airport, a Montreal-bound traveller realizes he's forgotten to pack his laptop's power cord. He turns to his cellphone and brings up Best Buy's wireless website. He orders a replacement cord, finds the store location closest to his hotel, and picks it up on his way to check in.

The above are examples of just a handful of customer interactions taking place today in the mobile commerce (*m-commerce*) channel. In each instance, a retailer uses mobile as a way to enhance customer engagement and loyalty. And it is the pervasiveness of cellphones, smartphones, and other mobile devices that is leading a growing number of retailers to explore what additional opportunities await in the mobile space.

Here's an example of how Sephora, the beauty products retailer, uses mobile strategy. It created a specific mobile website with thousands of product reviews intended to help shoppers evaluate and compare items on their smartphones

**merchant wholesalers**
Independently owned firms that take title to the merchandise they handle.

when they are in the stores. All the shopper has to do to retrieve the reviews is type in the SKU number or the name of the product in their smartphone.

The increasing number of shoppers arriving at stores with smartphones can also pose a threat for retailers. The threat comes from in-store shoppers using their phones to check prices at other retailers. Retailers that ignore the growing number of mobile Internet users will see their customers defect to competitors. A retailer's best defence for maintaining customer loyalty is to develop a mobile website, with information on the site that differentiates itself from competitors. This can take the form of such intangibles as product reviews, warranty information, customer service, product knowledge, and return policy.

Retailers should take note that their websites might have to be adapted for smartphones. Regular websites are not configured for mobile, which may lead to frustration as a shopper, for example, tries to read words that are too tiny to read on a phone. By providing mobile access to their extensive online product information, retailers can help customers feel more comfortable about making a purchase at that store as opposed to fleeing to another store solely for the low price.[36]

# WHOLESALING

**LO 8** Many retailers rely on intermediaries to provide them with selection and availability of the products sold in their retail operations. Many other businesses also use intermediaries to provide them with selection and availability, plus value-added services for products that they need to operate their businesses. Those intermediaries are commonly called wholesalers and agents (described briefly in Chapter 10), according to the functions that they fulfill in the distribution process. In addition, there are manufacturers' sales offices operated by the original manufacturers of the products. All of these wholesaling intermediaries play an important role in the retailing process and in helping other businesses get the products they need.

Truck jobbers are small wholesalers that have a small warehouse from which they stock their trucks for distribution to retailers.

© Digital Vision/Punchstock

## MERCHANT WHOLESALERS

**Merchant wholesalers** are independently owned firms that take title to—that is, they buy—the merchandise they handle. They go by various names, described in detail below. About 83 percent of the firms engaged in wholesaling activities are merchant wholesalers.

Merchant wholesalers are classified as either full-service or limited-service wholesalers, depending on the number of functions performed. Two major types of full-service wholesalers exist. General merchandise (or full-line) wholesalers carry a broad assortment of merchandise and perform all channel functions. This type of wholesaler is most prevalent in the hardware, drug, and clothing industries. However, these wholesalers do not maintain much depth of assortment within specific product lines. Specialty merchandise (or limited-line) wholesalers offer a relatively narrow range of products but have an extensive assortment within the product lines carried. They perform all channel functions and are found in the health foods, automotive parts, and seafood industries.

Four major types of limited-service wholesalers exist. Rack jobbers furnish the racks or shelves that display merchandise in retail stores and perform all channel functions. They sell on consignment to retailers, which means they retain the title to the products displayed and bill retailers only for the merchandise sold. Familiar products such as hosiery, toys, housewares, and health and beauty aids are sold by rack jobbers. Cash and carry wholesalers take title to merchandise but sell only to buyers who call on them, pay cash for merchandise, and furnish their own transportation for merchandise. They carry a limited product assortment and do not make deliveries, extend credit, or supply market information. This wholesaler commonly deals in electric supplies, office supplies, hardware products, and groceries. Drop shippers, or desk jobbers, are wholesalers that own the merchandise they sell but do not physically handle, stock, or deliver it. They simply solicit orders from retailers and other wholesalers and have the merchandise shipped directly from a producer to a buyer. Drop shippers are used for bulky products such as coal, lumber, and chemicals, which are sold in large quantities. Truck jobbers are small wholesalers that have a small warehouse from which they stock their trucks for distribution to retailers. They usually handle limited assortments of fast-moving or perishable items that are sold for cash directly from trucks in their original packages. Truck jobbers handle products such as bakery items, dairy products, and meat.

## AGENTS AND BROKERS

Unlike merchant wholesalers, agents and brokers do not take title to merchandise and typically provide fewer channel functions. They make their profit from commissions or fees paid for their services, whereas merchant wholesalers make their profit from the sale of the merchandise they have bought and resold.

Manufacturers' agents and selling agents are the two major types of agents used by producers. **Manufacturers' agents**, or manufacturers' representatives, work for several producers and carry non-competitive, complementary merchandise in an exclusive territory. Manufacturers' agents act as a producer's sales arm in a territory and are principally responsible for the transactional channel functions, primarily selling. They are used extensively in the automotive supply, footwear, and fabricated steel industries. By comparison, **selling agents** represent a single producer and are responsible for the entire marketing function of that producer. They design promotional plans, set prices, determine distribution policies, and make recommendations on product strategy. Selling agents are used by small producers in the textile, apparel, food, and home furnishing industries.

**Brokers** are independent firms or individuals whose main function is to bring buyers and sellers together to make sales. Brokers, unlike agents, usually have no continuous relationship with the buyer or seller but negotiate a contract between two parties and then move on to another task. Brokers are used extensively in the real estate industry.

A unique broker that acts in many ways like a manufacturer's agent is a food broker, representing buyers and sellers in the grocery industry. Food brokers differ from conventional brokers because they act on behalf of producers on a permanent basis and receive a commission for their services. For example, food giant Nabisco uses food brokers to sell its candies, margarine, and Planters peanuts, but it sells its line of cookies and crackers directly to retail stores.

# MANUFACTURER'S BRANCHES AND OFFICES

Unlike merchant wholesalers, agents, and brokers, manufacturer's branches and sales offices are wholly owned extensions of the producer that perform wholesaling activities. Producers assume wholesaling functions when there are no intermediaries to perform these activities, customers are few in number and geographically concentrated, orders are large or require significant attention, or they want to control the distribution of their products. A *manufacturer's branch office* carries a producer's inventory and performs the functions of a full-service wholesaler. A *manufacturer's sales office* does not carry inventory, typically performs only a sales function, and serves as an alternative to agents and brokers.

## ask YOURSELF

1. Describe how smartphones are being used by retailers to engage consumers and help them make better shopping choices.

2. What is the difference between merchant wholesalers and agents?

Used with permission of Indigo

1. *What do you think the strategy behind this ad is?*

2. *What is the main message you take away from this ad?*

3. *What would you change in the ad to make it more effective?*

**LO 1** • Retailing provides customer value in the form of various utilities: time, place, form, information, and possession.

• Economically, retailing is important in terms of the people employed and money exchanged in retail sales.

**LO 2** • Retailing outlets can be classified by forms of ownership, such as independent retailer, corporate chain, and contractual system.

**LO 3** • The first task in developing a retail strategy is to define the target market and positioning of the retail store.

**LO 4** • The retailing mix consists of goods and services, retail pricing, physical location, and communications.

• In retailing, the product P (of the 4 Ps of the marketing mix) includes level of service, merchandise mix, and store atmosphere.

• Stores vary in the level of service they provide. Three levels are self-service, limited service, or full service.

• Retail outlets vary in terms of the breadth and depth of their merchandise lines. Breadth refers to the number of different items carried, and depth refers to the assortment of each item offered.

• In retail pricing, retailers must decide on the markup. Off-price retailers offer brand-name merchandise at lower than regular prices.

• Retail store location is an important retail mix decision. The common alternatives are the central business district, regional shopping centre, community shopping centre, or strip location.

A variation of the strip location is the power centre, which is a strip location with multiple national anchor stores.

**LO 5** • Non-store retailing includes automatic vending, television home shopping, online retailing, and direct marketing (direct mail and catalogue retailing, telemarketing, and direct selling).

**LO 6** • Online retailing allows consumers to search for, evaluate, and purchase products and services online. The increasing sales and number of people purchasing online suggest that the profile of the online consumer is becoming more and more like the profile of the consumer of the traditional marketplace.

• Consumers refer to six reasons they shop and buy online: convenience, choice, communication, customization, cost, and control.

**LO 7** • Retailers are becoming increasingly aware of the value of smartphone-equipped customers:

– Retailers are looking at mobile as another important customer touch point.

– Cellphones, smartphones, and other handheld devices are a convenient way for customers to gather more information about a retailer's products or even conduct transactions on a mobile basis.

– Many retailers depend on the numerous types of intermediaries that engage in wholesaling activities.

**LO 8** • The main difference between the various types of wholesalers lies in whether they take title to the items they sell.

---

*key terms and concepts...* **A REFRESHER**

breadth of product line
brokers
central business district
community shopping centre
depth of product line
form of ownership
intertype competition
level of service

manufacturers' agents
merchandise mix
merchant wholesalers
multichannel retailers
off-price retailing
power centre
regional shopping centres
retailing

retailing mix
scrambled merchandising
selling agents
shrinkage
strip location
telemarketing

---

*hands-on...* **APPLY YOUR KNOWLEDGE**

**Online Retailing Assignment** A number of retailers like TELUS have alternate strategies to distribute their products. Online retailing is a key component to the strategy of most retailers. Interview an independent retailer in your local community to determine the benefits and challenges of providing an online retailing offering to the organization's clientele.

In the opening vignette of this chapter, the franchisee discusses how he can be an entrepreneur with a proven business model. In groups, research different potential franchises and identify the top three you want to pursue as a group. List the details of each franchise including its value proposition and initial investment.

infographic... **DATA ANALYSIS**

The Infographic, "Canada's Top Retail Trends for 2015," shows the continued opportunity for loyalty programs in Canada. List the loyalty programs you use currently and the current top five loyalty programs in Canada. Determine why the programs you use may be similar or different to the top five.

# Marketing Communications

The marketing communications tools available to marketers have evolved significantly over the last decade. This chapter looks at the offline marketing communications tools that are used to communicate with target audiences. Chapter 13 focuses on the evolving digital marketing space. Both offline and online approaches need to work in an integrated fashion to ensure maximum impact of marketing communication.

BIORÉ® is a trademark of Kao Corporation and is used with permission of Kao Canada Inc.

Kao Canada is recognized as an innovator in the development and manufacture of premium beauty care brands. They are known in Canada under the brands of Bioré®, John Frieda®, Curél®, Ban®, Jergens®, Goldwell®, and KMS California®.

The self-serve skincare category is a highly competitive one. Estimated to be worth $400 million in Canada, growth has been moderate over the past three years. This overall modest rate of growth is expected to continue as companies fight for market share by focusing on new product introductions and innovations.

The Bioré brand is best known for its iconic Deep Cleansing Pore Strips. If you aren't initially familiar with this product, it is a skincare product that comes in the form of a strip that you place over your nose (especially if you have blackheads). After ten minutes, you remove the strip, and your blackheads attach to the strip and are removed with it—it's that simple! Bioré's facial cleansing products come in liquid, powder, strip, mask, and bar formats to deep clean pores.

The Bioré brand is committed to offering new innovative products with unique forms and unique ingredients that appeal to the Canadian consumer. The original Bioré Deep Cleansing Pore Strips have seen the addition of a charcoal-based line of products launched in 2014 and the addition of a baking soda line in 2016. These product line extensions have further invigorated the brand.

Not surprisingly, Bioré targets a female audience, mainly between the ages of 15 and 29. It has broad distribution in food, drug, and mass retailers nationwide. While focusing on increasing brand awareness, brand relevancy is also a significant objective.

Bioré's mantra is "Free your pores!" To engage the target audience, Bioré uses funny, relatable headlines and vibrant colours. The company talks about pores in a fun and playful way, positioning Bioré products as the ultimate solution for clean, beautiful skin.

Bioré leverages all aspects of the promotional mix to reach target consumers and drive purchase, including traditional as well as online promotional vehicles. Integral to promotional planning at Bioré is the integration of brand messages across platforms and the alignment of the timing of promotional activities across all consumer touch points to maximize their impact.

**Advertising:** Out-of-home advertising has been used by Bioré to increase brand awareness. Bioré placed transit advertising in streetcars and buses in the top three Canadian cities (Toronto, Montreal, and Vancouver).

Bioré has found that a great vehicle to reach the 15-to-29 demographic is through a promotional partnership with Cineplex. Cineplex boasts over 70 percent reach for Bioré's targeted age group. Imagine walking to the lobby at a Cineplex theatre and seeing a Bioré ad on the digital lobby signage, reading the *Cineplex Magazine* while waiting for the show to begin and seeing a Bioré advertisement and sample, and then settling in as the lights dim and seeing a pre-show brand video spot highlighting the brand. This is the type of integrated and unexpected experience customers can have with the Bioré brand, at times when they are receptive to brand messages.

**Public relations:** Key media contacts are invited to exciting launch events introducing new product innovations with presentations from the company as well as beauty experts establishing the key benefits of the products.

**Event sponsorship and Bioré beauty ambassadors:** Bioré focuses on getting out and meeting its customers. Bioré beauty ambassadors regularly attend events and festivals to distribute samples or interact with customers as they take a photo in the Bioré Skincare Photo Booth. Color Me Rad is a premier event sponsored by Bioré. Color Me Rad involves

## CHAPTER FEATURES

**Bioré's "Free Your Pores" Campaign**
Bioré's integrated advertising campaign utilizes online and offline tools to increase sales.

**Canada—One of the World's Most Connected Nations**
People in Canada spend over 36 hours per month on the Internet.

**Nabob's Customers "Respect the Bean"**
Kraft re-established Nabob as a premier coffee brand in the eyes of its consumers.

**Is Sexism Alive and Well in Canadian Advertising?**
Advertising Standards Canada (Ad Standards) focused its latest consumer study on the perceptions of Canadians on sexism in advertising.

a series of races and other activities that take place across the country. The audience and tone surrounding its events are well-aligned with the brand, evoking a positive, colourful, and optimistic experience.

**Sampling and coupons:** Knowing that *Cineplex Magazine* was widely read by its target market, Bioré included a sample of a Deep Cleansing Pore Strip in the magazine to increase trial. In other situations, cleanser samples were distributed at Cineplex theatres with coupons for $2 off any Bioré product. Sample and coupon distribution is always aligned with key consumer activities to drive purchase.

**Trade promotion:** Kao works with its retail trade partners to feature Bioré products in its flyers and retail display units. Point-of-purchase displays keep Bioré front and centre while the customer is shopping in the store. Displays take the form of branded floor stands and counter displays that support product launches or promote key consumer programs such as Color Me Rad events. Bioré products are often featured in retail flyers distributed by retailers such as Shoppers Drug Mart, Walmart, and Loblaw.

**Brand ambassador:** *Pretty Little Liars* actress Shay Mitchell has adopted the role of brand ambassador for Bioré in the North American market. Shay is a relevant influencer for the Bioré target audience. She regularly tweets and post video blogs on her use of Bioré products.

**Digital:** In addition to the many traditional offline approaches used by the Bioré brand to reach its customers, Bioré has a strong digital marketing plan as well. The Bioré digital platforms will be discussed in more detail in Chapter 13, but it is important to note the role that digital plays in an integrated marketing communication plan. Mobile, social media, Internet advertising, search engine marketing strategies, website promotion, and e-mail communications all round out a fully integrated communication plan for the Bioré brand.

Erin Arthrell, brand manager for Bioré in Canada sums up the Bioré promotional plan, "The Bioré target consumer is bombarded by brand communication and highly aware of advertising messages. In order to break through the clutter and resonate with this consumer, it is crucial to reach them with a unique, relevant message when they are most receptive." This may be in the theatre, at the bus stop, or watching their favourite vlogger. Bioré focuses on offering a relevant but entertaining message to its key target audience in order to achieve its brand objectives.[1]

For further information on Bioré and Kao Canada, visit **www.biore.ca.**

## reality CHECK ✓

As you read Chapter 12, refer back to this Bioré vignette to answer the following questions:

- Why is the use of beauty and brand ambassadors a good choice for Bioré?
- What forms of offline communication tools were not used by Bioré in this campaign? Suggest the reasons why they were not considered appropriate.

# TRENDS IN MARKETING COMMUNICATIONS

**LO 1** The next two chapters provide readers with a realistic view of marketing communications, bringing to the forefront the offline and online approaches that are used by marketers to reach consumers. Chapter 12 focuses on the trends currently impacting marketing communications, it reviews the more traditional, offline approaches, and details the planning and evaluation of marketing communications programs. Chapter 13 examines how the online digital world continues to change and explains how these new digital approaches are used to reach ever-elusive consumers. Of utmost importance is the fact that offline and online marketing communications must work together, in an integrated fashion, to reach

*The lines are blurred between reality, entertainment, self-expression, and marketing communications.*

consumers in their worlds, relying on metrics and analytics to measure and evaluate success and to make improvements.

Today, consumers are bombarded with marketing messages. With the use of tags, bookmarks, opt-ins, and selective feeds, consumers can determine whether they receive marketing communication messages, and if so, when, where, and on what device. The lines are blurred between reality, entertainment, self-expression, and marketing communications.

## A CHANGING LANDSCAPE

We start by looking at the current trends impacting marketing communications.

**Connected Consumers** Affordable Internet technology provides consumers in Canada with easy-to-use services and devices that facilitate marketing communications. Free online services such as e-mail, search engines, and social media have made media more accessible so that two-way communication now exists between marketers and consumers, and between consumers and their friends. Many individuals multitask with the media, spending time on the Internet while watching TV, and using tablets and smartphones interchangeably, depending on the circumstance.[2]

The use of mobile devices in Canada (smartphones, tablets, e-readers, handheld gaming devices, and portable MP3 players) continues to grow. In 2016, there were over 30 million mobile subscribers in Canada.[3] Smartphone penetration in Canada has reached 73 percent and continues to climb. Smartphones are used for everything on the go, with usage including taking photos, messaging, social networking, listening to music, conducting searches, using apps, playing games, and shopping.[4] Chapter 13 reviews mobile marketing in detail.

Research studies tell us that consumers in Canada are among the most connected in the world. Data from comScore highlights that, on average, individuals in Canada spend 36.7 hours per month online. Online video viewing is particularly high, with 73 percent watching video on the Internet. Social networking is a popular online

activity, with people in Canada increasingly accessing social networks on their mobile devices.[5] **Social networks** are online websites that allow members to create a network of friends and contacts to share messages, comments, videos, and images as a form of self-expression.

The most popular social networking sites in Canada are Facebook, YouTube, Twitter, Pinterest, Google +, Instagram, and LinkedIn.[6] Chapter 13 provides an in-depth look at social media in Canada.

**Media Usage** The amount of time consumers spend with the media has changed significantly over the last few years, prompting marketers to take note and adapt marketing communications approaches. Adults in Canada spent 9 hours and 41 minutes per day using some form of media. Time spent on digital forms of media, including mobile and computer, is expected to continue increasing at rates between 3 and 6 percent per year until 2018. Time spent on all other forms of media is decreasing.[7]

*The most popular social networking sites in Canada are Facebook, YouTube, Twitter, Pinterest, Google +, Instagram, and LinkedIn.*

### Time Spent with Canadian Media

**Average Time Spent per Day by Adults**

| | Time Spent | % of Time |
|---|---|---|
| **TOTAL** | **9 hours and 41 minutes** | **100%** |
| Digital | 4 hours and 21 minutes | 45% |
| Desktop/ Laptop | 1 hour and 53 minutes | |
| Mobile | 2 hours and 28 minutes | |
| Television | 3 hours and 22 minutes | 35% |
| Radio | 1 hour and 34 minutes | 16% |
| Print | 24 minutes | 4% |

**Source:** "Mobile Drives Growth in Time Spent with Media in Canada, *eMarketer*, May 25, 2016, http://www.emarketer.com/Article /Mobile-Drives-Growth-Time-Spent-with-Media-Canada/1014003.

## Figure 12–1
Advertising expenditures in Canada (US$ millions)

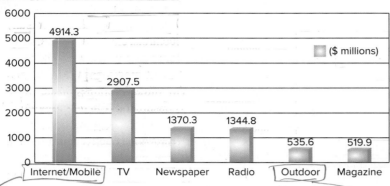

| Medium | ($ millions) |
|---|---|
| Internet/Mobile | 4914.3 |
| TV | 2907.5 |
| Newspaper | 1370.3 |
| Radio | 1344.8 |
| Outdoor | 535.6 |
| Magazine | 519.9 |

Internet/mobile advertising spending pulls away from other media.

**Source:** "AdSpend Database – Canada," WARC, accessed December 2016 at www.warc.com.

*[handwritten: Largest form of advertising in Canada (n.x. ads, ad within an email)]*

### Advertising Expenditures

Marketers are shifting advertising dollars online to respond to changing media habits. The Internet is now the largest recipient of advertising dollars in Canada, ahead of TV and newspaper. The latest data on advertising expenditures shows that the overall advertising spend in Canada in 2017 will reach the equivalent of US$11.6 billion (see Figures 12–1 and 12–2).[8]

### Evolving Media

The digital reality sees consumers spending more time online. Even the television industry is changing. Content is being produced strictly for streaming, and many television networks have made their content available online. Traditional media such as television, magazines, newspapers, and radio are creating their own online assets to remain competitive and relevant. News organizations, such as the CBC, use YouTube channels and apps to deliver content, despite having websites and TV channels of their own. Radio stations stream content online, create podcasts, and write articles for their websites, and there has been an

influx in Internet and satellite radio services such as Sirius. Magazines create content specifically for online reading, and in this new media universe, we see newspapers such as the *Globe and Mail* undergo digital redesigns to compete with online news and the 24/7 news cycle. Out-of-home advertising, such as billboards and transit advertising, are being replaced with digital boards, which provide the opportunity for video and interactive touchscreens. Digital advertising has also seen a shift from desktop- and laptop-formatted ads to mobile advertising.[9]

*[handwritten: or out-of-home (billboards, transit, posters, washroom ads, bus shelters)]*

# THE MARKETING COMMUNICATIONS INDUSTRY

**LO 2** The marketing communications industry consists of five main areas that work together to form an industry that is ethical, trustworthy, cohesive, and measurable. These areas include the

Popular social networking sites in Canada.

(Facebook): Craig Ruttle/AP Photo; (Twitter): Ingvar Björk/Alamy Stock Photo; (YouTube): TP/Alamy Stock Photo; (Instagram): © 2017 Instagram, Inc.; (LinkedIn): PRNewsFoto/PwC/AP Images; (Google+): © Google; (Pinterest): © Pinterest 2017

**Figure 12–2**

Trends—advertising expenditures by media (US$ millions) (2016–17 forecasted data)

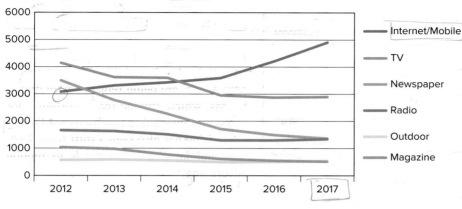

Source: "AdSpend Database – Canada," WARC, accessed December 2016 at www.warc.com.

following: (1) the media, (2) marketing communication agencies, (3) media research companies, (4) associations, and (5) regulatory bodies. Let's look at these areas in more detail.

# THE MEDIA

The main forms of media are Internet (including mobile), TV, newspaper, magazine, radio, and out-of-home (including billboards and transit).

**Paid media** is the media time that is purchased so that messages can be disseminated through channels that

## Looking for Media Data?

| | |
|---|---|
| Alliance for Audited Media (AAM) | auditedmedia.com |
| Numeris | www.numeris.ca |
| Canadian Out-of-Home Measurement Bureau (COMB) | www.comb.org |
| comScore | www.comscore.com |
| Forrester Research | www.forrester.com |
| Interactive Advertising Bureau of Canada (IAB) | www.iabcanada.com |
| Canadian Media Directors' Council | www.cmdc.ca |
| Nielsen Company | www.nielsen.com/ca |
| Television Bureau of Canada (TVB) | www.tvb.ca |
| ThinkTV | www.thinktv.ca |
| Vividata (amalgamation of NADbank and the Print Measurement Bureau (PMB)) | www.vividata.ca |

are controlled by others—TV advertising is an example. **Owned media** refers to the media channels that a company controls, either fully or partially, such as a website, microsite, or social media page that is used to directly communicate with consumers. **Earned media,** a term with origins in the public relations industry, refers to the free publicity secured through unpaid media mentions and consumers who spread the word through word of mouth or the Internet.

# MARKETING COMMUNICATION AGENCIES

**Marketing communication agencies** provide marketers with expertise on how best to communicate messages to their audiences. Agencies can be broad-spectrum and offer a variety of services to their clients, or they can be specialty agencies providing expertise in media, creative, public relations, event marketing, digital, product placement, direct marketing, or sales promotion. These terms are discussed in more detail later in this chapter.

# MEDIA RESEARCH COMPANIES

Metrics are central to the smooth functioning of the marketing communications industry. Data on audience measurement, readership, consumer trends, and the quality of communication messages is needed to provide transparent and reliable information to the media, agencies, and clients. Most major media sectors publish third-party data for the industry, which is used to determine advertising rates and trends. In addition, other media research companies, such as comScore and the Nielsen Company, provide data to keep the industry apprised on the latest developments.

# 4 ASSOCIATIONS

The marketing communications industry has a number of active associations that provide data and host informative events and educational workshops for the industry. Here are just a few that are active in keeping the industry:

- Canadian Marketing Association (**www.the-cma.org**)
- Institute of Communications Agencies (**www.icacanada.ca**)
- Interactive Advertising Bureau of Canada (**www.iabcanada.com**)
- Association of Canadian Advertisers (**www.acaweb.ca/en/**)

It is worth your time to investigate the resources and support available from each association.

# 5 REGULATORY BODIES

Prior to embarking on a marketing communications program, marketers need to be well-versed on the limitations and restrictions placed on them by regulatory bodies. Marketers are well-advised to become familiar with their specific industry associations and to stay up-to-date on marketing regulations, business restrictions, and best practices. Chapter 2 provides details on these regulatory bodies and the regulations that guide marketing communications in Canada. It is advisable at this point for you to re-visit these pages to obtain details. The following is only a brief reminder.

In Canada, there are six main regulatory groups that work toward limiting intentional and unintentional deceptive marketing practices: (1) Advertising Standards Canada (Ad Standards), (2) the Competition Bureau, (3) the Canadian Radio-television and Telecommunications Commission (CRTC), (4) the Canadian Marketing Association (CMA), (5) the Canadian Wireless Telecommunications Association (CWTA), and (6) the Mobile Marketing Association (MMA). Specialist areas and industry groups such as the public relations and health care industries also have regulatory bodies or associations that provide codes of ethics and guidelines on best practices to assist members.

- **Advertising Standards Canada (Ad Standards)** is the national, independent, not-for-profit advertising self-regulatory body that sets and regulates advertising standards. It uses a consumer-complaint process to review questionable ads that are withdrawn from the media if they contravene its guidelines and are not fixed. Ad Standards provides advice and pre-clearance services for advertisers but has no legal jurisdiction and does not levy fines. Detailed guidelines can be found at **www.adstandards.ca**. Ad Standards recently conducted a study that asked consumers about sexism in Canadian advertising. This topic is discussed further in the Focus on Ethics box, "Is Sexism Alive and Well in Canadian Advertising?"[10]

- The **Competition Bureau** is an independent law-enforcement agency with jurisdiction in many areas. In the marketing communications area, it looks at fraudulent advertising and misleading representation to sell products, including price and warranty claims. Deceptive price claims and contests that do not publish the required terms and conditions are illegal and heavily scrutinized. To see more about the Competition Bureau, visit its website at **http://competitionbureau.gc.ca**.

- The **Canadian Radio-television and Telecommunications Commission (CRTC)** is another government agency. It regulates the broadcast and telecommunications industry in Canada, including the licensing of stations. It also provides guidelines on Canadian content and sets limitations on the amount of advertising permitted during broadcasts. It oversees the advertising of alcoholic beverages and works with the Ad Standards on advertising to children. It also has jurisdiction over the national Do Not Call List (DNCL), which provides parameters for telemarketing in Canada. Find more about the CRTC at **www.crtc.gc.ca**.

- The **Canadian Marketing Association (CMA)** uses a code of ethics and standards of practice to guide the marketing industry in Canada on telemarketing, e-mail marketing, mobile marketing, Internet marketing, promotional contests, fundraising, database marketing, and marketing to children and teenagers. It also provides guidelines on privacy issues and anti-spam practices. Visit **www.the-cma.org** for more information.

**ADS HAVE CHANGED A LOT OVER THE YEARS** but one thing remains the same: truth in advertising matters.

Ad Standards™

Truthful, Fair, and Accurate.

adstandards.ca

This Ad Standards ad encourages truthful communications.

Reprinted with permission from Advertising Standards Canada

# Is Sexism Alive and Well in Canadian Advertising?

#HOWTODAD

General Mills avoided traditional stereotypes in its Cheerios advertising.
Courtesy of General Mills and Tribal Worldwide Canada

When LG Canada launched a social media campaign with advertisements that featured women at the salon and at the spa, Canadians were furious. Although LG was attempting to illustrate the time that could be saved by using its new, larger washing machine, consumers were asking a lot of questions. Is laundry done only by women? Is LG in a "1950s time warp"? Men were unhappy because the ads didn't represent the work that they do in the home. LG took down the ads and issued an apology.

Unilever, one of the world's biggest advertisers, conducted a global study on the issue of sexism in advertising. Unilever is the manufacturer of Dove and Axe. Dove's Real Beauty campaign has received acclaim for its positive portrayal of women in its ads. On the other hand, Axe has been renowned for its representation of men as primitive beings who are interested only in attracting young sexy women. Their research showed that only 2 percent of the ads studied showed modern, smart women. In addition, 40 percent of those surveyed couldn't relate to the images that they were exposed to in advertising. As a result, Unilever has committed to #unstereotype its

advertising. One of the first targets for this strategy is the Axe brand. The "Find Your Magic" theme updates the definition of masculinity by embracing individuality and expanding the boundaries of attractiveness.

Advertising Standards Canada (Ad Standards) focused a recent consumer study on the perceptions of Canadians on sexism in advertising. What did they find? Forty-seven percent of Canadians felt that women are treated unfairly in Canadian advertising; 31 percent felt men are treated unfairly. Forty-four percent of Canadians felt that ads have become less sexist versus ten years ago, while 20 percent believe they are more sexist. With women, sexism is depicted in advertisements by an unrealistic body image, by objectification, or by women being depicted in traditional roles only, the latter example being the one that LG was accused of portraying in its ads. And as we saw with the backlash to the LG ads, the study showed that sexist ads annoy people, and they blame not only the company and ad agency placing the ads but also society at large.

Men are also the victims of sexism in advertising. Showing an unrealistic body image is also a factor for men, but the most common sexist depiction

for men is as a stupid and unreliable character. And Canadians find sexist portrayals of men just as unacceptable as sexist portrayals of women. This has motivated companies such as General Mills to avoid traditional stereotypes of males in the household and portray men as an active caregiver in its Cheerios advertising.

How important should this issue be to marketers? Well, it is important to their consumers, and so companies need to be very aware of how their ads will be perceived. Close to 70 percent of Canadians stated that they are less likely to buy a product from a company with a sexist advertisement. ●

## Questions

1. Have you ever seen an advertisement that you felt was sexist?

2. As a marketer, how can you ensure that your ads properly represent your customer base?

---

- The **Canadian Wireless Telecommunications Association (CWTA)** administers the CWTA short code guidelines, a strict set of guidelines on pricing and practices for mobile text messaging. This includes pricing guidelines, the use of keyword protocols, opt-in rules, privacy requirements, and terms and conditions. To find out more about the CWTA, go to **www.cwta.ca.**

- The **Mobile Marketing Association (MMA)** is a global association that sets standards and guidelines for

mobile messaging, advertising, and promotion. It liaises with the Canadian Marketing Association to bring the best practices and ethical approaches in mobile marketing to marketers in Canada. For more information on the MMA, visit **http://www.mmaglobal.com/.**

Failure to abide by marketing communication regulations can have dire consequences for marketers—campaigns may be forced off air, companies and individuals may be fined, and legal action can result in jail time.

1. *How much time do you spend weekly searching the Internet, on mobile apps, listening to the radio, watching television, streaming video, and reading magazines or newspapers?*

2. *What are the most impactful trends in marketing communications?*

3. *How is marketing communications regulated in Canada?*

**outbound marketing**

Marketers seek out consumers by widely broadcasting messages using advertising, direct mail, e-mail marketing, telemarketing, and personal-selling approaches.

**inbound marketing**

When consumers find a product and its messaging by using online techniques that marketers facilitate, including search engine optimization, pay-per-click ads, and the use of social media to connect with consumers.

**integrated marketing communications (IMC)**

A communications approach that coordinates all promotional activities to provide a consistent message to a target audience.

**marketing communication tools**

Advertising, public relations, sales promotion, direct response marketing, event marketing and sponsorship, product placement and branded entertainment, personal selling, online marketing, social media marketing, and mobile marketing.

# APPROACHES TO MARKETING COMMUNICATIONS

## OUTBOUND AND INBOUND MARKETING COMMUNICATIONS

**LO 3** There are two terms that we need to understand in marketing communications: outbound marketing and inbound marketing. **Outbound marketing** refers to the traditional marketing approach where marketers seek out consumers by widely broadcasting messages using advertising, direct mail, e-mail marketing, telemarketing, and personal selling approaches. It includes advertising methods that consumers increasingly avoid, such as ads on TV and radio, ads in newspapers and magazines, and Internet display ads. **Inbound marketing** is when interested consumers find the product and its messaging by using online techniques that marketers facilitate. It involves search engine optimization, pay-per-click ads, and the use of social media to connect with consumers through social networks, blogs, social bookmarks, social media releases, and microsites.

These two approaches often work together to communicate with consumers in ways they prefer. Smaller businesses may rely more on inbound marketing, which is cheaper, while larger businesses, depending on the target market, may use a combination of both techniques.

# INTEGRATED MARKETING COMMUNICATIONS

The concept of designing a marketing communications program that coordinates all promotional activities to provide a consistent message to a target audience is referred to as **integrated marketing communications (IMC).**

The key to developing successful IMC programs is to use a process that makes it easy to design and evaluate. In an IMC program, each element has a distinct role as well as a purpose in the overall campaign. For example, TV ads and Internet display advertising might be used to build awareness and to drive consumers to a website; print advertising may be used to provide details on technical specifications; social media interactions may be used to encourage engagement; sales promotional offers may be needed to encourage product trial; e-mail marketing approaches may be required to create a database of the target market; and personal selling might be needed to complete a transaction. Each tool is used for a different reason and needs to be evaluated against that purpose and its contribution to the overall success of the marketing communications program.

Nabob's "Respect the Bean" campaign is an excellent example of a successful IMC program. See the Marketing NewsFlash box for more details.[11]

# MARKETING COMMUNICATION TOOLS

In this diverse media environment, a wide range of marketing communication tools is available. **Marketing communication tools**, also referred to as the promotional mix, consist of advertising, public relations, sales promotion, direct response marketing, event marketing and sponsorship, product placement and branded entertainment, personal selling, online marketing, social media marketing, and mobile marketing. Figure 12–3 summarizes the relative strengths and weaknesses of these elements.

# Nabob Respects the Bean

#RESPECTTHEBEAN

Nabob is a coffee brand steeped in Canadian heritage. It first came to market in the late 1800s in Vancouver, and 120 years later, with the introduction of premium coffee shops such as Starbucks and a vast array of premium coffees at the grocery store, Nabob's sales were in decline. Nabob is one of Kraft Canada's brands. Along with a rejuvenation of the product and packaging—including the introduction of Nabob Bold, Nabob Whole Bean, and Nabob Gastown Grind—Kraft needed to re-establish Nabob as a premium coffee brand in the eyes of its customers.

The solution was an integrated marketing communication (IMC) campaign under the umbrella concept of "Respect the Bean." The focus of the message was to reinforce the pleasure of a traditional cup of coffee. The message was the same, no matter what form of media was used. Each marketing communication tool presented a situation highlighting how ridiculous the "coffee culture" had become. The solution to this absurd situation was always Nabob.

Kraft Canada used a variety of different media to reinforce its "Respect the Bean" message, including TV commercials, online pre-roll, YouTube videos, digital banner ads, web page takeovers, out-of-home advertisements, print ads in magazines, and social media posts.

- **TV advertisement:** A 30-second commercial filmed in Colombian coffee fields was developed, showing the reactions of coffee farmers to the ridiculous drinks that have become part of the coffee culture in North America. The farmers have no time for whipped cream or extra flavouring, but they love the Nabob coffee they are given.
- **YouTube:** Nabob positioned itself on the cutting edge of coffee culture by responding to changing trends with videos on YouTube. They began a "Save the Pumpkin" from pumpkin-spiced lattes campaign and, in another video, highlighted the "complicated world of coffee" compared to the simple, great-tasting, quality beans in Nabob.
- **Out-of-home:** Transit ads and billboards were placed strategically close to coffee shops, reminding patrons of the other options available to them.
- **Digital banners and web page takeovers:** These reinforced the "Respect the Bean" mantra.
- **Magazine print ads:** With headlines such as "Never let a straw come between you and your coffee," print advertisements reinforced the customer's connection to the coffee.

Nabob re-established itself as a premium traditional coffee brand.

Courtesy of Kraft Heinz Foods Company. Used with permission.

- **Social media:** The Nabob Coffee Co. bombarded its customers with daily tweets united with the hashtag #RespectTheBean, encouraging customers to share how they enjoy their coffee.

Not only was Nabob able to achieve the corporate goal of maintaining its dollar share in the coffee market, both the Tim Hortons and Van Houtte brands lost dollar share over the same time frame. Nabob also experienced an increase in repeat buyers and spends per trip. The "Respect the Bean" campaign has been an ongoing theme for the brand for the past few years and is expected to continue its success into the future. ●

## Questions

1. What benefits does an integrated marketing campaign provide a brand?

2. How did Nabob shake up the premium coffee market?

3. What advantages does the social media channel provide?

# ADVERTISING

**LO 4** **Advertising** is a paid form of media used for non-personal communication to consumers about an organization, good, service, or idea. The *paid* aspect of this definition is important because advertising space is normally purchased, with the exception of some public service announcements, which may use donated media. The *non-personal* component of advertising is also important since advertising involves mass media (such as TV, radio, magazines, and the Internet), which are non-personal and do not have an immediate feedback loop available as does direct marketing or personal selling.

**advertising**
Paid form of media used for non-personal communication to consumers about an organization, good, service, or idea.

## Figure 12–3

Strengths and weaknesses of communication tools

| Promotional Tool | Strengths | Weaknesses |
|---|---|---|
| Advertising | • An efficient means of reaching large numbers of people both online and offline<br>• Many affordable online options exist for marketers with small budgets<br>• Online and offline options can work together to enhance messaging<br>• Advertisers control messaging | • Higher cost of offline approaches<br>• Difficult to evaluate offline approaches<br>• High clutter both online and offline<br>• Low credibility of messaging<br>• Viewers avoid both online and offline messaging |
| Public relations | • Highly credible messages when spread by the media<br>• Inexpensive, particularly when using social media<br>• New measurable tools available due to social media<br>• Can be well-integrated into IMC programs | • Unable to control media messaging<br>• Difficult to influence the number of messages spread through the media<br>• Results can be difficult to evaluate |
| Sales promotion | • Effective at increasing short-term sales<br>• Many options are available both online and offline<br>• Social media provides an affordable way to disseminate offers<br>• Results are measurable<br>• Can be well-integrated into IMC programs | • Fraud can occur<br>• Can lead to promotional wars<br>• Promotions can be easily duplicated by competitors<br>• Consumers may wait for a sales promotion before purchasing<br>• Legal regulations are complex |
| Direct response marketing | • Messages can be targeted through online and offline approaches<br>• Facilitates customer relationships<br>• Results are measurable | • High cost of offline and online approaches<br>• Negative customer reactions<br>• Clutter<br>• Requires a well-constucted database to be done properly |
| Event marketing and sponsorship | • Small branded events can be used to create a buzz and spread viral messages<br>• Major event sponsorships can reach large audiences and create positive associations<br>• Can be integrated into IMC programs<br>• Sponsorships can be carried into the online environment<br>• Buzz can be affordably created through microsites and social media | • Large event sponsorships can be limited to awareness-building messages<br>• Sponsorships can be costly and difficult to evaluate<br>• Results can be difficult to measure |
| Product placement and branded entertainment | • Seamless product integration into programming<br>• Can create a positive association for the brand with a particular movie or TV show | • Can be expensive<br>• Product placement is becoming ubiquitous |
| Personal selling | • Personal interactions can build lasting relationships with consumers<br>• Online approaches can be used to enhance relationships<br>• An important approach for expensive products<br>• Can be used in large and small businesses<br>• Can be a strong form of product differentiation | • Can become expensive when large sales-forces are involved<br>• Consistency in approach and messaging is difficult to achieve<br>• People may not want to engage |
| Online marketing (discussed in Chapter 13) | • Allows for two-way communication<br>• Can be used to implement most forms of marketing communication<br>• Can be relatively inexpensive | • Online message clutter<br>• Dependence on technology |
| Social media marketing (discussed in Chapter 13) | • Allows for two-way communication<br>• Can be relatively inexpensive<br>• Many platforms to select from | • Online message clutter<br>• Dependence on technology<br>• Potential immediate negative feedback |
| Mobile marketing (discussed in Chapter 13) | • Number of mobile users is increasing rapidly<br>• Can integrate mobile marketing programs with other promotion tools quite easily | • Mobile message clutter<br>• Dependence on technology<br>• Formatting challenges |

> *Marketers have a number of media options from which to choose. Selection is based on campaign objectives as well as the product, the target market, and budget constraints.*

Advertising can be very expensive. A one-time, national rate for a full-page, four-colour ad in the hard copy of *Maclean's* magazine, for example, costs $40,510, with digital tablet ads running at $3,237 per page.[12] Television ads are even more expensive, with average production costs running at approximately $200,000 and media prices running over $150,000 to run a 30-second spot during a top, prime-time, highly viewed TV broadcast. Media prices will vary, depending on when and where an advertiser wishes to run the spot.

### Advertising Media Choices

Marketers have a number of media options from which to choose. Selection is based on campaign objectives as well as the product, the target market, and budget constraints. Figure 12–4 summarizes the advantages and disadvantages of the major forms of advertising: Internet, TV, newspaper, magazine, radio, and out-of-home. These media choices are described in more detail in the following pages.

Media choice is an important decision for a marketer to make. Canadians are not always trusting of paid advertising messages (see the Infographic). While consumers seem to be more comfortable with the information presented in traditional media such as newspapers and brochures, they are less comfortable with messages delivered through digital media.[13]

**INTERNET, MOBILE, AND SOCIAL MEDIA** When it comes to online advertising, companies can create display ads that can be placed on various online destinations such as websites, web portals, blogs, social networks, e-mail platforms, and online gaming sites. Pay-per-click ads can also be placed on search engines, content networks, and social networks such as Facebook, LinkedIn, or YouTube. Forms of online advertising will be discussed in detail in Chapter 13.

**TELEVISION** Television is a valuable medium because it communicates with sight, sound, and motion and gets attention from large target audiences. Digital technology now allows TV viewing to be flexible, whether this means watching it on the go on a smartphone or tablet, time-shifting to watch it in a different time zone, or using a digital recording device to watch a program at a more convenient time. The rapid adoption of Internet-based services such as Netflix offers consumers more choices. Canadian Netflix subscriptions have now surpassed 5 million, and it is changing how consumers view TV-type programming and how marketers view TV as an advertising platform.[14]

When TV ads are well-designed and appropriately placed in the media, this tool can deliver very impactful and effective messages. Many TV advertisers complement their ads with other advertising options that meet target audiences online through online display ads or with pre-roll video ads that play before an online broadcast of a TV program. Marketers are aware that consumer behaviour is placing the effectiveness of stand-alone TV advertising into question. TV viewers frequently change channels when ads appear during commercial breaks, and many use digital recording devices to watch programs at a later date. Sometimes, people prefer to watch TV programs online where fewer ads exist, or catch a show at another time through on-demand digital programming. It is estimated that approximately 200,000 Canadians annually are "cord cutters" or people who decide to cancel TV cable or satellite and focus on online viewing. This number has been growing by 80 percent each year.[15]

*Maclean's* offers marketers a variety of advertising options.

™Trademarks of Rogers Communications Inc. or an affiliate, used with permission.

**NEWSPAPERS** The Canadian newspaper industry has undergone significant

## Figure 12–4

Advertising options—advantages and disadvantages

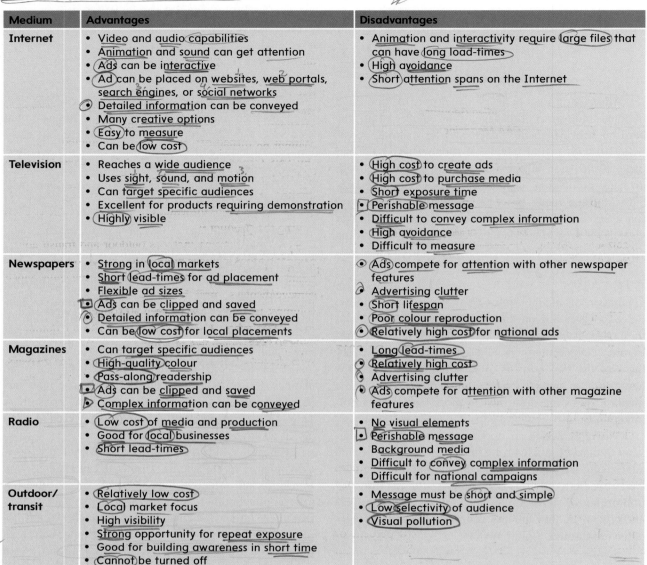

| Medium | Advantages | Disadvantages |
|---|---|---|
| Internet | • Video and audio capabilities<br>• Animation and sound can get attention<br>• Ads can be interactive<br>• Ad can be placed on websites, web portals, search engines, or social networks<br>• Detailed information can be conveyed<br>• Many creative options<br>• Easy to measure<br>• Can be low cost | • Animation and interactivity require large files that can have long load-times<br>• High avoidance<br>• Short attention spans on the Internet |
| Television | • Reaches a wide audience<br>• Uses sight, sound, and motion<br>• Can target specific audiences<br>• Excellent for products requiring demonstration<br>• Highly visible | • High cost to create ads<br>• High cost to purchase media<br>• Short exposure time<br>• Perishable message<br>• Difficult to convey complex information<br>• High avoidance<br>• Difficult to measure |
| Newspapers | • Strong in local markets<br>• Short lead-times for ad placement<br>• Flexible ad sizes<br>• Ads can be clipped and saved<br>• Detailed information can be conveyed<br>• Can be low cost for local placements | • Ads compete for attention with other newspaper features<br>• Advertising clutter<br>• Short lifespan<br>• Poor colour reproduction<br>• Relatively high cost for national ads |
| Magazines | • Can target specific audiences<br>• High-quality colour<br>• Pass-along readership<br>• Ads can be clipped and saved<br>• Complex information can be conveyed | • Long lead-times<br>• Relatively high cost<br>• Advertising clutter<br>• Ads compete for attention with other magazine features |
| Radio | • Low cost of media and production<br>• Good for local businesses<br>• Short lead-times | • No visual elements<br>• Perishable message<br>• Background media<br>• Difficult to convey complex information<br>• Difficult for national campaigns |
| Outdoor/transit | • Relatively low cost<br>• Local market focus<br>• High visibility<br>• Strong opportunity for repeat exposure<br>• Good for building awareness in short time<br>• Cannot be turned off | • Message must be short and simple<br>• Low selectivity of audience<br>• Visual pollution |

change over the last few years, with a decline in circulation rates and a concerted move to digital formats. In addition, newspapers are challenged with lower advertising revenues in this digital age where the news is accessible through multiple avenues.

However, newspapers are still an important advertising medium that are well-recognized in the market for providing reliable information. There are three types of newspapers: daily paid circulation newspapers, free daily newspapers, and free community newspapers. The highest daily circulation of a paid newspaper in Canada is the *Globe and Mail*, followed in order by the *Toronto Star*, *La Presse*, and *Le Journal de Montréal*. Two free daily newspapers, *Metro* and *24 Hours*, are enjoying high circulation numbers that rival some of the traditional paid circulation

newspapers.[16] Community newspapers are published either weekly or monthly and are an excellent media choice for local retailers and for community events.

MAGAZINES Magazines provide advertisers with a high-quality media environment and provide an excellent opportunity for advertisers to match magazines to their target market profile. Vividata readership and circulation figures show that 70 percent of Canadians read magazines.[17]

Magazines have adapted well to the online environment by providing added online content such as searchable databases, blogs, contests, and polls, as well as mobile versions that can be accessed on tablets and other mobile devices. As a result, almost half of all magazine readers are reading on a digital platform.

## Figure 12–5
Top magazines (readership in Canada)

| Ranking | Magazine |
|---------|----------|
| 1 | *Reader's Digest* |
| 2 | *Cineplex Magazine* |
| 3 | *Live Better* |
| 4 | *Canadian Living* |
| 5 | *Canadian Geographic* |
| 6 | *CAA Magazine* |
| 7 | *Chatelaine* |
| 8 | *Maclean's* |
| 9 | *People* |
| 10 | *Food and Drink* |

Source: "Magazine Topline Readership 2017-Q1 Adults 18+," Vividata, accessed July 2017 at https://vividata.ca/wp-content/uploads/2015/08/2017-Q1-Magazine-TOPLINE.pdf.

Vividata issues topline reports detailing circulation, readership, and target market information on many Canadian newspapers and magazines. The Q1-2017 report shows that Canadian magazines with the highest readership are *Reader's Digest* and *Cineplex Magazine*; the top ten magazines are noted in Figure 12–5.[18] Navigate to the Vividata website at **www.vividata.ca** to review its latest data.

5. **RADIO**   Canadians over the age of 12 listen to the radio for 16 hours per week on average. But listeners are utilizing different methods for listening to radio programming. Almost one quarter (22 percent) stream radio online. In addition, it is estimated that 16 percent of adult Canadians subscribe to satellite radio. The main characteristics of radio are that it is local and has a relatively low production cost. This makes it affordable for both small and large advertisers. There are 720 private commercial radio stations in Canada, many of which focus on specific listener interests, including news and talk, or music genres such as adult contemporary, country, contemporary hits, rock, classical, and the oldies. Stations also exist for specific ethnic groups that broadcast content in foreign languages. Radio stations have responded to the Internet with online broadcasts, downloadable podcasts, apps, and blogs.[19]

6. **OUT-OF-HOME**   **Out-of-home (OOH) advertising** reaches consumers outside the home in outdoor locations using media such as billboards, posters, bus shelter ads, transit ads, washroom ads, and a variety of nonconventional methods such as aerial advertising, closed-circuit TV, electronic signage, and street furniture.

Since consumers spend 70 percent of their time outside of their homes, OOH advertising is an effective medium for generating reach quickly to build awareness and interest in a product.[20] It is also an excellent reminder for current products. Over the last few years, this media has experienced slight increases due to its participation in IMC programs and the realization by marketers that this media cannot be turned off. In a survey completed by TNS Canada, 57 percent of adults indicated that they had taken action after seeing OOH advertising within the last six months. Actions included visiting a website, searching for more information, visiting a store, or even buying the product.[21]

OOH advertising includes outdoor and transit advertising. Outdoor includes billboards, back-lit posters, superboards (large billboards), mall posters, digital signs, video signage/displays, wall banners, murals, and street-level columns. Examples can be seen at Yonge-Dundas Square in Toronto where Canada's first media tower dominates with 20,000 square feet of advertising in the form of digital billboards, full-motion video, and customized displays.

**out-of-home (OOH) advertising**
Casually referred to as *outdoor;* reaches consumers outside the home in outdoor locations, in transit, or in commercial or business locations.

Corby Spirit and Wine grabbed the attention of consumers by placing outdoor transit ads for its Corby Safe Rides campaign.

Used with permission of Delvinia

# Infographic

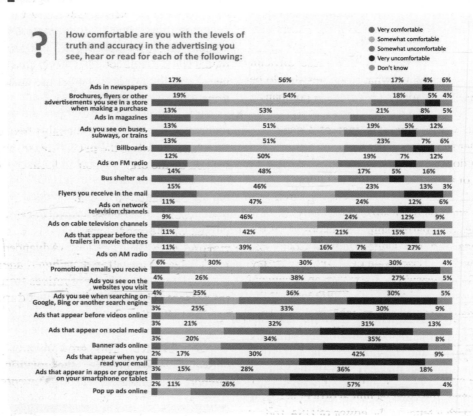

**?** How comfortable are you with the levels of truth and accuracy in the advertising you see, hear or read for each of the following:

● Very comfortable
○ Somewhat comfortable
◐ Somewhat uncomfortable
● Very uncomfortable
○ Don't know

| | | | | | |
|---|---|---|---|---|---|
| Ads in newspapers | 17% | 56% | 17% | 4% | 6% |
| Brochures, flyers or other advertisements you see in a store when making a purchase | 19% | 54% | 18% | 5% | 4% |
| Ads in magazines | 13% | 53% | 21% | 8% | 5% |
| Ads you see on buses, subways, or trains | 13% | 51% | 19% | 5% | 12% |
| Billboards | 13% | 51% | 23% | 7% | 6% |
| Ads on FM radio | 12% | 50% | 19% | 7% | 12% |
| Bus shelter ads | 14% | 48% | 17% | 5% | 16% |
| Flyers you receive in the mail | 15% | 46% | 23% | 13% | 3% |
| Ads on network television channels | 11% | 47% | 24% | 12% | 6% |
| Ads on cable television channels | 9% | 46% | 24% | 12% | 9% |
| Ads that appear before the trailers in movie theatres | 11% | 42% | 21% | 15% | 11% |
| Ads on AM radio | 11% | 39% | 16% | 7% | 27% |
| Promotional emails you receive | 6% | 30% | 30% | 30% | 4% |
| Ads you see on the websites you visit | 4% | 26% | 38% | 27% | 5% |
| Ads you see when searching on Google, Bing or another search engine | 4% | 25% | 36% | 30% | 5% |
| Ads that appear before videos online | 3% | 25% | 33% | 30% | 9% |
| Ads that appear on social media | 3% | 21% | 32% | 31% | 13% |
| Banner ads online | 3% | 20% | 34% | 35% | 8% |
| Ads that appear when you read your email | 2% | 17% | 30% | 42% | 9% |
| Ads that appear in apps or programs on your smartphone or tablet | 3% | 15% | 28% | 36% | 18% |
| Pop up ads online | 2% | 11% | 26% | 57% | 4% |

**Source:** Advertising Standards Canada, *Consumer Perspectives on Advertising 2016* (Toronto: Author, 2016), http://www.adstandards.com/en/ASCLibrary/2016ASCConsumerResearch.pdf. Reprinted with permission of Advertising Standards Canada.

---

**public relations**
A communications tool that seeks to influence the opinions and attitudes of target groups through the use of unpaid media exposure; targets the media in an attempt to generate positive publicity for a company, product, or individual.

It also includes place-based media where messages are placed in out-of-home destinations such as shopping malls, airports, parking lots, doctors' offices, health clubs, gas stations, elevators, and washrooms in restaurants, bars, and post-secondary schools. Transit advertising refers to ads placed on the interior and exterior of buses, subway cars, and taxis as well as in subway stations and on transit shelters.

## ask YOURSELF

1. *What types of advertising opportunities are available on the Internet?*

2. *How are newspapers in Canada dealing with the decline in advertising revenues?*

3. *Why is out-of-home advertising so effective?*

## PUBLIC RELATIONS

**LO 5** Public relations is an area that is increasingly used by marketers to deliver messages to consumers. While advertising may be viewed with suspicion, messages that come through a third party, such as the media, are often seen as more reliable and credible. In addition, for marketers with small budgets, public relations efforts can be a more affordable way to communicate with a wide audience.

**Public relations** is a communications tool that seeks to influence the opinions and attitudes of target groups through the use of unpaid media exposure. Public relations professionals build relationships with the media and stakeholders and use tools such as press releases, social media releases, press kits, news conferences, and events to spread the word. Public relations specialists target the media in an attempt to generate positive publicity for a company, product, or individual. Public relations can also take the form of crisis management and image management.

Crisis management can be an important aspect of public relations, as seen with various incidents over the last few years that have severely impacted people's lives and forced companies to answer to the public outcry. Public relations professionals, well-versed in crisis management, help companies navigate these difficult circumstances by advising on what strategies should be followed to rectify situations and salvage a company's image.

An example worth noting is that of Coca-Cola, which came under fire when it was uncovered that it had funded research downplaying the role that diet plays in obesity. As part of a partnership with the Global Energy Balance Network, funded by Coca-Cola, research was conducted that attempted to attribute obesity to lack of exercise. After this partnership was exposed by the media in Canada and the United States, Coca-Cola needed to deal with this corporate crisis by responding to its critics. When a crisis occurs within an organization, response must be rapid, with the CEO leading the charge. The organization needs to take responsibility and acknowledge any wrongdoing with transparency. It is also very important for the organization to present an action plan of next steps to confirm its commitment to rectifying the situation. Coke did all of these things. Within a couple days, the chief technical officer at Coca-Cola responded with a letter to the editor of *USA Today*, and this was followed by an editorial in the *Wall Street Journal* by Coca-Cola's CEO Muhtar Kent. Coca-Cola acknowledged that some of the decisions it had made to fund research and health programs were confusing to the public and created mistrust. In future, the company committed to more transparency and reinforced that both diet and exercise play an important role in combating obesity. Coca-Cola also committed to establishing an oversight committee of external experts to review any future research activities. By all accounts, Coca-Cola managed to handle this crisis in a professional manner, which reinforced its commitment to its customers.[22]

It is important to understand that while public relations efforts can yield positive results, ultimately the media decides if, what, and when it may spread a message about a company, brand, or individual. **Publicity** is a non-personal form of communication that appears in the media and is not paid for directly by the organization. The publicity is not controlled by the company itself, and the company has no control over what is discussed.

> Crisis management can be an important aspect of public relations.

## Public Relations Tools

Public relations activities need to be ethical and integrated into marketing communications efforts. Several tools and tactics are available for marketers, including press releases, press conferences, special events, and company reports. Social media releases and social media initiatives are relatively new tools that can come under the guise of public relations. Let's look at the tools.

**PRESS RELEASES**   One of the most frequently used public relations tools is the **press release**, an announcement written by the organization and sent to the media.

**PRESS CONFERENCES**   Another commonly used publicity tool is the **press conference**, when representatives of the media are invited to an informational meeting with the company. Advanced materials and press releases are often distributed ahead of time and external experts and/or executives from the company are present. This tool is often used during crisis management situations.

**SPECIAL EVENTS**   This growing area of public relations involves the creation, support, or sponsorship of special events such as company-sponsored seminars, conferences, and sporting or entertainment events. The goal of these events is to create a forum to disseminate company information and to create positive brand associations for participants or viewers.

**COMPANY REPORTS**   Formal company information that is published in annual reports, brochures, newsletters, or videos are also public relations tools that help spread positive messages.

**SOCIAL MEDIA RELEASES**   A **social media release** is a tool available for marketers to efficiently and effectively communicate information to the media and the public. Unlike press releases, which exist online and offline with mainly text-based information, social media releases use online multimedia to communicate with recipients. Video, images, and text are included in online releases, with comment areas and share buttons so that readers can easily share the release on blogs or social networks such as Twitter and Facebook.

**publicity**
A non-personal form of communication that appears in the media and is not paid for directly by the organization.

**press release**
An announcement written by an organization and sent to the media.

**press conference**
A planned event where representatives of the media are invited to an informational meeting with the company.

**social media release**
A multimedia, online press-release platform that includes video, text, and images, as well as social media buttons for sharing on social networks and comment areas where viewers can leave comments.

McDonald's Monopoly game has been a successful consumer promotion in Canada for 30 years.

CoCo Jones/Alamy Stock Photo

## 3. SALES PROMOTION

**sales promotion**
A communications tool that provides short-term incentives to generate interest in a product or cause and encourages purchase or support.

**consumer promotions**
Short-term marketing tools used to encourage immediate consumer purchase.

**trade promotions**
Short-term promotional tools used to generate support with wholesalers, distributors, or retailers.

**LO 6** **Sales promotion** is a communications tool that provides short-term incentives to generate interest in a product or cause and encourages purchase or support. There are two basic types of sales promotion: (1) consumer promotions and (2) trade promotions. **Consumer promotions** are short-term marketing tools used to encourage immediate consumer purchase. They include incentives such as coupons, premiums, contests, sweepstakes, samples, loyalty programs, rebates, bonus packs, and point-of-purchase materials, which are outlined in Figure 12–6.

McDonald's "Monopoly" game is one of Canada's most successful consumer promotions, and in 2017, it celebrates its 30th anniversary. The promotion is a result of a partnership between McDonald's and Hasbro, building on the popularity of the Monopoly board game. Consumers collect Monopoly properties as they purchase McDonald's products. They use the properties to win prizes. McDonald's has introduced an online component to the game for consumers to track their properties and claim prizes. Prizes range from cash and gift cards to cars and travel.[23]

**Trade promotions** are short-term promotional tools used to generate support with wholesalers, distributors, or retailers. Common approaches include trade shows, trade allowances and discounts, and cooperative advertising (see Figure 12–7).

## Figure 12–6

Consumer promotions

Consumer promotions are an effective way to increase short-term sales.

| Consumer Promotions | Promotional Tools | Explanation |
|---|---|---|
| **Short-term marketing tools used to encourage immediate consumer purchase** | Coupons | Price reductions offered in exchange for electronic or paper documents. Can be distributed online, on-pack, through flyers, or on shelf. |
| | Premiums | Offers that provide merchandise for free or at a significant savings in exchange for proof-of-purchase of a product. |
| | Contests | Offers where participants require a skill to win a prize such as creative submissions. |
| | Sweepstakes | Offers which are pure games-of-chance and where consumers often participate by completing an entry form and, if selected as a winner, answering a skill-testing question. |
| | Samples | The provision of free products to encourage consumers to try and purchase a product. |
| | Loyalty programs | Programs that encourage and reward customers for ongoing purchases with points that can be redeemed for rewards. |
| | Rebates | A price reduction supplied via mail in exchange for proof-of-purchase. |
| | Bonus packs/special packs | The provision of oversized packs or bonus items attached to the original product. |
| | Point-of-purchase materials | The use of in-store merchandising such as display materials, banners, floor decals, and posters to draw attention. |

## Figure 12–7

Trade promotions

Trade promotions are often required to encourage retail support.

| Trade Promotions | Promotional Tools | Explanation |
|---|---|---|
| Short-term promotional tools given to wholesalers, distributors, or retailers | Trade shows | Participation in industry events that showcase new products and initiatives. |
| | Off-invoice allowances | A price reduction taken off the invoice of a purchase that is made within a specific time frame. |
| | Merchandising allowances | A price reduction taken off a purchase in return for displaying the product. |
| | Co-op advertising | The contribution of funds for inclusion in a wholesaler, distributor, or retailer advertising program such as a flyer. |

### ask YOURSELF

1. What types of consumer promotions are available to marketers?

2. How do trade promotions differ from consumer promotions?

3. What trade promotional tools are available to marketers?

## DIRECT RESPONSE MARKETING

**LO 7**   **Direct response marketing** is a tool designed to communicate with consumers in a targeted and personalized way using either traditional or online approaches. In addition, unique to direct response marketing is the inclusion of a call to action for consumers.[24] In many instances, a direct response marketing program is multifaceted and designed with short-term communication blasts to build long-term relationships with the company and brand loyalty.

Offline approaches include direct mail, catalogues, telemarketing, and direct-response advertising on TV, radio, or print, where telephone numbers or web addresses drive an immediate call to action. Online approaches look to the Internet to facilitate one-on-one interactions and use tools such as e-mail campaigns and social media interactions to drive consumers to landing pages, websites, or microsites. In many instances, offline and online direct response approaches work together to encourage consumers to go to a store or an e-commerce site to complete a transaction.

Direct response marketing programs use metrics to evaluate success, such as business leads, traffic generation, and direct orders. **Lead generation** is the resultant request for additional information. **Traffic generation** is the resultant visit to a location or website.

A successful direct mail campaign was launched by BMW to mark the 40th anniversary of the M series vehicle. BMW sent existing and prospective customers an actual print of the wheel tread of an M series vehicle. In addition, the customer received a personalized URL to a YouTube video documenting the creation of the direct mail piece. The video itself received 500,000 hits and was shared extensively on social media. Owners of M series vehicles even started to post their own M series tire treads on social media.[25]

**direct response marketing**
A tool designed to communicate with consumers in a targeted and personalized way using either traditional or online approaches.

**lead generation**
The requests for additional information that result from direct response marketing.

**traffic generation**
The visits to a location or website that result from direct response marketing.

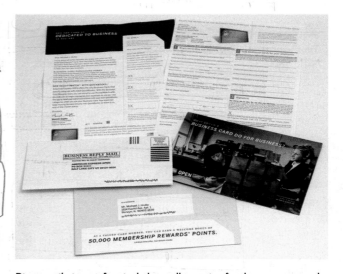

Direct mail pieces often include a call to action for the consumer and when integrated with other marketing communication vehicles, they can help a brand build a long-term relationship with the customer.

© Mike Hruby

Over 2 million people interact with the Toronto International Film Festival each year, providing valuable sponsorship opportunities.

Used with permission of TIFF

## 5. EVENT MARKETING AND SPONSORSHIP

**Event marketing** refers to the creation or involvement of a brand in an experience or occasion that heightens its awareness, creates positive associations, and generates a desired response. *Experiential marketing,* introduced in Chapter 1, can be based around an event, but it often combines public relations, event marketing, and promotions to break through the clutter of competing marketing messages. Event marketing and sponsorship often go hand-in-hand with brands lending their names to established events. Companies often weave event marketing into integrated campaigns to make connections with consumers and create a buzz.

**Sponsorship** involves a company paying a fee in exchange for inclusion in an event, involvement in its advertising opportunities, or exposure within the event itself. Sponsorship programs can encompass a multitude of approaches that range from placing ads or logos in brochures, to setting up banners at events, to the naming of the event itself.

**event marketing**
The creation or involvement of a brand in an experience or occasion that will heighten its awareness, create positive associations, and generate a desired response.

**sponsorship**
When an advertiser pays a fee in exchange for inclusion in an event, involvement in its advertising opportunities, or exposure within the event itself.

An example of sponsorship can be seen with the annual Toronto International Film Festival, or TIFF. The lead sponsor of TIFF is Bell. The 530,000 attendees at the event are only the tip of the iceberg. Over 2 million people interact in some way with TIFF each year. In addition, TIFF is able to provide a very clear description of its audience. Attendees are overwhelmingly younger individuals with a post-secondary education and an average household income of $91,000. For companies like Bell, the Royal Bank, and L'Oréal Paris, they can be sure that they will gain significant exposure with key target groups before, during, and after the event. TIFF not only offers opportunities for companies to entertain and host clients at the event, but there are a multitude of branding and promotional opportunities for sponsors as well, depending on the negotiated package. Media impressions hit 3.3 billion worldwide with over 1,000 media outlets.[26]

*Companies often weave event marketing into integrated campaigns.*

Personal selling plays a central role in many industries.

© Rob Melnychuk/Getty Images

## 6. PRODUCT PLACEMENT AND BRANDED ENTERTAINMENT

The fact that consumers avoid TV ads by muting the sound, changing the channel, or leaving the room is encouraging marketers to include products in TV shows and movies. This can be done through **product placement**, the inclusion of a product such as a soft drink in a movie or TV program, or the creation of an entire movie or TV episode around a brand, which is referred to as **branded entertainment**. When Ikea pays to have its furniture featured in a scene of *Deadpool*, this is an example of product placement. *The Lego Movie* and the Marvel franchise of movies are examples of branded entertainment.

## 7. PERSONAL SELLING

**LO 8**    **Personal selling** involves the two-way flow of communication between a buyer and seller, often face-to-face or facilitated through communication devices, to influence an individual or group purchase decision. Unlike advertising, personal selling is usually face-to-face communication, although telephone and electronic communication is also used.

Sales positions include account management positions, manufacturing sales personnel, real estate brokers, stockbrokers, and salesclerks who work in retail stores. In reality, virtually every occupation that involves customer contact has an element of personal selling with the salespeople representing the company.

The personal selling process consists of six stages: prospecting, pre-approach, approach, presentation, close, and follow-up, as detailed in Figure 12–8.

### ask YOURSELF

1. *What are the differences between advertising and public relations?*

2. *Which promotional tools can generate immediate responses?*

3. *What are the stages in the personal selling process?*

**product placement**
The inclusion of a product in a movie or TV program in return for payment.

**branded entertainment**
The creation of an entertainment program, such as a TV episode, that is highly focused on a brand in exchange for payment.

**personal selling**
The two-way flow of communication between a buyer and seller, often face-to-face or facilitated through communication devices, to influence an individual and group purchase decision.

### Figure 12–8
Stages and objectives in the personal selling process

| Stage | Objective | Comments |
|-------|-----------|----------|
| 1. Prospecting | Search for and qualify prospects | Start of the selling process; prospects generated through advertising, referrals, and cold canvassing |
| 2. Pre-approach | Gather information and decide how to approach the prospect | Information sources include personal observation, other customers, and company salespeople |
| 3. Approach | Gain prospect's attention, stimulate interest, and make transition to the presentation | First impression is critical; gain attention and interest through references to common acquaintances, a referral, or product demonstration |
| 4. Presentation | Begin converting a prospect into a customer by creating a desire for the product or service | Different presentation formats are possible; involving the customer is critical; responding to objections is key; a professional ethical approach is needed |
| 5. Close | Obtain a purchase commitment from the prospect and secure a customer | Salesperson asks for the order; different approaches include the trial close and assumptive close; trial close can be used at any stage |
| 6. Follow-up | Ensure that the customer is satisfied with the product or service | Resolve any problems faced by the customer to ensure customer satisfaction and future sales possibilities |

**push strategy**
When marketers focus communication on the distribution channel to gain support from retailers, distributors, and wholesalers.

**pull strategy**
When marketers focus communication efforts on ultimate consumers to build awareness, trial, and demand for a product.

# PLANNING AND EVALUATION

## DESIGNING MARKETING COMMUNICATION PROGRAMS

**LO 9** Marketing communications can be a fun yet daunting task for marketers. Its subjective nature can make it unnerving. However, the creativity required to pull it together, and the ability of metrics to measure success, can make it very rewarding.

Marketers turn to marketing communication experts to navigate this terrain. Communication agencies provide expertise on communication approaches with access to insights on new opportunities, consumer trends, and media research. They help guide strategy development, creative development, and media planning and buying, as well as program evaluation. Marketers shape the backdrop by providing company, product, and target market information, as well as insights into product positioning, previous campaigns, the competition, and budgetary constraints. They explain the balance between consumer and trade promotion, as well as how push and pull strategies are used. They are also involved in program creation and evaluation.

A **push strategy** is when marketers focus communication efforts on the distribution channel to gain support from retailers, distributors, and wholesalers through listings, sales, merchandising, featured pricing, and the inclusion in flyers. A **pull strategy** is when marketers focus communication efforts on ultimate consumers to build awareness, trial, and demand for a product. These approaches should work together (see Figure 12–9).

**Figure 12–9**
Push and pull communication strategies
Push and pull strategies need to work together.

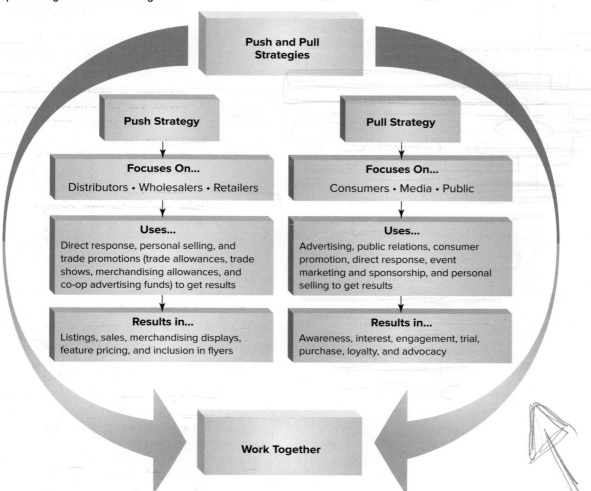

**Push and Pull Strategies**

**Push Strategy**

**Focuses On...**
Distributors • Wholesalers • Retailers

**Uses...**
Direct response, personal selling, and trade promotions (trade allowances, trade shows, merchandising allowances, and co-op advertising funds) to get results

**Results in...**
Listings, sales, merchandising displays, feature pricing, and inclusion in flyers

**Pull Strategy**

**Focuses On...**
Consumers • Media • Public

**Uses...**
Advertising, public relations, consumer promotion, direct response, event marketing and sponsorship, and personal selling to get results

**Results in...**
Awareness, interest, engagement, trial, purchase, loyalty, and advocacy

**Work Together**

# THE CUSTOMER ADVOCACY FUNNEL

Marketers use integrated marketing communications approaches to ensure that all communication elements speak with the same messaging and use a shared visual platform. This approach involves developing, executing, and evaluating each element of a promotional program so that it encourages customers to become loyal supporters that spread positive messages. We call this *advocacy*.

The **Customer Advocacy Funnel** (Figure 12–10) demonstrates how, over time, the positive connections that customers make with brands encourage them to become brand advocates who recommend the brand to others. This funnel has consumers moving from an initial awareness stage through to interest, engagement, trial, purchase, loyalty, and advocacy.

Let's try to understand how marketers can use specific tools in an integrated fashion to drive customers through the funnel:

- **Awareness:** A company trying to raise brand awareness may use a website, search engine, traditional, and online advertising to maximize consumer exposure to the product.

**Figure 12–10**
The Customer Advocacy Funnel

- **Awareness**: A company trying to raise online product awareness may use a website, search engine optimization, online video, and display ads to drive consumers to an online destination.
- **Interest**: Interesting product attributes are highlighted to entice potential customers to learn more.
- **Engagement**: Potential customers are invited to participate in the product experience and interact with its marketing.
- **Trial**: Customers obtain free samples or purchase the product as a limited trial or download.
- **Purchase**: Positive product experiences lead to product purchase.
- **Loyalty**: Ongoing positive product experiences lead to repeat purchases.
- **Advocacy**: Loyal customers are rewarded with additional experiences and become advocates who recommend the product to others.

- **Interest:** A company may use online video to increase interest in the product, this time using experts to demo the product and add credibility.
- **Engagement:** Social media can be added to the mix to encourage engagement by consumers.
- **Trial:** Contests, samples, and limited trials can be communicated through direct mail, product microsites, and social media networks.
- **Purchase:** Follow-up on product trial can be done through e-mail to reinforce a positive product experience, which can lead to product purchase.
- **Loyalty:** Customer loyalty can be encouraged through programs that reward continued purchases, such as loyalty programs. Social media can help encourage interaction with the brand.
- **Advocacy:** Ongoing communications, often one-to-one, through e-mail newsletters, social networks, branded communities, and blogs can solidify connections with loyal customers, providing them with information and experiences to share with others.

# STEPS IN THE MARKETING COMMUNICATIONS PROCESS

Today, with the multitude of communication tools available, and consumers fragmented over a wide array of touch points, marketers follow an integrated approach to marketing communications, making sure all elements work together to reach specific target audiences. The steps in this process, outlined in Figure 12–11, require a marketer to (1) specify the IMC objectives, (2) identify the target audience, (3) set the promotional budget, (4) design the promotional program, (5) schedule and run the IMC elements, and (6) evaluate the program and recommend changes. These steps are explained below.

## Step 1: Specify the IMC Objectives

The first step formalizes the purpose of the promotional program, such as building brand awareness, creating customer engagement, or increasing brand loyalty. Specific numerical targets are often included at this point and used later to evaluate the program. The Customer Advocacy Funnel noted earlier may help determine these objectives. Often a promotional plan includes objectives such as reach and frequency. **Reach** is the

**Customer Advocacy Funnel**
A communications approach that takes consumers from initial product awareness through to brand advocacy.

**reach**
The number of people who are exposed to a communication vehicle or message; is presented as percentage of the total number of people in a target audience.

## Figure 12–11

Steps in the marketing communications process

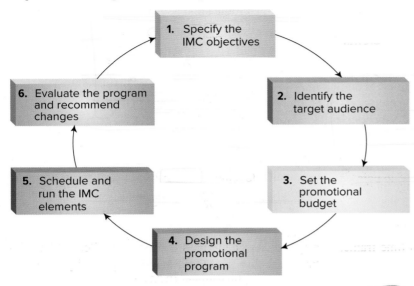

**All you can afford:** Allows money to be spent on promotion only after all other budget items—such as manufacturing costs—are covered.

**Objective and task:** The company determines the promotion objectives, outlines the tasks to accomplish those objectives, and determines the promotion cost of performing those tasks.

### Step 4: Design the Promotional Program

The key component of a promotional program is its messaging. It needs to be visible, resonate with its target audience, and be memorable. One of the major challenges of IMC is to design each promotional activity to communicate the same message.

Media and creative teams work hand-in-hand at this point to share ideas to ensure that opportunities are not overlooked and that the best possible promotional mix is created. The creative team brainstorms on programs that engage the target market, while media experts conduct thorough analyses to bring forward ideas and communication platforms that will effectively and efficiently reach target audiences. The **promotional mix** refers to the selection of promotional tools used to communicate with a target market. It can encompass online and offline approaches and include advertising, public relations, sales promotion, direct response marketing, event marketing and sponsorship, product placement and branded entertainment, personal selling, online marketing, social media marketing, and mobile marketing.

When determining the promotional program, marketers carefully consider their product's life cycle and the competitive nature of the market so that their programs are engaging and meaningful to target markets (see Figure 12–12). Product life cycle considerations include the knowledge that during introductory stages, marketing communication builds awareness, provides information, and encourages trial. In the growth stage, promotional focus changes and starts to persuade and differentiate the brand from the competition. In the maturity stage, promotional efforts are designed as a reminder of the brand and to encourage repeat purchases through special offers. The decline stage often has little to no promotion at all.

### Step 5: Schedule and Run the IMC Elements

The promotion schedule describes the order in which each promotional tool is introduced and

---

number of people who are exposed to a communication vehicle or message; it is presented as percentage of the total number of people in a target audience. **Frequency** is the number of times the target audience is exposed to the communication vehicle or the communication message.[27]

### Step 2: Identify the Target Audience

The second step in developing the promotion program involves identifying the target audience, the group of prospective buyers toward which a promotion program will be directed, using geographic, demographic, psychographic, and behavioural data. Information on media used by the target audience is also provided, as well as insights on consumer touch points. **Touch points** are any situation in which a customer comes into contact with a brand or company.

### Step 3: Set the Promotional Budget

Determining the budget is no easy task, particularly since the program has yet to be recommended. However, several methods can be used to set the promotion budget.[28]

- **Percentage of sales:** The amount of money spent on promotion is a percentage of past or anticipated sales.
- **Competitive parity:** Matches the competitor's absolute levels of spending or a proportion of their spend based on market shares.

**frequency**

The number of times the target audience is exposed to the communication vehicle or the communication message.

**touch points**

Any situation in which a customer comes into contact with a brand or company.

**promotional mix**

The selection of promotional tools used to communicate with a target market.

## Figure 12–12
Product life cycle considerations for promotional programs

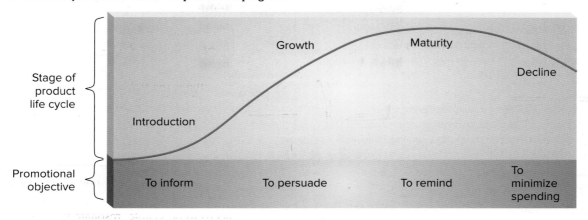

Stage of product life cycle

Introduction    Growth    Maturity    Decline

Promotional objective

To inform    To persuade    To remind    To minimize spending

the frequency of its use during a specified time frame. The order of promotional elements is carefully planned so that individual aspects seamlessly work together to communicate with target audiences. Throughout the campaign, marketers carefully monitor developments, particularly in social media, to immediately answer questions, respond to comments, and carefully deal with negative feedback.

### Step 6: Evaluate the Program and Recommend Changes
Promotional programs are evaluated on four levels. First, messaging is often evaluated before a program is fully developed to gauge responses so that adjustments can be made before launch.

Second, once the program is live, research may be fielded to measure campaign awareness and messaging elements such as *likability*, *message comprehension*, and *attitude changes* toward the brand.

Third, upon completion, each individual element will be evaluated against expectations. Online programs may look at page views and time on site. Public relations efforts may be measured on publicity mentions and return on investment (ROI).

Fourth, the promotional program will be evaluated against its objectives. This will look at business results such as sales, profitability, market share, and expected ROI.

All of these metrics will be used to determine campaign success and what elements can be strengthened in the future.

### ask YOURSELF

1. *What are the stages in the Customer Advocacy Funnel?*

2. *What approaches are used to set the promotional budget?*

3. *How are marketing communications programs evaluated?*

**LO 1** • The current trends impacting marketing communications include a more connected consumer, which has resulted in a shift to digital media from more traditional forms.

**LO 2** • The marketing communications industry consists of the media, marketing communications agencies, research companies, associations, and regulatory bodies.

• The marketing communications industry is regulated by Advertising Standards Canada (Ad Standards), the Competition Bureau, the Canadian Radio-television and Telecommunications Commission (CRTC), the Canadian Marketing Association (CMA), the Canadian Wireless Telecommunications Association (CWTA), and the Mobile Marketing Association (MMA).

**LO 3** • Marketing communications approaches can include inbound and outbound approaches with marketers commonly using an integrated marketing communications (IMC) approach.

• Marketing communication tools include advertising, public relations, sales promotion, direct response marketing, event marketing and sponsorship, product placement and branded entertainment, personal selling, online marketing, social media marketing, and mobile marketing.

**LO 4** • Advertising media choices include Internet/mobile, TV, newspaper, magazine, radio, and out-of-home.

**LO 5** • Public relations initiatives include press releases, press conferences, special events, company reports, and the use of social media releases.

**LO 6** • Consumer promotional tools include coupons, contests, sweepstakes, samples, premiums, loyalty programs, rebates, bonus packs, and point-of-sale materials.

• Trade promotions include trade shows, off-invoice allowances, merchandising allowances, and co-op advertising.

**LO 7** • Direct response marketing tools include direct mail, catalogues, telemarketing, and direct response advertising on TV, radio, and print, as well as e-mail marketing and social media interactions.

• Event marketing and sponsorship refers to the involvement of a brand in an event through either an advertising package or on-site involvement.

• Product placement is the inclusion of a product in a movie or TV program, while branded entertainment is the creation of an entertainment program highly focused on a brand.

**LO 8** • The personal selling process consists of six stages: prospecting, pre-approach, approach, presentation, close, and follow-up.

**LO 9** • The promotional planning process requires marketers to (1) specify the IMC objectives, (2) identify the target audience, (3) set the promotional budget, (4) design the promotional program, (5) schedule and run the IMC elements, and (6) evaluate the program and recommend changes.

• Evaluation approaches look at the program in general as well as each individual element.

---

*key terms and concepts...* **A REFRESHER**

advertising
branded entertainment
consumer promotions
Customer Advocacy Funnel
direct response marketing
earned media
event marketing
frequency
inbound marketing
integrated marketing communications (IMC)
lead generation

marketing communication agencies
marketing communication tools
outbound marketing
out-of-home (OOH) advertising
owned media
paid media
personal selling
press conference
press release
product placement
promotional mix
public relations

publicity
pull strategy
push strategy
reach
sales promotion
social media release
sponsorship
touch points
trade promotions
traffic generation

**Promotion Assignment** Using the information in the Marketing NewsFlash box regarding Nabob's "Respect the Bean" campaign, draft what you believe to be the following components of the campaign's promotional plan: (1) IMC objectives, (2) target market profile, (3) central promotional idea, (4) recommended promotional mix, and (5) methods to evaluate the campaign.

This chapter's opening vignette examines Kao Canada's integrated marketing campaign for the Bioré brand of products. Brainstorm other elements that you would add to the campaign to create additional touch points with the target audience.

Review the Infographic that details information on an Advertising Standards Canada (Ad Standards) study indicating the level of trust that individuals have with each media format. Why do you believe that some media formats are trusted more than others?

# CHAPTER **13**

## LEARNING OBJECTIVES

**LO 1** Explain the unique online approaches used in marketing communications

**LO 2** Describe social media marketing

**LO 3** Outline the main social networks and tools used in social media marketing

**LO 4** Summarize the best practices associated with the creation and monitoring of social media programs

**LO 5** Explain mobile marketing and its approaches

**LO 6** Describe the tools involved in mobile marketing

**LO 7** List the best practices and regulations that guide mobile marketing

# Digital Marketing Communications

**A**s discussed in the opening vignette for Chapter 12, Kao Canada is recognized as an innovator in the development and manufacture of premium beauty care brands. In the competitive skincare category, Kao is known for Bioré® face care. The brand is best known for the iconic Bioré Deep Cleansing Pore Strips. Bioré has been successful in this very competitive market by launching new product innovations through an integrated marketing communications program.

BIORÉ® is a trademark of Kao Corporation and is used with permission of Kao Canada Inc.

Kao has created an integrated campaign for Bioré Deep Cleansing Pore Strips. This campaign ensures multiple targeted consumer touch points that deliver a consistent message and imagery for the brand. Chapter 12 gave an overview of the more traditional approaches that Bioré uses to reach its young female audience. Promotional tools such as advertising, sampling, coupons, public relations, and trade promotions work together to build brand awareness and relevance.

Bioré has integrated a substantial digital marketing effort into its promotional mix. The target audience is composed of females between the ages of 15 and 29. Members of this demographic are digital natives, who are most comfortable communicating in a digital environment and rely on digital technology to connect with others and with their favourite brands.

Bioré is a brand made for the digital age. What better way to communicate with your customers in a relatable, funny, and colourful fashion than through digital technology? Another major advantage to digital marketing platforms is the ability to interact and build a relationship with customers. In order to reinforce Bioré's positioning as "the ultimate solution for clean, beautiful skin," the brand makes use of these digital tools:

**Mobile:** Bioré maximizes its activity on mobile platforms by distributing mobile coupon promotions directly to the customer's smartphone. Consumers in the target audience remain connected most often by using a smartphone. Bioré delivers coupon offers through apps such as Checkout 51 to drive the purchase of its products with targeted customers.

**Internet advertising:** Bioré analyzes the digital content that is most accessed by its target audience and layers its brand messages with targeted pre-roll video brand advertising on YouTube and other entertainment destinations such as Buzzfeed.

**Social media:** Bioré employs a comprehensive social media strategy with content based on its influencers and other generated content:

- **Facebook:** Year-round Facebook activity communicates key brand messages and amplifies other planned marketing activity (e.g., share influencer videos and Buzzfeed content). Bioré can also communicate with customers through the comment feature and offer coupons for $5 off any Bioré product to encourage trial.

- **YouTube:** Pre-roll video advertising is a great way to target ads to consumers with similar interests, or simply through demographic targeting. Bioré runs 15-second skippable and non-skippable ads on YouTube. Bioré has been able to reach consumers who are interested in women's beauty, lifestyle, and entertainment content, allowing targeting beyond simple demographics.

- **Brand influencers:** Brand influencers are an important part of Bioré's social media strategy. Bioré has partnerships with key YouTube vloggers/influencers for its target audience. These influencers demonstrate and review Bioré products, and Lauren (@laurDIY) is a great example. Lauren has 1.4 million views of a video where she declared the Bioré Deep Cleansing Pore Strip her "ride or die skincare product."

- **Twitter:** Twitter provides a flexible tool for Bioré to post new product information, links to coupons, and links to brand influencer posts, as well as to share Bioré reviews and comments posted by others.

- **Bioré brand ambassador:** Shay Mitchell, young award-winning actress, author, and blogger, signed on as brand ambassador for Bioré in the U.S. With cross-border social media, the impact of Shay's partnership, including national media interviews and brand content on her social media, is shared in Canada. Shay is the perfect brand ambassador to reach the younger female audience.

**Smartsource.ca:** Bioré posts coupons on SmartSource.ca, a one-stop shop for online/printable coupons for various manufacturers. Consumers can be linked to the site or go to the site on their own to select and print coupons for Bioré products.

**Search engine marketing:** Bioré utilizes year-round Google paid search, ratings, and reviews. Keywords are both brand-specific (e.g., Bioré, charcoal, pore strips) and focused on the skincare category (e.g., blackheads, acne, cleansers).

**E-mail:** Bioré uses e-mail to regularly provide loyal consumers with brand news and reward them with special offers before anyone else receives them. Consumers subscribe to e-mails by signing up on the Bioré website.

**Brand promotional website:** Biore.ca is the headquarters for all things Bioré. From the main web page, the consumer can link to social media, review Bioré products, find out where to buy Bioré products, and sign up for e-updates on products and promotions.

Digital marketing provides a breadth of tools to utilize with customers. The tricky part can be ensuring that messaging is consistent across each platform. Erin Arthrell, Canadian brand manager for Bioré, notes, "To establish awareness and understanding, and to keep the brand top of mind, it is important to reach the consumer with a consistent brand message at multiple touch points with an integrated campaign." Bioré provides us with an excellent example of how a campaign can integrate traditional offline platforms with unique online approaches to maximize messaging to and relationships with key customers.[1]

*reality* **CHECK** ⊘

As you read Chapter 13, refer back to the Bioré opening vignette on digital marketing to answer the following questions:

- Why is social media such a powerful communication tool for reaching millennials?
- What other digital tools would you recommend that Bioré integrate into its campaigns?

# DIGITAL MARKETING COMMUNICATION

Digital marketing communication tools are the most rapidly evolving areas in marketing, and a marketer needs to understand how consumers and marketers use them to stay connected and engaged. One of the first touch points that a brand may have with a consumer is through its website, where a consumer may go to find out more about a product or company. Consumers connect with each other and with brands using social media, whether this is with Facebook to locate an offer or Twitter to lodge a complaint. Mobile platforms are often used by consumers to reach out on social networks, checking statuses and posting updates to share with friends throughout the day and on the go. Marketers in turn connect brands with consumers on these networks and use mobile marketing approaches to reach consumers on their mobile devices.

This chapter is designed to provide students with an understanding of how digital communication tools are used for marketing purposes and how they can be integrated with offline marketing tools to create a truly integrated brand message. Recent data shows that Canadians spend over four hours per day on digital media, making it an important tool for any marketer.[2]

# ONLINE MARKETING TOOLS

**LO 1** The Internet has a number of unique online tools that marketers use to engage individuals—namely, websites and microsites, search engine marketing, display advertising, affiliate marketing, e-mail marketing, word-of-mouth marketing, social media marketing, and mobile marketing.

**transactional websites**
Electronic storefronts focused on converting an online browser into an online buyer.

The Walmart website has a focus on transactions.

Ed Endicott/Alamy Stock Photo

## WEBSITES

When it comes to websites, their design and content is central to successful ranking on search engines, which facilitates discovery by consumers. Content needs to be fresh and frequently updated. Many websites include blogs as a means of routinely adding fresh new content. Visual website appeal is also important. Consumers decide to click on a web page within seconds; therefore, content and visual appeal need to work together to present an appealing proposition. Websites can be transactional, promotional, or both. **Transactional websites** were discussed in Chapter 10. They are essentially electronic storefronts focused on converting an online searcher into an online buyer. **Promotional websites** focus on showcasing products and services.

**Microsites** are promotional websites created to showcase a specific brand or for short-term promotional purposes, often providing consumers with the ability to enter contests and access promotional offers. McCain Foods used a microsite to promote its #Modifry contest, encouraging customers to submit their innovative recipes using McCain French fries. **Corporate websites** are important destination sites for consumers and the media that want to quickly access company and product information.

*Microsites are promotional websites created to showcase a specific brand or for short-term promotional purposes.*

Websites often form the foundation of a company or brand's digital marketing strategy, providing links to social media as well as sign-up pages for newsletter and e-mail communications.

## SEARCH ENGINE MARKETING

**Search engine marketing (SEM)** is an Internet marketing approach that includes two areas: (1) search engine optimization and (2) pay-per-click advertising. **Search engine optimization (SEO)** looks at website design, technical coding, written content, incoming links, and website updates to ensure that websites are highly rated and properly indexed by search engines such as Google and Bing. Marketers often work with specialists to maximize search engine optimization.

An Internet advertising approach pioneered by search engines and now also used by a few websites, blogs, and social media sites is called **pay-per-click advertising (PPC)**. It is often referred to as *search advertising* because it primarily appears on search engines in the form of mini-text ads that are served during keyword searches on either the top or right-hand side of the search page. The search engine is paid by the PPC advertiser only when the ads are clicked. Pay-per-click image ads also exist on some blogs and social media sites.

## DISPLAY ADVERTISING

**Display advertising** refers to the use of online ads with images, audio, video, or animation. Display ads can be static or dynamic. Ads can be expandable and get larger as a page loads, they can float onto a page, or they can be transitional by appearing between the loading of two content pages. Display ads can also

**promotional websites**
Websites that focus on showcasing products and services.

**microsites**
Promotional websites created for short-term promotional purposes, often allowing consumers to enter contests and access promotional information.

**corporate websites**
Websites that provide company and brand information to consumers and the media.

**search engine marketing (SEM)**
Includes the use of search engine optimization and pay-per-click advertising to market on search engines.

**search engine optimization (SEO)**
Ensuring that websites are written, indexed, and coded so that they are highly rated and ranked by the search engines.

**pay-per-click advertising (PPC)**
Ads that appear in response to keyword triggers on search engines, as well as on some websites, blogs, and social media sites, where the advertiser pays only when the ad is clicked.

**display advertising**
The use of online ads with graphics or animation that are placed on websites.

be formatted as *home page takeovers* where an entire ad obscures a website home page.

Display ads are commonly called **banner ads**, and come in a variety of shapes and sizes—leaderboards, rectangles, squares, or skyscrapers. **Leaderboards** stretch across the top of a web page, while rectangles typically appear lower down, on the right-hand side of a webpage. **Skyscrapers** are tall, slim, vertical ads placed along the side of a web page. Figure 13–1 illustrates the types of display ads that can be purchased.

Gaming websites embed ads within their online games so that ads appear as billboards or posters within the games. This is called **advergaming**, an opportunity that allows marketers to dynamically rotate display ads as appropriate by time of day or day of the week. Ads can also be placed within offline games.

**In-stream advertising** refers to the use of video ads that play before (pre-roll), during (mid-roll), or after (post-roll) video segments that are watched online on social media sites such as YouTube. These types of ads are increasingly popular with marketers but have the disadvantage of being more expensive to produce than static or display ads. Many marketers extend the value of a television commercial by purchasing in-stream skippable or non-skippable video advertising.

## AFFILIATE MARKETING

**Affiliate marketing** is the term used when companies promote their businesses through a network of online associates (affiliates) to drive traffic, leads, and purchases. Affiliates are provided with ads and links to the business website and rewarded with commissions for resultant business activity. Affiliate commissions can be based on click-through rates, sales, or a combination of the two.[3] Walmart and Amazon use this business model, providing affiliates with online ads and links to display on their own websites or blogs.

## E-MAIL MARKETING

**E-mail marketing** includes the use of opt-in e-mail lists where consumers register and give permission to receive online communications. The Canadian Marketing Association (CMA) strictly advises members not to use spam. **Permission-based e-mail** is when a recipient chooses to receive e-mail from a marketer, while *spam* is unsolicited e-mail that clutters the Internet. The usage of e-mail marketing by Canadian marketers continues to grow. It was initially thought that the introduction of tougher anti-spam laws would severely limit the use of e-mail communication. However, marketers are finding that they have better quality e-mail lists to work with, and according to an Ipsos study, 80 percent of customers are willing to receive e-mails from companies.[4]

## WORD-OF-MOUTH MARKETING

**Word-of-mouth marketing** is based on the spread of positive messages about a product by listening to consumers, identifying influential individuals who can spread the word, and making it easier for them to do so. Research by the Word of Mouth Marketing Association showed the impact that word of mouth can exert, with 72 percent of respondents claiming that reviews from friends and family influence their decisions.[5]

Word-of-mouth communication works on several levels. On a viral level, it tries to create buzz through social media that seed fun

### Figure 13–1
Display ad formats
Internet display ads can be purchased in a variety of formats.

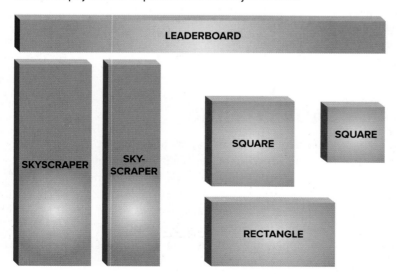

and interesting messages, many times with influential people who spread the word. On an influencer level, it identifies key communities, opinion leaders, and product advocates who get personally involved with the brand and have the ability to influence others.[6] In the opening vignette, Bioré identified @laurDIY as a key influencer in the beauty segment; followers depend on her advice when making decisions on beauty products. On a professional level, official referral programs may be put in place to reward satisfied customers who refer the brand to friends and contacts.

# THE SOCIAL MEDIA LANDSCAPE

**LO 2** Digital marketing tools are rapidly evolving, and we often find them working together to help brands make connections with consumers. We start by looking at the characteristics of social media and move into a discussion on social media marketing practices and tools. We continue by examining the top social media networks in Canada, and end this chapter by noting the best social media marketing practices.

# CHARACTERISTICS OF SOCIAL MEDIA

*Social media* is a form of online media that allows members to create their own network of friends and contacts to share comments, articles, opinions, videos, and images. It is helpful for marketers to understand that social media broadly falls into five areas, as shown in Figure 13–2. There are social communities such as Facebook, Twitter, and LinkedIn for sharing opinions, articles, images, and videos with friends, contacts, and associates; there are social bookmarking sites such as Pinterest for primarily sharing images; there are social review sites such as Zomato and TripAdvisor for posting reviews on local restaurants and travel services; there are social gaming sites such as Xbox Live for video games and Zynga for social games; and there are social creation and discovery sites such as YouTube, Snapchat, and Instagram for sharing video or image-based content. In all instances, members of these social media sites can share content and post comments to express their thoughts and opinions.

**Figure 13–2**
Social media categories and examples

**Social reviews**
Foursquare
Goodreads
TripAdvisor
Zomato
Yelp

**Social communities**
Facebook
Google+
LinkedIn
Path
Twitter

**Social bookmarks**
Delicious
Digg
Pinterest
Reddit
StumbleUpon

**Social creation and discovery**
Blogger
Etsy
Flickr
Instagram
Last.fm
SlideShare
Tumblr
YouTube
Vine
Wikipedia

**Social gaming**
Kongregate
QuizUp
Xbox Live
Zynga

The various forms of social media share common characteristics. They run off cloud-based software that does not have to be downloaded on a computer; they can be accessed from mobile or desktop devices; they often use apps for easy mobile access; they are generally free to join; they allow members to interact with content providers by sharing content, participating in conversations, and posting comments and opinions; they categorize content so it can be searched and accessed by others; and they continuously evolve with new elements for users. Many social networks allow marketers to place ads on the

What are the characteristics of social media networks?

© Ford Consulting Group

**affiliate marketing**
When companies promote their businesses through a network of online associates (affiliates) to drive traffic, leads, and purchases.

**e-mail marketing**
The use of e-mail to market products.

**permission-based e-mail**
When a recipient chooses to receive e-mail from a marketer.

**word-of-mouth marketing**
The spread of positive messages about a product by listening to consumers, identifying influential individuals that can spread the word, and making it easier for them to do so.

Coca-Cola's #ShareaCoke generated thousands of shared images of friends and their Cokes.

vadimguzhva/iStock/Getty Images Plus

social network to help build their social presence and to increase awareness; however, not all social networks have this opportunity.

A single social media site, such as Facebook or YouTube, is called a *social network*. The most popular social networks in Canada are Facebook, YouTube, Twitter, Pinterest, Google+, Instagram, LinkedIn, Snapchat, Tumblr, and Reddit, although numerous other niche social networks exist, built around particular topics of interest.[7] Social networks rely on users to share content that has been created by others, upload their own original content if they wish, and comment on content that has already been shared. Original online content that has been created by users is called **user-generated content (UGC)**. It can be in the form of blogs, posts, images, audio, or video. Coca-Cola's "Share a Coke" campaign showcased names and phrases on its Coke bottles and encouraged customers to share a Coke with a friend and post the picture on social media using the hashtag #ShareaCoke. This is an example of how UGC can support the marketing efforts for a brand.[8]

*Content marketing* is when brands or companies reach out by creating and sharing expertise and brand information that is designed to inform and engage with tools such as research papers, infographics, e-books, how-to videos, blogs, webinars, e-newsletters, case studies, and events. This information can be readily found by search engines. In the business-to-business market, the virtual meeting service provider GoToMeeting shares its own content around productive meetings, working from home, and other relevant topics to its business customers. It also shares other people's content to provide additional value to its followers.[9] Tangerine, the Canadian bank formerly known as ING, considers content marketing a core means of communicating with customers. Unlike its competitors, Tangerine doesn't have any bricks-and-mortar locations. Tangerine provides information that answers the questions and concerns that people have regarding banking and investing. Using tools such as social listening, Google search trends, and inbound inquiries, Tangerine has been able to provide valuable content such as "How I got over the intimidation of investing," and the "Return on investment of going back to school."[10] Check out the "Forward Thinking" section of the Tangerine website at **www.tangerine.ca** for some insightful articles.

Another form of user-generated content is a **blog**. Blog, a short form for "web log," is a web page in the form of an online diary that is used by organizations and individuals to post updates that include personal opinions, activities, and experiences. Readers can subscribe to blogs, post comments, and share content. A **vlog**, short form for a "video blog," is a blog that is posted in a video format. A **wiki** is a collaborative website (such as Wikipedia) that uses an application with which multiple users can create, add, edit, or delete content.

Brian Solis developed the Conversation Prism to visually demonstrate the vastness of the social media landscape and all that it has to offer. It tracks dominant, niche, and promising new social networks. It shows that social media is much larger than the popular sites that we hear about every day—Facebook, Twitter, LinkedIn, and YouTube. It shows that social media includes blogs and wikis as well as countless other social networks, such as Quora for asking questions, last.fm for listening to music, SlideShare for sharing presentations, Goodreads for book lovers, Foodspotting for food enthusiasts, Telfie for TV buffs, and so many more.

The Conversation Prism is a useful tool for marketers as it may point to social networks that may be useful for their brands. You can see more about this tool at **www.conversationprism.com**.

## COMPARING SOCIAL MEDIA WITH TRADITIONAL MEDIA

In Chapter 12, traditional media such as print, television, and radio were discussed. While both the more traditional forms of media and social media are effective at communicating brand messages, there are several inherent differences:[11]

- Social media is flexible and can be changed even after it is published.
- Social media is available immediately.
- Social media creates a conversation and so marketers do not have full control over the messaging.
- Social media can have less reliable demographic data about its audiences.
- Social media can be produced inexpensively.
- Social media needs dedicated attention.

There is the misconception that social media is free. While it is less expensive to produce, a company also needs to consider the time that needs to be dedicated to monitoring and managing a social media program.

## SOCIAL MEDIA MARKETING

*Social media marketing* is when brands reach out to consumers online through social networks where people connect with friends and contacts to share comments, articles, opinions, videos, and images as a form of self-expression. Brands engage on these platforms by hiring experts and social media managers to create brand pages on social media platforms, to join online conversations, to monitor and respond to questions and comments, to use metrics to measure performance and engagement, and to send out updates and offers.

The Conversation Prism shows the vastness of the social media landscape.

© Brian Solis (briansolis.com) and JESS3 (jess3.com)

Brands may also place ads on the social networks that accept advertising, as discussed earlier in the chapter.

The Social Media Examiner asked marketers what they felt the benefits of social media marketing were to their business. Figure 13–3 shows that

## Figure 13–3
Benefits of social media marketing

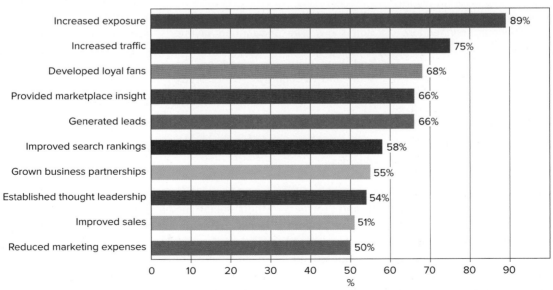

| Benefit | Percentage |
|---|---|
| Increased exposure | 89% |
| Increased traffic | 75% |
| Developed loyal fans | 68% |
| Provided marketplace insight | 66% |
| Generated leads | 66% |
| Improved search rankings | 58% |
| Grown business partnerships | 55% |
| Established thought leadership | 54% |
| Improved sales | 51% |
| Reduced marketing expenses | 50% |

**Source:** Michael Stelzner, "2016 Social Media Marketing Industry Report," *Social Media Examiner,* May 24, 2016, http://www.socialmediaexaminer.com/social-media-marketing-industry-report-2016/.

# McCain Superfries #Modifry the Frozen Food Category

McCain Foods is a Canadian success story. Established in 1957 in Florenceville, New Brunswick, McCain now employs 19,000 people across six continents, with sales of over $8 billion. It is estimated that one in every three French fries worldwide is a McCain French fry.

Current consumer trends indicate a move away from frozen and processed foods to fresher foods. This trend could have a significant impact on a company whose growth has been built on the sales of frozen desserts, French fries, and snacks. One component of the educational process for consumers was ensuring that they understood how McCain products are made. Key messages communicated were that McCain uses as few ingredients as possible, limits the use of artificial ingredients, and reduces the fat, sugar, and salt in its products. But this was only one piece of the puzzle. While a focus on real ingredients was a great start, this space is very crowded. McCain had to drive customer engagement with the brand, creating an emotional and behavioural connection.

McCain focused on a few key insights:

- Everyone loves fries!
- Foodie culture exists.

- Reinvention/elevation of "bad for you" foods such as bacon and burgers.
- Increased interest in "comfort" foods.
- Fries are normally eaten in the same way for the same occasions.

The opportunity became clear—elevate and inspire the consumption of Superfries!

McCain wanted to bring this vision to life using digital and social media channels. Facebook, Twitter, YouTube, the McCain website, and bloggers were used to get the message across. McCain partnered with chefs and other key influencers to develop inspirational recipes. Digital marketing channels were an important choice since consumers and foodies often use social media as a reference source for menu ideas. Kick-started by mouth-watering recipes developed by chefs such as Chili Lime Sweet Potato Fries and Loaded Nachos Supreme, followers were encouraged to post pictures of their own creative #Modifry dishes.

Each of the hosts on the television show, *The Social*, had unique #Modifry recipes created for them, and they were showcased on the show and through live Twitter feeds. Culinary influencers and vloggers

McCain's #Modifry campaign engaged consumers and influencers with exciting new recipes.

pilipphoto/Shutterstock

such as Lauren Toyota and Mike Ward were engaged to post their own #Modifry videos. These efforts were extended by the use of pre-roll video on YouTube and promoted posts.

A mix of user-generated content, key influencer engagement, and a multi-platform presence ensured that the campaign generated over 500,000 social interactions on social media with over 90 million impressions of #Modifry content. As a result, Superfries doubled its sales growth targets for the year. ●

## Questions

1. Why was social media an appropriate promotional channel for this campaign?

2. How could McCain integrate traditional media into the campaign?

89 percent of marketers believe that social media marketing generates brand exposure, and 75 percent indicate increased traffic is a major benefit. Interestingly, 68 percent mentioned that social media helped them develop loyal fans, and 66 percent believed that social media was responsible for providing market insights. All of these benefits can have a significant impact on a brand.[12]

On average, Canadians spend 18 percent of their social media time interacting with brands. The most common interactions include visiting corporate or brand websites; talking about companies with friends and family; reading permission-based content; following companies on Facebook, Twitter, Instagram, and/or LinkedIn; and posting comments on the same sites.[13]

Social media is a public venue, and marketers need to delicately deal with detractors and negative interactions, understanding that vehemently defending a brand in the court of public opinion can rapidly escalate on social media with negative repercussions. Unhappy consumers are most likely to take to Facebook or Twitter with their complaints.[14] In order to avoid negative situations on social media, companies create social media policies and guidelines to help guide programs and interactions.

Managing customers' comments, reviews, and complaints can be a very time-consuming process. Customers expect answers quickly. A recent study found that 72 percent of consumers expressing a complaint on Twitter expected an answer within an hour. However, only 11 percent of companies responded within an hour. The risk is that if companies aren't meeting customer expectations, they are likely to feel negatively about the brand. And this negativity is expressed in a very public social media forum.[15]

McCain did an excellent job at engaging its target audience with its brand and revitalizing the relevance of frozen French fries. The Marketing NewsFlash box, "McCain Superfries #Modifry the Frozen Food Category," discusses this campaign in more detail.[16]

## ask YOURSELF

1. *How is social media different from traditional media?*

2. *What is social media marketing?*

# SOCIAL MEDIA MARKETING NETWORKS AND TOOLS

**LO 3** Social media marketing requires knowledge of the social networks that can be used to drive engagement as well as an understanding of the tools that exist to help manage and measure these programs.

## SOCIAL MEDIA NETWORKS IN CANADA

Social media is used by marketers in many ways to help connect consumers with a brand. For example, Facebook can send out offers, updates, and contests; Twitter can post newsworthy updates and answer customer service questions; Pinterest and Instagram can post inspiring images and contests; YouTube can be used for storytelling, how-to content, and engaging videos; and LinkedIn can profile a company's expertise. The most developed social media programs use multiple social media sites to profile a brand in creative, engaging, and imaginative ways. Before creating social media marketing programs, marketers need to check any restrictions that these social media sites may have for running elements such as contests, which should also always adhere to the marketing regulations in Canada that were outlined in Chapter 2.

In 2016, the most popular social networks for Canadians were Facebook, YouTube, Twitter, Pinterest, Google+, Instagram, and LinkedIn.[17] The life cycle of social media sites can be rather fickle since these sites grow and die based on public perceptions, The databox below, "Comparing Social Media Networks," shows how social network usage compares globally.

## Comparing Social Media Networks—Global Users

Note: These are users of the network, not the number of registered profiles.

| | | |
|---|---|---|
| facebook | Facebook | 1.71 billion |
| You Tube | YouTube | 1 billion |
| Instagram | Instagram | 500 million |
| twitter | Twitter | 313 million |
| G+ | Google+ | 200 million |
| LinkedIn | LinkedIn | 106 million |
| Pinterest | Pinterest | 100 million |

**Source:** "Global Social Media Ranking," Statista website, accessed November 2016 at https://www.statista.com/; "YouTube site statistics," YouTube website, accessed November 2016 at https://www.youtube.com/yt/press/statistics.html; Joshua Barrie, "Nobody Is Using Google+," *Business Insider,* January 20, 2015, http://www.businessinsider.com/google-active-users-2015-1; "Here's How Many People are on Facebook, Instagram, Twitter and Other Big Social Networks," *AdWeek,* April 4, 2016, http://www.adweek.com/socialtimes/heres-how-many-people-are-on-facebook-instagram-twitter-other-big-social-networks/637205.

**Logos:** (Facebook): Craig Ruttle/AP Photo; (YouTube): TP/Alamy Stock Photo; (Instagram): © 2017 Instagram, Inc.; (Twitter): Ingvar Björk/Alamy Stock Photo; (Google+): © Google; (LinkedIn): PRNewsFoto/PwC/AP Images; (Pinterest): © Pinterest 2017

## Social Media Marketing Example: Game of Thrones*

**facebook** — "Like" if you're addicted to Game of Thrones

**twitter** — HBO releases season 7 #gameofthrones

**YouTube** — See HBO trailer for Game of Thrones Season 7

**LinkedIn** — Spruce up your networking skills by joining the LinkedIn group Game of Thrones Addicts

**(Instagram)** — Post a selfie watching #gameofthrones.

**Pinterest** — Find a map showing all the major land holdings from the houses on Game of Thrones.

**G+** — Read the best quotes from Jaime Lannister #gameofthrones #jaimequotes.

*This is a hypothetical example

Logos: (Facebook): Craig Ruttle/AP Photo; (Twitter): Ingvar Björk/Alamy Stock Photo; (YouTube): TP/Alamy Stock Photo; (LinkedIn): PRNewsFoto/PwC/AP Images; (Instagram): © 2017 Instagram, Inc.; (Pinterest): © Pinterest 2017; (Google+): © Google

While social media network usage is important, marketers tend to focus the majority of their time on specific networks: Facebook, Twitter, YouTube, Instagram, and LinkedIn.[18] Next, we look at these five mainstream social media networks to understand how they are used for marketing purposes. Figure 13–4 compares these major networks based on their usage and the ways they can be used for marketing.

**Facebook**  With over 1.7 billion users, Facebook is a free social network that is the top choice for people wanting to share photos, videos, and stories with their connections.[19] Facebook is the most used social networking site by marketers, with 93 percent indicating that they have a Facebook account.[20] Due to its dominance and well-developed platform, Facebook is usually the centre of a brand's social media program, and it accounts for most of its social media audience.

Facebook is a social network with three tracks. First, there is the *personal track,* which is how Facebook started, where users create a personal profile; add other users as friends; exchange comments, photos, videos, and "likes"; and receive updates through notifications in the News Feed feature. Private messages can also be sent, a popular feature that is used to quickly message people without using e-mail. Second, there is the *group track,* which uses Facebook Groups to allow Facebook members to create

## Figure 13–4
A comparison of social networks

|  | **Facebook** | **Twitter** | **YouTube** | **Instagram** | **LinkedIn** |
|---|---|---|---|---|---|
| **% of Canadian brands on network** | 93% | 78% | 68% | 60% | 35% |
| **What is it?** | Online sharing of photos, videos, and text | 140-character micro-blogging site | Video-sharing site | Mobile photo- and video-sharing site | Business networking site |
| **Communication tools** | Create company profile page that can be liked or followed; Facebook ads; sponsored posts | Track and plan tweets; sponsored tweets; use #hashtags | Brand YouTube channel; posting attention-getting and/or how-to videos | Publish visually appealing content | Company pages; paid sponsor updates |
| **Primary uses** | Build an audience of followers for your brand; two-way communication with your customers | Engage/interact with customers; make new connections; get messages out quickly | Gain attention for your brand; explain complex messages | Gain attention for your brand | Showcase your company; connect with other businesses; recruit employees |

Source: "The CMO's Guide to the 2015 Social Landscape," Aberdeen Group, March 9, 2015, http://www.cmo.com/features/articles/2015/3/4/cmos_guide_2015_social_landscape.html#gs.ryHIMTY; Lauren Maninigh, "A Breakdown of Social Media Platforms and Their Uses," Futurpreneur Canada, May 27, 2016, http://www.futurpreneur.ca/en/2016/a-breakdown-of-social-media-platforms-and-their-uses/; Emily Wexler, "The 2015 Marketer Survey," *Strategy,* December 11, 2015, http://strategyonline.ca/2015/12/11/the-2015-marketer-survey/.

Logos: (Facebook): Craig Ruttle/AP Photo; (Twitter): Ingvar Björk/Alamy Stock Photo; (YouTube): TP/Alamy Stock Photo; (Instagram): © 2017 Instagram, Inc.; (LinkedIn): PRNewsFoto/PwC/AP Images

public or private groups where members are focused on a particular interest, such as a high school reunion group or a group on pets, fitness, marketing, or an educational course. Facebook Groups allow members to post comments to everyone in the group at once. Facebook Groups provide members with notifications and have the added benefit of allowing people to upload documents. Third, there is the commercial *page track* that allows artists, public figures, businesses, brands, and non-profits to create pages that people can like and follow to receive notifications and updates in their News Feed. Figure 13–5 shows the components of Tim Hortons' Facebook page.

**FACEBOOK AS A PROMOTIONAL TOOL** Facebook Pages are used by organizations and brands to engage consumers with relevant updates, news, and offers that may be of interest to its followers. Facebook is also an excellent vehicle for a brand to ask questions of its customers and to allow ongoing two-way communication. Facebook Pages are provided with Page *insights*, a term Facebook uses to describe the metrics it provides for Facebook Pages. Metrics include likes, posts, reach, engagement, and visits. These insights also show which posts have the most traction, and the aggregated demographic profile of its users, including gender, age, country, city, and language data.

## Figure 13–5
Tim Hortons' Facebook page

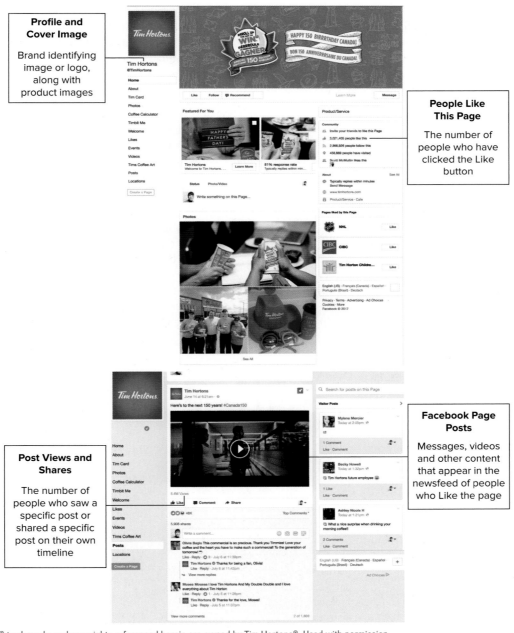

All Tim Hortons® trademarks and copyrights referenced herein are owned by Tim Hortons®. Used with permission.

Facebook Pages also provide page administrators with the ability to easily create and run ads on Facebook, with an area where images can be uploaded, and an interface to select the demographic that is being targeted by the ad. Administrators can select who will see the ad by choosing relevant descriptors such as gender, age, language, interests, location, lookalike audiences (people similar to those who like your page or shop on your website), and budget. Ads are paid for by a cost per click (CPC) or on a cost-per-thousand (CPM) impression basis, and using a bidding system, you have an opportunity to budget your spend per day. Ads can be deployed automatically from this interface and will only appear to the demographic that was selected.[21]

Facebook Live launched live video-streaming capabilities to the Canadian market in spring 2016, and many marketers are interested in using live video more frequently. The use of live video can increase a brand's reach and in some cases, it could take less time than a written post. Marketers can use live video for a range of activities, including more personal communication with customers in response to questions or postings, or to promote upcoming events.[22]

On Facebook, the marketer's challenge is to post and create fresh, creative, and engaging content that will be shared by its followers. This is often done by providing interesting updates and posting offers, contests, and images. Marketers also purchase ads on this network to rapidly increase followers. Tim Hortons® has the largest Canadian fan base on Facebook with close to 3 million total fans, including 2.1 million Canadian fans.[23] Marketers can use some of the following tips to maximize consumer engagement (comments, shares, and likes) with their brand on Facebook:[24]

- *Post when engagement is the highest,* not when the most users are logged in.
- *Learn about your customers* and share content that your customers want to see, not just what you want them to see.
- *Learn from the past* which content perform strongest and create more.
- *Use photos,* which are still the most posted and shared content. To make it even easier, post your Instagram photos to Facebook.
- *Engage by replying to comments.*
- *Create share-worthy content* with a headline that will grab attention.

- *Include a call to action* in your post by asking for a share, comment, or like.
- *Keep posts short,* between 0 and 50 words.

In order to promote its movie *Straight Outta Compton*, Universal Pictures and Beats by Dre launched the #StraightOutta campaign. This campaign started with over 100 celebrities from movies, music, and sports sharing their hometown using #StraightOutta and letting people know how their background influenced where they are today. An app was created to maximize engagement. People could upload a picture to the app and create their own custom #StraightOutta meme, highlighting their hometown and posting it to their Facebook timeline. Not only did celebrities get on board, but other companies jumped in to create their own meme. It became a true phenomenon, with Beat by Dre receiving 10 million shares. It was also the number 1 trending topic on Facebook and Instagram—a feat that hadn't been achieved by any other brand.[25]

**Twitter**  Twitter is a free social media site for individuals and organizations to post and receive short newsworthy text updates—*tweets*——and links in 140 characters from accounts of interest, whether this be from friends, journalists, media outlets, brands, or experts that are followed. Its advantage is the speed with which people can scan updates and decide whether they warrant additional reading. In this way, people are updated on developments in areas of interest, whether this be for business purposes or related to a passion or hobby. Twitter users can create lists, *favourite* tweets, send out other people's tweets through a *retweet,* and receive notifications recommending whom to follow. The platform encourages users to use hashtags (#) so that topics and conversations are searchable in the Twitter database. Twitter is home to 313 million global users, and it is supported in 40+ languages.[26]

**TWITTER AS A PROMOTIONAL TOOL** Organizations use Twitter for customer service and marketing purposes. While Facebook is the platform of choice for unhappy customers, Twitter is in second place, with 17 percent of consumers expressing their complaints with a company using Twitter.[27] Companies can use analytics platforms such as Hootsuite to

The #StraightOutta campaign was a partnership between Universal Pictures and Beats by Dre. It was the number 1 trending topic on Facebook and Instagram.

Artem Kovalenco/Shutterstock

monitor the Twitter landscape for brand and company mentions, to answer questions, and to respond to comments and suggestions in real time.

On Twitter, brands post newsworthy content related to areas of expertise and engage brand advocates that have influential social networks. Seventy-eight percent of Canadian brands have indicated a presence on Twitter.[28] Brand tweets may be pre-planned and pre-approved to coincide with marketing events and integrated into marketing communication programs, while others may task social media managers with the responsibility to deploy real-time tweets that respond to opportunities and buzz. Some marketers also use Twitter chats to profile their expertise and to build their following on social media platforms. These pre-scheduled chats revolve around a certain topic and occur on Twitter by using a pre-determined hashtag to monitor the conversations. These chats are hosted by a brand that could pose a few questions for discussion or bring an influencer into the chat to engage customers.

Marketers can use some of the following tips to make their tweets stand out in the crowd:[29]

Globally, YouTube is the second-largest social media network.

TP/Alamy Stock Photo

- Develop an *editorial calendar* and schedule events throughout the year.
- Create and reuse *graphic templates*.
- Use *videos and images* for Twitter promotion.
- Use *Twitter ads* that take the form of promoted accounts or promoted tweets. The advertiser pays only when followers are added or tweets are clicked, retweeted, or favourited, or when they result in a reply. Ads can be targeted by interest or by using your own e-mail contact list.

*Real-time marketing* is a planned tactical approach where brands make themselves relevant online during events or newsworthy occurrences by diving into conversations as they occur with aligned short-term messaging that takes advantage of the current buzz. This concept was introduced in Chapter 1. The best-known example of real-time marketing surfaced during the 2013 Super Bowl, when, during a lengthy power outage, Oreo cookies posted a tweet, "Power out? No problem," with a link to a visual showing an Oreo cookie with the caption, "You can still dunk in the dark." This real-time marketing tweet was retweeted almost 16,000 times, and generating over 20,000 likes on Facebook. This effort was not a fluke, Oreo had identified the Super Bowl as a focus and had a "command centre" set up, complete with marketers and advertising experts—with senior managers on call for

approvals. In this manner, Oreo was ready and poised to respond to whatever situation presented itself.[30]

Twitter has its own live-streaming service called Periscope. Similar to Facebook Live, it is available using the Periscope app or the Twitter app. It can be used to release brand videos, to talk directly to your customers, or for a regular weekly live broadcast. Given the large audiences available to marketers on Facebook, it makes sense to use Facebook Live as a live video-streaming platform, but Periscope is a great vehicle to reach out to a new audience using the base of Twitter.[31]

**YouTube** YouTube is a free video-sharing social network owned by Google, used by people to discover and be inspired by interesting, entertaining, and informative videos. Today it has more than 1 billion global users who collectively watch billions of hours of video per month. YouTube has been launched in more than 88 countries globally. The platform allows users to to create their own YouTube channels, subscribe to other channels, and to upload, watch, and share videos. The platform also allows users to post comments and share videos across other social media sites, such as Facebook, Twitter, Google+, and LinkedIn. YouTube is widely used by marketers who upload short films, how-to videos, and video ads on their products, relying on the platform to engage with storytelling. Marketers can also purchase advertising on this site.[32]

**YOUTUBE AS A PROMOTIONAL TOOL** Marketers understand that YouTube provides a robust marketing tool: Brands can create YouTube channels, upload videos, access YouTube analytics, and purchase advertising. Marketers target ads on YouTube in the form of banner ads, sponsored/featured videos, or in-stream video ads. They can also optimize their YouTube channels and videos for the search engines through the use of keywords.

Red Bull has one of the most popular brand YouTube channels. Its main YouTube channel strives to represent what it calls the "Red Bull lifestyle"; it is joined by a range of channels, including Red Bull Music, Red Bull eSports, and Red Bull Global Rallycross. Red Bull seeks to engage its subscribers by capturing exciting lifestyle-related programming, including ongoing series with key influencers and athletes.[33]

*Marketers understand that YouTube provides a robust marketing tool.*

Red Bull has one of the most popular brand YouTube channels.

(both): EvrenKalinbacak/Shutterstock.com

In a few instances, marketers use YouTube to upload videos that are designed to go *viral*. This is generally a carefully orchestrated approach that involves creating catchy content that is often humorous or very creative to appeal to a wide audience that will quickly view, share, and rate the video, sending it to the top of YouTube's recommended videos, which will immediately boost its popularity. Building on its "Red Bull gives you wings" slogan, Red Bull orchestrated the Red Bull Stratos Project. The Stratos videos are thought to be the most successful viral videos in history. Eight million viewers tuned in to watch Felix Baumgartner jump from a capsule 24 miles (38.6 km) in space, breaking the sound barrier and a world record for the highest jump. Not only did YouTube views break records, but longer term, the Red Bull YouTube channel subscriber base jumped. Social media engagement included over 900,000 Facebook interactions, and 83,000 shares. With Twitter, @redbullstratos received over 20,000 mentions in two days. It is estimated that the video could have reached up to 50 million people.[34]

**Instagram**  Instagram is a free social network that is owned by Facebook. It is a mobile app that is the world's largest photo-sharing site, with over 500 million active users who quickly and easily share their lives through photos and short videos that are taken with a mobile device, instantly adding filters and captions to customize the image before it is shared. Instagram's interface is very simple and allows users to add comments and likes, as well as use hashtags for easy search. Users can connect accounts to other social media sites so that images seamlessly appear on Facebook or Twitter—an element that makes Instagram very popular. Instagram is quickly being recognized by marketers as an essential tool to share visual content. It is estimated that 60 percent of brands in Canada use Instagram.[35]

Interesting images work for Sport Chek on Instagram.

Used with permission of FGL Sports

**INSTAGRAM AS A MARKETING TOOL**  Instagram can be used by marketers to post interesting behind-the-scenes footage from events, as well as stunning product shots and contests. Hashtags and captions can be added that invite people to engage with the brand by adding comments, liking the image, and posting their own images of the brand. Visual brands do well on Instagram: GoPro uses Instagram to showcase the adventures that can be captured on the GoPro camera. It posts stunning images of sand dunes, underwater vistas, and off-road adventures.[36] Marketers can build a more engaged Instagram following by observing these tips:[37]

- Include a *call to action*. Coca-Cola could ask their followers which flavour of Coke they prefer of the Coca-Cola Freestyle choices.
- *Leverage hashtags* that are already relevant to your audience. For example, #photooftheday is a commonly used hashtag on Instagram, Facebook, and Twitter. You may also consider using hashtags familiar to a particular interest. The #thesweatlife, is commonly utilized by a variety of fitness companies and fitness enthusiasts.
- *Share your Instagram pos*ts on Twitter, Facebook, and Snapchat.
- *Post at the right time*. Post when your audience can engage with your content. The use of Instagram tends to peak during off-work hours.

## LinkedIn

LinkedIn LinkedIn is a freemium (some services are free, and others require payment) business networking social media site for professionals that was launched in 2003. It has over 467 million global members, over 100 million active users, and is used in over 200 countries.[38] LinkedIn is free for its basic usage, which allows members to create professional profiles, connect to their network of business people, join business-oriented groups on particular interests, and use its job-search function to see recent job postings and company profiles. A free membership also allows members to post and share updates, endorse individuals, write recommendations, add comments, like articles, answer questions, contribute to discussions, follow companies, view profiles of individuals in their network, and see basic information on other LinkedIn members.

Premium LinkedIn services are offered for a monthly or annual fee and include upgraded services that range in price for recruiters, job seekers, and business professionals. These services include, among others, advanced search, increased e-mail capacity, and extended profile access. A premium service for job seekers moves a person to the top of a recruiter's list, provides comparisons with other applicants, and gives advice through its job seekers' group where webinars can be accessed. For a

> *LinkedIn provides upgraded services that range in price for recruiters, job seekers, and business professionals.*

fee, companies on LinkedIn can post job openings and receive real-time analytics on who has viewed the posting as well as profiles on the applicants.

LINKEDIN AS A PROMOTIONAL TOOL   In the business-to-business market, LinkedIn can be used as a successful marketing tool. It is used by organizations to profile their expertise and to target individuals, companies, and sectors who may be interested in their services. On the marketing front, LinkedIn allows companies to create company pages, access visitor analytics, and create groups that profile certain areas of interest or expertise. Companies can also run ads on LinkedIn with razor-sharp targeting, whether this is a job posting, a branded display ad, or a sponsored story. LinkedIn has the advantage of having fewer distractions than the other social networks as it is focused on business and work-related topics. LinkedIn display ads and sponsored stories are on a cost-per-click or a cost-per-impression basis. These ads can target by location,

LinkedIn is widely used by businesses to establish credibility.

PRNewsFoto/PwC/AP Images

keyword, and interest. They stand out for business-to-business marketers in that they also target by company, job title, job function, and group, which can result in very high-quality responses and business leads.

It is estimated that 35 percent of Canadian brands have a presence on LinkedIn and use their LinkedIn company page to drive engagement.[39] These organizations recognize the opportunity to use LinkedIn to share company values, expertise, and updates with current and potential customers. Marketers can use some of the following tips to increase engagement on their company pages:[40]

- Make the *headline* stand out.
- Post *videos*.
- Use *sponsored updates* to extend your reach beyond current followers.
- Leverage *company page analytics* to understand trends and optimize your content.
- Include your logo and an *impactful banner image* on your company page.

# Infographic

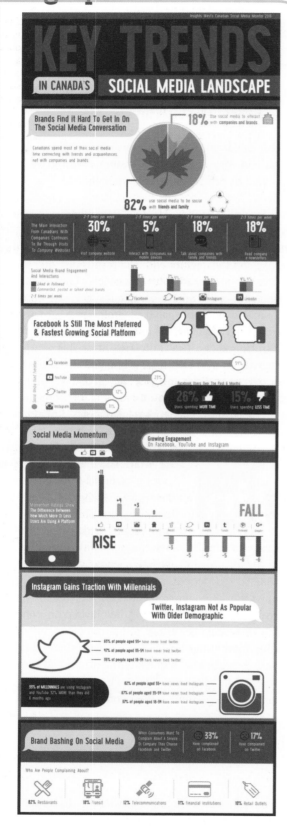

Source: "2016 Canadian Social Media Monitor," Insights West, May 2016, https://insightswest.com/wp-content/uploads/2016/05/IW_socmed_infographic1.pdf.

# BEST PRACTICES IN SOCIAL MEDIA MARKETING

**LO 4** The rapid adoption of digital technology and social media provides a great opportunity for marketers to develop strong customer relationships, improve their brand image, and help give customers the ability to engage with the brand.

## CREATING AND MEASURING SOCIAL MEDIA MARKETING PROGRAMS

Marketers need to carefully plan their social media marketing efforts to ensure that they are supportable and measurable, and can help drive brand engagement with a positive return on investment.

**Creating Social Media Marketing Programs** Marketers can start the process of building social media programs into their marketing initiatives by answering the questions outlined in Figure 13–6, which will help steer content and the tools of engagement. Questions refer to a range of elements such as understanding a company's social media policies, selecting which social networks are appropriate for a brand, and determining an analytics platform to monitor, measure, and deploy social media programs, as well as many other important elements.

**Measuring Social Media Marketing Programs** Social media monitoring and analytics platforms have surfaced to help marketers measure success in this environment. Social networks, such as Facebook and Twitter will often provide marketers with analytics on their accounts, but these cannot be aggregated across platforms. Third-party social media analytics and monitoring tools have surfaced to help marketers measure and manage multiple social media platforms, an important consideration since many brands engage across multiple platforms.

## Figure 13-6
Planning social media marketing

Answer these questions to help steer your social media marketing programs:

### Social Media Marketing Questions

1. What are your company's social media policies and guidelines?
2. How does your target market use social media and what drives engagement?
3. How can social media be integrated into other brand marketing programs?
4. What type of content is suitable for your brand on your selected social media sites?
5. Who will be creating social media content for your brand and what is the budget?
6. What are your daily/weekly targets for social media posts and interactions?
7. Who will be running and monitoring the social media programs?
8. What analytics platforms will be used to monitor, measure, and evaluate social media programs?
9. What social media networks are appropriate for your brand and target group?

**Social media analytics** and **social media monitoring** software vary by provider, but generally identify online brand mentions and monitor consumer sentiment, buzz, engagement, and amplification. These platforms often allow marketers to respond in real-time to customer questions and complaints, to pre-schedule posts, and to identify brand advocates with strong influence scores that can amplify and spread positive brand messages.

## Figure 13-7
Social media metrics

| Engagement Metrics | Optimization Metrics |
|---|---|
| • Followers | • Click through rate (CTR) |
| • Reach | • Cost per click (CPC) |
| • Comments | • Cost per thousand (CPM) |
| • Likes/Unlikes | • Cost per acquisition (CPA) |
| • Shares | • Cost per conversion |
| • Views | • Conversion rate |
| • Clicks | • Retention rate |
| • Sentiment | |
| • Buzz | |
| • Engagement | |
| • Brand awareness | |
| • Share of voice | |

**Source:** Adapted from Jay Shemenski, "The 3 Types of Social Media Metrics that Matter to You," SimplyMeasured [blog], December 1, 2016, http://simplymeasured.com/blog/the-3-types-of-social-media-metrics-that-matter-to-you/#sm.00000k61g84uecztxyp1birlwcur0.

Radian6 is an example of a paid social media monitoring and analytics tool that monitors 650 million Internet sources ranging from blogs to social networks to the mainstream media. It listens to and sifts through online conversations, allowing users to drill down into the comments by source, sentiment, and amplification, responding as needed. Summary dashboards routinely identify key metrics such as the number of conversations, demographic data, top influencers, trending topics, media sources, sentiment, and share of voice.[41] Free social media monitoring tools also exist, such as Hootsuite, which allows a marketer to monitor a brand's social media activity across social networks, including Twitter and Facebook.

Marketers should develop a set of engagement and performance metrics that are manageable and actionable. Figure 13-7 lists some of the frequently monitored metrics used to determine the success of a social media campaign. **Engagement metrics** measure how, how much, and how often consumers interact with social media content. Marketers can fairly easily track measures such as followers, likes, comments, shares, clicks, and views. Much of this data is available on the social media platform being utilized.

**Optimization metrics** provide data that can point to adjustments or changes that should be made to your social media program. Generally, marketers will look at **cost per thousand (CPM)**, the cost of reaching 1,000 people; **cost per acquisition (CPA)**, the cost of acquiring a new follower or sale; and **cost per click (CPC)**, the cost of getting someone to click on a link, image, or ad.

## BEST PRACTICES

Brands need to be seen as a trusted source of information on all platforms, and they need to use social media to connect. Organizations and brands are advised to use the following best practices when starting to use social media:

- Obtain senior management commitment.
- Set company-wide governance for social media.
- Create detailed social media policies, guidelines, and rules of engagement.

---

**social media analytics**
The real-time measurement, interaction, and analysis of social media to assess social media campaign performance, message resonation and amplification, consumer sentiment, and common themes.

**social media monitoring**
The monitoring of brand mentions, as well as consumer sentiment, buzz, and engagement, on the Internet

**engagement metrics**
Measures how much and how often consumers interact with social media content.

**optimization metrics**
Data that can point to adjustments or changes that should be made to your social media program.

**cost per thousand (CPM)**
The cost of reaching 1,000 people.

**cost per acquisition (CPA)**
The cost of acquiring a new follower or sale.

**cost per click (CPC)**
The cost of getting someone to click on a link or ad.

> Brands need to be seen as a trusted source of information on all platforms, and they need to use social media to connect.

- Set clearly defined and measurable social media marketing objectives.
- Select a platform that will be used to deploy, monitor, and measure social media activity.
- Identify the social networks that will be used.
- Establish metrics that will be used to evaluate approaches.
- Dedicate, train, and hire social media marketing experts.
- Understand that negative comments will surface on social networks and plan to handle them.
- Realize that mistakes will be made.
- Integrate social media programs into marketing practices.

These best practices will help organizations and brands reflect brand images and authentically communicate through multiple social networks. These best practices will also help organizations plan for negative situations that may surface and flag when scenarios should be escalated to a senior level. Social media marketing should be integrated into paid, owned, and earned media programs so that it positively impacts on the consumers' path-to-purchase.

**ask YOURSELF**

1. *What two type of metrics are used to measure social media marketing programs?*
2. *Which five of the best practices outlined would you prioritize for any organization?*

# THE MOBILE MARKETING LANDSCAPE

## THE MOBILE MARKET

**LO 5** Mobile has become a driving force in marketing, a central connector to other forms of media. It is used by consumers to communicate, to gather information, and to be entertained. It is a pillar in a multi-screen era where consumers connect in and out of home using portable devices such as tablets and smartphones, and use them to complement desktop/laptop usage and TV viewing. Mobile devices are no longer accessories, but tools that help manage daily lives.

Global data tell us that in 2016, there were 4.8 billion unique mobile subscribers and that this number is expected to grow to 5.7 billion by 2020. When focusing on devices, there are more mobile connections globally than the entire population.[42] Unlike other platforms, mobile devices are personal, portable, and usually on. They accompany us in the home, at work, and into our social spaces. They help manage our lives in real time, letting us access messages, set reminders, e-mail, text, and update calendars. They entertain us with photo apps, video viewing, and social networking. They help us find local restaurants, read product reviews, and shop for products.

Importantly, people use mobile devices to help in the path-to-purchase. People check mobile devices multiple times a day, providing numerous touch points for marketers to engage on this journey. Whether comparing product prices, looking for a store location, researching product features, or purchasing products and services, mobile devices have become relevant in the consumer path-to-purchase. Unlike other marketing tools, mobile marketing allows marketers to communicate directly with consumers at the point-of-purchase, which can be persuasive and compelling.

*Mobile marketing* is defined by the Mobile Marketing Association (MMA) as "a set of practices that enables organizations to communicate and engage with their audiences in an interactive and relevant manner through any mobile device or network."[43]

A wide range of mobile devices are available to keep consumers connected.

© Monicaodo | Dreamstime.com

*Mobile devices are used by over 4.8 billion unique subscribers worldwide.*

## MOBILE DEVICES

The mobile industry is complex due to the wide range of handsets, screen sizes, operating systems, browsers, and products that exist in this space. Devices include feature phones, smartphones, tablets, wearables, Internet-enabled handheld gaming devices, Internet-enabled MP3 players, and e-readers. Growth is currently driven by smartphones and tablets, but wearable devices are expected to increase in popularity once privacy issues are overcome.

A **feature phone** is a cellphone that is Internet-enabled and that allows for e-mailing, texting, and browsing, but unlike smartphones, it cannot download or use apps.[44] Feature phones tend to be cheaper and make the mobile landscape more complex as they are often built with their own unique technology, which makes consistent viewing across all devices difficult.

A **smartphone** is a more advanced cellphone that has similar functionality to a personal computer in addition to taking pictures, playing music and movies, offering GPS navigation, and using apps to enhance its features and capabilities.[45]

Smartwatches and other wearables are becoming very popular due the number of brands entering the market and the ease of use. The wearable electronics market in Canada has been growing rapidly, with 2.6 million units being worn by a variety of customer segments.[46] **Wearables** are devices that can be worn, either on clothes or on the body. They include smartwatches, health care monitors such as the Fitbit, smart clothing, and augmented reality devices such as Google Glass.[47]

From a platform perspective, there are three main mobile device platforms in Canada (Figure 13–8): Android (Google), iOS (Apple), and BlackBerry. In the smartphone market in Canada, Android is the market leader with a 50.5

### feature phone
Cellphone that is Internet-enabled and that allows for e-mailing, texting, and browsing but cannot download or use apps.

### smartphone
An advanced cellphone that has similar functionality to a personal computer in addition to taking pictures, playing music and movies, navigating with GPS, and using apps to enhance its features and capabilities.

### wearables
Devices that can be worn on the body or on clothes.

## Top Ten Activities on Mobile Devices for Canadians

| Smartphone | Tablet |
|---|---|
| 1. Send or receive e-mail | 1. Search the Internet |
| 2. Send or receive a text/instant message | 2. Watch a video |
| 3. Check weather | 3. Social networking |
| 4. Search the Internet | 4. Send or receive e-mail |
| 5. Social networking | 5. Check weather |
| 6. Watch a video | 6. Listen to music |
| 7. Access a map | 7. Access a map |
| 8. Listen to music | 8. Watch TV online |
| 9. Post photos | 9. Read reviews for products or services |
| 10. Play a game | 10. Send or receive a text/instant message |

**Source:** "Mobile Device Activities," Media Technology Monitor website, accessed December 2016 at https://mtm-otm.ca /Download.ashx?req=18-2-1.

### Figure 13–8
Smartphone platform market share in Canada

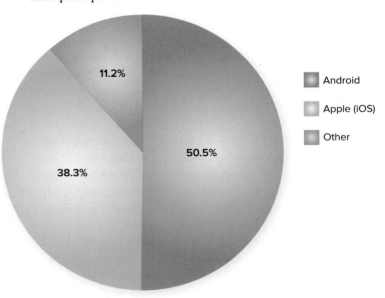

- 11.2%
- 38.3%
- 50.5%

Legend: Android, Apple (iOS), Other

**The Android platform leads the market in smartphones.**

**Source:** Paul Rich, Ben Martin, and Leah Jenkins, "2015 Canada Digital Future in Focus," comScore, March 27, 2015, https://www.comscore.com/Insights /Presentations-and-Whitepapers/2015/2015-Canada-Digital-Future-in-Focus. Used with permission.

## Figure 13–9
Mobile subscribers—Canada (millions)

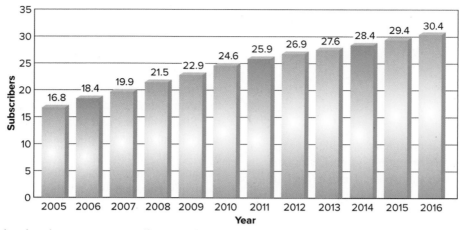

The number of mobile subscribers is growing rapidly in Canada.

**Source:** "Facts & Figures: Wireless phone subscribers in Canada," Canadian Wireless Telecommunications Association website, accessed December 2016 at http://cwta.ca/facts-figures.

percent market share, followed by Apple's iOS at 38.3 percent, and others (including BlackBerry) at 11.2 percent.[48]

In 2016, there were over 30 million mobile subscribers in Canada, with numbers expected to continue to climb (Figure 13–9). Smartphone ownership in Canada has reached over 73 percent.[49]

## CONSUMERS AND MOBILE DEVICES

Canadian demographic data (Figure 13–10) tell us that consumers who use a smartphone are equally divided, male and female, with 73 percent between the ages of 18 and 54 years and 74 percent with an annual household income over $50,000.[50]

Research from Internet analytics company comScore reveals that electronic devices play different roles throughout the day. A typical consumer starts the day at home checking e-mails on a smartphone, uses a desktop or laptop computer at work for business purposes, and returns home in the evening where relaxation often occurs in front of a TV, with a tablet and smartphone close at hand to respond to text messages, connect on social media, surf the Internet, and check apps. At all times during the day, a smartphone is close at hand and available for personal use.[51] People have become device-agnostic, switching seamlessly between devices depending on location, circumstance, and device availability.

 *Mobile devices have become relevant in the consumer path-to-purchase.*

Canadian technology researcher Media Technology Monitor reports that the top activities conducted on a smartphone are sending/receiving e-mails and texts, along with checking weather, using search engines, and interacting on social media. Tablets seems to be used more often for entertainment, with the most common activities focused on the use of search engines, watching videos, and social networking.[52]

What is "showrooming"?

Eva Katalin Kondoros/E+/Getty Images

## Figure 13–10

Canadian smartphone demographic breakdown

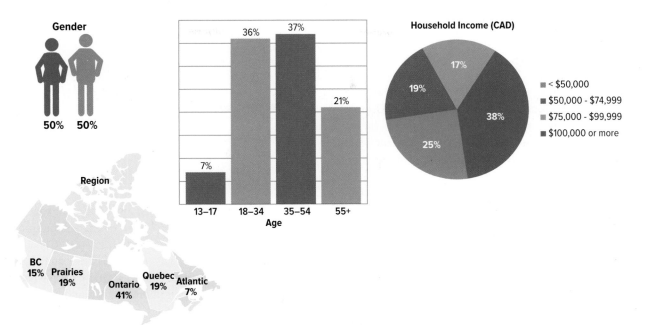

Canadian smartphone demographic breakdown.

**Source:** Paul Rich, Ben Martin, and Leah Jenkins, "2015 Canada Digital Future in Focus," comScore, March 27, 2015, https://www.comscore.com/Insights/Presentations-and-Whitepapers/2015/2015-Canada-Digital-Future-in-Focus. Used with permission.

**M-commerce** is the process of purchasing an item online through a mobile device. Smartphones are often used for researching products and gathering information. Most e-commerce purchases are completed on a personal computer, but purchases made from mobile devices are growing, especially with the 18- to 34-year-old age group.[53]

The widespread use of smartphones at retail is prompting a new consumer shopping habit known as *showrooming*, the practice of using mobile devices in-store to check competitive online product reviews and prices and to then purchase the cheaper product online. Marketers note that mobile devices are taking the store out of the store and making shopping accessible on the go, all hours of the day, and every day of the week.

### ask YOURSELF

1. *What is mobile marketing?*

2. *How does consumer behaviour differ on mobile devices throughout the day?*

3. *What is the importance of m-commerce to a brand?*

# MOBILE MARKETING TOOLS

**LO 6** Mobile marketing provides marketers with a platform for one-to-one personalized communications where targeting can be more precise, not only demographically but also by device, by interest, and in real time by exact location. Marketers note that consumers carefully guard their mobile devices and are cautious about inviting marketers in. Marketers are therefore advised to follow best practices, provide added value, show respect for the privacy of the mobile user, and in all instances, follow regulatory guidelines and ethical approaches. Remember that in most instances, consumers need to opt in to receive mobile messaging, so unless a mobile marketer can provide exceptional value and interest, a marketer will not want to opt in to your messages.

**m-commerce**
The process of purchasing an item online through a mobile device.

 *Consumers carefully guard their mobile devices and are cautious about inviting marketers in.*

Here we examine the mobile marketing tools that are used to engage consumers: mobile web, mobile applications, mobile advertising, and mobile sales promotional tools.

## MOBILE WEB

Websites that render on mobile devices need to be fast and functional and easier to use than a brand's desktop website. People do not want to scroll across screens on small mobile devices or pinch and zoom to read content. Mobile websites are created and designed for the smaller mobile screen with screens that load quickly, display clearly, and offer unique mobile features that satisfy the goal-oriented mobile user. **Mobile web** is when a website is designed for the smaller screens of mobile devices.

Research conducted by Nielsen showed that mobile users visit websites an average of six times before making a purchase, and 83 percent of those who use mobile to research a product want to make the purchase within one day.[54] These results highlight the importance of having a mobile website that is functional, engaging, and user-friendly.

It has been shown that companies use one of three approaches with mobile web. They either optimize a desktop website for the mobile web by using responsive design platforms that offer flexible layouts, flexible images, and flexible file options so that websites automatically adjust and resize to render on mobile devices. Alternatively, they can design separate mobile websites with streamlined content and finger- and thumb-friendly navigation. The third option uses a combination of these approaches. Some companies will create three different interfaces: one for a desktop site, which is information rich; one for tablets, which has heavy image-based content; and one for smartphones, which has less content and fewer images. Booking.com has a mobile site that is a variation of its desktop website, focused on providing the tools necessary for a customer to search for a hotel immediately upon landing on the page. Information is plentiful while the functionality and visual appeal is still strong.[55]

## MOBILE APPLICATIONS (APPS)

**Mobile applications (apps)** are software programs designed for mobile devices so that with a quick tap or click, they engage with information, entertainment, or other forms of interactivity. It is estimated that Google Play has 2.8 million apps available for the Android platform, the Apple App

Booking.com has a functional, yet appealing mobile website, mobile app, and tablet interface.

Used with permission of Booking.com B.V.

Store has 2.2 million, and Windows and Amazon offer over 600,000 apps each.[56] While there has been significant growth in the number of apps available to users, Canadians are more selective about which apps they use. In fact, app usage has started to decline overall. In 2014, people had an average of 26 apps on their phones; this number currently sits at just under 18, a decrease of 31 percent. The exceptions to this trend are online banking and e-mail apps. While Canadians are downloading apps at a slower pace, they are uninstalling them at a rapid rate.[57] Competition is fierce for the mobile consumer, reinforcing the need to provide value and quality to ensure app retention.

The most popular apps are for social networking, weather, maps, gaming, YouTube, and banking.[58]

Apps are most likely to be downloaded when they are recommended by friends and family if they sound interesting and fun, if the user is familiar with the company or brand, and if they offer exclusive offer. Most consumers expect apps to be free.[59]

### Popularity of Apps in Canada

| Type of App | Regularly Used by Percent of Smartphone Users |
|---|---|
| Facebook | 72% |
| Weather | 71% |
| Maps | 57% |
| Games | 53% |
| YouTube | 52% |
| Banks | 44% |
| Loyalty programs | 37% |

**Source:** "Canadian Shopper Study," BrandSpark, June 2016, p. 91, accessed December 2016 at www.brandspark.com.

**mobile web**
A website designed for the smaller screens of mobile devices.

**mobile applications (apps)**
Software programs that can be downloaded on a smartphone or tablet to engage consumers with information, entertainment, or interactivity.

*The most popular apps are for social networking, weather, maps, gaming, YouTube, and banking.*

Apps can be free or paid, and can also host ads, sell products, or just provide content. They are downloaded from online device-specific app stores. App developers pay small annual fees to these app stores, and typically pay a commission to the app stores from the revenues generated from the app (downloads, product sales, or ad revenues).

Technically, three types of apps can be created for marketing programs: (1) native apps, (2) web apps, or (3) hybrid apps. Depending on the choice, the app creation can become more or less expensive for marketers. For the end user, it is the app functionality that is important, and most users will not understand the nuances between these types of apps. Marketers, however, need to understand the differences:

- **Native apps** are created specifically to be hosted and run on a mobile device. They are downloaded from app stores and reside on mobile devices. They can provide a rich experience by interacting with mobile features such as the device's GPS, camera, or notification system. They can also work offline. Technology differences dictate that separate native apps need to be designed for iOS, Android, Windows, and BlackBerry devices. This can be an expensive undertaking.

- **Mobile web apps** are websites designed to simulate a native app experience. They run off browsers rather than the actual mobile device, and ask users to add a shortcut to the home screen. They can therefore run on any platform, making them cheaper to develop. The user experience is not as rich as on a native app, as these apps do not interact with the mobile device features. These apps do not pay app store developer fees, do not require app store approval, and do not share revenue with the app store.

- **Hybrid apps** combine the superior functionality of a native app with the flexibility of a web app. They can interact with mobile features, but render in a browser and so can be used across mobile platforms with minimal changes and therefore lower costs. Hybrid apps are generally cheaper to develop than native apps as they require minimal development changes for cross-platform use. Typically, hybrid apps do not provide the same rich experience as native apps, but they are becoming increasingly popular.[60]

Marketers use apps in various ways to engage with users. For example, Booking.com created an app to allow customers to research their destination, search for accommodations, and book hotel rooms; Facebook created an app to conveniently provide its service on the go; and Shoppers Drug Mart has an app for its loyalty card program. Other marketers use apps to provide functionality and to also generate revenue. For example, the Weather Network and the CTVNews apps both sell advertising space on their apps to marketers.

Starbucks is seen to have the premier branded mobile app. Starbucks was one of the first brands to initiate a mobile loyalty and payment system for its customers. With its "Mobile Order and Pay" system, a customer can open the app, decide on an order from the hundreds of options at Starbucks, pay for the order, and even tip the barista before arriving at the store. Once the customer arrives at the store, he or she can fast-track past the line and pick up the order without delay. The mobile payment system has been so successful that it is expected the app will account for 50 percent of all Starbucks transactions in the next few years.[61]

The functionality exists on many apps for consumers to be sent push notifications on their mobile phone. **Push notifications** are content that is sent to a mobile device. For example, the Weather Network allows users to select what type of weather notifications they would like to have sent to their phone. According to

**native apps**
Apps downloaded from app stores that are specifically created to be hosted and run on a mobile device.

**mobile web apps**
Websites designed to simulate an app experience by adding a shortcut that runs off a browser on a mobile device.

**hybrid apps**
Apps that combine the functionality of native apps with the flexibility of web apps.

**push notifications**
Any content sent to a mobile device that a customer must opt in to receive from a marketer.

Starbucks is seen to have the premier branded mobile app.

BestStockFoto/Shutterstock.com

Canada's Anti-Spam Legislation (CASL), consumers must opt in to consent to receive push notifications, and marketers must provide a clear method for consumers to unsubscribe or opt-out.

## MOBILE ADVERTISING

Advertising that renders on mobile devices is a rapidly growing area of mobile marketing, and it represents more than one-third of overall Internet advertising spending in Canada. Over half of the mobile advertising spend was for mobile search, followed by mobile display ads and mobile streaming video. Rather than cannibalizing other more traditional media formats, the spend on mobile seems to be an incremental spend.[62]

Research tells us that mobile ads are most effective in increasing brand awareness and purchase consideration. The next most common outcome when consumers click on mobile ads is that they are likely to make a purchase, followed by saving a page to their device, and adding to a product to their shopping list. While consumers indicate that they are most likely to pay attention to TV advertisements, mobile is second, with desktop, print, and radio far behind. This fact also reinforces the importance of implementing a multi-device marketing program, since a large number of consumers use mobile devices at the same time that they are watching television.[63]

Advertising options on mobile devices include placing displays ads on highly trafficked mobile-optimized websites, or placing ads within third-party apps such as the Weather Network app, which delivers ads for many companies such as the OLG lottery. Pay-per-click mobile ads can also be placed around mobile search results and takeover ads, and mobile video ads can be created to appear as pre-roll video ads that are seen before watching a video on a mobile device. The Marketing NewsFlash box, "Should Brands Invest More in Mobile?" looks that the value of mobile advertising from the perspective of Unilever's Magnum Ice Cream bars.[64]

An example of how marketers design ads for each device to maximize their impact is the Weather Network website properties:

- TheWeather Network desktop site at **www.thewea thernetwork.com/cahosts** display ads for companies such as BMO, Keurig, and Pampers that appear as banners, leaderboards and vertical ads in various sizes. The display ads change regularly and reflect the customer's views, browsing history, and interests.

- The Weather Network mobile site for cellphones can be downloaded from one of the app stores and is available in multiple formats. It has ads on its home page, but only as you scroll further down the page. This ensures that ads do not interfere with the ability to quickly obtain current weather conditions.

- The Weather Network tablet site focuses on weather information that needs to be communicated and has less space for any type of display advertising compared to the mobile and desktop versions. Small square display ads are interspersed with weather-related videos, and leaderboard-style ads are placed at the very bottom of the page.

The Weather Network app is very popular in Canada.

Used by permission of Pelmorex Media Inc.

# Should Brands Invest More in Mobile?

Consumers are adopting mobile devices at staggering rates, and marketers are jumping on board to use the mobile platform as a communication vehicle. However, there is little evidence to show that the mobile channel is effective in driving business outcomes. At the same time, corporations are increasing the pressure on their marketers to demonstrate return on their marketing investment.

The Mobile Marketing Association (MMA) initiated a study to help build the evidence base to support the mobile channel as a valid marketing tool. The MMA partnered with Unilever on the SMoX (SMoX stands for smart cross-marketing effectiveness research) study. Unilever is known for its premium quality Magnum Ice Cream bars that sell one billion units annually. Unilever was spending a portion of its advertising budget on digital and mobile platforms. Like many marketers, it wanted to understand the sales impact of each of the promotional tools that it employed. Equally important was gauging the effectiveness of each platform in generating brand awareness.

Magnum ran a campaign for the summer months and targeted women between the ages of 25 and 54. The campaign included traditional marketing media (TV, print), digital, and mobile. The mobile tools featured banner ads, in-app video, and mobile social media using demographic and weather targeting.

What did Unilever learn?

- **Increase investment:** The research concluded that mobile was a strong driver of sales for Magnum and that Unilever would benefit from reallocating additional spends to mobile. In a previous study completed by MMA across a variety of industries, it was estimated that an increased investment in mobile would improve the results of an overall campaign (based on the company's objectives) by between 4 and 12 percent.

- **Context and targeting matter:** Choosing the right targeting variables is important. For Magnum, targeting the ads during times when the weather was extremely hot meant increased brand awareness and sales that were 50 percent higher than the results from any other component of the campaign. Similarly, mobile ads for Magnum that ran at night delivered 40 percent higher results for purchase intent. Honing the mobile audience by location, context, and demographics consistently improved results.

- **Size, time, and creative matter:** Large banner ads performed better than smaller ones, and shorter videos were more effective than longer ones. Given the small size of a mobile screen, larger ads were not only more impactful, they offered the marketer the ability to include more images and create stopping power. The best solution is a mix of banner ads and audio/video ads, which can lead more directly to a change in perception and ultimately more sales.

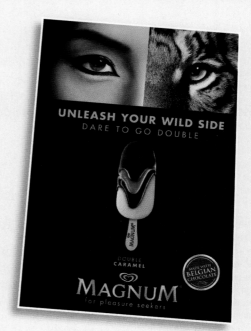

Unilever studied the success of its mobile marketing campaign for Magnum Ice Cream bars.

Reproduced with kind permission of Unilever PLC and group companies

The lesson learned by Unilever was that mobile is effective. Certainly the context, creative, and targeting can maximize results, but in the end mobile delivered better results, even with little investment. The trick with mobile is that you can reach the customer at any time, including at a time when they are potentially close to a point-of-purchase. This case study is really just the tip of the iceberg as marketers learn to optimize and ultimately trust the impact that mobile can have. ●

## Questions

1. What three important conclusions can you draw about mobile marketing from the Magnum case study?

2. What other targeting methods do you believe would benefit Magnum when advertising on mobile?

**mobile messaging**
Comes in the form of common short codes (CSC), short messaging services (SMS), multimedia messaging services (MMS), e-mail messaging, in-person voice phone calls, and voice messaging.

**common short codes (CSC)**
Dedicated short messaging codes of typically five to six digits that are used to trigger subscriptions, donations, alerts, or downloads, or to access promotional content.

**short messaging services (SMS)**
Standard text messaging that uses protocols of 160 characters per message.

**multimedia messaging services (MMS)**
Standard text messaging services that include audio, video, or images.

**mobile e-mail**
E-mail sent and/or received using a mobile device.

**matrix 2D barcode**
A two-dimensional response code that, when scanned by a mobile barcode reader or app, provides additional information, launches websites, prompts downloads, sends text messages, or deploys messages.

What is consistent across all platforms is a focus on functionality and consistent branding. However, the Weather Network offers a variety of advertising opportunities that best fit the format.

## MOBILE SALES PROMOTIONAL TOOLS

Sales promotions provide short-term incentives for people to interact with brands whether through a discount, an offer, or another form of engagement. These elements can be communicated through the advertising approaches mentioned above, but in the mobile space, other more direct tools can encourage engagement and interaction. In the sales promotion space, mobile marketers can use mobile messaging, matrix 2D barcodes, and proximity marketing approaches. Common examples include text message alerts, app notifications, and various mobile downloads (mobile coupons, wallpapers, ringtones, and games).

**Mobile Messaging** **Mobile messaging** comes in four main forms. There are (1) common short codes (CSC), (2) short messaging services (SMS), (3) multimedia messaging services (MMS), and (4) e-mail messaging.

**Common short codes (CSC)** are dedicated short messaging codes of typically five to six digits that trigger subscriptions, donations, alerts, downloads, or the ability to access promotional content. Mobile marketers often use these codes in conjunction with keywords to involve consumers in a program. CSC numbers are provided by the Canadian Wireless Telecommunications Association (CWTA). There are numerous examples of CSC programs in Canada, such as BMO which offers mobile alerts for any abnormal transactions on your bank account. Many charitable foundations also use CSC programs in Canada to fundraise. For example, a person can text the word "SUPPORT" to

*CSC programs in Canada must abide by the Canadian Wireless Telecommunications Association guidelines.*

the number 45678 to donate $10 to March of Dimes Canada, and this amount is then added to his or her mobile phone bill.

In terms of guidelines, all CSC programs in Canada must abide by the Canadian Wireless Telecommunications Association guidelines, which are discussed later in this chapter.

**Short messaging services (SMS)** and **multimedia messaging services (MMS)** are mobile communication approaches that allow marketers to send text messages or multimedia messages that contain graphics, video, or audio to an opted-in customer's mobile device. Customers must opt in to SMS/MMS programs to receive ongoing communication that might include, among other things, text message alerts, offers, discounts, or coupons. Airlines, such as Air Canada, regularly communicate flight information and check-in options to customers via SMS text.

**Mobile e-mail** is an important tool in a mobile marketer's arsenal. Mobile devices are personal communication gadgets, and retrieving and sending e-mails is widely used on these devices. As mentioned earlier in the chapter, while the overall use of apps has stagnated, app use for reading e-mails is still growing. When designing e-mails, marketers must consider that an e-mail may be viewed on a desktop, a laptop, a tablet, or a cellphone, which may render e-mails differently. E-mail marketing communications can be deployed by using e-mail service providers that provide analytics on open rates, forward rates, bounce rates, and clicks. These metrics allow marketers to test different subject lines, headlines, and content so that, over time, the most effective e-mail campaigns are deployed. When using e-mail campaigns, marketers must adhere to Canada's Anti-Spam Legislation and other marketing regulations as outlined in Chapter 2.

**Matrix 2D Barcodes** A **matrix 2D barcode** is a two-dimensional square or rectangular response code that, when scanned by a mobile barcode reader or app, provides additional information, launches websites, prompts downloads, or sends SMS or e-mail messages. A popular brand of matrix 2D barcode is the QR code.

> *A popular brand of matrix 2D barcode is the QR code.*

Matrix 2D barcodes can be placed on flat surfaces such as print ads, posters, business cards, or even at the bottom of TV screens so that they can be scanned by mobile devices. The use of QR codes was ubiquitous when smartphones were first brought to market. Currently, they are used less frequently but can be very effective tools for the marketer. Spotify launched a program whereby the customer could create a customized greeting card with a QR code printed on the card. When the recipient scanned the QR code with a mobile device, he or she would be able to enjoy a mixtape playlist selected by the card giver. Columbia Sportswear integrated QR codes into its corporate social responsibility campaign by including a QR code on reused or recycled packaging. When customers purchased a Columbia product online, they were asked whether they would like a new or reused box. If the customer selected reused, the product was delivered in a box with a QR code that has compiled all of the information regarding where this box had been, creating an interesting historical narrative in words and pictures. Eco-conscious customers loved the program, and it gained international attention.[65]

**Proximity Marketing** *Proximity marketing* is the local distribution of marketing content to mobile devices that have opted in at a specific geolocation. A shopping mall may use proximity marketing to provide mobile coupons to shoppers who are using its free WiFi network. A local coffee shop may use Bluetooth technology to invite people in the immediate vicinity to come in and try a new coffee. In research conducted by Unacast in 2016, retail, shopping malls, hotels/tourism, airports, stadiums/sports, and restaurants were the industries most likely to use proximity marketing.[66]

Yelp is a popular mobile discovery app.

dennizn/Shutterstock.com

Proximity marketing can be implemented using a number of different technologies such as Bluetooth beacons, near field communications (NFC), geofencing, and WiFi.

- **Bluetooth** or low-power radio waves are transmitted though beacons and wirelessly transfer text, images, and audio or video data through a local hotspot to Bluetooth-enabled and -activated devices. The Unacast research also estimated that there were 8.3 million beacons activated worldwide in 2016, a growth of over eight times the number of beacons deployed one year earlier.

- **Near field communications (NFC)** is the two-way radio communication between smartphones and smartphone-type devices that can transfer images, documents, or monetary transactions when the two devices touch or are within a few inches of each other. Unlike beacons, you cannot send push notifications with NFC, and it has a short range. The mobile wallet app Android Pay is an example of NFC. NFC approaches are used at industry events and conferences where NFC-enabled mobile devices can tap a centrally located hotspot to download complementary white papers, research studies, or speaker information.

- **Geofencing** uses global positioning systems (GPS) to trigger an event to happen when a device enters a certain geographic area.

- **WiFi hotspots** can be set up with free Internet access, and once customers log in to use the free WiFi, they can be sent location-specific content.[67]

Proximity marketing also includes mobile check-in services and mobile discovery apps that provide consumers with offers from local merchants. **Mobile check-in services** are when consumers check into locations using apps such as Foursquare or Yelp to post their whereabouts and then receive offers from local merchants on their mobile devices. **Mobile discovery** refers to the use of mobile

**Bluetooth**
Low-power radio waves that are transmitted though beacons and wirelessly transfer text, images, and audio or video data through a local hotspot to Bluetooth-enabled and -activated devices.

**near field communications (NFC)**
The two-way radio communication between smartphones and smartphone-type devices to transfer images, documents, or monetary transactions when the two devices touch or are within a few inches of each other.

**geofencing**
Uses global positioning system (GPS) to trigger an event to happen when a device enters a certain geographic area.

**WiFi hotspots**
Areas set up with free Internet access in which once customers log in to use the free WiFi, they can be sent location-specific content.

**mobile check-in services**
When consumers check into locations using apps to post their whereabouts and to receive offers from local merchants on their mobile device.

**mobile discovery**
The use of mobile apps to help find local businesses, services, and attractions.

Near field communications.

Artur Marciniec/Alamy Stock Photo

apps such as Google Maps, Yelp, or Zomato to find local services that are rated in the area.

## ask YOURSELF

1. *What types of apps exist and how do they differ?*

2. *What are common short codes (CSC) and how are they used in mobile marketing?*

3. *What forms of advertising are used on mobile devices?*

# MOBILE MARKETING REGULATIONS AND BEST PRACTICES

## MOBILE MARKETING REGULATIONS

**LO 7** The mobile marketing industry is regulated by the same guidelines that apply to the marketing industry in general, but with the addition of further regulations for mobile marketing practices. In this manner, the regulations, guidelines, and policies discussed in Chapter 2 all need to be followed. Mobile marketers need to be keenly aware of Canada's privacy legislation as well as Canada's anti-spam legislation (CASL).

In the mobile space, the Canadian Radio-television and Telecommunications Commission (CRTC), the Canadian Wireless Telecommunications Association (CWTA), and the Mobile Marketing Association (MMA) have additional regulations and codes of conduct to protect consumers and to help standardize the industry. The mobile marketing industry is rapidly changing, and so, in all instances, marketers are strongly advised to obtain regulatory updates and to consult with marketing lawyers and mobile marketing experts to ensure that approaches adhere to regulatory and legislative updates.

**The Wireless Code** In mobile marketing, the CRTC regulates the Wireless Code. This was introduced in 2013 as a mandatory code of conduct for all wireless service providers. It ensures that wireless contracts are easy to understand and that contracts can be cancelled after two years. In addition, data overages are capped for notification at $50 per month, roaming fees are capped at $100 per month, and data plan providers need to notify users when these limits are reached.[68]

For more details on the CRTC Wireless Code, navigate to **www.crtc.gc.ca/eng/phone/mobile/code .htm**. Complaints against wireless service providers can be lodged at the website for the Commissioner for Complaints for Telecommunications Services at **www .ccts-cprst.ca**.

**Common Short Code (CSC) Guidelines** These guidelines are administered by the CWTA to provide direction on CSC pricing and marketing

The CRTC Wireless Code helps protect consumers.

CRTC's Wireless Code Know Your Rights, http://www.crtc.gc.ca/eng/info_sht /t16.htm. Reproduced with the permission of the Canadian Readio-television and Telecommunications Commission on behalf of Her Majesty in Right of Canada, 2017.

practices. Mobile marketers must provide participants with mandatory keyword protocols (STOP/ARRET to stop participation, HELP/AIDE to access information on terms of use and privacy policies, and INFO to retrieve company and customer service information). In addition, consumers must double opt-in to some premium subscription CSC programs and be informed of its terms, conditions, and pricing.[69] Updates on CSC regulations can be found at **www.cwta.ca** and **www.txt.ca**.

The MMA Global Code of Conduct The MMA Global Code of Conduct is administered by the Mobile Marketing Association, which guides the industry with standards, guidelines, and best practices. The MMA has over 800 members and is represented in nearly 50 countries. The MMA Global Code of Conduct specifically notes that privacy policies and terms and conditions must be clear, and opt-in and opt-out protocols must be used. Messaging should be limited to its initial purpose, personal data must be protected, and all MMA members must demonstrate compliance with the code.[70] You can see more about the MMA and its code of conduct at **www.mmaglobal.com**.

## MOBILE MARKETING BEST PRACTICES

The mobile marketing industry is rapidly changing, with new technologies, devices, and regulations. Best practices start with marketers abiding by marketing regulations and using a mobile-first approach to make connections. A mobile-first approach means that mobile becomes a central element in a marketing program and is integrated throughout the consumer path-to-purchase. Mobile is not added as an afterthought, but instead it is integrated into marketing programs from the start.

Best practices also use market research to stay abreast of how technology impacts consumer behaviour and to learn how mobile devices are integrated into daily lives. Changes in shopping habits are noted and mobile analytics programs are used to glean insights on how best to approach, engage, and connect with consumers.

The Mobile Marketing Association (MMA) advises mobile marketers to keep the following best practices in mind:[71]

- Think *mobile first* and start with a mobile perspective.
- Generate *creative specifically for mobile*.
- *Communicate across multiple screens* to create a seamless experience as consumers switch between devices.
- *Target your audiences* more specifically using the rich dataset available from mobile interaction, including location.
- *Utilize a full spectrum of mobile tools* to interact with consumers.
- *Integrate mobile marketing programs* into traditional marketing campaigns.
- *Offer great service,* functionality, and benefits.
- *Leverage every stage of the path-to-purchase,* understanding that mobile is used for search and discovery as well as connecting and purchasing.
- Test your way to success by *tracking, measuring, and making adjustments* to improve results and ROI.

*A mobile-first approach means that mobile becomes a central element in a marketing program*

### ask YOURSELF

1. What is proximity marketing?
2. Which associations and commissions regulate mobile marketing in Canada?
3. What best practices have surfaced in mobile marketing?

**LO 1** • The Internet has a number of unique online tools including websites and microsites, search engine marketing, display advertising, affiliate marketing, e-mail marketing, word-of-mouth marketing, social media marketing, and mobile marketing.

**LO 2** • Social media marketing is when brands reach out to consumers online through social networks where people connect with friends and contacts to share comments, articles, opinions, videos, and images as a form of self-expression.

• On social media networks, brands post updates and offers, join online conversations, respond to questions and comments, and use metrics to measure performance and engagement.

• Brands can place ads on social networks that accept advertising.

**LO 3** • The main social networks used in Canada for marketing purposes are Facebook, Twitter, YouTube, Instagram, and LinkedIn.

**LO 4** • The best social media marketing practices include obtaining senior management commitment, setting company-wide governance, creating detailed social media policies, setting clearly defined and measurable social media marketing objectives, selecting social networks that will be used, establishing metrics, utilizing social media marketing experts, planning to handle negative comments, realizing that mistakes will be made, and integrating social media programs into marketing practices.

**LO 5** • Mobile marketing is a set of practices that enables organizations to communicate and engage with audiences in an interactive and relevant manner through any mobile device or network.

• Mobile marketing provides marketers with an additional platform to communicate with consumers one-to-one. It can target by location, by device, by interest, and by demographic.

• Mobile platforms are changing consumers' path-to-purchase with mobile devices used to gather information, to engage with brands, to make decisions, and to purchase products.

**LO 6** • Mobile marketing uses a variety of tools: the mobile web, mobile apps, mobile advertising, and mobile sales promotional tools. Mobile sales promotional tools include mobile messaging, matrix 2D barcodes, and proximity marketing approaches.

**LO 7** • Best practices for mobile marketing advise marketers to think mobile first, and to plan programs across devices and screens by using multiple mobile tools that can integrate offline and online approaches.

• Standard marketing regulations in Canada also apply to mobile marketing.

• Specific mobile marketing regulations are administered by the Canadian Radio-television and Telecommunications Commission (CRTC), the Canadian Wireless Telecommunications Association (CWTA), and the Mobile Marketing Association (MMA).

## key terms and concepts... A REFRESHER

advergaming
affiliate marketing
banner ads
blog
Bluetooth
common short codes (CSC)
corporate websites
cost per acquisition (CPA)
cost per click (CPC)
cost per thousand (CPM)
display advertising
engagement metrics
e-mail marketing
feature phone
geofencing
hybrid apps
in-stream advertising

leaderboards
matrix 2D barcode
m-commerce
microsites
mobile applications (apps)
mobile check-in services
mobile discovery
mobile e-mail
mobile messaging
mobile web
mobile web apps
multimedia messaging services (MMS)
native apps
near field communications (NFC)
optimization metrics
pay-per-click advertising (PPC)
permission-based e-mail

promotional websites
push notifications
search engine marketing (SEM)
search engine optimization (SEO)
short messaging services (SMS)
skyscrapers
smartphone
social media analytics
social media monitoring
transactional websites
user-generated content (UGC)
vlog
wearables
WiFi hotspots
wiki
word-of-mouth marketing

**Social Media Marketing Assignment** Pick your favourite brand and conduct a digital media audit for that brand. This involves monitoring which networks the brand is active on, the types of content posted on each network, and the level of consumer engagement. Based upon your research, do you believe that your favourite brand has a strong social media presence? Why or why not?

*chapter vignette...* **ACTIVITY**

This chapter's opening vignette outlined Kao Canada's digital campaign for the Bioré brand of products. Brainstorm additional social media and mobile elements that you would add to the campaign to create more touch points with the target audience.

*infographic...* **DATA ANALYSIS**

Review the Infographic on "Key Trends in Canada's Social Media Landscape" and navigate to the source of the research at **www.insightswest.com**. Review the latest information on social media usage in Canada and write a short analysis of industry changes that have occurred.

# Customer Relationship Management

**W**hether an organization is maintaining a fleet of one of Canada's airlines or providing recycling support services in Southern Ontario, building trusted relationships among customers and supporters is essential to an organization's success. Loyalty leads to deep relationships that yield multiple benefits for customers and companies. As an industry's landscape becomes more competitive, maintaining strong, long-term relationships becomes more challenging. In order to enhance customer relationships, organizations turn to two key strategies: customer relationship management (CRM) and customer experience management (CEM).

© Convisum | Dreamstime.com

For resource-strapped small businesses, implementing these strategies may be challenging. Fortunately for these companies, there are experts that can help them get started towards building customer loyalty.

Lukas Szczurowski, chief executive officer of Luxor CRM, offers such a service. Responsible for product development, sales and marketing activities, and the day-to-day operations of his organization, Lukas uses his experience in the CRM industry to help organizations build brand loyalty.

Companies use CRM databases to deepen relationships with customers. By collecting and analyzing customer needs, companies offer ideal solutions in their mutually beneficial relationships. Not all companies execute CRM strategies flawlessly. "Software is a key enabler," explains Lukas, "But for a CRM strategy to work, it needs to permeate through all areas of the organization."

Although a customer relationship management (CRM) strategy may begin with a software solution, in order to maximize the benefits of the software solution, the company's top management needs to creates a culture that incentivizes employees to execute the strategy. Effective execution of a CRM strategy offers faster and better results in sales and marketing. By leveraging CRM data, organizations place their customers in the centre of all business decisions. Furthermore, organizations need to ensure that they have an effective customer experience management (CEM) strategy in place. By creating positive experiences at all customer touch points, CEM facilitates a personalized experience for consumers. In essence, the two strategies work together to help organizations deepen relationships and retain customers.

Since CRM and CEM programs can be difficult to develop from scratch, Luxor CRM offers a number of components for companies to consider and integrates them within a company's culture. Lukas believes, "Each touch point with a customer is critical." With so many touch points for customers to engage with, companies need to evolve the one-to-one message into a multi-dimensional relationship driven by the customer. By placing the customer in the centre and allowing the customer to customize the information experience, organizations will create deeper relationships and better experiences.

When consumers make a purchase from a company, they are essentially aligning their personal brand and reputation with that company. "Consumers want to be engaged by the organization they trust with their business," shares Jeff Brettell, vice president of professional services at Luxor CRM. "That is why customer relationship management has to be a theme that permeates throughout the organization."

## CHAPTER OUTLINE

- Opening up the customer experience
- Customer relationship management (CRM)
- Social media and CRM
- Customer acquisition and retention
- Database marketing
- CRM and customer reacquisition

Luxor's CRM solution includes programs like contact management that organize contact information and build long-lasting relationships. Furthermore, its services automate the sales and marketing functions that allow for a consistent experience for the consumers. Finally, the tools Luxor provides business customers are supported by a customer support area providing exceptional service. "We need to ensure that our customer support area performs as an example that companies can emulate," explains Jeff.[1]

After consumers have initiated and completed their purchase decision, they become customers. Customer relationship management (CRM) considers the purchase decision from the point of view of the business. It engages three interactions with customers, including customer acquisition, customer retention, and customer reacquisition. To be executed effectively, CRM requires support from the company's top management.

# CUSTOMER RELATIONSHIP MANAGEMENT (CRM)

**LO 1**

*Customer relationship management (CRM)* is the overall process of building and maintaining profitable customer relationships by delivering superior customer value and satisfaction. Executing CRM may involve technology, business rules, and operational processes, as well as the cooperation of key stakeholders within the organization.[2] This involves many aspects within an organization, including how consumers become customers, how they are retained as customers, and how well a company manages information on customers. The strategies that companies put into place around how they manage data will help them be successful in the customer relationship management discipline.[3]

After consumers have initiated and completed their purchase decision, they become customers. Customer relationship management (CRM) considers the purchase decision from the point of view of the business. It engages three interactions with customers, including customer acquisition, customer retention, and customer reacquisition. To be executed effectively, CRM requires support from the company's top management.

## CUSTOMER SATISFACTION

Information about customers can be used to create marketing programs that result in customer satisfaction. Information technology and database systems are a great starting point for CRM; however, for CRM to be successful, there must be attitude changes in the organization. CRM started out as a tool to help the sales force keep track of customers and prospects, but it has evolved into so much more. A large corporation may spend tens of millions of dollars on a CRM system. Among the big suppliers are Oracle, SAP, and IBM; dozens of other companies specialize in components such as telephone call centre technology, database software, and Internet systems. The whole idea is to customize each system to a specific company's needs. Funnelling information to one place that otherwise would be dispersed in a big company allows all employees to access one customer profile instead of bits and pieces of information about the customer scattered throughout the company.

Call your local bank about your chequing account and you may discover that the person on the phone is looking at a screen that summarizes your previous calls and displays

Customer relationship management (CRM) strives to build and maintain profitable customer relationships.

© Andres Rodriguez/Alamy Stock Photo

Apple knows that customers dislike the touch point that consists of impersonal technical support calls, so it has created the Genius Bar in its retail stores.

© david pearson/Alamy Stock Photo; © Cliff Hide News/Alamy Stock Photo

information about your mortgage and credit card as well. Visit your local bank and you may be surveyed about your experiences and your likelihood to recommend the branch.

## CUSTOMER EXPERIENCE MANAGEMENT

A concept similar to CRM is a process called **customer experience management (CEM)**. CEM involves managing customer interactions to build brand equity and improve long-term profitability. It requires strategy to manage all points of the customer experience, as keeping customers satisfied will be more important than simply making a sale.[4] CEM focuses on customer interactions, or touch points. A **touch point** describes any customer interaction with the brand or company.

Customer interactions include every point in which the customer interacts with a business, product, or service. For the Starbucks customer, this may include the anticipation of going to Starbucks, walking up to a shop, opening the door, ordering and paying for the coffee, talking to the server, getting the coffee, and sitting down in

the relaxed atmosphere of the shop to enjoy the coffee. In the case of MacBooks, Apple ascertained that its customers disliked the touch point of impersonal technical support calls. Instead, Apple resolves this issue by creating Genius Bar touch points that offer face-to-face help at the Apple Store. Furthermore, your banking touch points include experiences with automatic bank machines (ABMs), online banking, and customer service representatives. Alternatively, read about how Target may have misread its consumers' touch points when it expanded into Canada in the Marketing NewsFlash box, "Off Target."[5]

Companies should measure and improve customer interactions on an ongoing basis. Levels of customer satisfaction at each touch point can be a better measure of customer loyalty than just measuring overall customer satisfaction. It starts by understanding and listing each individual interaction or touch point that influences customer satisfaction. Whether human (such as sales staff or a call centre), interactive (such as websites, e-mail, or Twitter), or static (such as radio or newspaper ads), each touch point is an opportunity to improve customer experience.[6]

CEM and touch points are used to maintain profitable relationships with customers and are used in various industries to enhance customer satisfaction. Canadian Pacific Hotels (CP Hotels) was not well-regarded by business travellers, a notoriously demanding and diverse group to serve, but also very lucrative and much coveted by other hotel chains. By investing

**customer experience management (CEM)**
Managing customer interactions with the goal of increasing satisfaction and loyalty.

**touch point**
Any situation in which a customer comes into contact with a brand or company.

## *marketing* **NewsFlash**

# Off Target

Target prides itself on customer satisfaction, summarized well by its tagline: "Our promise is simple: Expect More. Pay Less.®" It aims to create an environment in which team members and guests have an experience that exceeds their expectations. Part of the appeal of Target is that it partners with chic designer fashions and promotes their fashions at a reasonable price. This strategy led to a relatively high customer satisfaction index among its American customers and opportunities for further expansion into Canada.

When Target opened its first stores in Canada in 2013, it got off to a slow start with respect to customer satisfaction. By starting with 17 stores and with plans to expand to 124 stores, Target planned to bring the same customer experience it had in the United States to Canada. Shortly after its expansion, however, a Forum Research survey found that less than three out of ten consumers said they were "very satisfied" with Target. The main concerns of Canadian consumers included low inventory and high prices. Unfortunately, the touch points in the United States that attracted Canadians to the brand were not identical in the Canadian stores. The media companies that reported the findings also received feedback from their readers through social media. These comments offered a balanced view, yet commenters were split on their perspectives of Target.

The concerns from shoppers drove Target to the bottom of the Forum Research survey list among major retailers in Canada. With Costco Canada leading the pack and Target's main competitor Walmart Canada clearly improving, Target had a lot of opportunity for growth in this area. Unfortunately, attempting to roll out more than 100 stores at once was a challenge. Target had challenges with inventory that left dissatisfied with pricing and availability. The experience at a Target in Canada was very different from a Target in the United States.

Customer dissatisfaction contributed to poor sales, and profitability for the expansion was projected to 2021. Therefore, in 2015, Target decided to close its 133 Canadian locations. ●

Ken Wolter/Shutterstock.com

## Questions

1. Describe the attributes of a Canadian retailer that provides excellent customer service.

2. How do customer expectations affect customer relationship management and the future success of companies?

## Banking On Customer Satisfaction

J.D. Power creates a customer satisfaction index ranking based on a 1,000-point scale. The big 5 banks are ranked as follows:

| | |
|---|---|
| RBC Royal Bank | 760 |
| TD Canada Trust | 759 |
| Big 5 banks average | 755 |
| Bank of Montreal | 753 |
| CIBC | 750 |
| Scotiabank | 747 |

**Source:** "Mobile Banking in Canada Grows Rapidly as Satisfaction with Personal Service Drops, J.D. Power Finds," J.D. Power [news release], July 23, 2017, http://www.jdpower.com/press-releases/jd-power-2017-canadian-retail-banking-satisfaction-study.

time and money in learning what would most satisfy this segment, the company discovered that customers wanted recognition of their individual preferences and lots of flexibility with check-ins and check-outs. CP Hotels mapped each step of customer interactions from check-in to check-out, and set a standard of performance for each activity. Along the way, the management structure was revamped so that each hotel had a champion with broad cross-functional ability to ensure that the hotel lived up to its ambitious goals.[7]

Ideally CEM information is analyzed to gain insight into each customer's needs and behaviour, and then it is used to improve the customer's dealings with the company. This can be as simple as freeing the customer from having to repeat his mailing address every time he places an order, to something like being able to instantly tell the customer the status of a shipment. The analysis might guide promotion efforts so that the customer receives mailings, calls, e-mails, or website advertising tailored to his or her likes.

# CULTURAL CHANGES

CRM databases allow companies to get closer to their customers to establish a mutually beneficial relationship. A company's failure with CRM is often the result of approaching CRM as a software project rather than an overall company strategy. A company may spend millions of dollars on software, but doesn't bother changing the cultural attitudes of the organization. A company may be looking for a quick fix for its problems. Companies feel that if they purchase CRM software, their problems will disappear. Collecting and managing data is just one component of CRM. A more important component is the organizational culture and support from top management.

A hotel that is suffering from poor employee customer-service skills cannot use software alone to solve the issue. CRM requires a top-down long-run commitment and attitude change by management. If the hotel employees see that management treats them with respect and rewards customer satisfaction, there is a larger incentive for employees to treat customers with respect.

*A company's failure with CRM is often the result of approaching CRM as a software project rather than an overall company strategy.*

As seen in Chapter 3, BLUERUSH creates personalized digital customer experiences that generate leads, build loyalty, and increase sales. As an integral part of a customer life cycle management program, INDIVIDEO™ and ActivDialog, two proprietary BLUERUSH products, are significantly transforming online experiences and delivering real value to clients and their customers. These tools not only need to be adopted by client-facing individuals, they need to be driven by management.

In 1997, Xerox Canada refocused a 5,100-person organization with annual revenues over $1.1 billion and underwent a change in structure and compensation incentives to ensure that its employees focused on customer satisfaction. Although the change was not an easy one, it was necessary to achieve the result of customers being more satisfied with the company's service offerings.[8]

Although not always noticed by customers, the cultural change that organizations undergo requires an investment of time and resources. In the same year that Xerox Canada underwent its cultural change, the 407 ETR opened in the Greater Toronto Area, allowing an all-electronic tolling feature for drivers on this highway. Customer loyalty is increasing for this service due to a lack of competition and the additional convenience offered by the highway. Unfortunately, more resources should be allocated to understanding customer complaints from this organization.[9]

# CRM AT FOUR SEASONS HOTELS AND RESORTS

Four Seasons Hotels and Resorts grew from a modest hotel in downtown Toronto to a luxury hotel chain consisting of 91 hotels in 38 countries around the world. Founder Isadore Sharp has spent decades developing a culture in which all employees are empowered to take responsibility and make decisions, rather than exclusively relying on orders from management. Mr. Sharp says that culture has to start from the top, the person who really is able to control and make the decisions to reinforce the culture in a meaningful way. "The Golden Rule guides our interactions with our guests, our business partners and investors, but most importantly, with each other," says Sharp. "We also believe in investing in our employees and promoting from within. Many of our senior managers began their careers with Four Seasons and continue to be culture ambassadors." CRM involves tracking guest information and preferences, such as extra pillows, into a database. This information should be used by employees the next time the guest returns to the hotel. Satisfied employees will take this extra step to make guests feel important and recognized. However, if hotel employees are not feeling engaged or appreciated themselves, they may not take that extra step and may fail to enhance the guest experience. It has been estimated that in a 200- to 300-room luxury hotel, there are as many as 5,000 interactions between guests and staff per day; in other words, thousands of opportunities for high performance or for mishaps. Four Seasons Hotels and Resorts excels in making its interactions with guests very positive.[10]

The cultural attitudes of the organization must change internally to what is called a CRM culture if the company is really interested in instituting positive customer service. Management must understand the customer and drive its company to developing the best experience. Top-management support to align internal processes toward a company's CRM strategy is critical to a CRM program's success.[11]

Employees who take ownership in what they do have a heightened sense of customer service responsibility.

© Sean Locke/iStock.com

Gaining loyal customers is critical to a successful CRM strategy. In that strategy, you can ask questions similar to these below:

- Who are your most profitable customers?
- Why do your customers buy from you and not the competition?
- What percentage of your customers are profitable?
- How can you make profitable customers do more business with you?
- How do you plan on managing less profitable customers?

Ulitimately, a company should consider the answers to these questions to evaluate the state of the firm's CRM strategy and what culture changes need to be made in order to effectively execute the strategy. In the end, technology is an enabler of CRM, but a successful CRM strategy is executed by high-performing employees.[12]

## CRM AT WESTJET

WestJet is an excellent example of a company that has embraced CRM from the top management down. Every employee literally takes ownership in what they do. As shareholders of the company, WestJet employees have a heightened sense of customer service responsibility uncharacteristic of many employees. Seeing this as a differentiator, WestJet launched a series of ads that focused on WestJet's theme of ownership.

The average business executive goes into CRM thinking it's only about technology, but if cultural attitudes don't change, employees won't benefit from the information collected and analyzed. Without employees using the system, the software becomes useless. The most senior levels of management need to embrace the business strategy of CRM and move the message and tactics of CRM throughout the organization. CEOs need to get the message out to their VPs and have them get it out to their managers, down to supervisors, and down to the front line.

## CRM AT TD CANADA TRUST

Customer relationship management involves building and maintaining profitable customer relationships. After the merger of TD and Canada Trust banks, the newly formed organization invested $15 million in informing its clients of what to expect of the new company. The investment was part of its strategy of client retention and profitability. In recent TD Canada Trust customer loyalty polls, customers are expecting a higher level of customer service and are receiving it.[13]

But if they don't receive positive customer service, they may not be coming back. Businesses are constantly looking for ways to show customers that they care, such as through reward programs. Many customers appreciate the perks, but according to the findings of the TD Canada Trust loyalty poll, customers want to be treated well. When asked which form of appreciation they are most interested in, 49 percent ranked "just good customer service" as number one. This was followed by just 18 percent who cited reward programs. According to the results, respondents' definition of good service was friendly staff followed by quick and helpful service.

## SOCIAL MEDIA AND CRM

**LO 2** A growing number of companies are keeping track of what's said about their brands on social media platforms such as Facebook and Twitter. This activity falls in line with the process of CRM because it's an excellent way to build and maintain a relationship with customers. Dell, General Motors, H&R Block, Kodak, and Whole Foods Market are among a growing number of companies monitoring Twitter to see what people are saying about their brands as well as to provide solutions to customers' concerns. With the ability to create a conversation between companies and customers, social media provides an excellent platform for the consumer voice and a great resource for marketers. The attention to Twitter reflects the power of new social media tools in letting consumers shape public discussion over brands.[14] A single Twitter message—known informally as a tweet— sent in frustration over a product or a service's performance, can be read by hundreds or thousands of people. Similarly, positive interaction with a representative of the company can help turn an unhappy customer into a more loyal one.

Some companies are hiring social media analytics consultants to monitor social media sites such as Facebook and Twitter in order to digest and understand what consumers are saying about their brands. These consultants have developed specialized software for their clients to scour these sites in real time and to provide actionable insights for smarter business decisions.

## TOURISM AND SOCIAL MEDIA

Hotels and airlines were among the first industries to recognize the value of social media platforms such as Twitter and Facebook, and to monitor them to respond to angry customers. Increasingly, companies are taking the tactic to a new level, trying to listen in on every mention of their brands for a real-time gauge of what people think of their offerings, competitors, and industry trends.[15]

Consumers are increasingly using tools such as Twitter to contact an airline as opposed to the old way of phoning the company. For flyers who have lost luggage or missed a flight, the immediacy of social media–based feedback could render toll-free numbers and website feedback forms obsolete in the near future. In an industry where every airline essentially sells the same commoditized service, airlines that use social media to turn disappointed customers into happy ones, or to simply enhance the travel experience, are already setting themselves apart and building loyalty.

Consider this scenario, which actually took place at Porter Airlines. When an unhappy passenger found herself waiting in a check-in line that wasn't moving quickly enough, she tweeted her dissatisfaction from her smartphone. At the same time that this was occurring, Porter Airlines employees were scanning Twitter traffic and came across the woman's complaint. By the time that passenger got to the front of the line, Porter staff were on hand to directly deal with her complaint.[16]

The engagement created by social media cannot be ignored as it may have consequences. United Airlines baggage handlers damaged Halifax songwriter David Carroll's $3,500 custom-made bass guitar on a flight from Halifax to Chicago. Carroll spent nine months seeking compensation by sending e-mails, writing letters, and calling airline representatives, all to no avail. Carroll, deeply frustrated and out of options, wrote a song entitled "United Breaks Guitars" and uploaded it to YouTube. The catchy song went viral, with 150,000 views the day it went live and nearly 10 million since then. United Airlines finally relented and, at Carroll's request, donated the $1,200 he paid for repairs to charity. It's interesting to note that within four days of the song going online, the bad PR caused United Airlines' stock price to suffer a plunge of 10 percent, costing shareholders $180 million. After the incident, United Airlines created a Twitter presence, but approaches social media with a more controlled strategy.[17]

Ingvar Björk/Alamy Stock Photo

Porter Airlines employees scanned social media sites to help identify and resolve a customer complaint.

Used with permission from Porter Airlines Inc.

Dave Carroll got his revenge when United Airlines broke his guitar.

Christian Laforce/Halifax Chronicle Herald/The Canadian Press

## CREDIBILITY ISSUES OF SOCIAL MEDIA

One of the temptations for a company is to encourage consumers to say positive things about its brand on a social media platform. In 2009, Ford promoted its new Fiesta subcompact by letting 100 consumers drive the car for free for six months, gas included. All they had to do was blog, tweet, and post about the car. There exists the possibility that they were more likely to say good things about the car as a result of the freebie, instead of truly giving their unbiased opinions. Although credibility may have suffered as a result of this campaign, the underlying strategy for Ford was engagement. Even though there are not a lot of Fiestas on the road, Ford believes in social media as a means to attract the tech-savvy consumer, and it relaunched a similar social media campaign in 2014.[18]

Ford used social media to promote its Fiesta subcompact car.

Paceman/Shutterstock.com

### ask YOURSELF

1. *What is customer relationship management all about?*

2. *Describe how companies are using social media in their relationships with customers.*

# CUSTOMER ACQUISITION AND RETENTION

**LO 3** CRM starts by building customer relationships. Data-driven programs can examine the profiles of a company's most-popular customers and use these characteristics to find prospective customers. After a company has found commonalities among profitable customers, it can use this information to accurately target potential customers with the same profile.

Once customer relationships are established, CRM shifts to maintaining profitable customer relationships. A company that builds strong relationships with customers will retain these customers, resulting in more sales and profits than the company would have if it focused only on getting new customers. It's important to note that making a sale to a current customer is way less expensive than making a sale to a new customer.

> Listening to customers is as important as—if not more important than—talking to them.

Listening to customers is as important as—if not more important than—talking to them. Some business-to-business (B2B) companies are now making a special effort to ask customers when and how they would like to be contacted by the company. This information is placed in a database so that it is readily available. This practice shows respect for loyal customers' time and allows companies to direct the brand communication in a way that is appropriate.

The increased profitability that is associated with customer retention is due to several factors that occur after a relationship has been established with a customer. Furthermore, by choosing the right customer, nurturing the right customer, and allocating resources to the right customer, profitability can be further enhanced. Among

Canadian respondents in the financial services industry, more than three out of five say that the greatest benefit of CRM is in understanding, acquiring, and retaining customers. Why CRM can help increase profitability through customer retention is explained by the following factors:[19]

- The cost of acquiring a customer occurs only at the beginning of a relationship, so the longer the relationship, the lower the amortized cost.

- Long-term customers tend to be less inclined to switch, and also tend to be less price-sensitive.

- Long-term customers may initiate word-of-mouth activity and referrals.

## LOYALTY PROGRAMS

One way to retain customers is through **loyalty programs**. In Canada, customers have created emotional connections to loyalty programs such as the Air Miles Reward Program.[20] Air Miles is Canada's largest loyalty program; Air Miles can be earned through more than 100 different sponsors, and there are almost 1,000 different rewards that can be redeemed. BMO Bank of Montreal offers an Air Miles–sponsored program, and TD offers an Aeroplan program (see the Marketing NewsFlash box, "A Safe Landing for Aeroplan," for more detail).[21] Loyalty programs were not always as advanced as Air Miles. In fact, the oldest and best-known loyalty program in Canada is Canadian Tire Money.

Loblaw offers the President's Choice Financial MasterCard, with which consumers can get PC points that can be redeemed for groceries. And the Shoppers Drug Mart Optimum card is a very successful loyalty program. Loyalty programs have become a way for one company to differentiate itself from another, but these differentiations have high expectations from Canadians.[22]

Although businesses appreciate all their customers, CRM practices allow them to distinguish between the loyalty habits of their customers. In most product categories, a small number of heavy users accounts for a large percentage of a brand's sales and profits. Heavy users are customers who buy an above-average amount of a given brand. According to **Pareto's Rule**, a marketing rule of thumb named after Italian economist Vilfredo Pareto, 80 percent of a brand's sales come from 20 percent of its customers. Heavy users should be rewarded differently than light users. The implication here is to take special care of the 20 percent by offering them better rewards than the remaining 80 percent. Databases allow companies to do more than merely recognize their customers. Companies that surprise and delight their high-profit customers with reward programs are more likely to keep these customers in the long run.

Consider the loyalty program at Starwood Hotels & Resorts, which has such brands as Sheraton and Westin.

The chain offers a different twist on personalizing a loyalty program. As well as the usual system of accumulating points that can be redeemed for free rooms, Starwood Preferred Guest program members can use their points to bid for special experiences. The Moments program allows members to take part in online auctions to bid for "insider access" to red-carpet premieres, closed rehearsals with top musicians, private dinners with celebrity chefs, or rounds of golf with PGA Tour pros.

Members of the Moments program can hone their golf skills with a hands-on clinic led by PGA TOUR Professional Jason Gore. Members learn golfing techniques from Gore and then test out their new skills with 18 holes of challenging play, where Jason joins the member for several holes and offers tips along the way.[23]

Canadian banks have unique loyalty offerings as well. These can take the form of multiproduct rebates, as well as credit cards offering rewards programs. The rewards from these cards can be redeemed for travel and other incentives.[24]

In addition to rewarding customers, loyalty programs provide businesses with a wealth of information about their customers. This information is the raw material for data mining, which is discussed in the next section.

## PRIVACY

With technology becoming more pervasive in our culture and companies having access to more and more consumer information, the Canadian government has extended the responsibilities of the Office of the Privacy Commission of Canada to the private sector. This office acts as an advocate for Canadians on their rights to privacy. The *Personal Information Protection and Electronic Documents Act (PIPEDA)* established rules for how personal information

---

**Increased Loyalty, Decreased Activity**

|  | 2016 | 2015 |
|---|---|---|
| Loyalty programs enrollment per program member | 11.3 | 11.1 |
| Number of programs where program members are active | 7.3 | 7.4 |

**Source:** "The 2016 Bond Loyalty Report," Canadian Marketing Association, accessed at https://www.the-cma.org/resource/leadership/the-2016-bond-loyalty-report.

---

**loyalty programs**
Programs specifically designed for customer retention.

**Pareto's Rule**
The concept that 80 percent of a brand's sales come from 20 percent of its customers.

# A Safe Landing for Aeroplan

© Hemis/Alamy Stock Photo

Loyalty cards are normally associated with rewards. One of the more recognizable loyalty cards in Canada is Aeroplan. This consumer-facing brand allows travellers to collect points for travel rewards with Air Canada and its strategic alliances. Owned by Aimia, Aeroplan is considered Canada's premier coalition loyalty program since it has over 75 world-class partners and represents over 150 brands in the retail, travel, and financial industries.

With over 30 years in the loyalty business, Aeroplan has more than 4.6 million active members, making it a sought-after partner in a variety of industries. Well-known Canadian companies such as Esso, Home Hardware, and Sobeys were added as partners in 2005. In the financial services industry, Aeroplan partnered with American Express® and CIBC to offer rewards credit cards. Aeroplan's relationship with CIBC began in 1991

when Aeroplan and CIBC partnered to launch the CIBC Aerogold® VISA Card, considered one of the most popular credit cards in Canada.

Although the 20-year-plus partnership had been successful, Aeroplan had another suitor. In 2013, TD Bank entered into the Aeroplan loyalty business by becoming the primary credit card issuer for the Aeroplan loyalty rewards program. For a few months, this caused friction between all parties involved, including existing Aeroplan credit card holders. Fortunately, TD Bank Group and Canadian Imperial Bank of Commerce were able to reach an agreement.

With half of the Aeroplan card portfolio shifting from CIBC to TD, over 550,000 cardholder accounts were changing banks. As compensation for this change, CIBC received over $312.5 million from TD and Aimia, with Aimia paying $150 million of that figure.

A transition of this magnitude could be confusing to existing customers. However, understanding the importance of customer relationship management, TD added incentives to its TD Aeroplan cards to keep the transitioning customers satisfied. ●

## Questions

1. In terms of customer loyalty, why do you believe TD was so interested in becoming an Aeroplan partner?

2. What benefits does Aeroplan gain by expanding its partners in the financial services sector?

---

**database marketing**

The use of databases to customize communications to customers and potential customers for the purpose of promoting a product or service.

is handled during the course of business. Personal information can be collected only through lawful means. Consumers need to consent to the information being collected, while companies need to protect the information and cannot use it for purposes other than what was originally intended. Furthermore, in 2014, the Canadian government introduced anti-spam legislation. Given the ease of accessibility to consumer information, this legislation is intended to protect Canadians from unwanted communications and threats.[25]

> " *In addition to rewarding customers, loyalty programs provide businesses with a wealth of information about their customers.*

# DATABASE MARKETING

**LO 4** | **Database marketing** is an essential practice for enhancing the customer experience. It is significant to a company's success in identifying its customers and customizing its service offerings. Over time, company's collect, process, and analyze information on their customers, potential customers, and competitors. Through careful analysis, companies can better recognize customer needs and adjust accordingly to meet and exceed expectations. Whether through traditional means or social networks, database marketing can help companies improve customer loyalty.[26]

## DATA MINING

How does a company use the reams of information in its databases? One answer is data mining. *Data mining* is an efficient way to sort through large amounts of data to find relationships between variables. It is a process of analyzing customer patterns and insights to make better marketing

# Infographic

**Source:** "The Bond Brand Loyalty Report," Bond Brand Loyalty, accessed 2016 at http://info.bondbrandloyalty.com/2016-loyalty-report-canada.

decisions. By spotting trends and relationships among the reams of information, data mining can help specifically target customer segments to meet their needs. Since data mining is growing in its impact to customer satisfaction and developing business opportunities, companies need to place more emphasis in getting customer information in the hands of sales and support staff to make a difference. Effective integration of data mining in a company's CRM strategy will allow for improved customer service and sales performance.[27]

Loyalty programs supply a lot of information that can be used for data mining purposes. Information that customers supply when they apply for a loyalty program can be tied to their purchase behaviour. Data mining can then be used to find patterns in consumer behaviour and also help marketers with customer segmentation.

All the data about customers is stored in a central place, called the **data warehouse**. A data warehouse can be thought of as an electronics library where all the information is indexed. Once the data warehouse brings the data together, the company uses data mining techniques to find insights about customers.

There are multiple examples of how CRM and data mining techniques positively impact retail organizations in Canada. For example, Royal Bank of Canada has invested in its CRM strategy. It considers CRM a core strategy and attributes it having a positive impact to its revenue growth and profitability. The deeper the data can be analyzed, the better insights that can be made.[28]

A second example is Canadian Tire. Data mining enabled the retailer's credit card division to create psychological profiles of its cardholders that were built upon alarmingly precise correlations. Data mining revealed that cardholders who purchased carbon-monoxide detectors, premium birdseed, and felt pads for the bottoms of their chair legs rarely missed a payment. On the other hand, those who bought cheap motor oil and visited a Montreal pool bar called "Sharx" were a higher risk. Canadian Tire leveraged these learnings and is now quite an innovator in digital marketing.[29]

A third example of data mining involves Metro, a chain of supermarkets in Ontario and Quebec. Its bottled juices traditionally were placed on the shelves by brand.

> **data warehouse**
> A central repository of an organization's electronically stored data.

## ask YOURSELF

1. *What is Pareto's Rule?*
2. *Give some examples of loyalty programs.*
3. *What is data mining?*

But data mining information showed that consumers preferred the juices to be shelved by flavour. Metro made the change and sales of juices increased and continues to be flexible in its offer to the evolving consumer.[30]

## CUSTOMER LIFETIME VALUE

In customer relationship management, a company focuses on its relationship with customers with the ultimate goal of creating an unbreakable bond with its customers. Companies are starting to focus on the value of a customer if that customer remains loyal to the firm over the customer's lifetime. This is referred to as *customer lifetime value*.

Carl Sewell, a successful car dealer-owner and author of a book called *Customers for Life*, looks at each customer as an investment. If he can provide each customer with excellent customer service, that customer will likely remain loyal to Carl's dealership in the future. In a sense, that customer may have a lifetime value to Carl of hundreds of thousands of dollars. Knowing this, Carl keeps an insightful perspective in dealing with customers.[31]

An example of Carl's insight involved a customer who came to pick up his car after servicing and noticed that his tennis racquet, which he had left in the car, was gone. Under normal circumstances, a dealer would say that it is not responsible for items left in a car. Carl Sewell, on the other hand, went over to the customer and apologized for the mishap. He then proceeded to write a cheque for replacement of the racquet. Carl surmised that it was not worth jeopardizing an investment of hundreds of thousands of dollars over the price of a tennis racquet.

A concept very close to customer lifetime value is *share of wallet*. CRM techniques can help marketers get a larger share of a customer's purchases from that company. Here's an example of how a bank can increase its share of wallet. The bank that holds a customer's mortgage and chequing account may learn at some point that the customer has children and may then try to sell the customer a registered education savings plan. Another example of a company increasing share of wallet is Shoppers Drug Mart. A customer with an Optimum card who purchases cosmetics may receive subsequent communications from Shoppers that offer coupons for related cosmetic products.

## CRM AND CUSTOMER REACQUISITION

**LO 5** Companies are realizing that losing a customer means more than losing a sale. It means losing the entire future stream of purchases that the customer would make over a lifetime of patronage. Customers stop buying from a company for a variety of reasons. Very often, the reason can be poor customer service as opposed to something inherently wrong with the brand. The first step in customer recovery is to find the customer who is in jeopardy of being lost to the company. The longer customers stay away from a business, the less likely they are to return. Because customer databases capture purchases, computers can be programmed to periodically examine transaction frequencies and create a list of all customers who have not made a purchase within a set period of time. Because each customer generally has a certain purchase frequency, software can determine when each customer's purchase frequency has been broken. After lapsed customers are identified, the second step is to contact them to determine why they have stopped buying and potentially prepare an appropriate offer.[32] If the problem is resolved, the lapsed customer may become a very loyal customer because the firm has shown interest in the customer.

## RETAINING MARGINAL CUSTOMERS

CRM allows firms to use information technology to quantify the value of individual customers in terms of sales and profits. High-value customers are provided with better privileges, discounts, or other inducements. CRM analysis shows that a small proportion of customers contribute to a large percentage of profits, and that many customers are unprofitable. Many firms are beginning to jettison or fire their low-value customers and are focusing their time on their high-valued customers. In 2007, CNN reported that Sprint had dropped about 1,000 customers who were calling the customer-care centre too frequently—40 to 50 times more than the average customer every month over an extended period.[33]

Firing low-value customers seems to be a common-sense approach, but in some cases there is a danger. If a company is left with only high-value customers, this leaves the company open to poaching by competitors if they are aware of its customer base.

**LO 1**
- Customer relationship management (CRM) focuses on using information about customers to build and maintain profitable customer relationships.
- Customer experience management (CEM) involves managing customer interactions to build brand equity and improve long-term profitability.

**LO 2**
- A growing number of companies are keeping track of what's said about their brands on social media platforms such as Facebook and Twitter. This activity falls in line with the process of CRM, because it's an excellent way to build a relationship with customers.

**LO 3**
- One way to retain customers is through loyalty programs. It should be noted that all customers should be rewarded, but not all customers are the same. In most product categories, a small number of heavy users account for a large percentage of a brand's sales and profits.

**LO 4**
- Companies use database marketing to collect, process, and analyze information on their customers, potential customers, and competitors with a goal to improve customer loyalty.
- Data mining is an efficient way to sort through large amounts of data to find relationships between variables.
- Companies are starting to focus on the value of a customer if that customer remains loyal to the firm over the customer's lifetime.

**LO 5**
- Many firms are beginning to jettison or fire their low-value customers and are focusing their time on their high-value customers.
- Companies are instituting customer reacquisition programs to prevent losing customers.

## key terms and concepts... **A REFRESHER**

| | | |
|---|---|---|
| customer experience management (CEM) | data warehouse | Pareto's Rule |
| database marketing | loyalty programs | touch point |

## hands-on... **APPLY YOUR KNOWLEDGE**

**Online CRM Assignment**  Visit the Luxor CRM website at **www.luxorcrm.com/about-us/customer-case-studies.html**. Review two of the case studies and put into your own words how a Luxor customer relationship management solution helps companies.

## chapter vignette... **ACTIVITY**

In the opening vignette, customer relationship management and customer experience management are discussed. Answer the questions at the end of the vignette by reviewing the vignette as well as the Marketing NewsFlash boxes, "Off Target" and "A Safe Landing for Aeroplan."

## infographic... **DATA ANALYSIS**

More and more Canadians are expecting personalized communications. In order to offer this, marketers need to collect personal information on their audiences. What is interesting is that Canadians provide them with this information by joining loyalty programs, but they are not active in all the loyalty programs they belong to. Review the Infographic in this chapter and offer your thoughts about what loyalty marketers can do to increase activity.

# Strategic Marketing Planning

## LEARNING OBJECTIVES

**LO 1** Describe how strategy is developed at the corporate, business unit, and functional levels in an organization

**LO 2** Define the concepts of business, mission, and goals, and explain why they are important in organizations

**LO 3** Explain why managers use marketing dashboards and marketing metrics

**LO 4** Discuss how organizations formulate strategies

**LO 5** Outline the strategic marketing process

**P**ersonal finances can be challenging for Canadians. Whether it is managing on a fixed budget in college or university, or living on a fixed income in retirement, valuable advice from experts in the investment industry can help Canadians achieve their financial goals.

© Fredrick Kippe/Alamy Stock Photo

Whether it is a non-profit organization seeking donors or a business firm creating new customers, the right decisions and effective use of resources contribute to an organization's success. Always making the right decisions is challenging. Business leaders need guidelines and feedback mechanisms to support their direction. The strategy a business chooses helps define this framework. If developing and setting strategy seems like a daunting task, a good reference point is to start with the organization's mission statement.[1] For example, ESPN's mission is "to serve sports fans wherever sports are watched, listened to, discussed, debated, read about, or played."

More and more companies see talent in this industry as an important component to executing strategy. Finding the right people to execute business strategy well is a challenging and rewarding task, as the effective utilization of people, processes, and capital helps organizations achieve their long-term vision. Furthermore, once you acquire the talent, it is important for an organization to deliver the best onboarding and training possible for their new recruits.

Approximately 30 years ago, the Canadian banking industry designed services focused specifically on the future of Canada. By cultivating a youth market, banks began to reap the rewards from post-secondary graduates. The key to their strategy involved building a relationship at an early age that was difficult to break in future years. Education of Canadians at a young age is key to this strategy. In the competitive banking market, banks offer students access to loans to start early relationships for life. These strategies are intended to help win their long-term business; however, it is important for students to stay in control of debt.[2]

Fast forward 20 years and Canadians face a challenge with their growing household debt. Although challenging economies and high-risk lending products may contribute to this issue, certain trends have been identified with respect to demographic and geographic characteristics. Although warning signs were identified years ago, Canadians predilection to borrowing, a weak Canadian dollar, and shopping sprees have created an issue.

Why debt continues to grow could be due the speed at which decisions for purchases are now being made. Consumer purchase decisions can already be made quickly. And consumers have access to many credit facilities that facilitate their growing debt. Furthermore, options for individuals struggling with debt in Canada are unclear making it difficult for consumers to access the right advice.[3]

Primerica, one of SeeWhy Learning's many corporate clients, understands the financial challenges that Canadians face and provides advisors across Canada to help them. The fundamental financial principles taught by Primerica advisors can be life-changing. The company has offered Canadian families over $100 billion of life insurance coverage and administers over $10 billion of Canadian wealth.

"Primerica is an expert at attracting entrepreneurially minded individuals who wish to build their own practice with the support of a large respected financial institution," shares Cory Snyder, sales director at SeeWhy Learning. To begin a career with Primerica, representatives must obtain a life insurance licence, with many recruits eventually obtaining a mutual fund licence as well. This requires the successful completion of several challenging exams. That is where Primerica turns to partners like SeeWhy Learning.

SeeWhy Learning offers online study tools to prepare future financial industry professionals for their qualification examinations. Similar to many organizations, SeeWhy Learning's marketing plan involved completing a situation analysis. Once it understood its strengths and weaknesses, the organization began developing and positioning its product. It set goals and developed a marketing program that would allow it to achieve profits. It continues to execute and evaluate its marketing success as it acquires new clients and grows as an organization.

## CHAPTER FEATURES

**Preparing Future Advisors**
Leveraging technology to train our country's future advisors.

**Canada's Most Profitable**
Discover ten of Canada's most profitable companies.

**Board Diversity**
Review perspectives on gender diverse boards.

**Co-operative and Ethical**
Mountain Equipment Co-op ventures into corporate social responsibility.

**Changing Business Models**
Learn how Netflix changes its strategy to capitalize on its market.

**New Application**
The evolution of the job application process.

## CHAPTER OUTLINE

- Preparing future advisors
- Organizational structure and strategy
- Setting strategic directions
- The strategic marketing process

Since 2008, See Why Learning set a simple strategy to grow the number of corporate clients it works with. This required the company to increase the number of retail customers who independently purchase SeeWhy's tools via its online delivery channels. "Early on, we realized that large financial institutions were not receptive to cold calls," explains Cory. "We needed a different strategy. We decided to focus all our energies on developing excellent study tools. Our strategy was to build a better mouse trap and hope that corporate clients take notice and come to us for company-wide training solutions along with corporate pricing." The strategy proved successful as most of SeeWhy Learning's corporate clients were a direct result of feedback received from employees who purchased SeeWhy Learning tools independently. "We were confident we were on the right track when we secured our very first contract with a subsidiary of a big bank," recalls Cory. "We also work closely with several colleges as it gives us the opportunity to give back to the community. We understand that many of today's finance students will eventually become key decision makers at various institutions."

"We don't aim to sell our client's a product," explains academic director Andre Samuels. "We want to help them achieve a result." To fulfill that promise, SeeWhy Learning employs a success-based guarantee in its pricing model. Many of SeeWhy Learning products offer an unprecedented *If you don't pass, you don't pay* guarantee. This guarantee has very few conditions and is outlined on the company's website, **www.SeeWhyLearning.com**.

SeeWhy Learning actually structured its pricing model after the real estate industry, whose licensing exams it also supports. Much like how a real estate agent doesn't get paid until a house is bought or sold, SeeWhy Learning doesn't view its job as complete or the money earned until the student is successful on his or her exam. It realized that its clients do not come to SeeWhy Learning specifically for training tools; instead they want to achieve success. Therefore, SeeWhy's product is really exam success. The way it stands behind its products also demonstrates to clients that it believes in the quality of what it offers. It also holds the company accountable to continually improving its products and services.

"When we began operations, we implemented the innovative guarantee which would have been costly for established competitors to match. We absolutely stand behind our guarantee and do offer some refunds; albeit the refund rate is very low given the quality of our products. We believe the guarantee encouraged students to give us a try, and allowed us to gain market share at a critical point in the business. We believed it was only a matter of time before we were on our competitor's radar and needed to gain critical mass quickly," reflects Cory. "That was part of our strategy."

SeeWhy Learning also knew the success of the business relied on a strong Internet presence. "We were trainers first and foremost," says Andre, "So we knew we needed help. We wrestled with outsourcing this service versus the more expensive option of building our own dedicated internal IT team. We believed a strong Internet presence was vital to the success of the company, so we went with the costlier option and hired James (Jim) Cousineau, support and IT manager, to head up the team." Jim adds, "The team's remuneration is directly tied to sales, which gives us a vested interest in obtaining and maintaining good search engine rankings, etc. Our new corporate clients are also very impressed as we can build a custom intranet page within a few days, complete with the client's own branding, allowing it to securely offer negotiated pricing to their employees. It sets the tone for the level of service and support the client can expect to receive."

Today, SeeWhy Financial Learning is well-known for offering quality training solutions and has obtained credibility in the marketplace. Most recently it partnered with the IFSE Institute to develop training tools for the Harmonized Life Licensing Qualification Program, for which IFSE is one of the approved course providers. IFSE is the educational arm of the Investment Funds Institute of Canada (IFIC) and a leader in online learning delivery. They are dedicated to helping Canadians improve their financial literacy through best-in-class financial education and support. As a not-for-profit organization, IFSE makes its training affordable to ensure that financial education is widely accessible.

IFSE's goal is to empower the financial services industry as a whole, to benefit all whom the industry serves. They equip advisors with the tools they need to enhance their financial expertise and help inspire their clients' confidence. They are also dedicated to helping individuals improve their financial literacy through practical financial education and training courses. By building their financial knowledge, IFSE's students are also building a foundation for long-term financial success.

While the money back guarantee was implemented to gain market share quickly, it remains part of the SeeWhy's corporate strategy. The trainers and curriculum team enjoy being held accountable to such a high standard.[4]

## reality CHECK ⊘

As you read Chapter 15, refer back to the SeeWhy Learning vignette to answer the following questions:

- How is the strategic marketing process described by Andre Samuels and Cory Snyder aligned with the process described in the chapter?
- If SeeWhy Learning wanted to expand globally, what modifications (if any) would you make to its strategic marketing process?

# ORGANIZATIONAL STRUCTURE AND STRATEGY

**LO 1** This chapter describes how organizations set their mission and overall direction and link these activities to marketing strategies. As consumers become more concerned about a company's impact on society, marketing strategy may need to be linked to the social goals of the company's mission statement. This chapter also focuses on strategic planning and the role it plays in the marketing process.

## KINDS OF ORGANIZATIONS

Today's organizations can be divided into business firms and not-for-profit organizations. A *business firm* is an organization that serves its customers in order to earn a profit. **Profit** is the excess of revenues over costs, the reward to a business for the risk it undertakes in offering a product for sale. In contrast to business firms, a *not-for-profit organization* is an organization that serves its customers but does not have profit as an organizational goal. For simplicity, however, we use the terms *firm, company, corporation,* and *organization* to cover both business and not-for-profit operations.

## MARKETING AND THE THREE ORGANIZATIONAL LEVELS

All organizations should have a strategic direction—that is, they should have an idea of what they hope to achieve and how they plan to achieve it. Marketing not only helps set the direction but also helps the organization get there. Large organizations are complex and may consist of three organizational levels whose strategies are linked to marketing. Figure 15–1 illustrates the three levels of strategy in an optimal organization.

At the *corporate level,* top management directs overall strategy for the entire organization. Multimarket, multiproduct firms such as General Electric or Unilever really manage a group of different businesses, variously termed strategic business units (SBUs), strategic business segments, or product-market units (PMUs).[5] Each of these units markets a set of related products to a clearly defined group of customers. Management at the corporate level focuses on the interests of the shareholders of the firm, as measured by stock performance and profitability.

Similar to adjusting trajectory in the game Angry Birds, marketers make slight adjustments after executing their strategy.

© Ian Dagnall/Alamy Stock Photo

**profit**
The excess of revenues over costs, the reward to a business for the risk it undertakes in offering a product for sale.

The *business unit level* has business unit managers set the direction for individual products and markets. Strategic direction is more specific at the business unit level of an organization. For less complex firms with a single business focus, the corporate and business unit strategies may merge. Unilever has provided products such as Sunlight and Vaseline to Canadians for over 100 years. Another example of one of its strategic business units is Ben & Jerry's, a premium ice cream company with fun flavour names.[6]

At the *functional level,* each business unit has marketing and other specialized activities such as finance, manufacturing, or human resources. The name of a *department* generally refers to its specialized function, such as the marketing department or information systems department. At the functional level, the strategic direction becomes very specific and focused.

In a large corporation with multiple business units, marketing may be called on to assess consumer trends as an aid to corporate planning. At the business unit level, marketing may be asked to provide leadership in developing a new, integrated customer service program across all business units. At the functional level, marketing may implement an advertising campaign.

# STRATEGY ISSUES IN ORGANIZATIONS

**LO 2** Organizations need a reason for their existence—and a direction. This is where their business, mission, and goals converge. We'll discuss each below. Figure 15–1 illustrates the

different organizational levels in a business. Business and mission apply to the corporate and business unit levels, while goals relate to all levels.

## Strategy Defined for Business Plans and Marketing Plans

As discussed earlier, an organization has limited resources available to produce and market its offerings. Since it cannot possibly do everything, it must develop strategies to focus and direct the resources it has to achieve its goals. Unfortunately, the definition of strategy is debated among management and marketing theorists, so for our purposes, we will define **strategy** as an organization's long-term course of action designed to deliver a unique customer experience while achieving its goals.[7] Once the strategy of an organization or an organizational initiative is defined, business leaders collaborate to develop a marketing plan.

Getting ideas and goals down on paper is the first step to making them into reality. The business plan becomes a valuable tool for organizations to do this. It is a document that can help convey the value of your company to investors, employees, and future partners. Business plans help identify the strengths, weaknesses, opportunities, and threats of a business, as well as help develop accurate financial forecasts. Essential to the overall business plan, a marketing plan helps a business develop the right products to address customer needs, establish the best way to promote the business, and determine where the product will be distributed. Advertising and communications are also important components of the marketing plan.[8]

**The Business** Organizations such as Canadian Blood Services and your college or university exist for a purpose—to accomplish something for someone. At the beginning, most organizations have clear ideas about what "something" and "someone" mean. But as the organization grows over time, often its purpose becomes fuzzy and continually unclear.

**Figure 15–1**
The three levels of strategy in organizations: corporate, business unit, and functional

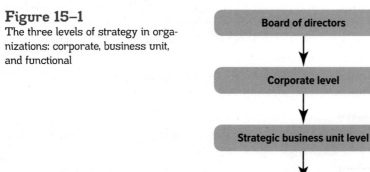
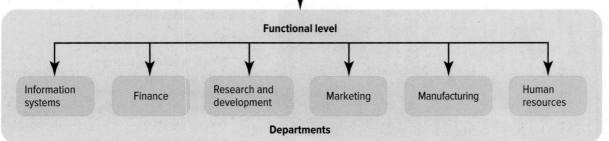

This is where the organization repeatedly asks some of the most difficult questions it ever faces: What business are we in? Who are our customers? What offerings should we provide to give these customers value? One guideline in defining the company's business is to try to understand the people served by the organization and the value they receive, which emphasizes the critical customer-driven focus that successful organizations have.

In a now-famous article entitled "Marketing Myopia," Harvard professor Theodore Levitt cited railroads as organizations that had a narrow, production-oriented statement of their business: "We are in the railroad business!" This narrow definition of their business lost sight of who their customers were and what their needs were. Railroads saw only other railroads as competitors and failed to design strategies to compete with airlines, barges, pipelines, trucks, bus lines, and cars and may have fared better over the past century by recognizing they are in "the transportation business." Examining business from a broader perspective allows you apply this concept to companies such as Disney. Disney is *not* in the movie and theme park business, but rather it *is* in the business of entertainment, creating fun and fantasy for customers.

**The Mission** By understanding its business, an organization can take steps to define its **mission**, a statement of the organization's scope, often identifying its customers, markets, products, technology, and values. Today often used interchangeably with *vision,* the *mission statement* frequently has an inspirational theme—something that can ignite the loyalty of customers, employees, and others with whom the organization comes in contact.

Inspiration and focus appear in the mission statements of business and non-profit organizations. Even if the businesses are different, their mission statements can exhibit similar qualities:

- **Ben & Jerry's (Product Mission):** "To make, distribute and sell the finest quality all natural ice cream and euphoric concoctions with a continued commitment to incorporating wholesome, natural ingredients and promoting business practices that respect the Earth and the Environment."
- **Canadian Blood Services:** "… operates Canada's blood supply in a manner that gains the trust, commitment and confidence of all Canadians by providing a safe, secure, cost-effective, affordable and accessible supply of quality blood, blood products and their alternatives."
- **Mountain Equipment Co-op:** "… to support our members to lead active outdoor lifestyles."

Each mission statement illustrates clear direction and challenging and compelling pictures for their futures. Ben & Jerry's goes so far as to add a mission focused on social responsibility as well as a mission for its product. IBM has put strategy in place to create a "smarter planet." It is driven by three core values that help it create its mission statement.

Organizations must connect not just with their customers but with all their *stakeholders.* Stakeholders are the people who are affected by what the company does and how well it performs. This group includes employees, owners, and board members, as well as suppliers, distributors, unions, local communities, governments, society in general, and, of course, customers. Communicating the mission statement is an important corporate-level marketing function. Some companies publish their mission statement on their website or in their annual reports. One British Columbia company has its mission statement on a huge wall poster in its manufacturing facility, and every employee reads and signs it! The Focus on Ethics box, "Board Diversity," discusses the value to a company of adhering to corporate values, in this case promoting diversity.[9]

**Goals** Goals or **objectives** take an organization's mission and translate it into targeted levels of performance to be achieved within a specific time frame. These goals measure how well the mission is being accomplished. Goals exist at the corporate, business unit, and functional levels, which were shown in Figure 15–1. All lower-level goals must contribute to achieving goals at the next highest level.

Business firms can pursue several different types of goals:

- **Profit:** Most firms seek to maximize profits—to get as high a financial return on investment (ROI) as possible.
- **Sales:** A firm may elect to maintain or increase its sales level even though profitability may not be maximized.
- **Market share:** A firm may choose to maintain or increase its market share, sometimes at the expense of greater profits if industry status or prestige is a desired goal. *Market share* is the ratio of sales revenue of the firm to the total sales revenue of all firms in the industry, including the firm itself.

**mission**
Statement of the organization's purpose and direction.

**goals (objectives)**
Targets of performance to be achieved within a specific time frame.

# Board Diversity

Correlation between the diversity of a board of directors and the financial performance of an organization is a good argument to encourage diversity in companies to increase shareholder value. Nonetheless, the progression of diverse boards is slow in Canada.

An organization's success depends on many factors. The organization's strategy set out by its leadership team is one of these important factors. This strategic direction will help identify what the organization hopes to achieve and how it plans to achieve it. Marketing may play a role in setting direction as well as executing plans. But as organizations increase in size, so may the complexity of the organizational structure. Large organizations normally have a board of directors that holds the top management accountable for the strategic direction set by the organization as well as the results achieved.

Canada is home to a diverse population. However, gender diversity on corporate boards has become a contentious issue between companies and their shareholders. In 2016, Restaurant Brands International, the parent company of Tim Hortons and Burger King, turned down a proposal to increase the number of women on its board of directors. At the time, there were no women on the board.

Before Tim Hortons merged with Burger King in 2014, a quarter of the Tim Hortons board were women. The combined company Restaurant Brands International (RBI) rolled out a ten-person all-male board of directors.

RBI does have two women in senior management, but some shareholders believe formal board diversity is required to ensure appropriate representation. Gender is one point of diversity, as are race, background, and experience. Tim Hortons may be the most recognizable brand in Canada where tension on gender diversity is apparent; however, other Canadian companies like BCE and

There is a correlation between diverse boards of directors and financial performance.

bowdenimages/iStock/Getty Images Plus

Dollarama have shareholders that also raise diversity issues. ●

## Questions

1. Other than financial performance, what other benefits are there to having a diverse board of directors in an organization?

2. If you do not agree with a company's strategy on governance or operations, what can you as a consumer do "voice" your opinion?

- **Quality:** A firm may target the highest quality, as Rolex does with its luxury wristwatches.

- **Customer satisfaction:** Customers are the key to an organization's success, so their perceptions and actions are of vital importance. Their satisfaction can be measured directly with surveys.

- **Employee welfare:** A firm may recognize the critical importance of its employees by having an explicit goal stating its commitment to good employment opportunities and working conditions.

- **Social responsibility:** A firm may seek to balance conflicting goals of stakeholders to promote overall welfare, even at the expense of profits. (See, for example, the discussion of the emphasis on corporate social responsibility at Mountain Equipment Co-op in the Focus on Ethics box, "MEC Believes Accountability Is Key to Corporate Social Responsibility.")[10]

## Canada's Most Profitable Companies

1. Royal Bank of Canada
2. Toronto-Dominion Bank
3. Bank of Nova Scotia
4. Bank of Montreal
5. CIBC
6. Canadian National Railway Co.
7. Brookfield Asset Management Inc.
8. BCE Inc.
9. Great-West Lifeco Inc.
10. Magna International Inc.

Source: Based on "Canada's top 15 most profitable companies: Investor 500 2016," *Canadian Business*, June 22, 2016, http://www.canadianbusiness.com/lists-and-rankings/best-stocks/2016-most-profitable-companies/.

# MEC Believes Accountability Is Key to Corporate Social Responsibility

Used with permission of Mountain Equipment Co-op (MEC)

**M**ountain Equipment Co-op (MEC) set challenging goals for itself in 2013. When sourcing its apparel materials, it focused on using facilities with environmental management systems and products with environmentally preferred materials. The additional steps MEC made for the benefit of the environment were not in vain. It surpassed its targets with respect to how it designs its products, how it operates as an organization, and how it supports the community.

MEC did not stop at achieving some of its goals. It held itself accountable through an accountability report shared with the public. This report highlighted where it succeeded and where it needed to improve. Furthermore, to ensure that results were conveyed in an unbiased yet fair manner, MEC looked to its stakeholders to form an accountability review panel to help compile and submit the findings. In 2016, it continues to increase and build on the goals it achieves. Mountain Equipment Co-op is not the only company focused on corporate social responsibility. According a recent article in *Maclean's,* applying socially responsible practices makes good business sense and adds to the bottom line of many Canadian companies. ●

## Questions

1. Give some examples of other companies practising corporate social responsibility.

2. Would you pay more for more environmentally friendly apparel? Discuss.

Many organizations (for example, museums, symphony orchestras, and private schools) do not seek profits as a primary goal. These organizations strive to serve consumers as efficiently as possible. Government agencies also perform marketing activities in trying to achieve their goal of serving the public good.

**Marketing Budgets and Financials** Clearly stating goals in a marketing plan is important. Aligning marketing objectives and financial objectives of a company is also important since discrepancies between chief marketing officer (CMO) and chief financial officer (CFO) activities can have a negative impact on financial results.[11]

The break-even analysis and profit equation, discussed in Chapter 9, help develop a pricing strategy for products and services. With key assumptions, marketing plans need to generate sales forecasts to determine the amount of money or sales that will be generated. These sales help the business's finance team forecast a company's cash flow and profit and loss for its overall business plan. Marketers rely on historical information, emerging trends, and assumptions to look forward, and then suggest the potential impact that marketing will have on the company's success.[12]

Determining how marketing spending impacts company profitability is an ongoing challenge for

CMOs.[13] With this challenge looming, marketers need to be able to prepare accurate budgets for their marketing plans. Since forecasts in marketing plans may be relied upon for other decisions, it is important for marketers to ensure that more than one forecast is created. Considering realistic, optimistic, and pessimistic forecasts helps decision makers see expected, best-case, and worst-case scenarios. Preparing forecasts and budgets provides an opportunity for companies to predict future revenues and expenses while looking for ways to cut costs. To help improve accuracy in budgeting and forecasting for marketing, marketers may review past sales, consider upcoming contracts, and propose predictions to potential changes in the market.[14]

# TRACKING STRATEGIC PERFORMANCE

**LO 3** Although marketing managers can set strategic directions for their organizations, how do they know if they are making progress in getting there? One answer is to measure performance by using marketing dashboards.

**marketing dashboard**

A visual computer display of essential marketing information.

**marketing metric**

A measure of the value or trend of a marketing activity or result.

Once the marketing plan is put into practice, it is immediately evaluated. Measuring the results of a marketing plan is a key step in achieving client satisfaction. As we review marketing metrics and dashboards, the tools and technology we are discussing today, may be obsolete in a few years. Notwithstanding, technology has added value to measuring the results from the investments made in marketing research and creative. When describing the importance of metrics, we can relate it to Angry Birds, the video game by Rovio. Before metrics and dashboards, marketing plans would be executed with a ready-aim-fire approach. That is, marketers would not receive feedback until the campaign was complete. The digital age we are in right now allows us to execute marketing plans with an aim-fire-adjust approach. After we execute a part of the recruitment marketing plan, we use the metrics to quickly adjust our plan and get closer to our desired result.

## Marketing Dashboards

A **marketing dashboard** is the visual display of the essential information related to achieving a marketing objective. Often, it is a computer-based display with real-time information and active hyperlinks to provide further detail. For example, a CMO may want to see daily what the effect of a new TV advertising campaign is on a product's sales in order to allocate future marketing resources effectively. Dashboards can track other parts of an organization's business, including the impact of its corporate social responsibility endeavours. Similar to a dashboard in a car, marketing dashboards can give feedback at a quick glance.

*What the marketing dashboard shows are the key marketing metrics that the organization believes will drive it to success.*

**Marketing Metrics** Most companies keep their marketing dashboards and metrics proprietary, as the information in the dashboard gives an indication as to the organization's strategy. Marketing dashboards are similar to the accountability report dashboard shown in Figure 15–2. The graphic displays of marketing dashboards are key performance measures of a product category, such as sales versus cost of sales. Each variable in a marketing dashboard is a **marketing metric**, which is a measure of the quantitative value or trend of a marketing activity or result. The choice of which marketing

### Figure 15–2

Example of a marketing dashboard

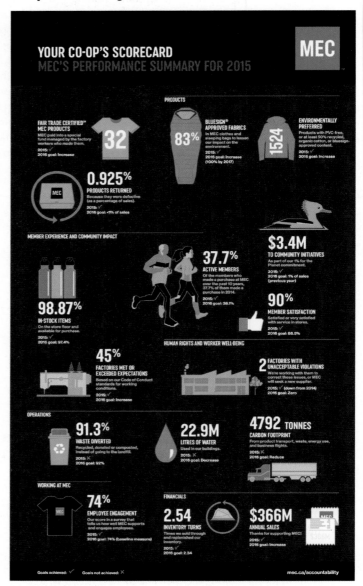

An effective dashboard, like this one from Mountain Equipment Co-op, helps managers assess their corporate social responsibility impact at a glance.

Used with permission of Mountain Equipment Co-op (MEC)

metrics to display is critical for a busy marketing manager, who can be overwhelmed with too much or inappropriate information.

Dashboard designers take great care to show graphs and tables in easy-to-understand formats to enable clear interpretation at a glance. What the marketing dashboard shows are the key marketing metrics that the organization believes will drive it to success.

Mountain Equipment Co-op distributes Garmin products, another company committed to being a good corporate citizen.
OvuOng/Shutterstock.com

# SETTING STRATEGIC DIRECTIONS

**LO 4** Setting strategic direction for drawing employees or consumers closer to an organization involves answering challenging questions: Where are we now? Where do we want to go? How will we get there?

## A LOOK AROUND: WHERE ARE WE NOW?

Asking an organization where it is at the present time involves identifying its customers, competencies, and competitors. More-detailed approaches of assessing "where are we now?" include SWOT analysis, discussed later in this chapter, and environmental scanning (Chapter 2). It is important for an organization to look internally and externally to assess its starting point. These approaches may be carried out at each of the three levels in the organization.

**Customers** Tilley Endurables is a Canadian retailer that knows that its customers appreciate the fine hats and travel clothing that Tilley makes. Tilley provides an example

**TOP 50**
**Socially Responsible Corporations · 2015**
**MACLEAN'S** ⊕ **SUSTAINALYTICS**

Each year, *Maclean's* recognizes companies and their socially responsible practices. Companies recognized in 2015 include Loblaw and Canadian Tire.

™Trademarks of Rogers Communications Inc. or an affiliate, used with permission.

of a clear focus on customers. Its stores and website give a remarkable statement about its commitments to customer relationships and the quality of its products. The Tilley guarantee for its legendary hats has always been an unconditional one: "Tilley Hats will be replaced free if they ever wear out, mildew, or shrink." The same guarantee applies to some of their shorts, vests, jackets, pants, and skirts. They are replaced free if they ever wear out.[15]

The crucial point: Strategic directions must be customer-focused and provide genuine value and benefits to existing and prospective customers.

**Competencies** "What do we do best?" asks about an organization's competencies—an organization's special capabilities, including skills, technologies, and resources that distinguish it from other organizations. Exploiting these competencies can lead to success.[16] In Tilley's case, its competencies include an obsession with quality. To quote the founder Alex Tilley, "I'll make travel clothing! I'll make it the best in the world! And then I'll make it even better!" Tilley Endurables is one of the last remaining companies to manufacture all its products in Canada.[17]

**Competitors** After understanding your business internally, it is important to set your analysis externally. In today's global competition, the lines among competitive sectors are increasingly blurred. This may not be as evident in the apparel industry, but consider Loblaws. Loblaws competes directly with other supermarkets such as Sobeys. At the same time, it also competes against mass merchandisers such as Walmart

Supercentres, which also carry groceries, and it competes with warehouse clubs such as Costco. Loblaws also carries many pharmacy items, which puts it into direct competition with pharmacies such as Shoppers Drug Mart and Pharma Plus. Shoppers Drug Mart carries many lines of cosmetics, which puts it in direct competition with department stores such as Hudson's Bay, which traditionally carries cosmetics.

# GROWTH STRATEGIES: WHERE DO WE WANT TO GO?

Knowing where the organization is at the present time enables managers to set a direction for the firm and commit resources to move in that direction. Two techniques to aid in these decisions are the business portfolio analysis and the market-product analysis.

**Business Portfolio Analysis** Developed by the Boston Consulting Group (BCG), *business portfolio analysis* uses quantified performance measures and market growth rates to analyze a firm's strategic business units as though they were a collection of separate investments.[18] While used at the business unit level here, the BCG analysis has also been applied at the product line or individual product or brand level. This kind of portfolio analysis is very popular; most large firms have used it in some form.

BCG, a leading management consulting firm, advises its clients to locate the position of each of its SBUs on a growth-share matrix (Figure 15–3). The vertical axis is the *market growth rate,* which is the annual rate of growth of the specific market or industry in which a given SBU is competing. The horizontal axis is the *relative market share,* defined as the sales of the SBU divided by the sales of the largest firm in the industry.

BCG has given specific names and descriptions to the four resulting quadrants in its growth-share matrix based on the amount of cash they generate for or require from the firm:

- *Cash cows* are SBUs that typically generate large amounts of cash, far more than they can invest profitably in their own product line. They have a dominant share of a slow-growth market and provide cash to pay large amounts of company overhead and to invest in other SBUs.

- *Stars* are SBUs with a high share of high-growth markets that may need extra cash to finance their own rapid future growth. When their growth slows, they are likely to become cash cows.

- *Question marks* or *problem children* are SBUs with a low share of high-growth markets. They require large injections of cash just to maintain their market share, and even more to increase it. Their name implies management's dilemma for these SBUs: choosing the right ones to invest in and phasing out the rest.

- *Dogs* are SBUs with a low share of low-growth markets. Although they may generate enough cash to sustain themselves, they do not hold the promise of ever becoming real winners for the firm. Dropping SBUs that are dogs may be required, except when relationships with other SBUs, competitive considerations, or potential strategic alliances exist.[19]

**Market-Product Analysis** Firms can also view growth opportunities in terms of markets and products. Think of it this way: For any product, there is both a current market (consisting of existing customers) and a new market (consisting of potential customers). And for any market, there is a current product (what they're now using) and a new product (something they might use if it were developed). Four possible market-product strategies are shown in Figure 15–4.

As Unilever attempts to increase sales revenues of its Ben & Jerry's business, it must consider all four of the alternative market-product strategies shown in Figure 15–4. For example, it can try to use a strategy of *market penetration*—increasing sales of present products in its existing markets, in this case by increasing sales of Ben & Jerry's present ice cream products to consumers. There is no change in either the basic product line or the market served, but increased sales are possible—either

## Figure 15–3

Boston Consulting Group's growth-share matrix for a strong, diversified firm showing some strategic plans

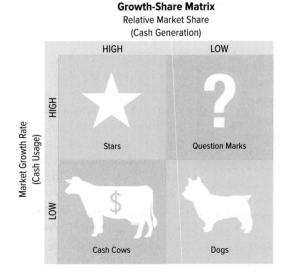

**Growth-Share Matrix**
Relative Market Share
(Cash Generation)

## Figure 15–4

Four market-product strategies: Alternative ways to expand sales revenues for Ben & Jerry's

| | Products | |
|---|---|---|
| **Markets** | **Current** | **New** |
| Current | **Market penetration** Selling more Ben & Jerry's super premium ice cream in North America | **Product development** Selling a new product such as frozen yogurt under the Ben & Jerry's brand in North America |
| New | **Market development** Selling Ben & Jerry's super premium ice cream in Brazil for the first time | **Diversification** Selling a new product such as breakfast cereal in China for the first time |

by selling more ice cream (through better promotion or distribution) or by selling the same amount of ice cream at a higher price to its existing customers.

*Market development* is a marketing strategy to sell current products to new markets. For Ben & Jerry's, Brazil is an attractive new market. There is good news and bad news for this strategy: As household incomes of Brazilians increase, consumers can buy more ice cream; however, the Ben & Jerry's brand may be unknown to Brazilian consumers.

An expansion strategy using *product development* involves selling a new product to existing markets. When Ben and Jerry's launched sorbet and frozen yogurt products, the firm was following a product development strategy. Figure 15–4 shows that the firm could try leveraging the Ben & Jerry's brand by selling its own frozen yogurt in North America.

*Diversification* involves developing new products and selling them in new markets. This is a potentially high-risk strategy for Ben & Jerry's—and for most firms—because the company has neither previous production experience nor marketing experience on which to draw. For example, in trying to sell a Ben & Jerry's brand of breakfast cereal in China, the company has expertise neither in producing cereals nor in marketing to consumers in China. Fast-food giant McDonald's has implemented diversification strategies to gauge success prior to introducing new product development in an established market. An example of this is its McCafé launch in Australia in 1993, many years before it came to North America.

Diversification can take different forms to open a company to new opportunities and threats. When Rogers purchased the Toronto Blue Jays, it got into a completely new area of business. Diversification can also consist of a company introducing a variation of a product to a new market. For example, McDonald's introduced product variations in India including the Veg McMuffin™ and the McVeggie™ to appeal to the high population of vegetarians.

### *ask* YOURSELF

1. *Why is it important to know what your competencies are?*

2. *How can you use business portfolio analysis to help improve your business?*

3. *What are the four market-product strategies?*

# THE STRATEGIC MARKETING PROCESS

**LO 5** The Marketing NewsFlash box, "The Netflix Launch and Its Continually Changing Business Model," describes how Netflix changed its business model to benefit from the digital age.[20] It is a great example of the strategic marketing process in action. In general, after an

McDonald's introduced McCafé in Australia, as well as the Veg McMuffin and the McVeggie in India, all examples of its diversification strategy.

© Alex Segre/Alamy Stock Photo

organization assesses where it's at and where it wants to go, it must work out how it will get there. Specifically, it must decide the following:

- How to allocate resources
- How to convert plans into actions
- How results compare with plans, and whether deviations (results that differ from expectations) require new plans and actions

This approach is used in the **strategic marketing process**, whereby an organization allocates its marketing mix resources to reach its target markets and achieve its goals. The strategic marketing process is so central to the activities of most organizations that they formalize it as a **marketing plan**, which is a road map for the marketing activities of an organization for a specified future period of time, such as one year or five years. The marketing plan is divided into three phases: planning, implementation, and evaluation (Figure 15–5).

See Appendix A for an example of a marketing plan, which also includes an executive summary.

This chapter's opening vignette focuses on the strategic marketing process for an information technology company supporting the financial services industry. Both profit and not-for-profit industries use this approach to help achieve their long-term visions and to satisfy stakeholders' requirements. The following sections give an overview of the marketing plan that puts Chapters 1 through 15 of this book in perspective.

# THE PLANNING PHASE OF THE MARKETING PLAN

As shown in Figure 15–5, the planning phase of the marketing plan consists of the three steps shown at the top of the figure: situation analysis, market-product focus and goal setting, and the marketing program. Let's use the recent marketing planning experiences of several companies to look at each of these steps.

**Figure 15–5**
Outline of a marketing plan

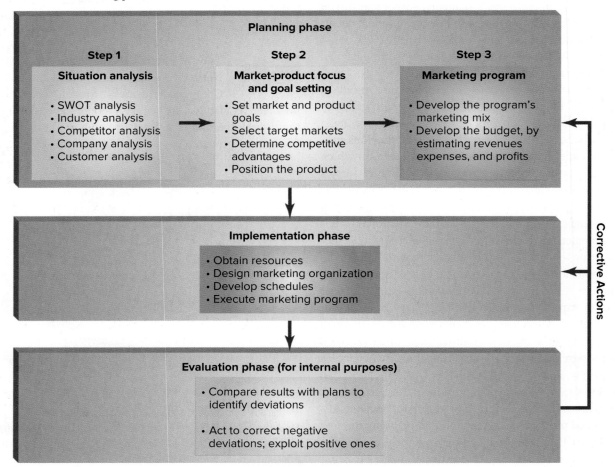

# The Netflix Launch and Its Continually Changing Business Model

I f in 1997 a customer had been charged a late fee of $40 for a VHS tape of *Apollo 13,* what might she or he have done? Maybe just grumble and pay it?

In the case of Reed Hastings, he was embarrassed, apparently paid the $40 late fee, and—this is where he's different—got to thinking that there's a big market out there. "So I started to investigate the idea of how to create a movie-rental business by mail," he told a *Fortune* magazine reviewer.

## The Original Business Model

"Early on, the first concept we launched was rental by mail, but it wasn't subscription-based so it worked more like Blockbuster," says Hastings, the founder and chief executive officer of Netflix. It wasn't very popular. So in 1999, he relaunched his idea with a new business model—as a subscription service, pretty much the mail business you see today. "We named the company Netflix, not DVDs by Mail, because we knew that eventually we would deliver movies directly over the Internet," Hastings says.

## Netflix's Changing Business Model

The Netflix DVDs-by-mail model delivered movies on DVD to customers for a fixed monthly fee—and drove Blockbuster to seek bankruptcy protection. But the Netflix business model changed over eight months in 2008: from "Watch Now," enabling subscribers to watch any of 1,000 streaming movies on a PC, to partnering with TiVo, Xbox, and others to enable their systems to let you see one of about 12,000 movies on your television.

The movie distribution channel has also expanded with web-ready TVs such as Sony's Bravia, game consoles such as Xbox 360, and tablets such as Apple's iPad.

With Netflix breaking a series of technology barriers, its "any movie, any time" business was just around the corner. In mid-2011, Netflix introduced controversial new pricing options: DVD only, streaming only, or both. Then in late-2011, when customer reaction exploded, Reed Hastings cancelled the plan to separate Netflix's DVD-by-mail business from its movie-streaming service. Change is a constant in the Netflix business model.

Netflix alters its "business model" to respond to changing consumer demand and technologies. Many organizations need to continually improve their businesses in order to stay ahead of the changes that are evident now and predicted for the future.

© Ian Dagnall/Alamy Stock Photo

In 2016, Netflix generated almost US$9 billion in revenue from its from domestic DVD sales, domestic streaming, and international streaming lines of business. Furthermore, the organization has begun creating its own content for its audiences. ●

## Questions

1. Netflix's leadership was able to foresee the change from watching movies on DVD to watching movies over the Internet. Why is foresight important when determining strategy.

2. What media do you access to get your news and entertainment? How can Netflix reach consumers like you?

---

**Step 1: Situation Analysis** The essence of a **situation analysis** is taking stock of the firm's or product's past performance, where it is now, and where it is headed in light of the organization's plans and the external factors and trends affecting it. The situation analysis box in Figure 15–5 is the first of the three steps in the planning phase.

Step 1 starts with a *SWOT analysis,* which describes an organization's appraisal of its internal **S**trengths and **W**eaknesses and its external **O**pportunities and **T**hreats. Both the situation and SWOT analyses can be done at the level of the entire organization, the business unit, the product line, or the specific product. As an analysis moves from the level of the entire organization to the specific product, it, of course, gets far more detailed. For small firms or

**situation analysis**
Taking stock of a firm's or product's past performance, where it is now, and where it is headed.

*A SWOT analysis helps a firm identify the strategy-related factors that can have a major effect on the firm.*

One of Ben & Jerry's 75 flavours of ice cream.

Keith Homan/ Shutterstock.com

those with basically a single product line, an analysis at the firm or product level is really the same thing.

Let's assume you are the Unilever vice president responsible for integrating Ben & Jerry's into Unilever's business. You might do the SWOT analysis shown in Figure 15–6. Note that your SWOT table has four cells formed by the combination of internal versus external factors (the rows) and favourable versus unfavourable factors (the columns) that summarize Ben & Jerry's strengths, weaknesses, opportunities, and threats.

A SWOT analysis helps a firm identify the strategy-related factors in these four cells that can have a major effect on the firm. The goal is not simply to develop the SWOT analysis but to translate the results of the analysis into specific actions to help the firm grow and succeed. The ultimate goal is to identify the critical factors affecting the firm and then build on vital strengths, correct glaring weaknesses, exploit significant opportunities, and avoid or prepare for disaster-laden threats. That is a big order.

The Ben and Jerry's SWOT analysis in Figure 15–6 can be the basis for these kinds of specific actions. An action in each of the four cells might be as follows:

- *Build on a strength.* Find specific efficiencies in distribution with Unilever's existing ice cream brands.

- *Correct a weakness.* Recruit experienced managers from other consumer product firms to help stimulate growth.

- *Exploit an opportunity.* Develop a new line of low-fat yogurts to respond to consumer health concerns.

- *Avoid or prepare for a disaster-laden threat.* Focus on less risky international markets, such as Mexico.

The next areas to consider in step 1 are as follows:

- The *industry analysis* section focuses on the industry and trends.

- The *competitor analysis* section looks at the firm's competitors.

- The *company analysis* section provides details of the company itself.

- The *customer analysis* section addresses the question: Who are the customers of the firm's products?

## Figure 15–6
Ben & Jerry's: A SWOT analysis

| Location of Factor | Type of Factor | | | |
|---|---|---|---|---|
| | **Favourable** | | **Unfavourable** | |
| **Internal** | **Strengths** | | **Weaknesses** | |
| | • Prestigious, well-known brand name among North American consumers | | • Danger that B&J's social responsibility actions may add costs, reduce focus on core business | |
| | • Major share of the super premium ice cream market | | • Need for experienced managers to help growth | |
| | • Can complement Unilever's existing ice cream brands | | • Flat sales and profits in recent years | |
| | • Widely recognized for its social responsibility actions | | | |
| **External** | **Opportunities** | | **Threats** | |
| | • Growing demand for quality ice cream in overseas markets | | • Consumer concern with fatty desserts; B&J customers are the type who read new government-ordered nutritional labels | |
| | • Increasing demand for frozen yogurt and other low-fat desserts | | • Competes with Haagen-Dazs brand | |
| | • Success of many firms in extending successful brand in one product category to others | | • Increased competition in international markets | |

**Step 2: Market-Product Focus and Goal Setting** Determining which products will be directed toward which customers (step 2 of the planning phase in Figure 15–5) is essential for developing an effective marketing program (step 3). This decision is often based on *market segmentation*, which involves considering prospective buyers in terms of groups, or segments. These groups have common needs and will respond similarly to a marketing program. Ideally, a firm can use market segmentation to identify the segments on which it will focus its efforts—its target market segments—and develop one or more marketing programs to reach them.

Goal setting involves setting measurable marketing objectives to be achieved. For organizations launching recruitment marketing campaign, the objective is applications and hires. Entertainment companies such as Netflix measure the number of members as well as the number of hours of television shows and movies that are downloaded. An organization selling apparel, such as Tilley Endurables, sets objectives for its product categories and offerings. When viewing the entire marketing program, objectives are often a series of actions to be implemented over several years.

Using the marketing plan outline shown in Figure 15–5, step 2 can be illustrated using Sleep Country Canada as an example:

- *Set market and product goals.* Based on listening to what is important to customers, Sleep Country Canada offers lots of choice in mattresses. It also makes each experience before, during, and after the sale an enjoyable one for the customer. One of its market goals may be to increase its market share by a certain percentage in the retailing mattress business in Canada. It's important to quantify the percentage so that the company can measure whether it successfully meets its goals.

- *Select target markets.* Sleep Country Canada targets consumers who want a quality mattress as well as a positive customer service experience.

- *Determine competitive advantages.* **Competitive advantages** are those characteristics of a product that make it superior to competing substitutes. Sleep Country Canada offers the mattress purchaser an enjoyable customer service experience unparalleled in this market. It offers clean, bright stores; sleep experts who put the customer's comfort and budget needs first; and courteous delivery people.

- *Position the product.* Sleep Country Canada is positioned as a mattress specialist that offers quality products with the added benefit of courteous and knowledgeable staff, an attractive in-store setting, and a convenient delivery service.

Details in these four elements of step 2 provide a solid foundation to use in developing the marketing program—the next step in the planning phase of the marketing plan.

---

## Ben & Jerry's Non-Dairy Debut

In Canada, Ben & Jerry's offers three new non-dairy, almond-based frozen treats in order to adapt to the changing dietary needs of consumers. There are additional flavours available in the United States.

1. Chocolate Fudge Brownie
2. P.B. Cookies
3. Coffee Caramel Fudge

Source: "Non-Dairy Pints," Ben & Jerry's website, accessed February 2017 at http://www.benjerry.com/flavors/non-dairy; "Ben & Jerry's Canada Debuts 3 New Non-Dairy Frozen Treat Flavors," *Canadify,* February 22, 2017, http://canadify.com/2017/02/22 /ben-jerrys-canada-debuts-3-new-non-dairy-frozen-treat-flavors/.

---

**Step 3: Marketing Program** Activities in step 2 tell the marketing manager which customers to target and which customer needs the firm's product offerings can satisfy—the *who* and *what* aspects of the marketing plan. The *how* aspect—step 3 in the marketing plan—involves developing the program's marketing mix and its budget.

Figure 15–7 shows components of each marketing mix element that are combined to provide a cohesive marketing program. For Sleep Country Canada, the marketing mix activities can include the following:

- **Product strategy:** Offer consumers one of the largest selections of top, name-brand mattresses.

- **Price strategy:** Offer consumers a low-price guarantee. If consumers find a comparable product at a competitor that is equal to or lower than Sleep Country Canada's price, the company will beat that figure by 5 percent.

- **Promotion strategy:** Sleep Country Canada uses mass media advertising to communicate its unique retail experience to prospective and current customers.

- **Place (distribution) strategy:** Sleep Country Canada is conveniently located in six Canadian provinces with 240 stores in total.

Putting a marketing program into effect requires that the firm commit time and money to it, prepare a sales forecast, and establish a budget that must be approved by top management. In some organizations, this is referred to as financial data and projections.

**competitive advantages**
Those characteristics of a product or service that make it superior to competing substitutes.

**Figure 15–7**

Elements of the marketing mix that comprise a cohesive marketing program

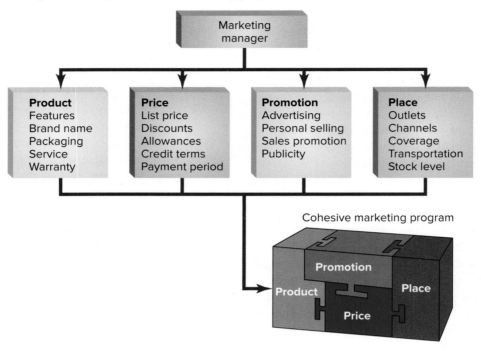

# THE IMPLEMENTATION PHASE OF THE MARKETING PLAN

A firm's marketing plan is the result of the many hours spent in the planning phase of the strategic marketing process. Implementation, the second phase of the marketing plan, involves implementing the marketing program that emerges from the planning phase. An organization needs to invest time and resources into the planning phase of the marketing plan, but just as is important is the implementation phase. The implementation phase is the part of the process that executes the individual tactics that support the marketing strategy. Figure 15–5 shows the four components of the implementation phase: obtaining resources, designing the marketing organization, developing schedules, and actually executing the marketing program designed in the planning phase.

**Obtaining Resources** Most companies have numerous options for growth. But such growth requires an investment. Corporate leadership within an organization determines the best options for growth and how they should be funded. Tying back to the three levels within an organization, it can sometimes be challenging to get support from all stakeholders. Ideally, this part of the process is already introduced during the planning phase and is more of a formality at this point.

**Designing the Marketing Organization** A marketing program needs marketing staff to implement it. Figure 15–8 shows the organization chart of a typical manufacturing firm, giving some details of the marketing department's structure. Four managers of marketing activities are shown to report to the vice president of marketing. Several regional sales managers and an international sales manager may report to the manager of sales. This marketing organization is responsible for converting marketing plans to reality.

**Developing Schedules** Effective implementation requires developing appropriate schedules and

## Figure 15-8

Organization of a typical manufacturing firm, showing a breakdown of the marketing department

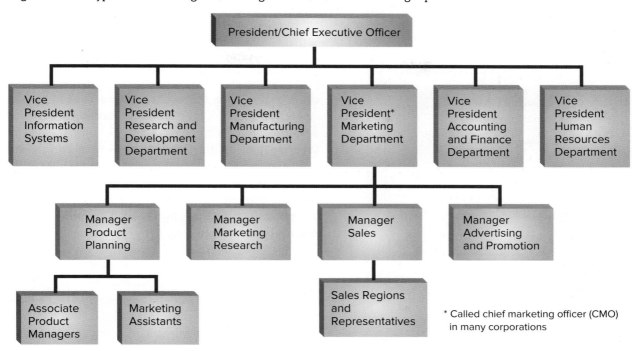

*Called chief marketing officer (CMO) in many corporations

determining specific deadlines for the creation and execution of marketing activities. For example, if a company wants to place an ad in the *Globe and Mail's Report on Business* magazine, it must reserve space a month prior to the date that the ad appears in the magazine. Also, the company must allow time for creating and producing the ad. Digital advertising allows for shorter advanced notice and tweaks to the creative process.

**Executing the Marketing Program**  Marketing plans are meaningless unless they are put into action. This requires attention to detail to both marketing strategies and marketing tactics. A **marketing strategy** is the means by which a marketing goal is to be achieved, usually characterized by a specified target market and a marketing program to reach it. Although the term strategy is often used loosely, it implies both the end sought (target market) and the means to achieve it (marketing program).

To implement a marketing program successfully, hundreds of detailed decisions are often required, such as writing ads or setting prices. These decisions, called **marketing tactics**, are detailed day-to-day operational decisions essential to the overall success of marketing strategies.

## THE EVALUATION PHASE OF THE MARKETING PLAN

The evaluation phase of the marketing plan is used to determine if the plan is moving in the right direction. The marketing manager compares the results of the marketing activities with the goals laid out in the marketing plan to identify deviations and to act on these deviations—correcting negative deviations and exploiting positive ones. Dashboards displaying marketing metrics will allow decisions makers to determine the next step.

**Identifying Deviations**  At this point of the marketing plan, dashboards and marketing metrics help evaluate the marketing plan. When a company sets goals and then compares them to actual results, it needs to research the reasons for the differences. Where plans are exceeded, the company determines the drivers of this success and identifies ways to build on them as it moves forward. When there is a shortfall (actual results less than planned—often referred

**marketing strategy**
Means by which a marketing goal is to be achieved.

**marketing tactics**
Detailed day-to-day operational decisions essential to the overall success of marketing strategies.

# Infographic

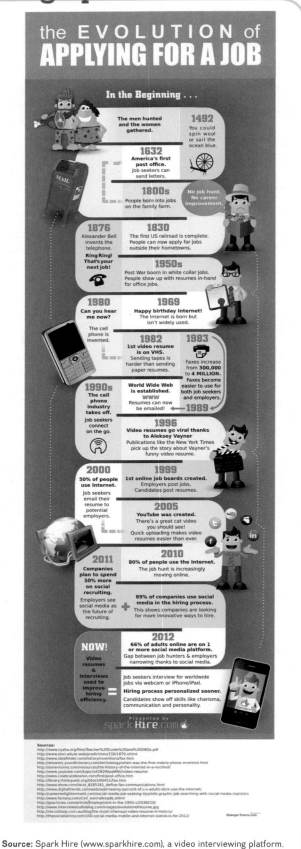

Source: Spark Hire (www.sparkhire.com), a video interviewing platform.

to as the *planning gap*), the company has to "fill in" this planning gap with a revised marketing program and possibly revised goals.

**Acting on Deviations** Generally speaking, results of a marketing plan will not be exactly as anticipated. Sometimes, the marketing program falls short of its goals. When this occurs, managers need to take corrective action. This is called *correcting a negative deviation.* For example, if Sleep Country Canada is experiencing less-than-desired sales from an Internet campaign, it may re-evaluate where they are advertising. Alternatively, when actual results are far better than the plan called for, creative managers find ways to exploit the situation. This is called *exploiting a positive deviation.* Continuing with the example, if Sleep Country Canada's sales are more than expected from certain digital media ads, it may consider investing more money into that part of the marketing program.

Whether an organization is selling ice cream, box-spring mattresses, or the opportunity to work at the company, technology impacts its strategic marketing process. The Infographic entitled "The Evolution of Applying for a Job" shares how job seekers changed the way they look for. Companies use this insight to review their recruitment marketing strategies. Furthermore, organizations focused on the strategic marketing process know that the business world is changing. Not only can we review results through dashboards quicker, but our world is changing so that strategy and marketing plans need to change with it.

## ask YOURSELF

1. *How would you distinguish a marketing strategy from a marketing tactic?*

2. *Describe the four components of the implementation phase of the marketing plan.*

**LO 1** • Large corporations can be complex. This complexity among business firms and not-for-profit organizations requires the division into three functional levels: the corporate, business unit, and functional levels.

- At the *corporate level,* top management directs overall strategy for the entire organization.
- The *business unit level* has business unit managers set the direction for individual products and markets.
- At the *functional level,* each business unit has marketing and other specialized activities such as finance, manufacturing, or human resources.

**LO 2** • Businesses exist for various purposes and establish missions and goals. A business's mission is the statement of its direction. Goals are the targets the organization has set to be achieved within a specific time frame.

- Missions and goals are important to businesses as they help them establish direction and maintain their course.

**LO 3** • In order to gauge the success of a marketing program, managers use marketing dashboards and marketing metrics to determine the performance of various elements of the marketing plan.

**LO 4** • An organization develops its strategy and direction by first understanding its current status. This involves asking "Where are we now?" to assess the organization's customers, competencies, and competitors. Asking "Where do we want to go" with techniques such as portfolio analysis and market-product analysis also help develop strategy. Furthermore, questions like "How will we get there?" helps create the marketing plan.

**LO 5** • The strategic marketing process involves an organization allocating its marketing mix resources to reach its target markets using three phases: planning, implementation, and evaluation.

- The planning phase of the marketing plan has three steps, each with more specific elements: situation (SWOT) analysis, market-product focus and goal setting, and marketing program.
- The implementation phase of the marketing plan has four key elements: obtaining resources, designing the marketing organization, developing schedules, and executing the marketing program.
- The evaluation phase of the marketing plan is used for internal purposes and involves comparing results with the planned targets to identify deviations and take actions to correct negative deviations and exploit positive ones.

*key terms and concepts...* **A REFRESHER**

competitive advantages
goals (objectives)
marketing dashboard
marketing metric

marketing plan
marketing strategy
marketing tactics
mission

profit
situation analysis
strategic marketing process
strategy

*hands-on...* **APPLY YOUR KNOWLEDGE**

**Strategic Marketing Planning Assignment** SeeWhy Learning developed its business through strategic planning and marketing. It now offers training solutions to financial services organizations. This chapter's opening vignette discusses components of the strategic planning process.

Assume you have a business that can make financial services companies across Canada more efficient in marketing to their customers. Using the ideas from the vignette and Figure 15–5 as a guide, outline a strategic marketing plan to gain more businesses as clients.

In this chapter's opening vignette, we learn how companies may partner with outside organizations to deliver specific training to their associates. Although the audience and desired result would be different, the strategic marketing process used in the vignette can also be used to develop loyal customers. Answer the Reality Check questions at the end of the vignette by reviewing the strategic marketing process in detail throughout the chapter.

The Infographic illustrates how the job application process has changed over the years. Companies need to be able to adjust their recruitment strategy to adapt to these new processes that are being adopted by candidates. Using more recent insights about job-seeking tactics, add them as extensions to the Infographic and suggest what future evolution recruitment advertisers may need to be ready for.

# Building an Effective Marketing Plan

**W**hen reviewing marketing plans of organizations, there are noticeable variations in strategy from company to company. Sustainability and greening are important to many, while market share are the priority of others. As established in the opening vignette in Chapter 15, SeeWhy Learning partners with financial services organizations to train talented individuals that require industry licensing. SeeWhy Learning's team is engaged when an organization needs expertise outside of its employee and executive base. A marketing plan is an excellent document to capture the marketing strategies and tactics of this organization.

Silvrshootr/E+/Getty Images

Marketing plans vary in strategy and can also vary in format. For small to medium-size businesses, if a marketing plan seems like an ominous task, consultants like Glenn Cressman of Share of Marketing can help. Glenn develops marketing plans for small to medium-size businesses and explains, "Every plan is customized to the needs of the business." There are some definite elements necessary to create a robust plan. "A good marketing plan identifies opportunities and uses practical, action-oriented tactics to capitalize on them."[1]

Applying Glenn's marketing plan framework, we can create a hypothetical example for SeeWhy Learning. In this example, we illustrate each component of the strategic marketing process, including potential examples of corrective actions. Although plans may deviate from this outline, generally there is a planning phase, an implementation phase, and an evaluation phase. In planning, marketers complete a situation analysis, decide on a market-product focus and goal setting, and then create a marketing program.

Small to medium-size businesses may be constrained by human and financial resources. Creating an effective marketing plan can allow the business to see more results in an efficient and effective manner. Following the marketing plan outline presented in Chapter 15, this section suggests some guidelines for creating an effective marketing plan.

# SAMPLE MARKETING PLAN FOR SEEWHY LEARNING

This is a **hypothetical** illustration of what SeeWhy Learning's marketing plan could look like. This plan is brief, given the hypothetical scenario and is not SeeWhy Learning's actual marketing plan, although it does identify key elements that are required to provide clear direction to an organization. Marketing plans can be more robust so long as the information provided enhances the strategy for the reviewer.

## 1. EXECUTIVE SUMMARY

The following marketing plan outlines strategies and tactics for SeeWhy Learning, an information technology company offering training solutions across Canada. The organization is located in Milton, Ontario. Despite being located outside of Toronto's financial district, SeeWhy Learning can service clients across Canada (or even globally) as most of its training solutions are offered remotely via online deliverables.

SeeWhy Learning has had success offering training and development solutions to financial services organizations, with preparatory study tools for over 20 different industry examinations, including securities, insurance, and even real estate licensing exams. SeeWhy Learning has ramped up training resources to some of the larger advisory companies in the investment industry. As the organization has grown, profits are reinvested into the company's infrastructure. SeeWhy Learning's goal is to reach its target client businesses in a cost-effective manner.

SeeWhy Learning is certain that financial advisory businesses in Canada will continue to have challenges with training recruits in challenging industry examinations. Regulatory requirements and exams tend to become *more* difficult with time, not easier.

Whether it is an entry-level examination or one with more complex concepts, the SeeWhy Learning offering addresses the business issues by clearly understanding the clients' needs. Its comprehensive and flexible solution allows customers to focus on their strengths and expertise while receiving access to exceptional training.

## 2. COMPANY DESCRIPTION

Established in 2008, SeeWhy Learning began offering preparation tools to the financial services industry, and a few years later, it expanded to also support the real estate licensing exams in Ontario. As industry examinations become more challenging, more organizations are deciding to outsource the examination preparation process. SeeWhy Learning is able to win more business with a client-centric service approach and added-value ancillary services.

According to the Government of Canada, Canada has one of "the strongest financial services sectors in the world." Target companies for SeeWhy Learning to partner with include banks, credit unions, securities dealers, and independent insurance agencies and brokers. SeeWhy Learning has expanded its team to service its growing client base. The staff is known for being able to provide support to new industry registrants in a consultative and collaborative fashion. Team members are experts in their field, but they make technical and non-technical clients alike feel comfortable with their approach.

This marketing plan describes how SeeWhy Learning can expand its presence within the financial services industry. It involves marketing strategies and tactics appropriate for an organization needing to maximize its resources.

# 3. STRATEGIC FOCUS AND PLAN

CORE VALUES   The core values of SeeWhy Learning are as follows:

1. To provide a continuously improving and learning environment for clients and team members.
2. To offer exceptional advice and service to its clients.

MISSION   The mission of SeeWhy Learning is to become the training partner for financial services advisory businesses, tailoring training solutions to the size of the business it is working with. This involves creating a collaborative and social environment among the company and the organizations that SeeWhy Learning serves.

NON-FINANCIAL OBJECTIVES

1. Open a satellite office in western Canada by December 2020 in order to better serve that market. Currently, SeeWhy Learning services these clients quite well by scheduling client meetings in western Canada on a regular and as needed basis.

2. Be recognized as the top training partner in the financial services industry.

FINANCIAL OBJECTIVES

1. Increase revenues by 10 to 15 percent on an annual basis.
2. Retain 20 percent of annual profits within the business to finance future growth. Historically, SeeWhy Learning has grown using internally generated funds instead of taking on corporate debt.

COMPETENCIES AND COMPETITIVE ADVANTAGE   The core competency of SeeWhy Learning is the expertise of its founders and the talent that they have hired. Essentially, its people are on the cutting edge of the financial services industry and are able to provide innovative, cost-effective training solutions for its clients. Given its size, SeeWhy Learning has mobility and flexibility in decision-making.

# 4. SWOT AND MARKET ANALYSIS

SWOT ANALYSIS   The SWOT analysis is summarized in Figure A-1. It shows internal and external factors that can affect the organization's success. The following statements help summarize the organization's situation:

**Figure A–1**
SeeWhy Learning SWOT Analysis

| Location of Factor | Type of Factor | |
| --- | --- | --- |
| | Favourable | Unfavourable |
| **Internal** | **Strengths**<br>• Success-based guarantee adds value to clients.<br>• Able to grow the client base and employees in line with corporate culture. | **Weaknesses**<br>• Running a lean team keeps costs down but additional resources may be required with rapid growth.<br>• Limited marketing budget as compared to larger training companies.<br>• Competitive market. |
| **External** | **Opportunities**<br>• Thousands of prospective corporate and retail clients.<br>• Continued growth in Ontario and western Canada. | **Threats**<br>• Larger companies are better equipped to compete on price.<br>• Clients' needs may become more demanding, requiring face-to-face training. |

- *SeeWhy Learning has an unmatched service offering.* Unlike its competitors, SeeWhy Learning offers a success guarantee on many of its training programs.

- *SeeWhy Learning is in a competitive marketplace.* Training companies have a low barrier to entry and continually enter the marketplace. SeeWhy Learning's biggest threat is that larger companies could attempt to beat it on price. To guard against this, SeeWhy runs a lean organization, which is why its head office is located in the suburbs and not downtown Toronto. This allows it to compete on price if required; however, it prefers to compete on quality.

- *SeeWhy Learning has the opportunity to grow nationally.* With well-established customers, and academic partners such as the IFSE Institute, the organization has the opportunity to expand its client base across Canada and find more target customers.

INDUSTRY ANALYSIS According to the Toronto Financial Services Alliance, "The Toronto region is home to over 40 percent of all financial services headquarters employment in Canada, including two of the world's largest life insurers."

SeeWhy Learning can continue to build its network in the Toronto area, understanding that there are more opportunities across Canada for expansion.

COMPETITIVE ANALYSIS SeeWhy Learning has several competitors, ranging from "Mom-and-Pop" type training outfits to larger organizations. Given the nature of the solutions, competitors outside of Ontario may also come into play. In order to compete in this marketplace, SeeWhy Learning needs to keep each proposal client-centric. It also has to perform nimbly enough to adjust to the competitive proposals. By focusing on its local clientele, SeeWhy Learning can definitely offer the benefit of more on-site presence than some of the larger, global organizations that may begin targeting its client base.

CUSTOMER ANALYSIS The ideal clients of SeeWhy Learning are financial services advisory businesses that either are growing the number of advisors or need to recruit and train replacement advisors. A company's stage in its life cycle will help determine the breadth of services sought from SeeWhy Learning. Businesses in Toronto that are in the growth stage of their life cycle are prime targets for SeeWhy Learning's services. These businesses have begun to generate income for their organization, and they need to focus on their core competencies for continued growth. By engaging SeeWhy Learning as a partner, they can expand their training expertise without having to invest as much to build their own training infrastructure.

# 5. MARKET-PRODUCT FOCUS AND GOAL SETTING

ONE-YEAR MARKETING OBJECTIVES

1. Improve brand awareness, specifically within the Greater Toronto Area as well as western Canada.

2. Increase market share, specifically in Toronto, where the majority of target customers have head office locations.

MARKETING AND PRODUCT OBJECTIVES SeeWhy Learning plans to take full advantage of its market potential in Canada while also considering expansion into the U.S. market. This plan is outlined in three areas below:

- **Established markets:** SeeWhy Learning will service and grow its existing client base with the intent of expanding its offering into new leading-edge training services.

- **New markets:** SeeWhy Learning will build the foundation for expansion into the U.S. This will involving building out prospective client lists while servicing its existing client base.

- **New services:** SeeWhy Learning will expand its exam preparatory service offering to include mobile technology.

POINTS OF DIFFERENCE SeeWhy Learning will have two distinguishing characteristics when compared to its competitors:

1. A success-based guarantee on specific training packages.

2. Easy access to the co-founders and/or senior staff.

POSITIONING In the exam preparatory marketplace, there are three areas that add value to clients: (1) operational excellence (cost-effective training solutions), (2) product leadership (best product), and (3) customer intimacy (truly customized service, based on deep customer knowledge). While it is imperative to be competent in all three disciplines, it is impossible to be viewed as superior in all three, since the market inherently distinguishes among all three. SeeWhy Learning is positioning itself to offer more customer intimacy than the larger consulting firms, while having greater operational excellence and product leadership than other consulting firms of its size. The company's ability to be nimble, while still offering advice at the same level of expertise of large consulting firms, positions it perfectly to the businesses it wants to serve.

# 6. MARKETING PROGRAM

**PRODUCT STRATEGY**  SeeWhy Learning will service and grow its existing client base with the intent of expanding its training offering into new leading-edge digital services.

**PRICE STRATEGY**  SeeWhy Learning plans to offer at-market pricing for its services. It will price-match firms of similar or smaller size. For bids against larger firms, the pricing strategy is to provide value-added services while maintaining a firm price. This is especially true when pursuing medium-size businesses with reasonable brand recognition.

**PROMOTION STRATEGY**  There are a number of initiatives that SeeWhy Learning can undertake to promote its business. These initiatives include pull and push marketing strategies that will enhance personal selling. Given the limited budget, the following is a marketing tactics list, recommended in order of priority:

1. Website upgrade
2. High-quality video production
3. Trade show booth
4. QR codes
5. Hard-copy marketing materials
6. Soft-copy marketing materials
7. YouTube channel
8. Twitter
9. Google pay-per-click marketing
10. LinkedIn

**PLACE STRATEGY**  Most SeeWhy Learning employees reside in or near the Halton or Peel regions. This makes accessibility for clients manageable. Servicing the Greater Toronto Area is also possible from the Milton office location, which also keeps down rental costs.

# 7. SALES FORECAST

As a privately held corporation, SeeWhy Learning does not publicly report sales and profitability figures. However, it reportedly strives to grow annual sales by an average of 10 to 15 percent per annum.

## Figure A–2
Marketing Budget
The marketing budget for year one is limited to $35,000.

| Marketing Costs | Budget |
|---|---|
| Website upgrade | $20,000 |
| Content production costs (e.g., video) | $40,000 |
| Advertising - print | $ 5,000 |
| Advertising - online | $ 7,500 |
| Give-away items | $ 5,000 |
| Entertainment | $ 5,000 |
| **Marketing Budget - Year One** | **$82,500** |

# 8. IMPLEMENTATION PLAN

**MARKETING ORGANIZATION**  Each quarter, in his capacity as sales director, Cory Snyder will lead his sales team to identify and reach out to five prospective corporate clients, with the goal of building a client relationship with at least one of them. These are usually warm leads as the sales team identifies companies whose employees are already purchasing SeeWhy Learning tools through its retail delivery channels. It turns the contact from a "sales call" to an opportunity to save the company's employees money through corporate pricing. During these sales calls, academic director Andre Samuels is responsible for listening to the client's needs and then working with the training team to offer an effective solution.

**MARKETING BUDGET**  Figure A-2 presents the marketing budget for year one of the plan implementation.

**MARKETING ACTIVITIES PLAN**  The marketing activities plan will consist of the various activities outlined in the promotion strategy and the personal selling activities of the sales team. All marketing materials and media placements need to be ready by December 2019.

# 9. EVALUATION PLAN

SeeWhy Learning will prepare an annual budget. Actual sales and expenses will be compared to the figures, and variances will be investigated and identified. Weekly sales activities and successes will also be tracked.

# Glossary

**actual product**  The physical good or the services that a consumer purchases.

**adoption curve**  The sequential diffusion and acceptance of an innovation into the market by consumers.

**advergaming**  Placing ads in online or offline video games.

**advertising**  Paid form of media used for non-personal communication to consumers about an organization, good, service, or idea.

**affiliate marketing**  When companies promote their businesses through a network of online associates (affiliates) to drive traffic, leads, and purchases.

**analytics**  The process of taking metrics data and applying smart thinking and technology to gain actionable insights that can help make better business decisions.

**attitude**  Tendency to respond to something in a consistently favourable or unfavourable way.

**augmented product**  The additional features and attributes that accompany a product.

**baby boomers**  Generation of people born between 1946 and 1965.

**back translation**  Retranslating a word or phrase back into the original language by a different interpreter to catch errors.

**banner ads**  Online ads that can stretch across the top of a web page or be formatted in various sizes, such as leaderboards, rectangles, big boxes, and skyscrapers.

**behaviouristics**  How and why consumers buy and use a product, including the desired product benefits, how frequently they buy, where they buy, and whether consumers are brand loyal in their purchase behaviour.

**beliefs**  Consumer's perceptions of how a product or brand performs.

**big data**  Massive amounts of data from traditional and online sources that are used for ongoing analysis.

**binge viewing**  Watching complete or partial seasons of TV shows over a few days.

**blog**  A website in the form of an online diary that is used by organizations and individuals to post updates that include personal opinions, activities, and experiences with readers able to subscribe and post comments.

**Bluetooth**  Low-power radio waves that are transmitted though beacons and wirelessly transfer text, images, and audio or video data through a local hotspot to Bluetooth-enabled and -activated devices.

**brand**  A name, phrase, symbol, or design uniquely given by a company to a product to distinguish it from the competition.

**brand development index (BDI)**  An index that shows how well a brand's sales are developed in a region relative to the region's population size.

**brand equity**  The value of a brand that results from the favourable exposure, interactions, associations, and experiences that consumers have with a brand over time.

**brand extension**  When new goods or services are introduced under an existing flagship brand name.

**brand loyalty**  Favourable attitude toward and consistent purchase of a single brand over time; the degree of target market commitment toward a brand over time that results in varying levels of purchase commitment.

**brand personality**  A set of human characteristics associated with a brand.

**branded entertainment**  The creation of an entertainment program, such as a TV episode, that is highly focused on a brand in exchange for payment.

**breadth of product line**  The variety of different items a store carries.

**break-even analysis**  Examines the relationship between total revenue and total cost to determine profitability at different levels of output.

**brokers**  Independent firms or individuals whose main function is to bring buyers and sellers together to make sales.

**business analysis**  Financial projections on the impact of bringing the new product to market and selling it in the future.

**business market**  Products that are purchased either to run a business or to be used as a component in another product or service.

**business marketing**  Marketing to firms, governments, or non-profit organizations.

**business products**  Products that are purchased either to run a business or to be used as a component in another product or service.

**buy classes**  Three types of organizational buying situations: straight rebuy, modified rebuy, or new buy.

**buying centre**  Group of people in an organization who participate in the buying process.

**causal research**  Research designed to identify cause-and-effect relationships among variables.

**central business district**  The oldest retail setting, the community's downtown area.

**channel conflict**  Arises when one channel member believes another channel member is engaged in behaviour that prevents it from achieving its goals.

**commercialization**  When the new product is brought to market with full-scale production, sales, and marketing support.

**common short codes (CSC)**  Dedicated short messaging codes of typically five to six digits that are used to trigger subscriptions, donations, alerts, or downloads, or to access promotional content.

**community shopping centre** Retail location that typically has one primary store and 20 to 40 smaller outlets, serving a population of consumers within a 2- to 5-km drive.

**competitive advantages** Those characteristics of a product or service that make it superior to competing substitutes.

**competitive forces** Alternative products that can satisfy a specific market's needs.

**concept tests** External evaluations of a new product idea, rather than the actual product itself.

**consumer behaviour** Actions a person takes when purchasing and using products and services.

**consumer market** Goods, services, and ideas that a person can purchase, use, or support for personal use.

**consumer products** Products purchased for their personal use by the ultimate consumer.

**consumer promotions** Short-term marketing tools used to encourage immediate consumer purchase.

**content marketing** Creating and sharing expertise, information, or branded content that is designed to inform and engage with tools such as research papers, e-books, infographics, how-to videos, blogs, webinars, e-newsletters, case studies, and events that can readily be found with search engines.

**continuous innovations** New products with more than just a minor product improvement, but that do not require radical changes by the consumer.

**convenience products** Items purchased frequently that are inexpensive and require minimum risk and shopping effort.

**copyrights** Used to legally protect original written works, sound recordings, or forms of communication from being copied by others.

**core product** The fundamental benefit that a consumer derives from having the product.

**corporate social responsibility (CSR)** When organizations voluntarily consider the well-being of society by taking responsibility for how their businesses impact consumers, customers, suppliers, employees, shareholders, communities, the environment, and society in general.

**corporate websites** Websites that provide company and brand information to consumers and the media.

**cost per acquisition (CPA)** The cost of acquiring a new follower or sale.

**cost per click (CPC)** The cost of getting someone to click on a link or ad.

**cost per thousand (CPM)** The cost of reaching 1,000 people.

**cross-channel shopper** An online consumer who researches products online and then purchases them at a retail store.

**cross-cultural analysis** Study of similarities and differences among consumers in two or more societies.

**cultural symbols** Objects, ideas, or processes that represent a particular group of people or society.

**culture** A set of values, ideas, and attitudes that are learned and shared among the members of a group.

**Customer Advocacy Funnel** A communications approach that takes consumers from initial product awareness through to brand advocacy.

**customer experience management (CEM)** Managing customer interactions with the goal of increasing satisfaction and loyalty.

**customer lifetime value** The potential sales that will be generated by a customer if that customer remains loyal to that company for a lifetime.

**customer relationship management (CRM)** The overall process of building and maintaining profitable customer relationships by delivering superior customer value and satisfaction.

**customer value proposition** The unique combination of benefits received by targeted buyers that will satisfy their needs; includes quality, price, convenience, delivery, and both before-sale and after-sale service.

**customs** Norms and expectations about the way people do things in a specific country or culture.

**dashboards** The visualization of data and key performance indicators using graphs, charts, and numbers so that numerical information tells a story that is insightful and easy to use and understand.

**data mining** The processing of large amounts of data using sophisticated software to find insightful correlations and patterns that lead to better business decisions.

**data warehouse** A central repository of an organization's electronically stored data.

**database marketing** The use of databases to customize communications to customers and potential customers for the purpose of promoting a product or service.

**delete** When a company discontinues a product.

**demand curve** Graph relating quantity sold and price, which shows how many units will be sold at a given price.

**demographics** The statistical data on a population according to characteristics such as gender, age, ethnicity, income, education, and occupation.

**depth of product line** The assortment of products within each product line.

**derived demand** Demand for industrial products and services driven by demand for consumer products and services.

**descriptive analytics** A type of analytics that focuses on what has happened.

**descriptive research** Research designed to describe basic characteristics of a given population or to clarify its usage and attitudes.

**development** The new product idea is turned into a prototype for further consumer research and manufacturing tests.

**digital marketing** Using digital technology to reach consumers through computers, gaming devices, out-of-home electronic screens, or mobile devices such as smartphones and tablets.

**direct competitors**  Similar products sold in the same category.

**direct response marketing**  A tool designed to communicate with consumers in a targeted and personalized way using either traditional or online approaches.

**discretionary income**  Money that consumers have left after paying taxes and buying necessities.

**disintermediation**  Vertical channel conflict that arises when a channel member bypasses another member and sells directly to consumers.

**display advertising**  The use of online ads with graphics or animation that are placed on websites.

**disposable income**  Balance of income left after paying taxes; income that is used for spending and savings.

**Do Not Call List (DNCL)**  Gives customers the ability to elect to not receive telemarketing calls on cellphones and landline phones by registering the numbers of their communication devices.

**dual distribution**  Arrangement whereby a firm reaches buyers by using two or more different types of channels for the same basic product.

**dumping**  Occurs when a firm sells a product in a foreign country below its domestic prices or below its actual cost.

**durable good**  An item that lasts over an extended number of uses.

**earned media**  The free publicity secured through unpaid media mentions and consumers who spread the word through word of mouth or the Internet.

**economy**  The collective income, expenditures, and resources that affect the cost of running a business or a household.

**electronic data interchange (EDI)**  A computer-to-computer exchange of business documents from a retailer to a supplier and back.

**electronic marketing channels**  Channels that use the Internet to make goods and services available to consumers or business buyers.

**e-mail marketing**  The use of e-mail to market products.

**e-marketplaces**  Online trading communities that bring together buyers and supplier organizations.

**engagement metrics**  Measures how much and how often consumers interact with social media content.

**environmental scan**  The process of continually acquiring information on events occurring outside an organization to identify trends, opportunities, and threats to a business.

**event marketing**  The creation or involvement of a brand in an experience or occasion that will heighten its awareness, create positive associations, and generate a desired response.

**exchange**  The trade of things of value between buyers and sellers so that each benefits.

**exclusive distribution**  Only one retail outlet in a specific geographical area carries the firm's products.

**experiential marketing**  Creating opportunities for consumers to directly interact with brands.

**experiment**  In marketing, changing a variable involved in a customer purchase to find out what happens.

**exploratory research**  Preliminary research conducted to clarify the scope and nature of the marketing problem or opportunity.

**fad**  Novelty products with very short product life cycles that experience immediate rapid growth, followed by an equally rapid decline.

**family brand**  When a company uses a brand name to cover a number of different product categories.

**family life cycle**  A family's progression from formation to retirement, with each phase bringing distinct needs and purchasing behaviours.

**fashion product**  The life cycle for fashion is relatively short and cyclical, going from introduction to decline within two to three years, only to resurface again a few years later.

**feature phone**  Cellphone that is Internet-enabled and that allows for e-mailing, texting, and browsing but cannot download or use apps.

**fixed cost**  Firm's expenses that are stable and do not change with the quantity of product that is produced and sold.

**fluctuating demand**  Demand for business products and services fluctuates more than demand for consumer products and services.

**focus group**  A qualitative research technique where a small group of people (usually six to ten) meet for a few hours with a trained moderator to discuss predetermined areas.

**form of ownership**  Distinguishes retail outlets on the basis of whether individuals, corporate chains, or contractual systems own the outlet.

**franchising**  Contractual arrangement in which a parent company (the franchiser) allows an individual or firm (the franchisee) to operate a certain type of business under an established name and according to specific rules set by the franchiser.

**frequency**  The number of times the target audience is exposed to the communication vehicle or the communication message.

**generation X**  People born between 1966 and 1980.

**generation Y**  People born between 1981 and 2000. This generation is also referred to as *millennials*.

**generation Z**  People born in 2001 and beyond.

**generic brand**  A product that has no branding and is produced as a cheap alternative to a manufacturer's brand and to branded private-label products.

**geofencing**  Uses global positioning system (GPS) to trigger an event to happen when a device enters a certain geographic area.

**geographics**  Where a target market lives, using variables such as country, region, province, city size, and population density, such as urban, suburban, or rural.

**global brands**  Brands that are sold in a variety of international markets and that enjoy wide recognition in these markets.

**goals (objectives)**  Targets of performance to be achieved within a specific time frame.

**good**  A product you can touch and own.

**greenwashing**  The deceptive use of marketing practices to give the

**impression** that a good, service, or organization is environmentally friendly.

**grey market** Situations where products are sold through unauthorized channels of distribution.

**gross domestic product (GDP)** The total dollar value of all goods and services produced in a country within a specified time period.

**gross income** Total amount of money made in one year by a person, household, or family unit, including taxes.

**harvest** When a company keeps a product but reduces marketing support in an attempt to reap some minor profits.

**high-learning product** Significant consumer education is required for these products, which have an extended introductory period.

**hybrid apps** Apps that combine the functionality of native apps with the flexibility of web apps.

**idea** A concept that typically looks for support.

**idea generation** Developing a pool of new product ideas.

**idle production capacity** When the supply of a service exceeds its demand.

**inbound marketing** When consumers find a product and its messaging by using online techniques that marketers facilitate, including search engine optimization, pay-per-click ads, and the use of social media to connect with consumers.

**in-depth interviews** Detailed interviews where a researcher questions an individual at length in a free-flowing conversational style in order to discover information that may help solve a marketing problem.

**indirect competitors** Products competing for the same buying dollar in a slightly different but related category.

**individual brand** When a company uses a brand name solely for a specific product category.

**individualized marketing** One-to-one marketing that involves customizing offers and, in some cases, products to fit individual needs.

**inelastic demand** Demand for products does not change because of increases or decreases in price.

**inflation** When the cost to produce and buy products and services gets higher as prices rise.

**in-stream advertising** The use of video ads that play before (pre-roll), during (mid-roll), or after (post-roll) video segments are watched online.

**integrated marketing communications (IMC)** A communications approach that coordinates all promotional activities to provide a consistent message to a target audience.

**intensive distribution** A firm tries to place its products or services in as many outlets as possible.

**interest rates** The amount charged for borrowing money, usually expressed as a percentage per year.

**intermediaries** Individuals or firms performing a role in the marketing channel, involved in making a product available.

**intertype competition** Competition between very dissimilar types of retail outlets.

**involvement** Personal, social, and economic significance of a purchase to the consumer.

**just-in-time (JIT) inventory system** A system designed to deliver less merchandise on a more frequent basis than traditional inventory systems.

**key performance indicators (KPIs)** Types of metric that are used to evaluate performance.

**lead generation** The requests for additional information that result from direct response marketing.

**leaderboards** Banner ads that stretch across the top of a web page.

**learning** Behaviours that result from repeated experience or reasoning.

**level of service** The degree of service provided to the customer by self-, limited-, and full-service retailers.

**line extension** The addition of a new item to an already existing product line.

**logistics** Activities that focus on getting the right amount of the right products to the right place at the right time at the lowest possible cost.

**low-learning product** Little consumer education is required, resulting

in a short introductory stage for the product.

**loyalty programs** Programs specifically designed for customer retention.

**macroeconomic forces** The state of a country's economy as a whole as indicated by its growth rates, inflation rates, unemployment rates, and consumer confidence indexes.

**manufacturer's brand** A brand owned and produced by the manufacturer.

**manufacturers' agents** Work for several producers and carry non-competitive, complementary merchandise in an exclusive territory.

**market** Potential consumers with both the willingness and the ability to buy.

**market research** The process of planning, collecting, and analyzing information in order to recommend actions to improve marketing activities.

**market segmentation** The aggregation of prospective buyers into groups that have common needs and respond similarly to marketing programs.

**market share** The percentage of sales volume for a product, relative to the entire sales volume of the category in which it competes; ratio of a firm's sales to the total sales of all firms in the industry.

**marketing** The process of planning and managing goods, services, or ideas to meet consumer needs and organizational objectives. It includes the conception of these products and the pricing, promotion, and distribution programs designed to make a profit and generate revenue or support for an organization.

**marketing channel** The set of individuals or firms involved in the process of making a product available.

**marketing communication agencies** Broad-spectrum integrated agencies or specialist agencies that provide marketers with expertise on how best to communicate messages to their audiences.

**marketing communication tools** Advertising, public relations, sales promotion, direct response marketing, event marketing and sponsorship, product placement and branded entertainment, personal selling, online marketing, social media marketing, and mobile marketing.

**marketing dashboard** A visual computer display of essential marketing information.

**marketing information system (MIS)** A set of procedures and processes for collecting, sorting, analyzing, and summarizing information on an ongoing basis.

**marketing metric** A measure of the value or trend of a marketing activity or result.

**marketing mix** The 4 Ps—product, price, place, and promotion.

**marketing orientation** Focusing organizational efforts to collect and use information about customers' needs to create customer value.

**marketing plan** Road map for the marketing activities of an organization for a specified future period of time.

**marketing process** The process of (1) identifying consumer needs, (2) managing the marketing mix to meet these needs, and (3) realizing profits.

**marketing strategy** Means by which a marketing goal is to be achieved.

**marketing tactics** Detailed day-to-day operational decisions essential to the overall success of marketing strategies.

**markup** The difference between selling price and cost, usually expressed as a percentage of cost.

**mass marketing** Marketing a product with broad appeal to the entire market without any product or marketing differentiation.

**matrix 2D barcode** A two-dimensional response code that, when scanned by a mobile barcode reader or app, provides additional information, launches websites, prompts downloads, sends text messages, or deploys messages.

**m-commerce** The process of purchasing an item online through a mobile device.

**merchandise mix** How many different types of products a store carries and in what assortment.

**merchant wholesalers** Independently owned firms that take title to the merchandise they handle.

**metrics** Numeric data that is collected and grouped to track performance, often presented in spreadsheets and dashboards.

**microeconomic forces** The supply and demand of goods and services and how this is impacted by individual, household, and company decisions to purchase.

**microsites** Promotional websites created for short-term promotional purposes, often allowing consumers to enter contests and access promotional information.

**millennials** People born between 1981 and 2000. This generation is also referred to as *generation Y*.

**minor innovations** Minor product modifications that require no adjustments on behalf of the consumer.

**mission** Statement of the organization's purpose and direction.

**mobile applications (apps)** Software programs that can be downloaded on a smartphone or tablet to engage consumers with information, entertainment, or interactivity.

**mobile check-in services** When consumers check into locations using apps to post their whereabouts and to receive offers from local merchants on their mobile device.

**mobile discovery** The use of mobile apps to help find local businesses, services, and attractions.

**mobile e-mail** E-mail sent and/or received using a mobile device.

**mobile marketing** A set of practices that enables organizations to communicate and engage with their audiences in an interactive and relevant manner through any mobile device or network.

**mobile messaging** Comes in the form of common short codes (CSC), short messaging services (SMS), multimedia messaging services (MMS), e-mail messaging, in-person voice phone calls, and voice messaging.

**mobile web** A website designed for the smaller screens of mobile devices.

**mobile web apps** Websites designed to simulate an app experience by adding a shortcut that runs off a browser on a mobile device.

**monopolistic competition** Type of competition where a large number of sellers compete with each other, offering customers similar or substitute products

**monopoly** When only one company sells in a particular market.

**motivation** Energizing force that stimulates behaviour to satisfy a need.

**multichannel marketing** Blending of different communication and delivery channels that are mutually reinforcing in attracting, retaining, and building relationships with customers.

**multichannel retailers** Use a combination of traditional store formats and non-store formats such as catalogues and online retailing.

**multimedia messaging services (MMS)** Standard text messaging services that include audio, video, or images.

**native apps** Apps downloaded from app stores that are specifically created to be hosted and run on a mobile device.

**near field communications (NFC)** The two-way radio communication between smartphones and smartphone-type devices to transfer images, documents, or monetary transactions when the two devices touch or are within a few inches of each other.

**need** Occurs when a person feels deprived of basic necessities.

**new product development process** Sequence of steps that a firm takes to develop a new product idea and take it to market.

**new product development strategy** Setting the new product strategic direction for the company as a whole, and the precise objectives for the project at hand.

**niche marketing** Marketing a limited product line to a narrow but profitable segment of the market that is of marginal interest to major competitors.

**non-durable good** An item that does not last and is consumed only once, or for a limited number of times.

**non-probability sampling** Selecting a sample so that the chance of selecting a particular element of a population is either unknown or zero.

**North American Industry Classification System (NAICS)** Provides common industry definitions for Canada, Mexico, and the United States.

**objectives** Specific, measurable, and achievable goals.

**observational research** Obtained by watching how people behave, in person or by using a machine to record the event.

**off-price retailing** Selling brand-name merchandise at lower than regular prices.

**oligopoly** Type of competition that occurs when a few companies control a market.

**omnibus survey** The voluntary participation of respondents in routine research surveys that allow marketers to add a small number of questions to an existing survey to receive cost-effective data.

**online behavioural advertising (OBA)** The use of web-based programs to track consumers' online activity so as to deliver ads that correspond to browsing interests.

**online research bulletin boards** Private online static forums, without real-time dialogue, where respondents can post their responses to questions posed by researchers.

**online research communities** The use of consumer groups, brought together privately in an online environment, to answer questions, respond to ideas, and collaborate with researchers in real time.

**opinion leaders** Individuals who have social influence over others.

**optimization metrics** Data that can point to adjustments or changes that should be made to your social media program.

**organizational buyers** Manufacturers, wholesalers, retailers, and government agencies that buy goods and services for their own use or for resale.

**organizational buying behaviour** Process by which organizations determine the need for goods and then choose among alternative suppliers.

**outbound marketing** Marketers seek out consumers by widely broadcasting messages using advertising, direct mail, e-mail marketing,

telemarketing, and personal-selling approaches.

**out-of-home (OOH) advertising** Casually referred to as *outdoor;* reaches consumers outside the home in outdoor locations, in transit, or in commercial or business locations.

**owned media** The media channels that a company controls, either fully or partially, such as a website, microsite, or social media page that is used to directly communicate with consumers.

**paid media** The media time purchased so that messages can be disseminated through channels that are controlled by others.

**panel** A large sample of respondents that voluntarily complete questionnaires on a regular basis so that researchers can assess changes in behaviour and attitudes.

**Pareto's Rule** The concept that 80 percent of a brand's sales come from 20 percent of its customers.

**partnership marketing** The creation of formal associations between brands that will result in incremental business for both brands that could not have been achieved separately.

**patents** Used to legally protect new technologies, unique processes, or formulations from usage by other companies.

**pay-per-click advertising (PPC)** Ads that appear in response to keyword triggers on search engines, as well as on some websites, blogs, and social media sites, where the advertiser pays only when the ad is clicked.

**perceived risk** Anxiety felt when a consumer cannot anticipate possible negative outcomes of a purchase.

**perception** Process by which someone selects, organizes, and interprets information to create a meaningful picture of the world

**perfect competition** Type of competition where there are many sellers with nearly identical products and little differentiation.

**permission-based e-mail** When a recipient chooses to receive e-mail from a marketer.

**personal selling** The two-way flow of communication between a buyer and seller, often face-to-face or facilitated through communication devices, to influence an individual and group purchase decision.

**personality** A person's character traits that influence behavioural responses.

**personas** Character descriptions of a typical customer in the form of fictional character narratives, complete with images that capture the personalities, values, attitudes, beliefs, demographics, and expected interactions with a brand.

**place** Distribution channels, retail formats, and merchandising used to sell a product.

**positioning maps** Visual representations of how products in a category are positioned in consumers' minds; also known as *perceptual maps*.

**positioning statement** A formalized statement that identifies the image a branded product represents in the market and what sets it apart from the competition.

**power centre** Large shopping strip with multiple anchor stores, a convenient location, and a supermarket.

**predictive analytics** The combination of data from varied sources to reveal patterns that are modelled to predict what might happen in the future.

**press conference** A planned event where representatives of the media are invited to an informational meeting with the company.

**press release** An announcement written by an organization and sent to the media.

**price** What is exchanged for a product, including the expected regular retail or sale price.

**pricing constraints** Factors that limit the range of price a firm may set.

**pricing objectives** Expectations that specify the role of price in an organization's marketing and strategic plans.

**primary data** Data that is original and specifically collected for a project.

**private-label brand** Otherwise known as a store brand, a brand owned by a retailer that contracts its manufacturing to major suppliers, and then sells the product at its own retail stores, under its own store-brand name.

**probability sampling**   Selecting a sample so that each element of a population has a specific known chance of being selected.

**product**   Attributes that make up a good, a service, or an idea, including product design, features, colour, packaging, warranty, and service levels.

**product differentiation**   Positioning a product to a target group so that it appears distinct from competitive offerings.

**product life cycle**   The stages that a new product goes through, starting with introduction and evolving into growth, maturity, and decline.

**product line**   A group of similar products that are closely related because they satisfy a similar need and are directed at the same general target market.

**product line depth**   The assortment of different versions of each product sold within its product lines.

**product line length**   The total number of products or brands in a product line.

**product mix**   All the product lines marketed by a company.

**product mix width**   The number of different product lines offered by a company.

**product placement**   The inclusion of a product in a movie or TV program in return for payment.

**product positioning**   The impression of the product you want to establish in consumers' minds relative to their needs and the competition.

**production orientation**   Focusing organizational efforts on the manufacture of goods.

**profit**   The excess of revenues over costs, the reward to a business for the risk it undertakes in offering a product for sale.

**profit equation**   Profit = total revenue – total cost.

**promotion**   Communication tools needed to inform consumers about a product, including advertising, public relations, sales promotion, direct response, event marketing, sponsorship, online approaches, and personal selling.

**promotional mix**   The selection of promotional tools used to communicate with a target market.

**promotional websites**   Websites that focus on showcasing products and services.

**proximity marketing**   The distribution of marketing content to mobile devices that have opted in at a particular local geo-location to receive information.

**psychographics**   Understanding consumers' attitudes to life, values, personalities, general interests, opinions, and activities.

**public relations**   A communications tool that seeks to influence the opinions and attitudes of target groups through the use of unpaid media exposure; targets the media in an attempt to generate positive publicity for a company, product, or individual.

**publicity**   A non-personal form of communication that appears in the media and is not paid for directly by the organization.

**pull strategy**   When marketers focus communication efforts on ultimate consumers to build awareness, trial, and demand for a product.

**purchase decision process**   Stages that a buyer passes through when making choices about which products or services to buy.

**push notifications**   Any content sent to a mobile device that a customer must opt in to receive from a marketer.

**push strategy**   When marketers focus communication on the distribution channel to gain support from retailers, distributors, and wholesalers.

**qualitative research**   A form of research that uses approaches such as focus groups, in-depth interviews, online communities, online bulletin boards, and social listening to provide insightful and directional information.

**quantitative research**   Statistically reliable information that uses observational and/or questioning techniques such as observations, surveys, and experiments.

**questionnaire**   Obtaining information by posing standardized questions through surveys that can be conducted in person, through the mail, on the telephone, or through the Internet.

**radical innovations**   New products that involve the introduction of a product that is entirely new and innovative to the market.

**reach**   The number of people who are exposed to a communication vehicle or message; is presented as percentage of the total number of people in a target audience.

**real-time marketing**   A planned tactical approach where brands make themselves relevant online during events or newsworthy occurrences by diving into conversations as they occur with aligned short-term messaging that takes advantage of the current buzz.

**recession**   A time of slow economic activity with two consecutive periods of negative growth.

**reference group**   A group of people who influence a person's attitudes, values, and behaviour.

**regional shopping centres**   Consist of 50 to 150 stores that typically attract customers who live within a 5- to 15-km range; often containing two or three anchor stores.

**regulations**   Restrictions placed on marketing practices by government and industry associations.

**relationship marketing**   When organizations create long-term links with customers, employees, suppliers, and other partners to increase loyalty and customer retention.

**repositioning**   Changing the place a product occupies in consumers' minds relative to competitive products to more accurately meet consumer needs.

**retailing**   All activities involved in selling, renting, and providing goods and services to ultimate consumers for personal, family, or household use.

**retailing mix**   The goods and services, pricing, physical distribution, and communications tactics chosen by a store.

**reverse auction**   Occurs when a buyer communicates a need for something and would-be suppliers bid in competition with each other.

**RFM analysis**   The rating of customers on the basis of how recently products were purchased (recency), how often products were purchased (frequency), and the dollar value of the transactions (monetary value)

**sales orientation**   Focusing organizational efforts on selling as many products as possible.

**sales promotion**   A communications tool that provides short-term incentives to generate interest in a product or cause and encourages purchase or support.

**sampling**   The process of gathering data from a subset of the total population rather than from all members of that particular group.

**scrambled merchandising**   Offering several unrelated product lines in a single retail store.

**screening and evaluation**   Reduces the list of ideas down to a list of promising concepts.

**search engine marketing (SEM)**   Includes the use of search engine optimization and pay-per-click advertising to market on search engines.

**search engine optimization (SEO)**   Ensuring that websites are written, indexed, and coded so that they are highly rated and ranked by the search engines.

**secondary data**   Facts and figures that have already been recorded by a third party.

**selective distribution**   A firm selects a few retail outlets in a specific geographical area to carry its products.

**selling agents**   Represent a single producer and are responsible for the entire marketing function of that producer.

**service**   A product that is intangible; an activity, benefit, or satisfaction that you cannot touch.

**service continuum**   A range from tangible goods to intangible services.

**share of wallet**   The percentage of a customer's purchases that a company has in a specific product category.

**shopping products**   Items that require comparison-shopping between different brands and an investment of shopping time.

**short messaging services (SMS)**   Standard text messaging that uses protocols of 160 characters per message.

**showrooming**   Using mobile devices in-store to check online competitive product reviews and prices, which results in the online purchase of a cheaper product.

**shrinkage**   Breakage and theft of merchandise by customers and employees.

**situation analysis**   Taking stock of a firm's or product's past performance, where it is now, and where it is headed.

**skyscrapers**   Banner ads that are tall, slim, and vertical and appear along the side of a web page.

**smartphone**   An advanced cellphone that has similar functionality to a personal computer in addition to taking pictures, playing music and movies, navigating with GPS, and using apps to enhance its features and capabilities.

**social analytics**   The real-time measurement, interaction, and analysis of social media to assess social media campaign performance, message resonation and amplification, consumer sentiment, and common themes.

**social listening**   Research that monitors public online consumer conversations on social media sites such as social networks, blogs, and forums.

**social media**   A form of online media that allows members to create their own network of friends and contacts to share comments, articles, opinions, videos, and images as a form of self-expression.

**social media analytics**   The real-time measurement, interaction, and analysis of social media to assess social media campaign performance, message resonation and amplification, consumer sentiment, and common themes.

**social media marketing**   Reaching out to consumers online through social media networks.

**social media monitoring**   The monitoring of brand mentions, as well as consumer sentiment, buzz, and engagement, on the Internet

**social media release**   A multimedia, online press-release platform that includes video, text, and images, as well as social media buttons for sharing on social networks and comment areas where viewers can leave comments.

**social networks**   Online websites that allow members to create a network of friends and contacts to share messages, comments, videos, and images as a form of self-expression.

**social TV**   Watching TV programming while adding comments on social networks.

**societal marketing concept**   Marketing programs that focus on the consumer *and* the well-being of society.

**socio-cultural forces**   Cultural values, ideas, and attitudes, as well as society's morals and beliefs.

**spam**   The dissemination of unsolicited electronic messages to recipients.

**specialty products**   Items for special occasions that require a specific product or brand and require considerable time and effort to purchase.

**sponsorship**   When an advertiser pays a fee in exchange for inclusion in an event, involvement in its advertising opportunities, or exposure within the event itself.

**strategic alliance**   Long-term arrangement between companies with similar values and marketing objectives that extends beyond short-term promotional offers into long-term formal business agreements.

**strategic marketing process**   Approach whereby an organization allocates its marketing mix.

**strategy**   An organization's long-term course of action that delivers a unique customer experience while achieving its goals.

**strip location**   A cluster of stores serving people who live within a 5- to 10-minute drive.

**structured data**   Data that can be easily tagged, stored, and searched in a database using consistently identifiable terms that are systematically organized into columns, rows, and tables.

**sub-brand**   A brand that uses the family brand name as well as its own brand name and identity so that it can take on the strengths of the parent brand but also differentiate itself.

**subcultures**  Subgroups within a larger culture that have unique values, ideas, and attitudes.

**supply chain**  Sequence of firms that perform activities required to create and deliver a product to consumers or industrial users.

**supply chain management**  Integration and organization of information and logistics activities across firms in a supply chain for the purpose of creating and delivering goods and services that provide value to consumers.

**supply partnership**  Relationship between a buyer and supplier that adopt mutually beneficial objectives, policies, and procedures.

**SWOT analysis**  The assessment of how well an organization or brand is servicing its businesses and target markets by evaluating its internal strengths and weaknesses, and its external opportunities and threats.

**syndicated studies**  A hybrid of primary and secondary research whereby the cost of a research study is shared among clients and made available at a price to interested parties.

**target market**  The specific group or segment(s) of existing and potential consumers to which marketers direct their marketing efforts.

**target market profile**  A description of the target market that contains specific information about the target group in four areas: geographics, demographics, psychographics, and behaviouristics.

**technological forces**  Inventions from science or engineering research.

**telemarketing**  Using the telephone to interact with and sell directly to consumers.

**test market**  An in-market localized approach, or short-term online destination, used to test the success of promotional offers, new services, or new product launches.

**test marketing**  Offering a new product for sale on a limited basis in a defined geographic area to assess its success.

**total cost**  Total expenses incurred by a firm in producing and marketing a product; total cost is the sum of fixed cost and variable costs.

**total revenue**  Total money received from the sale of a product.

**touch point**  Any situation in which a customer comes into contact with a brand or company.

**trade promotions**  Short-term promotional tools used to generate support with wholesalers, distributors, or retailers.

**trademarks**  Used by people or organizations to protect brand images, names, slogans, and designs from usage by others.

**traditional auction**  Occurs when a seller puts an item up for sale and would-be buyers bid in competition with each other.

**traffic generation**  The visits to a location or website that result from direct response marketing.

**transactional websites**  Electronic storefronts focused on converting an online browser into an online buyer.

**unemployment rate**  Measures the share of the labour force that is not working.

**unsought products**  Unknown items or those of no interest to the purchaser.

**unstructured data**  Data that comes from word-processed documents, presentations, audio files, images, video, and e-mail or social media messages that cannot be easily categorized and tagged in a database using fixed terms and definitions.

**user-generated content (UGC)**  Original online content that has been created by users in the form of blogs, posts, images, audio, or video.

**value**  The ratio of perceived benefits to price.

**variable cost**  Sum of the expenses of the firm that vary directly with the quantity of products that is produced and sold.

**vertical marketing systems**  Professionally managed and centrally coordinated marketing channels designed to achieve channel economies and maximum marketing impact.

**virtual services**  Services that exist only online and have no person-to-person interaction.

**vlog**  A blog posted in video format.

**want**  A need that is shaped by a person's knowledge, culture, and personality.

**wearables**  Devices that can be worn on the body or on clothes.

**web analytics**  The measurement and analysis of website data, looking at elements such as page views, time on site, bounce rate, new visitors, returning visitors, and referral traffic.

**WiFi hotspots**  Areas set up with free Internet access in which once customers log in to use the free WiFi, they can be sent location-specific content.

**wiki**  A collaborative website that uses an application with which multiple users can create, add, edit, or delete content.

**word of mouth**  People influencing each other in personal conversations.

**word-of-mouth marketing**  The spread of positive messages about a product by listening to consumers, identifying influential individuals that can spread the word, and making it easier for them to do so.

# Chapter Notes

## Chapter 1

1. Written input and interview with Jay Klein, founder and CEO of The PUR Company, May 2016; Mary Teresa Bitta, "Big Dragons' Den pitches, valuations from RosterBot and PUR Gum — but only one lands a clear deal," *Financial Post*, October 26, 2014, http://business.financialpost.com/entrepreneur/big-dragons-den-pitches-valuations-from-rosterbot-and-pur-gum-but-only-one-lands-a-clear-deal; Richard Blackwell, "Chewing gum losing grip on North American market," *Globe and Mail*, February 4, 2015, http://www.theglobeandmail.com/report-on-business/chewing-gum-losing-grip-on-north-american-market/article22796589/; Euromonitor International, "Gum in Canada," August 13, 2015, http://www.euromonitor.com/gum-in-canada/report; The PUR Company website, accessed May 2016 at https://thepurcompany.com/.

2. "Navigating the Connected Consumer's In-Store Shopping Cycle," Frank Mayer and Associates Inc., accessed May 2016 at www.frankmayer.com.

3. "Lowest Price Guarantee," Best Buy Canada, accessed June 2016 at http://www.bestbuy.ca/en-CA/help/lowest-price-guarantee/hc1001.aspx.

4. David P. Schulz, "Top 100 Retailers 2017," *Stores*, July 2017, http://stores.org/stores-top-retailers-2017/.

5. "2015 Annual Report," Amazon, http://phx.corporate-ir.net/phoenix.zhtml?c=97664&p=irol-reportsAnnual.

6. "Amazon Prime," Amazon.ca, accessed May 2016 at www.amazon.ca/gp/prime.

7. Paloma Aleman, "The Axe Effect," Media Literacy Project, 2013, https://medialiteracyproject.org/deconstructions/axe-effect/.

8. "Our Brands – Axe," Unilever Canada, accessed May 2016 at https://www.unilever.ca/brands/our-brands/axe.html.

9. Tim Nudd, "Ad of the Day: Axe Gets Inclusive in a Remarkable Ad That's Really Pretty Magical," *Adweek*, January 14, 2016, http://www.adweek.com/news/advertising-branding/ad-day-axe-gets-inclusive-remarkable-ad-thats-really-pretty-magical-168996.

10. Karen Mazurkewich, "Dove Story," *Strategy*, January 1, 2007, http://strategyonline.ca/2007/01/01/dove-20070101/.

11. "The Dove Campaign for Real Beauty," Unilever, accessed May 2016 at http://www.dove.us/Social-Mission/campaign-for-real-beauty.aspx.

12. "Amazon Prime," Amazon.ca, accessed May 2016 at www.amazon.ca/gp/prime.

13. Ryan Lunka, "Retail Data: 100 Stats About Retail, eCommerce & Digital Marketing," *nChannel*, July 9, 2015, https://www.nchannel.com/blog/retail-data-ecommerce-statistics/.

14. Laura Stevens, "'Free' Shipping Crowds Out Small Retailers," *Wall Street Journal*, April 27, 2016, http://www.wsj.com/articles/for-online-shoppers-free-shipping-reigns-supreme-1461789381.

15. "Amazon Prime," Amazon.ca, accessed May 2016 at www.amazon.ca/gp/prime.

16. JP Mangalindan, "Amazon's Prime and punishment," *Fortune*, February 21, 2012, http://fortune.com/2012/02/21/amazons-prime-and-punishment/.

17. Adapted from "Marketing," *Business Dictionary* website, accessed June 2016 at www.businessdictionary.com/definition/marketing.html.

18. "Join," SCENE.ca, accessed May 2016 at https://www.scene.ca/en-ca/enrollment.

19. "History and Impact," MADD Canada, accessed May 2016 at http://madd.ca/pages/about-us/what-we-do/history-and-impact/; and "Information for Parents," MADD Canada, accessed February 2017 at http://madd.ca/pages/programs/youth-services/information-for-parents/.

20. Rebecca Harris, "Movember Grows with Help from Visa and the NHL," *Marketing*, October 29, 2015, http://www.marketingmag.ca/brands/movember-grows-with-help-from-visa-and-the-nhl-160319; Canadian Press, "Movember Campaign Seeks to Draw More Moustached Men," *Marketing*, November 5, 2015, http://www.marketingmag.ca/brands/movember-campaign-seeks-to-draw-more-moustached-men-160757; Josh Kolm, "Beyond moustaches," *Strategy*, November 2, 2015, http://strategyonline.ca/2015/11/02/beyond-moustaches/; "Our Story," Movember Canada, accessed May 2016 at https://ca.movember.com/about/history; Josh Kolm, "Brands grow the mo, *Strategy*, November 5, 2014, http://strategyonline.ca/2014/11/05/growing-the-mo/; Richard Wassersug, John Oliffe, and Christina Han, "On manhood and Movember…or why the moustache works," *Global Health Promotion*, June 2015, vol. 22, no. 2, pp. 65–70; Alexis Dobranowski, "Gentlemen, Know They Nuts (To Check For Testicular Cancer)," *Huffington Post Canada*, April 27, 2016, http://www.huffingtonpost.ca/sunnybrook-health-sciences-centre/gentlemen-know-thy-nuts_b_9786290.html.

21. Brendan Sinclair, "Nintendo targeting Wii U marketing to kids, families," *gamesindustry.biz*, December 18, 2013, http://www.gamesindustry.biz/articles/2013-12-18-nintendo-targeting-wii-u-marketing-to-kids-families.

22. Frederick Crane, Roger Kerin, Steven Hartley, and William Rudelius, *Marketing*, Ninth Canadian Edition (Toronto: McGraw-Hill, 2014).

23. "Global consumers are willing to put their money where their heart is when it comes to goods and services from companies committed to social responsibility," Nielsen, news release, June 17, 2014, http://www.nielsen.com/us/en/press-room/2014/global-consumers-are-willing-to-put-their-money-where-their-heart-is.html; "Corporate Responsibility at TOMS," TOMS Shoes, accessed May 2016 at http://www.toms.ca/about-toms#corporateResponsibility; Kaitlyn McAvoy, "tentree: Finding a CSR Initiative With Roots, *Spend Matters*, October 14, 2015, http://spendmatters.com/2015/10/14/tentree-finding-a-csr-initiative-with-roots/; Chris Atchison, "Making a Difference: Why Social Responsibility Makes Smart Business Sense," *Profits*, (Business Development Bank of Canada), winter 2014, vol. 34, no. 1, pp. 12–15, https://www.bdc.ca/en/documents/profits/2014/profits_winter_2014.pdf; tentree corporate website, accessed May 2016 at http://tentree.com.

24. *Our Purpose: Live Life Well: 2016 Corporate Social Responsibility Report*, Loblaw Companies Limited, accessed June 2017 at http://www.loblaw.ca/en/responsibility/reports.html.

25. *Telus Sustainability Report 2015*, Telus, accessed May 2016 at https://telusdigital-sustainability-production.s3.amazonaws.com/uploads/2017/04/2015_Sustainability_Report-EN.pdf.

26. Julie Smyth, "Canada's top 50 socially responsible corporations: 2015," *Maclean's*, June 8, 2015, http://www.macleans.ca/economy/business/canadas-top-50-most-socially-responsible-companies/.

27. "Pampers and Unicef: A powerful partnership and a decade of achievement," Pampers.ca, accessed June 2017, https://www.pampers.ca/en-ca/about-pampers/pampers-unicef-partnership/article/pampers-and-unicef-the-journey-so-far-a-decade-of-achievement.

28. "10 worst household products for greenwashing," CBC News, September 14, 2012, http://www.cbc.ca/news/canada/10-worst -household-products-for-greenwashing-1.1200620.

29. "Our Commitments," The Body Shop, accessed May 2016 at http:// www.thebodyshop.ca/enrich-not-exploit/.

30. "Facts & Figures: 2016," Canadian Wireless and Telecommunications Association, accessed July 2017 at http://www.cwta.ca/facts-figures/.

31. Paul Rich, Ben Martin, and Leah Jenkins, "2015 Canada Digital Future in Focus," comScore, March 27, 2015, https://www .comscore.com/Insights/Presentations-and-Whitepapers/2015/2015 -Canada-Digital-Future-in-Focus.

32. "My Starbucks Idea," Starbucks, accessed May 2016 at http:// mystarbucksidea.force.com/.

33. Kate Taylor, "How Starbucks Went Digital—And Why You Should, Too," Entrepreneur, October 14, 2013, https://www .entrepreneur.com/article/229299.

34. "What Is Content Marketing?" Content Marketing Institute, ac- cessed June 2016 at http://contentmarketinginstitute.com/what-is -content-marketing.

35. For GE Reports in Canada, see https://gereports.ca/. For GE Reports YouTube channels, see https://www.youtube.com/user/ GEreports.

36. "MMA Updates Definition of Mobile Marketing," Mobile Marketing Association, November 17, 2009, www.mmaglobal.com/node/11102.

37. "2016 Canadian Social Media Monitor," Insights West, May 2016, http://www.insightswest.com/wp-content/uploads/2016/05/Rep _InsightsWest_CDNSocialMediaMonitor_2016.pdf.

38. "Most popular Facebook fan pages as of April 2016, based on number of fans (in millions)," Statista, accessed May 2016 at http://www.statista.com/statistics/269304/international-brands-on -facebook-by-number-of-fans/; David Moth, "How Coca-Cola uses Facebook, Twitter, Pinterest and Google+," Econsultancy, April 17, 2013, https://econsultancy.com/blog/62548-how-coca-cola-uses -facebook-twitter-pinterest-and-google/.

39. David Moth, "How Nike uses Facebook, Twitter, Pinterest and Google+," Econsultancy, March 27, 2013, https://econsultancy.com /blog/62412-how-nike-uses-facebook-twitter-pinterest-and-google; Nike Football Facebook page, accessed May 2016, www.facebook .com/nikefootball/.

40. Lianna Turchin, "Wait – What IS Real-Time Marketing?" Online Marketing Institute, November 9, 2015, https://www.onlinemarket inginstitute.org/blog/2015/11/wait-what-is-real-time-marketing/.

41. Richard O'Flynn, "The Way The Social Cookie Crumbles: The Ge- nius of Oreo's Social Media Marketing," 201:digital, April 23, 2015, http://www.201digital.co.uk/way-social-cookie-crumbles-genius -oreos-social-media-marketing-can-learn/; Oreo Facebook page, accessed May 2016, https://www.facebook.com/oreo/; Oreo Twitter account, accessed May 2016, https://twitter.com/oreo; Oreo Instagram Account, accessed May 2016, https://www.instagram.com/oreo/?hl=en.

42. Christopher Ratcliff, "Six inspiring new examples of experiential marketing," Econsultancy, May 13, 2015, https://econsultancy.com /blog/66431-six-inspiring-new-examples-of-experiential-marketing/.

43. Val Maloney, "Spotted! Nike's baller weekend," Media in Canada, February 16, 2016, http://mediaincanada.com/2016/02/16/spotted -nikes-baller-weekend/.

44. Joss Davidge, "The force is strong with Lego's brand experience," BEcause Experiential Marketing, November 25, 2015, https://www .becausexm.com/blog/the-force-is-strong-with-legos-brand-experience.

45. Lauren Johnson, "Nestlé Will Be the First Brand to Run a Sponsored Periscope Stream," Adweek, June 19, 2015, http://www.adweek.com /news/technology/nestl-will-be-first-brand-run-sponsored-periscope -stream-165443; "Periscope case study: Nestle turns camera on customers to generate social buzz," Digital Training Academy, accessed May 2016 at http://www.digitaltrainingacademy.com /casestudies/2016/04/periscope_case_study_nestle_turns_camera _on_customers_to_generate_social_buzz.php.

46. Jo Coughlin, "Creating the perfect blend in partnership marketing," The Drum, April 29, 2016, http://www.thedrum.com/opinion /2016/04/29/creating-perfect-blend-partnership-marketing.

47. Harmeet Singh, "Brand Partner of the Year: Nutella's pairings," Strategy, October 16, 2015, http://strategyonline.ca/2015/10/16 /brand-partner-of-the-year-nutellas-pairings/.

48. "Benefits of the Program," SCENE.ca, accessed June 2016 at https://www.scene.ca/programbenefits.aspx; Matt Semansky, "Sco- tiabank Takes Scene-ic Route to Youth," Marketing, July 27, 2008, http://www.marketingmag.ca/brands/scotiabank-takes-scene -ic-route-to-youth-16881.

49. Dan Taekema, "Poll finds rising Uber ridership — and satisfaction," Toronto Star, December 30, 2015, https://www.thestar.com/news/ gta/2015/12/30/poll-finds-rising-uber-idership-and-satisfaction.html; D. Satish and, Manish Agarwal, Uber: Rising Valuations Amidst Ethical Woes, IBS Centre for Management Research, July 2015, http://www.icmrindia.org/casestudies/catalogue/Business%20Ethics/ Uber_Rising_Valuations_Amidst_Ethical_Woes-Excerpts.htm; "Our Industry Matters," Canadian Taxi Association, accessed May 2016 at http://www.cantaxi.ca/taxi-industry-canada; Alec Scott, "Co -founding Uber made Calgary-born Garrett Camp a billionaire," Cana- dian Business, November 19, 2015, http://www.canadianbusiness.com /lists-and-rankings/richest-people/2016-garrett-camp-uber; Rebecca Harris, "Air Miles Hitches a Ride with Uber," Marketing, October 20, 2015, http://www.marketingmag.ca/brands/air-miles-hitches-a -ride-with-uber-159457; Danny Kucharsky, "Loblaw and Uber Partner on Click-And-Collect Offer," Marketing, April 14, 2015, http://www.marketingmag.ca/brands/loblaw-and-uber-partner-on -click-and-collect-offer-143442; "Shopper Innovation Awards: Uber gets seriously safe," Strategy, April 19, 2016, http://strategyonline. ca/2016/04/19/shopper-innovation-awards-uber-gets-seriously-safe; Jennifer Horn, "Newsmaker of the Year: Riding the Uber Wave," Strategy, October 19, 2015, http://strategyonline.ca/2015/10/19 /newsmaker-of-the-year-riding-the-uber-wave; Bruce Weinstein, "Opinion: Four other ways Uber is ethically challenged," CNN Money, November 21, 2014, http://money.cnn.com/2014/11/21 /technology/uber-ethics-oped/; Giuseppe Valiente, "Uber pushes Canadian cities to re-evaluate taxi industry," CBC News, July 19, 2015, http://www.cbc.ca/news/canada/montreal/uber-pushes-canadi- an-cities-to-re-evaluate-taxi-industry-1.3159212; "Newsroom," Uber, accessed June 2016 at https://www.uber.com/media/.

50. Lisa Quast, "Personal Branding 101," Forbes, April 22, 2013, http://www.forbes.com/sites/lisaquast/2013/04/22/personal -branding-101/#158f0cd615fa.

## Chapter 2

1. Personal interview with Jon Hamilton, general manager, communi- cations strategy, Canada Post, May 2016; personal communication with Rob Linke, director, writing services, Canada Post, June 2016; Ian Lee, "Is the Cheque Still in the Mail?" Macdonald-Laurier Insti- tute, July 2015, www.macdonaldlaurier.ca/files/pdf/MLI_PostOffice _F_web.pdf; What's in the Truck? 2015 Annual Report," Canada Post (Ottawa: Author, 2016), https://www.canadapost.ca/web/en /pages/aboutus/details.page?article=annual_report; "Housing starts by province," Statistics Canada, CANSIM, table 027-0008, April 22, 2016, http://www.statcan.gc.ca/tables-tableaux/sum-som/l01 /cst01/manuf05-eng.htm; "Homeownership and Shelter Costs in Canada: National Household Survey, 2011," Statistics Canada, Catalogue no. 99-014-X2011002 (Ottawa: Minister of Industry, 2013), http://www12.statcan.gc.ca/nhs-enm/2011/as-sa/99-014 -x/99-014-x2011002-eng.pdf; "Retail sales, by industry," Statistics Canada, CANSIM, table 080-0020, March 2016, http://www.statcan .gc.ca/tables-tableaux/sum-som/l01/cst01/trad42a-eng.htm; Murad Hemmadi, "Why Canada has a serious e-commerce problem, in one infographic," Canadian Business, November 27, 2014, http://www .canadianbusiness.com/innovation/canada-serious-e-commerce -problem-infographic/; Accenture Consulting, "Accenture Technol- ogy Vision for Postal Organizations: Five trends shaping the future" (Toronto: Author, 2015), https://www.accenture.com/us-en/insight -five-trends-shaping-future; David James Friend, "76% of Canadians shopped online last year, Canada Post says," Canadian Press, May

12, 2015, http://www.cbc.ca/news/business/76-of-canadians -shopped-online-last-year-canada-post-says-1.3070651; Canadian Internet Registration Authority (CIRA), "The State of e-Commerce in Canada: CIRA Internet Factbook," March 2016, https://cira.ca /sites/default/files/public/ecommerce-factbook-march-2016_0.pdf; Statistics Canada, "Digital technology and Internet use, 2013," *The Daily*, June 11, 2014, http://www.statcan.gc.ca/daily-quotidien /140611/dq140611a-eng.htm; Qasim Mohammad, "After years in the slow lane, Canada's e-commerce ecosystem is booming," *Canadian Business*, February 22, 2016, http://www.canadianbusiness. com/innovation/canada-ecommerce-innovators/; "Digital Canada 150 2.0," Industry Canada, December 2015, http://www.ic.gc.ca/eic /site/028.nsf/eng/home.

2.  Statistics Canada, "Population size and growth in Canada: Key results from the 2016 Census," *The Daily*, February 8, 2017, http://www. statcan.gc.ca/daily-quotidien/170208/dq170208a-eng.htm?HPA=1.

3.  Statistics Canada, "Age and sex, and type of dwelling data: Key results from the 2016 Census," *The Daily*, May 3, 2017, http://www .statcan.gc.ca/daily-quotidien/170503/dq170503a-eng.htm?HPA=1.

4.  Statistics Canada, "Population aged 0 to 14 and 65 years and older, as of July 1, 1995 to 2035, Canada," CANSIM tables 051-0001 and 052-0005, accessed February 2017, http://www.statcan.gc.ca/daily -quotidien/150929/cg-b003-eng.htm.

5.  Doug Norris, "Millenials: The Newest, Biggest and Most Diverse Target Market," paper presented at 9th Annual Environics Analytics User Conference, Toronto, November 4, 2015, http://www .environicsanalytics.ca/docs/default-source/eauc2015-presentations /dougnorris-afternoonplenary.pdf?sfvrsn=6.

6.  Statistics Canada, "Population by sex and age group," CANSIM, table 051-0001, accessed February 2017, http://www.statcan.gc.ca /tables-tableaux/sum-som/l01/cst01/demo10a-eng.htm; Doug Norris, "Millenials."

7.  Doug Norris, "Don't call us seniors: The Baby Boomers at 65," Environics Analytics, July 23, 2014, http://www.environicsanalytics .ca/blog-details/ea-blog/2014/07/23/don-t-call-us-seniors-the-baby -boomers-at-65.

8.  Sonya Fatah, "How boomers are consuming media," *Strategy*, January 25, 2016, http://strategyonline.ca/2016/01/25/diving-deep -into-boomers-media-consumption-habits/.

9.  Doug Norris, "Millenials"; Statistics Canada, "Population by sex and age group."

10. Doug Norris, "Millenials."

11. Ellie Williams, "Generation X Consumer Behavior," *AZCentral*, Business and Entrepreneurship, accessed May 2016, http://yourbusiness .azcentral.com/generation-x-consumer-behavior-9585.html.

12. Doug Norris, "Millenials"; Statistics Canada, "Population by sex and age group."

13. Doug Norris, "Millenials."

14. Ernst and Young, *Rise of Gen Z, a new challenge for retailers* (London: Author, 2015), http://www.ey.com/Publication/vwLUAssets/EY-rise -of-gen-znew-challenge-for-retailers/$FILE/EY-rise-of-gen-znew -challenge-for-retailers.pdf.

15. Doug Norris, "Millenials"; Statistics Canada, "Population by sex and age group."

16. Statistics Canada, "Population size and growth in Canada."

17. Ibid.

18. Ibid.

19. Statistics Canada, "Study: A look at immigration, ethnocultural diversity and languages in Canada up to 2036, 2011 to 2036," *The Daily*, January 25, 2017, http://www.statcan.gc.ca/daily -quotidien/170125/dq170125b-eng.htm.

20. Statistics Canada, "An increasingly diverse linguistic landscape: Highlights from the 2016 Census," *The Daily*, August 2, 2017, http:// www.statcan.gc.ca/daily-quotidien/170802/dq170802b-eng.htm.

21. Susan Krashinsky, "More Companies taking multicultural marketing to mainstream levels," *Globe and Mail*, October 8, 2015, http:// www.theglobeandmail.com/report-on-business/industry-news /marketing/more-companies-taking-multicultural-marketing-to -mainstream-levels/article26727716/.

22. Nancy Kwon, "Inside the mind of the ethnic consumer," *Canadian Grocer*, July 16, 2013, http://www.canadiangrocer.com /uncategorized/inside-the-mind-of-the-ethnic-consumer-29244; Raizel Robin, "Big grocers aim for authenticity with ethnic consumers," *Canadian Grocer*, February 2, 2016, http://www .canadiangrocer.com/top-stories/serving-a-taste-of-home-61569; Sarah Barmak, "New BrandSpark study shows how Canadian ethnic buyers shop," *Canadian Grocer*, July 22, 2014, http://www .canadiangrocer.com/top-stories/new-brandspark-study-shows-how -canadian-ethnic-buyers-shop-43031; Bernice Cheung, "Ethnic Opportunity—If Only I Knew," paper presented at Canadian Grocer 's Ethnic Insights Conference, Toronto, May 28, 2013, http://www .canadiangrocer.com/top-stories/canadian-grocers-ethnic-insights -conference-26888; Francine Kopun, "Loblaw's Superstore rolls out a diverse approach," *Toronto Star*, June 29, 2015, https://www .thestar.com/business/2015/06/29/loblaws-superstore-rolls-out -a-diverse-approach.html; John Chan, "Building relevance with ethnic consumers, *Canadian Grocer*, August 1, 2012, http://www .canadiangrocer.com/blog/building-relevance-with-eth-consumers -15044.

23. World Population Review, "Country Population 2016" and "Continent Population 2016," accessed May 2016, http:// worldpopulationreview.com/.

24. Statistics Canada, "Families, households, and marital status: Key results from the 2016 Census, *The Daily*, August 2, 2017, http://www.statcan.gc.ca/daily-quotidien/170802/dq170802a -eng.htm.

25. "Reflecting Canadian values," Canadian Index of Wellbeing, accessed May 2016, https://uwaterloo.ca/canadian-index-wellbeing /about-canadian-index-wellbeing/reflecting-canadian-values.

26. Sarah Radwanic, "An Average Monday in the UK: PCs for Lunch, Tablets for Dinner," comScore, February 17, 2013, http://www .comscore.com/Insights/Data-Mine/An-Average-Monday-in-the -UK-PCs-for-Lunch-Tablets-for-Dinner.

27. Rob Young, "Canada's Media Landscape," PHD Canada (prepared for Interactive Advertising Bureau), December 2015, https:// iabcanada.com/content/uploads/2017/02/1.-CMUST-2015-V3 -Total-Canada-Exec-Summary-Dec-2-2015.pdf.

28. Ellen Chang, "Showrooming Remains Unpopular With the Majority of Customers," *TheStreet*, May 26, 2016, https://www.thestreet .com/story/13587093/1/showrooming-remains-unpopular-with-the -majority-of-customers.html.

29. Larry Simmons, "Social Media & Consumer Behavior," *Houston Chronicle*, accessed May 2016, http://smallbusiness.chron.com /social-media-consumer-behavior-45733.html.

30. "Instagram tops in user satisfaction," Forum Research Inc., January 10, 2015, http://poll.forumresearch.com/post/213/facebook-leads -in-penetration-linkedin-shows-most-growth/; Melody McKinnon, "2015 Canadian Social Media Usage Statistics," *CanadiansInternet .com*, January 12, 2016, http://canadiansinternet.com/2015- canadian-social-media-usage-statistics/; Ron Cann, "Key Trends in Canada's Social Media Landscape," Insights West 2016 Canadian Social Media Monitor, May 2016, http://www.insightswest.com/wp -content/uploads/2016/05/Rep_InsightsWest_CDNSocialMedia Monitor_2016.pdf.

31. Canadian Radio-television and Telecommunications Commission (CRTC), *Communications Monitoring Report 2016* (Ottawa: Author, 2016), http://www.crtc.gc.ca/eng/publications/reports /policymonitoring/2016/cmrs.htm#exii.

32. Sophia Harris, "Cable cord-cutting numbers soar in Canada thanks to Netflix, high prices, says report," CBC News, April 8, 2016, http://www.cbc.ca/news/business/cable-costs-cord-cutting-canada -netflix-1.3525949.

33. Paul Rich, Ben Martin, and Leah Jenkins, "2015 Canada Digital Future in Focus," comScore, March 27, 2015, https://www .comscore.com/Insights/Presentations-and-Whitepapers/2015/2015 -Canada-Digital-Future-in-Focus.

34. Emily Jackson, "Netflix lands over a million new Canadian subscribers in less than one year: report," *Financial Post*, June 14,

2016, http://business.financialpost.com/technology/netflix-lands -over-a-million-new-canadian-subscribers-in-less-than-one-year -report/wcm/db9ff8aa-414d-41cb-8414-23bd49a38943.

35. "To Binge or Not to Binge, That is the Question," Solutions Research Group Consultants Inc., March 7, 2013, www.srgnet.com /index.php/2013/03/07/to-binge-or-not-that-is-the-question/.

36. Lu Ann Williams, "The 2015 Trends Impacting the Food Industry," *Canadian Food Business*, December 17, 2014, http:// canadianfoodinsights.com/2014/12/17/2015-trends-impacting -food-industry/.

37. Pete Evans, "Kraft Dinner to remove synthetic colours from macaroni and cheese," CBC News, April 20, 2015, http://www.cbc .ca/news/business/kraft-dinner-to-remove-synthetic-colours-from -macaroni-and-cheese-1.3040324.

38. Lu Ann Williams, "The 2015 Trends Impacting the Food Industry."

39. "Mapping Your Future Growth: Five Game-Changing Consumer Trends," Business Development Bank of Canada, October 2013, https://www.bdc.ca/consumertrend.

40. "Food Intolerance in Canada," Euromonitor International, April 2016, http://www.euromonitor.com/food-intolerance-in-canada /report.

41. Hollie Shaw, "Beyond chicken and fries: Loblaw seeks bigger bite of restaurant sales with new fresh-food offerings," *Financial Post*, August 2, 2014, http://business.financialpost.com/news/retail -marketing/loblaw-fresh-food.

42. Statistics Canada, *Population Projections for Canada, Provinces and Territories, 2009 to 2036*, Catalogue no. 91-520-X (Ottawa: Minister of Industy, 2010), http://www.statcan.gc.ca/pub/91 -520-x/2010001/aftertoc-aprestdm1-eng.htm.

43. Jonah Comstock, " IMS: Half of Android health apps have fewer than 500 downloads," *MobiHealthNews*, October 30, 2013, http:// mobihealthnews.com/26836/ims-half-of-android-health-apps-have -fewer-than-500-downloads.

44. "Mapping Your Future Growth: Five Game-Changing Consumer Trends," Business Development Bank of Canada.

45. "More than 52,000 Canadians travelled abroad for medical care in 2014: study," CTV News, March 17, 2015, http://www.ctvnews.ca /health/more-than-52-000-canadians-travelled-abroad-for-medical -care-in-2014-study-1.2283121.

46. Advertising Standards Canada, *The Canadian Children's Food and Beverage Advertising Initiative: 2014 Compliance Report*, (Toronto: Author, 2015, http://www.adstandards.com/en/childrensi nitiative/2014ComplianceReport.pdf; "Canadian Families Making Healthier Choices," H & K Perspectives, July 2014, http://www .adstandards.com/en/childrensinitiative/consumerResearch.html.

47. "Greendex 2014: Consumer Choice and the Environment," National Geographic, accessed May 2016, http://images.nationalgeographic.com /wpf/media-live/file/Greendex-Canadians_FINAL-cb1409255133.pdf.

48. "Mapping Your Future Growth: Five Game-Changing Consumer Trends," Business Development Bank of Canada.

49. "Understanding Green Claims," Industry Canada, Office of Consumer Affairs, accessed May 2016, https://www.ic.gc.ca/eic/site /oca-bc.nsf/eng/ca02523.html.

50. "Mapping Your Future Growth: Five Game-Changing Consumer Trends," Business Development Bank of Canada.

51. "Corporate Citizenship: Environmental Sustainability," Canadian Tire, accessed May 2016, http://corp.canadiantire.ca/EN/Corporate Citizenship/EnvironmentalSustainability/Pages/default.aspx.

52. "Canadian Lifestyles 2017: Pride and Purse Strings," Mintel, accessed July 2017, http://store.mintel.com/canadian-lifestyles -pride-and-purse-strings-canada-april-2017.

53. Rick Newman, "10 Products That Boomed During the Recession, *U.S. News & World Report*, October 20, 2009, http://money.usnews .com/money/blogs/flowchart/2009/10/20/10-products-that-boomed -during-the-recession.

54. Mark Koba, "Gross Domestic Product: CNBC Explains," CNBC, November 3, 2011, http://www.cnbc.com/id/44505017.

55. J.B. Maverick, "How do changes in interest rates affect the spending habits in the economy?" *Investopedia*, July 17, 2015, http://

www.investopedia.com/ask/answers/071715/how-do-changes -interest-rates-affect-spending-habits-economy.asp.

56. Sarah Radwanic, "An Average Monday in the UK."

57. Paul Rich et al., "2015 Canada Digital Future in Focus."

58. Karen J. Bannan, "Cross-Device Advertising: How to Navigate Mobile Marketing's Next Big Thing," Criteo, presented by Ad Age Content Strategy Studio, September 2014, http://www.criteo.com /resources/cross-device-advertising-how-to-navigate-the-next-big -opportunity-in-mobile-marketing/.

59. CIRA, "The State of e-Commerce in Canada."

60. Allison Enright, "Canada gets serious about e-commerce," *Internet Retailer*, September 1, 2015, https://www.internetretailer.com/2015 /09/01/canada-gets-serious-about-e-commerce.

61. David James Friend, "76% of Canadians shopped online last year."

62. K. Neilsen, "Deciphering Cloud Services for Consumers," November 21, 2011, accessed May 2016, http://cloud-services -review.toptenreviews.com/confused-about-the-cloud-deciphering -cloud-services-for-consumers.html; Kenneth Hess, "10 Cloud-Based Services You Can't Live Without," *ServerWatch*, January 13, 2011, http://www.serverwatch.com/trends/article.php/3920691/10 -CloudBased-Services-You-Cant-Live-Without.htm.

63. Alex Boutilier, "Canadians growing concerned over Internet privacy, poll shows," *Toronto Star*, November 24, 2014, https:// www.thestar.com/news/canada/2014/11/24/canadians_growing _concerned_over_internet_privacy_poll_shows.html.

64. Nick Patch, "How much will Canadians pay to stream music?" *Toronto Star*, June 8, 2015, https://www.thestar.com/business/tech_news /2015/06/08/how-much-will-canadians-pay-to-stream-music.html.

65. Paul Rich et al., "2015 Canada Digital Future in Focus."

66. Chris Powell, "Nearly 70% of Canadians watch YouTube monthly (report)," *Marketing*, November 11, 2015, http://www .marketingmag.ca/media/nearly-70-of-canadians-watch-youtube -monthly-report-161240.

67. Adam Lella, Andrew Lipsman, and Ben Martin, "The Global Mobile Report," comScore, July 14, 2016, https://www.comscore.com/Insights /Presentations-and-Whitepapers/2015/The-Global-Mobile-Report.

68. CRTC, *Communications Monitoring Report 2016*; Paul Rich et al., "2015 Canada Digital Future in Focus."

69. CRTC, *Communications Monitoring Report 2016*.

70. Jeff Fraser, "Mobile beacons' second wave will be all about data," *Marketing*, December 8, 2015, http://www.marketingmag.ca/tech /mobile-beacons-second-wave-will-be-all-about-data-163074.

71. Igor Bonifacic, "Mobile payments won't become mainstream in Canada before 2019: IDC," *MobileSyrup*, February 27, 2016, http:// mobilesyrup.com/2016/02/27/mobile-payments-wont-become -mainstream-in-canada-before-2019-idc/; Rose Behar, "What Apple Pay means for mobile payments in Canada," *MobileSyrup*, May 13, 2016, http://mobilesyrup.com/2016/05/13/what-apple-pay-means -for-mobile-payments-in-canada/?utm_content=bufferba271&utm _medium=social&utm_source=twitter.com&utm_campaign =buffer.

72. Competition Bureau Canada website, accessed February 2017, https://www.canada.ca/en/competition-bureau.html; Amy Judd, "Top 10 scams of 2016 reveal Canadians lost more than $90M last year," Global news, March 1, 2017, http://globalnews.ca/news /3280609/top-10-scams-of-2016-reveal-canadians-lost-more-than -90m-last-year/; Mike Laanela, "Canada's top 10 scams earned crooks $1.2B last year, says BBB," CBC News, March 1, 2016, http://www.cbc.ca/news/canada/british-columbia/canada-s-top -10-scams-earned-crooks-1-2b-last-year-says-bbb-1.3471279; Canadian Competition Bureau, *The Little Black Book of Scams* (Ottawa: Author, 2012), http://www.competitionbureau.gc.ca/eic /site/cb-bc.nsf/vwapj/Little-Black-Book-Scams-e.pdf/$file/Little -Black-Book-Scams-e.pdf.

73. Advertising Standards Canada, "The Canadian Code of Advertising Standards," accessed May 2016, http://www.adstandards.com/en /Standards/canCodeOfAdStandards.aspx.

74. "Report on the Operation of the National Do Not Call List(DNCL) for the period April 1, 2014 to March 31, 2015," Canadian

Radio-television and Telecommunications Commission (CRTC), September 30, 2015, http://www.crtc.gc.ca/eng/DNCL/rpt150930.htm.

75. "CMA Guides and Mini-Guides," Canadian Marketing Association, accessed May 2016, https://www.the-cma.org/regulatory/code-and-guidelines.

76. Canadian Wireless Telecommunications Association (CWTA) website, accessed May 2016, http://cwta.ca.

77. "Why Use Short Codes" CWTA, accessed May 2016, http://www.txt.ca/why-use-short-codes/.

78. "About Us," Mobile Marketing Association, accessed June 2016, http://www.mmaglobal.com/about.

79. "Fact Sheets, Privacy Legislation in Canada," Office of the Privacy Commissioner of Canada, accessed May 2016, at www.priv.gc.ca/resource/fs-fi/02_05_d_15_e.asp; Minister of Justice, *Privacy Act* as amended April 2016, accessed May 2016, http://laws-lois.justice.gc.ca/PDF/P-21.pdf and http://laws-lois.justice.gc.ca/eng/acts/P-21/index.html.

80. Office of the Privacy Commissioner of Canada, *Personal Information Protection and Electronic Document Act*, accessed May 2016, https://www.priv.gc.ca/en/privacy-topics/privacy-laws-in-canada/the-personal-information-protection-and-electronic-documents-act-pipeda/pipeda-compliance-help/guide_org/.

81. "Canada's Anti-Spam Legislation, Fast Facts," Government of Canada, accessed June 2017, http://fightspam.gc.ca/eic/site/030.nsf/eng/h_00039.html; "Canada's Anti-Spam Law Casts a Wide Net – Requires All Organizations to Take Action," Osler, Hoskin & Harcourt LLP, January 2014, https://www.osler.com/osler/media/Osler/reports/privacy-data/CASL-Canada-s-Anti-Spam-Law-Casts-a-Wide-Net.pdf.

82. "CMA Guide to Canada's Anti-Spam Law (CASL)," Canadian Marketing Association, April 2015, http://www.the-cma.org/regulatory/code-and-guidelines/cma-guide-to-canada-anti-spam-law.

83. "Online Behavioural Advertising," Office of the Privacy Commissioner of Canada, accessed May 2016 https://www.priv.gc.ca/resource/topic-sujet/oba-pcl/index_e.asp.

84. "Understanding Online Advertising," Digital Advertising Alliance of Canada, accessed May 2016, http://youradchoices.ca/understanding-online-advertising/.

## Chapter 3

1. Personal Interview with Larry Lubin, president and CEO, BLUERUSH, May 2016.

2. Alan Walks, "Mapping the urban debtscape: The geography of household debt in Canadian cities," *Urban Geography,* April 29, 2013, *34*(2), 153–187, doi:10.1080/02723638.2013.778647; Chris Sorensen, "Living beyond our means," *Maclean's,* March 22, 2014; Bryan Borzykowski, "Managing your debt-to-income ratio," *Maclean's,* November 19, 2012; Canada Country Profile, 2013, 1–82.

3. Jonathan Law, *A Dictionary of Business and Management* (5th ed.) (New York: Oxford University Press, 2009); Gordon C. Bruner II and Richard J. Pomazal, "Problem Recognition: The Crucial First Stage of the Consumer Decision Process," *Journal of Consumer Marketing 5* (1988), pp. 53–63; and James F. Engel, Roger D. Blackwell, and Paul Miniard, *Consumer Behavior,* 9th ed. (Fort Worth, TX: Dryden Press, 1998).

4. For a thorough description of consumer expertise, see Joseph W. Alba and J. Wesley Hutchinson, "Knowledge Calibration: What Consumers Know and What They Think They Know," *Journal of Consumer Research 27* (2000), pp. 123–156. For in-depth studies on external information search patterns, see Sridhar Moorthy, Brian T. Ratchford, and Debabrata Tulukdar, "Consumer Information Search Revisited: Theory and Empirical Analysis," *Journal of Consumer Research 23* (1997), pp. 263–277; and Joel E. Urbany, Peter R. Dickson, and William L. Wilkie, "Buyer Uncertainty and Information Search," *Journal of Consumer Research 16* (1989), pp. 208–215.

5. Patricia F. Phalen, Richard V. Ducey, "Audience Behavior in the Multi-Screen 'Video-Verse'," *International Journal on Media Management 14* (2012), pp. 141–156; Ginny Marvin, "Microsoft Study: Multi-Screen Behaviour and What It Means for Marketers," *Marketing Land*, March 18, 2013; and Philip Webb, "The New Multi-Screen World: Understanding Consumer Behaviour," *Mobify*, September 17, 2012.

6. Kristin Laird, "Reinventing retail," *Marketing*, March 28, 2013; "GroupM Next and Catalyst Release 'Showrooming in Canada' Report," *Wireless News* [news release], March 8, 2013; Megan Haynes, "Who's showrooming, and how?" *Strategy,* May 15, 2013, http://strategyonline.ca/2013/05/15/whos-showrooming-and-how/.

7. For an extended discussion on evaluative criteria, see Del J. Hawkins, Roger J. Best, and Kenneth A. Coney, *Consumer Behavior,* 8th ed. (New York: Irwin/McGraw-Hill, 2001), pp. 566–83.

8. Caroline Rouen-Mallet, Pascale Ezan, and Stéphane Mallet, "Toward a deeper understanding of the choice process in child consumers through the concept of the evoked set," *Recherche et Applications en Marketing* (English Edition), 29(4) (2014), pp. 60–88, doi:10.1177/2051570714558169; Jochen Wirtz and Anna S. Mattila, "The effects of consumer expertise on evoked set size and service loyalty," *Journal of Services Marketing 17* (2003), pp. 649–665; John A. Howard, *Buyer Behavior in Marketing Strategy,* 2nd ed. (Englewood Cliffs, NJ: Prentice Hall, 1994), pp. 101, 128–89.

9. Pantea Foroudi, T.C. Melewar, and Surashka Gupta, "Linking corporate logo, corporate image, and reputation: An examination of consumer perceptions in the financial setting," *Journal of Business Research 67* (2014), 2269–2281; Elyria Kemp, Carla Y. Childers, and Kim H. Williams, "Place branding: creating self-brand connections and brand advocacy," *Journal of Product & Brand Management 21* (2012), 508–515; Jesse Ferreras, "Canada real estate: Millennials aren't rushing to buy, BMO says," *Huffington Post*, April 28, 2016, http://www.huffingtonpost.ca/2016/04/28/canada-real-estate-millennial_n_9801542.html; Jason Heath, "Are Millenials better off renting? Why young Canadians may want to put off home ownership," *Financial Post*, August 7, 2015, http://business.financialpost.com/personal-finance/mortgages-real-estate/are-millennials-better-off-renting-why-young-canadians-may-want-to-put-off-home-ownership; Mike Valenti, "Welcome to the new breed of consumers," Glance Marketing, November 29, 2015, http://glancemarketing.ca/welcome-to-the-new-breed-of-consumers; Russ Martin, "What do Millennials value? Spotify's ad VP explains," *Marketing*, January 14, 2015, http://www.marketingmag.ca/brands/what-do-millennials-value-spotifys-ad-vp-explains-134882; Josh Fromm, "Secrets to win with affluent Millenials: Uber, Bose and brands getting traction," *Forbes*, November 2, 2015, http://www.forbes.com/sites/jefffromm/2015/11/02/secrets-to-win-with-affluent-millennials-uber-bose-and-brands-getting-traction/2/#3e924d2e47f8.

10. Peter Weill and Stephanie L. Woerner, "Optimizing your digital business model," *MIT Sloan Management Review,* March 19, 2013, pp. 71–78; Joerg Koenigstorfer and Andrea Groeppel-Klein, "Consumer acceptance of the mobile Internet," *Marketing Letters,* August 31, 2012, pp. 917–928; Sheena Leek and George Christodoulides, "Next-Generation Mobile Marketing: How Young Consumers React to Bluetooth-Enabled Advertising," *Journal of Advertising Research 49* (2009), pp. 44–53.

11. Nicole Fallon, "Why 'Webrooming' Could Bring Customers Back Into Stores," *Business News Daily*, June 9, 2014, http://www.businessnewsdaily.com/6565-webrooming-retail-stores.html; Adam Rapp, Thomas L. Baker, Daniel G. Bachrach, Jessica Ogilvie, and Lauren Skinner Beitelspacher, "Perceived customer showrooming behavior and the effect on retail salesperson self-efficacy and performance," *Journal of Retailing 91* (2015), 358–369; and Alan Wolf, "Best Buy Besting Walmart, Target at Showrooming," *TWICE*, July 7, 2013, http://www.twice.com/news/news/best-buy-besting-walmart-target-showrooming/42595.

12. Isabelle Goyette et al., "E-WOM Scale: Word-of-Mouth Measurement Scale for e-Services Context," *Canadian Journal of Administrative Sciences 27* (2010), pp. 5–23; Sun-Jung Moon, John P. Costello, and Dong-Mo Koo, "The impact of consumer confusion from eco-labels on negative WOM, distrust, and dissatisfaction,"

*International Journal of Advertising 36* (2016), pp. 246–271; Jagdish N. Sheth, Banwari Mitral, and Bruce Newman, *Consumer Behavior* (Fort Worth, TX: Dryden Press, 1999), p. 22.

13. Moti Salti, Imen El Karoui, Mathurin Maillet, and Lionel Naccache, "Cognitive Dissonance Resolution is Related to Episodic Memory," *PLoS One 9.9* (2014), e108579; Monika Koller and Thomas Salzberger, "Heterogeneous development of cognitive dissonance over time and its effect on satisfaction and loyalty," *Journal of Customer Behaviour 11* (2012), pp. 261–280; Thomas Salzberger and Monika Koller, "Investigating the impact of cognitive dissonance and customer satisfaction on loyalty and complaint behaviour," *REMark 9* (2010), pp. 5–16.

14. For an overview of research on involvement, see John C. Mowen and Michael Minor, *Consumer Behavior,* 6th ed. (Upper Saddle River, NJ: Prentice Hall, 2001), pp. 64–68; and Frank R. Kardes, *Consumer Behavior* (Reading, MA: Addison-Wesley, 1999), pp. 256–58.

15. For an overview on the three problem-solving variations, see Hawkins, Best, and Coney, *Consumer Behavior,* pp. 506–7; and Howard, *Buyer Behavior,* pp. 69–162.

16. Nelson Barber, Tim Dodd, and Natalia Kolyesiknova, "Gender differences in information search: implications for retailing," *Journal of Consumer Marketing 26* (2009), pp. 415–426; Kenneth C. Gehrt and Ruoh-Nan Yan, "Situational, consumer, and retailer factors affecting internet, catalog, and store shopping," *International Journal of Retail & Distribution Management 32* (2004), pp. 5–18; Sydney Roslow, Tiger Li, and J.A.F. Nicholls, "Impact of situational variables and demographic attributes in two seasons on purchase behaviour," *European Journal of Marketing 34* (2000), pp. 1167–1180; Russell Belk, "Situational Variables and Consumer Behavior," *Journal of Consumer Research 2* (1975), pp. 157–163.

17. "Shopping As Therapy: Good Health Comes in Small Packages," *Discover Fit & Health,* accessed June 2011 at http://health.howstuffworks.com/wellness/women/general/shopping-as-therapy.htm.

18. A. H. Maslow, *Motivation and Personality* (New York: Harper & Row, 1970).

19. "Brand Papers: Challenging Maslow," *Brand Strategy,* 2003; Francis Buttle, "The social construction of needs," *Psychology & Marketing,* September 15, 2006, p. 197.

20. Arthur Koponen, "The Personality Characteristics of Purchasers," *Journal of Advertising Research 1* (1960), pp. 89–92; Joel B. Cohen, "An Interpersonal Orientation to the Study of Consumer Behavior," *Journal of Marketing Research 4* (1967), pp. 270–78; and Rena Bartos, *Marketing to Women Around the World* (Cambridge, MA: Harvard Business School, 1989).

21. Michael R. Solomon, *Consumer Behavior,* 5th ed. (Upper Saddle River, NJ: Prentice Hall, 2002), p. 61.

22. "BMW Service and Warranties," BMW Canada website, accessed at www.bmw.ca/ca/en/owners/service/warranty/warranty_1.html.

23. Martin Fishbein and I. Aizen, *Belief, Attitude, Intention and Behavior: An Introduction to Theory and Research* (Reading, MA: Addison-Wesley, 1975), p. 6.

24. Richard J. Lutz, "Changing Brand Attitudes through Modification of Cognitive Structure," *Journal of Consumer Research 1* (1975), pp. 49–59; "Pepsi's Gamble Hits Freshness Dating Jackpot," *Advertising Age,* September 19, 1994, p. 50; and "Every Which Way to Color, Whiten, Brighten," *Brandweek,* June 17, 2002, p. 558.

25. "How many hours of sleep are enough?" Mayo Clinic website, accessed September 2014 at www.mayoclinic.com/health/how-many-hours-of-sleep-are-enough/AN01487.

26. "The VALS™ Types," www.strategicbusinessinsight.com, accessed July 2013.

27. Personal interview with Michael Weiss, chief marketing officer, Environics Analytics, July 2013.

28. "Maximizing the Market with Influentials," *American Demographics,* July 1995, p. 42; also see, "I'll Have What He's Having," *American Demographics,* July 2000, p. 22.

29. Representative recent work on positive and negative word of mouth can be found in Geok Theng Lau and Sophia Ng, "Individual and Situational Factors Influencing Negative Word-of-Mouth Behav-

iour," *Canadian Journal of Administrative Sciences 18* (2001), pp. 163–178; Robert E. Smith and Christine A. Vogt, "The Effects of Integrating Advertising and Negative Word-of-Mouth Communications on Message Processing and Response," *Journal of Consumer Psychology 4* (1995), pp. 133–151; Paula Bone, "Word-of-Mouth Effects on Short-Term and Long-Term Product Judgments," *Journal of Business Research 32* (1995), pp. 213–23; Chip Walker, "Word of Mouth," *American Demographics,* July 1995, pp. 38–45; and Dale F. Duhan, Scott D. Johnson, James B. Wilcox, and Gilbert D. Harrell, "Influences on Consumer Use of Word-of-Mouth Recommendation Sources," *Journal of the Academy of Marketing Science 25* (1997), pp. 283–295.

30. Weng Marc Lim, " The Influence of Internet Advertising and Electronic Word of Mouth on Consumer Perceptions and Intention: Some Evidence from Online Group Buying," *Journal of Computer Information Systems 55*(4) (2015), 81–89; Megan Haynes, "Hey brands, millennials want you to help out," *Strategy,* September 19, 2014, http://strategyonline.ca/2014/09/19/hey-brands-millennials-want-you-to-help-out/; Marta Tsimicalis, "Ethical consumerism is rampant amongst Canada's younger generation," *St. Joseph Communications* (n.d.), http://stjoseph.com/ethical-consumerism-and-youth/; and "Sowing the seeds of business success," *Globe and Mail* (Ottawa/Quebec Edition), September 30, 2015.

31. For an extended discussion on reference groups, see Wayne D. Hoyer and Deborah J. MacInnis, *Consumer Behavior,* 2nd ed. (Boston: Houghton Mifflin, 2001), chap. 15.

32. For an extensive review on consumer socialization of children, see Deborah Roedder John, "Consumer Socialization of Children: A Retrospective Look at Twenty-Five Years of Research," *Journal of Consumer Research 26* (1999), pp. 183–213.

33. This discussion is based on "The American Family in the 21st Century," *American Demographics,* August 2001, p. 20; and J. Paul Peter and Jerry C. Olson, *Consumer Behavior and Marketing Strategy,* 5th ed. (New York: Irwin/McGraw-Hill, 1999), pp. 341–43.

34. "Canadian households in 2011: Type and growth," Statistics Canada, September 2012, http://www12.statcan.gc.ca/census-recensement/2011/as-sa/98-312-x/98-312-x2011003_2-eng.pdf.

35. Diane Crispell, "Dual-Earner Diversity," *American Demographics,* July 1995, pp. 32–37.

36. "There She Is . . . ," *American Demographics,* August 2001, p. 6; "Wearing the Pants," *Brandweek,* October 20, 1997, pp. 20, 22; "Look Who's Shopping," *Progressive Grocer,* January 1998, p. 18.

37. Bridget Brennan, "Top 10 Things Everyone Should Know About Women Consumers," *Forbes,* January 21, 2015, http://www.forbes.com/sites/bridgetbrennan/2015/01/21/top-10-things-everyone-should-know-about-women-consumers/#7f28a29f2897; "Call It 'Kid-fluence,'" *U.S. News & World Report,* July 30, 2001, pp. 32–33; "Special Report: Superstars of Spending," *Advertising Age,* February 20, 2001, pp. S1, S10; Teen Research Unlimited, www.teenresearch.com, September 4, 2001.

38. "I.AM.Canadian by Molson," CBC Digital Archives, www.cbc.ca/archives/categories/economy-business/business/selling-suds-the-beer-industry-in-canada/i-am-canadian.html; and Susan Krashinsky, "I am Canadian, and so are they: Molson's new nationalist pitch," *Globe and Mail,* February 6, 2013, www.theglobeandmail.com/report-on-business/industry-news/marketing/i-am-canadian-and-so-are-they-molsons-new-nationalist-pitch/article8280376/.

39. "French and the francophonie in Canada," Statistics Canada, October 2012, www12.statcan.gc.ca/census-recensement/2011/as-sa/98-314-x/98-314-x2011003_1-eng.cfm.

40. Danny Kucharsky, "French Lessons," *Marketing,* March 27, 2006, p. 8.

41. Ed Crain, "Say 'Oui' to the Quebec Market," *Electronic Retailer,* August 2010, www.electronicretailermag.com/er0810_quebec.

42. Rebecca Harris, "Embrace and Prosper," *Marketing,* January 23, 2006.

43. For comprehensive references on cross-cultural aspects of marketing, see Paul A. Herbig, *Handbook of Cross-Cultural Marketing* (New York: Halworth Press, 1998); and Jean-Claude Usunier, *Marketing across Cultures,* 2nd ed. (London: Prentice Hall Europe,

1996). Unless otherwise indicated, examples found in this section appear in these excellent sources.

44. "McDonald's Adapts Mac Attack to Foreign Tastes with Expansion," *Dallas Morning News,* December 7, 1997, p. 3H; and "Taking Credit," *The Economist,* November 2, 1996, p. 75.

45. Patricia Adams, "Foreign aid corruption case puts Canada on trial," *National Post,* August 20, 1999.

46. These examples appear in Del I. Hawkins, Roger J. Best, and Kenneth A. Coney, *Consumer Behavior,* 8th ed. (Burr Ridge, IL: McGraw-Hill/Irwin, 2001), chap. 2.

47. "Greeks Protest Coke's Use of Parthenon," *Dallas Morning News,* August 17, 1992, p. D4.

48. Valentina Vescovi, "In Spain, Pepsi Becomes 'Pesi,'" *Advertising Age,* February 4, 2010, http://adage.com/article/global-news/marketing -spain-pepsi-pesi/141916/; and Valentina Vescovi and Aixa Rocca, "In Argentina, Pepsi Becomes 'Pecsi,'" *Advertising Age,* July 15, 2009, http://adage.com/globalnews/article?article_id=137946.

49. "Global Thinking Paces Computer Biz," *Advertising Age,* March 6, 1995, p. 10.

50. "If only Krispy Kreme makes you smarter," *Business 2.0,* August 2005, p. 108.

51. Anca Bucuta, "A review of the specific characteristics of the generation Y consumer," *The Proceedings of the International Conference, Marketing - from Information to Decision 8* (2015): 38; "The 'compassion effect,'" *USA Today,* Dec. 2015; Jeff Fromm, "Think Tank," *WWD,* July 22, 2015; "McDonald's Canada introduces self-serve ordering," *Toronto* Star, September 30, 2015, http://www.thestar .com/business/2015/09/30/mcdonalds-canada-introduces-self-serve -ordering.html; Brian Sozzi, "McDonald's rolling out self-ordering kiosks in Europe: Will the U.S. be next?" *The Street,* April 13, 2016, https://www.thestreet.com/story/13511123/1/mcdonald-s-rolling- out-self-ordering-kiosks-in-europe-will-u-s-be-next.html.

## Chapter 4

1. "Alcoholic Drinks in Canada," Euromonitor International, June 2016, accessed June 2016 at http://www.euromonitor.com/alcoholic -drinks-in-canada/report; Delvinia website, accessed June 2016 at www.delvinia.com; written input and personal communication with Susan O'Neill, director of communications, Delvinia, May/June 2016; written input from Corby Spirit and Wine Ltd.'s director, strategic planning, insights & innovation, June 2016.

2. For an expanded definition, consult the American Marketing Association's website at http://marketing-dictionary.org/ama.

3. "Population by year, by province and territory, 2015," Statistics Canada, CANSIM, table 051-0001, accessed June 2016 at http://www .statcan.gc.ca/tables-tableaux/sum-som/l01/cst01/demo02a-eng.htm.

4. Lisa Arthur, "What is Big Data?" *Forbes,* August, 15, 2013, http:// www.forbes.com/sites/lisaarthur/2013/08/15/what-is-big-data /#5329d8783487.

5. "Extracting business value from the 4 Vs of big data," IBM, accessed June 2016 at http://www.ibmbigdatahub.com/sites/default /files/infographic_file/4Vs_Infographic_final.pdf.

6. "The Zettabyte Era: Trends and Analysis," Cisco [white paper], June 2, 2016, http://www.cisco.com/c/en/us/solutions/collateral /service-provider/visual-networking-index-vni/vni-hyperconnectivity -wp.pdf.

7. Kit Smith, "Marketing: 96 Amazing Social Media Statistics and Facts," *Brandwatch,* March 7, 2016, https://www.brandwatch.com /2016/03/96-amazing-social-media-statistics-and-facts-for-2016/.

8. Sonya Fatah, "How boomers are consuming media," January 25, 2016, http://strategyonline.ca/2016/01/25/diving-deep-into -boomers-media-consumption-habits/; Courtney Rubin, "What Do Customers Want? Look at Their Selfies," *New York Times,* May 7, 2016, http://www.nytimes.com/2016/05/08/business/media /what-do-consumers-want-look-at-their-selfies.html?_r=0; Ira Kalb, "Selfies and Smartphone Video Are Changing Marketing," *Business Insider,* August 18, 2014, http://www.businessinsider.com/how -selfies-are-changing-marketing-2014-8; Douglas MacMillan and Elizabeth Dwoskin, "Smile! Marketing Firms Are Mining Your Selfies," *Wall Street Journal,* October 9, 2014, http://www.wsj .com/articles/smile-marketing-firms-are-mining-your-selfies -1412882222; Tom Sommers, "Selfies Disrupt Market-Research Industry," May 12, 2016, https://www.linkedin.com/pulse/ selfies-disrupt-market-research-industry-tom-sommers; Clayton M. Christensen and Bob Moesta, "Know the Job Your Product was Hired for (with Help from Customer Selfies)," *Harvard Business Review,* June 6, 2016, https://hbr.org/2016/06/know-the-job-your -product-is-doing-with-help-from-customer-selfies.

9. Bala Deshpande, "How to use RFM analysis for customer segmentation and classification," Simafore, December 3, 2013, http://www .simafore.com/blog/bid/159575/How-to-use-RFM-analysis-for -customer-segmentation-and-classification.

10. "RFM Analysis," IBM Knowledge Center, November 30, 2015, http://www.ibm.com/support/knowledgecenter/SSLVMB_20.0.0 /com.ibm.spss.statistics.help/rfm_intro.xml.htm.

11. "Bronze Canadian Advertising Success Stories," Institute of Communication Agencies," accessed June 2016 at https://cassies.ca /entry/viewcasepast/24934; Harmeet Singh, "Oikos dreams up a new campaign," *Strategy,* February 22, 2016, http://strategyonline .ca/2016/02/23/oikos-dreams-up-a-new-campaign/.

12. Anand Rao, "Social listening: How market sensing trumps market research," PwC, June 13 2016, http://www.pwc.com/gx/en/services /advisory/consulting/risk/resilience/publications/social-listening -how-market-sensing-trumps-market-research.html.

13. Matthew Klein, "Selling Pies, Driving ROI: Pizza Hut's Solid Social Listening Strategy," Falcon.IO, January 27, 2016, https:// www.falcon.io/insights-hub/case-stories/cs-social-media-roi /pizza-hut-social-listening-case-study/.

14. "Homescan," Nielsen Canada, accessed June 2016 at https://www .homescan.ca/panel/CA/EN/Login.htm.

15. Kira Vermond, "Why London, Ontario is the perfect test market," *Globe and Mail,* October 19, 2015, http://www.theglobeandmail .com/report-on-business/small-business/sb-managing/london-test -market/article26846284/.

## Chapter 5

1. Personal interview with Raffi Sarmazian, Sarmazian Brothers, June 2016.

2. Peter LaPlaca, "From the Editor," *Journal of Business and Industrial Marketing* 3 (1992); D. Lawin, "Business-to-business marketing: A defined strategy," *Franchising World* 36 (2004), pp. 24–25; Nicole E. Coviello and Roderick J. Brodie, "Contemporary marketing practices of consumer and business-to-business firms: How different are they?" *Journal of Business & Industrial Marketing* 16 (2001), pp. 382–400.

3. This figure is based on *Statistical Abstract of the United States: 2002,* 122nd ed. (Washington, DC: U.S. Census Bureau, 2002).

4. "Key Small Business Statistics (2013)," Industry Canada, September 2013, www.ic.gc.ca/eic/site/061.nsf/eng/02804.html.

5. "Federal Budget 2013: Government stays the course on cuts, 2015 balanced budget," Canadian Press, March 21, 2013, www .huffingtonpost.ca/2013/03/21/federal-budget-2013_n_2883904 .html; Joel Eastwood, "New database will allow Canadians to track government spending data," Canadian Press, April 22, 2013, http:// globalnews.ca/news/502224/new-database-will-allow-canadians -to-track-government-spending-data/; "Expenditure database," Treasury Board of Canada Secretariat, April 12, 2013, www.tbs-sct .gc.ca/ems-sgd/edb-bdd/edb-bdd-eng.asp.

6. "Charities Listings," Canada Revenue Agency, April 4, 2013, www.cra-arc.gc.ca/tax/charities/online_listings/canreg_interim-e .html; "Charities Program Update," Canada Revenue Agency, April 18, 2013, www.cra-arc.gc.ca/chrts-gvng/chrts/bt/chrtsprgrm_pdt -eng.html.

7. North American Industry Classification System (NAICS) Canada 2012, Statistics Canada, October 24, 2013, www23.statcan.gc.ca /imdb/p3VD.pl?Function=getVDPage1&TVD=118464.

8. Tessa Wegert, "Contently Case Story: How Content is helping Xerox Rebrand," *Contently,* October 6, 2015, https://contently.com /strategist/2015/10/06/contently-case-story-how-content-is-helping

-xerox-rebrand/; Chima Adiele, "Towards promoting interactivity in a B2B web community," *Information Systems Frontiers 13* (2011), pp. 237–249; Umberto Miletti, "B2B Companies Must Keep Pace with the Customer 2.0." *Social Media B2B,* June 7, 2010, http://socialmediab2b.com/2010/06/b2b-company-customer; "About," HealthBiz Decoded (n.d.), http://healthbizdecoded.com /about/; Kate Maddox, "BMA conference focuses on content, innovation," *B to B,* June 13, 2011; "2013 Content Marketing Awards," *B to B,* September 30, 2013, www.btobonline.com /article/20130930/CONTENTMARKETING01/309269992 /xerox-corp?template=CMAprofile.

9.  Joe Pulizzi, "The transformation of content marketing," *EContent,* December 2012, pp. 20–21; Joe Pulizzi, "2013 B2B Content Marketing Benchmarks, Budgets and Trends," Content Marketing Institute, October 24, 2012, http://contentmarketinginstitute.com/2012/10/2013 -b2b-content-marketing-research/; "What is content marketing?" Content Marketing Institute (n.d.), http://contentmarketinginstitute.com /what-is-content-marketing/; Sarah Johnson and Laura Sparks, "How to launch a content marketing strategy," *CPA Practice Management Forum* 9 (2013), pp. 5–7.

10. This listing and portions of the following discussion are based on F. Robert Dwyer and John F. Tanner, Jr., *Business Marketing,* 2nd ed. (Burr Ridge, IL: McGraw-Hill/Irwin, 2002); and Edward G. Brierty, Robert W. Eckles, and Robert R. Reeder, *Business Marketing,* 3rd ed. (Upper Saddle River, NJ: Prentice Hall, 1998); and Dominic F. Wilson, "Why divide consumer and organizational buyer behaviour?" *European Journal of Marketing* 34 (2000), pp. 780–796.

11. "TTC and Bombardier sign contract to build 204 new street cars," Toronto Transit Commission, news release, June 30, 2009, www .ttc.ca/News/2009/June/TTC_and_Bombardier_sign_contract _to_build_204_new_streetcars.jsp; J. T. Connelly, "Bombardier: 186 Subway Cars Ordered for Toronto Transit," *Business Review Canada,* May 13, 2010, www.businessreviewcanada.ca/news /transportation/bombardier-186-subway-cars-ordered-toronto -transit; Tess Kalinowski, " TTC unveils Toronto's new streetcars," *Toronto Star,* November 15, 2012, www.thestar.com/news/city _hall/2012/11/15/ttc_unveils_torontos_new_streetcars.html.

12. "The Changing B2B Buyer," Marketo (n.d.), accessed September 2014 at www.marketo.com/cheat-sheets/the-changing-b2b-buyer/; "What makes business-to-business marketing different," Proteus Marketing (n.d.), accessed September 2014 at www.proteusb2b .com/b2b-marketing/difference.php; R. B. Ferguson, "The uh-oh factor: Fundamental shifts in social business and what to do about it," *MIT Sloan Management Review* 54 (2012), pp. 1–4.

13. "Selling to the Government of Canada," Public Works and Government Services Canada; "The Procurement Process," Public Works and Government Services.; and "Key Small Business Statistics – August 2013," Innovation, Science and Economic Development Canada.

14. S. Andersson and P. Servais, "Combining industrial buyer and seller strategies for international supply and marketing management," *European Business Review* 22 (2010), pp. 64–81, doi:http:// dx.doi.org/10.1108/09555341011009016; J. H. Bantham, "An exploratory study of satisfaction in buyer-seller partnerships," *Journal of Consumer Satisfaction, Dissatisfaction and Complainin g Behavior* 23 (2010), p. 130; definitions adapted from F. E. Webster and Y. Wind, *Organizational Buying Behavior* (Englewood Cliffs, NJ: Prentice Hall, 1972).

15. T. V. Bonoma, "Major Sales: Who Really Does the Buying?" *Harvard Business Review,* July 2006, http://hbr.org/2006/07/major-sales-who -really-does-the-buying/ar/1.

16. Ibid.

17. Ibid.

18. Webster and Wind, *Organizational Buying Behavior;* F.E. Webster Jr. and Y. Wind, "A General Model for Understanding Organizational Buying Behavior," *Journal of Marketing* 36 (1972), pp. 12–19.

19. "Contract awarded for St. Lawrence project bridge," *Purchasing B2B,* October 21, 2013, www.canadianmanufacturing.com/purchasing-and -procurement/news/contract-awarded-for-st-lawrence-project-bridge

-120780; "Government of Canada awards contract for engineering and coordination services for the new bridge for the St. Lawrence project," Transport Canada, press release, October 18, 2013, www.tc.gc.ca/eng /mediaroom/releases-2013-h139e-7388.html.

20. Representative studies on the buy-class framework that document its usefulness include E. Anderson, W., Chu, and B. Weitz, "Industrial purchasing: An empirical exploration of the buy-class framework," *Journal of Marketing 51* (1987), pp. 71–86; M. Ghingold, "Testing the 'buy-grid' buying process model," *Journal of Purchasing and Materials Management 22* (1986), pp. 30–36; P. Matthyssens and W. Faes, "OEM buying process for new components: Purchasing and marketing implications," *Industrial Marketing Management 14* (1985), pp. 147–157; and T.W. Leight and A.J. Ethans, "A script-theoretic analysis of industrial purchasing behavior," *Journal of Marketing 48* (1984), pp. 22–32. Studies not supporting the buy-class framework include J.A. Bellizi and P. McVey, "How valid is the buy-grid model?" *Industrial Marketing Management 12* (1983), pp. 57–62; and D.W. Jackson, J.E. Keith, and R.K. Burdick, "Purchasing agents' perceptions of industrial buying center influences: A situational approach," *Journal of Marketing 48* (1984), pp. 75–83.

21. N. Weinberg, "Evolution, Not Revolution," *Forbes,* May 21, 2001, www.forbes.com/best/2001/0521/038.html; "Business connections: The wired way we work," *Newsweek,* April 30, 2001; V. Vijayasri, "Arriving at a systems paradigm: Measuring and managing the complexity of organizations and consumers online," Order No. 3019131, Syracuse University, ProQuest Dissertations and Theses (2001).

22. This discussion is based on M. Roberti, "General Electric's Spin Machine," *The Industry Standard* (2001), pp. 74–83; "Grainger lightens its 'digital load,'" *Industrial Distribution 90* (2001), pp. 21–24; and K. Kuryllowicz, "The future of the net: We called up the smartest internet users we know to ask where the net is headed next," *Profit,* May 1, 2001.

23. "Surprise upturn for online trading," *Supply Management* 6 (2001), p. 9; T. Gignac, "E-barter exchanges play matchmaker: Businesses are using online trading networks to swap services, save money and discover new customers," *Calgary Herald,* (May 28, 2001); J.O. Soo and S.W. Kim, "The effect of B2B e-marketplace type on buyer-supplier relational advantages of e-marketplace and firm performance," *Asian Journal on Quality* 12 (2011), pp. 189–203, doi: http://dx.doi.org/10.1108/15982681111158742

24. "Our Story," Ariba website (n.d.), www.ariba.com/ourstory.

25. "Etiquette guide to japan; know the rules that make the difference," rev. ed., *Reference and Research Book News 24* (2009); L. Laroche and S. Morey, "Minding your manners: Business etiquette and gift-giving are part and parcel of conducting business abroad," *CMA Management 74* (2000), pp. 38–41; B. Bradley, "Best behaviour: Business etiquette in Japan," *Report on Business Magazine,* March 2001; G. Cotton, "Do this, not that when doing business overseas," CNBC, April 6, 2013, www.cnbc.com/id/100588894; Chad Brooks, "Lost in Translation: 8 International Marketing Fails," *Business News Daily,* October 7, 2013, http://www.businessnewsdaily .com/5241-international-marketing-fails.html; Neil Kokemuller, "Marketing Blunders & Global Culture," *AZCentral* (n.d.), http:// yourbusiness.azcentral.com/marketing-blunders-global-culture -13505.html; "Nike tattoo leggings pulled after deemed exploitative of Samoan culture," *Huffington Post,* August 15, 2013, www .huffingtonpost.com/2013/08/15/nike-tattoo-leggings_n_3763591 .html; V. Tapaleao, "Nike commits cultural faux pas," *New Zealand Herald,* August 14, 2013, www.nzherald.co.nz/business/news /article.cfm?c_id=3&objectid=10912088; "Nike debuts athletic ware, offends all of Samoa, pulls athletic wear," MSN, August 14, 2013, http://now.msn.com/nike-apologizes-for-using-samoan -tattoo-as-inspiration-for-running-tights.

26. Christian McIntosh, "Online auctions push E-commerce," *PC World Online,* April 29, 1999; R. Bray, "Reverse auctions going full speed ahead," *Summit* 6 (2003); Olivia Korostelina, "Online reverse auctions: a cost-saving inspiration for businesses," *Dartmouth Business Journal,* March 17, 2012, http://dartmouthbusinessjournal.com

/2012/03/online-reverse-auctions-a-cost-saving-inspiration-for
-businesses/.

27. Mary Kwak, "Potential pitfalls of e-auctions: smart ideas on reverse auctions," *Working Knowledge for Business Leaders,* Harvard Business School, September 9, 2002, http://hbswk.hbs.edu/archive/3086 .html; Bob Tedeschi, "GE has a bright idea," *Smart Business,* September 25, 2001.

28. Sandy Jap, "Going, Going, Gone," *Harvard Business Review,* November 2000, http://hbr.org/2000/11/going-going-gone/ar/1; L. Wichmann, "Avoiding the pitfalls of e-procurement: Seminar lays down the pros and cons of internet commerce," *Plant* 59 (2000), p. 16; G. Cameron, "Reverse auctions remain high on OGCA hit list," *Daily Commercial News and Construction Record* 76 (2003), p. 5.

## Chapter 6

1. Personal and written communication with Allison Whiteside, director, business development, Environics Analytics Canada; written communication from Jason Easton, director, sales, service & marketing, Toronto/GTA for General Motors Canada; Jason Easton, "Driving Sales with Data-based Market Analytics, paper presented at 9th Annual Environics Analytics User Conference, Toronto, November 4, 2015, http://www.environicsanalytics.ca/docs/default -source/eauc2015-presentations/jasoneaston-gm.pdf?sfvrsn=4; Jeromy Lloyd, "Can data crack Toronto's tough car shoppers?" *Marketing,* February 23, 2016, http://www.marketingmag.ca/brands /can-data-crack-torontos-tough-car-shoppers-168500; "All-New 2016 Chevrolet Cruze Priced from $15,995," General Motors [press release], December 16, 2015, http://media.gm.ca/media/ca/en/gm /news.detail.html/content/Pages/news/ca/en/2015/Dec/1216-Cruze -Pricing.html; Chris Powell, "Chevrolet offering millennials their 'best Cruze ever,'" *Marketing,* December 16, 2015, http://www .marketingmag.ca/brands/chevrolet-offering-millennials-their-best -cruze-ever-164329; Dan Proudfoot, "Review: 2016 Chevrolet Cruze gets a long-overdue reworking," *Globe and Mail,* April 26, 2016, https://www.theglobeandmail.com/globe-drive/reviews/new -cars/review-2016-chevrolet-cruze-gets-a-long-overdue-facelift /article29751264/; "PRIZM5," Environics Analytics website, accessed September 2016 at http://www.environicsanalytics.ca /prizm5; "Canadian Car of the Year Winers (by Year), Automobile Journalists Association of Canada, accessed September 2016 at http://www.ajac.ca/web/ccoty/previous_byyear.asp.

2. "Development of Tide Synthetic Detergent," American Chemical Society, October 25, 2006, https://www.acs.org/content/acs/en /education/whatischemistry/landmarks/tidedetergent.html; "Explore Our Brands," P&G Canada website, accessed July 2016 at http://www .pg.com/en_CA/brands/all-brands.shtml; "I love Gain," P&G Canada website, accessed July 2016 at http://www.ilovegain.ca/en-ca; "Ivory Snow," P&G Canada website, accessed July 2016 at http://www .ivorysnow.ca/; "Tide laundry detergent," P&G Canada website, accessed July 2016 at http://www.tide.com/en-CA/index.jspx.

3. "Packaging product specs," French's Flavor Ingredients, accessed July 2016 at http://www.frenchsflavoringredients.com/products /packaging-product-specs/index.php; "French's Tomato Ketchup Packet," French's Foodservice, accessed May 2017 at http://www .frenchsfoodservice.com/frenchs/products/frenchs-tomato-ketchup -packet/.

4. Adapted from the American Marketing Association's dictionary, accessed July 2016 at https://www.ama.org/resources/Pages /Dictionary.aspx?dLetter=N.

5. "About Tesla," Tesla website, accessed July 2016 at https://www .teslamotors.com/en_CA/about; Katie Fehrenbacher, "7 Reasons why Tesla Insists on Selling its Own Cars," *Fortune,* January 19, 2016, http://fortune.com/2016/01/19/why-tesla-sells-directly/.

6. "About us," Eco-Max website, accessed July 2016 at http://eco-max .ca/consumer/about/.

7. Murhad Hemmadi, "Specialty TV channels just keep getting more and more profitable," *Marketing,* July 8, 2014, http://www .marketingmag.ca/media/specialty-tv-channels-just-keep-getting -more-and-more-profitable-119292; "Canadian Specialty Television

Channels," Canada TV Media website, accessed July 2016 at http:// www.canadatvmedia.com/specialty-programming.html.

8. Philip T. Kotler and Kevin Lane Keller, *Marketing Management,* 15th ed. (New York: Pearson Education, 2016).

9. "mi adidas," adidas website, accessed July 2016 at http://www .adidas.ca/en/customise.

10. "Coke Freestyle," Coca-Cola website, accessed July 2016 at http:// www.coca-colafreestyle.com.

11. "Build and Price," Mini Canada website, accessed July 2016 at http://mini.ca/en/shopping/buildandprice.

12. Car2Go, corporate website for Vancouver, Calgary, Toronto, and Montreal locations, accessed July 2016 at https://www.car2go.com /CA/en/toronto/; "Car2Go," Daimler website, accessed July 2017 at https://www.daimler.com/products/services/mobility-services /car2go/.

13. "Centrum Products," Centrum website, accessed July 2016 at http:// www.centrum.ca/products.

14. "About us," Euromonitor website, accessed July 2016 at www.euromonitor.com/.

15. "PRIZM5," Environics Analytics website.

16. Vito Di Filippis, "Omni-Channel Marketing: Not Your Father's Customer Journey," Environics Analytics [blog], June 10, 2016, http://www.environicsanalytics.ca/blog-details/ea-blog/2016/06/10 /omni-channel-marketing-not-your-fathers-customer-journey; "PRIZM5," Environics Analytics website.

17. PSYTE HD, Pitney Bowes Canada website, accessed July 2016 at http://www.pitneybowes.com/us/location-intelligence/gis-data-sets /psyte-hd-canada.html.

18. SuperDemographics website, accessed July 2016 at www.superde-mographics.com.

19. "Tennis in Canada continues remarkable growth in participation and popularity, recent study shows," Tennis Canada [news release], September 8, 2014, http://www.tenniscanada.com/tennis-in -canada-continues-remarkable-growth-in-participation-and -popularity-recent-study-shows/; "Global Tennis Racquet Market 2015–2019, *Tennis Industry Magazine,* January 13, 2015, http:// www.tennisindustrymag.com/news/2015/01/research_and_markets _global_te.html; "Products," Prince Tennis website, accessed July 2016 at www.princetennis.com.

20. Chris Powell, "TSN introduces "Champions Live Here" positioning," *Marketing,* February 11, 2016, http://www.marketingmag.ca /advertising/tsn-introduces-champions-live-here-positioning-167838.

21. Hayley Peterson "McDonald's turnaround strategy is in overdrive," *Business Insider,* September 19, 2015, http://www.businessinsider .com/changes-mcdonalds-made-this-year-2015-9; Tanya Dua, "Anatomy of a comeback: How McDonald's got its groove back," *Digiday,* January 14, 2016, http://digiday.com/brands/anatomy -comeback-mcdonalds-got-groove-back/; Jonathan Maze, "How McDonald's got its groove back," *National Restaurant News,* April 22, 2016, http://nrn.com/same-store-sales/how-mcdonald-s-got-its -groove-back; Jamie Sturgeon, "McDonald's to launch standalone McCafé coffee shops in Canada," Global News, December 9, 2015, http://globalnews.ca/news/2388325/mcdonalds-to-launch -standalone-mccafe-coffee-shops-in-canada/.

22. "Cassies Gold: A & W makes things better," *Strategy,* February 12, 2016, http://strategyonline.ca/2016/02/12/cassies-gold-aw-makes -things-better/; "The A&W Multi-Site Franchise Opportunity," AW Franchise website, April 27, 2015, http://awfranchise.ca /news/2015/04/inverview-vp-realestate-franchising-patti-parente/.

23. "Interac Be in the Black," Cassies website, accessed July 2016 at https://cassies.ca/entry/viewcasepast/24811; "Interac Debit is a low cost payment solution for merchants in Canada," Interac [press release], accessed July 2016 at https://interac.ca/en/interac-debit-is -a-low-cost-payment-solution-for-merchants-in-canada.html; "Our Company," Interac website, accessed July 2016 at https://interac .ca/en/about/our-company.html; Harmeet Singh, "Check it out: Interac's dog in debt," *Strategy,* April 11, 2016, http://strategyonline .ca/2016/04/11/check-it-out-interacs-dog-in-debt/; David Parkinson, "Canada's household debt holds near record; growth moderates,"

*Globe and Mail*, June 14, 2016, http://www.theglobeandmail.com /report-on-business/economy/canadas-household-debt-holds-near -record-levels-growth-moderates/article30444416/.

## Chapter 7

1. Personal communication with David Freeman, head of brand marketing at MLSE, and Dave Haggith, senior director communications at MLSE. "Toronto Raptors Logo History," Sports Team History website, accessed September 2016 at http://sportsteamhistory.com /toronto-raptors-logo-history; Murray Newlands, "How This Exec Rebranded the Toronto Raptors by Embracing Authenticity," *Forbes*, February 26, 2016, http://www.forbes.com/sites /mnewlands/2016/02/26/how-this-exec-rebranded-the-toronto -raptors-by-embracing-authenticity/#2c6cd8e75f8e; "We the North, Best Insight, Gold," Cassies website, accessed September 2016 at http://cassies.ca/entry/viewcasepast/24691; Rachel Brady, "How the Raptors redefined their brand – and took Toronto by the throat," *Globe and Mail*, October 28, 2014, http://www.theglobeandmail .com/sports/basketball/how-the-raptors-redefined-their-brand-and -took-toronto-by-the-throat/article21360335/; "Toronto Raptors "We The North" Events, Seasonal and Short-Term (SILVER)," Cassies website, accessed September 2016 at https://cassies.ca/entry /viewcasepast/17911; Sarah Niedoba, "Meet the marketer behind the Raptors' #WeTheNorth campaign," *Canadian Business*, May 13, 2016, http://www.canadianbusiness.com/leadership/shannon -hosford-mlse-we-the-north/; Karizza Sanchez, "Drake, the Raptors, and the Value of a 'Global Ambassador,'" *Complex Sports*, February 12, 2016, http://ca.complex.com/sports/2016/02/drake-raptors -partnership; Twitter, Facebook, and Instagram accounts for Toronto Raptors, accessed September 2016.

2. "Gross domestic product (GDP) by industry sector," Statistics Canada website, table 379-0031, accessed July 2016 at http://www .statcan.gc.ca/tables-tableaux/sum-som/l01/cst01/gdps04a-eng.htm.

3. Amanda Baltazar, "Why Transparent Packaging Works," *Marketing*, January 20, 2016, http://www.marketingmag.ca/brands/why -transparent-packaging-works-166129.

4. "Nutrition Labelling," Health Canada website, accessed July 2016 at http://www.hc-sc.gc.ca/fn-an/label-etiquet/nutrition/index-eng.php.

5. Susan Krashinsky, "Judging a beer by its bottle: How a craft brewer tripled sales," *Globe and Mail*, June 2, 2016, http://www.theglo beandmail.com/report-on-business/industry-news/marketing/in-the -crowded-craft-beer-market-branding-matters/article30254128/.

6. Chris Powell, "6 Packaging Trends for 2016," *Marketing*, January 5, 2016, http://www.marketingmag.ca/brands/6-packaging-trends-for -2016-164789; Mike Esterl, "'Share a Coke' Credited with a Pop in Sales," *Wall Street Journal*, September 25, 2014, http://www.wsj .com/articles/share-a-coke-credited-with-a-pop-in-sales-1411661519; Rick Lingle, "Game-changing Connected Package optimizes consumer interaction," *Packaging Digest*, July 11, 2016, http://www .packagingdigest.com/retail-packaging/game-changing-connected -package-optimizes-consumer-interaction1607; Nikki Clark, "4 fast-moving trends in food and beverage packaging," *Packaging Digest*, May 24, 2016, http://www.packagingdigest.com/food-packaging/4 -fast-moving-trends-in-food-and-beverage-packaging-2016-05-23; "More marketers personalise packaging," WARC [news release], October 7, 2015, http://www.warc.com/LatestNews/News/More _marketers_personalise_packaging.news?ID=35517; "Global Packaging Trends," Mintel website, accessed July 2016 at http:// www.mintel.com/global-packaging-trends; "Diet Coke Celebrates What Makes Us All One of a Kind," Coca-Cola [news release], September 6, 2016, http://www.coca-cola.ca/newsroom/press-releases /diet-coke-celebrates-what-makes-us-all-one-of-a-kind-with-millions -of-unique-colourful-package-designs.

7. "All Brands Canada," Coca-Cola Canada website, accessed July 2016 at http://www.coca-colacompany.com/brands/all.

8. "Google Ads - Reach customers when it matters," Google website, accessed July 2017 at https://www.google.com/ads/.

9. "All Brands," Procter & Gamble website, accessed July 2017 at http://www.pg.ca/en-CA/our-brands; "Dawn," Procter & Gamble website, accessed July 2017 at https://dawn-dish.com/en-us/coupons -and-offers/canada.

10. Russ Martin, "The 10 Most Influential Brands in Canada: Ipsos," *Marketing*, January 26, 2016, http://www.marketingmag.ca/brands /the-10-most-influential-brands-in-canada-ipsos-165968; "The Most Influential Brands," Ipsos, accessed July 2016 at http://www .ipsos.ca/en/products-tools/marketing/consumer-trends-product/ the-most-influential-brands.aspx; "ICA and Ipsos announce sixth annual Top 10 Most Influential Brands in Canada at FFWD," Ipsos North America [press release], January 31, 2017, http://www.ipsos -na.com/news-polls/pressrelease.aspx?id=7562.

11. "ICA and Ipsos announce sixth annual Top 10 Most Influential Brands in Canada at FFWD," Ipsos North America.

12. "2016 Global Best Brands," Interbrand website, accessed March 2017 at http://interbrand.com/best-brands/best-global-brands/2016/.

13. "What is a patent?" Canadian Intellectual Property Office website, accessed September 2016 at http://www.ic.gc.ca/eic/site/cipointernet -internetopic.nsf/eng/wr03716.html?Open&wt_src=cipo-patent-main.

14. "What is copyright?" Canadian Intellectual Property Office website, accessed September 2016 at http://www.ic.gc.ca/eic/site/cipointernet -internetopic.nsf/eng/wr03719.html?Open&wt_src=cipo-cpyrght-main.

15. "What is a trademark?" Canadian Intellectual Property Office website, accessed September 2016 at http://www.ic.gc.ca/eic /site/cipointernet-internetopic.nsf/eng/wr03718.html?Open&wt _src=cipo-tm-main.

16. "Number of monthly active Facebook users worldwide as of 1st quarter 2016 (in millions)," Statista website, accessed July 2016 at http://www.statista.com/statistics/264810/number-of-monthly -active-facebook-users-worldwide/; "Number of monthly active Twitter users worldwide from 1st quarter 2010 to 1st quarter 2016 (in millions)," Statista website, accessed July 2016 at http://www .statista.com/statistics/282087/number-of-monthly-active-twitter -users/; "CDRP Decisions," CIRA website, accessed July 2016 at https://cira.ca/legal-policy-compliance/cdrp-process-and-decisions /cdrp-decisions; Zach Brooke, "More Brands Getting a #Trademark on Hashtags," March 23, 2016, *Marketing News Weekly*, https:// www.ama.org/publications/eNewsletters/Marketing-News-Weekly /Pages/More-Brands-Getting-a-Trademark-on-Hashtags.aspx; "Trademark Policy" Twitter website, accessed July 2016 at https:// support.twitter.com/articles/18367; Eric Misterovich, "How to Claim Your Trademark as a Username on Instagram," *Revision/Legal*, July 30, 2015, https://revisionlegal.com/trademark-attorney/how-to-claim -your-trademark-as-a-username-on-instagram/; Trevor Little, "Protecting your brand in the social media environment," *Roundtable*, October/November 2012, http://www.worldtrademarkreview.com /Magazine/Issue/39/Roundtable/Protecting-your-brand-in-the-social -media-environment; Ethan Wall, "3 Necessary Steps to Protect Your Trademarks on Social Media," Maximize Social Business, July 17, 2016, http://maximizesocialbusiness.com/3-necessary-steps -protect-trademarks-social-media-22248/; Kyle-Beth Hilfer, "How to Secure Your Intellectual Property in Social Media" Maximize Social Business, accessed July 2016 at http://maximizesocialbusiness .com/secure-intellectual-property-in-social-media-8554/; Ted Roe, "Social Media and Trademark Law in the 21st Century: Presenting Opportunities and Problems," ThomsonReuters, accessed July 2016 at http://trademarks.thomsonreuters.com/fr/article/trademark -tweeting-social-media-opportunities-challenges?cid=98; "Coca-Cola applies to trademark hashtag slogans," Trademarks & Brands Online, June 1, 2015, http://www.trademarksandbrandsonline.com/news/ coca-cola-applies-to-trademark-hashtag-slogans-4231; "#likeagirl - Trademark details," Justia Trademarks website, accessed March 2017 at https://trademarks.justia.com/863/21/likeagirl-86321325. html; Jack Marshall, "Companies Increasingly Trademark Hashtags," *Wall Street Journal*, March 30, 2016, https://www.wsj.com/articles/ companies-increasingly-trademark-hashtags-1459333936.

17. "Brand Glossary - Brand Personality," Brandchannel website, accessed July 2016 at http://brandchannel.com/brand-glossary/?ap=b.

18. "Why Brand Personality Matters: Aligning Your Brand to Cultural Drivers of Success" Millward Brown, accessed July 2016 at http://

www.millwardbrown.com/docs/default-source/insight-documents/points-of-view/Millward_Brown_POV_Brand_Personality.pdf.

19. "Internet grows to 329.3.4 million domain names In the fourth quarter of 2016," Verisign [news release], February 28, 2017, http://www.businesswire.com/news/home/20170228006844/en/Internet-Grows-329.3-Million-Domain-Registrations-Fourth.

20. Zachary Crockett, "Microsoft vs. MikeRoweSoft," January 21, 2014, http://priceonomics.com/microsoft-vs-mikerowesoft/.

21. Joseph Peterson, "Cybersquatting complaints against.com domains are dropping," Domain Name Wire, June 28, 2016, http://domain-namewire.com/2016/06/28/cybersquatting-complaints-com-do-mains-dropping/.

22. Carman Allison, "Picking up private label," *Canadian Grocer*, March 24, 2015, http://www.canadiangrocer.com/blog/picking-up-private-label-51204.

23. Brad Tuttle, "Brand Names Don't Mean as Much Anymore, *Time*, November 1, 2012, http://business.time.com/2012/11/01/brand-names-just-dont-mean-as-much-anymore/.

## Chapter 8

1. Personal communication with Sameera Banduk, marketing director, Thalmic Labs; "How does the Myo armband work?" Myo Support, accessed August 2016 at https://support.getmyo.com/hc/en-us/articles/202532376-How-does-the-Myo-armband-work-; "Myo Market," Thalmic Labs website, accessed August 2016 at https://market.myo.com/; "Thalmic Labs Secures $14.5 Million in Series A Funding Led by Spark Capital and Intel Capital," Thalmic Labs [press release], June 5, 2013, accessed August 2016 at https://www.thalmic.com/press.

2. "Number of apps available in leading app stores as of March 2017," Statista website, accessed July 2017 at https://www.statista.com/statistics/276623/number-of-apps-available-in-leading-app-stores/; Luke Villapaz, "Apple iPhone: Six Years of a Stunningly Successful Advertising Campaign," *International Business Times*, April 10, 2013, http://www.ibtimes.com/apple-iphone-six-years-stunningly-successful-advertising-campaign-video-1414562; Mark Bergen, "A History of Apple's Product Launch Marketing," *Advertising Age*, September 8, 2014, http://adage.com/article/media/a-history-apple-s-product-launch-marketing/294843/; Lara O'Reilly, "The latest IPhone ad Is a strange spot all about onions," *Business Insider*, April 26, 2016, http://www.businessinsider.com/apple-iphone-6s-onions-ad-2016-4.

3. John Kirk, "Android's Penetration Vs. Apple's Skimming Marketing Strategies, Tech.pinions, March 21, 2013, https://techpinions.com/androidss-penetration-vs-apples-skimming-marketing-strategies/15255.

4. Aaron Tilley, "Apple Watch Scored an Estimated 1 Million Pre-Orders on Launch Day," *Forbes*, April 13, 2015, http://www.forbes.com/sites/aarontilley/2015/04/13/apple-watch-scored-an-estimated-1-million-pre-orders-on-launch-day/#749be4894f77; Doug Olenick, "Why the Apple Watch Launch is One for the History Books," *Forbes*, April 24, 2015, http://www.forbes.com/sites/dougolenick/2015/04/24/apple-watch-launch-is-one-for-the-history-books/print/; Don Reisinger, "Apple Watch Is Dominating the Global Smartwatch Market," *Fortune*, September 21, 2016, http://fortune.com/2016/09/21/apple-watch-market-share/.

5. "Worldwide Smartwatch Market Experiences Its First Decline as Shipments Fall 32% in the Second Quarter of 2016, According to IDC," IDC, July 21, 2016, https://www.idc.com/getdoc.jsp?containerId=prUS41611516; Ben Woods, "Smartwatch sales decline for the first time and Apple is hit hardest," *Wired*, July 21, 2016, http://www.wired.co.uk/article/smartwatch-sales-decline-for-first-time-but-apple-suffers-most.

6. Molly Raisch, "10 Most Improved Foods," *Prevention*, January 7, 2014, http://www.prevention.com/food/healthy-eating-tips/10-most-improved-foods/slide/1.

7. "P&G Everyday: Tide," P&G website, accessed August 2016 at https://www.pgeveryday.ca/tag/tide.

8. Canadian Business Staff and Bruce Philp, "Canada's Best Brands 2017: The Top 25," *Canadian Business*, October 11, 2016, http://www.canadianbusiness.com/lists-and-rankings/best-brands/canadas-best-brands-2017-the-top-25/; "How MEC scaled the heights to become Canada's best brand," *Canadian Business*, October 15, 2015, http://www.canadianbusiness.com/lists-and-rankings/best-brands/top-brand-2016-mec/.

9. Ian Kar, "The company that created Pokémon Go is now worth over $3 billion," *Quartz*, July 25, 2016, http://qz.com/741117/the-company-that-created-pokemon-go-is-now-worth-over-3-billion/; "Nintendo shares fall as game company says Pokémon Go won't lure big profits," CBC News, July 25, 2016, http://www.cbc.ca/news/business/pokemon-go-nintendo-share-price-1.3693978; Karen K. Ho, "Canadians and the Pokemon craze, in four charts," *Globe and Mail*, July 13, 2016, http://www.theglobeandmail.com/technology/canadians-and-the-pokemon-craze-in-four-charts/article30899687/; Darrell Etherington, "Pokemon Go estimated at over 75M downloads worldwide," *TechCrunch*, July 25, 2016, https://techcrunch.com/2016/07/25/pokemon-go-75m-downloads/; Matthew Lynley, "A brief history of Niantic Labs, the makers of Pokemon Go," *TechCrunch*, August 14, 2016, https://techcrunch.com/gallery/a-brief-history-of-niantic-labs-the-makers-of-pokemon-go/; Mahita Gajanan, "Nintendo stock slumps as investors realize it doesn't make Pokemon Go," Time, July 25, 2016, http://time.com/4421450/pokemon-go-nintendo-shares-tokyo/.

10. Hayley Peterson, "McDonald's turnaround strategy is in overdrive," *Business Insider*, September 19, 2015, http://www.businessinsider.com/changes-mcdonalds-made-this-year-2015-9.

11. Josh Kolm, "What drives Canadian purchase behaviour?" *Strategy*, August 24, 2016, http://strategyonline.ca/2016/08/24/what-drives-canadian-purchase-behaviour/?utm_source=rss&utm_medium=rss&utm_campaign=what-drives-canadian-purchase-behaviour.

12. "Winners of BrandSpark International's 2017 Best New Product Awards announced from a survey of 20,000 Canadians," BrandSpark International [news release], March 20, 2017, http://www.bestnewproductawards.biz/canada/pdf/2017/2017-BNPA-News-Release-FINAL.pdf.

13. Leslie Hayward, "Overcoming Barriers To Electric Vehicle Adoption," *The Fuse*, May 30, 2015, http://energyfuse.org/overcoming-barriers-to-electric-vehicle-adoption/.

14. Arthur Thomas, "Drones could be the next disruptive technology," *Milwaukee Business News*, April 4, 2016, https://www.biztimes.com/2016/04/04/drones-could-be-the-next-disruptive-technology/; John Patrick Pullen, "This is how drones work," *Time*, April 3, 2015, http://time.com/3769831/this-is-how-drones-work/; Peter Diamandis, "The top 10 reasons drones are disruptive," *Forbes*, August 11, 2014, http://www.forbes.com/sites/peterdiamandis/2014/08/11/top-10-reasons-drones-are-disruptive/#7300470728bd/.

15. Everett Rogers, *Diffusion of Innovations*, 5th ed. (New York: Free Press, 2003).

16. Jagdish Sheth and Banwari Mittal, *Consumer Behavior: A Managerial Perspective*, 2nd ed. (Mason, OH: South-Western College Publishing, 2003).

17. "Canada Electric Car Sales Face A Roadblock In 'Range Anxiety.' But What's That?" Canadian Press, June 20, 2016, accessed at http://www.huffingtonpost.ca/2016/06/20/canada-electric-car-sales-range-anxiety_n_10581332.html; Christina Rogers, "Demand Ebbs for Electric, Hybrid Cars," *Wall Street Journal*, September 3, 2014, http://www.wsj.com/articles/electric-hybrid-car-demand-stalls-1409785123.

18. Jonah Comstock, "IMS: Half of Android health apps have fewer than 500 downloads," *MobiHealthNews*, October 29, 2013, http://mobihealthnews.com/26836/ims-half-of-android-health-apps-have-fewer-than-500-downloads; "Technology-based Client Care," Equinoxe website, accessed August 2016 at http://equinoxelifecare.com/technology-based-care/; "Equinoxe Relaunches the EQ Virtual Clinic to Improve Access to Health Care," Equinoxe LifeCare [press release], February 23, 2016 accessed at PRNewswire (http://www.prnewswire.com/news-releases/equinoxe-relaunches-the-eq-virtual-clinic-to-improve-access-to-health-care-569797371.html);

Jocelyn Aspa, "EQ Virtual works to make online health services accessible to the Downtown Eastside," *Georgia Straight*, March 21, 2016, http://www.straight.com/life/662386/eq-virtual-works-make-online-health-services-accessible-downtown-eastside; "Virtual Healthcare App Akira Launches to Give Canadians a Doctor in Their Pocket," Akira [press release], May 18, 2016, http://www.newswire.ca/news-releases/virtual-healthcare-app-akira-launches-to-give-canadians-a-doctor-in-their-pocket-579937431.html; "How It Works" Askthedoctor website, accessed August 2016 at https://www.askthedoctor.com/ask-a-doctor; "Making care mobile: A roadmap to the virtualization of care," PwC website, accessed August 2016 at http://www.pwc.com/ca/en/industries/healthcare/publications/virtual-health-making-care-mobile-canada.html.

19. Elaine Watson, "Why do 85% of new CPG products fail within two years?" Food Navigator USA, July 31, 2014, http://www.foodnavigator-usa.com/Markets/Why-do-85-of-new-CPG-products-fail-within-two-years; Mike Collins, "Reducing the Failure Rate Of New Products," *Forbes*, April 30, 2015, http://www.forbes.com/sites/mikecollins/2015/04/30/reducing-the-failure-rate-of-new-products/#633f363361a4.

20. Michael E. Ross, "It seemed like a good idea at the time," NBC News, April 22, 2005, http://www.nbcnews.com/id/7209828/ns/us_news/t/it-seemed-good-idea-time/#.V8xgQ4-cHIU.

21. Julie Jargon, "Burger King Drops Lower-Calorie Fry 'Satisfries,'" *Wall Street Journal*, August 13, 2014, http://www.wsj.com/articles/burger-king-drops-lower-calorie-fries-1407964129; Brad Tuttle, "The Demise of 'Satisfries' and the Sad History of Healthy Fast Food," *Time*, August 14, 2014, http://time.com/money/3111817/burger-king-satisfries-healthy-fast-food/.

22. "Innovation Process," Stage-Gate website, accessed August 2016 at http://www.stage-gate.com/resources_stage-gate_full.php.

23. Bruce Brown and Scott Anthony, "How P&G tripled its innovation success rate," *Harvard Business Review*, June 2011, https://hbr.org/2011/06/how-pg-tripled-its-innovation-success-rate/.

24. Written communication with Sameera Banduk, marketing director, Thalmic Labs, August 2016.

25. Ibid.

26. Brown and Anthony, "How P&G tripled its innovation success rate,"; Barrett J. Brunsman, "P&G redesigns packaging, launches new ad campaign as poison concerns mount," *Cincinnati Business Courier*, April 21, 2016, http://www.bizjournals.com/cincinnati/news/2016/04/21/p-g-redesigns-packaging-launches-new-ad-campaign.html; Jack Neff, "P&G Reinvents Laundry With $150 Million Tide Pods Launch," *Advertising Age*, April 26, 2011, http://adage.com/article/news/p-g-reinvents-laundry-150-million-tide-pods-launch/227208/.

27. Written communication with Sameera Banduk, marketing director, Thalmic Labs, August 2016.

28. Ibid.

29. Kira Vermond, "Why London, Ontario is the perfect test market," *Globe and Mail*, October 19, 2015, http://www.theglobeandmail.com/report-on-business/small-business/sb-managing/london-test-market/article26846284/.

30. Written communication with Sameera Banduk, marketing director, Thalmic Labs, August 2016.

31. Ibid.

## Chapter 9

1. Personal interview with Mario Fleury, owner, Be Sweet Inc., July 2016.

2. Michael Gauthier, "Bugatti has announced the Veyron Grand Sport Vitesse has officially become the fastest convertible in the world. The company will celebrate the event by introducing a World Record Car (WRC) Edition at the Shanghai Motor Show," Motor1.com, April 11, 2013, http://www.motor1.com/news/38024/bugatti-veyron-grand-sport-vitesse-world-record-car-edition/; Juergen Zoellter, "2013 Bugatti Veyron 16.4 Grand Sport Vitesse," *Car and Driver*, April 2012, http://www.caranddriver.com/bugatti/veyron;

Aaron Robinson, "2011 Bugatti Veyron 16.4 Super Sport— First Drive Review," *Car and Driver*, October 2010, www.caranddriver.com/reviews/car/10q4/2011_bugatti_veyron_16.4_super_sport-first_drive_review.

3. Adapted from Kent B. Monroe, *Pricing: Making Profitable Decisions*, 3rd ed. (New York: McGraw-Hill, 2003); Krishnakumar Davey, Paul Markowitz, and Nagi Jonnalagadda, "The pricing opportunity: Discovering what customers actually value," *Strategy & Leadership* 34 (2006), pp. 23–30, doi:10.1108/10878570610660573

4. Roger A. Kerin and Robert A. Peterson, "Throckmorten Furniture (A)," *Strategic Marketing Problems: Cases and Comments*, 9th ed. (Englewood Cliffs, NJ: Prentice Hall, 1998), pp. 235–245; Jukti K. Kalita, Sharan Jagpal, and Donald R. Lehmann, "Do high prices signal high quality? A theoretical model and empirical results," *Journal of Product and Brand Management* 13 (2004), pp. 279–288.

5. "H&R Block Leads the Way with 100% Free Tax Software," H&R Block Canada [press release], February 2016, https://www.hrblock.ca/uploads/our_company-media_centre-press_releases/2016/100FreePersonalDownloadandOnlineTaxSoftware.pdf; Rob Carrick, "Save money this tax season by filing for free," *Globe and Mail*, March 11, 2015, http://www.theglobeandmail.com/globe-investor/personal-finance/taxes/save-money-at-tax-time-by-filing-for-free/article23412438/; "Filing online? A guide to the latest tax software," CBC News, February 21, 2013, http://www.cbc.ca/news/business/taxes/filing-online-a-guide-to-the-latest-tax-software-1.1285455.

6. For the classic description of skimming and penetration pricing, see Joel Dean, "Pricing Policies for New Products," *Harvard Business Review*, November–December 1976, pp. 141–53. See also, Reed K. Holden and Thomas T. Nagle, "Kamikaze Pricing," *Marketing Management*, Summer 1998, pp. 31–39.

7. Jean-Noel Kapferer, "Managing Luxury Brands," *Journal of Brand Management*, July 1997, pp. 251–60.

8. "Why That Deal Is Only $9.99," *BusinessWeek*, January 10, 2000, p. 36. For further reading on odd-even pricing, see Robert M. Schindler and Thomas M. Kilbarian, "Increased Consumer Sales Response through Use of 99-Ending Prices," *Journal of Retailing*, Summer 1996, pp. 187–99; Mark Stiving and Russell S. Winer, "An Empirical Analysis of Price Endings with Scanner Data," *Journal of Consumer Research*, June 1997, pp. 57–67; and Robert M. Schindler, "Patterns of Rightmost Digits Used in Advertised Prices: Implications for Nine-Ending Effects," *Journal of Consumer Research*, September 1997, pp. 192–201.

9. Thomas T. Nagle and Reed K. Holden, *The Strategy and Tactics of Pricing*, 3rd ed. (Englewood Cliffs, NJ: Prentice Hall, 2002), pp. 243–49.

10. Ibid., pp. 237–39.

11. Peter M. Noble and Thomas S. Gruca, "Industrial Pricing: Theory and Managerial Practice," *Marketing Science* 18, no. 3 (1999), pp. 435–54.

12. George E. Belch and Michael A. Belch, *Introduction to Advertising and Promotion*, 5th ed. (New York: Irwin/McGraw-Hill, 2001), p. 93.

13. Oliver Moore. "UberX will be allowed to operate legally in Toronto, city council decides," *Globe and Mail*, May 3, 2016, http://www.theglobeandmail.com/news/toronto/divided-toronto-council-seeks-middle-ground-as-uber-debate-begins/article29835110/; Matt Elliot, "Toronto's taxi debate points to issues far bigger than Uber," *Metro*, May 9, 2016, http://www.metronews.ca/views/toronto/torys-toronto-matt-elliott/2016/05/09/toronto-taxi-debate-points-to-issues-far-bigger-than-uber.html; "What is Uber and what should I think about the controversies?" *The Telegraph*, May 16, 2016, http://www.telegraph.co.uk/better/technology/what-is-uber-and-what-should-i-think-about-the-controversies/; Laura Perez. "The Uber controversy reveals the rottenness of the taxi industry," *In Defence of Marxism*, January 5, 2016, http://www.marxist.com/uber-controversy-reveals-rottenness-of-taxi-industry.htm.

14. S. Makridakis, "Forecasting: Issues challenges for marketing management," *Journal of Marketing* 41 (1977), p. 24.

15. S. Doyle, "Business application of forecasting with a campaign management content," *Journal of Database Marketing & Customer Strategy Management* 12 (2004), pp. 87–93.

16. M. Man and L. Gadau, "The profit and loss account in different approaches: Advantages and disadvantages," *Annales Universitatis Apulensis: Series Oeconomica* 12 (2010), pp. 152–160.

17. D. Peppers and M. Rogers, "Return on customer: A new metric of value creation—return on investment by itself is not good enough," *Journal of Direct, Data and Digital Marketing Practice* 7 (2006), pp. 318–331.

18. Frank Bruni, "Price of Newsweek? It Depends," *Dallas Times Herald*, August 14, 1986, pp. S1, S20.

19. Elizabeth Weise and Roger Yu, "'Newsweek' sold to 'International Business Times,'" *USA Today*, August 5, 2013, www.usatoday.com /story/money/business/2013/08/03/newsweek-sold-to-international -business-times/2615727/.

20. "Despite a strong preference for paper books, older readers actually have an easier time reading electronic tablets." *Review of Optometry*, March 2013.

21. Andrew J. Hawkins, "GM launches, a car-sharing service to compete with ZipCar," *The Verge*, January 21, 2016, http://www.theverge.com/2016/1/21/10802240/gm-maven-car-sharing-service-price -launch-date-michigan; Tyler Hamilton, "Sharing the Road," *Toronto Star*, February 20, 2010, www.thestar.com/business/article /768531; "Taking Car-sharing to the Max," *Toronto Star*, February 20, 2010, www.thestar.com/business/article/768533.

22. "Henderson jersey coming back to Canada: Buyer," CBC News, June 23, 2010, www.cbc.ca/canada/story/2010/06/23/henderson -hockey-canada.html.

23. "Will Tablets Close the Book on e-Readers?" *Knowledge @ Wharton*, July 7, 2010, accessed athttp://knowledge.wharton.upenn.edu /printer_friendly.cfm?articleid=2539.

24. Hollie Shaw, "Hershey Canada pleasds guilty to chocolate price-fixing," *Financial Post*, June 21, 2013, http://business.financialpost .com/legal-post/hershey-canada-pleads-guilty-to-chocolate-price -fixing; Brent Jang, "Airlines fined $1.1-billion over price-fixing," *Globe and Mail* , November 9, 2010, www.theglobeandmail .com/globe-investor/air-canada-others-fined-for-price-fixing /article1791755.

25. "Grafton-Fraser to pay $1.2M in misleading ads case," CBC News, July 27, 2016, http://www.cbc.ca/news/business/grafton-fraser -to-pay-1-2m-in-misleading-ads-case-1.623251; Marina Strauss, "Grafton-Fraser fined for misleading sale prices," *Globe and Mail*, July 28, 2006, http://www.theglobeandmail.com/report-on-business /grafton-fraser-fined-for-misleading-sale-prices/article18168771/.

26. "Stores Told to Lift Prices in Germany," *Wall Street Journal*, September 11, 2000, pp. A27.

27. "Rotten Apples," *Dallas Morning News*, April 7, 1998, p. 14A.

28. "When Grey Is Good," *The Economist*, August 22, 1998, p. 17; Neil Belmore, "Parallel Imports and Grey Market Issues," The Canadian Institute, December 5–6, 2001.

29. "How Dell Fine-Tunes Its PC Pricing to Gain Edge in a Slow Market," *Wall Street Journal*, June 8, 2001, pp. A1, A8.

30. For an extensive discussion on discounts, see Kent B. Monroe, *Pricing: Making Profitable Decisions*, 2nd ed. (New York: McGraw Hill, 1990), chaps. 14 and 15.

## Chapter 10

1. Personal interview with Tom Benson, co-founder and chief executive officer at WildPlay Limited, April 2017.

2. Patrick Gillespie, "Pepsi has a Venezuela problem: $1.4 billion," CNN, October 8, 2015, http://money.cnn.com/2015/10/06/investing /pepsi-hit-hard-in-venezuela/; Thomas T. Vogel Jr., "Pepsi Finds Bottler in Venezuela After Old Firm Defected to Coke," *Wall Street Journal*, November 14, 1996, https://www.wsj.com/articles /SB84792428752932500; Glenn Collins, "A Coke Coup in Venezuela Leaves Pepsi High and Dry," *New York Times*, August 17, 1996, www.nytimes.com/1996/08/17/business/a-coke-coup-in-venezuela -leaves-pepsi-high-and-dry.html; Elizabeth Fuhrman, "Bottler of

the year: Pepsi bottling ventures," *Beverage Industry* 100 (2009), pp. 24–26, 28, 30, 34.

3. This discussion is based on Bert Rosenbloom, *Marketing Channels: A Management View*, 6th edition. (Fort Worth: Dryden Press, 1999).

4. J.K. Johansson, "International alliances: Why now?" *Journal of the Academy of Marketing Science* (1995). pp. 301–304.

5. Allan J. Magrath, "Channel Vision: Getting Your Channels Right," *Ivey Business Journal*, November/December 2002, www.iveybusinessjournal .com/topics/innovation/channel-vision-getting-your-channels-right# .Uh6XMXbvzR1; Adrienne Mand, "Eddie Bauer's banner time of year," *Advertising Age*, October 1, 2001, http://adage.com/article/focus-design /databank-retail-eddie-bauer-s-banner-time-year/53693/; D.L. Duffy, "Case study: Multi-channel marketing in the retail environment," *Journal of Consumer Marketing* 21 (2004), pp. 356–359.

6. Melissa Chan, "Canadian Teens Cause an International Incident Playing *Pokémon Go*," *Time*, July 24, 2016, http://time.com /4420930/pokemon-go-teens-us-border-canada/; Associated Press, "Pokémon Go leads to International incident at U.S. border," July 23, 2016, accessed at http://ottawacitizen.com/news/national /pokemon-go-leads-to-international-incident-at-u-s-border; Canadian Press, "Pokémon Go officially launches in Canada, crashes app's servers," July 17, 2016, accessed at http://www.cbc .ca/news/technology/pokemon-go-launches-in-canada-1.3683087.

7. E. Brynjolfsson, Y.J. Hu, and M.S. Rahman, "Competing in the age of omnichannel retailing," *MIT Sloan Management Review* 54 (2013), pp. 23–29.

8. Andrea Stairs, "More and more shoppers are online, so where are the retailers?" *Globe and Mail*, June 24, 2015, http://www.theglobeandmail .com/report-on-business/rob-commentary/more-and-more-shoppers -are-online-so-where-are-the-retailers/article25078686/; Marina Strauss, "Gap expands Web shopping, eyes growth in Canada," *Globe and Mail*, August 23, 2012, http://www.theglobeandmail.com/globe-investor /gap-expands-web-shopping-eyes-growth-in-canada/article1378654/; Michael Krantz, "Click Till You Drop," *Time*, July 20, 1998, pp. 34–39; "Gap Inc. Creates Global Brand Management Structure to Drive the Company's Long-Term Growth," Gap Inc. [press release], October 16, 2012, www.gapinc.com/content/gapinc/html/media/pressrelease/2012 /med_pr_GPS_Global_Brand_Management_Structure101612.html.

9. Darrell Rigby and Michael O'Sullivan, *Fighting Fire with Water—From Channel Conflict to Confluence* (Cambridge, MA: Bain & Company); D. Peppers and M. Rogers, "'Tis the season for E-retailing," *Sales and Marketing Management* 151 (1999), pp. 30–32.

10. For an overview of vertical marketing systems, see Lou E. Pelton, David Strutton, and James R. Lumpkin, *Marketing Channels*, 2nd ed. (Burr Ridge, IL: McGraw-Hill/Irwin, 2003); and Peter R.J. Trim and L. Yang-Im, "Vertically integrated organisational marketing systems: A partnership approach for retailing organisations," *Journal of Business & Industrial Marketing* 21 (2006), p. 151.

11. M.R. Portmann, "Franchising the concept of the future," *World Trade* 13 (2000), pp. 46–50; L. Patton, "McDonald's Franchisees Rebel as Chain Raises Stores Fees," *Bloomberg*, August 6, 2013, www.bloomberg.com/news/2013-08-06/mcdonald-s-franchisees-go -rogue-with-meetings.html; "FAQs," McDonald's Canada website, accessed at www.mcdonalds.ca/ca/en/contact_us/faq.html.

12. "Apple to Open 25 Retail Stores in 2001," Apple Computer [press release], May 15, 2001, www.apple.com/pr/library/2001/05/15Apple -to-Open-25-Retail-Stores-in-2001.html; Kevin Anderson, "Apple unveils its offline strategy," BBC NewsOnline, May 19, 2001, http:// news.bbc.co.uk/2/hi/business/1339150.stm; Dennis Sellers, "Apple 'manifesto': 5 down, 95 to go," *Macworld*, May 15, 2001, www .macworld.com/article/1017497/manifesto.html.

13. For an extensive discussion on channel conflict, see Anne T. Coughlan, Erin Anderson, Louis W. Stern, and Adel I. El-Ansary, *Marketing Channels*, 6th ed. (Upper Saddle River, NJ: Prentice Hall, 2001); K.L. Webb and J.E. Hogan, "Hybrid channel conflict: Causes and effects on channel performance," *Journal of Business & Industrial Marketing* 17 (2002), pp. 338–356.

14. Sara Zucker, "Coke Returns to Costco with its Dignity Intact," *BrandChannel*, December 11, 2009, www.brandchannel.com/home

/post/2009/12/11/Coke-Returns-To-Costco-With-Its-Dignity-Intact
.aspx; Martinne Geller, "Costco to resume stocking Coca-Cola
drinks," Reuters, December 10, 2009, www.reuters.com/article
/2009/12/10/cocacola-costco-idUSN1020190520091210.

15. For an extensive discussion on power and influence in marketing
channels, see Coughlan, et al., *Marketing Channels.*

16. *What's It All About?* (Oakbrook, IL: Council of Logistics Manage-
ment, 1993); S.M. Rutner and C.J. Langley, "Logistics value:
Definition, process and measurement," *International Journal of
Logistics Management* 11 (2000), pp. 73–82.

17. This example is described in David Simchi-Levi, Philip Kaminsky,
and Edith Simchi-Levi, *Designing and Managing the Supply Chain*
(Burr Ridge, IL: McGraw-Hill/Irwin, 2000).

18. This discussion is based on Robyn Meredith, "Harder than the
Hype," *Forbes*, April 16, 2001, pp. 188–194; R.M. Monczka and
J. Morgan, "Supply Chain Management Strategies," *Purchasing*,
January 15, 1998, pp. 78–85; Robert B. Handfield and Ernest L.
Nichols, *Introduction to Supply Chain Management* (Upper Saddle
River, NJ: Prentice Hall, 1998); and P. Charan, "Supply chain per-
formance issues in an automobile company: A SAP-LAP analysis,"
*Measuring Business Excellence* 16 (2012), pp. 67–86.

19. Major portions of this discussion are based on Sunil Chopra and
Peter Meindl, *Supply Chain Management: Strategy, Planning, and
Operations* (Upper Saddle River, NJ: Prentice Hall, 2001); Mar-
shall Fisher, "What Is the Right Supply Chain for Your Product?"
*Harvard Business Review*, March 1997, pp. 105–117; and Pankaj
M. Madhani, "Value creation through integration of supply chain
management and marketing strategy," *IUP Journal of Business
Strategy* 9 (2012), pp. 7–26.

20. Sophia Harris, "Walmart quest to be Canada's No. 1 grocer,"
CBC News, August 13, 2016, http://www.cbc.ca/news/business
/walmart-grocery-store-1.3717480; Don Pitts, "Why Walmart hit
the bulls-eye Target missed: Don Pitts," CBC News, http://www
.cbc.ca/news/business/why-walmart-hit-the-bull-s-eye-target
-missed-don-pittis-1.2953293; "Managing Risk in Our Supply
Chain," Walmart, accessed at http://www.walmartcanada.ca
/product-sourcing/responsible-sourcing/managing-risk; "Case
Study: Why Walmart implemented cross-docking for supply chain
success," Crossdock Manitoba, December 13, 2012, http://www
.crossdock.mb.ca/blog/case-study-why-wal-mart-implemented
-cross-docking-for-supply-chain-success/; "Walmart selects Isotrak
to improve fleet visibility," *Isotrak*, March 14, 2015, http://isotrak
.com/walmart-canada-selects-isotrak-to-improve-fleet-visibility/;
Rebecca Walberg, "Never Lose Inventory Again," *Financial Post*,
July 6, 2010, www.financialpost.com/Never+lose+inventory+aga
in/3239772/story.html; Miguel Bustillo, "Wal-Mart Radio Tags to
Track Clothing," *Wall Street Journal*, July 23, 2010, https://www.wsj
.com/articles/SB10001424052748704421304575383213061198090.

21. "Truck Carriers - Join Smart Way," Natural Resources Canada
website, July 6, 2016, http://www.nrcan.gc.ca/energy/efficiency
/transportation/commercial-vehicles/smartway/trucks/7649;
"SmartWay Comes to Canada," Supply Chain & Logistics
Association of Canada website, accessed September 2014 at www
.scmanational.ca/en/tools-a-resources/smartway; "SmartWay in
Canada," Natural Resources Canada website, June 19, 2012, www
.nrcan.gc.ca/energy/efficiency/transportation/commercial-vehicles
/smartway/7615/.

## Chapter 11

1. Personal interview with Mike Drake, franchisee, 9Round and
Shannon Hudson, chief executive officer, 9Round, September 2016.

2. K. Cline, "The devil in the details," *Banking Strategies* 24 (1997);
R. Trap, "Design your own jeans," *The Independent*, October
18, 1998, p. 22; H. Cho and S.S. Fiorito, "Self-service technology in retailing: The case of retail kiosks," *Symphonya* 1 (2010),
pp. 42–54.

3. "Retail sales, by industry (unadjusted)," Statistics Canada, August
19, 2016, accessed at http://www.statcan.gc.ca/tables-tableaux/sum
-som/l01/cst01/trad15a-eng.htm.

4. Deloitte, *Global Powers of Retailing 2016*, accessed at http://www2
.deloitte.com/global/en/pages/consumer-business/articles/global
-powers-of-retailing.html.

5. "Target Canada closing, ending 2-year foray," CTV News, April 12,
2015, http://www.ctvnews.ca/business/target-canada-closing-ending
-2-year-foray-1.2323222; Marina Strauss and Jacquie McNish,
"With Target, Canada's retail landscape set for massive makeover,"
*Globe and Mail*, January 13, 2011, www.theglobeandmail.com
/globe-investor/with-target-canadas-retail-landscape-set-for-massive
-makeover/article1868308; Duncan Hood, "Target won't kill
Canadian retail: It will save it," *Canadian Business*, October 15,
2012, p. 4.

6. "Retail Trade-Establishments, Employees, and Payroll," *Statistical Abstract of the United States*, 120th ed. (Washington, DC: U.S.
Department of Commerce, Bureau of the Census, 2000); G. Koretz,
"Those Plucky Corner Stores," *Bloomberg Businessweek*, December
5, 1994, www.businessweek.com/stories/1994-12-04/those-plucky
-corner-stores; J. Fraser, "Mapping out the treasure hunt," *Canadian
Grocer* 122 (2008), p. 73.

7. "Foundations of Franchising," International Franchise Association
(n.d.), accessed at www.franchise.org/code.aspx.

8. Scott Shane and Chester Spell, "Factors for New Franchise Success," *MIT Sloan Management Review*, April 15, 1998, http://sloan
review.mit.edu/article/factors-for-new-franchise-success/; Richard
Branson, "Richard Branson on Building a Strong Reputation," *Entrepreneur*, April 8, 2013, www.entrepreneur.com/article/226296.

9. Alexandra Lopez-Pacheco, "Customers expect quality even in recession," *National Post*, January 27, 2008, p. FP7; Carol Stephenson,
"Thriving in turbulent times," *Ivey Business Journal*, May/June 2009,
http://iveybusinessjournal.com/publication/thriving-in-turbulent
-times/; Hollie Shaw, "Online sales complement brick-and-mortar retail, Harry Rosen CEO says," *Financial Post*, August 1, 2013, http://
business.financialpost.com/2013/08/01/online-sales-complement
-brick-and-mortar-retail-harry-rosen-ceo-says/.

10. Tim Manners, "Shopper Marketing," *Fast Company*, June 14, 2008,
accessed at https://www.fastcompany.com/890025/shopper-marketing;
"With U.S. consumers watching their wallets more than ever, tuning
into shoppers' mindsets key to warding off brand switching," Nielsen
[news release], October 16, 2008, www.nielsen.com/content/dam
/corporate/us/en/newswire/uploads/2008/10/press_release18.pdf;
"Shopper marketing," *Marketing*, 116 (2011), p. 29.

11. Marina Strauss, "Holt's opens doors a little more widely,"
*Globe and Mail*, September 1, 2010, www.theglobeandmail
.com/report-on-business/holts-opens-doors-a-little-more-widely
/article1693204/?cmpid=tgc; Hollie Shaw, "Holt Renfrew wants
to make you feel welcome," *National Post*, September 2, 2010;
Sarah Kelsey, "Holt Renfrew celebrates 175 years: Luxury retailer
announces major expansion plans," *Huffington Post Canada*,
September 7, 2012, www.huffingtonpost.ca/2012/09/07/holt
-renfrew-celebrates-1_n_1864421.html.

12. R. Eagan, "The green capitalist," *Library Journal* 134 (2009);
"Defining the Green Economy," ECO Canada, 2010, www.eco.ca
/pdf/Defining-the-Green-Economy-2010.pdf; J.G. Hae, "Are fashion-conscious consumers more likely to adopt eco-friendly clothing?" *Journal of Fashion Marketing and Management* 15 (2011),
pp. 178–193, doi:10.1108/13612021111132627; Dixie Gong, "10
Best Canadian Eco-Shops," *Flare*, March 28, 2013, www.flare.com
/fashion/10-best-canadian-eco-shops/; "Corporate Social Responsibility," Foreign Affairs, Trade and Development Canada, October
22, 2013, www.international.gc.ca/trade-agreements-accords
-commerciaux/topics-domaines/other-autre/csr-rse.aspx?lang=eng;
"The Greening of Roots," Roots (n.d.), accessed at http://about.
roots.com/on/demandware.store/Sites-RootsCorporate-Site/default
/Link-Page?cid=THE_ENVIRONMENT_OurCommitment.

13. Francine Kopun, "Shoppers Drug Mart deal helps Loblaw more
than double profit," *Toronto Star*, February 26, 2015, https://www
.thestar.com/business/2015/02/26/shoppers-drug-deal-helps-loblaw
-more-than-double-profit.html; Canadian Press, "Loblaw closes
deal to buy Shoppers Drug Mart," March 28, 2014, accessed at http://

www.theglobeandmail.com/report-on-business/loblaw-closes-deal-to-buy-shoppers-drug-mart/article17723887/; Lisa Wright, "Craft beer flying off shelves at Loblaws," *Toronto Star*, June 29, 2016, https://www.thestar.com/business/2016/06/29/craft-beer-flying-off-shelves-at-loblaws.html; "Beer sales in grocery stores," Government of Ontario (n.d.), accessed at https://www.ontario.ca/page/beer-sales-grocery-stores; "Full list of Ontario grocery stores," CBC News, December 16, 2015, http://www.cbc.ca/news/canada/toronto/ontario-grocery-stores-that-sell-beer-list-1.3365796; Canadian Press, "How alcohol is sold in provinces across Canada," April 16, 2015, accessed at http://www.citynews.ca/2015/04/16/how-alcohol-is-sold-in-provinces-across-canada/; James Cowan, "Retail: The genius of Dollarama," *Canadian Business*, April 7, 2011, www.canadianbusiness.com/business-strategy/retail-the-genius-of-dollarama/; John Daly, "How Dollarama turns pocket change into billions," *Globe and Mail*, March 29, 2012, www.theglobeandmail.com/report-on-business/rob-magazine/how-dollarama-turns-pocket-change-into-billions/article4097813/; Jim McElgunn and Kim Shiffman, "Canada's entrepreneurs of the decade," *Profit*, December 2010, pp. 44–53.

14. Valentina Palladino, "Apple Store receives trademark for 'distinctive design and layout,'" *Wired*, January 30, 2013, www.wired.com/design/2013/01/apple-store-trademark/; "Canadian Trade-Mark Data," Canadian Intellectual Property Office, October 22, 2013, www.cipo.ic.gc.ca/app/opic-cipo/trdmrks/srch/vwTrdmrk.do;jsessionid=0001aVzIlRWXB-TRtDf81OHAa5I:3UAPV7CT3?lang=eng&status=OK&fileNumber=1503650&extension=0&startingDocumentIndexOnPage=1.

15. F.J. Mulhern and R.P. Leon, "Implicit Price Bundling of Retail Products: A Multiproduct Approach to Maximizing Store Profitability," *Journal of Marketing* 55 (1991), pp. 63–76; Scott Hamilton, "U.K. retail sales increase as discounts spur consumer demand," *Bloomberg*, July 18, 2013, https://www.bloomberg.com/amp/news/articles/2013-07-18/u-k-retail-sales-increase-as-discounts-spur-consumer-demand-1-.

16. F.S. By, "The 'sale' is fading as a retailing tactic—in pricing shift, 'everyday lows' replace specials," *Wall Street Journal*, March 1, 1989; G.K. Ortmeyer, J.A. Quelch, and W.J. Salmon, "Restoring Credibility to Retail Pricing," *MIT Sloan Management Review* 33 (1991), pp. 55–66; T. Busillo, "Bed, bath & more: A Canada first," *Home Textiles Today* 19 (1998), pp. 8, 23; Andria Cheng, "Wal-Mart pitches 'everyday low prices' overseas," *MarketWatch*, June 1, 2011, www.marketwatch.com/story/wal-mart-pitches-everyday-low-prices-overseas-2011-06-01.

17. W.B. Dodds, "In Search of Value: How Price and Store Name Information Influence Buyers' Product Perceptions," *Journal of Services Marketing* 5 (1991), pp. 27–36; D. Grewal, R. Krishnan, J. Baker, and N. Borin, "The effect of store name, brand name and price discounts on consumers' evaluations and purchase intentions," *Journal of Retailing* 74 (1998), pp. 331–352; N. Williams, "Profile: GM shifting gears from price to brand image," *Strategy* (2005), p. 53.

18. B. Brown, "Edmonton Makes Size Pay Off in Down Market," *Advertising Age*, January 27, 1992, pp. 4–5; "Facts," West Edmonton Mall website (n.d.), accessed at www.wem.ca/about-wem/facts; R. Warnica, "Taking West Edmonton Mall to New Jersey," *Maclean's*, October 3, 2011, p. 41.

19. N. Ramage, "Edo Japan leaves the malls behind," *Marketing* 108 (2003), p. 2; A.G. Hallsworth, K.G. Jones, and R. Muncaster, "The planning implications of new retail format introductions in Canada and Britain," *Service Industries Journal* 15 (1995), p. 148; B.J. Lorch, "Big Boxes, Power Centres and the Evolving Retail Landscape of Winnipeg: A Geographical Perspective," Institute for Urban Studies, University of Winnipeg, 2004.

20. Hollie Shaw, "McDonald's Canada to add build-your-own burgers, table service," *Financial Post*, September 30, 2015, http://business.financialpost.com/news/retail-marketing/mcdonalds-canada-to-add-build-your-own-burgers-table-service; Marina Strauss, "McDonald's rolls out upscale options," *Globe and Mail,* September 30, 2015, http://www.theglobeandmail.com/report-on-business/mcdonalds-rolls-out-table-service-customized-burgers-in-upscale-shift/article26601464/.

21. K. Buscemi, "Vending gets smarter," *Appliance Manufacturer* 52 (2004), pp. 25–26; "Vending embraces growth and technology," *Beverage Industry* 102 (2011), pp. 118–119.

22. Christopher Brown-Humes, "Ikea creates a challenge for postmen of the world: The store catalogue is published in 36 countries and is free, writes Christopher Brown-Humes," *Financial Times*, August 14, 2003; "IKEA appoints McCann New York as global agency of record to re-invent the IKEA catalogue," *Marketing Weekly News* [news release], August 2, 2011; "2014 IKEA Catalogue Comes to Life with Augmented Reality," IKEA Canada [press release], August 12, 2013, accessed at www.newswire.ca/en/story/1209085/2014-ikea-catalogue-comes-to-life-with-augmented-reality.

23. "Knockout strategies of the 90s: Telemarketing and direct marketing," *Canadian Business*, advertising supplement, March 1993, pp. 45–54; "Canada's Do Not Call Registry," *The Gazette*, December 29, 2007.

24. Nanette Byrnes, "Avon's new calling," *Bloomberg Businessweek*, September 18, 2000, accessed at www.businessweek.com/2000/00_38/b3699001.htm; D.B. Van, "Avon calling on global ad effort to change its image," *Marketing* 105 (2000), p. 6; "About Avon," Avon website (n.d.), accessed at www.avoncompany.com/aboutavon/avonmarkets.html.

25. M. Schifrin, "Okay, big mouth," *Forbes*, October 9, 1995, p. 47; V. Byrd and W. Zellner, "The Avon Lady of the Amazon," *Business Week*, October 23, 1994, www.businessweek.com/stories/1994-10-23/the-avon-lady-of-the-amazon; D.L. Duffy, "Direct selling as the next channel," *Journal of Consumer Marketing* 22 (2005), pp. 43–45; C. Rawlins and P.R. Johnson, "Let's party: The remarkable growth in direct sales," Allied Academies International Conference, Academy of Organizational Culture, Communications and Conflict Proceedings 10 (2005), pp. 47–50.

26. Tavia Grant, "More Canadians Shopping on Net," *Globe and Mail*, September 28, 2010, www.theglobeandmail.com/report-on-business/more-canadians-shopping-on-net/article1727434; Canadian Press, "Canadian retailers running out of time on e-commerce, report says," May 6, 2013, accessed at www.cbc.ca/news/business/canadian-retailers-running-out-of-time-in-e-commerce-report-says-1.1410261; Hollie Shaw, "Online retail sales to hit $34-billion in Canada by 2018," *Financial Post*, July 23, 2013, http://business.financialpost.com/2013/07/23/online-retail-sales-to-hit-40-billion-in-canada-by-2018/.

27. B. Hameed, "Facebook, Twitter Influences up to 28% of Online Buying Decisions," Startup Meme [blog], December 14, 2009, http://startupmeme.com/facebook-twitter-influences-upto-28-of-online-buying-decisions; L.P. Forbes, "Does social media influence consumer buying behavior? An investigation of recommendations and purchases," *Journal of Business & Economics Research* 11 (2013), p. 107; Lara O'Reilly, "Women make friends with 'liked' brands on Facebook," *Marketing Week*, August 9, 2012, p. 6.

28. S. Casimiro, "Shop Till You Crash: Just in time for Christmas, online retailing is getting bigger, smarter, faster, and easier. You'll notice we're not calling it flawless. Yet," *Fortune*, December 21, 1998, http://money.cnn.com/magazines/fortune/fortune_archive/1998/12/21/252661/index.htm; D.A. Pitta, "Internet currency," *Journal of Consumer Marketing* 19 (2002), pp. 539–540; "Lands' end improves online profitability via my virtual model technology," *Direct Marketing* 64 (2001), p. 11.

29. Wen-Jang Jih, "Effects of consumer-perceived convenience on shopping intention in mobile commerce: An empirical study," *International Journal of E-Business Research* 3 (2007), pp. 33–40, 43–48; J. Ramaprasad, "Online social influence and consumer choice: Evidence from the music industry," (Order No. 3364967, University of California, Irvine). ProQuest Dissertations and Theses (2009); "Consumers and Changing Retail Markets," Office of Consumer Affairs, Industry Canada, July 27, 2012, www.ic.gc.ca/eic/site/oca-bc.nsf/eng/ca02096.html#a21; "5 Canadian consumer trends to shape the future of retail," CBC News, October 21, 2013, www.cbc.ca/news/business/5-canadian-consumer-trends-to-shape-the-future-of-retail-1.2129072.

30. Brad Tuttle, "Why Monday is e-retailers' favorite day of the week," *Time*, January 9, 2012, http://business.time.com/2012/01/09/why-monday-is-e-retailers-favorite-day-of-the-week/; Sean Silcoff, "What keeps online retail in Canada from clicking?" *Globe and Mail*, May 12, 2012, www.theglobeandmail.com/report-on-business/what-keeps-online-retail-in-canada-from-clicking/article4178807/?page=all; Ashante Infantry, "Not all Canadians love to shop online: study," *Toronto Star*, August 21, 2013, www.thestar.com/business/tech_news/2013/08/21/not_all_canadians_love_to_shop_online_study.html; Kevin Duong, "2014 Canada Digital Future in Focus," comScore, April 2014, www.comscore.com/Insights/Presentations_and_Whitepapers/2014/2014_Canada_Digital_Future_in_Focus.

31. Alexandra Lopez-Pacheco, "Welcome the New Consumer," *Financial Post*, October 5, 2010, www.canada.com/business/fp/money/Welcome+consumer/3551652/story.html.

32. Naresh Kumar, "Social Media Recommendations May Increase Online Purchases," PSFK.com, July 1, 2010, www.psfk.com/2010/07/social-media-recommendations-may-increase-online-purchases.html.

33. "Global Advertising: Consumers Trust Real Friends and Virtual Strangers the Most," Nielsen [news release], July 7, 2009, www.nielsen.com/us/en/newswire/2009/global-advertising-consumers-trust-real-friends-and-virtual-strangers-the-most.html.

34. J. Weidauer, "QR codes: Building a mobile loyalty program beyond key tags," Retail Customer Experience, April 20, 2010, www.retailcustomerexperience.com/article/21622/QR-codes-Building-a-mobile-loyalty-program-beyond-key-tags; C. Sherburne, "Are QR codes for real?" *Printing Impressions* 52 (2010), p. 36; M. Partee, "Everyone's going crazy for QR codes!" *Credit Union Management* 34 (2011), pp. 32–33.

35. "Retail's Mobility Imperative: A Measured Approach to the Emerging Channel," *Forbes Insight* (2010), www.forbes.com/forbesinsights/retailmobility/.

36. J. Boyd, "The web goes wireless—popular site operators set their sights on mobile users," *InternetWeek* 828 (2000), pp. 20–27; R. Shields, "Digital strategy: Are you making the most from mobile?" *Marketing Week*, November 2010, pp. 69–71; J. Wisniewski, "Mobile websites with minimum effort," *Online* 34 (2010), pp. 54–57; C. Murphy, "Mistakes," *InformationWeek* 1345 (2012), pp. 32–35.

## Chapter 12

1. Personal and written communication with Erin Arthrell, Bioré brand manager, Kao Canada, November 2016; "Beauty and Personal Care in Canada," Euromonitor International, April 27, 2016, www.euromonitor.com; "Digital Signage in Cinema Lobby," Cineplex website, accessed November 2016 at http://media.cineplex.com/digital-signage; *Cineplex Magazine*, Cineplex, accessed November 2016 at http://media.cineplex.com/magazine; "The pre-movie ads go on, and on...," *Maclean's*, August 16, 2013, http://www.macleans.ca/politics/the-pre-movie-ads-go-on-and-on/.

2. Rob Young, "Canada's Media Landscape," PHD Canada (prepared for Interactive Advertising Bureau), December 2015, https://iabcanada.com/content/uploads/2017/02/1.-CMUST-2015-V3-Total-Canada-Exec-Summary-Dec-2-2015.pdf.

3. "Facts & Figures: 2016," Canadian Wireless and Telecommunications Association website, accessed July 2017 at http://www.cwta.ca/facts-figures/.

4. "Communications Monitoring Report 2016," CRTC website, accessed July 2017 at http://www.crtc.gc.ca/eng/publications/reports/policymonitoring/2016/cmrs.htm#exii; Paul Rich, Ben Martin, and Leah Jenkins, "2015 Canada Digital Future in Focus," comScore, March 27, 2015, https://www.comscore.com/Insights/Presentations-and-Whitepapers/2015/2015-Canada-Digital-Future-in-Focus.

5. Rich et al., "Digital Future in Focus Canada 2015."

6. "2016 Canadian Social Media Monitor," Insights West, May 2016, http://www.insightswest.com/wp-content/uploads/2016/05/Rep_InsightsWest_CDNSocialMediaMonitor_2016.pdf.

7. "Mobile Drives Growth in Time Spent with Media in Canada, *eMarketer*, May 25, 2016, http://www.emarketer.com/Article/Mobile-Drives-Growth-Time-Spent-with-Media-Canada/1014003.

8. "AdSpend Database – Canada," WARC, accessed December 2016 at www.warc.com.

9. "Canadian Media Investment Trends: Where are ad budgets headed?" Canada Media Insights, February 26, 2016, http://media-corps.com/canadian-media-investments/.

10. Susan Krashinsky, "Sexism in advertising: What Canadian men and women find unacceptable," *Globe and Mail*, May 5, 2016, http://www.theglobeandmail.com/report-on-business/industry-news/marketing/sexism-in-advertising-what-canadian-men-and-women-find-unacceptable/article29907652/; "LG Canada accused of sexism for washing machine ads," CBC News, April 12, 2016, http://www.cbc.ca/news/trending/sexism-lg-canada-1.3532536; Jeromy Lloyd, "The long road to fixing advertising's sexism problem, *Marketing*, May 6, 2016, http://www.marketingmag.ca/advertising/the-long-road-to-fixing-advertisings-sexism-problem-173874; Christine Birkner, "Q&A: Unilever's Global Marketing Chief on Busting Gender Stereotypes in Advertising," *AdWeek*, October 24, 2016, http://www.adweek.com/news/advertising-branding/qa-unilevers-global-marketing-chief-busting-gender-stereotypes-advertising-174242; Mark Sweney, "Unilever vows to drop sexist stereotypes from its ads," *The Guardian*, June 22, 2016, https://www.theguardian.com/media/2016/jun/22/unilever-sexist-stereotypes-ads-sunsilk-dove-lynx; "Unilever to #unstereotype Portrayals of Gender in Advertising," *Marketing Communications News*, June 23, 2016, http://www.marcomm.news/unilever-to-unstereotype-portrayals-of-gender-in-advertising/; Advertising Standards Canada, *Consumer Perspectives on Advertising 2016* (Toronto: Author, 2016), http://www.adstandards.com/en/ASCLibrary/2016ASCConsumerResearch.pdf.

11. "Nabob – Respect the Bean (Packaged Goods Gold)," Cassies website, accessed November 2016 at http://cassies.ca/entry/viewcasepast/24988#_ftn1; David Brown, "Kraft's simple solution for building a coffee brand," *Marketing*, November 27, 2014, http://marketingmag.ca/brands/krafts-simple-solution-for-building-a-coffee-brand-131387/.

12. "Maclean's 2016 rate card," *Maclean's* website, accessed October 2016 at http://www.rogersmedia.com/wp-content/uploads/2013/03/15-528_MAC_MediaKit_FINAL.pdf.

13. Advertising Standards Canada, *Consumer Perspectives on Advertising 2016*, p. 7.

14. Emily Jackson, "Netflix lands over a million new Canadian subscribers in less than one year: report," *Financial Post*, June 14, 2016, http://business.financialpost.com/technology/netflix-lands-over-a-million-new-canadian-subscribers-in-less-than-one-year-report/wcm/db9ff8aa-414d-41cb-8414-23bd49a38943.

15. Sophia Harris, "Cable cord-cutting numbers soar in Canada thanks to Netflix, high prices, says report," CBC News, April 8, 2016, http://www.cbc.ca/news/business/cable-costs-cord-cutting-canada-netflix-1.3525949.

16. "Circulation Report: Daily Newspapers 2015," Newspapers Canada, accessed November 2016 at http://newspaperscanada.ca/wp-content/uploads/2016/06/2015-Daily-Newspaper-Circulation-Report-REPORT_FINAL.pdf.

17. Chris Powell, "Vividata reveals readership stats on Canadian media," *Marketing*, April 15, 2016, http://marketingmag.ca/media/vividata-reveals-readership-stats-on-canadian-media-172483/.

18. "Magazine Topline Readership 2017-Q1 Adults 18+," Vividata, accessed July 2017 at https://vividata.ca/wp-content/uploads/2015/08/2017-Q1-Magazine-TOPLINE.pdf.

19. "Communications Monitoring Report 2015: Broadcasting sector overview," Canadian Radio and Television Corporation website, November 11, 2016, http://www.crtc.gc.ca/eng/publications/reports/policymonitoring/2015/cmr4.htm.

20. "FAQ," Out-of-Home Marketing Association of Canada website, accessed November 2016 at http://www.omaccanada.ca/faq/.

21. "Strengths of OOH," Out-of-Home Marketing Association of Canada website, accessed November 2016 at http://www.omaccanada.ca/strengths-of-ooh/.

22. "Coca-Cola's research funding criticized by obesity expert," CBC News, August 10, 2015, http://www.cbc.ca/news/health/coca-cola-s

-research-funding-criticized-by-obesity-expert-1.3186279; Ed Hays, "Coca-Cola: We stand for quality, integrity," *USA Today*, August 16, 2015, http://www.usatoday.com/story/opinion/2015/08/16/coca -cola-company-ed-hays-editorials-debates/31818829/; Muhtar Kent, "Coca-Cola: We'll Do Better," *Wall Street Journal*, August 19, 2015, http://www.wsj.com/articles/coca-cola-well-do-better-1440024365; W. Comcowich, "Case Study: Coca-Cola PR Crisis Management," August 25, 2015, accessed November 2016 at http://www.cyberalert .com/blog/index.php/case-study-coca-cola-pr-crisis-management/.

23. "Canada Coast to Coast Monopoly," McDonald's Canada website, accessed November 2016 at https://mcdpromotion.ca/en-ca; Jordan Twiss, "More than chance: 25 years of McDonald's Monopoly," *Strategy*, October 30, 2012, http://strategyonline.ca/2012/10/30 /more-than-chance-25-years-of-mcdonalds-monopoly/.

24. "What is direct marketing?" Direct Marketing Association of Canada website, accessed November 2016 at http://www.directmac .org/direct-marketing1.

25. "From zero to 60 in 4 seconds: BMW wins big with sensory cross-media marketing," Canada Post Corporation [blog], August 8, 2013, https://www.canadapost.ca/web/en/blogs/business/details. page?article=2013/08/08/from_zero_to_60_in_4&cattype=busines s&cat=directmail; "The Making of a BMW M Print," BMW USA, November 19, 2012, https://youtu.be/aYuk64NMYLM.

26. "Corporate Partners," Toronto International Film Festival website, accessed November 2016 at http://www.tiff.net/partnerships/; "Sponsorship," Toronto International Film Festival website, accessed November 2016 at http://content.tiff.net.s3.amazonaws.com /documents/Sponsorship_Festival_2016.pdf; "Sponsorship Festival 2016," Toronto International Film Festival website, accessed November 2016 at http://content.tiff.net.s3.amazonaws.com /documents/Sponsorship_Festival_2016.pdf.

27. Adapted from the American Marketing Association's dictionary, accessed November 2016 at https://www.ama.org/resources/Pages /Dictionary.aspx.

28. "Advertising Budget," Inc. website, accessed November 2016 at http://www.inc.com/encyclopedia/advertising-budget.html.

## Chapter 13

1. Personal and written communication with Erin Arthrell, Bioré brand manager, Kao Canada, November 2016; Biore Canada Facebook Page, accessed November 2016 at https://www.facebook.com/BioreCanada/; Biore Canada website, accessed November 2016 at http://www.biore .ca/en-CA/biore-skincare; Biore Canada Twitter account, accessed November 2016 at https://twitter.com/biorecanada; "Getting Engaged in Paris??" Laur DIY, October 2, 2016, https://www.youtube.com/ watch?v=rrx-4LeOMZ0; "Bioré® Skincare Announces Shay Mitchell As New Brand Ambassador For Launch Of Baking Soda Cleansers," PR Newswire [news release], April 5, 2016, http://www.multivu.com /players/English/7793151-biore-ambassador-shay-mitchell/.

2. "Mobile Drives Growth in Time Spent with Media in Canada, *eMarketer*, May 25, 2016, http://www.emarketer.com/Article /Mobile-Drives-Growth-Time-Spent-with-Media-Canada/1014003.

3. Adapted from the American Marketing Association's dictionary, "Affiliate Marketing," accessed November 2016 at https://www .ama.org/resources/pages/dictionary.aspx?dLetter=A.

4. Russ Martin, "Email marketing is on the rise in Canada," *Marketing*, March 9, 2016, http://www.marketingmag.ca/tech/email -marketing-is-on-the-rise-in-canada-169813.

5. "Wommapedia: Why Word of Mouth Marketing?" Word of Mouth Marketing Association website, accessed December 2016 at http:// wommapedia.org/.

6. Ibid.

7. "2016 Canadian Social Media Monitor," Insights West, May 2016, http://www.insightswest.com/wp-content/uploads/2016/05/Rep _InsightsWest_CDNSocialMediaMonitor_2016.pdf.

8. "Coke's "Share a Coke" Campaign: An Integrated Marketing Success," Incitrio [press release], October 1, 2014, http:// incitrio.com/cokes-share-a-coke-campaign-an-integrated -marketing-success/.

9. Meghan Keaney Anderson, "The Best of B2B Marketing Content: 9 Examples," HubSpot [blog], June 9, 2015, http://blog.hubspot .com/blog/tabid/6307/bid/33505/10-b2b-companies-that-create -exceptional-content.aspx#sm.00000k61g84uecztxyp1birlwcur0.

10. "Tangerine Dreams of Fully Integrated Content Marketing," *Marketing*, August 22, 2016, http://www.marketingmag.ca/sponsored /tangerine-dreams-of-fully-integrated-content-marketing-181688; "Forward Thinking," Tangerine website, accessed November 2016 at https://www.tangerine.ca/forwardthinking/.

11. Bailey Roy, "Social vs. Traditional Media: Has the Battle Already Ended?" *MyPRSA*, April 1, 2016, https://www.prsa.org/Intelligence /Tactics/Articles/view/11445/1124/Social_vs_Traditional_Media _Has_the_Battle_Already#.WDzXJ_krLIU.

12. Michael Stelzner, "2016 Social Media Marketing Industry Report," *Social Media Examiner*, May 24, 2016, http://www.socialmediaexaminer .com/social-media-marketing-industry-report-2016/.

13. "2016 Canadian Social Media Monitor," Insights West.

14. Ibid.

15. Iris Vermeren, "Marketing: How to Provide Great Customer Service Via Social Media," Brandwatch [blog], February 25, 2015, https://www.brandwatch.com/blog/marketing-provide-great -customer-service-via-social/.

16. "About us," McCain Foods website, accessed November 2016 at http://www.mccain.com/about-us; "Ingredients and Processes," McCain Foods website, accessed November 2016 at http://www .mccain.com/good-food/ingredients-and-processes; "New Recipes and Meal Inspiration," McCain Foods website, accessed November 2016 at http://mccain.ca/en/recipes/modifry?utm_campaign =superfries&utm_medium=multiimage&utm_source=twitter &utm_content=superfriesmodifry; "McCain Superfries – Modifry: Off to a Good Start," Cassies website, accessed November 2016 at http://cassies.ca/entry/viewcasepast/24493.

17. "2016 Canadian Social Media Monitor," Insights West.

18. Emily Wexler, "The 2015 Marketer Survey," *Strategy*, December 11, 2015, http://strategyonline.ca/2015/12/11/the-2015-marketer-survey/.

19. "Global Social Media Ranking," Statista, accessed November 2016 at https://www.statista.com/statistics/272014/global-social- networks-ranked-by-number-of-users/.

20. Wexler, "The 2015 Marketer Survey."

21. "Facebook Business – Facebook Ads Basic," Facebook website, accessed December 2016 at https://www.facebook.com/business /learn/facebook-ads-basics.

22. Christian Karasiewicz, "6 Ways to Use Facebook Live Video for Your Business," *Social Media Examiner*, July 25, 2016, http://www .socialmediaexaminer.com/6-ways-to-use-facebook-live-video-for -your-business/.

23. "Facebook Pages Stats in Canada," Socialbakers website, accessed at https://www.socialbakers.com/statistics/facebook/pages/local /canada/brands/.

24. Dominique Jackson, "10 Ways Marketers Can Increase Facebook Engagement," SproutSocial [blog], March 21, 2016, http:// sproutsocial.com/insights/facebook-engagement/.

25. "Facebook Awards 2016 Winners - Beats by Dre," Facebook website, accessed December 2016 at https://www.facebook-studio .com/awards/winners#/gallery/submission/beats-by-dre.

26. "Company," Twitter website, accessed December 2016 at https:// about.twitter.com/company.

27. "2016 Canadian Social Media Monitor," Insights West.

28. Wexler, "The 2015 Marketer Survey."

29. Jenn Chen, "Twitter Tips for Your Business to Follow Into 2017," SproutSocial [blog], November 30, 2016, http://sproutsocial.com /insights/twitter-tips/.

30. Richard O'Flynn, "The Way The Social Cookie Crumbles: The Genius of Oreo's Social Media Marketing," *201:digital*, April 23, 2015, http://www.201digital.co.uk/way-social-cookie-crumbles -genius-oreos-social-media-marketing-can-learn/.

31. Steve Olenski, "What Is Periscope And How Can You Use It For Business Video Streaming?" *Forbes*, December 5, 2015, http://www .forbes.com/sites/steveolenski/2015/12/05/what-is-periscope-and-how

-can-you-use-it-for-business-video-streaming/print/; Therese, "Facebook Live vs. Periscope: What's the difference?" *Social Media Hound*, September 20, 2016, http://www.socialmediahound.com /2016/09/20/facebook-live-vs-periscope/.

32. "Statistics," YouTube website, accessed December 2016 at https:// www.youtube.com/yt/press/statistics.html.

33. "Red Bull YouTube channel," accessed December 2016 at https:// www.youtube.com/user/redbull; "Red Bull's YouTube Presence," The Shorty Awards website, accessed December 2016 at http:// shortyawards.com/7th/red-bulls-youtube-channel; "Most popular YouTube channels as of October 2016," Statista website, accessed December 2016 at https://www.statista.com/statistics/277765/most -popular-youtube-brand-channels-ranked-by-subscribers/.

34. "Socialbakers Mini-Report: Red Bull Stratos on Social Media," Socialbakers, accessed December 2016 at https://cdn.socialbakers .com/www/archive/storage/www/red-bull-stratos-case-study.pdf.

35. Wexler, "The 2015 Marketer Survey."

36. "Official GoPro Instagram page," GoPro, accessed December 2016 at https://www.instagram.com/gopro/.

37. Neil Patel, "6 Tactics That Will Instantly Improve Your Instagram Engagement," *Forbes*, May 12, 2016, http://www.forbes.com /sites/neilpatel/2016/05/12/6-tactics-that-will-instantly-improve -your-instagram-following/2/#4be885fa533f; Ross Simmonds, "7 Ways to Build an Engaged Instagram Following," *Social Media Examiner*, May 25, 2015, http://www.socialmediaexaminer.com /build-an-engaged-instagram-following/.

38. "LinkedIn Statistics and Facts," Statista website, accessed December 2016 at https://www.statista.com/topics/951/linkedin/.

39. Wexler, "The 2015 Marketer Survey."

40. Danielle Thibault, "8 Ways to Increase Engagement on LinkedIn Company Pages," July 3, 2015, accessed December 2016 at https:// www.linkedin.com/pulse/8-ways-increase-engagement-linkedin -company-pages-danielle-thibault.

41. "Radian6," Salesforce Marketing Cloud, accessed December 2016 at https://www.marketingcloud.com/au/products/social-media -marketing/radian6/.

42. "Mobile Economy 2017," GSMA website, accessed April 2017 at http://www.gsma.com/mobileeconomy/.

43. "MMA Glossary – Mobile Marketing," Mobile Marketing Association website, accessed December 2016 at http://www.mmaglobal .com/wiki/mobile-marketing.

44. "PC Magazine Encyclopedia – Feature Phone," PC Magazine website, accessed December 2016 at http://www.pcmag.com/encyclopedia.

45. "PC Magazine Encyclopedia – Smartphone," PC Magazine website, accessed December 2016 at http://www.pcmag.com/encyclopedia.

46. "Wearable Electronics in Canada," Euromonitor International website, accessed December 2016 at euromonitor.com.

47. "PC Magazine Encyclopedia – Wearable Computing," PC Magazine website, accessed December 2016 at http://www.pcmag.com /encyclopedia.

48. Paul Rich, Ben Martin, and Leah Jenkins, "2015 Canada Digital Future in Focus," comScore, March 27, 2015, https://www .comscore.com/Insights/Presentations-and-Whitepapers/2015/2015 -Canada-Digital-Future-in-Focus.

49. "Facts & Figures: Wireless phone subscribers in Canada," Canadian Wireless Telecommunications Association website, accessed December 2016 at http://cwta.ca/facts-figures; Rich et al., "2015 Canada Digital Future in Focus."

50. Rich et al., "2015 Canada Digital Future in Focus."

51. Sarah Radwanic, "An Average Monday in the UK: PCs for Lunch, Tablets for Dinner," comScore, February 17, 2013, http://www .comscore.com/Insights/Data-Mine/An-Average-Monday-in-the -UK-PCs-for-Lunch-Tablets-for-Dinner.

52. "Mobile Device Activities," Media Technology Monitor website, accessed December 2016 at https://mtm-otm.ca/Download .ashx?req=18-2-1.

53. "The State of e-Commerce in Canada," CIRA, March 2016, https://cira.ca/sites/default/files/public/Ecommerce-Factbook -March-2016.pdf.

54. "Mobile Path to Purchase: Five Key Findings," Google/Nielsen Company, November 2013, https://ssl.gstatic.com/think/docs /mobile-path-to-purchase-5-key-findings_research-studies.pdf.

55. Christine Austin, "8 Awesome Examples of Effective Mobile Web Design," June 26, 2017, https://www.impactbnd.com/8-awesome -examples-of-effective-mobile-website-design.

56. "Number of apps available in leading app stores as of June 2016," Statista website, accessed December 2016 at https://www.statista .com/statistics/276623/number-of-apps-available-in-leading-app -stores/.

57. "Smartphone behaviour in Canada and the implications for marketers in 2016," Catalyst website, accessed April 2017 at http://catalyst .ca/2016-canadian-smartphone-behaviour/.

58. "Leading apps used on smartphones in Canada as of January 2016," Statista website, accessed December 2016 at https://www.statista .com/statistics/495992/canada-popular-smartphone-apps/.

59. "Mobile App Marketing Insights: How Consumers Really Find and Use Your Apps," Google/Ipsos, May 2015, https://think.storage .googleapis.com/docs/mobile-app-marketing-insights.pdf.

60. Raluca Budiu, "Mobile: Native Apps, Web Apps, and Hybrid Apps," Nielsen Norman Group, September 14, 2013, www.nngroup .com/articles/mobile-native-apps/.

61. Olga Kharif and Leslie Patton, "Starbucks Takes its Pioneering Mobile-Phone App to a Grande Level," *Bloomberg*, March 30, 2016, https://www.bloomberg.com/news/articles/2016-03-30 /starbucks-takes-its-pioneering-mobile-phone-app-to-grande-level.

62. "Annual Online Advertising Revenue Reports," IAB Canada, accessed December 2016 at http://iabcanada.com/annual-internet -advertising-revenue-reports/; "Canada Digital Ad Spending Forecast 2016: Mobile, Video and Social Pushing Investment to New Heights," *eMarketer*, December 21, 2015, https://www.emarketer .com/Report/Canada-Digital-Ad-Spending-Forecast-2016-Mobile -Video-Social-Pushing-Investment-New-Heights/2001706.

63. Stephen Jenkins, "What's My Worth? How Ads Appeal to Consumers," Millennial Media [blog], August 27, 2015, http:// www.millennialmedia.com/mobile-insights/blog/whats-my -worth-how-ads-appeal-to-consumers.

64. "A SMoX Executive Summary on Cross-Marketing Effectiveness: Unilever's Magnum Ice Cream Bars," Mobile Marketing Association, October 2016, http://www.mmaglobal.com/documents/smox -executive-summary-cross-marketing-effectiveness-unilevers -magnum-ice-cream-bars; Vassilis Bakopoulos, Greg Stuart, and Rex Briggs, "Measuring the value of mobile advertising in driving business outcomes: Empirical data from Coca-Cola, AT&T, MasterCard and Walmart," *Applied Marketing Analytics*, vol. 2, no. 2, pp. 169–179, accessed at http://www.mmaglobal.com/files /documents/ama0068_stuart_2_2.pdf.

65. Lynn Bates, "Are QR Codes Still Relevant in 2016?" Mobilozophy [blog], February 2, 2016, http://blog.mobilozophy.com/are-qr-codes -still-relevant-in-2016.

66. "More Marketers Use Proximity Tech, Beacons to Get Closer to the Action," *eMarketer*, September 1, 2016, https://www.emarketer. com/Articles/Print.aspx?R=1014428.

67. Romet Kallas, "Proximity Marketing - What, How, Why?" Unacast [blog], March 23, 2016, https://unacast.com/post/proximity-marketing -what-how-why.

68. "The Wireless Code, Simplified," Canadian Radio-television and Telecommunications Commission website, accessed December 2016 at http://crtc.gc.ca/eng/phone/mobile/codesimpl.htm.

69. "Canadian Common Short Code Application Guidelines. Version 3.0," Canadian Wireless Telecommunications Association, March 11, 2015, http://www.txt.ca/wp-content/uploads/2015/06/Canadian -Common-Short-Code-Application-Guidelines.pdf.

70. "About Us," Mobile Marketing Association website, accessed April 2017 at http://www.mmaglobal.com/about; "Global Code of Conduct," Mobile Marketing Association, July 15, 2008, http://www .mmaglobal.com/files/codeofconduct.pdf.

71. "Winning in Mobile: 8 New Principles for Today's Marketers," Mobile Marketing Association, November 2015, http://www

.mmaglobal.com/documents/winning-mobile-8-new-principles
-todays-marketers; "A SMoX Executive Summary on Cross
-Marketing Effectiveness," Mobile Marketing Association.

## Chapter 14

1. Personal interview with Jeff Brettell, vice president, professional services, Luxor CRM, December 2016.

2. Michael J. Cunningham, *Customer Relationship Management: Marketing*, 1st ed. (Oxford: Capstone Publishing, 2002); M.R. Ciraulo and K.S. Auman, "Insurers can unlock value via CRM," *National Underwriter* 106 (2002), pp. 27:29; Philip Kotler et al., *Principles of Marketing*, 7th Canadian edition (Toronto: Pearson, 2008).

3. Angela Reid and Daragh O'Brien, "Case study: Creating a single view of the customer for CRM strategy," *Interactive Marketing* 6 (2005), pp. 357–365.

4. Dhruv Grewal, Michael Levy, and V. Kumar, "Customer experience management in retailing: An organizing framework," *Journal of Retailing* 85 (2009), pp. 1–14. doi:10.1016/j.jretai.2009.01.001

5. Matthew Townsend, "Why Target Is Raking Up Its Maple Leaves,"*Bloomberg BusinessWeek*, January 22, 2015, http://www .bloomberg.com/news/articles/2015-01-22/why-target-is-closing -up-shop-in-canada; "Target Canada Last In Forum Research Customer Satisfaction Survey," *Huffington Post Canada*, August 19, 2013, www.huffingtonpost.ca/2013/08/19/target-canada-customer -satisfaction_n_3779175.html#slide=2815273; Marina Strauss, "Target's Canadian effort receives a poor grade from shoppers," *Globe and Mail*, August 18, 2013, www.theglobeandmail.com /report-on-business/targets-canadian-effort-receives-a-poor-grade -from-shoppers/article13832051/; Marina Strauss, "Talking Target: A bullseye for a reader response," *Globe and Mail*, August 23, 2013, www.theglobeandmail.com/commentary/a-bullseye-for -reader-response/article13950239/; "About Target: Our Passion and Commitments," Target website, accessed at https://corporate.target .com/about/.

6. Michael Hinshaw, "Customer Satisfaction Is Not Enough—Why High Satisfaction Scores May Actually Spell Danger for Your Brand,"*Brandchannel*, November 19, 2010; John Ozimek, "The disloyalty ladder—two rungs further down," *Journal of Direct, Data and Digital Marketing Practice* 11 (2010), pp. 207–218. doi:10.1057/dddmp.2009.45; Lucy Kimbell, "Designing for Service as One Way of Designing Services," *International Journal of Design* 5(2) (2011), pp. 41–52.

7. "Why Some Companies Succeed at CRM (and Many Fail)," *Knowledge@Wharton*, January 15, 2003, accessed at http:// knowledge.wharton.upenn.edu/article.cfm?articleid=699.

8. Susan E. Robinson, "Customer satisfaction: The Xerox Canada story," *Managing Service Quality* 7 (1997), pp. 12–15.

9. Brent McKenzie, "Customer relationship management and customer recovery and retention: The case of the 407 express toll route," *Knowledge Management Research & Practice* 6 (2008), pp. 155–163. doi:10.1057/kmrp.2008.5

10. Barbara M. Talbott, "The Power of Personal Service : Why It Matters What Makes It Possible How It Creates Competitive Advantage," The Centre for Hospitality Research, Cornell University, 2006, pp. 6–14; "The Story of the Four Seasons," Four Seasons Hotels and Resorts, August 7, 2013, http://press.fourseasons.com /trending-now/corporate/the-story-of-four-seasons/.

11. K.W. Li, "The critical success factors of customer relationship management (CRM) technological initiatives," (Order No. MQ68423, Concordia University (Canada)). ProQuest Dissertations and Theses (2002); Soumaya Ben Letaifa and Jean Perrien, "The impact of E-CRM on organisational and individual behavior: The effect of the remuneration and reward system," *International Journal of E-Business Research* 3 (2007), pp. 13–16, 18, 20–23.

12. Darrell Rigby, Frederick Reicheld, and Chris Dawson, "Winning customer loyalty is the key to a winning CRM strategy," *Ivey Business Journal*, 2003, accessed at http://iveybusinessjournal.com /topics/social-responsibility/winning-customer-loyalty-is-the-key -to-a-winning-crm-strategy#.Ujj8fhbvzR0.

13. Mario Johne, "Brand building after the merge," *CMA Management* 77 (2003), p. 32; Eric Beauchesne, "Customers Want Friendly Service Most," *Star Phoenix*, June 20, 2008.

14. A. Darling, "Social media & CRM: Conversation starter," *New Media Age*, 2010, pp. 20–21; Rachael King, "How Companies Use Twitter to Bolster Their Brands," *Bloomberg Businessweek*, September 6, 2008, www.businessweek.com/technology/content /sep2008/tc2008095_320491.htm.

15. Colin Campbell, "Tuning into Twitter," *Maclean's*, October 7. 2010, www2.macleans.ca/2010/10/07/tuning-in-to-twitter/.

16. Carmi Levy, "Airlines use Twitter, other social tools to revolutionize customer service," *Toronto Star*, October 10, 2010, www.thestar .com/business/companies/porter/article/871979--airlines-use -twitter-other-social-tools-to-revolutionize-customer-service; N. Sreenivasan, C. Lee, and D. Goh, "Tweeting the friendly skies: Investigating information exchange among Twitter users about airlines," *Program: Electronic Library & Information Systems* 46 (2012), pp. 21–42. doi:10.1108/00330331211204548

17. Ravi Sawhney, "Broken Guitar Has United Playing the Blues to the Tune of $180 Million," *Fast Company*, July 28, 2009, www .fastcompany.com/blog/ravi-sawhney/design-reach/youtube-serves -180-million-heartbreak; M. Unnikrishnan and R. Wall, "All That Twitters," *Aviation Week & Space Technology* 172 (2010), pp. 42–44.

18. K. Barry, "Ford Bets the Fiesta on Social Networking," *Wired*, April 17, 2009, www.wired.com/autopia/2009/04/how-the-fiesta/ all/1; "Power to the People! Fiesta Movement: A Social Remix Gives Control of New Ford Fiesta Ad Campaign to the People," Ford, press release, February 19, 2013, http://corporate.ford. com/news-center/press-releases-detail/pr-power-to-the-people- fiesta-37706; Stephen Edelstein, "Ford relaunches Fiesta movement Social Media marketing campaign," *Digital Trends*, February 20, 2013, accessed at www.digitaltrends.com/social-media/2014-ford- fiesta-goes-viral-with-fiesta-movement-social-media-campaign/.

19. Robin W.T. Buchanan and Crawford S. Gillies, "Value Managed Relationship: The Key to Customer Retention and Profitability," *European Management Journal* 8 (1990); Vikki Spencer, "Customer relationship management: Who is your customer?" *Canadian Underwriter* 68 (2001), pp. 12–16; V. Kumar, R. Venkatesan, and B. Rajan, "Implementing profitability through a customer lifetime value management framework," *GfK Marketing Intelligence Review* 1 (2009), pp. 32–43,64.

20. Caroline Papadatos, "The art of storytelling: How loyalty marketers can build emotional connections to their brands," *Journal of Consumer Marketing* 23 (2006), pp. 382–384. doi:10.1108/07363760610712902

21. Mark Brown, "The best Aeroplan credit card in the migration from CIBC to TD," *MoneySense*, January 21, 2014, http://www.moneysense .ca/save/debt/the-best-aeroplan-credit-card-in-the-migration-from-cibc -to-td/; Tim Kiladze, "TD, CIBC battle for Aeroplan loyalty," *Globe and Mail*, June 27, 2013, www.theglobeandmail.com/report-on-busi- ness/td-to-take-over-as-aeroplan-provider-as-parent-to-split-with-cibc /article12852318/; Ross Marowits, "TD Bank wins battle for Aeroplan," *Metro*, August 12, 2013, http://metronews.ca/news/canada/763882 /td-bank-wins-battle-for-aeroplan/; "About Aeroplan," Aimia website, 2013, accessed at www.aimia.com/English/About/Our-Businesses /Aeroplan/default.aspx; Canadian Press, "TD, CIBC reach deal on Aeroplan credit card migration," CBC News, September 16, 2013, www.cbc.ca/news/business/td-cibc-reach-deal-on-aeroplan-credit -card-migration-1.1855664.

22. David Friend, "Canadian companies aim for balance as customers expect more for loyalty," *Globe and Mail*, July 21, 2013, www .theglobeandmail.com/report-on-business/canadian-companies -aim-for-balance-as-customers-expect-more-for-loyalty /article13332480.

23. "About Us," Starwood Hotels and Resorts website (n.d.), Moments, accessed at http://auction.starwoodhotels.com/cgi-bin/ncommerce3 /ExecMacro/static/aboutus.d2w/report?wl=67280009; "Loyalty is a virtue and it's rewarded when you travel," *National Post*, March 22,

2013, http://nationalpost.com/luxury-living/loyalty-is-a-virtue -and-its-rewarding-when-you-travel/wcm/6f2b32d2-ad70-4c6f -821a-7e1f53658c30.

24. "Reward yourself in style with RBC Rewards and Saks Fifth Avenue," RBC [press release], February 3, 2016, http://www.rbc .com/newsroom/news/2016/20160203-rewards-saks.html; Mark Brown, "Best retail rewards credit cards of 2016," *MoneySense*, August 24, 2016, http://www.moneysense.ca/spend/credit-cards /best-retail-rewards-credit-cards-of-2016/; and Rob Carrick, "How to rid yourself of those pesky monthly banking fees," *Globe and Mail*, April 17, 2014, http://www.theglobeandmail.com/globe -investor/personal-finance/household-finances/free-banking -options-are-there/article18045437/.

25. "A Guide for Individuals Protecting Your Privacy," Office of the Privacy Commission of Canada, 2014, accessed at www.priv.gc.ca /information/pub/guide_ind_e.asp.; Canada's Anti-Spam Legislation website, 2014, accessed at http://fightspam.gc.ca/eic/site/030. nsf/eng/home.

26. J. Łodziana-Grabowska," Significance of database marketing in the process of target segments identification and service," *Problems of Management in the 21st Century* (2013), pp. 640–647; I. Gregurec, T. Ević, and D. Dobrinić, "The importance of database marketing in social network advertising," *International Journal of Management Cases* 13 (2011), pp. 165–172.

27. Thomas J. Siragusa, "Implementing data mining for better CRM," *Customer Inter@ction Solutions* 19 (2001), pp. 38–41; Jayanthi Ranjan and Vishal Bhatnagar, "Role of knowledge management and analytical CRM in business: Data mining based framework," *The Learning Organization* 18 (2011), pp. 131–148. doi:10.1108/09696471111103731; Vikas Saraf, MBA, PhD., P. Thakur, and L. Yadav, "CRM with data mining & warehouse: 'Optimizes customer insight,'" *International Journal of Marketing and Technology* 3 (2013), pp. 177–187.

28. N. Sutton, "RBC creates e-marketing council to assess client data," *Computing Canada*, June 20, 2003, p. 6; Lawrence Ang and Francis Buttle, "CRM software applications and business performance," *Journal of Database Marketing & Customer Strategy Management* 14 (2006), pp. 4–16.

29. John Lorinc, "How Canadian Tire is pioneering tomorrow's retail experience now," *Canadian Business*, February 29, 2016, http:// www.canadianbusiness.com/lists-and-rankings/most-innovative -companies/canadian-tire/; Dana Flavelle, "What the data crunchers know about you," *The Toronto Star*, April 23, 2010, https://www .thestar.com/business/tech_news/2010/04/23/what_the_data _crunchers_know_about_you.html.

30. Ross Marowitz, "Metro preps for future of online grocery," *Canadian Grocer*, May 20, 2015, http://www.canadiangrocer.com/top-stories /metro-preps-for-future-of-online-grocery-53510; Peter Hadekel, "Loyalty Programs Start to Pay Off for Grocer Metro," *The Gazette*, November 24, 2010, www.montrealgazette.com/columnists/Loyalty+ program+starts+grocer+Metro/3875329/story.html.

31. Carl Sewell and Paul Brown, *Customers for Life*, Doubleday Publishing, 2002.

32. "Winning Back Lost Customers," *Harvard Business Review,* April 2016, https://hbr.org/2016/03/winning-back-lost-customers; Tom Duncan, *Principles of Advertising + IMC*, 2nd Edition (New York: McGraw-Hill/Irwin, 2005); Mert Tokman, Lenita Davis, and Katherine N. Lemon, "The WOW factor: Creating value through win-back offers to reacquire lost customers," *Journal of Retailing* 83 (2007), pp. 47–64. doi:10.1016/j.jretai.2006.10.005

33. Reuters, "Sprint hangs up on high-maintenance customers," FoxNews.com, July 9, 2007, www.foxnews.com/story/2007/07/09 /sprint-hangs-up-on-high-maintenance-customers/; "Why firing your worst customers isn't such a great idea," *Knowledge @Wharton*, December 12, 2007, http://knowledge.wharton.upenn.edu/article .cfm?articleid=1870.

## Chapter 15

1. John A. Pearce, II, "The company mission as a strategic tool," *Sloan Management Review* 23 (1982), p. 15.

2. Gregory H. Watson, "Design and execution of a collaborative business strategy," *Journal for Quality and Participation* 28 (2005), pp. 4–9; M. Campbell, "Customers of the future," *Canadian Banker 103*(3) (1996, May-June), 15+; and H. Schachter, "Course 101: managing debt," *Canadian Banker 104*(2) (1997, March-April), 23+.

3. Alan Walks, "Mapping the urban debtscape: The geography of household debt in Canadian cities," *Urban Geography 34* (2013), 153–187, doi:10.1080/02723638.2013.778647; Amy Cameron, "The Debt Bomb: 'Tis the season to use plastic -- but watch out: Canadians are already borrowing way too much," *Maclean's*, December 10, 2001; Milica Milosavljevic, Christof Koch, and Antonio Rangel, "Consumers can make Decisions as Little as a Third of a Second," *Judgment and Decision Making 6* (2011), 520–530; Stephanie Ben-Ishai and Saul Schwartz, "Credit Counselling in Canada: An Empirical Examination," *Canadian Journal of Law and Society 29* (2014), 1–20.

4. Personal interview with Andre Samuels, academic director, See-Why Learning and Cory Snyder, sales director, SeeWhy Learning, December 2016.

5. Roger A. Kerin, Vijay Mahajan, and P. Rajan Varadarajan, *Contemporary Perspectives on Strategic Marketing Planning* (Boston: Allyn & Bacon, 1990), chap. 1; and Orville C. Walker, Jr., Harper W. Boyd, Jr., and Jean-Claude Larreche, *Marketing Strategy* (Burr Ridge, IL: Richard D. Irwin, 1992), chaps. 1 and 2.

6. "Ben & Jerry's," Unilever website (n.d.), accessed at www.unilever .com/brands-in-action/detail/ben-and-jerrys/291995/?WT.content type=view%20brands.

7. The definition of *strategy* reflects thoughts appearing in Michael E. Porter, "What Is Strategy," *Harvard Business Review*, November 1, 1996, pp. 4,8.

8. "Why do you need a business plan," Canada Business Network, 2014, accessed at www.canadabusiness.ca/eng/page/3426/; "Developing a marketing plan," Canada Business Network, 2014, accessed at www.canadabusiness.ca/eng/page/2690/.

9. "Companies With More Women Board Directors Experience Higher Financial Performance, According to Latest Catalyst Bottom Line Report," *Catalyst* (n.d.), accessed at http://www.catalyst.org/ media/companies-more-women-board-directors-experience-higher -financial-performance-according-latest; Aleksandra Sagan, "Tim Hortons parent company shareholders reject gender diversity proposal," *Toronto Star*, June 9, 2016, https://www.thestar.com /business/2016/06/09/tim-hortons-parent-company-shareholders -reject-gender-diversity-proposal.html; David Milstead, "With no women on its board, shareholder calls for diversity policy at Tim Hortons owner RBI," *Globe and Mail*, June 8, 2016, http://www .theglobeandmail.com/report-on-business/with-no-women-on-its -board-shareholder-calls-for-diversity-policy-at-tim-hortons-owner -rbi/article30346961/; Jesse Ferreras, "Tim Hortons owner has no women on its board. It's an easy fix," *Huffington Post Canada*, June 8, 2016, http://www.huffingtonpost.ca/2016/06/08/tim-hortons -women-board-of-directors_n_10360366.html.

10. "Accountability," MEC website, accessed at https://www.mec.ca /en/explore/accountability/; "Things That Matter," MEC website, accessed 2016 at www.mec.ca/AST/ContentPrimary/Sustainabil ity/AccountabilityReport.jsp; Alex Ballingall, "How corporate social responsibility improved these companies' bottom lines," *Maclean's*, June 14, 2012, www2.macleans.ca/2012/06/14/how -corporate-social-responsibility-improved-these-companies -bottom-lines/.

11. "CMOs and CFOs Are Misaligned," *Investor's Business Daily*, June 9, 2014, p. A07.

12. "Writing your business plan," Canada Business Network, 2014, accessed at www.canadabusiness.ca/eng/page/2753/#toc-_financial _forecasts_and_other_information.

13. Christine Moorman, "From Marketing Spend to Marketing Accountability," *Marketing News* 48 (2014), pp. 24–25, https://www .ama.org/publications/MarketingNews/Pages/from-marketing -spend-marketing-accountability.aspx.

14. "Budgeting and forecasting," Canada Business Network, 2014, accessed at www.canadabusiness.ca/eng/page/2642/.

15. Tilley Endurables website, accessed at www.tilley.com/home.asp.

16. George Stalk, Phillip Evans, and Lawrence E. Shulman, "Competing on Capabilities. The New Rules of Corporate Strategy," *Harvard Business Review*, March–April 1992, pp. 57–69.

17. Tilley Endurables website, accessed at www.tilley.com/home.asp.

18. Adapted from "The Experience Curve Reviewed, IV. The Growth Share Matrix of the Product Portfolio" (Boston: The Boston Consulting Group, 1973).

19. Kerin, Mahajan, and Vardarajan, *Contemporary Perspectives*, p. 52.

20. Aneri Pattani, "Why Spotify, Netflix and HBO nailed business model of the future", CNBC, October 31, 2016, http://www.cnbc.com/2016/10/31/why-spotify-netflix-and-hbo-nailed-business-model-of-the-future.html; Michelle Castillo, "Netflix plans to spend $6 billion on new shows, blowing away all but one of its rivals", *CNBC*, October 17, 2016, http://www.cnbc.com/2016/10/17/netflixs-6-billion-content-budget-in-2017-makes-it-one-of-the-top-spenders.html; Peter Cohan, "How Netflix Reinvented Itself," *Forbes*, April 23, 2013, https://www.forbes.com/sites/petercohan/2013/04/23/how-netflix-reinvented-itself/#5f3907242886.

## Appendix

1. Personal interview with Glenn Cressman, Share of Marketing, April 2017.

# Name Index

# Company/Product Index

# Subject Index

lifestyle, 74–75
likeability, 311
limited line wholesalers, 283
limited access to buyers, 198
limited problem-solving, 68, 68f
limited service, 271
limited-service wholesalers, 283
line extensions, **191**
linguistic diversity, 36–37
LinkedIn, 329, 329f
list price, 229–231
*The Little Black Book of Scams*, 47, 49
logistical function, 240, 257–259
logistics, **253**
logistics management, 253
long-run profits, 224
long-term customer relationships, 14
loss, 217, 218
loss-leader pricing, 217–218
lottery scams, 49
low-learning product, **190**
loyalty programs, 14, 22–23, 97, 304f, **355**, 356,
        357

# M
*MacLean's* top 50 socially responsible companies,
        17, 272
macroeconomic forces, **42**
magazines, 300–301, 300f, 301f
mail survey, 101, 108f
management ability, 250
manufacturers' agents, **284**
manufacturer's branches and offices, 284
manufacturer's brand, **177–178**
manufacturer's representatives, 284
manufacturer-sponsored retail franchise systems,
        248
manufacturer-sponsored wholesale franchise
        systems, 248
marginal customers, 358
markdown, 274
market, **11**
    business market, 139
    common characteristics, 153, 155
    consumer market, 139
    the mobile market, 332
    target market. *See* target market
    type of, and channel choice, 249
market attractiveness, 198
market development, 371
market factors, and channel choice, 249–250
market follower, 227
market growth rate, 370
market leader, 227
market penetration, 199f, 371
market research, **91**
    causal research, 98
    descriptive research, 98
    exploratory research, 98, 102–106
    future of, 110
    observational research, 106
    primary data, 102, 104–106
    primary qualitative research, 103
    primary quantitative research, 103
    qualitative research, 102–106
    quantitative primary research, 106–109, 107f
    secondary data, 102, **103**–104, 103f, 104f
    secondary research, 103
    six-step market research approach, 98–110
    types of, 97–98
market research process, 98–110
    compile, analyze and interpret data, 109–110
    define the problem/issue/opportunity, 101
    design the research plan, 101–102
    exploratory and qualitative research, 102–106
    generation of reports and recommendations, 110
    quantitative primary research, 106–109

market researcher, 98
market segmentation, **139**–143, 375
    B2B market segmentation, 128–129
    forms of, 140–143
    individualized marketing, 142–143
    mass marketing, 140
    niche marketing, 141–142
    one-to-one marketing, 142–143
    personalized marketing, 142–143
    segment marketing, 140–141
    segmentation analytics, 146–149
    steps in, 149–151, 150f
market share, **91**, 225, 365
market support, 198
marketer-dominated sources, 63
marketing, **10**
    buzz marketing, 77
    content marketing, 19
    customer needs, focus on, 6–7
    customer value, creation of, 7–8
    environmental scan, 6
    event marketing, 296, 298f
    evolution of, 13
    experiential marketing, 22
    external stakeholders, 5
    human resources, 5
    individualized marketing, 142–143
    information systems, 5
    internal stakeholders, 5
    manufacturing, 5
    marketing mix, coordination of, 8–9
    mass marketing, 140
    mobile marketing. *See* mobile marketing
    multichannel marketing, 243–245
    new and evolving marketing practices, 18–25
    niche marketing, 141–142
    omni-channel marketing, 244
    one-to-one marketing, 142–143
    and organizational levels, 363–364, 364f
    partnership marketing, 22–23
    personalized marketing, 142–143
    proximity marketing, 20
    real-time marketing, 21
    research and development, 5
    return on investment, 5
    reverse marketing, 124
    role of, 5–8
    segment marketing, 140–141
    social media marketing. *See* social media
        marketing
    stakeholders, 5
    target markets, appealing to, 4, 8
    viral marketing, 77
marketing blogs, 26
marketing budgets, 367
marketing careers, 25–26
marketing channel, **238**
    business goods and services, 242, 242f
    channel design considerations, 250–252
    channel relationships, 252–253
    channel structure and organization, 241–246
    choice and management, 249–253
    company factors, 250
    conflict, 252
    consumer goods and services, 241–242, 241f
    cooperation, 253
    desire for channel control, 250
    direct channel, 241
    electronic marketing channels, 242–243, 243f
    factors affecting channel choice, 249–250
    global channel strategy, 245–246, 246f
    how distribution channels work, 254f
    importance of, 238–241
    indirect channels, 241
    integrated channels, 276
    intermediaries, 238, 239–241, 239f, 240f
    market factors, 249–250

multichannel retailers, 276
multiple channels and strategic alliances, 243
nature of, 238–241
online consumer, multichannel marketing to,
        243–245
product factors, 250
vs. supply chain, 254
vertical marketing systems, 246–249, 246f
marketing communication agencies, **293**
marketing communication tools, **296**–302
    advertising, 297–302
    direct response, 305
    event marketing, 305
    personal selling, 307, 307f
    public relations, 302–303
    sales promotion, 304–305
    sponsorship, 306
    strengths and weaknesses, 298f
marketing communications
    approaches to, 296
    branded entertainment, 307
    changing landscape, 291–292
    Customer Advocacy Funnel, 309, 309f
    design of marketing communication programs,
        308–309
    developments in, 290–292
    evaluation, 308–311
    inbound marketing, 296
    industry. *See* marketing communications industry
    integrated marketing communications (IMC), 296
    marketing communication tools. *See* marketing
        communication tools
    labelling, 167
    and online retailing, 280
    outbound marketing, 296
    packaging, 167
    planning, 308–311
    product placement, 307
    and retailing, 275–276
    steps in marketing communications process,
        309–311
marketing communications industry, 292–296
    associations, 294
    marketing communication agencies, 293
    the media, 293
    regulatory bodies, 294–295
    research companies, 293
marketing communications process, 309–311
    design of promotional program, 310
    evaluation of program, 311
    IMC objectives, 309–310
    promotional budget, 310
    recommendation of changes, 311
    schedule and run of IMC elements, 310–311
    steps in, 310f
    target audience, 310
marketing concept, 13
marketing dashboard, 368, 368f
marketing department, 377f
marketing environment, 33
marketing environment scan, 6, 33–34, 53f, 54f,
        55f, 56f
    assessment of ideas, 54
    brainstorming, 54
    cluster information into facts and trends, 53
    competitive forces, 6, 45–47
    competitive reviews, 53
    data and information collection, 53
    demographic forces, 6, 34–38
    economic forces, 6, 42–43
    evaluation of alternatives, 54
    evaluation of ideas, 54
    external demographic forces, 6
    regulatory forces, 6, 47–52
    socio-cultural forces, 6, 38–42
    steps in, 52–54
    technological forces, 6, 43–45

marketing fraud, 47
marketing information system (MIS), **91**
marketing intermediaries. *See* intermediaries
marketing metrics, 92, **368**–369
    key, 92*f*, 94
    role of, 92*f*
marketing mishaps in global economy, 131
marketing mix, **8**, 47, 270
    *see also* specific elements of marketing mix
    coordination of, 8–9
    elements of, 8
    place, 4, 8, 10
    price, 4, 8, 10, 211–212
    product, 4, 8, 10
    promotion, 4, 8, 10
    target market, 4
"Marketing Myopia" (Levitt), 365
marketing orientation, **13**–14
marketing plan, 364, **372**
    evaluation phase, 377–378
    implementation phase, 376–377
    outline of, 372*f*
    planning phase, 372–376
marketing process, 10–13, 10*f*
    market, 12–13
    what can be marketed, 11
marketing program, 151, 377
marketing publications, 26
marketing regulations, 24–25, 110
marketing strategy, **377**
    *see also* strategic marketing planning
    extended usage strategies, 191
    global pricing strategy, 228
    market-product strategies, 371*f*
    new product development strategy, 200
    place (distribution) strategy, 376, 376*f*
    price strategy, 376, 376*f*
    product life cycle strategies,
      190–194
    product strategy, 376, 376*f*
    promotion strategy, 376, 376*f*
    pull strategy, 308, 308*f*
    push strategy, 308, 308*f*
    and supply chain management,
      255–257
marketing tactics, **377**
market-product analysis, 370–371
market-product focus, 375
market-product strategies, 371*f*
marketspace, 243
markup, **214**–215, 214*f*
Maslow's hierarchy of needs, 70, 70*f*
mass marketing, **140**
matrix 2D barcodes, **340**, 341
maturity stage, 185, 188–189
maximization of current profit, 224
McMillennial, 84
m-commerce, 282, **335**
media
    earned media, 293
    evolving media habits, 38–40
    forms of, 292–293
    multiple devices, 38
    owned media, 293
    paid media, 293
    social media. *See* social media
    as socio-cultural force, 38–40
    TV and video viewing, 39–40
    usage, 291
media buzz, 4
media data, 293
medical tourism, 41
membership group, **78**
merchandise mix, 271–274
merchandising allowance, 305*f*
merchant wholesalers, **283**
mergers and acquisitions, 47

message comprehension, 311
metrics, **23**–24, 91–92, 92*f*
Mexico, 119
microeconomic forces, **43**
microsites, **317**
middle-aged married couples, 79
middleman, 239*f*
millennials, **35**, 36, 66, 84, 101
minor innovations, **194**
misleading pricing practices, 48
mission, **365**
mission statement, 365
MMA Global Code of Conduct, 343
mobile advertising, 338–340
mobile applications (apps), 19, 45, 336–338
mobile banking, 279
mobile channel, 281–282
mobile check-in services, **341**
mobile commerce, 282, 335
mobile devices, 19, 43, 66, 333–334
mobile discovery, **341**
mobile e-mail, **340**
the mobile market, 332
mobile marketing, **19**–20, 298*f*, 316, 318, 319
    best practices, 343
    branded games, 19–20
    landscape, 319–320
    mobile devices, 333–334
    mobile first approach, 343
    the mobile market, 332
    proximity marketing, 20–21
    regulations, 342–343
    tools, 335–342
Mobile Marketing Association (MMA), 51
mobile marketing tools, 335–342
    mobile advertising, 338–340
    mobile applications (apps), 336–338
    mobile sales promotional tools, 340–342
    mobile web, 336
mobile messaging, **340**
mobile sales promotional tools, 340–342
    matrix 2D barcodes, 340–341
    mobile messaging, 340
    proximity marketing, 341–342
mobile subscribers, 334*f*
mobile technology, and purchase behaviour, 66, 168
mobile web, **336**
mobile web apps, **337**
modified rebuy, 127–128
monetary value, 150
monopolistic competition, **46**–47, 46*f*
monopoly, **46**, 46*f*
most influential brands, 172–173
motivation, **70**
movement along a demand curve, 221
multichannel marketing, **243**–245
multichannel retailers, **276**
multiculturalism, 36–37
multifunction devices, 44
multimedia messaging services (MMS), **340**
multiple channels, 243
multiple devices, 38
multiple market environments, 243
music, 44
mutual reinforcement, 244

### N

native apps, **337**
near field communications (NFC), 168, 341
needs, **6**, 153, 155
negative deviation, 378
negative reinforcement, 73
Net Generation, 36
new and evolving marketing practices, 18–25
    content marketing, 19
    ethical considerations, 24–25
    marketing regulations, 24–25

metrics and analytics, 23–24
mobile marketing, 19–20
partnership marketing, 22–23
proximity marketing, 20
real-time marketing, 21
social media marketing, 20–21
new buy, 128, 129
new marketing approaches, 190
new product development, 199–203
    *see also* new products
    approaches to, 199
    company structure, 199
    new product development process,
      199–203
    team-based approach, 199
new product development process, **199**–203
    business analysis, 201–202
    commercialization, 203
    development, 202
    elements in each stage of, 200*f*
    idea generation, 200–201
    new product development strategy, 200
    screening and evaluation, 201
    steps in, 200*f*
    test marketing, 202–203
new product development strategy, **200**
new products
    *see also* new product development
    adoption curve, 195–196, 196*f*
    degree of product innovation, 194*f*
    drivers of product success, 193–194
    failure, reasons for, 198
    introduction of, 193–194
    successful new products, 198
    types of new products, 194–195
new uses for a product, 192
new-concept definition, 198
new-product failure
    bad timing, 198, 198*f*
    inadequate market support, 198, 198*f*
    incomplete new-concept definition,
      198, 198*f*
    insensitivity to critical customer needs, 198
    insignificant point of difference, 198, 198*f*
    insufficient market attractiveness, 198, 198*f*
    limited access to buyers, 198
news websites, 11
newspapers, 299–300, 300*f*
New Zealand, 131
niche marketing, 141–**142**
non-durable good, **163**
non-durable items, 79
non-probability sampling, **102**
non-profit organizations, 118
non-store retailing, 276–279
    automatic vending, 276
    direct marketing, 276–279
    television home shopping, 276
    non-traditional families, 38
North America, 83
North American Free Trade Agreement
    (NAFTA), 119
North American Industry Classification System
    (NAICS), 115, **119**, 119*f*
not-for-profit organization, 118, 363

### O

objectives, **101**, **365**
    IMC objectives, 309–310
    organizational buying, 123
    organizational objectives, 365–366
    pricing objectives, 224–228
    strategic company objectives, 151
observational research, 103, **106**, 107*f*
odd-even pricing, 213
Office of the Privacy Commissioner of Canada,
    51, 51*f*, 52

official languages, 83
off-invoice allowances, 305*f*
off-price retailing, **275**
oligopoly, **46**, 46*f*
omnibus surveys, **108**
omni-channel marketing, 244
one-price policy, 229
one-to-one marketing, 142–143
online auction, 130, 132
online behavioural advertising (OBA), **52**
online banking, 31–32
online bulletin boards, 102, 103
online buying in organizational markets, 129–132
online communities, 102, 103
online consumer, 280–281
online dating, 49
online marketing, 298*f*
online research bulletin boards, **105**
online research communities, **105**
online retailing, 279–281
   cashless future, 279
   mobile banking, 279
   the online consumer, 280–281
   reasons for shopping online, 279–280
   top online shopping sites in Canada, 280
   what online consumers buy, 281
   when online consumer shop and buy, 280
   where online consumer shop and buy, 280
online video, 44, 292
opinion leaders, **76**
optimization metrics, **331**
opportunities, 373, 374
order processing, 258
order size, 123, 249
organization, 363
organizational buyers, **116**
organizational buying
   buyer-seller relationships, 124–125
   buying criteria, 124
   buying process characteristics, 121*f*
   characteristics of, 120–125, 121*f*
   derived demand, 120, 122*f*
   direct demand, 122*f*
   fear in organizational buying behaviour, 124
   fluctuating demand, 122
   inelastic demand, 122
   key behavioural characteristics, 121*f*
   market characteristics, 121*f*
   marketing mix characteristics, 121*f*
   number of potential buyers, 123
   objectives, 123
   product characteristics, 121*f*
   service characteristics, 121*f*
   size of order or purchase, 123
   supply partnerships, 124–125
organizational buying behaviour, 121*f*, **125**
organizational buying process, 126, 127*f*
organizational levels, 363–364, 364*f*
organizational markets
   e-marketplaces, 129–132
   government markets, 117–118
   industrial markets, 117
   measurement of, 119
   nature of, 116–119
   non-profit organizations, 118
   North American Industry Classification System
     (NAICS), 119
   online auction, 130, 132
   online buying, 129–132
   reseller markets, 117
   size of, 116–119
organizational products, 170
organizational strategy, 364–367
   the business, 364–365
   business plans, 364
   goals or objectives, 365–367
   marketing budgets and financials, 367

marketing plans, 364
   mission, 365
organizational structure, 363–364
organizations
   kinds of, 363
   organizational levels, 363–364, 364*f*
   strategy issues, 364–367
outbound marketing, **296**
outdoor advertising, 300*f*, 301
out-of-home advertising, 297, 301
owned media, **293**

## P

packaging, 166–169
packaging decisions, 167, 168
page track, 325
paid media, **293**
panel, **108**
panel surveys, **108**
parallel importing, 228
Pareto's Rule, **355**
partnership marketing, **22**–23
patents, **174**, 177
payoffs, 82
pay-per-click advertising (PPC), 109, **317**, 338
peer-to-peer car sharing, 220
penetration pricing, 212–213
perceived risk, **72**
perception, **71**–72
   perceived risk, 72
   selective perception, 71–72
perceptual maps, 153
perfect competition, 46*f*, **47**
performance-based culture, 23
perishability, 164, 250
permission-based e-mail, **318**
personal influences, 76–77
*Personal Information Protection and Electronic
   Documents Act* (PIPEDA), 51, 110, 355
personal interviews, 101, 108*f*
personal questionnaires, 101
personal risk, 124
personal selling, 115, 298*f*, **307**, 307*f*
personal sources, 63
personal track, 324–325
personal values, 73
personality, **71**
personalized marketing, 142–143, 168
personas, **146**
phishing e-mails, 49
physical location, 275
physical surroundings, 69
physiological needs, 70, 70*f*
place, 8, 10, 148
   *see also* distribution
place (distribution) strategy, 376, 376*f*
place utility, 240
place-based media, 302
planning phase of the marketing plan, 372–376
planograms, 273–274
point of difference, 198*f*
point-of-purchase materials, 304*f*
Poland, 83
Ponzi schemes, 49
positioning, 139, 375
   deceptive positioning, 17
   positioning maps, 153, 155
   product positioning, 151–155
   repositioning, 152–155
positioning maps, **153**
positioning statement, 152
positive deviation, 378
possession utility, 241
post-purchase behaviour, 66–67
potential buyers, 123, 249
power centre, **275**

pre-approach, 307*f*
*Precious Metals Marking Act*, 47
predatory pricing, 48, 228
predictive analytics, 97
premium, 208
prepared food, 40
pre-roll video advertising, 315
presence, 172
presentation, 307f
press conference, **303**
press release, **303**
prestige pricing, 213
price, 6, 8, 10, 148, 152, 208
   *see also* pricing
   break-even analysis, 223
   competitors' prices, 226–227
   costs, controlling, 222
   demand, estimate of, 219–222
   final price, 229–231
   importance of, 208–212
   as indicator of value, 210–211
   list price, 229–231
   in marketing mix,
     211–212
   nature of, 208–212
   quoted price, 229–231
   revenue, estimate of, 222
   of similar products, 219–220
price comparisons, 227*f*
price discrimination, 227
price elasticity of demand, 221–222
price equation, 208, 210
price fixing, 47, 227
price level, 228–229
price lining, 213
price skimming, 187
price strategy, 376, 376*f*
pricing, 6
   *see also* price
   above-market pricing, 216–217
   at-market pricing, 216–217
   below-market pricing, 216–217
   bundle pricing, 214
   competition-oriented approaches, 216–218
   constraints, 226–227
   cost-oriented approaches, 214–215
   cost-plus pricing, 215
   customary pricing, 216
   demand-oriented approaches, 212–214
   dynamic pricing, 280
   ethical considerations, 227–228
   FOB origin pricing, 231
   general pricing approaches, 212–218, 212*f*
   global pricing strategy, 228
   legal considerations, 227–228
   loss-leader pricing, 217–218
   objectives, 224–228
   odd-even pricing, 213
   penetration pricing, 212–213
   prestige pricing, 213
   price lining, 213
   profit-oriented approaches, 215–216
   retail pricing, 274–275
   setting a final price, 228–231
   skimming pricing, 212
   standard markup pricing, 214–215
   target pricing, 213–214
   target profit pricing, 215–216
   target return-on-investment pricing, 216
   target return-on-sales pricing, 216
   uniform delivered pricing, 231
   yield management pricing, 214
pricing constraints, **226**–227
   brand, demand for, 226
   competitors' prices, 226–227
   cost of producing and marketing the product,
     226

customers, 369
  growth strategies, 370–371
  marketing dashboard, 368, 368*f*
  marketing metrics, 368–369
  market-product analysis, 370–371
  setting strategic directions, 369–371
  strategic marketing process, 371–378
  tracking strategic performance, 367–369
strategic marketing process, 371, **372**–378
  evaluation phase of marketing plan, 377–378
  goal setting, 375
  implementation phase of the marketing plan, 376–377
  marketing program, 375
  market-product focus, 375
  planning phase of the marketing plan, 372–376
  situation analysis, 373–374
strategy, **364**
  *see also* marketing strategy
strengths, 373, 374
strip location, **275**
structured data, **94**
sub-brand, **174**
subcultures, **80**–81
successful new products, 198
supplementary services, 163
supplies, 172
supply chain, 254
  alignment with marketing strategy, 255
  automotive supply chain, 254–255, 254*f*
  Dell Computer, 255–256
  harmonization with marketing strategy, 255
  key logistics functions, 257–259
  vs. marketing channels, 254
  responsive supply chain, 255–256
  understanding, 255
  Walmart, Inc., 259
supply chain management, **254**, 255–257
supply partnerships, 124–**125**
support goods and services, 171–172
surcharges, 208
surveys, 101, 106–108, 107*f*, 108*f*
survival, 225
sweepstakes, 304*f*
SWOT analysis, 26, **34**, 369, 373–374, 374*f*
symbols, cultural, 83
syndicated studies, **107**–108

**T**

tablets, 18, 44
target audience, 310
target market, 4, **8**, 143
  appealing to, 8
  for automobile industry, 136, 137
  coverage, 250–251
  personas, 146
  selection, 269, 375
  target market profile, 143–146, 144*f*
  typical variables in Canadian consumer markets, 144*f*
target market profile, 143–146, 144*f*
  behaviouristics, 144*f*, 145–146
  demographics, 144*f*, 145
  geographics, 143–145, 144*f*
  psychographics, 144*f*, 145
target pricing, 213–214

target profit pricing, 215–216
target return, 224
target return-on-investment pricing, 216
target return-on-sales pricing, 216
targeting, 139
tastes, 219
tax advantages, 118
team-based approach, 199
teaser advertising campaigns, 76
technical factors, and channel choice, 250
technological factors, 6, 31–32
technological forces, 6, 33, 43–45
technological innovations, 187
technology, 110, 203
teenagers, influence of, 79–80
*Telecommunications Act*, 48
telemarketing, **278**
telephone survey, 108*f*
television, 299, 300*f*
television home shopping, 276
temporal effects, 69
test market, 108, **109**
test marketing, **202**–203
test cities, 109
*Textile Labelling Act*, 47
threats, 373, 374
"thumbs-up," 83
time utility, 240
tipping etiquette, 221*f*
total cost, **222**, 222*f*
total cost concept, 222*f*
total product concept, 165–166, 166*f*
total profit, 222
total revenue, **222**
total revenue concept, 222*f*
touch point, **310**, **349**
tourism, and social media, 353
trackers, 44–45
trade discounts, 230, 231*f*
trade promotions, 290, **304**, 305*f*
trade-in allowances, 231
trade shows, 305*f*
trademarks, **174**, 175, 177
traditional auction, **130**
traditional distribution centre, 259
traditional marketplace, 244
traffic generation, **305**
transactional function, 239–240
transactional websites, 244–245, **317**
transit advertising, 301*f*, 301, 302
transportation, 258
trial, 309
truck jobbers, 283
trustworthiness, 172
tuition, 208
TV viewing, 39–40, 44
tweet, 326
Twitter, 326–327
2D barcodes, 20

**U**

unemployment rate, **42**
uniform delivered pricing, 231
unit value, 250
United Kingdom, 34, 34*f*
United States, 34, 34*f*, 38*f*, 119

unsought products, **171**
unstructured data, **94**
user, 79
user-generated content (UGC), **320**
users, 127*f*

**V**

VALS system, 74
value, **210**
  assessment of, 65
  buying value, 65–66
  in consumption or use, 66–67
  intermediaries, created by, 238–241
  monetary value, 150
  price as indicator of value, 210–211
  seeking value, 63
value pricing, 210
values, 73–74, 82
variable cost, 222, 222*f*
variety, 93, 93*f*, 252
velocity, 93, 93*f*
vending machines, 276
veracity, 93, 93*f*,
vertical conflict, 252
vertical marketing systems, 246–249, 246*f*
  administered vertical marketing systems, 249
  contractual vertical marketing system, 247–249
  corporate vertical marketing system, 246–247
video testimonials, 164
video viewing, 39–40
viral marketing, 77
virtual services, **163**
vision, 365
vlog, **320**
volume, 93, 93*f*, 225

**W**

want, **6**
warehousing, 258–259
warranties, 72
weaknesses, 373, 374
wearables, **333**
web analytics, 94, **96**
web apps, 337
web pages, 297
websites, 317
wholesaler, 239*f*
wholesaler-sponsored voluntary chains, 247, 268
wholesaling, 282–284
  agents, 282, 283–284
  brokers, 282, 283–284
  manufacturer's branches and offices, 284
  merchant wholesalers, 283
wiki, **320**
Wireless Code, 48, 342–343
women's beauty, portrayal of, 295
word of mouth, 4, 22, 67, **76**, 77

**Y**

yield management pricing, 214
YouTube, 327–328